AP®
U.S. History
Prep Plus
2020 & 2021

Lead Editor:

Katy Haynicz-Smith, MA

Special thanks to our writers and reviewers on this edition: Thomas Darragh, Mark Feery, Peter Haynicz-Smith, and Melissa McLaughlin.

Additional special thanks to the following for their contributions to this text: Laura Aitcheson, Steve Bartley, Leslie Buchanan, Naomi Beesen, Lauren Claus, Sherri Couillard, M. Dominic Eggert, Tim Eich, Caity Gillooley, Joanna Graham, Adam Grey, Rebecca Knauer, Liz Laub, Mandy Luk, Emily Moore, Camellia Mukherjee, Monica Ostolaza, Aishwarya Pillai, Kathy Schreiner, Rebecca Truong, Ethan Underhill, Oscar Velazquez, Robert Verini, Shayna Webb-Dray, Jessica Yee, and Amy Zarkos.

AP® is a registered trademark of the College Board, which was not involved in the production of, and does not endorse, this product.

Published by Kaplan Publishing, a division of Kaplan, Inc.
750 Third Avenue
New York, NY 10017

10 9 8 7 6 5 4 3 2

Retail ISBN: 978-1-5062-4810-3
Course ISBN: 978-1-5062-4941-4

Kaplan Publishing print books are available at special quantity discounts to use for sales promotions, employee premiums, or educational purposes. For more information or to purchase books, please call the Simon & Schuster special sales department at 866-506-1949.

TABLE OF CONTENTS

PART 3: COMPREHENSIVE REVIEW

PART 4: PRACTICE EXAMS

PART 1

Getting Started

CHAPTER 1

What You Need to Know About the AP U.S. History Exam

Congratulations—you have chosen Kaplan to help you get a top score on your AP U.S. History exam. Kaplan understands your goals and what you're up against: conquering a tough exam while participating in everything else that high school has to offer.

You expect realistic practice, authoritative advice, and accurate, up-to-the-minute information on the exam. And that's exactly what you'll find in this book.

In preparing for the AP exam, you certainly will have built a solid foundation of U.S. history knowledge. While this knowledge is critical to your learning, keep in mind that just being able to recall isolated facts, dates, and events does not ensure success on the exam. U.S. history is about big ideas, such as: how America became a country; how various regions have developed distinct identities; how economics, politics, and social structures have developed; how the United States interacts with the rest of world. The College Board (the maker of the AP exam) asks you to apply the knowledge you've learned at a higher level in order to show evidence of college-level abilities.

That's where this book comes in. This guide offers much more than a review of basic content. We'll show you how to put your knowledge to brilliant use on the AP exam through structured practice and efficient review of the areas you need to work on most. We'll explain the ins and outs of the exam structure and question formats so you won't experience any surprises. We'll even give you test-taking strategies that successful students use to earn high scores.

Are you ready for your adventure in the study and mastery of everything AP U.S. History? Good luck!

EXAM STRUCTURE

The main goal of the College Board is to help students think like historians. To that end, some skills and methods you'll be expected to demonstrate are:

- analyzing primary and secondary sources
- explaining and analyzing historical processes, developments, and events
- making connections using historical reasoning (specifically, comparison, causation, continuity, and change)
- developing historical arguments

AP U.S. History is broken down into nine historical periods:

Period	Exam Weighting
1491–1607	4–6%
1607–1754	6–8%
1754–1800	10–17%
1800–1848	10–17%
1844–1877	10–17%
1865–1898	10–17%
1890–1945	10–17%
1945–1980	10–17%
1980–Present	4–6%

The exam is 3 hours and 15 minutes long and is divided into two sections:

Section	Part	Exam Weighting	Timing
I	Part A: Multiple-Choice (55 Questions)	40%	55 minutes
	Part B: Short-Answer (3 Questions)	20%	40 minutes
II	Part A: Document-Based (1 Question)	25%	60 minutes (includes a recommended 15-minute reading period)
	Part B: Long Essay (1 Question)	15%	40 minutes

EXAM SCORING

Once you complete your AP exam, it will be sent to the College Board for grading. Student answer sheets for the multiple-choice section (Section I, Part A) are scored by machine. Scores are based on the number of questions answered correctly. No points are deducted for wrong answers, and no points are awarded for unanswered questions.

The free-response sections (Section I, Part B and Section II) are evaluated and scored by hand by trained AP readers. Rubrics based on each specific free-response prompt are released on the AP central website after the exams are administered.

After your total scores from Sections I and II are calculated, your results are converted to a scaled score from 1 to 5. The range of points for each scaled score varies depending on the difficulty of the exam in a particular year, but the significance of each value is constant from year to year. According to the College Board, AP scores should be interpreted as follows:

5 = Extremely well qualified

4 = Very well qualified

3 = Qualified

2 = Possibly qualified

1 = No recommendation

Colleges will generally not award course credit for any score below a 3, with more selective schools requiring a 4 or 5. Note that some schools will not award college credit regardless of your score. Be sure to research schools that you plan to apply to so you can determine the score you need to aim for on the AP exam.

Registration and Fees

To register for the exam, contact your school guidance counselor or AP Coordinator. If your school does not administer the AP exam, contact the College Board for a listing of schools that do.

There is a fee for taking AP exams. The current cost can be found at the official exam website listed below. For students with acute financial need, the College Board offers a fee reduction equal to about one-third of the cost of the exam. In addition, most states offer exam subsidies to cover all or part of the remaining cost for eligible students. To learn about other sources of financial aid, contact your AP Coordinator.

For more information on all things AP, contact the Advanced Placement Program:

Phone: (888) 225-5427 or (212) 632-1780

Email: apstudents@info.collegeboard.org

Website: https://apstudent.collegeboard.org/home

CHAPTER 2

How to Get the Score You Need

HOW TO GET THE MOST OUT OF THIS BOOK

Kaplan's *AP U.S. History Prep Plus* contains precisely what you'll need to get the score you want in the time you have to study. The unique format of this book allows you to customize your prep experience to make the most of your time.

Start by going to kaptest.com/moreonline to register your book and get a glimpse of the additional online resources available to you.

Book Features

Specific Strategies

This chapter features both general test-taking strategies and strategies tailored specifically to the AP U.S. History exam. You'll learn about the types of questions you'll see on the official exam and how to best approach them to achieve a top score.

Customizable Study Plans

We recognize that every student is a unique individual, and there is no single recipe for success that works for everyone. To give you the best chance to succeed, we have developed three customizable study plans. Each offers guidance on how to make the most of your available study time. In addition, we have split this book into "Rapid Review and Practice" and "Comprehensive Review" sections for each historical period. There is guidance in both the study plans and the Rapid Review sections to help you determine how to best move through this book and optimize your study time.

Rapid Review

Chapters 3–11 aim to cover the most high-yield content in the shortest amount of time. Each Rapid Review and Practice chapter begins with a "Test What You Already Know" section containing a multiple-choice quiz and a checklist of key terms; this combination allows you to see where you stand with this historical period before you even begin studying the content. The "Next Steps" chart (example shown below) will guide you in customizing your further study. In the middle of the Rapid Review chapter, the section entitled "Essential Content" contains a summary of key takeaways and a complete list of definitions for all of the key terms. Finally, the "Test What You Learned" section contains another multiple-choice quiz and the same key terms checklist so you can see how you're doing after some studying.

If You Got...	Do This
80% or more of the Test What You Already Know assessment correct	• Read definitions in this chapter for all the key terms you didn't check off. • Complete the Test What You Learned assessment in this chapter.
50% or less of the Test What You Already Know assessment correct	• Read the comprehensive review for this period. • If you are short on time, read only the High-Yield sections. • Read through all of the key term definitions in this chapter. • Complete the Test What You Learned assessment in this chapter.
Any other result	• Read the High-Yield sections in the comprehensive review of this period. • Read definitions in this chapter for all the key terms you didn't check off. • Complete the Test What You Learned assessment in this chapter.

Comprehensive Review

Chapters 12–20 feature the same time periods as the Rapid Review and Practice chapters, but they offer a more detailed look at all of the important topics tested on the AP exam. You'll be directed to these Comprehensive Review chapters, for studying the High-Yield topics or for reading the complete chapter, based on your results in the corresponding Rapid Review chapter.

The Comprehensive Review chapters are like an abbreviated version of a textbook you would use in class. The key terms in bold are the same (and appear in the same order) as the terms in the Rapid Review and Practice chapters. Chapter 21 is an in-depth review of the free-response section of the exam, including sample essays and grading rubrics. High-Yield icons appear throughout the Comprehensive Review chapters to help you recognize when information is absolutely essential to know. You will also see AP Expert Notes that highlight important connections between topics and provide tips about how to better apply your knowledge on the official exam.

Full-Length Practice Exams

In addition to all of the exam-like practice questions featured in the chapter quizzes, we have provided three full-length practice exams. These full-length exams mimic the multiple-choice and free-response questions on the real AP exam. Taking a practice full-length gives you an idea of what it's like to answer exam-like questions for about three hours. Granted, that's not exactly a fun experience, but it is a helpful one. And the best part is that it doesn't count; mistakes you make on our practice exams are mistakes you won't make on your real exam.

After taking each practice exam, you'll score your multiple-choice and free-response sections using the answers and explanations. Then, you'll navigate to the scoring section in your online resources and input your raw scores to see what your overall score would be with a similar performance on the official exam.

Online Quizzes

While this book contains dozens of exam-like multiple-choice questions, you may still find yourself wanting additional practice on particular topics. That's what the online quizzes are for! Your online resources contain additional quizzes for each historical period. Go to kaptest.com/moreonline to find them all.

HOW TO CHOOSE THE BEST STUDY PLAN FOR YOU

There's a lot of material to review before the AP exam, so it's essential to have a solid game plan that optimizes your available study time. The tear-out sheet in the front of the book consists of three separable bookmarks, each of which covers a specific, customizable study plan. You can use one of these bookmarks both to hold your place in the book and to keep track of your progress in completing one of these study plans. But how do you choose the study plan that's right for you?

Fortunately, all you need to know to make this decision is how much time you have to prep. If you have two months or more with plenty of time to study, then we recommend using the Two-Month Study Plan. If you only have about a month, or if you have more than a month but your time will be split among competing priorities, you should probably choose the One-Month Study Plan. Finally, if you have less than a month to prep, your best bet is the Two-Week Study Plan.

Regardless of your chosen plan, you have flexibility in how you follow the instructions. You can stick to the order and timing that the plan recommends or tailor those recommendations to fit your particular study schedule. For example, if you have six weeks before your exam, you could use the One-Month Study Plan but spread out the recommended activities more.

After you've made your selection, tear out the perforated study plan page, separate the bookmark that contains your choice of plan, and use it to keep track of both your place in the book and your progress in the plan. You can further customize any of the study plans by skipping over chapters or sections that you've already mastered or by adjusting the recommended time to better suit your schedule. Don't forget to also use the guidelines in the Rapid Review chapters to further customize how you study.

STRATEGIES FOR EACH QUESTION TYPE

The AP U.S. History exam can be challenging, but with the right strategic mindset, you can get yourself on track for earning the score you need to qualify for college credit or advanced placement. Let's review some strategies that, along with the content review and practice questions in the rest of this book, will help you succeed on the AP exam.

Section I

Multiple-Choice Questions

Part A of Section I consists of multiple-choice question sets that typically contain three or four questions and can focus on any historical period. A primary or secondary source is provided for each question set, which could be a passage, image, graph, or map. The questions assess your ability to understand and analyze historical texts and interpretations, as well as your ability to make larger historical connections. Keep in mind that even if a question set is based on a specific historical period, the individual questions may require you to make connections to other periods and events.

The questions range from easy and medium to difficult with no distinct pattern to their appearance within the exam. In other words, the easiest question may be the last one, so make sure to go through all of the exam questions! A solid strategy for the multiple-choice section is to do multiple passes:

1. On your first pass, answer all of the questions that you know and are sure about.

2. Next, go back through the remaining questions. If you can eliminate at least two answer choices and the topic is familiar, take your best educated guess as to the answer. If you look at the question and do not remember the topic, mark the question with an X in your exam booklet and move on. (If you skip a question, make sure that you skip that line on the answer grid!)

3. Go back through the exam for a third time to answer the questions you marked with an X. Again, try to eliminate at least two choices, and take an educated guess. If you're still not sure, at this point, just bubble in an answer for the question; remember that there is no penalty for guessing on the AP exam multiple-choice questions.

4. With the time remaining, remove any extraneous marks in your answer grid (such as any X's you may have left), and make sure that the answers you have bubbled in correspond to the correct numbers in the test booklet.

✔ **AP Expert Note**

Know when and how to guess

The AP exam does not deduct points for wrong answers, so never leave a multiple-choice question unanswered! A blind guess gives you a 1 in 4 (25 percent) chance of getting the correct answer. Even better, every incorrect answer you can confidently eliminate increases those odds: eliminate one answer choice and your chances improve to 33 percent, two and you're at 50 percent.

When eliminating incorrect choices, look for ones that are out of the given time period or region or are not related to specific categories (e.g., the question asked for economic factors, and the answer choice is about cultural trends).

Lastly, do not change an answer you have made unless you are absolutely sure that your initial answer is incorrect. Research shows that your first attempt is usually the correct one.

Short-Answer Questions

In Part B of Section I, you will have three short-answer questions to answer, each of which will have multiple parts. The short-answer section allows you to demonstrate what you know best since you get to choose which historical examples to discuss in relation to the prompts. While two of the short-answer prompts are required, for the third and final question, you get to choose between two prompts.

According to the College Board, a high-scoring response to a short-answer question will accomplish all tasks outlined in the question. You must answer each part of the question with complete sentences and provide specific historical examples in order to receive full credit. Make sure you go beyond simply quoting or paraphrasing historical evidence and really explain its meaning or significance. In composing your answer, you do not need to develop and support a thesis statement, but you do need to synthesize your ideas into cohesive paragraphs.

In Chapter 21, you'll learn a straightforward Kaplan Method you can apply to every free-response question. In general, take time to analyze all of the parts of each short-answer question. Then, before you begin writing your response, create a plan of which historical examples you will be using for each part. You will have plenty of opportunities to practice writing responses to short-answer questions on the practice exams, so be sure to complete those sections to the best of your ability for the most exam-like experience.

Section II

The Document-Based Question

The first part of Section II is the document-based question (DBQ). This essay asks you to think like a historian and develop an argument based on evidence. You will be provided a specific prompt and seven related documents; these will vary in length and format, including text, graphs, and images. Essentially, you must take these sources and draw conclusions based on your analytical skills. The task at hand is less about remembering facts and more about organizing information in an analytical manner. You are expected to make sophisticated connections; therefore, it is essential to demonstrate your knowledge of larger historical themes (rather than just isolated events, dates, and people) in order to earn the highest scores.

If the DBQ prompt and accompanying documents cover something well outside the mainstream, don't panic! The exam writers do this on purpose. The other essay on the exam—the long essay question—will evaluate your knowledge of history, but the DBQ evaluates your ability to work with historical material, even material with which you're less familiar. Writing the DBQ is a skill that can be learned much like any other skill, and this book will help you hone that skill.

The Long Essay Question

The second part of Section II is the long essay question (LEQ). You will answer one of three prompts, each of which focuses on different time periods. Make sure to choose the prompt that best show-cases the extent of your knowledge.

The LEQ assesses your ability to apply knowledge of history in a complex, analytical manner. You will be asked to develop an argument about a historical process or development—thus, you will need to supply relevant historical examples as evidence to support a claim you make about the long essay question prompt. High-scoring long essay responses do not merely list information that is related to the prompt; the critical component of the long essay is your ability to develop a sup-ported argument. See Chapter 21 for scoring rubrics and special strategies for both the DBQ and LEQ.

Pacing

The multiple-choice section, Part A of Section I, consists of 55 questions to be completed in 55 minutes. Since you will need to analyze primary and secondary sources for each question set, you'll want to move quickly but thoroughly through the multiple-choice section; don't linger on any one question for more than 30 seconds or so.

In Part B of Section I, you have 40 minutes to answer three short-answer questions. Aim to spend about 13 minutes on each question, including both planning and writing. Apply any extra time you have at the end of the section to reread your responses, looking for quick errors to fix (such as a missing word or punctuation mark).

The 100 minutes for Section II of the exam is divided into two parts. The first 15 minutes is the suggested reading and organizing time for the document-based question, and the last 85 minutes is the suggested essay writing time, to be split between the two essays. It is recommended that you spend 45 minutes writing the document-based question and 40 minutes writing the long essay question. The proctor may make timing announcements, but you will not be forced to move from reading and planning to writing, or from the DBQ to the LEQ, if you're not yet ready.

Practice, Practice, Practice

Now you've learned about the structure of the exam sections and the types of questions you'll encounter, but to maximize your scoring potential, you'll need to practice these question types. The quizzes in the Rapid Review section (Chapters 3–11), the free-response chapter (Chapter 21), the full-length exams, and the additional quizzes in your online resources provide the perfect opportunity to practice your skills with hundreds of exam-like questions!

> ✔ **AP Expert Note**
>
> **Practice your Test Day mindset**
>
> Having the right mindset plays a large part in how well people do on a test. Students who practice consciously reframing feelings of nervousness as excitement when taking tests can approach their AP exams with a more confident attitude; this helps sharpen their focus and often leads to higher scores. Practice developing a confident mindset—no matter what, you've prepared for this exam and you can do well. As you work your way through the exam, devote your attention to just one question at a time, and don't be afraid to pause and take a few refocusing deep breaths as needed. You've got this!

COUNTDOWN TO THE EXAM

This book contains detailed review, guidance, and practice for you to utilize in the weeks leading up to your AP exam. In the final few days before your exam, we recommend the following steps.

Three Days Before the Exam

Take a full-length practice exam under timed conditions. Use the techniques and strategies you've learned in this book. Approach the exam strategically, actively, and confidently. (Note that you should *not* take a full-length practice exam with fewer than 48 hours left before your real exam. Doing so will probably exhaust you and hurt your score.)

Two Days Before the Exam

Go over the results of your latest practice exam. Don't worry too much about your score or whether you got a specific question right or wrong. Instead, examine your overall performance on the different topics, choose a few of the topics where you struggled the most, and brush up on them one final time.

Know exactly where you're going to take the official exam, how you're getting there, and how long it takes to get there. It's probably a good idea to visit your testing center sometime before the day of your exam so that you know what to expect: what the rooms are like, how the desks are set up, and so on.

The Night Before the Exam

Do not study! You cannot cram for a test as extensive as the AP exam. Worse, pulling an all-nighter will simply deplete your stamina ahead of the exam. If you feel you must review some AP material, only do so for a little while and stick to broad review (such as the Essential Content sections of this book). The best, most effective way to prepare for the AP exam at this point is to rest the night beforehand.

Get together an "AP Exam Kit" containing the following items:

- A few No. 2 pencils (Pencils with slightly dull points fill the ovals better; mechanical pencils are NOT permitted.)

- A few pens with black or dark blue ink (for the free-response questions)

- Erasers

- A watch (as long as it doesn't have Internet access, have an alarm, or make noise)

- Your 6-digit school code (Home-schooled students will be provided with their state's or country's home-school code at the time of the exam.)

- Photo ID card

- Your AP Student Pack

- If applicable, your Student Accommodation Letter verifying that you have been approved for a testing accommodation such as braille or large-type exams

Make sure that you don't bring anything that is *not* allowed in the exam room. You can find a complete list at the College Board's website (https://apstudent.collegeboard.org/home). Your school may have additional restrictions, so make sure you get this information from your school's AP Coordinator prior to the exam.

Again, try to relax. Read a good book, take a hot shower, watch something you enjoy. Go to bed early and get a good night's sleep.

The Morning of the Exam

Wake up early, leaving yourself plenty of time to get ready without rushing. Dress in layers so that you can adjust to the temperature of the testing room. Eat a solid breakfast: something substantial, but nothing too heavy or greasy. Don't drink a lot of coffee, especially if you're not used to it; bathroom breaks cut into your time, and too much caffeine is a bad idea. Read something as you eat breakfast, such as a newspaper or a magazine; you shouldn't let the exam be the first thing you read that day.

Leave extra early so that you can ensure you are on time to the testing location. Allow yourself extra time for any traffic, mass transit delays, and/or detours.

During the Exam

Breathe. Don't get shaken up. If you find your confidence slipping, remind yourself how well you've prepared. You know the structure of the exam; you know the material covered on it; you've had practice with every question type.

If something goes really wrong, do not panic! If you accidentally misgrid your answer page or put the answers in the wrong section, raise your hand and tell the proctor. He or she may be able to arrange for you to regrid your exam after it's over, when it won't cost you any time.

After the Exam

You might walk out of the AP exam thinking that you blew it. This is a normal reaction. Lots of people—even the highest scorers—feel that way. You tend to remember the questions that stumped you, not the ones that you knew. Keep in mind that almost nobody gets everything correct. You can still score a 4 or 5 even if you get some multiple-choice questions incorrect or miss several points on a free-response question.

We're positive that you will have performed well and scored your best on the exam because you followed the Kaplan strategies outlined in this chapter and reviewed all the content provided in the rest of this book. Be confident and celebrate the fact that, after many hours of hard work and preparation, you have just completed the AP U.S. History exam!

PART 2

Rapid Review and Practice

CHAPTER 3

Period 1: 1491–1607

LEARNING OBJECTIVES

After studying this time period, you will be able to:

- Explain how environmental and geographic factors, as well as competition for resources, affected various communities and impacted government policies

- Explain immigrants' effects on society and the reasons for migration to North America

- Describe how conflict and cooperation among empires, nations, and individuals have affected North American development

- Describe labor systems in North America and their effects on workers and society

- Describe the rise of, and changes in, group identities over time

TIMELINE

Date	Event
1492	Christopher Columbus sails to the Western Hemisphere.
1494	Spain and Portugal sign the Treaty of Tordesillas to divide territory.
1499	Amerigo Vespucci reaches Brazil.
1501	Transatlantic slave trade begins.
1513	Spanish Requirement of 1513 asserts Spain's divine right to conquer the New World.
1521	Hernán Cortés leads Spanish forces to defeat Montezuma and the Mexican people.
1524	French explorers arrive in North America.
1550	The *encomienda* system is replaced with the *repartimiento* system.
1585	Sir Walter Raleigh founds Roanoke, "The Lost Colony."
1598	Juan de Oñate leads a revolt in Florida.
1607	Jamestown colony is founded in Virginia.

TEST WHAT YOU ALREADY KNOW

Part A: Quiz

Questions 1 and 2 refer to the image below.

The town of Pomeiock and true forme of their howses, couered and enclosed some wth matts, and some wth barcks of trees. All compassed abowt wth smale poles stock thick together in stedd of a wall.

The drawing depicts an Algonquin village, circa 1585

1. The drawing most directly reflects the

   (A) militaristic nature of the Algonquin peoples

   (B) nomadic lifestyle of the Algonquin peoples

   (C) organized social structure of the Algonquin peoples

   (D) highly developed trade system of the Algonquin peoples

2. The Algonquin and other eastern North American tribes most typically

   (A) depended on trade with other indigenous peoples for survival

   (B) believed in human sacrifice to appease their gods

   (C) relied on farming, hunting, and fishing as sources of food

   (D) depended on military conquest to obtain goods and food resources

Questions 3–5 refer to the excerpt below.

"At the time the first Europeans arrived, the Indians of the Great Plains between the Rocky Mountains and the forested areas bordering on the Mississippi lived partly by corn culture but mostly by the buffalo on foot with bow and arrow. Although Europeans regarded all Indians as nomads (a convenient excuse for denying them the land they occupied), only the Plains Indian really were nomadic. Even they did not become so until about A.D. 1550, when they began to break wild mustangs, offspring of European horses turned loose by the Spaniards."

Samuel Eliot Morison, *The Oxford History of the American People*, 1965.

3. During the Columbian Exchange, the societies of Great Plains tribes were most significantly impacted by

   (A) the introduction of corn as a staple crop

   (B) the European concept of land ownership

   (C) the development of a vast network of trade with Europeans

   (D) the introduction of horses

4. The excerpt suggests that Europeans used the lifestyle of American Indian tribes to justify

   (A) warfare and eradication of the native population

   (B) the creation of an extensive trade network

   (C) expansion into native lands

   (D) the creation of the *encomienda* system

5. Which of the following claims most directly supports Morison's assertions?

   (A) The American Indians of the Great Plains had a developed social structure.

   (B) The American Indians of the Great Plains lived in small, democratic communities.

   (C) Although nomadic, the American Indians of the Great Plains typically remained in two seasonal locations.

   (D) The American Indians of the Great Plains depended upon river systems for trade.

Questions 6–8 refer to the excerpt below.

"The great Cahokia, or better known as Monk's Mound, together with many smaller mounds are located on a 204 acre farm. . . . [Cahokia] covers more ground than any pyramid of Egypt . . . or the Aztec temple mound of Mexico excepted. . . . The variety and nature of material formed around the great Cahokia group clearly indicate that the mound builders . . . had access to or traded with other tribes or people located at the headquarters of the Mississippi and Missouri Rivers, also on the Gulf of Mexico, and possibly from the Atlantic to the Pacific Oceans, as evidenced by the vast quantities and nature of . . . such material as flint, jasper, pipe stone, granite, agate, galena, obsidian, hematite, copper, quartz, crystal, deep sea conch shells and much other material foreign to this section of Illinois."

E. A. Allen, *The Prehistoric World*, 1885

6. The excerpt most directly illustrates that Cahokia's culture

    (A) developed in response to its residents acting as hunter-gatherers

    (B) was not as advanced as the cultures of other American Indian nations

    (C) reinforced a social structure that did not prioritize familial relationships

    (D) developed in response to its residents' complex society

7. The lifestyle of Cahokia's residents was most similar to that of which American Indian peoples?

    (A) American Indians of the Great Plains

    (B) North American Indian peoples on the eastern seaboard

    (C) Isolated tribes that depended on local crops and self-sufficiency

    (D) Inuits

8. Before the Columbian Exchange impacted American Indian peoples, these societies

    (A) largely coexisted peacefully

    (B) were predominantly nomadic

    (C) were highly influenced by their natural environment

    (D) only engaged in local trading

Questions 9 and 10 refer to the excerpt below.

"A [Spanish] royal edict of 1501 permitted African slaves, born in slavery among Christians, to be transported. Within two years there were such numbers of Africans in Hispaniola that Ovando, the governor of the island, requested that their coming might be restrained. . . . But, after the culture of sugar was begun, the system of slavery easily overcame the scruples of men in power . . . The benevolent Las Casas, who felt for the native inhabitants of the New World all that the purest missionary zeal could inspire, and who had seen them vanish away like dew before the cruelties of the Spaniards while the African thrived under the tropical sun, in 1517 suggested that they might still further be employed to perform the severe toils which they alone could endure."

George Bancroft, *A History of the United States of America (Vol. 1)*, 1882

9. Which of the following best serves as evidence for the claim that American Indians "vanish away like dew"?

(A) Spanish colonizers lacked a local and readily available source of labor.

(B) The European demand for tobacco increased dramatically.

(C) Spanish explorers and colonizers introduced Old World diseases.

(D) The number of immigrants from Spain to the colonies remained small.

10. During the sixteenth century, the number of European immigrants who settled in Spain's New World colonies

(A) exponentially grew during each decade

(B) remained small

(C) fluctuated wildly due to the frequent wars

(D) remained higher than 10,000 individuals per year

Part B: Key Terms

The following is a list of the major people, places, and events for 1491–1607. You will likely see many of these on the AP U.S. History exam.

For each key term ask yourself the following questions:

- Can I describe this key term?
- Can I discuss this key term in the context of other events?
- Could I correctly answer a multiple-choice question about this key term?
- Could I correctly answer a free-response question about this key term?

Check off the key terms if you can answer "yes" to at least three of these questions.

Populations in the Americas before European Arrival

☐ Three Sisters   ☐ American Indians of the Great Plains   ☐ American Indians of the Northeast

The Columbian Exchange

☐ Columbian Exchange

European Expansion

☐ Treaty of Tordesillas   ☐ Conquistadores   ☐ *Repartimiento* system

☐ Spanish Requirement of 1513   ☐ *Encomienda* system

3

Next Steps

Step 1: Tally your correct answers from Part A and review the quiz explanations at the end of this chapter.

1.	C	6.	D
2.	C	7.	B
3.	D	8.	C
4.	C	9.	C
5.	A	10.	B

_____ out of 10 questions

Step 2: Count the number of key terms you checked off in Part B.

_____ out of 9 key terms

Step 3: Read the Key Takeaways in this chapter.

Step 4: Consult the table below and follow the instructions based on your performance.

If You Got...	Do This
80% or more of the Test What You Already Know assessment correct (8 or more questions from Part A and 7 or more key terms from Part B)	• Read definitions in this chapter for all the key terms you didn't check off. • Complete the Test What You Learned assessment in this chapter.
50% or less of the Test What You Already Know assessment correct (5 or fewer questions from Part A and 5 or fewer key terms from Part B)	• Read the comprehensive review for this period in Chapter 12. • If you are short on time, read only the High-Yield sections. • Read through all of the key term definitions in this chapter. • Complete the Test What You Learned assessment in this chapter.
Any other result	• Read the High-Yield sections in the comprehensive review of this period in Chapter 12. • Read definitions in this chapter for all the key terms you didn't check off. • Complete the Test What You Learned assessment in this chapter.

ESSENTIAL CONTENT

Key Takeaways: 1491–1607

1. Before the Europeans arrived in the Americas, there were many American Indian tribes scattered across North and South America. These tribes had complex societies with unique religious, political, and cultural beliefs.

2. European countries sought to conquer the New World in order to gain wealth and military status and to spread the ideas of Christianity. European exploration often resulted in negative consequences for native populations, such as widespread epidemics and forced labor systems like the Spanish *encomienda* system.

3. Relationships between the Europeans and American Indians were often fraught with misunderstandings and conflict regarding not only land and resources but also differing cultural beliefs.

4. The Columbian Exchange resulted in tremendous social, cultural, and political change for both the Europeans and the American Indians. New food crops and new sources of mineral wealth brought about extensive demographic, economic, and social change in Europe. The introduction of new food crops and animals also impacted the Americas.

5. As native populations dwindled, Europeans turned to Africa as a new source of forced labor, giving rise to the early plantation system and widespread system of slavery in the Americas.

Key Terms: 1491–1607

Remember that the AP U.S. History exam tests you on the depth of your knowledge, not just your ability to recall facts. While we have provided brief definitions here, you will need to know these terms in even more depth for the AP exam, including how terms connect to broader historical themes and understandings.

Populations in the Americas before European Arrival

Three Sisters: Three staple crops—maize (corn), beans, and squash—favored by many native tribes in North America. Their collective name references their interdependence: the cornstalks provided a structure for the beans to grow up, and the squash held moisture in the soil for all three.

American Indians of the Great Plains: Mostly nomadic tribes residing in the American Great Plains west of the Mississippi River and east of the Rocky Mountains. Relied on hunting and gathering, following the seasonal migration of the America bison or buffalo; integrated the use of horses after introduction by European explorers. Developed Plains Indian Sign Language (PLSI) to foster communication and trade among tribes.

American Indians of the Northeast: Relied on agriculture, as well as hunting and fishing. Lacked concept of land ownership, and had a matrilineal society. Five tribes formed a political confederation known as the Great League of Peace.

The Columbian Exchange

Columbian Exchange: The transmission and interchange of plants, animals, diseases, cultures, human populations (including slaves), and technologies between the New World and the Old World. Greatly benefited Europe and Asia while simultaneously bringing catastrophe to American Indian populations and cultures.

European Expansion

Treaty of Tordesillas: Signed between Spain and Portugal in 1494, it decided how Christopher Columbus's discoveries of the New World would be divided. It established the zone of Portuguese influence in what would become Brazil.

Spanish Requirement of 1513: Spain's assertion of its divine right to conquer the New World, stating that its main concern was to convert indigenous peoples to Catholicism.

Conquistadores: Generalized term for soldiers and explorers of the Spanish and Portuguese Empires. Colonized what became Latin America in the sixteenth through eighteenth centuries.

***Encomienda* system:** A legal system established by the Spanish crown. Conquistadores or other officials were given a set number of American Indians from whom they would extract tribute while instructing in the Roman Catholic faith. In practice, it was a form of slavery.

***Repartimiento* system:** Replaced the *encomienda* system. American Indians living in native villages were legally free. This system legally rendered indigenous slavery nonexistent; natives were allowed land, received pay for labor, and could not be bought and sold. However, they were still abused by Spanish authorities, and working conditions could still be brutal.

TEST WHAT YOU LEARNED

Questions 1–3 refer to the image below.

AN OLD-TIME BUFFALO HUNT, 1898

1. The individuals depicted in the painting most likely represent

   (A) the Cahokia Nation located around the Mississippi River

   (B) the Seminole Nation located in the southeastern region of the modern United States

   (C) the Great Plains Indians located west of the Mississippi River and east of the Rocky Mountains

   (D) the Navajo Nation located in the southwestern region of the modern United States

2. Sixteenth-century Europeans transformed the American Indian tribes of the Great Plains by

   (A) introducing grain crops, which allowed the tribes to become more sedentary

   (B) introducing the horse, which allowed nomadic tribes to move more efficiently

   (C) introducing firearms, which allowed the tribes to conquer territories belonging to their traditional enemies

   (D) introducing transportation mechanisms that allowed the tribes to develop a more advanced trade system

3

3. Prior to the beginning of the Columbian Exchange, American Indian nations on the Atlantic coast

(A) organized into nomadic communities, which followed various crops' growing seasons

(B) developed trade agreements to provide necessary resources for all on the Atlantic coast

(C) established sedentary communities, with economic systems that were based on hunting and gathering

(D) remained in small and relatively unorganized settlements, which depended on agriculture and nomadic hunting practices

Questions 4–6 refer to the excerpt below.

"Columbus was the natural outcome of conditions which had been in course of preparation for years. The Old World, with its prejudices and barbarism, was unfit for the planting of the germ of freedom, and so Providence guided the bark of Columbus to the shores of America. Here the tree of liberty was planted under circumstances which encouraged its growth and insured its life. Nowhere is the providence of God more visible. Here was the virgin soil to be conquered. . . . [Settlers] did not come here to enrich themselves with gold. They did not come here to plunder the soil and return to Spain to spend the proceeds in riot. They were men in whose hearts liberty never died. They sought this continent that they might create liberty, and they did it. Their labor was fruitful."

Senator Bourke Cockran, *True American Patriotism*, 1894

4. Which of the following most directly caused the trend of European colonization described in the excerpt?

   (A) The European colonists' intentional efforts to spread diseases in order to gain additional territory

   (B) The lack of knowledge in American Indian societies

   (C) The American Indian societies' failure to prosper despite the fertility of their extensive lands

   (D) The diseases which decreased many American Indian populations

5. During the period of cultural exchange discussed in the excerpt, American Indian societies were most significantly impacted by the arrival of

   (A) companion planting techniques

   (B) tomato and cabbage plants

   (C) horses and sheep

   (D) fur-producing animals, such as beavers

6. Which of the following represents the largest population flow during the sixteenth, seventeenth, and eighteenth centuries?

   (A) The slave trade from Africa to North America

   (B) Immigration from the British Isles and Western Europe to North America

   (C) Immigration from Spain and Portugal to Central and South America

   (D) The forced migration of American Indian tribes from the southeastern United States to west of the Mississippi River

3

Questions 7 and 8 refer to the excerpt below.

"On the part of the King, Don Fernando, and of Doña Juana, his daughter, Queen of Castille and León, subduers of the barbarous nations, we their servants notify and make known to you, as best we can, that the Lord our God, living and eternal, created the heaven and the earth, and . . . [has] made donation of these isles and Terra Firma to the aforesaid King and Queen and to their successors, our lords, with all that there are in these territories, Wherefore, as best we can, we ask and require you that you consider what we have said to you, and you take the time that shall be necessary to understand and deliberate upon it, and that you acknowledge the Church as the ruler and superior of the whole world, But if you do not do this, and maliciously make delay in it, I certify to you that, with the help of God, we shall powerfully enter into your country, and shall make war against you in all ways and manners that we can, and shall subject you to the yoke and obedience of the Church and of their highnesses; we shall take you, and your wives, and your children, and shall make slaves of them, and as such shall sell and dispose of them as their highnesses may command; and we shall take away your goods, and shall do you all the mischief and damage that we can . . . and we protest that the deaths and losses which shall accrue from this are your fault, and not that of their highnesses, or ours, nor of these cavaliers who come with us."

Spanish Requirement of 1513 (translation courtesy of the U.S. National Library of Medicine)

7. According to the excerpt, the Spanish Requirement of 1513

    (A) mandated that an interpreter communicate the ideas of the document to native peoples

    (B) declared that the Spanish monarchy has the divine right to conquer New World territories

    (C) detailed the rights of native peoples to practice their own religions

    (D) offered an explanation for the Spaniards' emphasis on teaching the native peoples about Catholicism

8. Spanish colonists used the Requirement of 1513 to justify which of the following?

    (A) The *encomienda* system

    (B) The *hacienda* system

    (C) The *repartimiento* system

    (D) The taxation of native peoples

Questions 9 and 10 refer to the excerpt below.

"Why will you take by force what you may obtain by love? Why will you destroy us who supply you with food? What can you get by war? . . . We are unarmed, and willing to give you what you ask, if you come in a friendly manner . . .

I am not so simple as to not to know it is better to eat good meat, sleep comfortably, live quietly with my women and children and laugh and be merry with the English, and being their friend, trade for their copper and hatchets, than to run away from them . . .

Take away your guns and swords, the cause of all our jealousy, or you may die in the same manner."

Chief Powhatan, speech to English settlers in Jamestown, circa 1609

9. Which of the following constituted a major cultural difference between American Indian people and the English settlers?

   (A) Willingness to trade

   (B) Willingness to engage in warfare

   (C) Perceptions of government

   (D) Perceptions of land ownership

10. Which of the following groups of European colonists had the least conflict with American Indian tribes?

    (A) The Dutch

    (B) The Spanish

    (C) The English

    (D) The French

3

Part B: Key Terms

This key terms list is the same as the list in the Test What You Already Know section earlier in this chapter. Based on what you have now learned, again ask yourself the following questions:

- Can I define this key term and use it in a sentence?
- Can I provide an example related to this key term?
- Could I correctly answer a multiple-choice question about this key term?
- Could I correctly answer a free-response question about this key term?

Check off the key terms if you can answer "yes" to at least three of these questions.

Populations in the Americas before European Arrival

☐ Three Sisters   ☐ American Indians of the Great Plains   ☐ American Indians of the Northeast

The Columbian Exchange

☐ Columbian Exchange

European Expansion

☐ Treaty of Tordesillas   ☐ Conquistadores   ☐ *Repartimiento* system

☐ Spanish Requirement of 1513   ☐ *Encomienda* system

Next Steps

Step 1: Tally your correct answers from Part A and review the quiz explanations at the end of this chapter.

1.	C	6.	A
2.	B	7.	B
3.	C	8.	A
4.	D	9.	D
5.	C	10.	A

_____ out of 10 questions

Step 2: Count the number of key terms you checked off in Part B.

_____ out of 9 key terms

Step 3: Compare your Test What You Already Know results to these Test What You Learned results to see how exam-ready you are for this period.

For More Practice:

- Read (or reread) the comprehensive review for this period in Chapter 12.
- Go to kaptest.com to complete the online quiz questions for 1491–1607.
  - Haven't registered your book yet? Go to kaptest.com/moreonline to begin.

ANSWERS AND EXPLANATIONS

Test What You Already Know

1. C

The picture depicts a permanent settlement, with the community buildings organized around a shared central area; these aspects suggest that these Algonquins had an organized community structure. Therefore, **(C)** is correct. The stakes around the village, which help establish the boundary of the settlement, do not appear to be militaristic in nature; (A) is incorrect. The sturdy buildings and number of people gathered in the central plaza do not support the idea that this tribe was nomadic, making (B) incorrect. While it might be possible that the village had a well-developed system of trade, the picture provides no evidence of that concept, so (D) is also incorrect.

2. C

Historians have determined that the American Indians who lived in the eastern half of North America primarily relied on farming for their livelihood; they supplemented their harvests with hunting, fishing, and gathering. Therefore, **(C)** is correct. Tribes engaged in trade but did not rely on this trade for their survival, making (A) incorrect. (B) is incorrect because eastern North American tribes did not believe in or practice human sacrifice. They were occasionally at war, but they did not rely on conquest as their main source of goods or food; thus, (D) is incorrect.

3. D

Of the four possible answers, the introduction of the horse by the Spanish during the sixteenth century had the greatest impact on the Great Plains tribes. Using horses allowed tribal members, who had previously hunted on foot, to become more efficient hunters and to follow their main prey, the buffalo, for longer distances. As a result, the American Indians of the Great Plains adopted a nomadic lifestyle. **(D)** is correct. While the introduction of corn and trade with Europeans benefited the Great Plains tribes, neither came close to having the same impact on their livelihood and lifestyle as the introduction of the horse; (A) and (C) are incorrect. Because these tribes adopted a nomadic lifestyle, they were likely less bothered by

the European concept of land ownership than the more settled tribes to the east were, making (B) incorrect.

4. C

American Indian tribes believed that groups collectively possessed the lands to farm and hunt. In fact, their culture had no concept of the private ownership of land by individuals. In contrast, Europeans valued land as a possession owned by an individual or a family, and they regarded land as a source of wealth. It was convenient for Europeans to assume that nomadic tribes did not claim ownership of any land; **(C)** is correct. Europeans often took over native lands without eradicating their native population, making (A) incorrect. (B) is incorrect because trade networks were not relevant to enforcing the concept of land ownership. The Spanish *encomienda* system, in which the Spanish crown granted the colonists the right to use native labor to develop an area of land, was not operational in the territory of the Great Plains tribes, making (D) incorrect.

5. A

The American Indians of the Great Plains held organized hunts for buffalo and did, to some extent, farm corn as a staple crop; these actions suggest that they maintained a formal social structure; **(A)** is correct. The Great Plains tribes were not run democratically, making (B) incorrect. While some tribes had permanent land that they used to grow crops, they did not limit themselves to a certain number of locations, making (C) incorrect. Although there was trade between tribes, their trading system was not river-based; (D) is also incorrect.

6. D

Even preliminary archaeological studies of Cahokia indicated that it was one of the most advanced societies in pre-Columbian North America. The excerpt mentions evidence of Cahokia's extensive trading network and the sheer size of the mounds constructed. Thus, **(D)** is correct and (B) is incorrect. Such a sprawling society could not have been fed solely with hunter-gatherer activities, eliminating (A). There is no evidence in the excerpt to support the idea that the Cahokia did not prioritize familial relationships; (C) is incorrect.

7. B

The lifestyle in Cahokia was most similar to other eastern tribes that had permanent settlements and relied on farming for food; **(B)** is correct. Cahokia's residents were not nomadic like the Great Plains tribes were, making (A) incorrect. Cahokia was a trading center, and its residents traded frequently, eliminating (C). The Inuits lived in the tundra region south of the Arctic Ocean. Though the Inuits built homes composed of turf and stone, in addition to their temporary igloos, the Inuits' architecture was not as complex as Cahokia's architecture. Also, the Inuits primarily relied on hunting for food, while residents of Cahokia lived in a more temperate environment and could cultivate crops. Therefore, (D) is incorrect.

8. C

Each American Indian community adapted to its natural surroundings. For example, if a tribe was located on a river system, it would likely participate in trade, set up permanent settlements, and grow crops; however, if a tribe lived on the Great Plains and hunted buffalo, it might adopt a more nomadic lifestyle. Thus, **(C)** is correct. While various tribes traded and interacted, they also conducted raids and waged war, making (A) incorrect. Most of the North American Indian communities maintained permanent settlements and made their living by farming, hunting, and fishing, eliminating (B). Additionally, pre-Columbian American Indians participated in extensive trading networks, so (D) is incorrect.

9. C

The arrival of Old World diseases devastated the indigenous populations of the Americas, and they were at increased risk of exposure to such diseases as forced laborers to the Spanish. Thus, **(C)** is correct. Spanish colonizers turned to African slave labor when they could not find other labor sources, including labor sources among their own small population. However, neither of those facts explains the claim made in the excerpt about American Indians; (A) and (D) are incorrect. The dramatic increase in tobacco production in response to European demand did not occur until after 1607, while the excerpt references events in the early sixteenth century. Also, for several decades after the initial increase in demand for tobacco, it was indentured servants, not slaves, who were the principal labor force in the tobacco fields of the Chesapeake. (B) is incorrect.

10. B

The number of Europeans who immigrated to Spain's New World colonies was small, not only during the sixteenth century, but also for several centuries thereafter. Thus, **(B)** is correct and (A) is incorrect. Spain struggled to defend its colonies against the English, and later the Americans, because it had so few colonists to occupy the land or serve as soldiers; (C) and (D) are incorrect.

Test What You Learned

1. C

The American Indian nations of the Great Plains depended upon buffalo hunting, which is depicted in the painting, for survival. The Great Plains Indians were nomadic groups that followed their food supply. Therefore, **(C)** is correct. The Cahokia Nation hunted mammoths, bison, and deer, eliminating (A). Unlike the American Great Plains, other ecosystems within the Americas only consisted of smaller animals. The Seminole Nation hunted deer, wild turkeys, rabbits, and alligators, and the Navajo Nation hunted deer, antelope, and small game; thus, (B) and (D) are incorrect.

2. B

The horse was accidentally introduced to American Indians of the Great Plains when runaway horses from Spanish exploration parties eventually traveled into the North American Plains. The Great Plains tribes learned to tame these horses and utilize them for speedier transportation. This allowed them to hunt buffalo in less time, which gave them more time to develop their cultural traditions. **(B)** is correct. Although Europeans introduced grain crops to the American Indians of the Great Plains, these tribes continued their nomadic lifestyle, including hunting; (A) is incorrect. While some trade for firearms was conducted, the introduction of the horse had far wider-ranging social and cultural ramifications for tribes on the Great Plains, making (C) incorrect. The introduction of the horse was the primary form of transportation that the Spaniards brought to the New World, but Great Plains tribes mainly used them to hunt, in part due to the ongoing disruption to American Indian societies due to rampant disease. (D) is incorrect.

3. C

The American Indian nations of the modern-day northeastern United States were highly organized and were sedentary, as they had developed a productive agricultural system. Thus, **(C)** is correct. Because American Indian settlements along the Atlantic coast were permanent and organized, (A) and (D) are incorrect. Prior to encountering Europeans, American Indian nations had not developed a method of trade to provide necessary resources to the entire Atlantic coast, making (B) incorrect.

4. D

At the time, and for many years thereafter, Europeans attributed their ability to defeat the native peoples of the Americas to the superiority of their weapons and civilization. However, more recent research has demonstrated that the American Indians' high disease rate most significantly contributed to their decline; **(D)** is correct. While there were some documented instances of biological warfare (such as the smallpox blankets at the English Fort Pitt), this was not a common practice and was not widespread among all of the European colonies. Native peoples typically contracted novel diseases through casual contact with colonizers. Thus, (A) is incorrect. (B) and (C) are incorrect because the native peoples had a vast knowledge of the land and natural resources and were largely organized in tribes.

5. C

European colonizers brought domesticated animals, such as horses and sheep, to the Americas. The American Indians were able to make use of these animals to improve their lifestyles and to resist further European encroachments. Therefore, **(C)** is correct. (A) and (B) are both incorrect because companion planting techniques and certain plants such as tomatoes were exports from the New World to the Old. Indigenous peoples in the New World were already trading furs prior to the arrival of European colonizers, so (D) is also incorrect.

6. A

British colonists recognized that African slaves best served their demand for labor, and they imported hundreds of thousands of African slaves to the colonies as the tobacco and rice economies continued to grow. **(A)** is correct.

Immigrants from the British Isles and Western Europe typically came to North America in small groups, the largest being 20,000 people during the Great Migration, making (B) incorrect. The Spaniards and Portuguese immigrated to Central and South America in smaller numbers over time, so (C) is incorrect. The forced migration of American Indian tribes known as the Trail of Tears did not occur until the nineteenth century; (D) is also incorrect.

7. B

In the Requirement of 1513, the Spanish monarchy announced that it had a divine right to take ownership of territories in the New World thus, **(B)** is correct. While the Spanish conquistadors were encouraged to use interpreters, this practice was not mandated; (A) is incorrect. The Requirement of 1513 provided a religious justification for the Spaniards' actions; it described their duty to convert indigenous peoples to Catholicism; (C) is incorrect. While the Requirement of 1513 did not force the native peoples to accept Catholicism, Spaniards often used it as a justification to take aggressive action, including enslavement and killing, in the face of any perceived rebellion; (D) is incorrect.

8. A

Spanish conquistadors forced American Indians into labor through the *encomienda* system. The Requirement of 1513 justified taking natives as captives, under the argument that it was Spain's divine right to conquer and convert the New World. Therefore, **(A)** is correct. The *hacienda* system refers to the system of larger land ownership that included mines, factories, and plantations; (B) is incorrect. The *repartimiento* system was a labor system that did not utilize slavery, and which replaced the *encomienda* system; (C) is incorrect. In the early 1500s, the Spanish focused on exploiting the native peoples in terms of labor, not taxation, making (D) incorrect.

9. D

Many American Indian tribes did not believe that land could be owned, while the English settlers strongly believed in land ownership; this cultural difference led to many conflicts between the two populations. Therefore, **(D)** is correct. (A) is incorrect; upon the English settlers' arrival, the native peoples began to trade with them. While Powhatan emphasizes the virtues of peace in this speech, he also makes it clear that his people will readily go to war with the Europeans if needed. Additionally, American Indian tribes often fought each other for land and resources. Therefore, (B) is incorrect. (C) is also incorrect; although the English and American Indians maintained different forms of government, this political difference was not as major of a cultural difference as land ownership was.

10. A

The Dutch began exploring America with modest commercial goals in mind. Dutch merchants regularly exchanged goods with the natives for furs, and they generally practiced tolerance of other cultures. Thus, **(A)** is correct. (B), (C), and (D) are incorrect, as the other colonizers used aggressive tactics, such as enslaving native people, taking over native lands, or creating conflict by trading with warring tribes.

CHAPTER 4

Period 2: 1607–1754

LEARNING OBJECTIVES

After studying this time period, you will be able to:

- Explain immigrants' effects on society and the reasons for migration to North America

- Explain how environmental and geographic factors, as well as competition for resources, affected various communities and impacted government policies

- Describe how conflict and cooperation among empires, nations, and individuals have affected North American development

- Describe the reasons for internal U.S. migration and settlement and the effect of such migration on American life

- Chart the development of, and changes in, American politics

- Describe labor systems in North America and their effects on workers and society

- Describe the rise of, and changes in, group identities over time

- Explain the development of economic patterns and the government's response to economic issues

TIMELINE

Date	Event
1608	Samuel de Champlain founds Quebec for the French.
1610	The Spanish establish a settlement at Santa Fe.
1619	The first captured Africans are brought to Virginia. Virginia establishes the House of Burgesses, the first legislative assembly in the New World.
1620	Pilgrims sail on the *Mayflower* to the New World.
1624	Virginia becomes a royal colony.
1630	Massachusetts Bay Colony is founded by the Puritans.
1632	Maryland is founded as a proprietary colony.
1636	The Pequot War occurs in New England.
1675–1676	King Philip's War is fought in New England.
1676	Bacon's Rebellion occurs in Virginia.
1680	Popé leads the Pueblo Revolt in Sante Fe.
1682	La Salle and Cavalier explore the Mississippi River and the Gulf of Mexico.
1692	The Salem Witch Trials occur in Massachusetts.
1733	The Georgia colony is founded.
1734	The Great Awakening begins with the sermons of Jonathan Edwards.
1739	A slave revolt called the Stono Rebellion occurs in South Carolina.

TEST WHAT YOU ALREADY KNOW

Part A: Quiz

Questions 1–3 refer to the excerpt below.

"It was the spaniards good hap to happen upon those parts where were infinite numbers of people, whoe had manured the ground with that providence that it afforded victuall at all times; and time had brought them to that perfection (that) they had the use of gold and silver, and (of) the most of such commodities as their countries affoorded; so that what the Spanaird got was only the spoile and pillage of those countrie people, and not the labours of their owne hands.

But had those fruitfull Countries beene as savage, as barbarous, as ill-peopled, as little planted laboured and manured, as Virginia; their proper labors, it is likely would have produced as small a profit as ours."

William Simmonds, *The Proceedings of the English Colonie in Virginia Since Their First Beginning*, 1612

1. Which of the following developments is most directly depicted in the excerpt?

   (A) Enlightenment

   (B) Monarchism

   (C) Democratization

   (D) Mercantilism

2. Which of the following groups would be the least likely to support the belief which Simmonds expressed in the excerpt?

   (A) Traders in Quebec

   (B) Settlers in Jamestown

   (C) Colonizers in Santa Fe

   (D) Pilgrims in Plymouth

3. All of the following contributed to the economic hardship that colonists in Jamestown experienced EXCEPT

   (A) the contagious nature of typhoid and dysentery

   (B) the frailty of the tobacco plant

   (C) the colonists' limited population

   (D) the swamp that surrounded the colony

Questions 4–7 refer to the image below.

The illustration depicts a courtroom hearing during the Salem witch trials.

4. Which of the following statements about the Salem witch trials is supported by the image?

   (A) They were conducted like religious ceremonies.

   (B) They were overseen by both men and women.

   (C) They were characterized by emotion and hysteria.

   (D) They were led by an impartial judge.

5. The controversy surrounding the Salem witch trials most likely led to

   (A) the establishment of United States courts of law

   (B) increased criticism of Puritan clergy

   (C) increased belief in witchcraft

   (D) improved rights for Puritan women

6. During the decades leading to the Salem witch trials, the population of the Massachusetts Bay Colony

   (A) rapidly increased

   (B) drastically declined

   (C) assimilated with American Indian tribes

   (D) incorporated African Americans as slaves

7. Which of the following movements developed in direct contradiction to the practices of the Salem witch trials?

   (A) The Reformation

   (B) The Enlightenment

   (C) The Great Awakening

   (D) The Inquisition

Questions 8–10 refer to the excerpt below.

"Act XII. Children got by an Englishman upon a Negro woman shall be bond or free according to the condition of the mother, and if any Christian shall commit fornication with a Negro man or woman, he shall pay double the fines of a former act."

Acts of the Virginia Commonwealth, 1662

8. The Acts of the Virginia Commonwealth were most directly intended to

    (A) control the rapidly growing slave population

    (B) affirm the privileged status of biracial children

    (C) prohibit interracial sexual relations

    (D) establish Virginia as the first colony to legalize slavery

9. The wording of the excerpt suggests that by 1662, slavery in Virginia

    (A) was analogous to slavery in the West Indies

    (B) was punishable by fines

    (C) was mentioned in legal acts

    (D) was threatened by slave rebellions

10. Which of the following colonies initially banned the practice of slavery?

    (A) Massachusetts

    (B) New York

    (C) Georgia

    (D) Virginia

Part B: Key Terms

The following is a list of the major people, places, and events for 1607–1754. You will likely see many of these on the AP U.S. History exam.

For each key term ask yourself the following questions:

- Can I describe this key term?
- Can I discuss this key term in the context of other events?
- Could I correctly answer a multiple-choice question about this key term?
- Could I correctly answer a free-response question about this key term?

Check off the key terms if you can answer "yes" to at least three of these questions.

European Colonization in the New World

- ☐ New France
- ☐ Dutch East India Company
- ☐ New Amsterdam
- ☐ Pueblo Revolt
- ☐ Jamestown
- ☐ Virginia Company

Indentured Servitude

- ☐ Indentured servants
- ☐ Bacon's Rebellion

Slavery

- ☐ Atlantic slave trade
- ☐ Stono Rebellion

English Conflicts with American Indians

- ☐ Pequot War
- ☐ King Philip's War

The Development of English Colonial Societies in North America

- ☐ Puritans
- ☐ Plymouth
- ☐ Mayflower Compact
- ☐ Massachusetts Bay Company
- ☐ Great Migration of the 1630s
- ☐ Salem witch trials
- ☐ Fundamental Orders of Connecticut
- ☐ Charter of Liberties and Privileges
- ☐ Fundamental Constitutions of Carolina
- ☐ Quakers

Characteristics of English Colonial Societies

- ☐ Mercantilism
- ☐ Great Awakening

Next Steps

Step 1: Tally your correct answers from Part A and review the quiz explanations at the end of this chapter.

1.	D	6.	A
2.	C	7.	B
3.	B	8.	C
4.	C	9.	C
5.	B	10.	C

____ out of 10 questions

Step 2: Count the number of key terms you checked off in Part B.

____ out of 24 key terms

Step 3: Read the Key Takeaways in this chapter.

Step 4: Consult the table below and follow the instructions based on your performance.

If You Got...	Do This
80% or more of the Test What You Already Know assessment correct (8 or more questions from Part A and 19 or more key terms from Part B)	• Read definitions in this chapter for all the key terms you didn't check off. • Complete the Test What You Learned assessment in this chapter.
50% or less of the Test What You Already Know assessment correct (5 or fewer questions from Part A and 12 or fewer key terms from Part B)	• Read the comprehensive review for this period in Chapter 13. • If you are short on time, read only the High-Yield sections. • Read through all of the key term definitions in this chapter. • Complete the Test What You Learned assessment in this chapter.
Any other result	• Read the High-Yield sections in the comprehensive review of this period in Chapter 13. • Read definitions in this chapter for all the key terms you didn't check off. • Complete the Test What You Learned assessment in this chapter.

ESSENTIAL CONTENT

Key Takeaways: 1607–1754

1. Spanish, French, Dutch, and British colonizers had different goals that impacted the economic, political, and cultural development of their colonies and shaped colonizers' interactions with American Indian populations.

2. Conflict arose due to competition for resources among European rivals. It also arose between the Europeans and American Indians. Examples of American Indian resistance to colonizers were the Pueblo Revolt, the Pequot War, and King Philip's War.

3. Early British colonies developed along the Atlantic coast with some regional differences. New England colonies were settled by the Puritans, who lived in small towns. The middle colonies were characterized by the export of cash crops, less social rigidity, and more religious tolerance. The southern colonies developed a plantation-based economy.

4. The African slave trade grew extensively throughout the eighteenth century. The trading of slaves, cash crops, and manufactured goods between Africa, the Americas, and Europe became known as Triangular Trade.

5. England used its colonies to obtain raw materials for its own manufacturing purposes and wealth creation. There were, consequently, early examples of colonial resentment and resistance. From Bacon's Rebellion in 1676 to the Great Awakening starting in the 1730s, the colonists begin to carve out a distinct American identity.

Key Terms: 1607–1754

Remember that the AP U.S. History exam tests you on the depth of your knowledge, not just your ability to recall facts. While we have provided brief definitions here, you will need to know these terms in even more depth for the AP exam, including how terms connect to broader historical themes and understandings.

European Colonization in the New World

New France: The area colonized by France in North America, including lands in both modern-day Canada and the United States. Its primary purpose was economic: gaining wealth through natural resources (such as furs) and trade with indigenous peoples.

Dutch East India Company: The vehicle for the commercial ambitions of the Netherlands in the New World, especially with regards to the fur trade. Led to the founding of New Netherlands and New Amsterdam.

New Amsterdam: The Dutch capital of their New Netherland colony. Noted for its tolerance of religious practices. It failed to attract enough settlers to compete with the surrounding English colonies. Conquered by the English in 1664, who renamed it New York City.

Pueblo Revolt: A 1680 revolt against Spanish settlers in the modern-day American Southwest. Led by a Pueblo man named Popé, it forced the Spanish to abandon Santa Fe. A rare, decisive American Indian victory against European colonization.

Jamestown: Founded in Virginia in 1607, it was the first permanent English settlement in the New World. Several waves of colonists struggled to survive, but eventually the English started to gain more of a foothold, aided in part by the leadership of John Smith and tobacco cultivation headed up by John Rolfe.

Virginia Company: Chartered in 1606 by King James I in order to settle the North American eastern coastline. Established a headright system (1618) and the legislative body, the House of Burgesses (1619). By 1624, a lack of profit forced the company to concede its charter to the crown, who appointed a royal governor.

Indentured Servitude

Indentured servants: People who offered up five to seven years of their freedom in exchange for passage to the New World. They had limited rights while servants, but were considered free members of society upon release. During the seventeenth century, nearly two-thirds of English immigrants were indentured servants. Declined in favor of slavery, which was more profitable to planters.

Bacon's Rebellion: A failed 1676 rebellion in Jamestown. Led by Nathaniel Bacon, indentured servants and slaves revolted against the Virginia Colony's aristocracy. It led to a strengthening of racially coded laws, such as the Virginia Slave Codes of 1705, in order to divide impoverished white and black slaves, thus safeguarding the planter aristocracy from future rebellions.

Slavery

Atlantic slave trade: A transatlantic trade network, also known as Triangular Trade. New World colonies exported raw materials such as sugar and cotton to England. There, these materials were transformed into rum and textiles. Europeans sold these manufactured goods, including at African ports, in exchange for slaves, who would then be sold in the colonies as farm workers, thus completing the triangle.

Stono Rebellion: A 1739 slave uprising in Stono, South Carolina. Led to the deaths of more than four dozen colonists and as many as 200 African slaves. Prompted South Carolina's proprietors to create a stricter slave code.

English Conflicts with American Indians

Pequot War: A war in New England in 1636–1638. Fought between the Pequot tribe and the English colonists with their American Indian allies. A catastrophic defeat for the Pequot tribe. Famous for the Mystic massacre, where over 500 Pequot were slaughtered in a blaze.

King Philip's War: Also known as Metacom's War, King Philip's War (1675–1678) was an ongoing battle between English colonists and the American Indian inhabitants of New England. The English victory expanded their access to land that was previously inhabited by the natives.

The Development of English Colonial Societies in North America

Puritans: Religious group who split off from the Church of England, believing that its ceremonies and teachings were too reminiscent of Catholicism. The first Puritans to colonize the New World were the Pilgrims, a minority group of Puritans known as separatists.

4

Plymouth: A colony in modern-day Cape Cod and southeastern Massachusetts, founded by the Pilgrims in 1620. By 1691, it was merged with the Massachusetts Bay Colony to form the crown colony of the Province of Massachusetts Bay.

Mayflower Compact: The first written form of government in the modern-day United States. Drafted by the Pilgrims, it was an agreement to establish a secular body that would administer the leadership of the Plymouth colony.

Massachusetts Bay Company: Founded in 1629 by a collective of London financiers, who advocated for the Puritan cause and wanted to profit from American Indian trade.

Great Migration of the 1630s: A period in which many Puritan families moved across the Atlantic. By 1642, approximately 20,000 Puritans had immigrated to Massachusetts.

Salem witch trials: An infamous 1692 instance of mass hysteria. A group of young girls in Salem, Massachusetts, accused older wealthy members of the community of witchcraft. Twenty were executed, five died in prison, and the Puritan clergy's prestige was irreversibly damaged.

Fundamental Orders of Connecticut: The first constitution in colonial America, which fully established the Hartford government in 1639. While it modeled itself after the government of the Massachusetts Bay Colony, the document—in a key innovation—called for the power of government to be derived from the governed, who did not need to be church members to vote.

Charter of Liberties and Privileges: Drafted in 1683 by a New York assembly, following the colony's takeover by the English. It mandated elections and reinforced traditional English liberties such as trial by jury, security of property, and religious tolerance for Protestant churches.

Fundamental Constitutions of Carolina: Issued by the proprietors of Carolina in 1669, who aimed to create a feudal society composed of nobles, serfs, and slaves. Four-fifths of the land was owned by the planters. Colonial leaders established an elected assembly and a head-right system to attract immigrants, who were allowed to own the remaining land. It allowed for religious tolerance, both for Christian dissenters and Jewish people.

Quakers: Formally known as the Society of Friends. A Protestant church that advocated that everyone was equal, including women, Africans, and American Indians.

Characteristics of English Colonial Societies

Mercantilism: The theory that a government should control economic pursuits to further a nation's national power, especially in the acquisition of silver and gold. Prominent in Europe from the sixteenth to the eighteenth centuries. Replaced by free trade.

Great Awakening: A Protestant religious movement that took place across the Thirteen Colonies during the 1730s and 1740s. It indirectly helped spur religious tolerance and led to the founding of many universities.

TEST WHAT YOU LEARNED

Questions 1–4 refer to the image below.

This painting depicts New Netherland colonists and American Indians in 1626.

1. The Dutch relationship with American Indians can best be described as one based on

   (A) conquest

   (B) one-sided trade

   (C) mutually beneficial exchange

   (D) an alliance against the French

2. Dutch colonists were primarily motivated to establish settlements because

   (A) they wanted to establish permanent colonies that would become part of their global empire

   (B) they pursued economic gains

   (C) they needed additional territory, due to overpopulation in the Netherlands

   (D) they desired to challenge Spanish naval supremacy

3. Both Dutch and French colonies adopted which of the following colonization practices?

   (A) Intermarriage with Native Americans

   (B) Development and promotion of the slave trade

   (C) Establishment of permanent colonies for entire families

   (D) Establishment of colonies that promoted religious tolerance

4. Which of the following English colonies shared the religious tolerance of Dutch colonies?

   (A) Georgia

   (B) Massachusetts Bay

   (C) Plymouth

   (D) Pennsylvania

Questions 5–7 refer to the excerpt below.

". . . if enslaving our fellow creatures be a practice agreeable to Christianity, it is answered in a great measure in many treatises at home, to which I refer you . . .

. . . we are all apt to shift off the blame from ourselves and lay it upon others, how justly in our case you may judge. The Negroes are enslaved by the Negroes themselves before they are purchased by the masters of the ships who bring them here. It is, to be sure, at our choice whether we buy them or not, so this then is our crime, folly, or whatever you will please to call it."

Reverend Peter Fontaine, "A Defense of Slavery in Virginia," 1757

5. Fontaine's ideas suggest that British colonists justified slavery by

   (A) emphasizing how slavery was based upon Christian principles

   (B) underscoring how the system of slavery already existed outside of North America

   (C) relying on the concept that slavery was part of the "natural order" of the human races

   (D) maintaining that "inferior people" were destined to serve as slaves, according to English law

6. Slavery evolved in seventeenth century British North America because

   (A) slaves were brought with the first settlers to Jamestown

   (B) slavery was developed after the deaths of thousands of enslaved American Indians from Old World diseases

   (C) the Anglican Church actively encouraged the transport of slaves to the colonies in North America as a source of cheap labor

   (D) the developing plantation system required a source of cheap labor after the initial influx of indentured servants decreased

7. Which of the following individuals would most likely reject Fontaine's arguments?

   (A) A former indentured servant in Virginia

   (B) A plantation owner in Carolina

   (C) A Quaker in Pennsylvania

   (D) An Anglican in Massachusetts

Questions 8–10 refer to the excerpt below.

". . . the Enlightenment slowly helped undermine the power of traditional authority—something the Great Awakening did as well. But unlike the Great Awakening, the Enlightenment encouraged men and women to look to themselves—not to God—for guidance as to how to live their lives and to shape society. Enlightenment thought, with its emphasis on human rationality, encouraged a new emphasis on education and a heightened interest in politics and government. Most Enlightenment figures did not challenge religion and insisted that rational inquiry would support, not undermine, Christianity."

Alan Brinkley, *American History: Connecting with the Past*, 2014

8. Which of the following would most directly oppose the sentiments of the Enlightenment as described by Brinkley?

    (A) Deist religious views

    (B) Puritan sermons

    (C) Benjamin Franklin's *Poor Richard's Almanack*

    (D) Anne Hutchinson's arguments at her trial

9. Advocates of Enlightenment ideals, such as those expressed in the excerpt, would have most likely supported which of the following movements?

    (A) Mercantilism

    (B) Empiricism

    (C) Monarchism

    (D) Colonialism

10. Enlightenment ideals would inspire the American colonies through which of the following events?

    (A) The passage of the Navigation Acts

    (B) The creation of the Dominion of New England

    (C) The outcome of Bacon's Rebellion

    (D) The Glorious Revolution

Part B: Key Terms

This key terms list is the same as the list in the Test What You Already Know section earlier in this chapter. Based on what you have now learned, again ask yourself the following questions:

- Can I define this key term and use it in a sentence?
- Can I provide an example related to this key term?
- Could I correctly answer a multiple-choice question about this key term?
- Could I correctly answer a free-response question about this key term?

Check off the key terms if you can answer "yes" to at least three of these questions.

European Colonization in the New World

☐ New France   ☐ New Amsterdam   ☐ Jamestown

☐ Dutch East India Company   ☐ Pueblo Revolt   ☐ Virginia Company

Indentured Servitude

☐ Indentured servants   ☐ Bacon's Rebellion

Slavery

☐ Atlantic slave trade   ☐ Stono Rebellion

English Conflicts with American Indians

☐ Pequot War   ☐ King Philip's War

The Development of English Colonial Societies in North America

☐ Puritans   ☐ Great Migration of the 1630s   ☐ Charter of Liberties and Privileges

☐ Plymouth

☐ Mayflower Compact   ☐ Salem witch trials   ☐ Fundamental Constitutions of Carolina

☐ Massachusetts Bay Company   ☐ Fundamental Orders of Connecticut   ☐ Quakers

Characteristics of English Colonial Societies

☐ Mercantilism   ☐ Great Awakening

Next Steps

Step 1: Tally your correct answers from Part A and review the quiz explanations at the end of this chapter.

1. C
2. B
3. A
4. D
5. B

6. D
7. C
8. B
9. B
10. D

____ out of 10 questions

Step 2: Count the number of key terms you checked off in Part B.

____ out of 24 key terms

Step 3: Compare your Test What You Already Know results to these Test What You Learned results to see how exam-ready you are for this period.

For More Practice:

- Read (or reread) the comprehensive review for this period in Chapter 13.
- Go to kaptest.com to complete the online quiz questions for 1607–1754.
  - Haven't registered your book yet? Go to kaptest.com/moreonline to begin.

ANSWERS AND EXPLANATIONS

Test What You Already Know

1. D

The excerpt describes how the Spanish colonizers achieved more economic success in the New World than English colonizers did in the seventeenth century. Mercantilism was the theory that a government should control its economic pursuits and take advantage of its colonies, to advance its own power. Therefore, **(D)** is correct. (A) is incorrect because the Enlightenment was an intellectual movement that promoted reason. Monarchism and democratization are political systems, but the excerpt focuses on economic developments, making (B) and (C) incorrect.

2. C

Simmonds claims that Spanish conquistadors achieved economic success because the American Indian settlements in Spain's New World were populous and sophisticated. However, Spanish colonizers likely attributed their success to their own skill and religious zeal and would disagree with Simmonds's assessment. Spanish colonizers founded Santa Fe, making **(C)** correct. (A) is incorrect because Quebec was primarily populated by French traders, for whom Simmonds's argument would be largely irrelevant. (B) and (D) are incorrect because Jamestown and Plymouth were primarily populated by English settlers, who would likely agree with Simmonds's justifications.

3. B

Colonists in Jamestown achieved economic success after John Rolfe improved their methods for cultivating the tobacco plant, making tobacco a prosperous cash crop. Therefore, **(B)** is correct, because the question is asking what factor did *not* contribute to economic hardship. The contagious nature of diseases such as typhoid and dysentery decreased the population of English settlers in Jamestown, which lowered their pool of laborers and added to their economic challenges; (A) and (C) are incorrect. (D) is also incorrect; the swamp that surrounded the colony made Jamestown a difficult area to settle, contributing to the colony's economic difficulties.

4. C

Historical accounts describe the Salem witch trials as filled with emotion and hysteria, which is also supported by the facial expressions and gestures of the individuals in the image. Thus, **(C)** is correct. While there were religious motivations, the trials did not mirror religious ceremonies; therefore, (A) is incorrect. The magistrates overseeing the trial were strictly male, as was the norm in Puritan society; (B) is incorrect. The image does not present evidence that the judge is impartial, and the courtroom depicted shows a one-sided mob with no counterpoint offered in favor of the defendants. Thus, (D) is incorrect.

5. B

The way in which the Puritan clergy handled the Salem witch trials was widely criticized in the colonies and in Europe; in fact, the trials caused colonists to shift away from church-controlled governments. Therefore, **(B)** is correct. Now viewed as a classic example of mass hysteria, the Salem witch trials caused many colonists to begin questioning the existence of witchcraft; (C) is incorrect. The Salem witch trials did not lead to the establishment of United States courts of law, so (A) is incorrect. Colonial courts of law eventually evolved into the United States legal system, well after the Salem witch trials had concluded. Also, there is no evidence that the controversy resulting from the Salem witch trials led to improved rights for Puritan women; Puritan women continued to hold subservient roles in Puritan society. Thus, (D) is also incorrect.

6. A

During the seventeenth century, the population of the Massachusetts Bay colony grew rapidly. In the Great Migration of the 1630s, nearly 20,000 Puritan families immigrated across the Atlantic Ocean to Massachusetts. Before the Salem witch trials began in 1692, this population continued to grow because it had a balanced gender distribution and the climate of Massachusetts was analogous to that of Western Europe. Thus, **(A)** is correct and (B) is incorrect. The Massachusetts Bay Colony did not significantly assimilate with American Indians or incorporate African Americans as slaves, so (C) and (D) are incorrect.

7. B

Beginning in the Renaissance, European philosophers began to emphasize the importance of science and reason, looking beyond religious beliefs to better understand their lives. This led to the seventeenth-century movement known as the Enlightenment. Enlightenment principles directly contradicted the practices of trying and executing people for witchcraft. Thus, **(B)** is correct. During the Reformation, witch hunting actually became more popular, especially in areas contested by both Protestants and Catholics; therefore, (A) is incorrect. During the First Great Awakening, theocratic attitudes further declined. However, leaders of this Great Awakening prized spiritual matters as paramount; therefore, it is unlikely that they would have separated religious leadership from community trials. (C) is incorrect. During the Inquisition, supposed heretics encountered aggressive persecution; members of the Inquisition would have likely been open to investigating accusations of witchcraft. (D) is incorrect.

8. C

Slaves were brought to the English colonies in North America as early as 1619, and the system of slavery was legalized in Virginia by the 1660s. Accordingly, the statute excerpt indicates that some of slavery's defining features had been written into law by 1662. The excerpt specifically mentions that engaging in sexual relations with slaves would result in punishment in the form of fines; thus, **(C)** is correct. The act did not directly attempt to control the growing slave population; in fact, many slave owners forced slaves to reproduce in order to build up their workforce. (A) is incorrect. Although the excerpt addresses the status of mixed-race children, children did not necessarily receive any particular privileges if they had mixed-race heritage, making (B) incorrect. Lastly, Massachusetts was actually the first colony to legalize slavery (in 1634), making (D) incorrect.

9. C

The 1662 statute established hereditary slavery, to address the issue of children born to white male colonists and African American women. According to this statute, children of female slaves and male colonists were slaves. Thus, **(C)** is correct. During the period prior to Bacon's Rebellion in 1676, indentured servants continued to dominate the labor force in Virginia; the African American slave population was less than 1,000 when the 1662 statute was passed. Slavery was much more common in the West Indies. Also, slaves in the West Indies engaged in more strenuous labor in a hotter climate. Therefore, (A) is incorrect. White colonists could be fined for engaging in sexual relations with slaves, not for owning slaves, according to the 1662 statue, so (B) is incorrect as well. Major slave rebellions occurred in the eighteenth century, not the seventeenth century. Therefore, (D) is incorrect.

10. C

Georgia was established in 1733 as a haven for English prisoners who were in debt. The proprietors of Georgia were unique in banning slavery when they founded the colony; **(C)** is correct. The governments of Massachusetts, New York, and Virginia did not initially ban slavery; in fact, Massachusetts was the first colony to legalize slavery in 1634. Therefore, (A), (B), and (D) are incorrect.

Test What You Learned

1. C

The Dutch were primarily concerned with acquiring wealth in the New World, and they sought to trade with American Indians. Therefore, **(C)** is correct. (A) is incorrect; the Dutch were not interested in conquest or territorial expansion in North America, although other European empires were. (B) is incorrect because the Dutch freely and fairly traded with the American Indians for resources like furs. (D) is incorrect because France's holdings in the New World were primarily in the northern regions of North America, in modern-day Canada; the French were not in direct competition with the Dutch or their American Indian trading partners.

2. B

The Dutch primarily sought wealth in the New World. Therefore, the Dutch claimed New Netherland, now New York, as a trading outpost; **(B)** is correct. (A) is incorrect, as the Dutch were interested in lucrative trade, not in territorial expansion. Inhabitants of the Netherlands had a high standard of living, and this region maintained enough resources to support its population; thus, (C) is also incorrect. While the Dutch had recently escaped Spanish domination, they secured their continued freedom through trade rather than direct military pursuits; therefore, (D) is incorrect.

3. A

Both French and Dutch male colonists intermarried with Native American groups in North America; **(A)** is correct. While all European colonizers were active in the slave trade to some extent, France and the Netherlands were the least involved; (B) is incorrect. The French and the Dutch did not adopt the English strategy of sending entire families to live in the colonies, so (C) is incorrect. While the Dutch colonies did promote religious tolerance, the French colonies established Catholicism as the only acceptable religion. Therefore, (D) is incorrect.

4. D

Pennsylvania most closely resembled the Dutch colonies when it came to broad religious tolerance. While Pennsylvania did not formally extend protection to Judaism, it offered religious liberty to all Christian denominations; **(D)** is correct. Georgia provided religious liberty to all Protestants, but it specifically excluded Catholics; thus, (A) is incorrect. Both Massachusetts Bay and the Plymouth colonies were founded by Puritans who disapproved of other forms of Protestantism and deeply disapproved of Catholicism and Judaism; therefore, (B) and (C) are incorrect.

5. B

Slavery was viewed as a business transaction and a necessity for plantation owners, who had to compete with other colonies that used slave labor. The fact that American colonists did not themselves enslave Africans, but rather purchased already-enslaved people, was used as a justification for plantation owners who wanted to "shift off the blame" from themselves. Therefore, **(B)** is correct. (A) is incorrect because Fontaine, who was a minister, implies that purchasing slaves from the ships that brought them from Africa might be labeled a "crime" or "folly." According to this excerpt, Fontaine does not appear to accept slavery as the "natural order," so (C) is incorrect. Fontaine also does not shift the blame to any English law, so (D) is incorrect.

6. D

As jobs became available in England, fewer individuals and families sought to travel to North America in order to work as indentured servants. At the same time that prosperity was returning to England, the English colonies' plantations required more labor. Therefore, by the 1660s, different colonies began to pass legislation that made persons of African descent slaves for life. **(D)** is correct. While the first Africans to come to British North America did arrive in Jamestown in 1619, the concept of slavery did not yet formally exist in the American colonies; (A) is incorrect. It is true that the deaths of many American Indians thwarted Spain's original plan to use them for plantation labor. However, this was not a reason for the rise of slavery in British North America, so (B) is incorrect. The Anglican Church did not endorse slavery as a source of cheap labor, so (C) is also incorrect.

7. C

Quakers were the first group to publicly declare that slavery was immoral because one human could not

own another human. Therefore, **(C)** is correct. Some former indentured servants who received grants of land after their indenture bought slaves themselves, so (A) is incorrect. Plantation owners in Carolina relied heavily on slave labor for their livelihood, so (B) is incorrect. (D) is incorrect because Massachusetts was actually the first colony in British North America to legalize slavery in 1643.

8. B

Puritan ministers believed that God's hand guided their lives. Therefore, their religious views did not align with the Enlightenment's emphasis on individual education and introspection; **(B)** is correct. Deists' view of God's role in the world is reflected in the excerpt; (A) is incorrect. Benjamin Franklin's focus on practical and scientific thinking was directly aligned with Enlightenment ideas; (C) is incorrect. Anne Hutchinson used reasoning similar to Enlightenment philosophy to interrogate her faith and challenge the views of the Puritan clergy in the Massachusetts Bay Colony; (D) is also incorrect.

9. B

Empiricism was the view that knowledge comes from experience and observation of the world, one of the core concepts of the Enlightenment, so **(B)** is correct. Mercantilism (the economic strategy of adding colonies to benefit an empire), monarchism (the system of government in which a monarchy leads the state), and colonialism (the policy in which a mother country makes decisions for its colonies) were British systems that were in opposition to Enlightenment thinking. Therefore, (A), (C), and (D) are incorrect.

10. D

The Glorious Revolution occurred in 1688 when King William III and Queen Mary I were brought to the throne in England, replacing the absolute rule of King James II. With Parliament, William and Mary enacted the English Bill of Rights, which became the foundation of English law and later inspired American colonists during their revolution. Therefore, **(D)** is correct. The Navigation Acts and the Dominion of New England placed restrictions on American colonists; (A) and (B) are incorrect. Although Bacon's Rebellion shared ideals similar to the Glorious Revolution, democratic measures passed by the House of Burgesses were rescinded after the rebellion's failure; thus, (C) is incorrect.

CHAPTER 5

Period 3: 1754–1800

LEARNING OBJECTIVES

After studying this time period, you will be able to:

- Describe how conflict and cooperation among empires, nations, and individuals have affected North American development

- Describe the reasons for internal U.S. migration and settlement and the effect of such migration on American life

- Describe the role of political philosophies in the developing American identity

- Describe how reformers and activists have changed American society

- Explain the causes and effects of U.S. economic, diplomatic, and military initiatives in North America and globally

- Explain the impact on U.S. politics of conflicting views of the federal government's role

- Chart the development of, and changes in, American politics

TIMELINE

Date	Event
1754–1763	The Seven Years' War takes place.
1764	The British pass the Sugar Act.
1765	The British enact the Quartering Act and the Stamp Act.
1770	The Boston Massacre occurs.
1773	The Boston Tea Party occurs as a reaction against the Tea Act.
1774	The British impose the Intolerable Acts (the Coercive Acts). The First Continental Congress meets in Philadelphia.
1775	The America Revolution begins. The Battles of Lexington and Concord take place. The Second Continental Congress meets. The Battle of Bunker Hill is fought.
1776	Thomas Paine's *Common Sense* is published. The Declaration of Independence is signed.
1777	The Americans win the Battle of Saratoga.
1781	The Articles of Confederation are ratified. The Battle of Yorktown is the final major battle of the Revolution.
1783	The Treaty of Paris formally ends the American Revolution.
1787	Shays' Rebellion occurs in Springfield, Massachusetts. The Constitutional Convention takes place in Philadelphia.
1788	The U.S. Constitution is ratified.
1789	George Washington becomes the first president.
1791	The Bill of Rights is ratified.
1794	The Whiskey Rebellion occurs in Pennsylvania.
1797	John Adams becomes the second president.

TEST WHAT YOU ALREADY KNOW

Part A: Quiz

Questions 1–3 refer to the excerpt below.

"And We do further declare it to be Our Royal Will and Pleasure, for the present as aforesaid, to reserve under our Sovereignty, Protection, and Dominion . . . all the Lands and Territories not included within the Limits of Our said Three new Governments, or within the Limits of the Territory granted to the Hudson's Bay Company, as also all the Lands and Territories lying to the Westward of the Sources of the Rivers which fall into the Sea from the West and North West as aforesaid.

And We do hereby strictly forbid, on Pain of our Displeasure, all our loving Subjects from making any Purchases or Settlements whatever, or taking Possession of any of the Lands above reserved without our especial leave and Licence for that Purpose first obtained.

And We do further strictly enjoin and require all Persons whatever who have either wilfully or inadvertently seated themselves upon any Lands within the Countries above described . . . forthwith to remove themselves from such Settlements."

The Royal Proclamation, 1763

1. As described in the excerpt, after The Seven Years' War, the British sought to

    (A) create a lasting peace with the French still residing in their new land acquisitions

    (B) settle the newly acquired lands to establish commerce with American Indians

    (C) prevent westward expansion in order to mend relations with natives previously allied with the French

    (D) establish local governments that could control French Quebec and Spanish Florida

2. Immediately following The Seven Years' War, American colonists were determined to

    (A) declare independence from Great Britain

    (B) settle lands in the Ohio River Valley

    (C) create commercial relationships with American Indians

    (D) repay debt incurred during the war

3. Which of the following was a result of colonial encroachment on native lands in the Great Lakes region?

    (A) A renewed tension between French traders and American colonists

    (B) An uprising led by Pontiac

    (C) Hostilities between British regulars on the frontiers and American settlers

    (D) Taxes on colonists to prevent their westward expansion

Questions 4–7 refer to the excerpt below.

"ARTICLE 2. His Majesty consents to withdraw all his troops and garrisons from all posts and places within the boundary lines assigned by the treaty of peace to the United States. The evacuation is to take place on or before the 1st of June, 1796. All settlers in those parts to enjoy private property rights and become citizens of the United States in one year unless allegiance is declared to His Britannic Majesty.

ARTICLE 6. Gives to British subjects the power of recovering debts due to them by American citizens previous to the treaty of peace; which debts have not been recovered hitherto, on account of some legal impediments. The United States agree to make full and complete compensation to the creditors who have suffered by those impediments. The amount of the losses and damages is to be ascertained by five commissioners — two to be appointed by Great Britain, two by the President of the United States, and one by the other four."

Treaty of Amity, Commerce, and Navigation (Jay's Treaty), 1794

4. One of the major terms of Jay's Treaty was that the British would

    (A) remove troops and garrisons from American homes and buildings

    (B) repay debts they had collected from Americans after the war

    (C) remove British soldiers from forts in American territories according to the Treaty of Paris

    (D) evacuate British citizens from the Northwest territory

5. As a stipulation of the treaty, America

    (A) guaranteed partial payment to British merchants for debts that existed before the war

    (B) agreed to assume the debts of its citizens and pay the British

    (C) argued that the British merchants were falsifying claims and refused to acknowledge them

    (D) insisted that British merchants relinquish all debt claims held with the Americans

6. Which of the following was a result of the provisions of the treaty?

   (A) The British immediately began evacuating their forts and posts in the Old Northwest.

   (B) Citizen Edmund Genet, a French minister, began advocating war against the British.

   (C) Many Americans were angry because they saw the treaty as a sign of weakness against their former enemy.

   (D) John Jay was hailed as a hero in America because of his efforts to prevent another war.

7. Which of the following statements is true regarding the years following the passage of Jay's Treaty?

   (A) Britain upheld its agreements with the United States as set forth in the treaty.

   (B) Britain failed to follow through with its commitments outlined in the treaty.

   (C) Spain became more hostile to American commercial interests because it saw the United States as a British ally.

   (D) France sought to compete with Britain by strengthening its own ties with American commercial interests.

5

Questions 8–10 refer to the excerpt below.

"SECTION 1. Be it enacted by the Senate and House of Representatives of the United States of America, in Congress assembled, That if any persons shall unlawfully combine or conspire together, with intent to oppose any measure or measures of the government of the United States, which are or shall be directed by proper authority, or to impede the operation of any law of the United States, or to intimidate or prevent any person holding a place or office in or under the government of the United States, from undertaking, performing or executing his trust or duty, and if any person or persons, with intent as aforesaid, shall counsel, advise or attempt to procure any insurrection, riot, unlawful assembly, or combination . . ."

Alien and Sedition Acts, 1798

8. The Alien and Sedition Acts were passed in response to which event?

   (A) Jay's Treaty

   (B) Pinckney's Treaty

   (C) The Louisiana Purchase

   (D) The XYZ Affair

9. The underlying purpose of the Alien and Sedition Acts was to

   (A) prevent Federalists from controlling Congress

   (B) silence anti-Federalist critics of the current government's policies

   (C) restrict the president's ability to deport immigrants

   (D) eliminate political corruption within federal offices

10. What was the main purpose of the Virginia and Kentucky Resolutions?

    (A) To counter laws that encroached on the rights of individual Americans

    (B) To advocate state secession from the federal government

    (C) To promote open relations with Britain to check the power of the Federalists

    (D) To suggest an alliance with the French in opposition to the federal government

Part B: Key Terms

The following is a list of the major people, places, and events for 1754–1800. You will likely see many of these on the AP U.S. History exam.

For each key term ask yourself the following questions:

- Can I describe this key term?
- Can I discuss this key term in the context of other events?
- Could I correctly answer a multiple-choice question about this key term?
- Could I correctly answer a free-response question about this key term?

Check off the key terms if you can answer "yes" to at least three of these questions.

The Seven Years' War

- ☐ The Seven Years' War
- ☐ Albany Plan of Union
- ☐ Treaty of Paris (1763)

Effects of the Seven Years' War

- ☐ Proclamation of 1763
- ☐ Currency Act
- ☐ Sugar Act
- ☐ Quartering Act
- ☐ Stamp Act
- ☐ Stamp Act Congress
- ☐ Sons and Daughters of Liberty
- ☐ Declaratory Act
- ☐ Townshend Acts
- ☐ Boston Massacre
- ☐ Committees of Correspondence
- ☐ *Gaspee* Affair
- ☐ Tea Act
- ☐ Boston Tea Party
- ☐ Quebec Act
- ☐ Intolerable Acts

The American Revolution

- ☐ Declaration and Resolves
- ☐ First Continental Congress
- ☐ American Revolution
- ☐ Enlightenment
- ☐ Second Continental Congress
- ☐ Declaration of Independence
- ☐ Loyalists
- ☐ Patriots
- ☐ Battle of Saratoga
- ☐ Treaty of Paris (1783)

American Indians during and after the Revolution

- ☐ Northwest Indian War

The Impact of the Enlightenment

☐ Separation of powers   ☐ Direct democracy

The Articles of Confederation

☐ Articles of Confederation   ☐ Northwest Ordinance of 1787   ☐ Shays' Rebellion

The Constitutional Convention

☐ Constitutional Convention   ☐ House of Representatives   ☐ Electoral College

☐ Connecticut Compromise   ☐ Senate   ☐ Three-Fifths Compromise

The Debate over Ratification

☐ Ratification   ☐ Anti-Federalists   ☐ Bill of Rights

☐ Federalists

Washington's Presidency and the New Republic

☐ George Washington   ☐ Bank of the United States   ☐ Republican Motherhood

☐ Whiskey Rebellion

Development of Foreign Policy

☐ French Revolution   ☐ Farewell Address

Adams as Second President

☐ John Adams   ☐ Kentucky Resolution   ☐ Virginia Resolution

☐ Alien and Sedition Acts

Next Steps

Step 1: Tally your correct answers from Part A and review the quiz explanations at the end of this chapter.

1.	C	6.	C
2.	B	7.	B
3.	B	8.	D
4.	C	9.	B
5.	B	10.	A

____ out of 10 questions

Step 2: Count the number of key terms you checked off in Part B.

____ out of 55 key terms

Step 3: Read the Key Takeaways in this chapter.

Step 4: Consult the table below and follow the instructions based on your performance.

If You Got...	Do This
80% or more of the Test What You Already Know assessment correct (8 or more questions from Part A and 44 or more key terms from Part B)	• Read definitions in this chapter for all the key terms you didn't check off. • Complete the Test What You Learned assessment in this chapter.
50% or less of the Test What You Already Know assessment correct (5 or fewer questions from Part A and 28 or fewer key terms from Part B)	• Read the comprehensive review for this period in Chapter 14. • If you are short on time, read only the High-Yield sections. • Read through all of the key term definitions in this chapter. • Complete the Test What You Learned assessment in this chapter.
Any other result	• Read the High-Yield sections in the comprehensive review of this period in Chapter 14. • Read definitions in this chapter for all the key terms you didn't check off. • Complete the Test What You Learned assessment in this chapter.

ESSENTIAL CONTENT

Key Takeaways: 1754–1800

1. After the British and the colonists won the French and Indian War, England faced enormous debt. The resulting taxation of the colonists led to resentment and tension with England. The Boston Massacre and Boston Tea Party were two notable examples of this increasingly troubled relationship.

2. Colonial leaders called for resistance to imperial rule and demanded that their rights be respected. New experiments with democracy and republican forms of government came about with the Continental Congress, the ideas of Benjamin Franklin and Thomas Paine, and, ultimately, the Declaration of Independence.

3. After the American Revolution, the Articles of Confederation united the newly formed states. However, the federal government remained very weak, which was made evident by Shays' Rebellion. Debates on how to govern the new country culminated in the calling of the Constitutional Convention.

4. Throughout the presidencies of George Washington and John Adams, the Federalists and Anti-Federalists debated on how the young nation should manage its economy, foreign affairs, and internal relations with the new states. The Federalists, led by Alexander Hamilton, favored a stronger central government. The Anti-Federalists, led by Thomas Jefferson, favored giving more power to the individual states.

5. The development of a distinct American foreign policy emerged. George Washington warned against becoming entangled in foreign affairs, such as the French Revolution, and preferred diplomatic initiatives, like Jay's Treaty and Pinckney's Treaty, to deal with continued European presence in America.

6. Migration trends and competition over boundaries, resources, and trade fueled ethnic tensions and sparked nativist sentiments. The relationship of the United States with American Indian groups continued to evolve, often centering on conflict regarding native lands.

Key Terms: 1754–1800

Remember that the AP U.S. History exam tests you on the depth of your knowledge, not just your ability to recall facts. While we have provided brief definitions here, you will need to know these terms in even more depth for the AP exam, including how terms connect to broader historical themes and understandings.

The Seven Years' War

The Seven Years' War: 1754–1763. Featured Britain and France, and their colonial and native allies, fighting for control of North America east of the Mississippi. Although the British won, they incurred massive debts in the process. This led to trouble down the road for them.

Albany Plan of Union: A proposal by the Albany Congress, under the guidance of Benjamin Franklin, during the French and Indian War. It called for a confederation of colonies to defend against attack by European and native foes. Rejected by the colonial assemblies due to concern over the central consolidation of power and by the British government due to concern that it allowed for too much colonial independence.

Effects of the Seven Years' War

Proclamation of 1763: In reaction to Pontiac's Rebellion, King George III barred American colonists from settling west of the Appalachian Mountains. The British saw this as a quick and easy way to make peace while securing the fur trade. Colonists, however, were incensed by the crown's interference in their ability to settle land they had won in the French and Indian War. This was an important contributing factor to the American Revolution.

Currency Act: A law passed by Parliament in 1764. It limited the use of colonial paper money, in order to protect British merchants from depreciation. While not a major contributing factor to the American Revolution, it did signify growing British interest in regulating the colonies.

Sugar Act: A 1764 law that raised the previous amount demanded on sweeteners (molasses and sugar). Part of British attempts to pay off debt from the French and Indian War.

Quartering Act: A 1765 act of Parliament that required colonial citizens to provide room and board for British soldiers stationed in America. Wildly unpopular. This practice was later banned by the Third Amendment to the Constitution.

Stamp Act: A pivotal 1765 law. It required that all paper in the colonies, from death and marriage certificates to newspapers, have a stamp affixed signifying that the required tax had been paid.

Stamp Act Congress: A meeting of representatives of nine of the Thirteen Colonies. They sent word to England that only colonial legislatures had the authority to tax the colonists. Repealed in 1766 and replaced with the Declaratory Act.

Treaty of Paris (1763): Treaty that capped off the French and Indian War. The British took control of French Canada and Spanish Florida, effectively removing France's presence from North America.

Sons and Daughters of Liberty: A group of Patriot activists who intimidated tax collectors by attacking their homes, burning them in effigy, and even tarring and feathering them. They also ransacked warehouses that held stamps and burned them to the ground.

Declaratory Act: Replaced the Stamp Act. A 1766 law that maintained the right of the crown to tax the colonies, as Parliament's authority was identical in both Britain and North America.

Townshend Acts: A revenue plan passed by Parliament in 1767. It imposed harsher taxes on the purveyors of imported goods such as glass, paper, and tea. In addition, a special board of customs officials was appointed to enforce writs of assistance. Repealed in 1770.

Boston Massacre: A landmark incident on March 5, 1770, that helped alienate the American people from Parliament and King George III. Angered by the Quartering Act, a crowd of Bostonians harassed the British troops guarding a local customs house. The guards fired upon the crowd, killing five and wounding six protesters. John Adams would defend the guards tried for this incident and secure their acquittal.

Committees of Correspondence: A means by which Patriots could circulate letters of protest against British policies. It functioned as a kind of shadow opposition government in the run-up to the American Revolutionary War. Vital in organizing the Continental Congress.

***Gaspee* Affair:** The *Gaspee* was a British warship commissioned to capture vessels carrying smuggled goods before they reached the colonies. The *Gaspee* ran aground on the shores of Rhode Island. The Sons of Liberty set fire to the boat, an event celebrated throughout coastal colonial towns as a victory for the tax-burdened consumer.

Tea Act: A 1773 law that actually lowered the price of tea, but colonists were now wary of any British attempt to collect revenue. They refused to purchase the tea.

Boston Tea Party: In protest of the Tea Act, Bostonians dressed as American Indians boarded British merchant ship and dumped their tea into Boston Harbor. Resulted in closure of the harbor, the colonial charter of Massachusetts being revoked, and the Quartering Act.

Quebec Act: A 1774 act of Parliament that allowed the former French region to expand its borders, taking away potential lands from colonists in the Ohio River Valley. Even more offensive to the largely Protestant colonists, it also allowed Quebec citizens to practice Catholicism freely.

Intolerable Acts: A colonial term for a number of punitive laws passed by the British Parliament in response to the Boston Tea Party. Also called the Coercive Acts.

The American Revolution

Declaration and Resolves: An attempt by the First Continental Congress to reconcile the Thirteen Colonies with the British Empire. Addressed to King George III, it urged him to correct the wrongs incurred by the colonists while simultaneously acknowledging the authority of Parliament to regulate colonial trade and commerce.

First Continental Congress: Organized in 1774 as a response to the Intolerable Acts, colonial leaders managed to urge their colonies to expand military reserves and organize boycotts of British goods in the meantime.

American Revolution: An anti-colonial revolt (1765–1773) in which the Thirteen Colonies threw off the yoke of the British Empire and established the United States of America. Distinct from but related to the American Revolutionary War (1775–1783). Its beginning is traced to the aftermath of the French and Indian War, when Britain sought to resolve the debt that war had created.

Enlightenment: An eighteenth-century philosophical and intellectual movement that prized reason. It challenged traditional notions of reflexive obedience to the Church and to monarchy, and laid the groundwork for the scientific revolution and Industrial Revolution.

Second Continental Congress: An assembly of delegates from across the Thirteen Colonies (1775–1781). It passed the Declaration of Independence and the Articles of Confederation.

Declaration of Independence: Announced the colonies' official break from England, making the United States a country in its own right. It contained a preamble that heavily reflected Enlightenment philosophy regarding natural rights, as well as 27 grievances and charges of wrongdoing directed at the crown and Parliament.

Loyalists: Colonists who disagreed with the Patriots and wanted to preserve ties with England. Often older, wealthy, educated citizens of the Middle or Southern colonies whose allegiance to England benefited their social, economic, and/or political standing.

Patriots: Activists for independence from the British Empire. Mostly young New Englanders and Virginians. Often did not have significant status in society. Many volunteered their time to the Continental Army, typically without pay.

Battle of Saratoga: An umbrella term for two battles fought 18 days apart in autumn 1777. British forces under General Burgoyne attacked U.S. forces led by Horatio Gates and Benedict

Arnold. The British were eventually forced to retreat. News of the American victory led to the introduction of French aid, reshaping the entire war.

Treaty of Paris (1783): Treaty that officially ended the American Revolutionary War. The United States agreed to repay debts to British merchants and promised not to punish Loyalists who chose to remain in the United States. Formal recognition of the United States as an independent country. Set the geographic boundaries between the British Empire and the United States.

American Indians during and after the Revolution

Northwest Indian War: One of the most notable conflicts between the natives and Americans that took place in and around the Ohio River Valley, 1785–1795. A military alliance led by Little Turtle and Blue Jacket attempted to resist the expansion of the United States into the Old Northwest territory. Came to an end in 1794, when 3,000 American soldiers won a sweeping defeat of Little Turtle's forces at the Battle of Fallen Timbers.

The Impact of the Enlightenment

Separation of powers: An Enlightenment concept advocated by the French philosopher Montesquieu in his seminal 1748 work *The Spirit of the Laws*. It is the idea that a government's power should be divided into multiple branches that balance and check each other.

Direct democracy: A form of democracy in which the people directly vote on matters of policy, rather than electing delegates to decide for them as in representative democracy.

The Articles of Confederation

Articles of Confederation: The first constitution of the United States, drafted alongside the Declaration of Independence but by a separate committee. It strongly favored states' rights and forbade Congress from levying taxes. Ratified in 1781. Replaced by the Constitution following Shays' Rebellion.

Northwest Ordinance of 1787: A rare triumph under the Articles of Confederation, it established guidelines for attaining statehood: territories with at least 60,000 people could apply for statehood. If accepted by Congress, the new state would have equal status with other states. It banned slavery north of the Ohio River and east of the Mississippi, thereby guaranteeing future free states in the Midwest.

Shays' Rebellion: An insurrection in Massachusetts (1786–1787) over oppressive taxes and debt collectors. Led by Daniel Shays. It helped spur the Constitutional Convention.

The Constitutional Convention

Constitutional Convention: A meeting that took place in Philadelphia from May 25 to September 17, 1787. Ostensibly called to amend the Articles of Confederation, the majority of the delegates arrived with the intention to simply draft a new constitution, one which is still in use to the present day.

Connecticut Compromise: Agreement that provided the basis for the structure of the legislative branch; also known as the Great Compromise of 1787, or Sherman Compromise. It bridged the gap between the Virginia Plan, which called for representation in both legislative houses to be based on population (proportional representation) and the New Jersey Plan, which called for equal representation in legislative branch, regardless of state population.

House of Representatives: The lower chamber of the United States Congress. Representation is proportional to population. Its size varied over the decades, but was fixed at the current membership of 435 seats by the Reapportionment Act of 1929.

Senate: The upper chamber of the United States Congress. Representation is by state. Each state has two senators regardless of population. Until 1913, senators were appointed by state legislatures. Named for the Roman Senate, upon which it is based.

Electoral College: A compromise at the Constitutional Convention regarding how to elect the president. Electors cast votes as representatives of their states, which delegates believed would protect the election process from corruption and the influence of factions (political parties).

Three-Fifths Compromise: Infamous compromise at the Constitutional Convention. It held that an enslaved person in the South was counted as three-fifths of a person. In addition, the South conceded to the end of the legal importation of slaves in 1808.

The Debate over Ratification

Ratification: The act of giving official certification to a law or treaty. In this period, it often refers to the process of ratifying the U.S. Constitution. Approval from at least nine states was required to ratify the new Constitution, an infringement on state sovereignty as seen by the Anti-Federalists.

Federalists: Supporters of the Constitution. Many of its members later formed the Federalist Party. Leaders included John Jay, Alexander Hamilton, and James Madison, the authors of the *Federalist Papers*; one of the more famous letters is *Federalist No. 10*, which claimed that political parties could not be prevented, but that their influence could be mitigated in a large republic.

Anti-Federalists: A post-revolutionary political faction that was wary of centralization and infringements upon individual liberties, especially when it came to taxation. This criticism spurred the creation of the Bill of Rights and would go on to contribute to the formation of the Democratic-Republicans.

Bill of Rights: Umbrella term for the first 10 Amendments to the U.S. Constitution. It explicitly lists protections for individual rights and state sovereignty. Created to secure the support of Anti-Federalists in ratifying the U.S. Constitution, which initially had no such guarantees.

Washington's Presidency and the New Republic

George Washington: First President. Served 1789–1797. A land surveyor from Virginia, he led colonial militia as an officer in the Seven Years' War. Led the Continental Army during the American Revolutionary War at battles such as Valley Forge and Yorktown. Later presided over the Continental Congress. Among many other acts, he established the informal two-term limit for presidents by declining to run for reelection in 1796.

Whiskey Rebellion: An early test of the American government's power under the new Constitution. Angered by the Federalist government's excise tax imposed on distilled liquors such as whiskey, farmers in western Pennsylvania rebelled over being taxed by a government that seemingly did not represent them. Quickly defeated, it proved the new central government's power to stop rebellions and maintain peace.

Bank of the United States: A national bank in which the federal government held the major financial interest. The national treasury would keep its deposits in the bank, keeping the funds safe and available as loanable funds. The brainchild of Alexander Hamilton. Opposed by Thomas Jefferson on Constitutional grounds.

Republican Motherhood: Ideal that took hold in response to many women's participation in the American Revolution and subsequent desire for expanded roles. Women were now charged with teaching republican values to their children, giving them a new significance in American culture.

Development of Foreign Policy

French Revolution: A period of massive upheaval in 1789–1799 in which the French overthrew their monarchy and established a republic, which in turn gave rise to Napoleon. One of the most important events in world history, it led to the spread of republicanism and Enlightenment ideas. Partly triggered by the debts incurred by France aiding American revolutionaries.

Farewell Address: An open letter penned by George Washington in 1797. It warned the American people to remain neutral with regard to European affairs, to avoid entangling alliances, and to refrain from the formation of political parties.

Adams as Second President

John Adams: Second president. Served 1791–1801. First vice president (1789–1797). Lobbied for declaring independence at the Continental Congress. Signed the Alien and Sedition Acts, and built up the armed forces during the Quasi-War. Died on July 4, 1826, the same day as his friend and political rival Thomas Jefferson.

Alien and Sedition Acts: Laws passed by Congress in 1789. The Alien Acts increased the residency requirement for citizenship from 5 to 14 years and gave the president power to detain and/or deport enemy aliens during wartime. The Sedition Act criminalized the making of false statements that were critical of the president or of Congress.

Kentucky Resolution: One of two notable responses to the Alien and Sedition Acts. Covertly written by Thomas Jefferson, it declared that states could overrule federal law, as the U.S. Constitution drew its powers only from what the sovereign states delegated to it. An important precedent for later acts of nullification.

Virginia Resolution: One of two notable responses to the Alien and Sedition Acts. Covertly written by James Madison, it declared that states could overrule federal law, as the U.S. Constitution drew its powers only from what the sovereign states delegated to it. An important precedent for later acts of nullification.

TEST WHAT YOU LEARNED

Questions 1–3 refer to the excerpt below.

"To these grievous acts and measures Americans cannot submit, but in hopes that their fellow subjects in Great Britain will, on a revision of them, restore us to that state in which both countries found happiness and prosperity, we have for the present only resolved to pursue the following peaceable measures:

To enter into a non-importation, non-consumption, and non-exportation agreement or association.

To prepare an address to the people of Great Britain, and a memorial to the inhabitants of British America, and

To prepare a loyal address to his Majesty, agreeable to resolutions already entered into."

Declaration and Resolves of the First Continental Congress, 1774

1. Unlike previous attempts to unify the British North American colonies, the Declaration and Resolves

   (A) blamed the king for the issues faced by the colonists

   (B) threatened to hurt the British economy

   (C) was formally introduced in Congress

   (D) demonstrated unanimous agreement about how to interact with Britain

2. The main idea expressed in the excerpt was also expressed in which of the following?

   (A) The Virginia and Kentucky Resolutions

   (B) The *Federalist Papers*

   (C) The debate over the admission of Missouri as a state

   (D) The Constitutional Convention of 1787

3. The Revolutionary War began soon after the Declaration and Resolves was sent to Britain. All of the following seemed to favor a British victory EXCEPT

   (A) ample funding

   (B) a powerful navy

   (C) efficient communication

   (D) conflict among colonial troops

Questions 4–6 refer to the image below.

This engraving, by Paul Revere, depicts the Boston Massacre of 1770.

4. Which of the following is true regarding the Boston Massacre?

   (A) It quickly led to the outbreak of war between the British and the American colonists.

   (B) It had relatively little immediate impact because it coincided with the repeal of several Townshend duties.

   (C) It was strongly condemned by John Adams, winning him the admiration of the Patriots.

   (D) It was a result of protests of the Molasses Act.

5. In the immediate aftermath of the Boston Massacre, many of the citizens of the city of Boston

   (A) decided to enlist in the British army in order to obtain weapons to defend themselves

   (B) organized the Boston Tea Party

   (C) circulated propaganda in the form of pamphlets and prints

   (D) looked to George Washington to organize and lead a new colonial military force

6. When John Adams described the victims of the massacre as "a motley rabble of saucy boys, negroes and mulattoes, Irish teagues and outlandish jack tarrs," he was

   (A) implying that one motive behind the disturbance might have been resentment between the social classes

   (B) affirming the right of the common people to organize a demonstration against oppressive British policies

   (C) making a plea to his fellow colonists to respect the rights of immigrants and members of racial and ethnic minority groups

   (D) criticizing the British soldiers for firing on a group of innocent victims

Questions 7–10 refer to the excerpt below.

"One of the expedients of party to acquire influence within particular districts is to misrepresent the opinions and aims of other districts . . . The inhabitants of our Western country have lately had a useful lesson on this head; they have seen, in the negotiation by the Executive, and in the unanimous ratification by the Senate, of the treaty with Spain, . . . decisive proof how unfounded were the suspicions propagated among them of a policy in the General Government and in the Atlantic States unfriendly to their interests in regard to the Mississippi; . . . the . . . two treaties, that with Great Britain, and that with Spain, . . . secure to them everything they could desire, in respect to our foreign relations, towards confirming their prosperity."

George Washington, Farewell Address, 1796

7. Washington's Farewell Address makes reference to both Jay's Treaty and Pinckney's Treaty, in part for the purpose of

   (A) emphasizing the president's accomplishments in office

   (B) encouraging the development of a stronger national identity and foreign policy

   (C) discrediting criticisms of the president made by Federalists

   (D) discouraging radical New Englanders from seceding from the Union

8. President Washington's references to "the expedients of party" and to "the inhabitants of our Western country" indicate what fear?

   (A) The Federalist Party might lose seats in Congress in the next election.

   (B) People living in the West might form a new political party.

   (C) Attacks by American Indians might devastate frontier settlements.

   (D) Westerners' regional identity might be exploited for partisan political purposes.

9. In his Farewell Address, Washington was careful to allude to the fact that Pinckney's Treaty

   (A) guaranteed United States navigation rights on the Mississippi

   (B) contained several provisions unfriendly to England

   (C) stopped the Atlantic states from discriminating against Westerners

   (D) protected the United States from the threat of a French invasion

10. Another important argument within Washington's Farewell Address was his warning against political parties. At this point, all of the following were true EXCEPT

   (A) the Federalists and Anti-Federalists were divided on topics such as the Bank of the United States

   (B) the Federalists had become known as the Democratic-Republican party

   (C) the Anti-Federalists criticized the Proclamation of Neutrality of 1793

   (D) the Democratic-Republican party had been established

Part B: Key Terms

This key terms list is the same as the list in the Test What You Already Know section earlier in this chapter. Based on what you have now learned, again ask yourself the following questions:

- Can I define this key term and use it in a sentence?
- Can I provide an example related to this key term?
- Could I correctly answer a multiple-choice question about this key term?
- Could I correctly answer a free-response question about this key term?

Check off the key terms if you can answer "yes" to at least three of these questions.

The Seven Years' War

- ☐ The Seven Years' War
- ☐ Albany Plan of Union
- ☐ Treaty of Paris (1763)

Effects of the Seven Years' War

- ☐ Proclamation of 1763
- ☐ Currency Act
- ☐ Sugar Act
- ☐ Quartering Act
- ☐ Stamp Act
- ☐ Stamp Act Congress
- ☐ Sons and Daughters of Liberty
- ☐ Declaratory Act
- ☐ Townshend Acts
- ☐ Boston Massacre
- ☐ Committees of Correspondence
- ☐ *Gaspee* Affair
- ☐ Tea Act
- ☐ Boston Tea Party
- ☐ Quebec Act
- ☐ Intolerable Acts

The American Revolution

- ☐ Declaration and Resolves
- ☐ First Continental Congress
- ☐ American Revolution
- ☐ Enlightenment
- ☐ Second Continental Congress
- ☐ Declaration of Independence
- ☐ Loyalists
- ☐ Patriots
- ☐ Battle of Saratoga
- ☐ Treaty of Paris (1783)

American Indians during and after the Revolution

- ☐ Northwest Indian War

The Impact of the Enlightenment

- ☐ Separation of powers
- ☐ Direct democracy

The Articles of Confederation

☐ Articles of Confederation   ☐ Northwest Ordinance of 1787   ☐ Shays' Rebellion

The Constitutional Convention

☐ Constitutional Convention   ☐ House of Representatives   ☐ Electoral College

☐ Connecticut Compromise   ☐ Senate   ☐ Three-Fifths Compromise

The Debate over Ratification

☐ Ratification   ☐ Anti-Federalists   ☐ Bill of Rights

☐ Federalists

Washington's Presidency and the New Republic

☐ George Washington   ☐ Bank of the United States   ☐ Republican Motherhood

☐ Whiskey Rebellion

Development of Foreign Policy

☐ French Revolution   ☐ Farewell Address

Adams as Second President

☐ John Adams   ☐ Kentucky Resolution   ☐ Virginia Resolution

☐ Alien and Sedition Acts

5

Next Steps

Step 1: Tally your correct answers from Part A and review the quiz explanations at the end of this chapter.

1.	B	6.	A
2.	A	7.	B
3.	C	8.	D
4.	B	9.	A
5.	C	10.	B

_____ out of 10 questions

Step 2: Count the number of key terms you checked off in Part B.

_____ out of 55 key terms

Step 3: Compare your Test What You Already Know results to these Test What You Learned results to see how exam-ready you are for this period.

For More Practice:

- Read (or reread) the comprehensive review for this period in Chapter 14.
- Go to kaptest.com to complete the online quiz questions for 1754–1800.
  - Haven't registered your book yet? Go to kaptest.com/moreonline to begin.

ANSWERS AND EXPLANATIONS

Test What You Already Know

1. C

The British intended to conciliate the American Indians who had fought against the British in The Seven Years' War and who resided in the territories Britain acquired in 1763. Preventing expansion would shield the American Indians from violent encroachment by colonists; **(C)** is correct. (A) is incorrect because the British were primarily concerned with the large numbers of American Indians, not French people, living in the new land acquisitions. (B) is incorrect because the British wanted to create peace with the tribes rather than attempt to establish commerce. (D) is incorrect because the British did not struggle with any major challenges with establishing governments in these regions.

2. B

After the war, Americans believed they had fought for and were entitled to settle lands west of the Appalachian Mountains, which included the Ohio River Valley; **(B)** is correct. (A) is incorrect because at this time the colonies still relied on Great Britain; the Declaration of Independence was not signed until 13 years later. The primary financial concern of the colonists was to expand farming settlements in the fertile Ohio River Valley, not to establish economic relationships with American Indians; (C) is incorrect. (D) is incorrect because the colonists did not believe they were responsible for this debt; in fact, tensions arose due to the British efforts to collect funds from the colonies, ultimately leading to the Revolutionary War.

3. B

Although the Proclamation of 1763 forbade settlement past the Appalachian Mountains, it was difficult to enforce and American settlers flooded into Indian lands. **(B)** is correct because this encroachment caused a major uprising led by Pontiac, an Ottawa chief. (A) is incorrect because the American settlers did not experience further conflicts with the French when encroaching on native lands. (C) and (D) are incorrect because this encroachment did not result in hostility toward or taxes from the British.

4. C

According to the terms of the Treaty of Paris of 1783, the British were supposed to evacuate their forts and posts in the Great Lakes region. They did not, which led Supreme Court Justice John Jay to once again call on them to follow the previous terms; therefore, **(C)** is correct. (A) is incorrect because Article 2 of Jay's Treaty does not describe removing troops from American homes, just the forts and posts; following the end of the Revolutionary War and the passage of the Constitution, Americans were no longer required to house British troops. While the Treaty did seek to settle wartime debts, the issue was resolved by issuing trade rights to Americans, not by requiring Britain to repay war debts, making (B) incorrect. (D) is incorrect because the treaty only required the withdrawal of British Army units from forts in the Northwest Territory, not citizens.

5. B

Before the American Revolution, the commercial relationship between British and American merchants was intertwined, so many British merchants were still owed money by Americans after the war. **(B)** is correct because the American government agreed to assume these debts and pay the British in exchange for the British meeting the terms of the treaty. (A), (C), and (D) are incorrect because Article 6 of Jay's Treaty acknowledges the debts and agrees to pay them in exchange for British compliance with the treaty's terms.

6. C

John Jay was seen as a traitor once the public became aware of the treaty; **(C)** is correct. (A) is incorrect, as most of the terms of the treaty were never upheld by the British. The frustration this treaty caused was directed toward Jay rather than the British, making (B) incorrect. (D) is incorrect because Jay was considered a traitor; in fact, his body was burned in effigy in the streets by the angry American public.

7. B

The British never fully upheld their end of Jay's Treaty, and relations eventually deteriorated to the point of another war; therefore, **(B)** is correct. The British failed to evacuate forts or respect American interests and continued to arm hostile Indians in the Old Northwest, making (A) incorrect. While Spain was concerned about Jay's Treaty, it did not become more hostile, but instead negotiated with the United States through Pinckney's Treaty; (C) is incorrect. (D) is incorrect because France did not seek to strengthen its ties to America; in fact, the United States and France were engaged in a naval quasi-war from 1798 to 1800.

8. D

The XYZ Affair of 1797, in which French agents demanded bribe money from American diplomats, angered the American public. The Federalists were able to seize on this anger to win a majority of Congressional seats in the 1798 election, at which time they immediately passed the Alien and Sedition Acts. **(D)** is correct. (A) and (B) are both incorrect; while these treaties both had to do with foreign diplomatic relations (with Britain and Spain, respectively), they were not catalysts for the Alien and Sedition Acts. (C) is incorrect because the Louisiana Purchase occurred in 1803, after the Alien and Sedition Acts.

9. B

The Alien and Sedition Acts were aimed at the anti-Federalist critics of Adams's presidency and his approach to French relations during the XYZ Affair and resulting quasi-war; **(B)** is correct. The Acts were actually put into place by Federalists, who already controlled Congress at this time, making (A) incorrect. (C) is incorrect because the Acts actually allowed the president to imprison and deport noncitizens who were thought dangerous. (D) is incorrect because the legislation punished any government critics not just federal officials.

10. A

The Virginia and Kentucky Resolutions argued that states could nullify, within their borders, laws that were thought to be unconstitutional; **(A)** is correct. (B) is incorrect because the resolutions did not go so far as to suggest that the states would secede from the federal government. Both (C) and (D) are incorrect because these resolutions themselves were not specifically related to foreign policy, although they were passed in response to the Alien and Sedition Acts.

Test What You Learned

1. B

Based on the demands of the First Continental Congress, the Americans promised not to import British goods, purchase or use British goods, or export goods to England to be processed in their factories. Previously, the colonies had maintained healthy economic ties with the British Crown; it wasn't until predatory tax policies went into place that colonists boycotted and otherwise broke ties with Britain. Therefore, **(B)** is correct. (A) is incorrect because the colonists actually appealed to the King to convince Parliament to listen to their demands, looking to him for support. (C) is incorrect because the Declaration and Resolves was not the first attempt at unification to be introduced in Congress. Benjamin Franklin had introduced the Albany Plan to Congress earlier (which was reviewed and eventually rejected). While colonial leaders agreed that they had to demand that Britain repeal the Intolerable Acts, they disagreed on many other points, including how to interact with Britain in the future, making (D) incorrect.

2. A

Much like the First Continental Congress believed their essential rights were being violated, Virginians and Kentuckians believed that their rights to nullify a federal law (specifically, the Alien and Sedition Acts) were being violated. **(A)** is correct. (B) is incorrect because the *Federalist Papers* were written primarily to influence citizens to ratify the Constitution. When Missouri applied for statehood in 1819, the debate centered upon the balance between free and slave states, not essential rights, making (C) incorrect. Finally, (D) is incorrect because, while the ideals of the Constitutional Convention did include popular sovereignty, they also included federalism and a balance of power across all branches of government.

3. C

One of Britain's weaknesses during the Revolutionary War was the ability to communicate quickly and efficiently to its troops; given the distance between England and America, it took a long time for British orders to be communicated and carried out. Therefore, **(C)** is correct. The British army's robust finances and powerful navy were both advantages in the war; (A) and (B) are incorrect. (D) is incorrect because, as various colonies vied for power, infighting occurred among the colonial troops, and this disunity benefited the British military.

4. B

The Boston Massacre occurred in March 1770, but actual fighting between British troops and colonial militia did not begin until April 1775; thus, **(B)** is correct and (A) is incorrect. In the immediate aftermath of the massacre, another event had an even more decisive short-term impact: the repeal of four of the five Townshend duties, an action that helped reduce tensions for the next two to three years. (C) is incorrect because John Adams actually defended the accused British soldiers in a court of law. Lastly, the Molasses Act, while especially egregious to colonists, was passed in 1733, decades before the Boston Massacre; (D) is incorrect.

5. C

Days and weeks after the incident, a propaganda battle was waged between radicals seeking rebellion and loyalists trying to influence opinion back in England; **(C)** is correct. The engraving above was used to make prints that were circulated in the *Boston Gazette*. Few citizens of Boston, including loyalist Tories, decided to enlist in any military force in 1770, much less in the British army, which makes (A) incorrect. (B) is incorrect because the Boston Tea Party was a response to the Tea Act of May 1773, not the Boston Massacre of March 1770. (D) is incorrect because, while citizens would eventually know him as a great leader, George Washington's appointment to lead a new colonial military force did not occur until June 1775.

6. A

John Adams's characterization of the victims is a direct comparison between the uniformed, higher-class British soldiers and the working-class colonists. The context was the animosity that the presence of British troops in Boston had caused, particularly the resentment on the part of many laborers. They resented the competition that British soldiers caused in the search for menial jobs, as well as the Intolerable Acts decree that allowed soldiers to be quartered in the houses of colonists. Therefore, **(A)** is correct. (B) is incorrect because the right to organize had not yet been asserted. (C) is incorrect because Adams himself was a lawyer and a member of a higher class; he was not

advocating specifically for these minority groups. Adams defended the British soldiers in court, so he would not accuse them of actions as described in (D).

7. B

President Washington referenced both treaties as examples of diplomatic initiatives that were preferable to becoming entangled in foreign wars. Additionally, he argued that these treaties benefited the settlers living in the West, in an attempt to further unite the country; **(B)** is correct. Washington wrote his address near the end of his second term with the intention of retiring from office. While he did defend his administration's record, the address was intended to inspire confidence in the federal government, not himself personally; (A) is incorrect. Washington was broadly sympathetic to the Federalist Party, and was not criticized by them, making (C) incorrect. Finally, New Englanders did not consider seceding from the Union until the Hartford Convention in 1814, long after Washington had left office; (D) is incorrect.

8. D

President Washington warned his countrymen not to be swayed by inauthentic appeals to one's regional identity for partisan political purposes; **(D)** is correct. (A) is incorrect because Washington was eager to retire from politics, and he was not concerned with Federalist representation in Congress. While Washington was always wary of "factions," or political parties, he does not specifically reference Westerners forming their own party, but was rather concerned with outsiders manipulating people in the West; (B) is incorrect. (C) is incorrect because Washington's address focused on politics and policy, not security from attacks by American Indians.

9. A

President Washington was aware that Westerners, much like the rest of the American public, had been critical of former treaties with foreign nations (for example, Jay's Treaty). Therefore, Washington's reference to securing for Westerners "everything they could desire, in respect to our foreign relations, towards confirming their prosperity" was to remind them of their newly guaranteed navigation rights on the Mississippi, as granted in the Pinckney Treaty. **(A)** is correct. Westerners weren't uniquely concerned with relations with England, which makes (B) incorrect. Pinckney's Treaty did not relate to alliances between the states or threats of a French invasion, so (C) and (D) are incorrect.

10. B

The Democratic-Republican party was comprised primarily of Anti-Federalists, not Federalists, making **(B)** correct. (Remember that the question is asking which of the answer choices is *not* true.) For years, the Federalists and Anti-Federalists had debated the role of central government versus state government. Hotly contested topics, such as the Bank of the United States, further drove a wedge between these two groups. By the election of 1792, disparate Anti-Federalists had formed a group they named Democratic-Republicans, or Jeffersonian Republicans. Therefore, (A) and (D) are incorrect. (C) is also incorrect, because the Proclamation of Neutrality was indeed criticized by Anti-Federalists, such as Jefferson and Madison, who denounced the Federalists' neutrality regarding the French Revolution.

5

CHAPTER 6

Period 4: 1800–1848

LEARNING OBJECTIVES

After studying this time period, you will be able to:

- Describe the effects on American life of differing interpretations of the Constitution

- Chart the development of, and changes in, American politics

- Analyze relationships among various social, ethnic, and racial groups and their effect on U.S. national identity

- Describe the impact of religion on American life

- Analyze how U.S. growth and global involvement have changed ideas about national identity

- Describe how reformers and activists have changed American society

- Describe the role of political philosophies in the developing American identity

- Explain how technological developments have impacted American economy and society

TIMELINE

Date	Event
1800	Thomas Jefferson is elected the third president.
1803	The Supreme Court hears the landmark case *Marbury v. Madison*. The Louisiana Purchase more than doubles the size of the United States.
1804	The Lewis and Clark expedition begins.
1807	Robert Fulton invents the steamboat.
1808	James Madison is elected president.
1812	The United States declares war on Great Britain.
1814	The Treaty of Ghent is signed to end the War of 1812.
1816	James Monroe is elected president.
1819	A major financial crisis, the Panic of 1819, threatens the Era of Good Feelings.
1820	The Missouri Compromise is accepted by both the North and South, admitting Missouri and Maine to the Union.
1823	The Monroe Doctrine is issued.
1828	Andrew Jackson is elected president. The Tariff of 1828 ("Tariff of Abominations") is enacted.
1831	Nat Turner's slave rebellion takes place in Virginia.
1832	The Tariff of 1832 escalates states' rights tensions, prompting the Nullification Crisis.
1833	William Lloyd Garrison founds the American Antislavery Society.
1838–1839	The Cherokee Indians are forcibly moved west along the Trail of Tears.
1841	President William Henry Harrison dies while in office, and John Tyler assumes the presidency.
1848	The Seneca Falls Convention occurs to promote women's rights.

TEST WHAT YOU ALREADY KNOW

Part A: Quiz

Questions 1 and 2 refer to the excerpt below.

"I am aware that the necessity of a few removals for legal, oppressions, delinquencies and other official malversations, may be misconstrued as done for political opinions, & produce hesitation in the coalition so much to be desired . . . in the class of removals however I do not rank the new appointments . . . crouded in with whip & spur from the 12th of Dec. when the event of the election was known, (and consequently that he was making appointments, not for himself, but his successor) until 9 aclock of the night, at 12 aclock of which he was to go out of office. This outrage on decency, shall not have it's affect . . . I consider the nominations as nullities & will not view the persons appointed as even candidates for their office, much less as possessing it by any title meriting respect."

Thomas Jefferson, Letter to Henry Knox, 1801

1. The excerpt describes Thomas Jefferson's resentment toward which political event?

    (A) Alexander Burr's appointment as governor of New York by the Essex Junto

    (B) Alexander Burr's appointment as vice presidential running mate to Jefferson

    (C) President John Adams's appointment of "midnight judges"

    (D) President John Adams's appointment of Cabinet members

2. Which Supreme Court case resulted from the event described in the excerpt?

    (A) *McCulloch v. Maryland*

    (B) *Marbury v. Madison*

    (C) *Worcester v. Georgia*

    (D) *Dred Scott v. Sandford*

6

Questions 3–5 refer to the image below.

This political cartoon is from 1807. The man on the right is a merchant being held back by a turtle called an "Ograbme," which is "embargo" spelled backward.

3. This political cartoon refers to

    (A) the French demand for bribes during the XYZ Affair

    (B) American reaction to the writs of assistance

    (C) New England's reaction to the passage of a "no trade" law

    (D) the ban on American trade with Haiti after the Haitian Revolution

4. Which of the following best describes the regional unrest that resulted from events such as those illustrated in the cartoon?

    (A) Southern states demanded secession unless economic restrictions on trade were lifted.

    (B) Western territories threatened to establish an independent republic.

    (C) Some New England states demanded several changes to the U.S. Constitution and an immediate halt to a war.

    (D) Some New England states called for secession and joining the Canadian Confederation.

5. Which of the following best describes the change in American politics between 1798 and 1816?

    (A) The members of the Democratic-Republican Party, once for strict trade regulation, became stalwarts of free trade.

    (B) The Federalist Party supported the concepts of states' rights versus a strong central government.

    (C) The Federalists advocated an expansionist philosophy, hoping to spread their political ideas westward.

    (D) The Whig Party emerged as a plausible third-party choice.

Questions 6–8 refer to the map below.

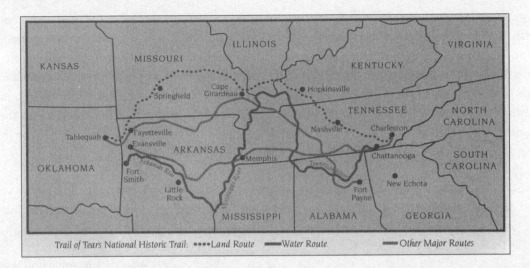

Trail of Tears National Historic Trail: ••••Land Route ━━Water Route ━━Other Major Routes

6. Which of the following best explains President Jackson's reasoning for authorizing the Indian Removal Act of 1830?

   (A) He was eager to protect the native settlers by keeping white colonists from immigrating into the area.

   (B) He wished to punish the American Indians for their alliances to the British and French in previous wars.

   (C) He was convinced that the violent Five Civilized Tribes posed the greatest challenge to land claimed by Americans in Southern states.

   (D) He believed that white settlers had rights to the fertile farmland that the American Indians inhabited.

7. Which American Indian tribe attempted to use legal and political channels to oppose their forced removal?

   (A) The Creek tribe

   (B) The Seminole tribe

   (C) The Choctaw tribe

   (D) The Cherokee tribe

8. Which of the following statements best reflects the consequences of the Indian Removal Act of 1830?

   (A) The American Indians were provided protection and supplies from the United States government to ease their transition.

   (B) Many American Indians perished due to the harsh winter and lack of food and supplies during their westward journey.

   (C) The American Indians were removed from fertile farmland and placed in a similar environment in western territory.

   (D) American Indians who willingly assimilated into American culture were allowed to stay in their original territory.

Questions 9 and 10 refer to the excerpt below.

"[T]he traveller who floats down the current of the Ohio to the spot where that river falls into the Mississippi may be said to sail between liberty and servitude. . . . Upon the left bank of the stream the population is rare; from time to time one discerns a troop of slaves loitering in the half-desert fields; the primaeval forest recurs at every turn; society seems to be asleep, man to be idle, and nature alone offers a scene of activity and of life. From the right bank, on the contrary, a confused hum is heard which proclaims the presence of industry; the fields are covered with abundant harvests, the elegance of the dwellings announces the taste and activity of the laborer, and man appears to be in the enjoyment of that wealth and contentment which is the reward of labor.

The State of Kentucky was founded in 1775, the State of Ohio only twelve years later; but twelve years are more in America than half a century in Europe, and, at the present day, the population of Ohio exceeds that of Kentucky by two hundred and fifty thousand souls."

Alexis de Tocqueville, *Democracy in America* (Vol. 1), 1835

9. The excerpt best illustrates which of the following developments?

   (A) The growing national influence of southern planters

   (B) The passage of the Northwest Ordinance

   (C) The economic consequences of the Erie Canal

   (D) The U.S. victory in the Northwest Indian War

10. The excerpt most directly reflects which of the following developments during the early 1800s?

    (A) The fierce debates over the spread of slavery into the Northwest

    (B) The rise of Jacksonian Democracy

    (C) The economic shift of the Market Revolution

    (D) The growth of "King Cotton" in the South

6

Part B: Key Terms

The following is a list of the major people, places, and events for 1800–1848. You will likely see many of these on the AP U.S. History exam.

For each key term ask yourself the following questions:

- Can I describe this key term?
- Can I discuss this key term in the context of other events?
- Could I correctly answer a multiple-choice question about this key term?
- Could I correctly answer a free-response question about this key term?

Check off the key terms if you can answer "yes" to at least three of these questions.

The Election of Thomas Jefferson

☐ Federalist Party   ☐ Thomas Jefferson   ☐ Democratic-Republican Party

The Louisiana Purchase

☐ Louisiana Territory

The Marshall Court

☐ Judiciary Act of 1789   ☐ *Marbury v. Madison*   ☐ Impeachment
☐ Supreme Court

Jefferson's Challenges

☐ Napoleonic Wars   ☐ Embargo Act of 1807   ☐ Non-Intercourse Act of 1809

The War of 1812

☐ James Madison   ☐ War of 1812   ☐ Battle of New Orleans
☐ Battle of Tippecanoe   ☐ The Star-Spangled Banner   ☐ Treaty of Ghent

Ideological Divides in the United States

☐ Hartford Convention   ☐ Missouri Compromise

Monroe and the Era of Good Feelings

☐ James Monroe   ☐ Tariff of 1816   ☐ Second Bank of the United States
☐ Monroe Doctrine   ☐ American System

The Rise of the Two-Party System

- ☐ Rise of the Common Man
- ☐ John Quincy Adams
- ☐ Andrew Jackson
- ☐ Democrats
- ☐ National Republicans

Challenges to Federal Authority

- ☐ *McCulloch v. Maryland*
- ☐ Panic of 1837
- ☐ Tariff of 1828
- ☐ Tariff of 1832
- ☐ Spoils system
- ☐ Indian Removal Act
- ☐ *Cherokee Nation v. Georgia*
- ☐ *Worcester v. Georgia*

Religious Revival and Reform Movements

- ☐ Second Great Awakening
- ☐ Cult of domesticity
- ☐ Abolitionists
- ☐ Declaration of Sentiments
- ☐ Underground Railroad
- ☐ Nat Turner's Rebellion

Economic and Social Revolution

- ☐ Market Revolution
- ☐ American Party (Know-Nothing Party)
- ☐ King Cotton

Next Steps

Step 1: Tally your correct answers from Part A and review the quiz explanations at the end of this chapter.

1. C

2. B

3. C

4. C

5. B

6. D

7. D

8. B

9. B

10. C

_____ out of 10 questions

Step 2: Count the number of key terms you checked off in Part B.

_____ out of 46 key terms

Step 3: Read the Key Takeaways in this chapter.

Step 4: Consult the table below and follow the instructions based on your performance.

If You Got...	Do This
80% or more of the Test What You Already Know assessment correct (8 or more questions from Part A and 37 or more key terms from Part B)	• Read definitions in this chapter for all the key terms you didn't check off. • Complete the Test What You Learned assessment in this chapter.
50% or less of the Test What You Already Know assessment correct (5 or fewer questions from Part A and 23 or fewer key terms from Part B)	• Read the comprehensive review for this period in Chapter 15. • If you are short on time, read only the High-Yield sections. • Read through all of the key term definitions in this chapter. • Complete the Test What You Learned assessment in this chapter.
Any other result	• Read the High-Yield sections in the comprehensive review of this period in Chapter 15. • Read definitions in this chapter for all the key terms you didn't check off. • Complete the Test What You Learned assessment in this chapter.

ESSENTIAL CONTENT

Key Takeaways: 1800–1848

1. The United States continued to develop its own democratic ideals, sparking debates about the role of federal government and leading to the formation of various political parties.

2. The U.S. Supreme Court established the principle that federal laws take precedence over state laws. Through *Marbury v. Madison* (1803), the Court also established the principle of judicial review, which allowed courts to check the power of the legislative and executive branches of government, further solidifying a separation of powers.

3. America developed a national culture, especially after the War of 1812, and various religious and social reform groups emerged. The temperance movement sought to ban alcohol. The abolition movement worked to end slavery and to assist African Americans. The women's rights movement's efforts culminated in the Seneca Falls Convention.

4. America underwent an economic and technological revolution. Major developments included the cotton gin, the steam engine, the factory system, and the expansion of railroads and canals. America moved away from a small subsistence-based economy and into an era of increasing industrialization, which impacted societal and family structures.

5. Expanding westward after the Louisiana Purchase, the United States sought to expand its borders and to be seen as a major player in foreign trade. The Monroe Doctrine and military actions against American Indian tribes demonstrated the desire for more control in North America.

6. As new states joined the United States, the debate over slavery raged on. In an attempt to appease both the North and South, Henry Clay crafted the Missouri Compromise, resolving some tension for the next three decades.

Key Terms: 1800–1848

Remember that the AP U.S. History exam tests you on the depth of your knowledge, not just your ability to recall facts. While we have provided brief definitions here, you will need to know these terms in even more depth for the AP exam, including how terms connect to broader historical themes and understandings.

The Election of Thomas Jefferson

Federalist Party: Early political party, led by Alexander Hamilton. Supported an orderly, efficient central government.

Thomas Jefferson: Third president. Served 1801–1809. Authored the Declaration of the Independence. He led the United States through the Tripolitanian War and avoided involvement in the Napoleonic Wars. In some cases, Jefferson adhered to the letter of the Constitution, while at other times (such as with the Louisiana Purchase) he adopted a loose interpretation. For example, he kept many of the hallmarks of the Federalist Era intact (such as Hamilton's economic system), but he had the citizenship requirement of the Alien Act reduced to five years and abolished the excise tax.

Democratic-Republican Party: Early political party that opposed the Federalist Party. Led by Thomas Jefferson and James Madison. Supported states' rights and favored agrarianism.

The Louisiana Purchase

Louisiana Territory: Lands purchased by Jefferson in 1803 from France; they stretched from the Gulf of Mexico to the Hudson Bay and from the Mississippi River to the Rocky Mountains, greatly increasing America's holdings.

The Marshall Court

Judiciary Act of 1789: Established the structure of the judiciary branch, with the Supreme Court consisting of one presiding chief justice and five associate justices. It also provided for the establishment of 13 district courts and three circuit courts of appeal.

Supreme Court: The highest court in the judicial branch. In the present day, there are nine justices seated at it, with one of the nine serving as chief justice, although this number fluctuated in the early years of the United States. The president nominates a justice, and the Senate votes on that nomination. If confirmed, the justice has a lifetime appointment, serving until their death or retirement.

Marbury v. Madison: 1803 ruling that stated Congress cannot pass laws that are contrary to the Constitution and that it is the judicial system's job to interpret what the Constitution permits. Overturned a clause in the Judiciary Act of 1789 that granted the Supreme Court the power to command any subordinate government authority to take or not take an action that is that authority's legal duty.

Impeachment: The process of a legislative body removing a government official from their appointed office. Impeachment is often mistaken for being successfully removed. In fact, it is merely the name for the overall process.

Jefferson's Challenges

Napoleonic Wars: The umbrella term for seven major European conflicts between 1803 and 1815, which spun out of the French Revolution and its various wars. In the end, following a failed invasion of Russia, Napoleon was defeated. The resulting Congress of Vienna redrew Europe's borders, established a conservative anti-nationalistic, pro-monarchy consensus for several decades, and established the supremacy of the British Empire and the *Pax Britannica* until World War I.

Embargo Act of 1807: A general ban on trade and economic activities between the United States and England and France. Passed by Congress in response to the British attack on the USS *Chesapeake* off the coast of Virginia, which killed three Americans.

Non-Intercourse Act of 1809: Replaced the unpopular Embargo Act of 1807. This law allowed the United States to trade with foreign nations except Britain and France. Like its predecessor, the Embargo Act, it was difficult to enforce and mostly ineffective.

The War of 1812

James Madison: Fourth President. Served 1809–1817. A Virginian and Democratic-Republican, he served as Jefferson's secretary of state (1801–1809) and helped negotiate the Louisiana Purchase. He led the United States through the War of 1812. Due to the war's difficulties, he shifted toward supporting a stronger centralized state, a rechartered national bank, and various internal improvements.

Battle of Tippecanoe: A battle that took place in the Indiana Territory on November 7, 1811; caused many members of Congress from the frontier to feel justified in their call for war. American forces under the command of Governor William Henry Harrison battled Tecumseh's Confederacy, an American Indian force of various tribes led by the Shawnee leader Tecumseh and his brother the Prophet.

War of 1812: Often called the Second War of Independence. Fought from 1812–1815. The war went poorly and nearly led to New England's secession at the Hartford Convention. However, the United States managed not to lose territory before the Treaty of Ghent was signed, and the Battle of New Orleans reinvigorated U.S. morale.

The Star-Spangled Banner: The U.S. national anthem. Written by Francis Scott Key after witnessing the bombardment of Fort McHenry during the War of 1812. It was made the official national anthem in 1931 during the twilight of the Hoover administration, but had gained some official recognition as a national anthem by the Wilson administration in 1916.

Battle of New Orleans: 1815 battle in which U.S. General Andrew Jackson led American troops through Alabama to New Orleans and successfully prevented the English from gaining control over the Mississippi River. Jackson emerged as an American war hero.

Treaty of Ghent: It ended the War of 1812, and was signed by American envoys and British diplomats in Belgium on December 24, 1814. The provisions of the treaty provided for the return of any conquered territories to their rightful owners, and the settlement of a boundary between Canada and the United States. Essentially, the war ended in a draw—neither side gained any major concessions, restitution, or apologies. Most Americans were pleased, however, because they had expected to lose territory.

Ideological Divides in the United States

Hartford Convention: During the winter of 1814–1815, a radical group of New England Federalists met to discuss ways to demand that the federal government pay them for the loss of trade due to the Embargo Act and the War of 1812. The group also proposed amending the Constitution to limit the U.S. president to one term; require a two-thirds vote to enact an embargo, declare war, and admit new states; and repeal the Three-Fifths Compromise. Some even suggested secession.

Missouri Compromise: Proposed by Henry Clay of Kentucky, it constituted three bills which collectively allowed for the admission of Missouri as a slave state while also admitting Maine as a free state, maintaining the balance of power in the Senate. In addition, slavery would not be permitted in states admitted above the latitude 36° 30′ (with the exception of Missouri, which lay above the line). Functionally repealed by the Kansas-Nebraska Act, but not officially overturned until the *Dred Scott v. Sandford* ruling declared it was unconstitutional.

Monroe and the Era of Good Feelings

James Monroe: Fifth President. Served 1817–1825. A Virginian and Democratic-Republican, he helped secure the Louisiana Purchase. During the War of 1812, he served as both secretary of state (1811–1817) and secretary of war (1814–1815). The Era of Good Feelings, a period of national unity following the War of 1812, largely overlaps with his presidency. He dealt with the Panic of 1819 as well as the Missouri Compromise. In 1823, he issued the Monroe Doctrine, a long-lasting foreign policy of the United States.

Monroe Doctrine: Proposed by President Monroe in his annual address to Congress in 1823, it quickly became the basis of U.S. foreign policy in Latin America. The doctrine called for nonintervention in Latin America and an end to European colonization. Though the United States did not actually have a strong enough military to defend the doctrine if necessary, it remained firm and adhered to the doctrine throughout the nineteenth and twentieth centuries.

Tariff of 1816: Because of a postwar upsurge in nationalism after the War of 1812, there was a strong desire to protect all things American, especially the burgeoning industrial economy. To prevent cheap British goods from flooding the market and injuring American manufacturing, Congress passed the Tariff of 1816, which imposed a 20 percent duty on all imported goods and became the first truly "protective tariff" in American history. However, the passage of the tariff was unpopular in the South due to its export-oriented agricultural economy. The tariff was allowed to lapse in 1820.

American System: Proposed by Henry Clay of Kentucky, it sought to establish manufacturing and bring in much needed revenue for internal improvements throughout the country. It included the recharter of the Bank of the United States; protective tariffs, such as the one passed in 1816; and improvements on American infrastructure, such as turnpikes, roads, and canals. The South did not support the plan, as plantations made their money on export (especially of cotton). Internal improvements also required a stronger federal government, which potentially threatened the South's control over its slave population.

Second Bank of the United States: A national bank, patterned on Alexander Hamilton's design for the original. It existed from 1818–1824. The BUS was charted by James Madison in 1816, as he felt the need to strengthen the central government after the problems encountered during the War of 1812. However, the bank contributed to the Panic of 1819, infuriating many and leading to Andrew Jackson's successful effort to kill it.

The Rise of the Two-Party System

Rise of the Common Man: An aspect of what became the Jacksonian Democrats. By 1820, many states had adopted universal male suffrage for whites, eliminating the property-owning requirement to be able to vote. This era signaled a retreat from exclusive rule by the well-to-do and a shift to a more democratic society.

John Quincy Adams: Sixth president. Served from 1825–1829. Son of John Adams. In his lifetime, JQA was a member of basically every major political party at some point. He was elected after striking a deal with Henry Clay in the disputed 1824 election. Following his presidency, JQA was elected to the House in 1830 and served until his death in 1848. He became increasingly opposed to slavery, even arguing before the Supreme Court in 1841 on behalf of African slaves in the *Amistad* case, winning them their freedom. He criticized the Mexican-American War.

Andrew Jackson: Seventh president. Served from 1829–1837. He gained fame for his defense of New Orleans during the War of 1812, a rare outright U.S. victory in that conflict. Jackson advocated for the common man against established interests, and supported universal male suffrage for whites, nixing the existing property requirement that barred the poor from participating in democracy. He also pushed for a spoils system to reward supporters, opposed abolitionism, and killed the Second Bank of the United States. He forcefully quashed South Carolina during the Nullification Crisis. Jackson is infamous for creating the Trail of Tears.

Democrats: During the Era of Good Feelings, the Democratic-Republicans fragmented. In the 1828 election, the Democrats supported Andrew Jackson and the National Republican faction supported Henry Clay. The (Jacksonian) Democrats of this time period favored an agrarian economy, ending the national bank, lowering tariffs, and increasing the political power of the common man, such as through universal male suffrage for whites. They also supported states' rights and federal restraint in social affairs.

National Republicans: A faction of the splintering Democratic-Republicans during the 1828 election. They supported Henry Clay and opposed Andrew Jackson. The National Republicans eventually became the Whig Party in 1836. Whig ideology was very similar to the platform of the old Federalist Party, favoring economic nationalism, a strong central government, and the rechartering of the national bank.

Challenges to Federal Authority

McCulloch v. Maryland: An 1819 case that challenged the doctrine of federalism. It involved the state of Maryland attempting to collect a tax from the Second Bank of the United States. Marshall invoked the "necessary and proper" clause of the Constitution to rule that the federal government had an implied power to establish the bank. He also declared that the state had no right to tax a federal institution; he argued that "the power to tax was the power to destroy" and would signal the end of federalism. Most importantly, the ruling established that federal laws were the supreme law of the land, superseding state laws.

Panic of 1837: A financial crisis that lasted from 1837 until the mid-1840s. Caused, in part, by Andrew Jackson killing the Bank of the United States and issuing the Specie Circular; the latter caused the value of paper money to plummet.

Tariff of 1828: This tariff came about in response to New England merchants who had been pushing for stronger protection from foreign competitors. However, the new tariff was incredibly damaging to the Southern economy, causing Vice President John C. Calhoun to secretly write "The Southern Carolina Exposition and Protest," which threatened South Carolina's secession. Calling the tariff the "Tariff of Abominations," Calhoun recommended that the Southern states declare it to be null and void (nullification) if the federal government refused to lower the duty requirement.

Tariff of 1832: It lowered the Tariff of 1828's rate from 45 percent to 35 percent in a failed attempt to placate the South. Calhoun resigned from the vice presidency in response. South Carolina voted to nullify the Tariff of 1832 and threatened to secede if Jackson attempted to collect the duties by force. In response, Jackson encouraged Congress to lower tariffs even more. However, he also asked Congress to pass the Force Bill, which gave the president the power to use the military to collect tariffs. This signaled to the South that their threats would not be tolerated. In response, South Carolina rescinded the nullification. However, the tensions between the North and the South would continue to escalate, culminating in the Civil War.

Spoils system: A form of political corruption in which a political party rewards its supporters with favors, often posts to public office. Andrew Jackson was a proponent of the spoils system, in which he appointed those who supported his campaign to government positions. Jackson created jobs and appointed many friends to his unofficial Cabinet, earning it the name "Kitchen Cabinet" from critics.

Indian Removal Act: This law provided for the immediate forced resettlement of American Indians living in Alabama, Florida, Georgia, Mississippi, and present-day Illinois. By 1835, some 100,000 Cherokee, Chickasaw, Choctaw, Creek, and Seminole American Indians had been forcibly removed from their homelands.

Cherokee Nation v. Georgia: A Supreme Court case from 1831. The Marshall Court ruled that the Cherokee Tribe was not a sovereign foreign nation and, therefore, had no right to sue for jurisdiction over its homelands.

Worcester v. Georgia: A Supreme Court case (1832) which ruled that the state of Georgia could not infringe on the Cherokee Nation's sovereignty, thus nullifying Georgia state laws within the tribe's territory. President Jackson, incensed, allegedly said, "John Marshall has made his decision; now let him enforce it." The expulsion of the Cherokee resulted in the Trail of Tears. Also notable as being one of the few times a president ignored a Supreme Court ruling.

Religious Revival and Reform Movements

Second Great Awakening: A Protestant religious movement that took place across the United States between the 1790s and the 1840s, peaking in the 1820s. Known for its church revivals, or "camp meetings," and inspirational sermons. Sparked a great number of reform movements, most notably movements for temperance, public education, women's rights, and abolition.

Cult of domesticity: After the market revolution and transportation boom of the 1820s, the nature of "women's work" shifted. The growth of industry moved men out of the fields and into factories, while women were defined as homemakers and mothers.

Abolitionists: People who advocated for ending slavery. Aside from the influence of Enlightenment ideas about freedom, many abolitionists believed that slavery was sinful and, therefore, must be eliminated.

Declaration of Sentiments: The women at the Seneca Falls Convention (1848) drafted this document. Modeled after the Declaration of Independence, it declared that "all men and women are created equal" and demanded suffrage for women. Much like the earlier temperance movement, the women's crusade soon became eclipsed by the abolitionist movement and did not resurface until closer to the turn of the twentieth century.

Underground Railroad: A network of abolitionists and abolitionist sympathizers who helped slaves escape into free states and Canada. Members included Sojourner Truth and Harriet Tubman, among many others. The Underground Railroad gained greater support after the Compromise of 1850. At its peak, approximately 1,000 slaves per year escaped.

Nat Turner's Rebellion: Turner, an enslaved African American from Virginia, organized a massive slave uprising in 1831. It resulted in the deaths of over 50 white men, women, and children and the retaliatory killings of hundreds of slaves. Afterwards, states across the South passed laws restricting civil rights for all African Americans, free or slave, and banned their education as well.

Economic and Social Revolution

Market Revolution: The economic process in which America shifted away from localized economies and small-scale farming and toward an interlocking national economy with specialized regions (cash crops and raw materials in the South, factories and processing in the North, agriculture in the West).

American Party (Know-Nothing Party): Nativists, who were largely Protestants of English ancestry, disliked the large numbers of Irish and Germans that began to arrive in the 1840s, especially due to their Roman Catholic faith; many Central Europeans were also leftists fleeing from prosecution after the failed Revolutions of 1848. These nativists formed the American Party, or Know-Nothing Party, to advance their anti-immigrant agenda.

King Cotton: Made possible by Eli Whitney's cotton gin, King Cotton was the name for the era in which the lucrative cotton export business caused an expansion of slavery as more workers were needed in the fields; the number increased from one million slaves to four million in 50 year. This exacerbated regional tensions that led to the Civil War, because slaveowners now had increased investment in the institution of slavery.

TEST WHAT YOU LEARNED

Questions 1–4 refer to the excerpt below.

"SECTION 8. And be it further enacted, That in all that territory ceded by France to the United States, under the name of Louisiana, which lies north of thirty-six degrees and thirty minutes north latitude, not included within the limits of the state, contemplated by this act, slavery and involuntary servitude, otherwise than in the punishment of crimes, whereof the parties shall have been duly convicted, shall be, and is hereby, forever prohibited: Provided always, That any person escaping into the same, from whom labour or service is lawfully claimed, in any state or territory of the United States, such fugitive may be lawfully reclaimed and conveyed to the person claiming his or her labour or service as aforesaid."

Missouri Compromise, 1820

1. The Missouri Compromise was drafted primarily as a response to

   (A) Missouri's desire to enter the Union as a slave state

   (B) Missouri's desire to enter the Union as a free state

   (C) conflict between rival state governments in Missouri

   (D) the ban on slavery in the Missouri Territory due to the Northwest Ordinance

2. Which politician earned the title the Great Compromiser?

   (A) William H. Seward

   (B) Daniel Webster

   (C) Henry Clay

   (D) John C. Calhoun

3. The Missouri Compromise is known for accomplishing all of the following EXCEPT

   (A) the termination of fugitive slave laws within land previously owned by France

   (B) the prohibition of slavery north of the 36° 30′ line within land obtained in the Louisiana Purchase

   (C) the entrance of Missouri and Maine to the Union as a slave state and free state, respectively

   (D) the temporary cessation of sectional tensions between pro- and antislavery supporters

4. The Missouri Compromise was eventually overturned by

   (A) the *Dred Scott* decision of 1857

   (B) the Compromise of 1850

   (C) the raid on Harper's Ferry in 1859

   (D) the Kansas-Nebraska Act of 1854

Questions 5–8 refer to the two tables below.

Table 1: Percentage of Urban Population

Year	Percentage Urban
1790	5.1%
1800	6.1%
1810	7.3%
1820	7.2%
1830	8.8%
1840	10.8%
1850	15.3%
1860	19.8%

Data from: W. Elliot Brownlee, *Dynamics of Ascent: A History of the American Economy*, 1979

Table 2: Shares of Agriculture and Manufacturing in Total Labor Force Participation

Year	Agriculture	Manufacturing
1800	82.6%	Not Available
1810	83.7%	3.2%
1820	79.0%	Not Available
1830	70.7%	Not Available
1840	63.4%	8.8%
1850	54.8%	14.5%
1860	53.2%	13.7%

Data from: Paul David, "The Growth of Real Product in the United States Before 1840: New Evidence, Controlled Conjectures," *Journal of Economic History*, 1967

5. Which region of the U.S. benefited most from the industrialization and increase in urbanization reflected in these two tables?

   (A) Old Northwest

   (B) New England

   (C) Southwest

   (D) Southeast

6. The increase in textile manufacturing, especially the construction of large factories devoted to textiles, is most directly reflected in the

   (A) large percentage of the labor force engaged in manufacturing by 1860

   (B) increase in the percentage of the labor force engaged in manufacturing by 1840

   (C) increase in the percentage of the labor force engaged in manufacturing between 1840 and 1850

   (D) increase in urban percentage between 1850 and 1860

7. Both the increasing use of steamboats on major rivers and the boom in canal building are best reflected by the

    (A) sustained growth of the urban percentage between 1820 and 1860

    (B) increase in manufacturing between 1840 and 1850

    (C) increase in the urban percentage between 1850 and 1860

    (D) increase in the agricultural labor force between 1800 and 1810

8. The great increase in railroad building in the United States is most directly reflected in the

    (A) substantial increase in the manufacturing workforce between 1840 and 1850

    (B) sharp increase in the urban percentage between 1820 and 1830

    (C) sharp decline of the agricultural labor force between 1830 and 1840

    (D) substantial increase in the urban percentage between 1840 and 1860

Questions 9 and 10 refer to the excerpt below.

"*Resolved*, That such laws as conflict, in any way, with the true and substantial happiness of woman, are contrary to the great precept of nature, and of no validity; for this is superior in obligation to any other.

Resolved, That all laws which prevent woman from occupying such a station in society as her conscience shall dictate, or which place her in a position inferior to that of man, are contrary to the great precept of nature, and therefore of no force or authority.

Resolved, That woman is man's equal—was intended to be so by the Creator, and the highest good of the race demands that she should be recognized as such.

Resolved, That the women of this country ought to be enlightened in regard to the laws under which they live, that they may no longer publish their degradation, by declaring themselves satisfied with their present position, nor their ignorance, by asserting that they have all the rights they want.

Resolved, That inasmuch as man, while claiming for himself intellectual superiority, does accord to woman moral superiority, it is pre-eminently his duty to encourage her to speak, and teach, as she has an opportunity, in all religious assemblies."

Declaration of Rights and Sentiments, Seneca Falls Convention, 1848

9. The main purpose of the Seneca Falls Convention was to

   (A) claim the right to vote for women

   (B) advocate for the creation of all-female colleges

   (C) assert the rights of women as equals to men morally, socially, and politically

   (D) demand that the word *women* be added to the Declaration of Independence alongside the word *men*

10. Which of the following was NOT a key factor for women gaining increased civil rights during the Second Great Awakening?

   (A) Institutions for women's higher education, such as Mt. Holyoke and Wesleyan College, were founded.

   (B) Women gained social importance as the leaders of reform movements, such as abolitionism.

   (C) Women were elected to political offices, empowering them to advocate for more rights, like suffrage.

   (D) Women became more involved in religion, such as taking on a larger role in the church hierarchy.

Part B: Key Terms

This key terms list is the same as the list in the Test What You Already Know section earlier in this chapter. Based on what you have now learned, again ask yourself the following questions:

- Can I define this key term and use it in a sentence?
- Can I provide an example related to this key term?
- Could I correctly answer a multiple-choice question about this key term?
- Could I correctly answer a free-response question about this key term?

Check off the key terms if you can answer "yes" to at least three of these questions.

The Election of Thomas Jefferson

☐ Federalist Party ☐ Thomas Jefferson ☐ Democratic-Republican Party

The Louisiana Purchase

☐ Louisiana Territory

The Marshall Court

☐ Judiciary Act of 1789 ☐ *Marbury v. Madison* ☐ Impeachment
☐ Supreme Court

Jefferson's Challenges

☐ Napoleonic Wars ☐ Embargo Act of 1807 ☐ Non-Intercourse Act of 1809

The War of 1812

☐ James Madison ☐ War of 1812 ☐ Battle of New Orleans
☐ Battle of Tippecanoe ☐ The Star-Spangled Banner ☐ Treaty of Ghent

Ideological Divides in the United States

☐ Hartford Convention ☐ Missouri Compromise

6

Monroe and the Era of Good Feelings

- ☐ James Monroe
- ☐ Monroe Doctrine
- ☐ Tariff of 1816
- ☐ American System
- ☐ Second Bank of the United States

The Rise of the Two-Party System

- ☐ Rise of the Common Man
- ☐ John Quincy Adams
- ☐ Andrew Jackson
- ☐ Democrats
- ☐ National Republicans

Challenges to Federal Authority

- ☐ *McCulloch v. Maryland*
- ☐ Panic of 1837
- ☐ Tariff of 1828
- ☐ Tariff of 1832
- ☐ Spoils system
- ☐ Indian Removal Act
- ☐ *Cherokee Nation v. Georgia*
- ☐ *Worcester v. Georgia*

Religious Revival and Reform Movements

- ☐ Second Great Awakening
- ☐ Cult of domesticity
- ☐ Abolitionists
- ☐ Declaration of Sentiments
- ☐ Underground Railroad
- ☐ Nat Turner's Rebellion

Economic and Social Revolution

- ☐ Market Revolution
- ☐ American Party (Know-Nothing Party)
- ☐ King Cotton

Next Steps

Step 1: Tally your correct answers from Part A and review the quiz explanations at the end of this chapter.

1.	A	6.	C
2.	C	7.	A
3.	A	8.	D
4.	D	9.	C
5.	B	10.	C

_____ out of 10 questions

Step 2: Count the number of key terms you checked off in Part B.

_____ out of 46 key terms

Step 3: Compare your Test What You Already Know results to these Test What You Learned results to see how exam-ready you are for this period.

For More Practice:

- Read (or reread) the comprehensive review for this period in Chapter 15.
- Go to kaptest.com to complete the online quiz questions for 1800–1848.
  - Haven't registered your book yet? Go to kaptest.com/moreonline to begin.

ANSWERS AND EXPLANATIONS

Test What You Already Know

1.   C

Just before Thomas Jefferson took office, former President John Adams appointed 16 new judges, dubbed the "midnight judges" because of the last-minute nature of these appointments. Jefferson balked at the idea that his predecessor would choose so many judges who would then serve on the bench for life, including during Jefferson's administration. **(C)** is correct. Burr was indeed nominated for governor by the radical group, the Essex Junto, in a bid for New England state secession; however, this occurred after this letter was written, so (A) is incorrect. Burr was considered for Jefferson's vice presidential running mate in the 1804 election, but the Democratic-Republicans decided not to select him; (B) is also incorrect. (D) is incorrect because Adams did not appoint Cabinet members; additionally, the sitting president chooses his Cabinet and can also dismiss Cabinet members without cause.

2.   B

When Jefferson purposefully ignored the appointments of the "midnight judges," one of them, William Marbury, took the case to the Supreme Court. The resulting case, *Marbury v. Madison*, was a landmark case that established the power of the Supreme Court and its ability to check the legislative and executive branches. **(B)** is correct. *McCulloch v. Maryland* also involved the role of the federal government, but focused around the constitutionality of a national bank; it did not result from the event described in the excerpt, so (A) is incorrect. Both (C) and (D) are incorrect, because these Supreme Court cases were much later than Jefferson's letter and had to do with separate issues (American Indian rights and African American rights, respectively).

3.   C

New England merchants protested the Embargo Act of 1807 because their regional economy greatly depended upon trade, especially with Great Britain. The Jefferson administration had passed the law as a failed bid to stop the British practice of impressment. Thus, **(C)** is correct. The XYZ Affair, in which French agents demanded

bribes ahead of formal negotiations, took place in 1797–1798. Likewise, the scandal involving writs of assistance took place around 1760, well before the cartoon's 1807 publication. Thus, (A) and (B) are incorrect. The Haitian embargo took place at the same time as this cartoon, but the British were not involved with that matter. Haiti was formerly a French colony. Thus, (D) is incorrect.

4.   C

The Embargo Act of 1807 and War of 1812 led to the Hartford Convention. In December 1814, the five New England states met and discussed several issues, even entertaining secession. Ultimately, they issued several demands for constitutional changes and demanded an immediate end to the war with Great Britain. However, the war had ended by the time the Hartford Convention's demands were made public. Thus, **(C)** is correct. New England states were the ones making demands, not the South or West; (A) and (B) are incorrect. (D) is incorrect because the New England states did not consider joining the Canadian Confederation, which did not exist until 1867.

5.   B

In its Hartford Convention statement, the Federalist Party, which initially supported the concept of a strong central government, alluded to the concepts of the Kentucky and Virginia Resolutions of 1798. These were authored by Democratic-Republicans, who advocated for states' rights. The Federalists feared that a strong central government led by the Democratic-Republicans would marginalize their influence; **(B)** is correct. The Democratic-Republican Party always feared increased trade would undermine the republican character of the United States. Thus, (A) is incorrect. The Federalists sought to slow westward expansion as they feared it would dilute their political power; (C) is incorrect. (D) is incorrect because the Whig Party was not formed until the early 1830s.

6.   D

The Indian Removal Act authorized President Andrew Jackson to negotiate land-exchange treaties with American Indians east of the Mississippi. The act paved the way for the reluctant, often forcible immigration of over 100,000 American Indians to a newly defined Indian

Territory in present-day Oklahoma. This allowed white settlers to take ownership of the fertile farmland left behind; **(D)** is correct. President Jackson had no interest in protecting American Indians; (A) is incorrect. Though ill treatment of American Indians was certainly a consequence of President Jackson's actions, his specific motivation was not to punish native people; (B) is incorrect. The Five Civilized Tribes actually coexisted more peacefully with white settlers than with other nations, eliminating (C).

7. D

The Cherokees, Creeks, Choctaws, Chickasaws, and Seminoles all adopted a constitution and a form of legal government. When faced with the prospect of removal, the Cherokees sought to utilize their established government as proof that they were an independent country. John Ross, the principal chief of the Cherokee Nation, asked Congress to enforce the boundary between Georgia and the Cherokee Nation's historic tribal lands. After this effort failed, a Cherokee delegation asked the Supreme Court for an injunction against Georgia. Thus, **(D)** is correct. Even though the other tribes also protested relocation, they used other methods, including violence or simply refusing relocation, rather than pursuing legislative alternatives; (A), (B), and (C) are incorrect.

8. B

During the 116-day march from North Carolina and Georgia to present-day Oklahoma, thousands of Cherokees died of exposure, disease, and lack of food. This march became known as the Trail of Tears; **(B)** is correct. While the government promised protection and supplies for their journey, they did not actually provide assistance; (A) is incorrect. The Indian Removal Act of 1830 falsely promised American Indians territory west of the Mississippi comparable to the land they were to be removed from; instead, the new land was significantly smaller and less fertile. Thus, (C) is incorrect. The Five Civilized Tribes were highly assimilated into white culture; however, because they also possessed the most sought-after farmland, they were still removed against their will. Thus, (D) is also incorrect.

9. B

The excerpt best illustrates the results of the Northwest Ordinance, which prohibited the expansion of slavery into the present-day Upper Midwest. Alexis de Tocqueville's description of Ohio and Kentucky conveys to the reader how slavery, or the lack thereof, influenced the economic development and settlement of both states. Thus, **(B)** is correct. (A) is incorrect because, if anything, the excerpt illustrates the eventual declining national influence of southern planters by contrasting the population growth of Ohio and Kentucky. With its growing population, the Midwest would eventually join with the Northern states to politically outgun the slave-holding South. (C) is incorrect because the Erie Canal, which connected the Great Lakes with the Hudson River in New York, was not directly related to the scene of Alexis de Tocqueville's voyage, which was along the Ohio River where it intersected with the Mississippi. (D) is tempting but incorrect; while the U.S. victory in the Northwest Indian War secured the Ohio River Valley for settlement, slavery might have been allowed in those settlements if not for the Northwest Ordinance.

10. C

The excerpt reflects the development of the Market Revolution, which was a shift away from localized economies and small-scale farming toward interlocking, specialized regions. The excerpt makes clear that the economic specialization of South and West was already well underway. Thus, **(C)** is correct. There were no major debates about prohibiting slavery in the Northwest Territory; (A) is incorrect. There is no discussion of democracy in the excerpt; (B) is incorrect. Alexis de Tocqueville describes fields tended to by slaves, not what those slaves were growing. Furthermore, Kentucky is located in the Upper South, while cotton plantations were largely a feature of the Deep South. Therefore, (D) is incorrect.

Test What You Learned

1. A

In 1819, the Union consisted of 11 free and 11 slave states. When Missouri petitioned to join the Union as a slave state, Northerners worried it would lead to an imbalance favoring slave-holding states. To resolve this issue, Henry Clay created the Missouri Compromise, allowing Missouri to enter as a slave state and permitting Maine to break away from Massachusetts in order to enter as a free state; therefore, **(A)** is correct and (B) is incorrect. (C) is incorrect because Missouri did not have rival state governments at the time it sought admission into the Union. The Northwest Ordinance did not cover territory on the western bank of the Mississippi River where Missouri is located; (D) is incorrect.

2. C

Senator Henry Clay of Kentucky was nicknamed "the Great Compromiser" because he played a major role in formulating legislative compromises, most notably the Missouri Compromise and the Compromise of 1850. Thus, **(C)** is correct. These agreements temporarily calmed sectional tension between pro- and antislavery factions. Seward, a leading antislavery advocate, opposed the Compromise of 1850 and repealed the Missouri Compromise through his Kansas-Nebraska Act. Thus, (A) is incorrect. While Daniel Webster worked alongside Clay in seeking compromises, he was not involved with the Missouri Compromise; (B) is incorrect. John C. Calhoun actually opposed the Compromise of 1850 because it limited the expansion of slavery westward; (D) is incorrect.

3. A

The Missouri Compromise did not address the issue of how fugitive slaves would be treated in the new territory acquired from France; **(A)** is correct. In 1819, the Union consisted of 11 free and 11 slave states. (B), (C), and (D) are all incorrect, because the Missouri Compromise did accomplish all of those things.

4. D

The *Dred Scott* Supreme Court decision protected slave owners' rights to slaves as property, no matter where they resided, and would have voided the Missouri Compromise. However, this had already been overturned three years earlier by the Kansas-Nebraska Act of 1854, which enforced popular sovereignty upon new territories. Thus, **(D)** is correct and (A) is incorrect. The Compromise of 1850 accomplished many things, including admitting California as a free state, banning the slave trade (but not slavery) in Washington, D.C., and enforcing a stricter Fugitive Slave Act; it did not, however, overturn the Missouri Compromise. Thus, (B) is incorrect. The raid on Harper's Ferry was an effort by abolitionist John Brown to initiate an armed slave revolt; (C) is incorrect.

5. B

New England was the only U.S. region that contained significant numbers of factories prior to 1860. By the eve of the American Civil War, industrialization had begun to contribute to major urban growth. Therefore, **(B)** is correct. The Old Northwest is the modern Midwest, and it would significantly industrialize only in the 1860s and 1870s; (A) is incorrect. (C) is also incorrect, as the Southwest was sparsely settled by 1860. Lastly, the Southeast, which would form the core of the Confederacy in the 1860s, relied on plantation agriculture for its economy rather than urbanized industry. Thus, (D) is incorrect.

6. C

Labor force participation in manufacturing increased by more than 50 percent between 1840 and 1850; **(C)** is correct. However, in terms of real numbers, less than 14 percent of the total U.S. labor force was involved in manufacturing by 1860, making (A) incorrect. The growth of manufacturing initially took place in rural, not urban, areas. It did not accelerate significantly until the 1840s; (B) is incorrect. The economy's agricultural sector continued to expand significantly as late as the 1850s thanks to westward expansion. This fact ensured that, relatively speaking, the growth of manufacturing slowed during the final decade before the Civil War; (D) is incorrect.

7. A

The increased use of steamboats on major rivers stimulated the growth of river cities such as Cincinnati and St. Louis. The opening of the Erie Canal fed the growth of cities on the Great Lakes, such as Buffalo and Chicago, from the 1820s onward. Therefore, **(A)** is correct. (B) is incorrect because its increase in manufacturing was merely an outgrowth of the trends described for (A). The urban percentage was growing each decade starting in 1820. Thus, the urban percentage growth between 1850 and 1860 was an extension of an existing phenomenon and not something new; (C) is incorrect. The agricultural labor force only grew 1 percent between 1800 and 1810, which is not significant, and then it shrunk almost 4 percent by 1820. This does not indicate the influence of steamboats and new canals, which would have aided the transport of goods to market; (D) is incorrect.

8. D

The great increase in railroad building did not reach its peak until the 1850s, when it contributed greatly to urban growth by connecting towns and cities along major rail routes. Thus, **(D)** is correct. The increase in the manufacturing workforce between 1840 and 1850 is also reflective of this, but it is a secondary effect of the increasing urbanization and ease of transporting goods. Therefore, (A) does not most directly reflect the growth of railroad building in the United States. The urban percentage grew 1.6 percent between 1820 and 1830, which was only a small increase; (B) is incorrect. The agricultural labor force had experienced a sharper decline between 1820 and 1830, which indicates that railroad building is not most directly reflected in the 1830–1840 decline. (C) is also incorrect.

9. C

The Seneca Falls Convention in 1848 was the first women's rights convention, held to allow both men and women to discuss the overall rights of women; **(C)** is correct. While voting and access to college were two of the rights discussed, neither was the main focus of the convention, eliminating (A) and (B). The convention lasted two days and resulted in the creation of the Declaration of Rights and Sentiments, which was directly modeled after the Declaration of Independence, but discussed the equality of both men and women explicitly. (D) is incorrect because the convention attendees did not wish to edit the Declaration of Independence itself.

10. C

Women were not elected to any political positions during the Second Great Awakening; **(C)** is correct. The Second Great Awakening lasted from approximately 1790 to 1840, renewing America's religious intensity and also initiating various reform movements. The fervor of religious revivalism contributed to female students gaining access to higher educational opportunities. Women's seminaries and colleges were established to provide mothers with a sufficient education that would allow them to properly form their children's moral characters. Thus, (A) is incorrect. Given that women were in charge of spiritual and moral well-being, they began to organize reform movements, such as prison reform and abolitionism, which caused their social importance to increase drastically. After seeing what they were able to accomplish through other reform movements, many women banded together to begin their own movement toward equality. Thus, (B) is incorrect. Finally, many more women than men converted to Christian denominations and devoted significant amounts of their time to helping the church. As a result, women were placed in more important roles than ever before; (D) is incorrect.

CHAPTER 7

Period 5: 1844–1877

LEARNING OBJECTIVES

After studying this time period, you will be able to:

- Describe the reasons for internal U.S. migration and settlement and the effect of such migration on American life

- Explain how environmental and geographic factors, as well as competition for resources, affected various communities and impacted government policies

- Explain the causes and effects of U.S. economic, diplomatic, and military initiatives in North America and globally

- Describe labor systems in North America and their effects on workers and society

- Explain the development of economic patterns and the government's response to, and influence on, economic issues

- Analyze relationships among various social, ethnic, and racial groups and their effect on U.S. national identity

- Describe how reformers and activists have changed American society

- Chart the development of, and changes in, American politics

- Describe the effects of differing interpretations of the Constitution on American life

TIMELINE

Date	Event
1844	James Polk is elected president.
1845	The United States annexes Texas.
1846	The Mexican-American War begins. California becomes an independent republic.
1848	The Treaty of Guadalupe Hidalgo ends the Mexican-American War.
1849	The California Gold Rush spurs mass westward migration.
1850	The Compromise of 1850 averts a national crisis over slavery while enacting a stricter Fugitive Slave Act.
1852	Harriet Beecher Stowe publishes *Uncle Tom's Cabin*.
1854	The Kansas-Nebraska Act repeals the Missouri Compromise of 1820. The Republican Party is created.
1856–1861	Mass violence breaks out in Kansas (Bleeding Kansas) over the issue of slavery.
1857	The *Dred Scott* decision is issued by the Supreme Court.
1859	John Brown leads the raid on Harper's Ferry.
1860	Abraham Lincoln is elected president. South Carolina leaves the Union.
1861	Seven states in the South form the Confederate States of America. Confederate troops fire on Fort Sumter. The First Battle of Bull Run is fought.
1862	The Second Battle of Bull Run takes place. The Battle of Antietam is fought. The Battle of Fredericksburg is fought.
1863	Lincoln issues Emancipation Proclamation. The Battle of Gettysburg takes place.
1865	Lee surrenders to Grant at Appomattox Court House in Virginia. President Lincoln is assassinated. The Thirteenth Amendment is ratified, abolishing slavery.
1866	The Fourteenth Amendment grants citizenship to African Americans.
1867	President Andrew Johnson is impeached by the House of Representatives.
1868	Ulysses S. Grant is elected president.
1870	The Fifteenth Amendment grants African Americans the right to vote.
1876	The presidential election between Rutherford B. Hayes and Samuel Tilden results in no clear winner.
1877	The Compromise of 1877 settles the presidential election, allowing Hayes to take office, and ends Reconstruction in the South.

7

TEST WHAT YOU ALREADY KNOW

Part A: Quiz

Questions 1–3 refer to the image below.

This political cartoon from 1861 depicts the Union defeating the secession of Southern states.

1. Which of the following political events most directly led to the secession of the South?

   (A) The presidential election of 1860

   (B) The *Dred Scott v. Sandford* case

   (C) The Kansas-Nebraska Act

   (D) The Ten Percent Plan

2. Which of the following did Southern states use to justify seceding from the United States?

   (A) The Lecompton Constitution

   (B) The Force Acts

   (C) The Kentucky and Virginia Resolutions

   (D) The Kansas-Nebraska Act

3. The Compromise of 1850 initially alleviated tension between the North and the South and delayed secession. Which of the following was not included in this Compromise?

   (A) The admission of California as a free state

   (B) The creation of the Utah and New Mexico territories

   (C) A ban on the slave trade in Virginia and Maryland

   (D) The enactment of a stricter Fugitive Slave Law

Questions 4–7 refer to the excerpt below.

"I am naturally anti-slavery. If slavery is not wrong, nothing is wrong . . . And yet I have never understood that the Presidency conferred upon me an unrestricted right to act officially upon this judgment and feeling . . . I did understand however, that my oath to preserve the constitution to the best of my ability, imposed upon me the duty of preserving, by every indispensable means, that government—that nation—of which that constitution was the organic law . . . I was, in my best judgment, driven to the alternative of either surrendering the Union, and with it, the Constitution, or of laying strong hand upon the colored element . . . it shows a gain of quite a hundred and thirty thousand soldiers, seamen, and laborers. These are palpable facts, about which, as facts, there can be no cavilling."

Letter from Abraham Lincoln to Albert G. Hodges, outlining Lincoln's
reasoning for the Emancipation Proclamation, April 4, 1864

4. Abraham Lincoln's intended purpose in issuing the Emancipation Proclamation was to

(A) establish the preservation of the Union as the goal for the Civil War

(B) abolish slavery across the United States

(C) assert the end of slavery as a major outcome of the Civil War

(D) advocate for a peaceful era of Reconstruction

5. Lincoln's Emancipation Proclamation most directly followed which of the following events?

(A) The Union victory at the Battle of Antietam

(B) The Union victory at the Battle of Gettysburg

(C) The implementation of a Union draft

(D) The attack on Fort Sumter

6. The immediate reaction of many Northerners after the issuance of the Emancipation Proclamation was most similar to

(A) Southern reaction to the War of 1812

(B) Northern reaction to the War of 1812

(C) Southern reaction to the Mexican-American War

(D) Northern reaction to the Mexican-American War

7. The Emancipation Proclamation benefited the Union war effort in which of the following ways?

(A) The Union gained control of more railroads and factories.

(B) European countries decided not to back the Confederacy.

(C) More African Americans joined Union troops.

(D) More citizens of border states supported the war.

Questions 8–10 refer to the excerpt below.

"With malice toward none, with charity for all, with firmness in the right as God gives us to see the right, let us strive on to finish the work we are in, to bind up the nation's wounds, to care for him who shall have borne the battle and for his widow and his orphan, to do all which may achieve and cherish a just and lasting peace among ourselves and with all nations."

Abraham Lincoln, Second Inaugural Address, 1865

8. Which of the following groups would most likely object to the perspective in this excerpt?

   (A) Radical Republicans

   (B) Moderate Republicans

   (C) Southern Democrats

   (D) Northern Democrats

9. Which of the following events officially abolished slavery in the United States?

   (A) The Emancipation Proclamation

   (B) Robert E. Lee's surrender at Appomattox

   (C) The passage of the Thirteenth Amendment

   (D) The Civil Rights Act of 1875

10. After President Lincoln was assassinated, President Andrew Johnson was in office from 1865 to 1869. He faced all of the following issues EXCEPT

    (A) the passage of Black Codes in the South

    (B) opposition from Republicans in Congress

    (C) impeachment by the Senate

    (D) rejection of his Reconstruction plan

7

Part B: Key Terms

The following is a list of the major people, places, and events for 1844–1877. You will likely see many of these on the AP U.S. History exam.

For each key term ask yourself the following questions:

- Can I describe this key term?
- Can I discuss this key term in the context of other events?
- Could I correctly answer a multiple-choice question about this key term?
- Could I correctly answer a free-response question about this key term?

Check off the key terms if you can answer "yes" to at least three of these questions.

The Impacts of Manifest Destiny

- ☐ Manifest Destiny
- ☐ Oregon Trail
- ☐ Martin Van Buren
- ☐ Panic of 1837
- ☐ Whig Party
- ☐ William Henry Harrison
- ☐ John Tyler
- ☐ James K. Polk

The Mexican-American War

- ☐ Mexican-American War
- ☐ Wilmot Proviso

Continued Debate over Slavery

- ☐ Gadsden Purchase
- ☐ Free Soil Party
- ☐ Zachary Taylor
- ☐ Gold Rush
- ☐ Compromise of 1850
- ☐ Fugitive Slave Act
- ☐ Millard Fillmore
- ☐ Franklin Pierce
- ☐ Kansas-Nebraska Act
- ☐ Republican Party
- ☐ James Buchanan
- ☐ *Dred Scott v. Sandford*

The Rise of Lincoln and the Election of 1860

- ☐ Abraham Lincoln
- ☐ Freeport Doctrine
- ☐ Confederate States of America
- ☐ Jefferson Davis

The Civil War

- ☐ Civil War
- ☐ Fort Sumter
- ☐ Battle of Bull Run (Battle of Manassas)
- ☐ Second Battle of Bull Run
- ☐ Antietam
- ☐ Battle of Fredericksburg
- ☐ Battle of Gettysburg
- ☐ Gettysburg Address

The End of Slavery

☐ Emancipation Proclamation   ☐ Thirteenth Amendment

Consequences of the Civil War

☐ Suspension of the writ of   ☐ Pacific Railway Act
     habeas corpus

Reconstruction

☐ Reconstruction

☐ Andrew Johnson

☐ Ten Percent Plan

☐ Wade-Davis Bill

☐ Freedman's Bureau

☐ Black Codes

☐ Sharecropping

☐ Civil Rights Bill of 1866

☐ Fourteenth Amendment

☐ Radical Republicans

☐ Ulysses S. Grant

☐ Fifteenth Amendment

☐ Civil Rights Act of 1875

☐ National Woman Suffrage Association (NWSA)

☐ American Woman Suffrage Association (AWSA)

☐ Ku Klux Klan (KKK)

☐ Rutherford B. Hayes

Next Steps

Step 1: Tally your correct answers from Part A and review the quiz explanations at the end of this chapter.

1.	A	6.	D
2.	C	7.	C
3.	C	8.	A
4.	C	9.	C
5.	A	10.	C

_____ out of 10 questions

Step 2: Count the number of key terms you checked off in Part B.

_____ out of 55 key terms

Step 3: Read the Key Takeaways in this chapter.

Step 4: Consult the table below and follow the instructions based on your performance.

If You Got...	Do This
80% or more of the Test What You Already Know assessment correct (8 or more questions from Part A and 44 or more key terms from Part B)	• Read definitions in this chapter for all the key terms you didn't check off. • Complete the Test What You Learned assessment in this chapter.
50% or less of the Test What You Already Know assessment correct (5 or fewer questions from Part A and 28 or fewer key terms from Part B)	• Read the comprehensive review for this period in Chapter 16. • If you are short on time, read only the High-Yield sections. • Read through all of the key term definitions in this chapter. • Complete the Test What You Learned assessment in this chapter.
Any other result	• Read the High-Yield sections in the comprehensive review of this period in Chapter 16. • Read definitions in this chapter for all the key terms you didn't check off. • Complete the Test What You Learned assessment in this chapter.

ESSENTIAL CONTENT

Key Takeaways: 1844–1877

1. Americans enthusiastically supported western expansion in hopes of finding new economic opportunities. The philosophy of Manifest Destiny emerged as motivation for this westward migration. America's expansionist philosophy extended into foreign policy as well, as evidenced by conflict over the Oregon territory with Britain and involvement in the Mexican-American War.

2. The Compromise of 1850, the Kansas-Nebraska Act, and the *Dred Scott* decision were all important attempts made by national leaders and the courts to resolve the issues surrounding slavery.

3. Debates about slavery—as well as economic, political, and cultural differences—led to a widening gap between the North and South. Despite various efforts at compromise, the South (11 states in all) seceded from the United States to form the Confederate States of America. America would soon afterward become embroiled in the Civil War.

4. Due to superior military strategy, more resources, a larger population, and stronger infrastructure, the Union defeated the Confederacy. During the war, President Lincoln declared an end to slavery with the Emancipation Proclamation, and after the war worked to rebuild the country. After his assassination, many questions remained, however, about the role of the federal government and citizens' rights, including those of women, African Americans, and other minorities.

5. After the Civil War, the Thirteenth Amendment officially ended slavery, and the Fourteenth and Fifteenth Amendments further expanded the rights of African Americans. Despite these efforts, African Americans faced great hardships in gaining equal rights and employment.

Key Terms: 1844–1877

Remember that the AP U.S. History exam tests you on the depth of your knowledge, not just your ability to recall facts. While we have provided brief definitions here, you will need to know these terms in even more depth for the AP exam, including how terms connect to broader historical themes and understandings.

The Impacts of Manifest Destiny

Manifest Destiny: Coined by journalist John O'Sullivan in 1845 to describe the belief that it was God's will for the United States to expand westward to the Pacific Ocean. It also describes a more general expansionism, such as the dispute over the Oregon Territory that Polk campaigned on and the U.S. expansion into the Southwest following the Mexican-American War.

Oregon Trail: Throughout the 1840s, a flood of settlers began traversing the dangerous Oregon Trail. Families traveled up to six months in caravans, covering only about 15 miles per day with good weather. While living on the trail, some women began to run prayer meetings and schools to maintain some vestiges of home. Women also began to take on new roles outside of homemaking and childcare, such as repairing wagon wheels and tending to livestock.

Martin Van Buren: Eighth president. Served from 1837–1841. Van Buren's presidency was marred by an economic depression resulting from the policies of his predecessor, Andrew

Jackson. The Panic of 1837 dogged his administration. Van Buren was the first president to be born a U.S. citizen, and the only president to speak English as a second language (Dutch being the primary language spoken in his childhood home).

Panic of 1837: A financial crisis that lasted from 1837 until the mid-1840s. Caused, in part, by Andrew Jackson killing the Bank of the United States and issuing the Specie Circular; also caused by overspeculation and faulty loans from "wildcat" western banks.

Whig Party: The Whig Party was born out of opposition to Jacksonian Democrats. The Whigs favored economic nationalism, a strong central government, and rechartering the national bank. They believed in protectionist measures such as tariffs to support American industrialization. They also promoted Clay's American System as a way to improve the roads, canals, and infrastructure of the country. The party collapsed over the question of slavery's expansion into newly acquired territories.

William Henry Harrison: Ninth president. Served from March 4 to April 4, 1841, famously dying after 31 days in office. A hero of the War of 1812, specifically the Battle of Tippecanoe, his lively campaign saw the Whigs cart model log cabins to towns and distribute hard cider to boast of Harrison's poor background. His "Tippecanoe and Tyler, too" ticket easily defeated Van Buren in 1840. However, he gave his inaugural address on a cold, rainy day and neglected to wear a warm coat. He contracted pneumonia and died.

John Tyler: Tenth president. Served April 4, 1841, to 1845. A Virginian Whig, Tyler was that first vice president to ascend to the presidency upon the death of the incumbent. This act set the precedent that all future vice presidents would follow, as the issue was something of a legal gray area constitutionally. Tyler sought the annexation of Texas but was unable to secure it. Nicknamed "His Accidency."

James K. Polk: Eleventh president. Served from 1845–1849. An heir of sorts to Andrew Jackson, he advocated for Manifest Destiny. His campaign slogan was "Fifty-four forty or fight!" Yet while that slogan advocated a hardline position on the disputed Oregon Territory, he instead reached a diplomatic agreement with Britain. The border was drawn at the 49th parallel, which ceded what is now British Columbia, including Vancouver Island. He then oversaw the controversial Mexican-American War, expanding the United States into the Southwest. Having pledged to only serve one term, he declined to run for reelection in 1848.

The Mexican-American War

Mexican-American War: A conflict between the United States and Mexico. It took place from April 1846 to February 1848. Following the 1845 American annexation of Texas, war broke out between the two nations. The war was deeply controversial in its time, illustrating the deepening divide between free and slave states. Many political and military leaders of the Civil War fought in this war. It also led to a major U.S. territorial expansion, as the United States gained California and most of the Southwest (including current-day New Mexico, Arizona, Utah, and Nevada).

Wilmot Proviso: Following the Mexican-American War, Representative David Wilmot proposed that slavery would be forbidden in any new lands acquired by the war with Mexico. The final bill passed in the House but failed in the Senate. This bill, the Wilmot Proviso, signaled the start of an even deeper crisis that would pit the North against the South over issues of slavery's expansion, states' rights, and government representation.

7

Continued Debate over Slavery

Gadsden Purchase: An 1853 treaty between the United States and Mexico. It was ratified in 1854. The treaty resolved a border issue lingering from the Treaty of Guadalupe Hidalgo. In exchange for $10 million, the United States purchased a chunk of modern-day Arizona and a small portion of southwest New Mexico. This was the last notable expansion of the continental United States.

Free Soil Party: Inspired by the Wilmot Proviso, antislavery advocates from various political parties founded the Free Soil Party to oppose the expansion of slavery into the new western territories. Martin Van Buren ran for president as a Free Soil candidate in 1848. The Free Soil Party's membership was later absorbed into the new Republican Party.

Zachary Taylor: Twelfth president. Served from 1849–1850. Died of a stomach ailment. Tayler was a Mexican-American War general. The Whigs nominated him in the 1848 election. Although he was a slave-owner, he did not advocate the expansion of slavery, believing that the practice wasn't economically viable in the West.

Gold Rush: Commonly refers to the California Gold Rush, which took place between 1848 and roughly 1855. The population of California ballooned as prospectors flocked to the state to seek a fortune in mining gold; those who came were often called Forty-Niners (referring to 1849).

Compromise of 1850: A package of several bills that alleviated some of the tension between the North and South, delaying the Civil War for another decade. Orchestrated by Henry Clay. Its key points were: California was admitted as a free state; it created the New Mexico and Utah Territories, and popular sovereignty would determine slavery's status in them; it banned the slave trade in Washington, D.C.; it enacted a stricter Fugitive Slave Act; it give Texas monetary compensation to drop its claims to part of New Mexico's territory.

Fugitive Slave Act: A controversial law that constituted part of the Compromise of 1850. It required that escaped slaves, upon their capture, would be returned to their masters, and that the authorities in a free state had to cooperate with this process. Nicknamed "the Bloodhound Law" by abolitionists for the common use of such dogs in hunting down slaves.

Millard Fillmore: Thirteenth president. Served 1850–1853. Took office after the sickness and death of Zachary Taylor. A longtime House member, Fillmore worked to help pass the Compromise of 1850. Notably, he dispatched the Perry Expedition to Japan. After failing to gain the Whig nomination in 1852, he served as the Know-Nothing Party nominee in 1856.

Franklin Pierce: Fourteenth president. Served from 1853–1857. A northern Democrat, Pierce signed the Kansas-Nebraska Act into law, which inflamed regional tensions and helped lead to the creation of the Republican Party. He also signed the Gadsden Purchase. Pierce lost his party's renomination in 1856 to James Buchanan.

Kansas-Nebraska Act: Proposed by Senator Stephen A. Douglas in 1854, it functionally repealed the Missouri Compromise. The act proposed the Nebraska Territory be divided into two regions, Nebraska and Kansas, and each would vote by popular sovereignty on the issue of slavery. It was presumed that Nebraska would become a free state, while Kansas would become a slave state. Douglas was able to push his bill through Congress, and President Pierce signed it into law in 1854. It helped spur the formation of the Republican Party.

Republican Party: Also known as the GOP, for Grand Old Party, it emerged from the renewed sectional tension of the 1850s. The GOP was founded in 1854 by antislavery Whigs, Democrats, Free Soilers, and Know-Nothings from the North and West. Although the GOP lost the 1856 presidential election, the popular John C. Fremont garnered many votes and won 11 of the 16 free states in the Electoral College.

James Buchanan: Fifteenth president. Served from 1857–1861. A Pennsylvania Democrat, Buchanan had a storied career as a U.S. senator and representative, a secretary of state, and an ambassador to both Russia and Britain. He essentially won his party's nomination due to being abroad for so long, meaning he wasn't tied to any of the contentious domestic issues of the 1850s. He supported the *Dred Scott* ruling and the entry of Kansas into the Union as a slave state. Declined to run for a second term. Often ranked as the worst president for exacerbating regional tensions in the run-up to the Civil War and then doing nothing to stop secession.

Dred Scott v. Sandford: A landmark 1857 Supreme Court case that was a major contributing factor in the outbreak of the Civil War. Dred Scott, a slave in Missouri, spent years in Wisconsin and Illinois with his master. After his master's death, Dred Scott sued for freedom. The Court ruled that all African Americans (free or slave) were not citizens. The chief justice also ruled that Congress had no right to deny citizens of their individual property, and therefore the Missouri Compromise was unconstitutional for stripping slave owners of their rightful property once they moved north.

The Rise of Lincoln and the Election of 1860

Abraham Lincoln: Sixteenth President. Served 1861 to his assassination on April 15, 1865. A former Whig who had opposed the Mexican-American War, he joined the newly formed Republican Party. His 1860 election triggered the secession of several states, and he deftly led the Union through the ensuing Civil War.

Freeport Doctrine: During the Lincoln-Douglas debates, Lincoln challenged Douglas to rationalize the concept of popular sovereignty with the decision of the *Dred Scott* case. Douglas stated that territories would have to pass and enforce laws to protect slavery. In essence, he argued that *Dred Scott* would still be the law of the land but that, by willfully choosing to not arm themselves with the means to police the issue, territories could still functionally be free soil. This attempt to appease both wings of the Democratic Party alienated supporters in the South, dwindling the chances of Douglas to win the presidency in 1860.

Confederate States of America: A bloc of states that attempted to secede from the United States. It was led by Jefferson Davis and its capital was in Richmond, Virginia. Its members included: Alabama, Arkansas, Florida, Georgia, Louisiana, Mississippi, North Carolina, South Carolina, Tennessee, Texas, and Virginia.

Jefferson Davis: The sole president of the Confederate States. Served February 22, 1862, to May 10, 1865. Davis was a Democrat from Mississippi. A veteran of the Mexican-American War, he had served in the House (1845–1856) and Senate (1847–1851, 1857–1861), as well as secretary of war (1853–1857) under Franklin Pierce. Davis was a micromanager who hampered the Confederate war effort by refusing to delegate issues or authority to his subordinates. He also lacked the political skill to overcome the decentralized states' rights structure of the Confederacy, which made him reliant on state governors in a way Lincoln was not.

The Civil War

Civil War: Also known as the American Civil War, it was fought from 1861 to 1865. Several states seceded to form the Confederate States of America, an illegal act. The Confederacy sought to protect the institution of slavery from perceived interference by Lincoln, who had won the 1860 election without his name even being on the ballot in many Southern states, thus showcasing the relative declining power of the South over U.S. domestic policy. The war cemented the supremacy of the federal government over the states. The death toll is estimated to be over 620,000.

Fort Sumter: A sea fort near Charleston, South Carolina. On April 12–13, 1861, the first shots of the Civil War were fired there. The Confederate Army fired upon the unarmed merchant vessel *Star of the West*, which was attempting to resupply the U.S. forces stationed at the fort.

Battle of Bull Run (Battle of Manassas): Known as Manassas in Confederate histories, the (First) Battle of Bull Run took place on July 21, 1861. It was an early Confederate victory in the Civil War, showing the North that this would be a long and bloody war, while Southerners felt emboldened by their victory. Union forces had expected an easy victory; many congressmen and D.C. elites actually brought their families along to hold picnics to watch the battle.

Second Battle of Bull Run: A Confederate victory in August 1862. John Pope's defeat created an opening for Robert E. Lee's Maryland Campaign, which culminated in the Battle of Antietam.

Antietam: A Civil War battle that took place on September 17, 1862. The bloodiest single-day battle in U.S. history, it saw 22,717 killed. Despite stopping Lee's invasion of Maryland, McClellan failed to exploit an opening to destroy Lee's army and shorten the war, leading to Lincoln removing him as general-in-chief of the Union Army. Nevertheless, Antietam offered good enough news to allow Lincoln to issue the Emancipation Proclamation.

Battle of Fredericksburg: A Civil War battle fought December 11–15, 1862. A lopsided Confederate victory, it saw Union forces suffer 3-to-1 casualties. Lincoln removed General Burnside as a result, replacing him with Joseph Hooker.

Battle of Gettysburg: Arguably the most significant battle of the Civil War. Fought July 1–3, 1863, in southern Pennsylvania. Over 50,000 men died there. It was the final major Confederate push into the North, and Lee's defeat ended any hope of Britain or France recognizing the Confederacy as a legitimate nation. General Meade's failure to chase and destroy Lee's retreating army, however, lengthened the war.

Gettysburg Address: A brief, poignant address by Abraham Lincoln commemorating the Battle of Gettysburg. It was delivered on November 19, 1863. Hearkening back to the Declaration of Independence 87 years prior, Lincoln proposed the idea of equality—"all men are created equal"—as the core spirit of the Declaration and the Constitution. He went on to reframe the context of the Civil War as a trial to see if equality could endure, rather than framing it solely as an issue of preserving the Union.

The End of Slavery

Emancipation Proclamation: Issued on January 1, 1863, it was an executive order that freed any slave in areas in open rebellion against the United States government. Slavery in the border states was still legal. Despite its limitations, the proclamation did much to bolster the morale of Union troops and supporters at home. However, some Unionists felt betrayed, believing they had been duped into fighting a war for emancipation instead of merely for the Union's preservation. The Proclamation also served to dissuade Britain and France from recognizing the Confederacy, as it reframed the moral context for the war as opposition to slavery.

Abolitionism was popular with the voters in Britain and France.

Thirteenth Amendment: It banned slavery and involuntary servitude, and functionally repealed the Three-Fifths Clause. Passed in early 1865 and ratified later that year, this amendment was one of Lincoln's last major achievements prior to his assassination.

Consequences of the Civil War

Suspension of the writ of habeas corpus: During the Civil War, Lincoln exercised his executive power to limit Americans' civil rights and liberties in order to protect the Union. He suspended the writ of habeas corpus, which meant that the federal government could hold an individual in jail with no charges levied against him or her. For many alleged traitors, this meant long jail terms with no charges ever filed.

Pacific Railway Act: This 1862 act approved building a transcontinental railroad that would transform the West by linking the Atlantic Ocean with the Pacific. An example of infrastructure spending, it had been held up for several years by arguments over whether the route should be from the South or the North, given the economic opportunity such a rail line would provide.

Reconstruction

Reconstruction: A period (1865–1877) of rebuilding and reforming the South following the Civil War. It is considered a failure, as African Americans were left destitute and disenfranchised for another century.

Andrew Johnson: Seventeenth president. Served from 1865–1869. One of only two presidents to be impeached; like Bill Clinton, he was not convicted. Took office after Lincoln's assassination. A Democrat who had run with the Republican Lincoln, he was disliked by Congress, especially for his mild terms for Reconstruction and disinterest in protecting newly freed slaves; this all led to Radical Republicans passing the Civil Rights Bill of 1866 and the Fourteenth Amendment.

Ten Percent Plan: Also known as the Proclamation of Amnesty and Reconstruction, Lincoln proposed this plan in 1863 as a way to bring Southern states back under the wing of the

federal government. The plan reestablished state governments and required at least 10 percent of the states' voters to swear an oath of loyalty to the United States and the Constitution. Lincoln was also prepared to grant complete pardons to any former Confederate, but required an oath of allegiance and agreement to eliminate slavery.

Wade-Davis Bill: Passed by both houses in 1864 in response to Lincoln's Ten Percent Plan. It required that 50 percent of Southern state voters take the loyalty oath, and it allowed only those citizens who had not been active members or supporters of the Confederacy to approve of the new state constitutions. Exercising his executive power, Lincoln pocket-vetoed the bill by refusing to sign it.

Freedman's Bureau: A government program created in 1865 to help manage and assist newly emancipated slaves. The bureau provided assistance in the form of food, shelter, and medical attention to African Americans. Eventually, the bureau would establish schools across the South to help educate large numbers of former slaves. The Freedman's Bureau struggled as Congress refused to increase its funding, which expired in 1872.

Black Codes: Laws passed by Southern legislatures in response to legal emancipation of slaves. These codes restricted the actions, movements, and freedoms of African Americans. Under these codes, African Americans could not own land, so they were tied instead to small plots leased from a landowner. This began the system of sharecropping.

Sharecropping: Sharecroppers would lease land and borrow supplies to till their plots, while giving a significant portion of their harvest to the landowner as payment for the loan. This exploitative system ensured that farmers were never able to harvest enough to pay the landlord and feed their families. Generations of African Americans remained tied to their plot of land until the civil rights movement of the 1950s and 1960s.

Civil Rights Bill of 1866: It was designed to end the Black Codes by giving African Americans full citizenship. As expected, Johnson vetoed the bill, and Congress overturned his veto. Many Republicans were concerned that a future return of a Democratic majority might mean the end of the bill they had worked so hard to pass. Therefore, they needed a more permanent solution in the form of the Fourteenth Amendment.

Fourteenth Amendment: A response to the lackluster Reconstruction efforts by President Johnson. Proposed in 1866 and ratified in 1868, it protected the rights of all U.S. citizens, granted all African Americans full citizenship and civil rights, and required states to adhere to the due process and equal protection clauses of the Constitution. Furthermore, it disallowed former Confederate officers from holding state or federal office. It would decrease the proportional representation of any state that denied suffrage to any able citizen.

Radical Republicans: A group within the Republican Party of the United States from around 1854 until the end of Reconstruction in 1877. Their goal was the eradication of slavery, without compromise. In 1867, they passed the Military Reconstruction Act, placing the South under martial law; the act was a response to the leniency displayed by President Johnson toward the Confederacy.

Ulysses S. Grant: Eighteenth president. Served from 1869–1877. Grant served in the Mexican-American War, where he worked as a quartermaster. During the Civil War, he led Union forces in the West, winning famous victories at Shiloh and Vicksburg. He eventually was placed in command of the whole U.S. Army in 1864, and he fought several engagements with Lee. He supervised Reconstruction and prosecuted efforts against the KKK. He served two terms as president, to decidedly mixed results. The cronyism of his administration led to a push for civil service reform.

Fifteenth Amendment: Ratified in 1870, it barred any state from denying a citizen's right to vote on the basis of race, color, or previous servitude. However, it did not ban poll taxes or literacy tests, which would be a loophole exploited by whites after the end of Reconstruction to suppress African American voters.

Civil Rights Act of 1875: The last of the Reconstruction-era civil rights reform made it a crime for any person to be denied full and equal use of public places, such as hotels, rail cars, restaurants, and theaters. Unfortunately, this act lacked any wording to enforce it, and it was therefore ignored by most states, both Northern and Southern.

National Woman Suffrage Association (NWSA): The Fourteenth and Fifteenth amendment split the women's suffrage movement in two, leading to decades of bitter partisanship between the two wings. One faction, the NWSA, was an all-female organization that favored a federal solution to women's suffrage, namely an amendment. Overall, the NWSA was considered the more liberal in nature of the two splinter groups.

American Woman Suffrage Association (AWSA): The other suffragist faction, the AWSA, admitted that the Reconstruction amendments disadvantaged women, but held that the needs of former slaves were more critical. In contrast to the NWSA, the AWSA favored a state-by-state effort at securing women's suffrage, accepted male members, and remained focused on suffrage to the exclusion of other issues. It was considered more conservative.

Ku Klux Klan (KKK): An underground society of whites who ruthlessly and successfully used terrorist tactics to frighten both white and black Republicans in the South. While quashed by the Force Acts of 1870 and 1871, the organization survived, resurfacing and spreading throughout the country in later years.

Rutherford B. Hayes: Nineteenth president. Served from 1877–1881. While a Civil War veteran and a Republican, he ended Reconstruction as part of the Compromise of 1877 to resolve the disputed 1876 election. Enacted modest civil service reform. Ordered federal troops to break up the Great Railroad Strike of 1877. Pledged not to run for reelection and returned to Ohio.

TEST WHAT YOU LEARNED

Questions 1 and 2 refer to the excerpt below.

"Whereas the President of the United States, in his message of May 11, 1846, has declared that 'the Mexican Government not only refused to receive him, [the envoy of the United States,] or listen to his propositions, but, after a long-continued series of menaces, has at last invaded *our territory* and shed the blood of our fellow-citizens on our *own soil* . . .'

And again, in his message of December 8, 1846, that 'we had ample cause of war against Mexico long before the breaking out of hostilities; but even then we forbore to take redress into our own hands until Mexico herself became the aggressor, by invading *our soil* in hostile array, and shedding the blood of our citizens . . .'"

Abraham Lincoln, speech before the U.S. House of Representatives, 1847

1. Lincoln's speech to Congress challenged

   (A) America's justification for declaring war against Mexico

   (B) America's claim that the Rio Grande River was the official border between the United States and Mexico

   (C) the idea that Texas should be considered United States territory when it had not yet been officially admitted as a state

   (D) the authority of the president to declare war on a nonhostile nation

2. Which of the following was a reason the Democratic Party supported the Mexican-American War?

   (A) The potential to gain territory could help fulfill Manifest Destiny.

   (B) Additional free territory could counterbalance the large slave territory established by the Missouri Compromise.

   (C) The American public was eager and willing to go to war with a neighboring power.

   (D) A victory could counteract the humiliating defeat of the United States in the War of 1812.

7

Questions 3–6 refer to the map below.

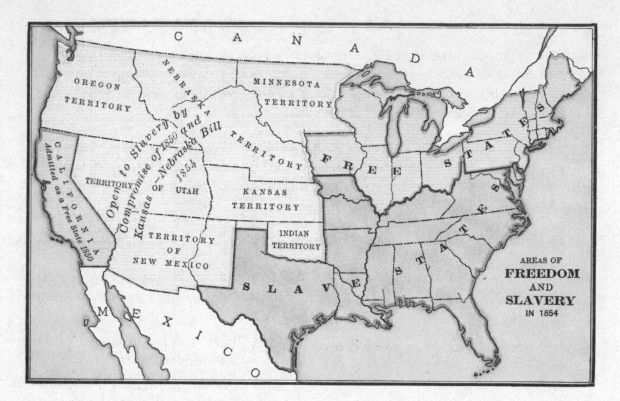

3. The proportion of free and slaves states shown on the map directly led to

    (A) the passage of the Northwest Ordinance

    (B) the formation of the Republican Party

    (C) a backlash against Manifest Destiny

    (D) an increase in nativist sentiment

4. Texas was a source of conflict for all of the following reasons EXCEPT its

    (A) application for annexation

    (B) disputed borders

    (C) rejection of the Compromise of 1850

    (D) refusal to abide by Mexican laws

5. The Compromise of 1850 and the Kansas-Nebraska Act were

    (A) a source of increased sectional conflict in the antebellum years

    (B) an example of tensions resolved by the *Dred Scott* case

    (C) a direct cause of U.S. entry into the Mexican-American War

    (D) a catalyst for greater political party unity

6. Opponents of the Kansas-Nebraska Act most likely supported

    (A) an extension of the Missouri Compromise

    (B) a free-soil position

    (C) expansion of slavery

    (D) annexation of additional territory

Questions 7–10 refer to the excerpt below.

"Disloyalty . . . of any kind was a punishable offense . . . If a newspaper promulgated disloyal sentiments, the paper was suppressed and the editor imprisoned. If a clergyman was disloyal in prayer or sermon, or if he failed to utter a prescribed prayer, he was liable to be treated in the same manner, and was sometimes so treated. A learned and eloquent Lutheran clergyman came to me for advice because he had been summoned before the provost marshal for saying that a nation which incurred a heavy debt in the prosecution of war laid violent hands on the harvests of the future; but his offense was condoned, because it appeared that he had referred to the 'Thirty Years' War' and had made no direct reference to the debt of the United States, and perhaps for a better reason—that he had strong Republican friends among his congregation."

George William Brown, Mayor of Baltimore, *Baltimore and the Nineteenth of April, 1861: A Study of the War*, 2001

7. The situations described in the excerpt most clearly relate to

   (A) Reconstruction plans by Radical Republicans

   (B) religious tolerance in the mid-nineteenth century

   (C) Republican support for the Confederate cause

   (D) Union concern over the allegiance of the border states

8. The controversy highlighted in the passage above most directly led to

   (A) widespread civilian protests over religious freedom

   (B) the issuance of the Emancipation Proclamation

   (C) the establishment of martial law in the border states

   (D) collaboration between Northern Democrats and Republicans

9. All of the following plans for Reconstruction included the requirement of a loyalty oath EXCEPT

   (A) the Military Reconstruction Acts

   (B) Lincoln's Ten Percent Plan

   (C) the Wade-Davis Bill

   (D) Johnson's Reconstruction plan

10. The excerpt most clearly reflects which of the following themes present throughout the history of the United States?

   (A) Tensions between liberty and authority

   (B) Changing relationships among the branches of the federal government

   (C) Competition for territory and resources

   (D) Expansion of religious freedom and toleration

Part B: Key Terms

This key terms list is the same as the list in the Test What You Already Know section earlier in this chapter. Based on what you have now learned, again ask yourself the following questions:

- Can I define this key term and use it in a sentence?

- Can I provide an example related to this key term?

- Could I correctly answer a multiple-choice question about this key term?

- Could I correctly answer a free-response question about this key term?

Check off the key terms if you can answer "yes" to at least three of these questions.

The Impacts of Manifest Destiny

- ☐ Manifest Destiny
- ☐ Panic of 1837
- ☐ John Tyler
- ☐ Oregon Trail
- ☐ Whig Party
- ☐ James K. Polk
- ☐ Martin Van Buren
- ☐ William Henry Harrison

The Mexican-American War

- ☐ Mexican-American War
- ☐ Wilmot Proviso

Continued Debate over Slavery

- ☐ Gadsden Purchase
- ☐ Compromise of 1850
- ☐ Kansas-Nebraska Act
- ☐ Free Soil Party
- ☐ Fugitive Slave Act
- ☐ Republican Party
- ☐ Zachary Taylor
- ☐ Millard Fillmore
- ☐ James Buchanan
- ☐ Gold Rush
- ☐ Franklin Pierce
- ☐ *Dred Scott v. Sandford*

The Rise of Lincoln and the Election of 1860

- ☐ Abraham Lincoln
- ☐ Confederate States of America
- ☐ Jefferson Davis
- ☐ Freeport Doctrine

The Civil War

- ☐ Civil War
- ☐ Second Battle of Bull Run
- ☐ Battle of Gettysburg
- ☐ Fort Sumter
- ☐ Antietam
- ☐ Gettysburg Address
- ☐ Battle of Bull Run (Battle of Manassas)
- ☐ Battle of Fredericksburg

The End of Slavery

- [ ] Emancipation Proclamation
- [ ] Thirteenth Amendment

Consequences of the Civil War

- [ ] Suspension of the writ of habeas corpus
- [ ] Pacific Railway Act

Reconstruction

- [ ] Reconstruction
- [ ] Andrew Johnson
- [ ] Ten Percent Plan
- [ ] Wade-Davis Bill
- [ ] Freedman's Bureau
- [ ] Black Codes
- [ ] Sharecropping

- [ ] Civil Rights Bill of 1866
- [ ] Fourteenth Amendment
- [ ] Radical Republicans
- [ ] Ulysses S. Grant
- [ ] Fifteenth Amendment
- [ ] Civil Rights Act of 1875

- [ ] National Woman Suffrage Association (NWSA)
- [ ] American Woman Suffrage Association (AWSA)
- [ ] Ku Klux Klan (KKK)
- [ ] Rutherford B. Hayes

Next Steps

Step 1: Tally your correct answers from Part A and review the quiz explanations at the end of this chapter.

1.	A	6.	B
2.	A	7.	D
3.	B	8.	C
4.	C	9.	A
5.	A	10.	A

____ out of 10 questions

Step 2: Count the number of key terms you checked off in Part B.

____ out of 55 key terms

Step 3: Compare your Test What You Already Know results to these Test What You Learned results to see how exam-ready you are for this period.

For More Practice:

- Read (or reread) the comprehensive review for this period in Chapter 16.
- Go to kaptest.com to complete the online quiz questions for 1844–1877.
  - Haven't registered your book yet? Go to kaptest.com/moreonline to begin.

ANSWERS AND EXPLANATIONS

Test What You Already Know

1. A

Lincoln's nomination and election as president directly prompted Southern states to secede. Six more states soon joined South Carolina to leave the Union; therefore, **(A)** is correct. Both (B) and (C) are incorrect because these events were favorable to Southern states and temporarily appeased their desire for secession. (D) is incorrect because Lincoln's Ten Percent Plan (also known as the Proclamation of Amnesty and Reconstruction) occurred after the Civil War and was an attempt to reintegrate the Southern states.

2. C

The South drew upon the Kentucky and Virginia Resolutions, as well as speeches by South Carolina's John C. Calhoun regarding nullification, to justify seceding from the United States. They argued that states had formed the Union as part of a social contract and that individual states had the right to leave that contract if the government no longer served the needs of their people. **(C)** is correct. While both the Lecompton Constitution and the Kansas-Nebraska Act fueled the escalating conflicts between the North and South about slavery and states' rights, the South did not cite them as major reasons for secession; (A) and (D) are incorrect. (B) is also incorrect because the Force Acts, which authorized the use of federal troops to quell violence, were passed after the Civil War.

3. C

The Compromise of 1850 specified that the slave trade (but not slavery itself) would be banned only in Washington, D.C.; this ban did not extend to neighboring states Virginia and Maryland. Therefore, **(C)** is correct. (A), (B), and (D) are incorrect, as they were all components of the Compromise of 1850 as proposed by Henry Clay.

4. C

Lincoln's initial goal in fighting the Civil War was to preserve the Union. The Emancipation Proclamation enlarged the purpose of the war to include the end of slavery. Therefore, **(C)** is correct and (A) is incorrect. The proclamation applied only to slaves living in Confederate states, and slavery in the border states was still legal; (B) is incorrect. While Lincoln did eventually advocate for Reconstruction efforts, including pardoning and reintegrating Southern states, this was not the purpose of the Emancipation Proclamation, making (D) incorrect.

5. A

By July of 1862, Lincoln had already decided to issue what would become the Emancipation Proclamation. The timing of this announcement was important, to both win the support of conservative Northerners and to avoid seeming militarily desperate. After the strategic Union victory at Antietam in September of 1862, the timing was right, and the Emancipation Proclamation was issued on January 1, 1863, making **(A)** correct. The Battle of Gettysburg, while significant, was fought in July 1863, after the Emancipation Proclamation, eliminating (B). (C) is incorrect; although the Union draft was met with deadly rioting in New York City, it did not prompt a direct response from Lincoln. (D) marked the beginning of the war.

6. D

Many Northerners reacted negatively to Lincoln's Emancipation Proclamation, which included ending slavery as a purpose of the Civil War. Some felt Lincoln had led them into a major war and then abruptly shifted its purpose. Similarly, the Mexican-American War resulted in negative reactions. Many Northerners accused Polk of waging war under false pretenses by dishonestly claiming that American blood had been shed on American soil when Mexican forces crossed the Rio Grande. Therefore, **(D)** is the best match and is correct. Southerners did not have a unified negative response to the Mexican-American War; some even saw it as a way to add to America's total of slave states. Thus, (C) is incorrect. While the War of 1812 had its critics, a heightened sense of nationalism caused many Americans to support the war, making (A) and (B) incorrect.

7. C

Some African American soldiers fought for the North early in the war, but those numbers increased significantly (to approximately 180,000) after the Emancipation Proclamation; therefore, **(C)** is correct. (A) and (B) are incorrect because both of these Union advantages were true before the Civil War began, and they were not caused by the Emancipation Proclamation. People in the border states did not support Lincoln's proclamation, so it did not lead to increased support for the war; (D) is also incorrect.

8. A

In contrast to Lincoln's call for ending Reconstruction as quickly and amicably as possible, radicals within his own Republican party wanted to treat the South as "conquered provinces" and advocated for a much harsher policy in dealing with the South. Thus, **(A)** is correct. Moderates initially sided with Lincoln, making (B) incorrect. (C) and (D) are incorrect because Democrats in both the North and South preferred Lincoln's position to that of his critics.

9. C

The Emancipation Proclamation did not actually end slavery, because it only freed slaves in Confederate states. In addition, the Constitution's language left the legal status of slavery ambiguous. An amendment to the Constitution was needed to legally achieve complete emancipation of all slaves. In 1865, the Thirteenth Amendment was ratified by Congress and officially abolished slavery in the United States; **(C)** is correct and (A) is incorrect. Though Lee's surrender marks the end of the war, it did not legally abolish slavery, making (B) incorrect. The Civil Rights Act of 1875 came after slavery was abolished; (D) is also incorrect.

10. C

President Johnson was impeached by the House of Representatives, but was acquitted by the Senate by just one vote; therefore, **(C)** is correct. (A), (B), and (D) were all issues that Johnson faced during his presidency. The Black Codes of the South, which legalized discriminatory policies against African Americans, caused controversy in Congress and nationwide. The Republican-led Congress rejected Johnson's proposal for handling Reconstruction and repeatedly opposed him on other issues as well.

Test What You Learned

1. A

The breakout of the Mexican-American War due to the annexation of Texas sparked controversy across the United States. Northern Whigs, including Lincoln, opposed going

to war over the supposed shedding of American blood on American soil that Polk claimed had occurred. Opponents of the war suspected Polk was using the incident as an excuse to gain Mexican territory through war. Therefore, **(A)** is correct. Lincoln was more concerned about America's justification for going to war, rather than the specific boundaries it was going to war over; therefore, (B) is incorrect. (C) is incorrect because Texas had formally been admitted as a state in 1846, which helped spark the Mexican-American War. Lincoln did not express any concerns about the president's legal authority to declare war. Instead, he questioned whether Polk was justified in doing so; (D) is also incorrect.

2. A

The Democratic Party desired the territorial expansion of the United States based on the philosophy of Manifest Destiny. **(A)** is correct. However, this expansion would also allow for more slave territory, making the Mexican-American War a bitterly partisan issue and leading to an increase in sectional tensions ahead of the American Civil War. Thus, (B) and (C) are incorrect. The United States did not perceive a loss of national honor in the War of 1812. On the contrary, a majority of Americans saw a moral victory in not losing to the more powerful British Empire. Thus, (D) is incorrect.

3. B

Increasing tension over the possible expansion of slavery into the Kansas and Nebraska territories, due to the popular sovereignty provision in the Kansas-Nebraska Act, led to a major party realignment in the 1850s. The new Republican Party was founded by antislavery Whigs, Democrats, Free-Soilers, and Know-Nothings from the North and West, making **(B)** correct. While the Northwest Ordinance did outline rules for free and slave states, banning slavery north of the Ohio River, it was passed in 1787, prior to the events depicted in the map, making (A) incorrect. (C) is incorrect because Manifest Destiny was still a popular national ideology at this time. Nativist sentiments against foreigners would plague America in the years to come, but they were not the direct result of the free state/slave state controversy of this time. Therefore, (D) is also incorrect.

4. C

While Texas was forced to cede some of its disputed territory back to Mexico as part of the Compromise of 1850, it received compensation for doing so and accepted the compromise's terms, making **(C)** correct. (A), (B), and (D) were all sources of conflict involving Texas. Its application for annexation and its bid to join the United States ultimately led to the Mexican-American War. Also, annexation, as well as its disputed borders, contributed to Mexican-American conflict and reignited debates about the balance of slave and free states. Lastly, when Texas was still part of Mexico, American settlers openly refused to follow Mexican laws, particularly those outlawing slavery.

5. A

Concern over the free or slave status of the territory gained from Mexico increased sectional tensions in the late 1840s. After 1850, when California came in as a free state, this upset the sectional balance in the U.S. Senate. The slave or free status of future states ultimately led to the outbreak of violence in Kansas. Thus, **(A)** is correct. The *Dred Scott v. Sandford* case did not resolve any tension, but was instead an additional source of antebellum conflict; (B) is incorrect. The Mexican-American War actually led to the Compromise of 1850 and the Kansas-Nebraska Act, not the other way around, which makes (C) incorrect. Lastly, these events caused major political party conflicts and realignments, so (D) is incorrect.

6. B

Opponents of the Kansas-Nebraska Act included Republicans and others who wanted free soil; in other words, no extension of slavery into any additional territories that were either gained from Mexico or previously acquired in other territorial acquisitions. Thus, **(B)** is correct and (C) is incorrect. Opponents of the Kansas-Nebraska Act would not have supported the annexation of additional territory, or the extension of the Missouri Compromise to the Pacific border. This would have paved the way for the continuation of slavery into the West, as long as the territory was south of the 36° 30′ line. Therefore, (A) and (D) are incorrect.

7. D

The loyalty of the border states—slave states that remained in the Union during the Civil War, which included Maryland—led to actions that challenged the constitutional rights of residents; **(D)** is correct. Radical

Republican planning for Reconstruction would develop years after the Civil War ended, making (A) incorrect. While the excerpt discusses civil liberties in a religious setting, it is not primarily centered on religious tolerance; therefore, (B) is also incorrect. (C) is incorrect because the Republican party supported the Union, not the Confederacy.

8. C

Concern over the loyalty of the border states led to Maryland being placed under martial law (military rule) in 1861, making **(C)** correct. While citizens did express concern over the federal government's extended reach during the war, this concern was unrelated to religious freedom; (A) is incorrect. The issuance of the Emancipation Proclamation was largely unrelated to the federal government's management of the border states; (B) is incorrect. (D) is also incorrect because government censorship and martial law actually led to further dissent within Congress, with some Northern Democrats criticizing President Lincoln's broad use of executive power and demanding an end to the "unjust war."

9. A

The Military Reconstruction Acts, passed by Radical Republicans, had many strict requirements for the South, such as martial law by Union generals and universal suffrage for all men, including former slaves. However, these acts did not explicitly require that Southern states take loyalty oaths; **(A)** is therefore correct. (B), (C), and (D) are incorrect: 10 percent of Southern states' voters had to swear an oath of loyalty in Lincoln's Ten Percent Plan; that number was increased to 50 percent of voters in the Wade-Davis Bill; and despite the ways in which Johnson's Reconstruction plans diverged significantly from Lincoln's, Johnson did include the loyalty oath as a requirement.

10. A

During the Civil War, President Lincoln exercised his executive power to limit Americans' civil rights and liberties to protect the Union. Challenges to freedom of speech, freedom of the press, and freedom of expression became part of an effort to ensure that the border states remained in the Union during the Civil War. Lincoln also suspended the writ of habeas corpus, which meant that the federal government could hold an individual in jail with no charges levied against him or her. This tension between civil liberties and the authority of the nation often appears during wartime (e.g., the Alien and Sedition Acts of 1798 and the Sedition Act passed during World War I). Thus, **(A)** is correct. While this excerpt relates to the federal government's authority, it is not about the branches of government, so (B) is incorrect. (C) is incorrect because, although war involves competition for land and resources, the primary theme of the excerpt is civil liberties during wartime. Similarly, even though a Lutheran clergyman is the focus of the excerpt, his concern is with freedom of expression, not religious freedom; (D) is also incorrect.

CHAPTER 8

Period 6: 1865–1898

LEARNING OBJECTIVES

After studying this time period, you will be able to:

- Explain the development of economic patterns and the government's response to economic issues

- Explain how technological developments have impacted the economy and society

- Explain the impact on U.S. politics of conflicting views of the federal government's role

- Describe the reasons for internal U.S. migration and settlement and the effect of such migration on American life

- Describe how reformers and activists have changed American society

- Explain the effects of the arts and sciences on American life

- Describe how conflict and cooperation among empires, nations, and individuals have affected North American development

- Describe the rise of, and changes in, group identities over time

TIMELINE

Date	Event
1865	The Civil War ends.
1869	The Transcontinental Railroad is completed at Promontory Point, Utah.
1870	John D. Rockefeller organizes the Standard Oil Company.
1874	Frances Willard forms the Woman's Christian Temperance Union.
1876	Alexander Graham Bell patents the first telephone. The U.S. Army is defeated at the Battle of Little Bighorn.
1877	The Great Railroad Strike occurs.
1881	Booker T. Washington becomes the head of Tuskegee Institute.
1886	The Haymarket Square Riot takes place. The American Federation of Labor is formed.
1887	The Interstate Commerce Act is enacted. The Dawes Severalty Act strips rights away from Native Americans.
1889	Andrew Carnegie writes the "Gospel of Wealth" essay. Jane Addams founds Hull House in Chicago.
1890	The Sherman Antitrust Act is enacted.
1891	The Battle of Wounded Knee takes place.
1893	A major financial crisis, the Panic of 1893, impacts the nation's economy.
1896	The Supreme Court hears the landmark case *Plessy v. Ferguson*.
1898	The Spanish-American War occurs.

8

TEST WHAT YOU ALREADY KNOW

Part A: Quiz

Questions 1–3 refer to the excerpt below.

"Be it enacted by [Congress] . . . SEC. 6. That upon the completion of said allotments and the patenting of the lands to said allottees, each and every member of the respective bands or tribes of Indians to whom allotments have been made shall have the benefit of and be subject to the laws, both civil and criminal, of the State or Territory in which they may reside; . . . And every Indian born within the territorial limits of the United States to whom allotments shall have been made under the provisions of this act, or under any law or treaty, and every Indian born within the territorial limits of the United States who has voluntarily taken up, within said limits, his residence separate and apart from any tribe of Indians therein, and has adopted the habits of civilized life, is hereby declared to be a citizen of the United States, and is entitled to all the rights, privileges, and immunities of such citizens, whether said Indian has been or not, by birth or otherwise, a member of any tribe of Indians within the territorial limits of the United States without in any manner impairing or otherwise affecting the right of any such Indian to tribal or other property . . ."

Dawes Severalty Act, 1887

1. Which of the following was a result of the Dawes Severalty Act of 1887?

    (A) An increase in American Indian tribal lands

    (B) An increase in federal American Indian reservations

    (C) A decrease in federal intervention in American Indian affairs

    (D) A decrease in tribal autonomy

2. A counterexample to the ideology behind the Dawes Severalty Act would be

    (A) the Homestead Act of 1862

    (B) *Cherokee Nation v. Georgia*

    (C) Jim Crow laws

    (D) Booker T. Washington's philosophy

3. The Dawes Severalty Act most directly reflects which of the following continuities in United States history?

    (A) Debates about expansion of voting rights

    (B) Debates about national identity

    (C) Debates about the growth of executive power

    (D) Debates about globalization

Questions 4–7 refer to the excerpt below.

"THE PLATFORM OF DEMANDS [of the Farmers' Alliance] . . .

Fifth . . . 'equal rights to all and special privileges to none,' that our national legislation . . . not build up one industry at the expense of another, . . . remove existing heavy tariff; . . . a just and equitable system of graduated tax on incomes

Sixth . . . State and National government control and supervision of the means of public communication and transportation . . . [or] government ownership of such

Seventh . . . an amendment . . . providing for the [direct] election of United States Senators . . ."

Thomas Campbell-Copeland, *Cleveland and Stevenson: Their Lives and Record,* 1892

4. Which of the following groups would be most likely to support the demands in this excerpt?

   (A) Opponents of the Grangers

   (B) Supporters of the Populist (People's) Party

   (C) Advocates of business consolidation

   (D) Sharecroppers in the New South

5. Which of the following events benefited small farmers in the nineteenth century?

   (A) The government's adoption of a laissez-faire policy

   (B) The *Munn v. Illinois* court case

   (C) The Great Railroad Strike of 1877

   (D) The *In re Debs* decision

6. In the second half of the nineteenth century, America's economy shifted from local and rural to national and industrial. One of the ways railroads aided this change was by

   (A) transporting raw materials to consumer markets

   (B) connecting the East, West, and South regions of the United states

   (C) utilizing private funding for the Transcontinental Railroad

   (D) increasing the consumption of steel

7. All of the following methods contributed to the rise of big business in America EXCEPT

   (A) collective bargaining

   (B) vertical integration

   (C) horizontal integration

   (D) trusts and monopolies

8

Questions 8–10 refer to the image below.

This 1896 political cartoon, by William Jennings Bryan, is in support of "Free Silver."

8. Expanding the money supply became a topic of debate during the Gilded Age for all of the following reasons EXCEPT

(A) the silver rush of 1859

(B) the government's outdated bimetal standard

(C) the fluctuation of gold and silver values

(D) limited circulation of gold-backed dollars

9. Divisions over the currency issue, among others, would lead to the formation of which political party?

(A) Whig Party

(B) Free Soil Party

(C) Populist Party

(D) Liberty Party

10. People who agreed with the argument for free silver would most likely also recommend which economic stance?

(A) Laws to increase the federal government's power in the economy

(B) A return to a laissez-faire economic approach by the federal government

(C) An end to the "separate but equal" position established by *Plessy v. Ferguson*

(D) Laws to limit the power of labor unions

8

Part B: Key Terms

The following is a list of the major people, places, and events for 1865–1898. You will likely see many of these on the AP U.S. History exam.

For each key term ask yourself the following questions:

- Can I describe this key term?
- Can I discuss this key term in the context of other events?
- Could I correctly answer a multiple-choice question about this key term?
- Could I correctly answer a free-response question about this key term?

Check off the key terms if you can answer "yes" to at least three of these questions.

The Industrialization of America

- ☐ Transcontinental Railroad
- ☐ Robber barons
- ☐ Carnegie Steel Company
- ☐ Vertical integration
- ☐ U.S. Steel
- ☐ Standard Oil Company
- ☐ Horizontal integration
- ☐ Trust
- ☐ Panic of 1893
- ☐ Monopolies
- ☐ Laissez-faire
- ☐ Social Darwinism

Industrialization and Organized Labor

- ☐ Great Railroad Strike of 1877
- ☐ Rutherford B. Hayes
- ☐ National Labor Union
- ☐ Panic of 1873
- ☐ Knights of Labor
- ☐ Haymarket Square Riot
- ☐ American Federation of Labor (AFL)
- ☐ Strikebreaking
- ☐ Grover Cleveland
- ☐ *In re Debs*

Expansion and Conflict in the West

- ☐ Greenback Party
- ☐ Homestead Act of 1862

The Farmer's Plight

- ☐ Mechanized agriculture
- ☐ National Grange of the Patrons of Husbandry (Grangers)
- ☐ *Munn v. Illinois*
- ☐ Interstate Commerce Act

Impacts on American Indians in the West

☐ Battle of Little Bighorn ☐ Battle of Wounded Knee ☐ Dawes Severalty Act

The New South

☐ The New South ☐ *Plessy v. Ferguson* ☐ Jim Crow laws

Urbanization and Social Change

☐ Nativists ☐ Political machine

A Wave of Reform in the Gilded Age

☐ Gilded Age ☐ Temperance movement ☐ National American Woman Suffrage Association
☐ Social Gospel ☐ Gospel of Wealth
☐ Settlement house movement

Next Steps

Step 1: Tally your correct answers from Part A and review the quiz explanations at the end of this chapter.

1.	D	6.	D
2.	C	7.	A
3.	B	8.	B
4.	B	9.	C
5.	B	10.	A

_____ out of 10 questions

Step 2: Count the number of key terms you checked off in Part B.

_____ out of 42 key terms

Step 3: Read the Key Takeaways in this chapter.

Step 4: Consult the table below and follow the instructions based on your performance.

If You Got...	Do This
80% or more of the Test What You Already Know assessment correct (8 or more questions from Part A and 34 or more key terms from Part B)	• Read definitions in this chapter for all the key terms you didn't check off. • Complete the Test What You Learned assessment in this chapter.
50% or less of the Test What You Already Know assessment correct (5 or fewer questions from Part A and 21 or fewer key terms from Part B)	• Read the comprehensive review for this period in Chapter 17. • If you are short on time, read only the High-Yield sections. • Read through all of the key term definitions in this chapter. • Complete the Test What You Learned assessment in this chapter.
Any other result	• Read the High-Yield sections in the comprehensive review of this period in Chapter 17. • Read definitions in this chapter for all the key terms you didn't check off. • Complete the Test What You Learned assessment in this chapter.

ESSENTIAL CONTENT

Key Takeaways: 1865–1898

1. Large-scale production due to technological advances, improvements in railroads and transportation, and the opening of new markets led to the rise of industrialism and capitalism during this era. Business leaders such as Cornelius Vanderbilt, Andrew Carnegie, and John D. Rockefeller amassed huge fortunes. Aggressive financial methods caused multiple economic downturns and financial panics.

2. Due to the rise of big business, many groups, such as farmers and labor unions, called for stronger governmental protections to regulate the economy and safeguard the rights of workers. The government often sided with business, however, as evidenced by federally supported strikebreaking.

3. Migration increased, both to and within the United States. Cities became areas of economic growth that attracted African Americans and migrants from Asia and Europe. Multiple ethnic groups vied for control of the western frontier, and cultural tensions continued nationwide.

4. New intellectual and cultural movements arose during this period, often dubbed the Gilded Age. One view, called Social Darwinism, attempted to justify a wealthy elite class as natural and inevitable. Another view, known as the Gospel of Wealth, urged big business and the wealthy to help the less fortunate.

5. Debates intensified over citizens' rights, especially in relation to gender and race. The Supreme Court case *Plessy v. Ferguson* (1896) marked a major setback for African Americans, as it upheld racial segregation and ended some of the progress made in the decades following the Civil War. African American reformers continued to strive for political and social equality in the face of escalating violence and discrimination.

Key Terms: 1865–1898

Remember that the AP U.S. History exam tests you on the depth of your knowledge, not just your ability to recall facts. While we have provided brief definitions here, you will need to know these terms in even more depth for the AP exam, including how terms connect to broader historical themes and understandings.

The Industrialization of America

Transcontinental Railroad: The Transcontinental Railroad linked the United States from Atlantic to Pacific by both rail and telegraph, and accelerated the development and eventual closure of the frontier. Contained various rail lines, including the Union Pacific Railroad and Central Pacific railroad, which meet at Promontory Point in Utah.

Robber barons: A pejorative name for investors who artificially inflated the value of their company's stock, sold the stock to the public, and pocketed the profits. The company would then go bankrupt, leaving stockholders with nothing. The fierce competition of the Gilded Age coupled with lack of federal regulation often led to dishonest business practices.

Carnegie Steel Company: A company founded and owned by Andrew Carnegie. At its height, it supplied over half the world's steel. Sold to J. P. Morgan to form U.S. Steel.

Vertical integration: The process of controlling every aspect of the production process for a product, from the acquisition of raw materials to the distribution of the final product. A favored practice by Andrew Carnegie.

U.S. Steel: The first corporation in history with a capitalization of over one billion dollars, at a time when the entire U.S. stock market was worth roughly nine billion dollars. It was formed by J. P. Morgan, who purchased Andrew Carnegie's steel business and then went on to consolidate that whole industry.

Standard Oil Company: An oil refining company owned by John D. Rockefeller. At its height, it controlled 95 percent of U.S. refineries through consolidation. This business strategy is called horizontal integration. In 1911, the Supreme Court ruled it an illegal monopoly under the Sherman Antitrust Act and split it into 34 companies.

Horizontal integration: The process of merging companies that all compete in one aspect of a long production process, such as refinement in the oil industry, thereby creating either a monopoly (total control by one company) or an oligopoly (control by few companies).

Trust: Also called a corporate trust, it was a common form of monopoly around the turn of the twentieth century. Essentially, the stockholders of several companies would sell their stock to the owner of a larger company in exchange for trust certificates, which entitled them to a share of the profits as silent partners. The several companies still technically existed but were now effectively one entity. Later on, government policies would attempt to break up these trusts.

Panic of 1893: An economic depression caused by the failure of the Reading Railroad company and by overspeculation artificially inflating the price of stocks. The market did not recover for almost four years. Investors began trading in their silver for more valuable gold, depleting the already dangerously low supply of gold.

Monopolies: The total or near-total domination of an industry by one business. Monopolies can artificially fix prices and stifle innovation, as a lack of competition means they have little reason to reinvest their profits in improving their products.

Laissez-faire: First articulated by the economist Adam Smith in his treatise *The Wealth of Nations*, laissez-faire economics states that natural market forces, not government regulations or subsidies, should control the marketplace. However, the growth of monopolies during the Gilded Age prevented any natural competition from occurring, leading to antitrust laws. The term derives from the French for "let do," or in essence "Let the economy run itself."

Social Darwinism: The application of Charles Darwin's theory of evolution to society, specifically the concept of survival of the fittest. It attempted to explain economic and social differences by arguing that wealth belonged in the hands of those who were most fit to manage it. Many Social Darwinists believed that giving assistance to the poor went against the natural order.

Industrialization and Organized Labor

Great Railroad Strike of 1877: A nationwide strike that took place from July 14 to September 4, 1877. More than 100,000 railroad workers were ultimately involved, and the strike affected such cities as Baltimore, Newark, Pittsburgh, St. Louis, and Chicago. The state National Guardsmen

8

were often called in, but most militia members (and local residents) were sympathetic to the strikers. Ultimately, President Rutherford B. Hayes authorized the use of federal troops to break the strike. More than 100 workers were killed in the crackdown, and the strikers gained nothing. However, it led to more organized unionizing efforts.

Rutherford B. Hayes: Nineteenth president. Served from 1877–1881. While a Civil War veteran and a Republican, he ended Reconstruction as part of the Compromise of 1877 to resolve the disputed 1876 election. Enacted modest civil service reform. Ordered federal troops in to break up the Great Railroad Strike of 1877. Pledged not to run for reelection and returned to Ohio.

National Labor Union: The first attempt to organize all workers nationwide. Founded in 1866, its goals included better working conditions, higher wages, an eight-hour workday, and equal rights for women and African Americans (but at the exclusion of Chinese-Americans). Members included skilled and unskilled workers as well as farmers; these groups had different, sometimes incompatible, needs. The Panic of 1873 contributed to its decline, as did the failure of Great Railroad Strike of 1877.

Panic of 1873: A financial crisis that created an economic depression (1873–1879). It had several interlocking causes that reflected the period's increasingly globalized economy. Initially referred to as the Great Depression until the far more severe economic crisis of that name in the 1930s.

Knights of Labor: Founded as a secret society in 1869. Elected Terence V. Powderly its leader in 1879, and under his leadership, the union announced itself in 1881. One of its strengths was that it was a broad industrial union: all wage workers (skilled, unskilled, women, and minorities) were invited to join. The Knights advocated

for both economic and social reforms, such as the development of labor cooperatives, an eight-hour workday, and federal regulation of business. It preferred to use arbitration rather than violent strikes. Entered terminal decline after the Haymarket Square Riot.

Haymarket Square Riot: On May 4, 1886, a rally in support of the eight-hour workday was held in Chicago's Haymarket Square. When police began to break up what had been a peaceful public meeting, someone in the crowd threw a bomb at the police, and police fired into the crowd. Several dozens were killed. Rumors circulated that alleged the Knights of Labor were tied to the anarchist bombing, which fatally weakened the Knights. However, Haymarket Square ultimately became a global rallying point for the eight-hour workday. May Day began, in part, as an international commemoration for Haymarket Square.

American Federation of Labor (AFL): Founded in 1886, the AFL was a federation of 20 craft unions (unions of skilled workers, each representing a particular trade). The AFL concentrated on what it considered to be basic economic issues, such as the eight-hour workday and higher wages, rather than social change. Because the AFL was made up of skilled rather than unskilled laborers, its workers could not be as easily replaced if a strike were called.

Strikebreaking: The process of breaking a strike to avoid making concessions to workers, either through violence or through the use of replacement workers. In the nineteenth century, the government often sided with businesses and would authorize the use of the National Guard or U.S. Army troops on striking workers.

Grover Cleveland: Twenty-second and twenty-fourth president. Only president to serve nonconsecutive terms, in 1885–1889 and 1893–1897. The first Democratic Party president since before the Civil War. Supported the gold standard. His second term was defined by the Panic of 1893, which caused a severe depression. Sent federal troops in to break up the Pullman Strike. His resolution of the Venezuelan crisis of 1895 began the reconciliation between the United States and British Empire.

In re Debs: A landmark 1895 Supreme Court case. It ruled that the use of court injunctions to break strikes was justified in the support of interstate commerce. In effect, the federal government had permitted employers to not deal with labor unions.

Expansion and Conflict in the West

Greenback Party: A third party formed in 1874 and disbanded in 1889. It existed alongside the Farmers' Alliance. Its elements later merged into the Populist Party.

Homestead Act of 1862: A law that provided a settler with 160 acres of land if he promised to live on it and work it for at least five years.

About 500,000 families took advantage of the Homestead Act, while many more bought land from private purveyors. Unfortunately, the parcels of land on the Great Plains were difficult to farm, owing to lack of rain and hard-packed soil. Many homesteaders left the land behind and returned home.

The Farmer's Plight

Mechanized agriculture: Using machines to do the work of farming. This greatly increases agricultural yields and productivity, but the machinery is expensive to purchase and maintain, which gives large commercial farms a big advantage over small local farms.

National Grange of the Patrons of Husbandry (Grangers): Founded in 1867 by Oliver H. Kelley, it was a kind of fraternity of farmers and their families. The Grange sought to break the hold of railroad owners and middlemen who kept raising the cost of farming by charging exorbitant prices for shipping and storage. The Grangers gained significant political power, and they played an important part in the rise of the Populist Party.

Munn v. Illinois: Supreme Court ruling (1877) that held that a state had the right to regulate the practices of a business if that business served the public interest. Because railroad transportation was very much in the public's interest, according to the Court, state regulation of rates was appropriate. Despite these successes on the state level, federal laws still protected interstate commerce and allowed railroad companies to raise their long-haul rates in order to offset the losses on short hauls.

Interstate Commerce Act: An 1887 law that would regulate and investigate railroad companies that participated in interstate rail trafficking. The first example of the federal government regulating private industry in U.S. history.

Impacts on American Indians in the West

Battle of Little Bighorn: Sometimes called Custer's Last Stand, it is the most famous victory of American Indian forces over the U.S. military (although not the largest in death toll). The Sioux killed over 260 troops and their leader, Lieutenant Colonel George Armstrong Custer.

The Sioux were hunted down and killed by other U.S. forces.

Battle of Wounded Knee: A massacre of over 200 American Indian men, women, and children that took place in December 1890 in South

Dakota. Over 20 soldiers involved were awarded the Medal of Honor.

Dawes Severalty Act: An 1887 act which stripped tribes of their official federal recognition and land rights and would only grant individual families land and citizenship in 25 years if they properly assimilated. Former reservation land was sold, and the proceeds funded "civilizing" ventures for natives, such as so-called Indian Schools which were rampant with abuse and neglect. This forced-assimilation policy remained the federal government's way of dealing with American Indians until 1934.

The New South

The New South: After the Civil War, the South suffered from slow economic progress. Southern leaders called for a new era in which the South shifted from an exclusively agricultural society to industrialization. The concept of the New South struggled to catch on, and sharecropping and tenant farming continued to be the primary economic activities.

Plessy v. Ferguson: Landmark Supreme Court case (1896) that upheld segregation, codifying the doctrine of separate but equal. Partially overturned by *Brown v. Board of Education*. Functionally overturned by the Civil Rights Act of 1964 and the Voting Rights Act of 1965.

Jim Crow laws: Laws that enforced segregation, primarily but not exclusively in the South. The name references a famous nineteenth-century blackface act called Jump Jim Crow.

Urbanization and Social Change

Nativists: Anti-immigrant activists in the nineteenth century. Many nativists, much like the Know-Nothings during the first wave of immigration, feared domination by a Catholic population. Labor unions feared a loss of jobs to an eager immigrant work pool who would accept lower wages and worse working conditions. On the West Coast, Chinese immigrants prompted similar xenophobic sentiments, including the Chinese Exclusion Act, which restricted Chinese immigration to the United States.

Political machine: An authoritarian or oligarchical political organization that commands political influence, voting blocs, and corporate influence in such a way that it can decide (or strongly influence) the outcome of elections. Often corrupt and prone to political patronage. Usually active at the city level, but sometimes extends statewide. A famous political machine in New York City was Tammany Hall, led by Boss Tweed. A target of reform during the Gilded Age.

A Wave of Reform in the Gilded Age

Gilded Age: A period from the 1870s to 1900; the term was coined by author Mark Twain. While marked by massive economic growth due to industrialization, it also led to equally massive economic inequality. Backlash to this period manifested in the reforms of the Progressive Era.

Social Gospel: An influential Protestant social justice movement in the late nineteenth and early twentieth centuries. It stated that Christians had an obligation to improve the lives of those less fortunate, especially the poor. Its leaders encouraged many middle-class Protestants to join reform efforts, such as those calling for laws banning child labor and making school compulsory for children. Essentially, it was the religious wing of the Progressive movement.

Settlement house movement: A social reform movement led by young female activists, as they could not become involved in the political process. It aimed to achieve social reform through mixed-income housing, with people of different classes living in one house. These houses often offered education and daycare. The most famous of the settlement houses was Hull House in Chicago (1889).

Temperance movement: A long-running social justice movement that sought to reduce the consumption of alcohol. The Victorian ideal of strict moral decorum and the concern over Catholic immigration led to its revival after the Civil War. The movement eventually hardened into a prohibition movement. Served as a stand-in for social issues that could not be discussed openly, such as domestic violence, and also as a soft form of nativism against German and Irish Americans.

Gospel of Wealth: Economic philosophy developed by Andrew Carnegie; it asserted that wealth was a result of God's will and that, in turn, the wealthy had an obligation to give money away to better society.

National American Woman Suffrage Association: Formed in 1890, it combined the once rival National Woman Suffrage Association and American Woman Suffrage Association to fight for a woman's right to vote. The NAWSA organized several hundred state and local chapters.

TEST WHAT YOU LEARNED

Questions 1–4 refer to the image below.

This photograph depicts a crowded New York City street in the nineteenth century.

1. The influx of immigrants in the late nineteenth century to cities like New York most directly led to

   (A) widespread movement of Southern and Eastern Europeans to rural areas

   (B) the growth in power of urban political machines

   (C) ethnic diversity in urban neighborhoods

   (D) a backlash against Protestant immigrants

2. Which of the following groups would be most likely to support the interests of immigrants?

   (A) Promoters of the New South

   (B) Opponents of the settlement house movement

   (C) Organizers for national unions

   (D) Advocates of Social Darwinism

3. Which of the following issues from the mid-nineteenth century most clearly parallels the issues surrounding immigration in the late nineteenth century?

   (A) Increased nativism connected to Irish and German immigration

   (B) Political upheaval connected to Manifest Destiny

   (C) Displacement of native groups connected to territorial expansion

   (D) States' rights in connection to the growth of federal power

4. Along with increased immigration, all of the following cultural changes occurred in the late nineteenth century EXCEPT

   (A) the growth of the working class

   (B) the decline of the middle class

   (C) increased independence for women

   (D) increased literacy rates

8

Questions 5–7 refer to the excerpt below.

"The first count in the declaration . . . [charges] that the Wabash, St. Louis & Pacific Railway Company had, in violation of a statute of the state of Illinois, been guilty of an unjust discrimination in its rates or charges of toll and compensation for the transportation of freight [from Illinois to New York State] . . . [The court] holds as law that said act . . . cannot apply to transportation service rendered partly without the state . . . and cannot operate beyond the limits of the state of Illinois. The court further holds as matter of law that the transportation in question falls within the proper description of 'commerce among the states' . . ."

Decision from *Wabash, St. Louis and Pacific Railway Company v. State of Illinois*, 1886

5. The Supreme Court's decision in the *Wabash* case directly led to

   (A) an increase in states' powers to regulate interstate commerce

   (B) a decrease in federal intervention in state economics

   (C) stricter enforcement of economic regulations in the railroad industry

   (D) the creation of the Interstate Commerce Commission

6. Economic issues arose again in a later Supreme Court case, *In re Debs*, which centered on the federal government's

   (A) support of labor unions

   (B) curtailing of big businesses

   (C) role in strikebreaking

   (D) laissez-faire approach

7. The reasoning expressed in the Supreme Court's decision most directly reflects which of the following continuities in United States history?

   (A) Debates over the effects of territorial expansion

   (B) Debates over industry's impact on the environment

   (C) Debates over the role of government

   (D) Debates over competition for land and resources

Questions 8–10 refer to the image below.

This photograph from 1898 depicts cotton being bundled for sale in New Orleans

8. Which of the following features of the South in the late nineteenth century is most clearly illustrated in the photograph?

    (A) The limited economic progress of the New South

    (B) Southern opposition to the *Plessy v. Ferguson* decision

    (C) The South's economic independence from the North

    (D) The dominance of mechanized agriculture in the South

9. Which of the following statements is NOT true regarding the South's post–Civil War economy in the nineteenth century?

    (A) Tenant farmers were largely unable to escape the cycle of debt.

    (B) Most Southerners, both black and white, were impoverished.

    (C) Land-owning farmers profited from the crop-lien system.

    (D) The price of cotton hit an all-time low by the end of the nineteenth century.

10. Along with the economy, another major issue for the late nineteenth century South was race relations. The Supreme Court case *Plessy v. Ferguson* led directly to

    (A) the repeal of Jim Crow laws

    (B) the establishment of Black Codes

    (C) the formation of the Ku Klux Klan

    (D) the Great Migration

Part B: Key Terms

This key terms list is the same as the list in the Test What You Already Know section earlier in this chapter. Based on what you have now learned, again ask yourself the following questions:

- Can I define this key term and use it in a sentence?

- Can I provide an example related to this key term?

- Could I correctly answer a multiple-choice question about this key term?

- Could I correctly answer a free-response question about this key term?

Check off the key terms if you can answer "yes" to at least three of these questions.

The Industrialization of America

☐ Transcontinental Railroad   ☐ U.S. Steel   ☐ Panic of 1893

☐ Robber barons   ☐ Standard Oil Company   ☐ Monopolies

☐ Carnegie Steel Company   ☐ Horizontal integration   ☐ Laissez-faire

☐ Vertical integration   ☐ Trust   ☐ Social Darwinism

Industrialization and Organized Labor

☐ Great Railroad Strike of 1877   ☐ Knights of Labor   ☐ Strikebreaking

☐ Rutherford B. Hayes   ☐ Haymarket Square Riot   ☐ Grover Cleveland

☐ National Labor Union   ☐ American Federation of Labor (AFL)   ☐ *In re Debs*

☐ Panic of 1873

Expansion and Conflict in the West

☐ Greenback Party   ☐ Homestead Act of 1862

The Farmer's Plight

☐ Mechanized agriculture   ☐ National Grange of the Patrons of Husbandry (Grangers)   ☐ *Munn v. Illinois*

☐ Interstate Commerce Act

Impacts on American Indians in the West

☐ Battle of Little Bighorn   ☐ Battle of Wounded Knee   ☐ Dawes Severalty Act

The New South

☐ The New South   ☐ *Plessy v. Ferguson*   ☐ Jim Crow laws

Urbanization and Social Change

☐ Nativists   ☐ Political machine

A Wave of Reform in the Gilded Age

☐ Gilded Age   ☐ Temperance movement   ☐ National American Woman Suffrage Association

☐ Social Gospel   ☐ Gospel of Wealth

☐ Settlement house movement

Next Steps

Step 1: Tally your correct answers from Part A and review the quiz explanations at the end of this chapter.

1.	B	6.	C
2.	C	7.	C
3.	A	8.	A
4.	B	9.	C
5.	D	10.	D

____ out of 10 questions

Step 2: Count the number of key terms you checked off in Part B.

____ out of 42 key terms

Step 3: Compare your Test What You Already Know results to these Test What You Learned results to see how exam-ready you are for this period.

For More Practice:

- Read (or reread) the comprehensive review for this period in Chapter 17.

- Go to kaptest.com to complete the online quiz questions for 1865–1898.

  ○ Haven't registered your book yet? Go to kaptest.com/moreonline to begin.

ANSWERS AND EXPLANATIONS

Test What You Already Know

1. D

While earlier government policy toward American Indians sought to remove them from their homelands and place them on reservations, the Dawes Severalty Act sought to divide reservation land and create smaller farmsteads for individual American Indians. Excess tribal land could then be sold off to the increasing number of white settlers looking to move onto the Great Plains. The Dawes Severalty Act served to destroy tribal organization. Therefore, **(D)** is correct and (B) is incorrect. (A) is incorrect because the Dawes Severalty Act stripped natives of land they had previously been legally deeded by the U.S. government. The federal government also continued to intervene in native affairs, with the new goal being to forcibly assimilate American Indians into mainstream white society; thus, (C) is also incorrect.

2. C

The Jim Crow laws passed after the Civil War legalized segregation between African Americans and white Americans, which further separated black and white people both physically and culturally. Conversely, much of the impetus behind the Dawes Severalty Act was to assimilate American Indians into white society. Thus, **(C)** is correct. The Homestead Act of 1862 was similar to the Dawes Severalty Act in that it granted parcels of land based on certain requirements; (A) is incorrect. (B) is incorrect because the Supreme Court denied the Cherokee Nation's argument that it was a sovereign nation, stating instead that it was part of the United States and had to abide by U.S. laws and norms. Booker T. Washington encouraged African Americans to educate themselves in order to work within the existing system; like the Dawes Severalty Act, he advocated assimilation into mainstream society. (D) is also incorrect.

3. B

The Dawes Severalty Act attempted to alter the traditional tribal structure and governance of American Indians and to assimilate native peoples into mainstream American society. The positioning and treatment of different ethnic groups has been a theme throughout American history and directly relates to debates about what constitutes national identity; **(B)** is correct. While the Dawes Severalty

Act dealt with civil rights issues and autonomous native governments, voting rights were not a central focus; (A) is incorrect. (C) is incorrect because, although the act is related to the power of the federal government, it does not reflect the growth of executive branch power in particular. Lastly, the Dawes Severalty Act dealt with national issues, not global ones, making (D) incorrect.

4. B

The demands made in this excerpt by the Farmers' Alliance center on American farmers' struggles with the negative effects of industrial capitalism, including high transportation and storage rates. In the 1890s, the Populist (or People's) Party was created, and it advocated for many of the demands listed in the excerpt. Thus, **(B)** is correct. Grangers were midwestern farmers who banded together to fight against these same issues and would likely support these demands; opponents of the Grangers would not support the demands in the excerpt, so (A) is incorrect. Advocates of business consolidation were the same industry leaders that the Farmers' Alliance was trying to combat; (C) is incorrect. While sharecroppers in the post–Civil War New South were also farmers, they dealt with other issues, such as the cycle of crushing debt caused by the tenant farming system.

5. B

In the court case *Munn v. Illinois* (1877), the Supreme Court ruled that a state had the right to regulate the practices of a business if that business served the public interest. By extension, this meant that states could regulate railroad transportation and ensure that railroad companies did not charge farmers exorbitant rates. **(B)** is correct. The government's laissez-faire economic stance helped big business, not small farmers, so (A) is incorrect. While the Great Railroad Strike of 1877 was in support of workers' rights, it caused the halt of all trains, which would have hurt farmers' ability to make a profit from their shipped crops; (C) is incorrect. The Supreme Court's *In re Debs* ruling in 1895 had to do with the government's role in labor conflicts and was not relevant to farmers' issues; (D) is also incorrect.

6. D

The growth of railroads had a major influence on the growth of the national economy; one of the major reasons was the enormous consumption of steel to make safer and stronger rails. Railroads stimulated the steel industry, which became one of the largest business ventures in America, led by tycoons such as Cornelius Vanderbilt and Andrew Carnegie. Therefore, **(D)** is correct. Railroads transported raw materials to factories, not consumer markets (which were the recipients of finished goods); (A) is incorrect. The railroad network connected the East with the West, but did not connect with or benefit the South, making (B) incorrect. Lastly, while some railroads were privately funded, the Transcontinental Railroad was federally funded, including both land grants and loans; thus, (C) is also incorrect.

7. A

Collective bargaining was a tactic used by labor unions to make gains against big business; **(A)** is correct. (B), (C), and (D) are all incorrect; all of these methods contributed to the expansion of businesses, such as oil and steel, and facilitated the increase of industrialists' unchecked power.

8. B

During the Gilded Age, the United States government used only gold to back its money supply. According to some, this gold standard was the cause of the Panic of 1873 due to restricted money supply, and adopting a bimetal standard to include silver would prevent future economic crises. Therefore, **(B)** is correct. (Remember that the question is asking which was *not* a reason for the currency debate.) (D) is incorrect because the limited circulation of gold-backed currency was in fact an issue. The silver rush in 1859, and the consequent increase in mining silver as well as gold, negatively impacted the economy and caused greater fluctuation in gold and silver values, making both (A) and (C) incorrect.

9. C

The debate over including silver in a bimetal standard was one of the most important issues around which the Populist Party united in 1892. Members of the Populist Party argued that an unlimited, or free, supply of silver would loosen up the nation's tight money supply. **(C)** is correct. The Whig Party had already been formed in the 1830s, before currency became a major issue; (A) is incorrect. The Free Soil Party was created to oppose the expansion of slavery into western territories; similarly, the Liberty Party's platform was based on the abolition of slavery. Neither the Free Soil Party nor the Liberty Party included currency as a major issue, so both (B) and (D) are incorrect.

10. A

People who supported free silver and a bimetal standard also tended to advocate for stricter government regulation of railroads, banks, and big businesses; later, these were two major issues that the Populist Party would include in its platform. Therefore, **(A)** is correct. (B) is incorrect because the laissez-faire economic approach benefited big businesses. *Plessy v. Ferguson* was not primarily economic in nature, making (C) incorrect. (D) is incorrect because supporters of free silver would likely also support labor unions and the ways in which they challenged big industry's ruthless tactics.

Test What You Learned

1. B

The influx of immigrants to the cities of the Northeast increased the importance of urban political machines, such as Tammany Hall in New York City, which provided aid and assistance to immigrants in exchange for political support; therefore, **(B)** is correct. the Southern and Eastern European immigrants who came to the United States settled predominantly in cities, where they could more easily find jobs and build a support system; (A) is incorrect. (C) is incorrect, because city neighborhoods actually became more segregated during this time period, with ethnic communities all adhering to their own respective cultural traditions. The new wave of immigrants of the late nineteenth century were often Catholic, Jewish, or Greek Orthodox Christians, whereas the relatively older wave of immigrants were predominantly English Protestants. The nativist movements that subsequently gained traction discriminated against non-Protestant immigrant groups; thus, (D) is incorrect.

2. C

Unions, especially industrial ones, sought to represent the interests of labor, including the recently arrived immigrants, in a rapidly changing industrial world emerging in the United States during the late nineteenth and early twentieth centuries; therefore, **(C)** is correct. (A) is incorrect because the New South was removed from the

8

influx of immigrants into northeastern cities. Settlement houses deliberately catered to the urban poor, including immigrants, making (B) incorrect. Finally, advocates of Social Darwinism, believing in the survival of the fittest, opposed any kind of social assistance to immigrants or other groups, making (D) incorrect.

3.   A

The increase in Southern and Eastern European immigrants in the late nineteenth century prompted renewed calls for immigration restrictions. This nativist sentiment was also seen when large amounts of Irish and German immigrants came to America between the 1830s and 1860s; **(A)** is correct. The boom in immigration during the late nineteenth century was concentrated in small urban areas, and it caused different issues than the vast territorial expansion of the mid-nineteenth century; for this reason, both (B) and (C) are incorrect. While states' rights continued to be an issue throughout the nineteenth century and onward, the issues related to immigration did not echo the mid-nineteenth century tension between state and federal power; (D) is also incorrect.

4.   B

The late nineteenth century actually saw an expansion of the middle class, due to factors such as the movement of workers from farms to factories; the creation of managerial positions within factories; and the growth of the professional service industry in areas such as medicine, law, and education. Therefore, **(B)** is correct. (A), (C), and (D) were all cultural changes that did occur in the late nineteenth century. The working class grew as more blue-collar workers were needed for industrial jobs. Women became more independent, holding pink-collar jobs (such as clerical work), at the same time as the women's suffrage movement experienced renewed vigor. Lastly, education changes, such as publicly funded high schools and compulsory elementary attendance laws, increased the literacy rate of Americans to almost 90 percent.

5.   D

The *Wabash* case was a prime example of how federal laws protected interstate commerce, making states powerless to keep railroad companies from charging exorbitant shipping rates. Soon after the *Wabash* ruling, Congress responded by passing the Interstate Commerce Act in 1887 and creating the Interstate Commerce Commission (ICC), which would regulate and investigate railroad companies that transported goods across different states. Therefore, **(D)** is correct and (A) is incorrect. The ICC was one of the first modern regulatory agencies, and it set a precedent for federal intervention in economic issues that had previously only been dealt with at the state level; thus, (B) is incorrect. While the ICC was important symbolically, it ultimately lacked enforcement powers to regulate large businesses like the railroad industry, making (C) incorrect.

6.   C

The end of the nineteenth century was difficult for organized labor, as the government decisively sided with big business. One example of this was the practice of strikebreaking. In 1893, workers for the Pullman Palace Car Company went on strike, and they were soon joined by rail workers across the nation, who all refused to load, link, or carry any train with a Pullman car. In the resulting case *In re Debs*, the Supreme Court ruled that the use of court injunctions to break strikes was justified and that the government could regulate interstate commerce when the industry involved the general welfare of the public. This decision opened the door for employers to break strikes and to refuse to deal with labor unions. Thus, **(C)** is correct, and (A) and (B) are incorrect. By getting involved in this case, the federal government had moved away from a hands-off, or laissez-faire, approach, making (D) incorrect.

7.   C

The controversial role of both state and federal governments has been a constant theme in American history, and it is clearly evident in the *Wabash* decision regarding the regulation of America's evolving market economy. Supporters of a free-market laissez-faire economy tend to want no government regulation, whereas other parties (in this case, farmers and laborers) tend to look to the government to help control the power of big businesses. **(C)** is correct. (A) is incorrect because although railroad companies were tied to territorial expansion, the effects of expansion were not the primary theme in the *Wabash* case. The impact of industrialization on the environment was not yet a major theme in the nineteenth century, although it would become a prominent issue in the next century and beyond; (B) is incorrect. The *Wabash* case had to do with competition for resources,

8

but it was not about access to or competition for land, making (D) incorrect.

8. A

Despite the goals of some Southerners to create a New South based on a growing economy and increased industrialization, the Southern economy remained heavily agricultural. This picture demonstrates farmers' reliance on the same cash crops of the antebellum years. Therefore, **(A)** is correct and (D) is incorrect. The image does not provide any evidence of opposition to the "separate but equal" doctrine established by the *Plessy v. Ferguson* case, so (B) is incorrect. While the South sought to be economically independent from the North, the Civil War had had the opposite effect. Any postwar economic recovery was partially if not mostly financed by the North, and the South relied on supplying raw goods such as cotton to Northern industries such as textile mills, making (C) incorrect.

9. C

The South faced many economic hardships after the Civil War. Most farmers remained tied to the land because of the use of crop liens, which allowed farmers to pay for goods on credit; this would be paid back with the harvest of their next crop. Farmers almost never made any significant profits because one poor harvest could drive both tenant and land-owning farmers deeper into debt. Therefore, **(C)** is correct. (A), (B), and (D) were all realities of the Southern economy. For the most part, Southern citizens remained some of the most impoverished in the nation. The majority of Southerners, both black and white, subsisted as sharecroppers and farmers. As in the antebellum economy, cotton remained a major cash crop for the South, and more and more farmers converted land to till cotton. They eventually flooded the worldwide marketplace with cotton, driving the price to an all-time low in the 1890s.

10. D

The open discrimination, harassment, and lynchings that occurred after the *Plessy v. Ferguson* case led many African Americans to leave the South for Northern cities; this trend was dubbed the Great Migration. **(D)** is correct. The Supreme Court justices used the separate but equal doctrine to justify their *Plessy v. Ferguson* decision, which paved the way for legal segregation on the basis of color in all public places. Jim Crow laws, which segregated public facilities, were immediately adopted by cities across the South, not repealed; (A) is incorrect. The discriminatory laws called the Black Codes, as well as the formation of the Ku Klux Klan, occurred in the 1860s, well before the 1896 *Plessy v. Ferguson* case; (B) and (C) are incorrect.

CHAPTER 9

Period 7: 1890–1945

LEARNING OBJECTIVES

After studying this time period, you will be able to:

- Explain the development of economic patterns and the government's response to economic issues

- Describe how reformers and activists have changed American society

- Analyze the impact ideas about women and gender roles had on politics and society

- Describe labor systems in North America and their effects on workers and society

- Describe the reasons for internal U.S. migration and settlement and the effect of such migration on American life

- Explain the causes and effects of U.S. economic, diplomatic, and military initiatives in North America and globally

- Analyze how U.S. growth and global involvement have changed ideas about national identity

- Analyze relationships among various social, ethnic, and racial groups and their effect on U.S. national identity

TIMELINE

Date	Event
1896	William McKinley is elected president.
1898	The Spanish-American War occurs.
1901	President McKinley is assassinated, and Teddy Roosevelt takes office.
1908	The NAACP is created.
1912	Woodrow Wilson is elected president.
1913	The Federal Reserve Act creates the Federal Reserve System.
1914	World War I begins in Europe. The Clayton Antitrust Act curbs the power of monopolies.
1917	The United States enters World War I. The Bolshevik Revolution starts in Russia.
1918	Wilson delivers his Fourteen Points address, calling for the creation of a League of Nations.
1919	Paris Peace Conference creates the Treaty of Versailles, the formal end to World War I. The Red Scare breaks out in America.
1920	The Nineteenth Amendment gives women the right to vote. The beginning of the Jazz Age, or the Roaring Twenties.
1923	The Teapot Dome Scandal takes place. President Harding dies in office, and Calvin Coolidge takes office.
1929	The stock market crashes on Black Tuesday, triggering the Great Depression.
1933	The first part of FDR's New Deal is implemented.
1939	Hitler invades Poland, starting World War II.
1940	France falls to Hitler. The United States implements the first peacetime draft.
1941	Japan attacks the U.S. military installation at Pearl Harbor. The United States declares war on Japan. Germany declares war on the United States.
1942	The United States sends Japanese-Americans to internment camps. The Battles of the Coral Sea and Midway are victories for the Allies.
1944	The GI Bill is signed into law. D-Day invasion occurs on the beaches of Normandy in France.
1945	Germany surrenders to the Allied Powers. FDR, Stalin, and Churchill meet at the Yalta Conference. President Roosevelt dies while still in office. Harry Truman becomes president. The United States drops atomic bombs on Japan, bringing an end to World War II.

TEST WHAT YOU ALREADY KNOW

Part A: Quiz

Questions 1–4 refer to the excerpt below.

"Laws Passed as a Result of the Commission's Second Year's Work

1. Reorganization of Labor Department . . .
5. Fire escapes and exits; limitation of number of occupants . . .
7. Prohibition of employment of children under fourteen, in cannery sheds or tenement houses . . .
8. Physical examination of children employed in factories . . .
11. Night work of women in factories . . .
12. Seats for women in factories . . .

The enactment of these laws marked a new era in labor legislation . . . It placed the State of New York in the lead in legislation for the protection of wage earners."

Fourth Report of the Factory Investigation Commission, 1913

1. Which of the following terms most clearly reflects the goals described in the excerpt?

   (A) Social Gospel
   (B) Americanization
   (C) Social Darwinism
   (D) Gilded Age

2. Which of the following political concepts from the 1930s parallels the ideas of the excerpt?

   (A) Isolationism
   (B) Socialism
   (C) Laissez-faire
   (D) The New Deal

3. The actions in the excerpt were most likely the result of an alliance between which of the following?

   (A) African American activists and Southern Democrats
   (B) Urban political machines and progressive reformers
   (C) Industrial capitalists and labor unions
   (D) Republicans and industrial capitalists

4. The actions in the excerpt most clearly reflect which of the following continuities in United States history?

   (A) Debates over the proper degree of government activism
   (B) Debates over gender inequality
   (C) Debates over the challenges of urbanization
   (D) Debates over increased consumerism

Questions 5–7 refer to the image below.

This poster from 1919 called upon all Americans to buy war bonds.

5. Which change in American society in the early twentieth century most directly led to the stance depicted in the poster?

    (A) Increased support for American imperialism

    (B) A demographic shift in immigration patterns

    (C) Decreased support for immigration quotas

    (D) Increased xenophobia

6. Which event of the post–World War I era most directly challenged the sentiment in the poster?

    (A) The Great Migration out of the South

    (B) Unrestricted immigration from the Western Hemisphere

    (C) The first Red Scare

    (D) The "closing" of the American frontier

7. The ideas expressed in the poster most clearly show the influence of which of the following?

    (A) Violations of civil liberties

    (B) Wartime patriotism

    (C) Support for women's suffrage

    (D) Nativism

Questions 8–10 refer to the excerpt below.

"The President of the United States of America and the Prime Minister . . . met together . . . [and] make known . . . their hopes for a better future . . .

First, their countries seek no aggrandizement, territorial or other;
Second, . . . no territorial changes that do not accord with the freely expressed wishes of the peoples . . . ;
Third, . . . the right of all peoples to choose [their] form of government . . . ;
Fourth, . . . access, on equal terms, to the trade and to the raw materials of the world . . . ;
Fifth, . . . the fullest [economic] collaboration between all nations . . . ;
Sixth, after the final destruction of the Nazi tyranny, . . . freedom from fear and want;
Seventh, . . . traverse the high seas and oceans without hindrance;
Eighth, . . . the establishment of a . . . permanent system of general security, [and] disarmament . . ."

The Atlantic Charter, 1941

8. Which of the following events of the early twentieth century most clearly represents a continuation of the ideas illustrated in the passage?

   (A) The creation of the League of Nations

   (B) The development of a unilateral foreign policy

   (C) Violations of civil liberties during wartime

   (D) Support for isolationism

9. The ideas expressed in the Atlantic Charter of 1941 echo which of the following?

   (A) Woodrow Wilson's Fourteen Points

   (B) William Jennings Bryan's "Cross of Gold" speech

   (C) Theodore Roosevelt's New Nationalism

   (D) Franklin Roosevelt's New Deal programs

10. The ideas expressed in the passage most directly reflect which of the following continuities in United States history?

   (A) The impact migration and population patterns had on American life

   (B) The impact changes in transportation and technology had on American society

   (C) The difficulty of maintaining a balance between liberty and order

   (D) The difficulty of finding acceptable ways to pursue international and domestic goals

9

Part B: Key Terms

The following is a list of the major people, places, and events for 1890–1945. You will likely see many of these on the AP U.S. History exam.

For each key term ask yourself the following questions:

- Can I describe this key term?
- Can I discuss this key term in the context of other events?
- Could I correctly answer a multiple-choice question about this key term?
- Could I correctly answer a free-response question about this key term?

Check off the key terms if you can answer "yes" to at least three of these questions.

The "Forgettable" Administrations

- ☐ Rutherford B. Hayes
- ☐ Chester A. Arthur
- ☐ Grover Cleveland
- ☐ James Garfield

Agrarian Discontent

- ☐ Benjamin Harrison
- ☐ Panic of 1893
- ☐ William McKinley
- ☐ Populist Party

New Imperialism

- ☐ New imperialism
- ☐ Treaty of Paris (1898)
- ☐ Theodore Roosevelt
- ☐ Spanish-American War
- ☐ Open Door Policy
- ☐ Roosevelt Corollary

The Progressive Era

- ☐ Progressive Era
- ☐ Woodrow Wilson
- ☐ Clayton Antitrust Act
- ☐ Square Deal
- ☐ Muckrakers
- ☐ Federal Trade Commission (FTC)
- ☐ William Howard Taft
- ☐ Federal Reserve System

African Americans at the Turn of the Century

- ☐ National Association for the Advancement of Colored People
- ☐ Great Migration

Women's Roles and Suffrage

- ☐ National Woman's Party
- ☐ Nineteenth Amendment

World War I

- ☐ Zimmermann Telegram
- ☐ *Schenck v. United States*
- ☐ League of Nations

Post-World War I Recovery

- ☐ Red Scare

American Business and Consumerism

- ☐ Warren G. Harding
- ☐ Herbert Hoover
- ☐ Kellogg-Briand Pact
- ☐ Calvin Coolidge
- ☐ Rugged individualism
- ☐ Good Neighbor Policy
- ☐ Dawes Plan

Culture in the Interwar Period

- ☐ Jazz Age (Roaring Twenties)
- ☐ Harlem Renaissance
- ☐ American Civil Liberties Union

The Great Depression

- ☐ Black Tuesday
- ☐ Eighteenth Amendment
- ☐ First Hundred Days
- ☐ Great Depression
- ☐ New Deal
- ☐ Second New Deal
- ☐ Franklin Delano Roosevelt

New Deal Support and Criticism

- ☐ Judicial Procedures Reform Bill (1937)
- ☐ National Labor Relations Act
- ☐ Fair Labor Standards Act
- ☐ National Industrial Recovery Act

International Problems and World War II

- ☐ Treaty of Versailles
- ☐ Pearl Harbor

World War II: A Two-Front War

- ☐ Yalta Conference
- ☐ D-Day
- ☐ Harry S. Truman
- ☐ United Nations
- ☐ Battle of the Bulge
- ☐ Atomic bomb

9

World War II's Impact on American Society

☐ Office of War Information   ☐ Harlem Riot of 1943   ☐ Executive Order 9066

☐ Navajo code talkers   ☐ Zoot Suit Riots

Next Steps

Step 1: Tally your correct answers from Part A and review the quiz explanations at the end of this chapter.

1. A   6. C

2. D   7. B

3. B   8. A

4. A   9. A

5. B   10. D

_____ out of 10 questions

Step 2: Count the number of key terms you checked off in Part B.

_____ out of 64 key terms

Step 3: Read the Key Takeaways in this chapter.

Step 4: Consult the table below and follow the instructions based on your performance.

If You Got...	Do This
80% or more of the Test What You Already Know assessment correct (8 or more questions from Part A and 51 or more key terms from Part B)	• Read definitions in this chapter for all the key terms you didn't check off. • Complete the Test What You Learned assessment in this chapter.
50% or less of the Test What You Already Know assessment correct (5 or fewer questions from Part A and 32 or fewer key terms from Part B)	• Read the comprehensive review for this period in Chapter 18. • If you are short on time, read only the High-Yield sections. • Read through all of the key term definitions in this chapter. • Complete the Test What You Learned assessment in this chapter.
Any other result	• Read the High-Yield sections in the comprehensive review of this period in Chapter 18. • Read definitions in this chapter for all the key terms you didn't check off. • Complete the Test What You Learned assessment in this chapter.

ESSENTIAL CONTENT

Key Takeaways: 1890–1945

1. The United States continued its transition from an agricultural economy to an industrial economy. In the 1920s, urban areas grew and employment opportunities were on the rise. However, the United States would soon plunge into the Great Depression.

2. Progressives across the country responded to political and economic uncertainty; they called for greater government action regarding social issues such as women's suffrage, the prohibition of alcohol, political corruption, and economic inequality.

3. With new forms of mass media, modern culture was born in an era known as the Roaring Twenties, also dubbed the Jazz Age. Americans debated larger social issues such as science, religion, gender roles, race, and immigration.

4. Major changes in migration occurred, as Americans and migrants from Asia and Europe increasingly moved into urban areas. Nativist campaigns succeeded in convincing the government to pass quotas and restrictions on immigration. The Great Migration saw African Americans leave the racial violence and segregation of the South and move to the North, where they sought better economic opportunities.

5. In an attempt to end the Great Depression, President Franklin Roosevelt promoted his New Deal plan to assist the poor, provide employment, and revitalize a stalling, weak economy. Through the New Deal, Roosevelt helped define modern American liberalism and left a long-lasting legacy of political, social, and economic reform.

6. America fought in three major wars during this period. The U.S. victory in the Spanish-American War resulted in increased overseas territory. After a period of relative peace, America entered World War I in 1917. The United States then entered a short-lived period of isolationism before World War II.

Key Terms: 1890–1945

Remember that the AP U.S. History exam tests you on the depth of your knowledge, not just your ability to recall facts. While we have provided brief definitions here, you will need to know these terms in even more depth for the AP exam, including how terms connect to broader historical themes and understandings.

The "Forgettable" Administrations

Rutherford B. Hayes: Nineteenth president. Served from 1877–1881. Even though he was a Civil War veteran and a Republican, he ended Reconstruction as part of the Compromise of 1877 to resolve the disputed 1876 election. Enacted modest civil service reform. Ordered federal troops in to break up the Great Railroad Strike of 1877. Pledged not to run for reelection and returned to Ohio.

James Garfield: Twentieth president. Served from March 4, 1881, until his death on September 19, 1881. He was shot on July 2, 1881, and unsanitary medical treatment caused a fatal infection to take root. Otherwise not notable.

Chester A. Arthur: Twenty-first president. Served from 1881–1885, but only assumed office after President Garfield's assassination. Mainly remembered for the Pendleton Civil Service Reform Act, which encouraged a merit-based system for the civil service. Declined to run for reelection in 1884 due to poor health. He died in November 1886 from a cerebral hemorrhage.

Grover Cleveland: Twenty-second and twenty-fourth president. Only president to serve nonconsecutive terms, in 1885–1889 and 1893–1897. The first Democratic Party president since before the Civil War. Supported the gold standard. His second term was defined by the Panic of 1893, which caused a severe depression. Sent federal troops in to break up the Pullman Strike. His resolution of the Venezuelan crisis of 1895 began the reconciliation between the United States and British Empire.

Agrarian Discontent

Benjamin Harrison: Twenty-third president. Served from 1889–1893 and was bookended by Cleveland's two nonconsecutive terms. Harrison supported the passage of the Sherman Antitrust Act but did little to enforce it. His attempt at securing voting rights for African Americans was unsuccessful. Modernized the U.S. Navy with new warships.

Populist Party: Also known as the People's Party. Its 1892 policy platform advocated for a silver standard, a graduated income tax, direct election of U.S. senators, and ownership of railroads, telegraph, and telephone lines. While the Populists won five western states in the 1892 election, the Democrats absorbed their policies thanks to William Jennings Bryan.

Panic of 1893: An economic depression caused by the failure of the Reading Railroad company and by overspeculation artificially inflating the price of stocks. The market did not recover for almost four years. Investors began trading in their silver for more valuable gold, depleting the already dangerously low supply of gold.

William McKinley: Twenty-fifth president. Served from 1897–1901. A proponent of the gold standard and a moderate between business and labor interests, McKinley was assassinated six months into his second term by an anarchist. McKinley oversaw U.S. involvement in the Spanish-American War, as well as the subsequent extension of American control over Cuba and the Philippines.

New Imperialism

New imperialism: A wave of U.S. imperialism spurred by an aggressive foreign policy stance, the desire to find new markets in which to sell American goods, and the philosophy of social Darwinism.

Spanish-American War: A war between the United States and Spain (April 21, 1898–August 13, 1898). Ostensibly triggered by the alleged sinking of the *Maine* by Spanish forces, it involved the United States aiding independence efforts in Cuba to protect financial investments there. It was also to safeguard the Gulf Coast from a free Cuba potentially leasing its ports to foreign powers. The United States took control of Cuba, the Philippines, Puerto Rico, and several other islands. Also led to the Philippine-American War and subsequent Moro Rebellion (1899–1913).

Treaty of Paris (1898): The peace treaty that ended the Spanish-American War. It turned Cuba, Guam, the Philippines, and Puerto Rico over to the United States. The treaty also signaled the end of Spain as a world power and the beginning of the United States as a rising one.

Open Door Policy: A policy articulated by Secretary of State John Hay, who served in both the McKinley and Roosevelt administrations. It declared that China would be open and free to trade equally with any nation. The policy was wildly popular in the United States, as it kept Chinese markets open to American business while outwardly avoiding the taint of imperialism. Unsurprisingly, it was denounced and resisted in China due to its thinly veiled justification for violating China's sovereignty. Contributed to the outbreak of the Boxer Rebellion.

Theodore Roosevelt: Twenty-sixth president. Served from 1901–1909. A reformist New York governor, Roosevelt was kicked upstairs by party bosses to the vice presidency, which was seen as an unimportant office. After McKinley was assassinated, Roosevelt became president at 42, the youngest ever. He pursued a progressive domestic agenda called the Square Deal. In terms of foreign policy, he forced through construction of the Panama Canal. He brokered an end to the Russo-Japanese War, which secured him the 1906 Nobel Peace Prize. He unsuccessfully attempted to run for a third, nonconsecutive term in 1912.

Roosevelt Corollary: An amendment to the Monroe Doctrine issued by Theodore Roosevelt. It stated that the United States would come to the aid of any Latin American nation experiencing financial trouble. In essence, the United States gained total control of Latin America through the corollary.

The Progressive Era

Progressive Era: An era of social and political reform that began in the 1890s and lasted until the beginning of U.S. involvement in World War I in 1917. The goals of the Progressive movement were protecting social welfare, promoting moral improvement, and spurring economic reform. Antitrust legislation and labor reform were key aspects of this era, along with support for women's suffrage, direct election of U.S. senators, and prohibition of alcohol.

Square Deal: A progressive policy platform advocated by President Theodore Roosevelt. It involved breaking up trusts, increasing government regulation of business, pro-labor laws, and promoting environmental conservation. The New Deal took its name from it.

William Howard Taft: Twenty-seventh president. Served from 1909–1913. Tenth chief justice (1921–1930). While a trust-busting Republican in Theodore Roosevelt's mold, he also had some sympathies with the party's conservative wing. Split the vote with Roosevelt's Bull Moose Party in the 1912 election, allowing Woodrow Wilson to win the White House. Later appointed to the Supreme Court, he became the only person to have led both the executive and judicial branches.

Woodrow Wilson: Twenty-eighth president. Served from 1913–1921, although a series of near-fatal strokes in late 1919 incapacitated him for the rest of his life, and the remainder of his presidency was essentially run by his wife Edith. The first Southern president since before the Civil War. When healthy, Wilson supported a number of progressive reforms, such as the Federal Reserve Act and the Clayton Antitrust Act. Implemented segregation throughout the executive branch offices, including the Navy, which had never been segregated. Internationally, he is famous for the Fourteen Points as well as his brainchild, the League of Nations. Died in 1924.

Muckrakers: A nickname for investigative journalists who seek to spur reform and expose corruption. Originated during the Progressive Era. The term comes from Theodore Roosevelt, who said: ". . . the men with the muck rakes are often indispensable to the well-being of society; but only if they know when to stop raking the muck." An example is Upton Sinclair, who wrote the 1906 novel *The Jungle*, illustrating the poor conditions at a Chicago meatpacking plant.

Federal Reserve System: Created in 1913 in reaction to the Panic of 1907, it consists of 12 regional banks that are publicly controlled by the Federal Reserve Board but privately owned by member banks. The system serves as the lender of last resort for all private banks, holds and sells the nation's bonds, and issues Federal Reserve Notes—otherwise known as dollar bills—for consumers to purchase goods and services.

Clayton Antitrust Act: A 1914 law which strengthened provisions for breaking up trusts and protected labor unions from prosecution under the Sherman Antitrust Act. Labor leader Samuel Gompers hailed the bill as labor's Magna Carta.

Federal Trade Commission (FTC): Created in 1914, the FTC is a regulatory agency that monitors interstate business activities and forces companies who break laws to comply with government's cease and desist orders.

African Americans at the Turn of the Century

National Association for the Advancement of Colored People: The NAACP was founded on February 12, 1908. It seeks to end all racial discrimination, segregation, and disenfranchisement.

Great Migration: A period beginning around 1910 that saw millions of African Americans move from the South to northern cities. This was to take advantage of economic opportunities in the North, often to escape from the exploitative system of sharecropping.

Women's Roles and Suffrage

National Woman's Party: A splinter group of the National American Woman Suffrage Association, led by Alice Paul. Founded in 1916 and disbanded in 1997. It focused on the ratification of a constitutional amendment securing women's suffrage nationwide. Later sought to secure equal rights for women, such as with the Equal Pay Act of 1963.

Nineteenth Amendment: Ratified in 1920, it granted women the right to vote.

World War I

Zimmermann Telegram: A diplomatic letter from German Foreign Secretary Zimmermann to the Mexican president, promising him that if his country assisted Germany in a possible war against the United States, Mexico would be given back the territory lost in the Mexican-American War. A contributing factor to U.S. entry into World War I.

Schenck v. United States: Pivotal Supreme Court ruling that stated that Congress could limit the right of free speech if it represented a "clear and present danger" that would bring about evils the government was seeking to stop. This was an example of the curbing of American civil liberties that took place during wartime.

League of Nations: A precursor to the United Nations, proposed by Woodrow Wilson in his Fourteen Points speech. Article X of the League's charter called for members to stand at the ready if another member nation's sovereignty was being threatened. This killed the charter's chances of ratification in the United States, as it seemed to promise future wars.

Post-World War I Recovery

Red Scare: Ran from 1917 through the 1920s. A period of social anxiety and paranoia concerned with communist and anarchist infiltration of society. Driven by the nationalism of World War I, labor unrest, nativism, and most especially the 1917 Russian Revolution that established the world's first communist state in the Soviet Union. Led to a series of mass arrests and deportations in 1919–1920 known as the Palmer Raids.

American Business and Consumerism

Warren G. Harding: Twenty-ninth president. Served from 1921 until August 2, 1923. Initially popular, various scandals (such as Teapot Dome) uncovered after his death destroyed Harding's reputation. Oversaw the Washington Naval Conference.

Calvin Coolidge: Thirtieth president. Served from 1923–1929. Assumed the presidency following Warren G. Harding's death. Elected in 1924. Nicknamed "Silent Cal" for his tight-lipped nature. He was a small-government conservative and supported laissez-faire economics. Unsuccessfully called on Congress to make lynching a federal crime.

Dawes Plan: A loan program crafted by Charles Dawes that enabled Germany to pay its World War I reparations, thus lessening the financial crisis in Europe. It was successful until the program ended with the U.S. stock market crash in 1929.

Herbert Hoover: Thirty-first president. Served from 1929–1933. A Quaker and humanitarian, he famously led famine relief efforts in Europe after World War I, as well as oversaw the response to the Great Mississippi Flood of 1927. However, his response (or lack thereof) to the Great Depression destroyed his popularity. Homeless encampments were mockingly dubbed Hoovervilles. He signed the Smoot–Hawley Act into law and supported Prohibition.

Rugged individualism: A belief articulated by Herbert Hoover, which stated that anyone could become successful in life through hard work. Influenced his response to the Great Depression.

Kellogg-Briand Pact: A 1928 pact that sought to foster world peace by making offensive wars illegal throughout the world. Unfortunately, the pact did not have any teeth: it did not prohibit defensive warfare or provide for punishment of countries that disobeyed the pact.

Good Neighbor Policy: A foreign policy initiative by FDR. Centered on Latin America, it saw the withdrawal of American forces from Nicaragua and the establishment of normalized relations between the United States and the nations of Latin America. Its non-interference, non-interventionist doctrine lasted until the start of the Cold War.

Culture in the Interwar Period

Jazz Age (Roaring Twenties): An era from 1920 to 1929 that experienced a cultural explosion similar to that of the antebellum period. Jazz music became the music of choice for young people and urbanites. As leisure time increased, radio and movies became popular. The Lost

Generation was made up of authors and poets, such as F. Scott Fitzgerald, who reacted to the impact of technology and business by creating realist or early surrealist works that portrayed America without the glitter of consumerism.

Harlem Renaissance: A term for a cultural flowering in the New York City neighborhood of Harlem during the 1920s. Harlem became the center of African American culture during this period. It helped to change the perception of African Americans.

American Civil Liberties Union: Founded in 1920, the ACLU is an organization dedicated to the absolutist protection of Constitutional liberties, especially those of the First Amendment. In the 1920s, they appointed Clarence Darrow as defense in the Scopes Monkey Trial.

The Great Depression

Black Tuesday: The name for the worst stock market crash in U.S. history, which occurred on October 29, 1929. A common starting point for the Great Depression.

Great Depression: The name for a global economic depression that took place from 1929 and lasted until the outbreak of World War II. The massive social and political disruption it caused due to the loss of wealth and a spike in unemployment contributed to instability throughout the world and led to the rise of the Nazi Party in Germany.

Franklin Delano Roosevelt: Thirty-second president. Served from 1933–1945. He was the only president to be elected to four terms. FDR oversaw the response to the Great Depression with the New Deal, led the United States through most of World War II, approved the Manhattan Project, and laid the groundwork for the postwar international system. Paralyzed after a 1921 bout with polio, FDR carefully hid his disability with the help of the press. He died in office and was succeeded by Harry Truman.

Eighteenth Amendment: The "noble experiment" in banning alcohol in the United States. This period was known as Prohibition. In practice, narrow exemptions were made for medical necessity or for religious rites that required sacramental wine. Took effect in 1920 and was repealed by the Twenty-First Amendment in December 1933.

New Deal: A series of domestic policy initiatives and social welfare programs proposed by Franklin Delano Roosevelt. It sought to alleviate the suffering of the Great Depression with massive government spending, thus avoiding a potential communist or fascist revolution.

First Hundred Days: A common term for the breakneck pace of New Deal legislation passed during FDR's first hundred days in office as president. Often used as a measuring stick for the perceived success or failure of new presidents, as the common perception is that they enjoy a honeymoon period in both public and opposition opinion early in their presidency.

Second New Deal: Ran from 1935 to 1938. Focused more on relief and reform. Among several programs passed during this period, the most famous is the Social Security Act.

New Deal Support and Criticism

Judicial Procedures Reform Bill (1937): An attempt by FDR to add more justices to the Supreme Court (6 more, for a total of 15), with the goal to receive more favorable decisions for New Deal legislation that the Court had deemed unconstitutional. Frequently termed the the "court-packing plan." While the bill itself did not pass, Roosevelt eventually was able to make eight appointments to the Supreme Court during his presidency.

National Industrial Recovery Act: Part of the First New Deal, the NIRA was the most proactive legislation to date (circa 1933) in protecting the rights of workers and organized labor. Its board set maximum work hours, minimum wages, and price floors. It was also responsible for setting production quotas and inventories to prevent overproduction or price gouging. Later ruled unconstitutional in 1935. Importantly for organized labor, the NIRA guaranteed labor the right to organize and collectively bargain.

National Labor Relations Act: Also called the Wagner Act, it strengthened the language of the NIRA. It still stands as the foundation of U.S. labor law and created the National Labor Relations Board.

Fair Labor Standards Act: A law passed during the Second New Deal. It established a federal minimum wage and set the maximum hours for workers employed by interstate businesses. It also ensured an end to child labor.

International Problems and World War II

Treaty of Versailles: The peace treaty that officially ended World War I, but not ratified by the United States, which secured a separate peace in 1921. The treaty's terms were extremely harsh but laxly enforced as time went by, resulting in the worst of both worlds. They contributed to Germany's postwar economic turmoil while allowing for the rise of Adolf Hitler and the Nazi Party.

Pearl Harbor: A lagoon harbor located on the island of Oahu, Hawaii. Home to a major U.S. Navy base. On December 7, 1941, it was the target of an infamous surprise attack by Japan. Several U.S. Navy ships were destroyed and 2,403 Americans were killed. Inflamed a previously lukewarm American public opinion about involvement in World War II.

World War II: A Two-Front War

Yalta Conference: A February 1945 meeting of the Big Three (Winston Churchill, Franklin D. Roosevelt, and Joseph Stalin). It finalized their plans for postwar Europe, with the division of Germany into four occupied military zones and Stalin agreeing to allow free elections in Eastern Europe. Stalin also agreed to enter the war against Japan within three months of Germany's surrender. Yalta also yielded the skeleton framework for the United Nations.

United Nations: An intergovernmental organization chartered in October 1945 to mediate disputes between nations. Its headquarters is located in New York City. All recognized nations are granted seats in the General Assembly.

However, veto power is reserved to the five permanent members of the Security Council, which represent the victorious world powers of World War II: Nationalist China (now held by the People's Republic of China), France, the Soviet Union (now held by Russia), the United Kingdom, and the United States.

D-Day: A common name for the Normandy landings, although it technically only refers to the initial landing operation on June 6, 1944. The Western Allies invaded along five beachheads, gaining a foothold in Nazi-occupied France. Out of 4,414 total Allied fatalities, 2,499 Americans died. Often dramatized in movies and video games.

9

Battle of the Bulge: The last major German offensive on the Western Front. It took place in December 1944 and aimed to encircle the Allied armies, hold them hostage to force a peace treaty, and thus allow Germany to focus its full attention on the Soviets. Despite suffering heavy losses, the Allies were able to recover and continue their push toward Germany.

Harry S. Truman: World War I veteran who led an artillery regiment. Missouri senator (1935–1945) elected with aid of the Pendergast machine. He later gained a reputation for investigating military waste. Vice president from January 20, 1945, to April 12, 1945. Ascended to the presidency upon FDR's death. He ordered the dropping of two atomic bombs on Japan and oversaw the final phases of both the Western and Pacific Fronts.

Atomic bomb: Nuclear weapon that was dropped on the Japanese cities of Hiroshima and Nagasaki in 1945. Hiroshima was struck on August 6, killing 80,000 instantly and 135,000 in the long-term total. Nagasaki was struck on August 9, killing another 80,000 in total. The use of the atomic bomb on largely civilian populations would have a lasting impact on warfare.

World War II's Impact on American Society

Office of War Information: The OWI was organized during World War II to produce radio shows and news reels to keep Americans apprised of events overseas. It aimed to keep American morale high and to increase support for the war.

Navajo code talkers: A group of American Indian volunteers during World War II. They translated U.S. documents and orders into their native language so that enemy forces could not decipher their content.

Harlem Riot of 1943: Violent conflict that took place in Harlem, New York, after a white police officer shot and wounded a black soldier. It was one of at least six riots that occurred in that same year across the country, due to ongoing racial tensions between black and white populations.

Zoot Suit Riots: A series of California race riots in the summer of 1943. Mainly occurred between white sailors and Mexican American teens who wore flashy, long "zoot suits."

Executive Order 9066: An order issued by President Roosevelt in 1942 in reaction to the paranoia that American citizens of Japanese ancestry might turn against their adopted country to aid Japan in an invasion of the West Coast. The Supreme Court upheld the decision to forcibly relocate these citizens to internment camps in the case *Korematsu v. United States* (1944), stating that in times of war, the curbing of civil rights was justified and that the court could not second-guess military decisions.

TEST WHAT YOU LEARNED

Questions 1–3 refer to the image below.

WHERE WOULD WE BE? (1898)

Original caption: "If the real Americans had held Lodge's view of immigration there would be no Lodge Bill now — nor anything else."

1. The debate illustrated by this cartoon was the result of an influx of immigrant groups from

    (A) Northern and Western Europe

    (B) Central and South America

    (C) Eastern and Central Asia

    (D) Southern and Eastern Europe

2. The 1891 Immigration Act

    (A) granted responsibility for immigration to the states

    (B) repealed the Chinese Exclusion Act of 1882

    (C) created a federal office to supervise immigration at U.S. ports of entry

    (D) specifically limited immigration from Latin America

3. Which of the following groups from the twentieth century would be most likely to oppose the perspective of the cartoon?

    (A) African Americans migrating away from the South

    (B) Immigrants from Europe hoping to achieve the American dream

    (C) Citizens opposed to government actions during the Red Scare

    (D) Supporters of the immigration laws passed in the 1920s

Questions 4–6 refer to the excerpt below.

"The northward migration of African-Americans accelerated after the war, thanks to the advent of the mechanical cotton picker—an invention whose impact rivaled that of Eli Whitney's cotton gin . . . Overnight, the Cotton South's historic need for cheap labor disappeared. Their muscle no longer required in Dixie, some 5 million black tenant farmers and sharecroppers headed north in the three decades after the war. Theirs was one of the great migrations in American history . . . Within a single generation, a near majority of African-Americans gave up their historic homeland and their rural way of life . . . The speed and scale of these changes jolted the migrants and sometimes convulsed the communities that received them."

David M. Kennedy and Lizabeth Cohen, *The American Pageant*, 2013

4. What was the major motivation for the Great Migration?

    (A) Assistance programs subsidized by the federal government

    (B) An escape from economic depression in the South

    (C) The lack of racial violence in the North

    (D) Industrial jobs with good pay

5. The Great Migration is most similar to which of the following events?

    (A) The Exodusters' migration to Kansas in the 1870s and 1880s

    (B) The migration of runaway slaves using the Underground Railroad in the 1840s and 1850s

    (C) The Back to Africa movement led by Black Nationalists in the 1920s

    (D) The California Gold Rush in the 1840s

6. Which of the following African American institutions rose to prominence during the time of the Great Migration?

    (A) The Tuskegee Institute

    (B) The National Association for the Advancement of Colored People (NAACP)

    (C) The Freedman's Bureau

    (D) The Congress of Racial Equality (CORE)

9

Questions 7–10 refer to the image below.

7. The ideas illustrated in the poster most clearly show the influence of which of the following?

   (A) Federal power as defined by the Articles of Confederation

   (B) American cultural pride demonstrated by Manifest Destiny

   (C) The Constitutional amendments of the Reconstruction era

   (D) The social justice reforms of the Progressive Era

8. Which change in American society most directly led to the Social Security Act?

   (A) A rise in political corruption

   (B) The result of unrestricted immigration

   (C) The impact of severe business cycle fluctuation

   (D) Massive internal migrations

9. Which of the following was a direct result of legislation such as the Social Security Act?

   (A) The Great Depression

   (B) Increased support for laissez-faire economic policies

   (C) The electoral dominance of the Republican Party

   (D) The rise of a limited welfare state

10. Roosevelt's Second New Deal policies exemplified which of the following philosophies?

   (A) Upholding laissez-faire economics

   (B) Increasing government spending

   (C) Decreasing government spending

   (D) Balancing the national budget

9

Part B: Key Terms

This key terms list is the same as the list in the Test What You Already Know section earlier in this chapter. Based on what you have now learned, again ask yourself the following questions:

- Can I define this key term and use it in a sentence?
- Can I provide an example related to this key term?
- Could I correctly answer a multiple-choice question about this key term?
- Could I correctly answer a free-response question about this key term?

Check off the key terms if you can answer "yes" to at least three of these questions.

The "Forgettable" Administrations

- ☐ Rutherford B. Hayes
- ☐ Chester A. Arthur
- ☐ Grover Cleveland
- ☐ James Garfield

Agrarian Discontent

- ☐ Benjamin Harrison
- ☐ Panic of 1893
- ☐ William McKinley
- ☐ Populist Party

New Imperialism

- ☐ New imperialism
- ☐ Treaty of Paris (1898)
- ☐ Theodore Roosevelt
- ☐ Spanish-American War
- ☐ Open Door Policy
- ☐ Roosevelt Corollary

The Progressive Era

- ☐ Progressive Era
- ☐ Woodrow Wilson
- ☐ Clayton Antitrust Act
- ☐ Square Deal
- ☐ Muckrakers
- ☐ Federal Trade Commission (FTC)
- ☐ William Howard Taft
- ☐ Federal Reserve System

African Americans at the Turn of the Century

- ☐ National Association for the Advancement of Colored People
- ☐ Great Migration

Women's Roles and Suffrage

- ☐ National Woman's Party
- ☐ Nineteenth Amendment

World War I

- ☐ Zimmermann Telegram
- ☐ *Schenck v. United States*
- ☐ League of Nations

Post-World War I Recovery

- ☐ Red Scare

American Business and Consumerism

- ☐ Warren G. Harding
- ☐ Herbert Hoover
- ☐ Kellogg-Briand Pact
- ☐ Calvin Coolidge
- ☐ Rugged individualism
- ☐ Good Neighbor Policy
- ☐ Dawes Plan

Culture in the Interwar Period

- ☐ Jazz Age (Roaring Twenties)
- ☐ Harlem Renaissance
- ☐ American Civil Liberties Union

The Great Depression

- ☐ Black Tuesday
- ☐ Eighteenth Amendment
- ☐ First Hundred Days
- ☐ Great Depression
- ☐ New Deal
- ☐ Second New Deal
- ☐ Franklin Delano Roosevelt

New Deal Support and Criticism

- ☐ Judicial Procedures Reform Bill (1937)
- ☐ National Labor Relations Act
- ☐ Fair Labor Standards Act
- ☐ National Industrial Recovery Act

International Problems and World War II

- ☐ Treaty of Versailles
- ☐ Pearl Harbor

World War II: A Two-Front War

- ☐ Yalta Conference
- ☐ D-Day
- ☐ Harry S. Truman
- ☐ United Nations
- ☐ Battle of the Bulge
- ☐ Atomic bomb

9

World War II's Impact on American Society

- ☐ Office of War Information
- ☐ Navajo code talkers
- ☐ Harlem Riot of 1943
- ☐ Zoot Suit Riots
- ☐ Executive Order 9066

Next Steps

Step 1: Tally your correct answers from Part A and review the quiz explanations at the end of this chapter.

1.	D	6.	B
2.	C	7.	D
3.	D	8.	C
4.	D	9.	D
5.	A	10.	B

_____ out of 10 questions

Step 2: Count the number of key terms you checked off in Part B.

_____ out of 64 key terms

Step 3: Compare your Test What You Already Know results to these Test What You Learned results to see how exam-ready you are for this period.

For More Practice:

- Read (or reread) the comprehensive review for this period in Chapter 18.
- Go to kaptest.com to complete the online quiz questions for 1890–1945.
  - Haven't registered your book yet? Go to kaptest.com/moreonline to begin.

ANSWERS AND EXPLANATIONS

Test What You Already Know

1. A

In the aftermath of the Triangle Shirtwaist Factory fire in New York City, New York State created a series of investigating commissions to look into working conditions across the industries in the state. Supporters of the Social Gospel focused on social justice and lessening the problems of industrialization, including poverty and political corruption. **(A)** is correct. *Americanization* is a term used to describe how American culture influences other countries' practices; (B) is incorrect. Social Darwinism is the belief that living creatures are subject to natural selection and that existence is ruled by survival of the fittest. Instead of looking into whether a specific demographic is more fit to survive, the investigation analyzed working conditions, making (C) incorrect. (D) is incorrect because the Gilded Age was a period in history when the American economy transitioned from primarily agrarian-based to primarily industrial-based.

2. D

Just as the investigation yielded new laws to improve working conditions in response to the Triangle Shirtwaist fire, the New Deal was enacted in the 1930s in response to the Great Depression. New Deal programs were created to assist the unemployed, recover the economy, and reform the financial system, making **(D)** correct. (A) is incorrect because isolationists, who did not support involvement in international politics, may or may not have been interested in workers' rights. The Socialist Party of America was established in 1901 and declined in popularity in the 1920s, eliminating (B). Laissez-faire was a popular economic philosophy in the 1920s and 1930s among those who wished to avoid interference with the economy, making (C) incorrect.

3. B

By the Progressive era, urban political machines, especially Tammany Hall in New York City, realized that much of their political support came from immigrant communities demanding government action. These voters, combined with the actions of urban middle class reformers, swayed political machines to support reform that would impact working conditions in order to retain political power, making **(B)** correct. (A) is incorrect because African American activists and Southern Democrats disagreed on civil rights and racial reform. (C) is incorrect because labor unions were constantly at odds with industrial capitalists over wages, hours, and working conditions throughout the early 1900s until business began to prosper in the wake of the Great Depression. Republicans often benefited from the support of industrial capitalists; however, this support did not lead to bettering working conditions in factories, making (D) incorrect.

4. A

As American capitalism developed, debates occurred over the role of government in the economy and the proper amount of government intervention necessary to limit the worst abuses of capitalism; **(A)** is correct. While the majority of garment workers who died in the Triangle Shirtwaist fire were women, the resulting laws affected working conditions of both genders, making (B) incorrect. Though this fire was one of the deadliest industrial accidents in U.S. history, the government became increasingly responsible for protecting urban workers, eliminating (C). Instead of increasing the protection or interests of consumers, the fire led to increased protection of workers; (D) is incorrect.

5. B

This World War I era poster calls upon all Americans, whatever their ethnic background, to participate in a bond drive to fund the war effort. After 1890, more immigrants came from Southern and Eastern Europe than from Northern and Western Europe, which is illustrated by the listing of names; **(B)** is correct. (A) is incorrect; while the United States followed the policy of imperialism during World War I, the poster does not communicate the intention to take over another country. (C) is incorrect because the poster celebrates assimilation by addressing everyone as "Americans all!" Xenophobia is a fear of foreigners, which is the opposite of what the poster represents, making (D) incorrect.

6. C

Shortly after World War I and the Bolshevik Revolution, concern over the spread of communism and anarchism led to the first Red Scare in the United States, which was marked by increased xenophobia and a limitation on civil liberties; **(C)** is correct. The Great Migration out of the South, which refers to the relocation of more than six million African Americans from the South to the North, Midwest, and West, directly relates to the poster's message of assimilation and immigration, eliminating (A). (B) is incorrect because unrestricted immigration also relates to the poster's sentiment. In 1890, the U.S. Census stated that the frontier had been settled and, in effect, "closed." However, this did not exclude immigrants from moving to the West and occurred before WWI began, making (D) incorrect.

7. B

With posters like this, the American government appealed to the wartime patriotism of its entire population, including its large immigrant population, making **(B)** correct. (A) is incorrect because the poster focused on addressing Americans as a group, not the factions that violations of civil liberties would create. While Lady Liberty is featured on the poster, the message is not one of women's suffrage, making (C) incorrect. (D) is incorrect because liberty bond drives raised money for the war effort from across a wide demographic of the American population, including immigrants and natives alike.

8. A

Prior to American entry into World War II, President Roosevelt met with British Prime Minister Winston Churchill off the coast of Newfoundland and agreed to a general statement of war principles. This Atlantic Charter articulated many of the goals of President Wilson's Fourteen Points prior to U.S. entry into World War I, including an organization to promote general security, namely the League of Nations; **(A)** is correct. (B) is incorrect because the charter involved more than one country. Roosevelt and Churchill focused on supporting the restoration of self-governments for all countries that had been occupied instead of violations of civil liberties that may have occurred in war; (C) is incorrect. Because the Atlantic Charter was a joint declaration between the United States and Great Britain that provided war aims, (D) is incorrect.

9. A

The Atlantic Charter reflected many of Wilson's Fourteen Points, including freedom of the seas and the principle of self-determination. Therefore, **(A)** is correct. William Jennings Bryan delivered his "Cross of Gold" speech in support of making both gold and silver legal forms of currency, which is not relevant to the Allies' ideal goals of war as outlined in the Atlantic Charter; (B) is incorrect. Theodore Roosevelt's New Nationalism philosophy and Franklin Roosevelt's New Deal programs called for change within America, while the Atlantic Charter focused on global issues; this eliminates (C) and (D).

10. D

While the Atlantic Charter established an idealized set of world goals, the decision to act on those goals involved complex questions of federal policy, public opinion, and the economic resources necessary to achieve public policy goals at home and abroad. **(D)** is correct. (A) and (B) are incorrect because neither address the international affairs of the United States. While the Atlantic Charter outlined Roosevelt and Churchill's intention to ensure the liberty of men, (C) is incorrect because it did not directly lead to difficulty maintaining a balance between liberty and order in the United States.

Test What You Learned

1. D

The number of immigrants from Southern and Eastern Europe greatly increased during the mid-1880s. The influx of so many Jews and Roman Catholics was a source of concern for many Americans, who were predominantly Protestant in this era. Thus, **(D)** is correct. Immigrants from Northern and Western Europe arrived in America in the early nineteenth century, eliminating (A). During this time period, Central and South America were popular destinations for European immigrants; (B) is incorrect. The Chinese Exclusion Act of 1882 had already been passed in response to immigrants from Eastern and Central Asia, eliminating (C).

2. C

The 1891 Immigration Act created the Office of the Superintendent of Immigration to oversee basic immigration procedures. The service collected passenger lists from incoming ships and, after questioning, admitted or rejected the immigrants. **(C)** is correct. Because the 1891 Immigration Act created a federal office responsible for overseeing immigration for the entire country, (A) is incorrect. The Chinese Exclusion Act was actually renewed the following year, eliminating (B).

Immigration from Southern and Eastern Europe, not Latin America, was the main concern in the 1890s, making (D) incorrect.

3.   D

The cartoonist was criticizing the descendants of previous immigrants for their hypocrisy in opposing new immigrants. Later, during the 1920s, nativists viewed the increase in immigration from Southern and Eastern Europe as a threat to America's stability. Immigration laws passed in that decade placed quotas on the number of immigrants admitted into the county, so nativists and other supporters of these laws would have disagreed with the cartoonist's perspective; **(D)** is correct. African Americans leaving the South as part of the Great Migration faced many challenges during this period and would likely have been able to sympathize with immigrants, making (A) incorrect. European immigrants would likely have agreed with the pro-immigrant perspective of the cartoon, eliminating (B). The government often took an anti-immigrant stance during the Red Scare, so those in opposition to such actions would likely have sided with the perspective of the cartoon, making (C) incorrect.

4.   D

After the outbreak of the World War I, many African Americans moved northward to take jobs in the factories that were gearing up for the war effort; **(D)** is correct. While the factory jobs in the North had to do with the war effort, they were not supported by the federal government, and government assistance programs were not prevalent; (A) is incorrect. The South was still undergoing economic difficulties, but this was not the major driver for the Great Migration, making (B) incorrect. (D) is incorrect because, unfortunately, African Americans in the North also experienced racial discrimination, including intimidation and riots.

5.   A

Freedmen from the South were attracted to Kansas with the (false) promise of free land and work animals; they were called Exodusters because their mass migration was much like that described in Exodus in the Bible. Similarly, African Americans who migrated to the North did so because of the promises of good-paying jobs and less

discrimination, both of which proved false. Therefore, **(A)** is correct. (B) and (C) are incorrect because, though these events involved African Americans, the respective motivations of freedom from slavery and forming a separate African community were different from the details of the Great Migration. The economic lure of the Gold Rush is similar to that of the Great Migration, but the other factors differed too much for this to be the best match; (D) is also incorrect.

6.   B

The Great Migration started around 1910. In 1905, Du Bois held a meeting in Niagara Falls to discuss possible forms of protest against racial discrimination and violence. This group, called the Niagara Movement, joined forces with other concerned African Americans and whites to form the National Association for the Advancement of Colored People (NAACP) in 1908, which gained prominence in the 1910s and onward. **(B)** is correct. Booker T. Washington's Tuskegee Institute was founded in the 1880s and gained popularity in the 1890s, before the Great Migration had occurred, making (A) incorrect. The Freedman's Bureau, founded by the federal government in 1865, also pre-dated the Great Migration, making (C) incorrect. The Congress of Racial Equality (CORE) was an African American civil rights organization that was founded in 1942, after the Great Migration; (D) is also incorrect.

7.   D

During the early twentieth century, Progressive Era reformers at the local, state, and national levels sought to increase the role of government to protect American consumers, workers, and citizens. They hoped to curb the worst abuses of industrial and finance capitalism. **(D)** is correct. This time period marked an increase in the government's dealings with the economy, whereas the Articles of Confederation created a weak central government with less involvement in issues like the economy; (A) is incorrect. (B) is incorrect because Manifest Destiny referred to the settlers' responsibility to expand into the West, and the period of the New Deal did not focus on further expansion. (C) is incorrect because the constitutional amendments of the Reconstruction era focused on abolishing slavery, establishing citizenship rights, and enacting voting rights.

9

8. C

The boom-bust cycle of the late nineteenth century continued into the twentieth century with the Great Depression. The reform legislation of the Second New Deal, including the Social Security Act, attempted to make the population more economically secure through federal government action. Therefore, **(C)** is correct. (A) is incorrect because the Social Security Act benefited workers by requiring the current generation of workers to pay into a fund, which would pay them a monthly amount based on what they contributed upon the age of 65. In effect, the Social Security system was a national program created as a type of social insurance to combat unemployment, not to discourage migrations or immigration, eliminating (B) and (D).

9. D

The reform legislation that created various agencies during the Second New Deal, including the Social Security Act, the National Labor Relations Act, and the Federal Deposit Insurance Corporation, made the national government more responsible for the economic safety and well-being of its citizens. Not without controversy, this increased role for government formed the basis for a limited welfare state, which matches **(D)**. (A) is incorrect because the New Deal was Roosevelt's plan to stabilize the economy following the Great Depression. In the 1920s, President Coolidge adopted laissez-faire economic policies, which contributed to the Great Depression; (B) is incorrect. Roosevelt's election in 1932 ended the Republican Party's dominance of national politics and began a period of Democratic dominance, making (C) incorrect.

10. B

In line with Keynesian theory, Franklin D. Roosevelt initiated an increase in spending on public works projects and other programs as part of the Second New Deal to help the economy; **(B)** is correct. FDR's New Deal programs were the opposite of laissez-faire; the government took an active role in the economy, increasing its spending in order to spur more demand that would eventually increase the need for employees. Therefore, (A) is incorrect. The Roosevelt Recession occurred in 1937 and 1938 because the president had decided to do less government spending, making (C) incorrect. Keynesian theory proposed that instead of attempting to balance the budget and imposing new taxes on an already taxed system, the government should resort to deficit spending; this eliminates (D).

CHAPTER 10

Period 8: 1945–1980

LEARNING OBJECTIVES

After studying this time period, you will be able to:

- Explain the causes and effects of U.S. economic, diplomatic, and military initiatives in North America and globally

- Describe the role of political philosophies in the developing American identity

- Explain how environmental and geographic factors, as well as competition for resources, affected various communities and impacted government policies

- Describe the effects on American life of differing interpretations of the Constitution

- Analyze relationships among various social, ethnic, and racial groups and their effect on U.S. national identity

- Describe how reformers and activists have changed American society

- Describe the rise of, and changes in, group identities over time

- Explain the impact on U.S. politics of conflicting views of the federal government's role

TIMELINE

Date	Event
1945	World War II ends.
1947	The Truman Doctrine attempts to counter the spread of communism. The Marshall Plan assists the rebuilding of Western Europe after World War II.
1949	NATO is created. Communists under the leadership of Mao Tse-Tung defeat the nationalists in China.
1950–1953	The Korean War takes place.
1952	General Dwight D. Eisenhower is elected president.
1954	*Brown v. Board of Education* overturns the earlier landmark court case *Plessy v. Ferguson*.
1955	Rosa Parks refuses to give up her bus seat to a white man. The Soviet Union forms the Warsaw Pact.
1957	Black students, known as the Little Rock Nine, face violent protests as they enter an all-white school in Arkansas.
1960	John F. Kennedy defeats Richard Nixon to become president.
1961	The Berlin Wall is built to separate East and West Germany. The Bay of Pigs invasion takes place in Cuba.
1962	Cold War tensions escalate with the Cuban Missile Crisis.
1963	Martin Luther King Jr. delivers his "I Have a Dream" speech. President Kennedy is assassinated, and Lyndon Johnson takes office.
1964	The Civil Rights Act passes. President Johnson declares a War on Poverty.
1965	President Johnson's Great Society legislative program begins. The Voting Rights Act is enacted.
1968	The Tet Offensive is launched by the Viet Cong. The My Lai Massacre occurs in Vietnam. Martin Luther King Jr. is assassinated in Memphis.
1969	The musical festival Woodstock takes place in New York state.
1970	Deadly protests at Kent State and Jackson State take place.
1972	Nixon visits China and the Soviet Union, promoting his policy of *détente*.
1973	The last U.S. troops leave Vietnam, ending direct U.S. involvement in the war.
1974	Nixon resigns from office as a result of the Watergate Scandal. Gerald Ford becomes the president and pardons Nixon.
1975	South Vietnam falls to the communists.
1976	Jimmy Carter is elected president.
1978	President Carter negotiates the Camp David Accords, a significant first step in the Middle East peace process.

TEST WHAT YOU ALREADY KNOW

Part A: Quiz

Questions 1–4 refer to the excerpt below.

"A vital element in keeping the peace is our military establishment. Our arms must be mighty, ready for instant action . . . Our military organization today bears little relation to that known by any of my predecessors . . .

Until the latest of our world conflicts, the United States had no armaments industry. American makers of plowshares could, with time and as required, make swords as well. But now we can no longer risk emergency improvisation of national defense . . .

This conjunction of an immense military establishment and a large arms industry . . . we must not fail to comprehend its grave implications . . . In the councils of government, we must guard against the acquisition of unwarranted influence, . . . by the military-industrial complex. The potential for the disastrous rise of misplaced power exists . . ."

President Dwight D. Eisenhower, Farewell Address, 1961

1. Which United States governmental stance most directly led to the situation described in the passage?

    (A) Increased internationalism after World War II

    (B) Development of the New Deal programs

    (C) Expansion of opportunities for minorities after the *Brown v. Board of Education* decision

    (D) Increased isolationism after the Korean War

2. Which action from the second half of the twentieth century most clearly supported the position stated in the passage above?

    (A) Elimination of United States factory jobs in the 1980s

    (B) Lyndon Johnson's Great Society programs

    (C) Development of a homogeneous mass culture

    (D) Vietnam era protests

3. The reasoning expressed in the passage most directly reflects which of the following continuities in United States history?

    (A) Debates about the role of the federal government in the economy

    (B) Debates about the changing relationships among the federal branches

    (C) Debates about the balance between liberty and security

    (D) Debates about the impact of American foreign policy on the world community

4. Which of the following from the first half of the twentieth century most closely resembles the argument raised in the passage?

    (A) Reasons for the first Red Scare

    (B) Reasons for economic collapse during the Great Depression

    (C) Reasons for American interventions in Latin America

    (D) Reasons for United States entry into World War I

Questions 5 and 6 refer to the image below.

These two United States postal stamps from 1975 depict the Apollo-Soyuz mission, which was a Russian space program.

5. Which of the following events from the second half of the twentieth century most clearly parallels the Russian Apollo-Soyuz mission?

   (A) President Reagan's negotiations with Soviet leader Mikhail Gorbachev

   (B) The containment policy of the Korean War

   (C) The collective security agreement which created NATO

   (D) President Kennedy's negotiations with Soviet leader Nikita Khrushchev

6. The idea expressed in the images above most directly reflects which of the following continuities in United States history?

   (A) Debates over economic values and role of the federal government in economy

   (B) Debates over separation of powers as contained in the U.S. Constitution

   (C) Debates over the impact of immigration policy

   (D) Debates over public support of the arts

Questions 7–10 refer to the excerpt below.

"Mr. Speaker, I rise today to commemorate the 65th anniversary of my hometown, Levittown, Pennsylvania . . . which is one of the first planned communities built in the U.S.

Between 1952 and 1958, Levitt & Sons built 17,311 single-family houses with lawns. There were six models a family could choose from: the Levittowner, the Rancher, the Jubilee, the Pennsylvanian, the Colonial, and the Country Clubber. Levitt & Sons pushed the boundaries of housing construction by perfecting the homebuilding assembly line. Levittown remains a special place in Bucks County. Originally designed as a completed community, Levittown grew into the model middle-class community."

Representative Brian Fitzpatrick on the founding of Levittown, June 27, 2017

7. Which change in American society most directly led to increased suburban growth as exhibited by Levittown?

   (A) Expansion of the electorate to include women

   (B) Decreasing social and economic mobility

   (C) Growth of a car culture

   (D) Increasingly restrictive immigration laws

8. Which of the following groups most likely benefited from suburban growth?

   (A) Smart-growth planners

   (B) World War II veterans

   (C) Mass transit users

   (D) Civil rights activists

9. Suburban growth in America most directly led to the

   (A) increasingly homogeneous mass culture of the 1960s

   (B) dominance of the Democratic Party in the 1950s

   (C) passage of new immigration laws in the 1960s

   (D) rapid expansion in higher education in the 1960s

10. Which of the following innovations from the early twentieth century was most clearly demonstrated in suburbs such as Levittown?

   (A) Efficiencies in production techniques

   (B) The first electronic computers improving urban planning

   (C) Increased opportunity for women in the workforce

   (D) Development of mass media

10

Part B: Key Terms

The following is a list of the major people, places, and events for 1945–1980. You will likely see many of these on the AP U.S. History exam.

For each key term ask yourself the following questions:

- Can I describe this key term?
- Can I discuss this key term in the context of other events?
- Could I correctly answer a multiple-choice question about this key term?
- Could I correctly answer a free-response question about this key term?

Check off the key terms if you can answer "yes" to at least three of these questions.

The Early Cold War

- ☐ Cold War
- ☐ Harry S. Truman
- ☐ Truman Doctrine
- ☐ Marshall Plan
- ☐ Berlin Airlift
- ☐ North Atlantic Treaty Organization (NATO)
- ☐ Warsaw Pact
- ☐ National Security Act

Cold War Policy in Asia

- ☐ Korean War

The Second Red Scare

- ☐ Second Red Scare
- ☐ McCarthyism

American Foreign Policy and Attitudes in the Cold War

- ☐ Dwight D. "Ike" Eisenhower
- ☐ Brinksmanship
- ☐ Massive retaliation
- ☐ U-2 Incident
- ☐ John F. Kennedy
- ☐ Bay of Pigs
- ☐ Berlin Wall
- ☐ Cuban Missile Crisis
- ☐ Space Race
- ☐ Military-industrial complex

The Vietnam War

- ☐ Geneva Convention
- ☐ Domino theory
- ☐ Lyndon B. Johnson
- ☐ Vietnam War
- ☐ Operation Rolling Thunder
- ☐ Viet Cong
- ☐ Tet Offensive
- ☐ Pentagon Papers
- ☐ War Powers Act

The "Affluent Society"

- ☐ Beatniks
- ☐ Counterculture movement
- ☐ Equal Rights Amendment
- ☐ Suburbanization

From the New Frontier to the Great Society

- ☐ New Frontier
- ☐ Great Society

The Civil Rights Movement

- ☐ *Brown v. Board of Education*
- ☐ Montgomery Bus Boycott
- ☐ Student Nonviolent Coordinating Committee (SNCC)
- ☐ Civil Rights Act of 1964
- ☐ Voting Rights Act of 1965
- ☐ Black Panthers
- ☐ Kerner Commission

Social Justice Movements

- ☐ *Hernandez v. Texas*
- ☐ United Farm Workers (UFW)
- ☐ League of United Latin American Citizens (LULAC)
- ☐ Indian termination
- ☐ American Indian Movement (AIM)
- ☐ Lavender Scare
- ☐ Stonewall Riots

The Nixon Administration

- ☐ Richard M. Nixon
- ☐ Drug Enforcement Administration
- ☐ *Silent Spring*
- ☐ *Détente*
- ☐ Strategic Arms Limitation Treaty (SALT I)
- ☐ Organization of Petroleum Exporting Countries (OPEC)
- ☐ Watergate
- ☐ Gerald R. Ford

The Carter Administration

- ☐ Jimmy Carter
- ☐ Camp David Accords
- ☐ SALT II
- ☐ Three Mile Island

New Conservatism

- ☐ Conservatism
- ☐ STOP ERA

10

Next Steps

Step 1: Tally your correct answers from Part A and review the quiz explanations at the end of this chapter.

1.	A	6.	A
2.	D	7.	C
3.	C	8.	B
4.	D	9.	D
5.	A	10.	A

____ out of 10 questions

Step 2: Count the number of key terms you checked off in Part B.

____ out of 64 key terms

Step 3: Read the Key Takeaways in this chapter.

Step 4: Consult the table below and follow the instructions based on your performance.

If You Got...	Do This
80% or more of the Test What You Already Know assessment correct (8 or more questions from Part A and 51 or more key terms from Part B)	• Read definitions in this chapter for all the key terms you didn't check off. • Complete the Test What You Learned assessment in this chapter.
50% or less of the Test What You Already Know assessment correct (5 or fewer questions from Part A and 32 or fewer key terms from Part B)	• Read the comprehensive review for this period in Chapter 19. • If you are short on time, read only the High-Yield sections. • Read through all of the key term definitions in this chapter. • Complete the Test What You Learned assessment in this chapter.
Any other result	• Read the High-Yield sections in the comprehensive review of this period in Chapter 19. • Read definitions in this chapter for all the key terms you didn't check off. • Complete the Test What You Learned assessment in this chapter.

ESSENTIAL CONTENT

Key Takeaways: 1945–1980

1. The United States positioned itself as a global leader. The Cold War, an escalating struggle between the United States and the Soviet Union, defined this period. Fearing the expansion of communism, the United States got involved in two major military engagements in Korea and Vietnam.

2. Initially, there was major American support for an anti-communist foreign policy. As the war in Vietnam dragged on, however, mass antiwar protests broke out across the United States. Passionate debates over war in Southeast Asia, the proliferation of nuclear weapons, and the power of the executive branch were all central to the politics of this period.

3. Civil rights activists energized a new nationwide movement for racial progress. Martin Luther King Jr. used the strategies of nonviolent protests, direct action, and legal battles. The landmark Supreme Court case of *Brown v. Board of Education* (1954) was a significant achievement for civil rights activists, but progress was slow and resistance was high.

4. Spurred by the civil rights movement, other social movements advocated their causes. Debates raged over issues such as sexuality, gender, the environment, and economic equality, and the counterculture of the 1960s emerged.

5. In the 1960s, President Johnson's Great Society program attempted to use the power of the federal government to eliminate poverty, end racial discrimination, and promote social justice. Fearing a cultural and moral decline, conservatives challenged such actions and sought to limit the role of the federal government.

6. In the 1970s, the public grew increasingly distrustful of the government's ability to solve problems. This distrust reached a peak with the Watergate scandal, the stalemate in Vietnam, and President Nixon's resignation from office.

Key Terms: 1945–1980

Remember that the AP U.S. History exam tests you on the depth of your knowledge, not just your ability to recall facts. While we have provided brief definitions here, you will need to know these terms in even more depth for the AP exam, including how terms connect to broader historical themes and understandings.

The Early Cold War

Cold War: A geopolitical struggle between rival blocs led by the United States and the Soviet Union. Lasted from 1946 to 1991. While it primarily featured an ongoing arms race and proxy wars, direct nuclear conflict between the two blocs almost occurred on several occasions.

Harry S. Truman: Thirty-third president. Served from 1945–1953. Desegregated the U.S. military. Help found the United Nations and pushed for the Marshall Plan. Reformed U.S. foreign policy toward internationalism, with a focus on containment of communism. Oversaw early Cold War conflicts, like the Berlin Airlift and the Korean War. Ordered the use of atomic weapons on the cities of Hiroshima and Nagasaki. Narrowly won reelection in a 1952 upset.

10

Truman Doctrine: A 1947 policy articulated by Harry Truman, stating the United States had a duty to aid free nations under communist threat. The cornerstone of U.S. Cold War policy.

Marshall Plan: A program proposed by George Marshall in 1947. Supplied $13 billion to Western Europe, enabling its postwar economic boom and ending the threat of mass starvation.

Berlin Airlift: A major crisis in the early Cold War. From June 1948 to May 1949, the Soviet Union blockaded the West's land access to Berlin. President Truman responded by airlifting in supplies around the clock, putting the onus for starting another world war on the Soviets.

North Atlantic Treaty Organization (NATO): A military alliance formed by the Western Allies of World War II to deter Soviet aggression. It guaranteed collective defense under the rule that an attack on one member is an attack on all members.

Warsaw Pact: A collective defense arrangement similar to NATO, to protect the Eastern bloc from Western aggression. It also served to solidify Soviet control over Eastern Europe. Dissolved in 1991.

National Security Act: A landmark 1947 act that restructured the U.S. government's military and national security agencies. Created the Department of Defense (formally the Department of War), the National Security Council, and the Central Intelligence Agency (CIA), as well as an independent U.S. Air Force.

Cold War Policy in Asia

Korean War: Nicknamed "the Forgotten War." Ran from June 1950 to July 1953 de facto, but the lack of a formal peace treaty means it is still technically ongoing. Principally a war fought between North and South Korea, with the North backed by the People's Republic of China and the South backed by a UN coalition. Despite wild swings in fortune by both sides throughout the war, it ultimately ended in a stalemate. Borders were fixed at the prewar status quo.

The Second Red Scare

Second Red Scare: Lasted from 1947 to 1956. A period of social anxiety and paranoia concerned with communist infiltration. Driven by events such as the Rosenbergs' trial, the Soviet occupation of Eastern Europe, and the victory of Mao's communists in the Chinese Civil War. The Smith Act of 1940 authorized the arrest of people advocating the U.S. government's overthrow even if they had no intention of ever doing so. The House Un-American Activities Committee (HUAC) was established in 1938 to investigate domestic subversives with either fascist or communist ties.

McCarthyism: A term originating in the Second Red Scare; refers to senator Joseph McCarthy. It is the practice of making accusations of disloyalty and treason without providing concrete evidence, with the intent of suppressing dissent and strengthening the accuser's position.

American Foreign Policy and Attitudes in the Cold War

Dwight D. "Ike" Eisenhower: Thirty-fourth president. Served from 1953–1961. A former five-star general, Ike acted as Supreme Commander of the Western Allies in Europe. He oversaw the invasion of North Africa and the Normandy landings. A moderate conservative,

10

Ike preserved the New Deal programs and established NASA. His signature achievement is the Interstate Highway System. In terms of foreign policy, he ended the Korean War, began American involvement in Vietnam, and directed the overthrow of democratic governments in Iran and Guatemala.

Brinksmanship: The practice of achieving a goal by escalating events to one step shy of open conflict in order to force a rival party to knuckle under for fear of catastrophe. A common tactic in the Cold War period.

Massive retaliation: A defense strategy pursued by President Eisenhower for budgetary reasons, due to the financial burden of maintaining conventional forces alongside nuclear arms. Rather than fight a conventional war, the United States pledged to use nuclear weapons against any nation that attacked it. Criticized as too aggressive. Abandoned by the Kennedy administration for the policy of flexible response, which resumed investment in conventional forces.

U-2 Incident: A May 1960 incident where the Soviet Union shot down a U.S. U-2 spy plane and captured its pilot alive. Resulted in Eisenhower's public humiliation, ending a tentative thaw between the two superpowers that had been underway.

John F. Kennedy: Thirty-fifth president. Served from 1961–1963. First Roman Catholic president. Narrowly elected over Richard Nixon, his term in office was dominated by the rising civil rights movement and escalating Cold War tensions. The early months of his presidency saw such events as the Bay of the Pigs and the building of the Berlin Wall. In October 1962, he dealt with the Cuban Missile Crisis. Assassinated on November 22, 1963, in Dallas, Texas, by Lee Harvey Oswald.

Bay of Pigs: A failed intervention by CIA-backed rebels in communist Cuba during April 1961. A public humiliation for President Kennedy, it bolstered Castro's position at home and abroad.

Berlin Wall: A militarized concrete barrier separating East and West Berlin. Existed from 1961 to 1989. Constructed by the Soviets to halt a brain drain of East Germans. Its fall heralded German reunification and the twilight of the Cold War.

Cuban Missile Crisis: A confrontation between the United States and the Soviet Union over the placement of Soviet nuclear missiles in Cuba. Occurred October 16–28, 1962. Considered one of the Cold War's tensest events. Resolved diplomatically, it bolstered President Kennedy's then-shaky reputation but led to the overthrow of Nikita Khrushchev.

Space Race: In 1957, the Soviet union launched the first satellite, *Sputnik*. This sparked the Space Race, as well as a massive investment in the American education system. Americans were convinced that they had better keep up with Soviet technology, and Congress responded by allocating millions of dollars to schools and universities across the nation to prepare students in mathematics, science, and foreign languages. Eisenhower also urged the creation of the National Aeronautics and Space Administration (NASA).

Military-industrial complex: A term coined by President Eisenhower in his farewell address. It refers to the vested interest the American military and arms industry have in influencing public policy, especially as it relates to defense spending and military conflicts. In the original draft of his speech, Eisenhower referred to it as the "military-industrial-congressional complex" but dropped the third term for fear of offending his political contemporaries.

10

The Vietnam War

Geneva Convention: A series of international treaties and protocols negotiated in the aftermath of World War II, which established humanitarian standards for wartime, updating protocols originally agreed to in 1929. Contested in the 2000s with the rise of non-state actors.

Domino theory: The idea that political revolutions in one country will cause similar revolutions in neighboring countries, akin to only one domino being necessary to topple over a whole chain of dominos. Typically associated with the spread of communism, although a variant associated with spreading democracy gained currency during the 2003 Iraq War.

Lyndon B. Johnson: Thirty-sixth president. Served from 1963–1969. Senate majority leader from 1955–1961. Vice president from 1961–1963. Assumed the presidency upon the assassination of John F. Kennedy. Oversaw the Civil Rights Act of 1964 and Voting Rights Act of 1965, as well as a series of landmark domestic legislation known as the Great Society. Escalated the Vietnam War. Declined to run for reelection in 1968. A domestic policy maestro but a foreign policy.

Vietnam War: Also called the Second Indochina War. Direct American involvement in Vietnam began in 1955 and ended on April 30, 1975, with the Fall of Saigon. However, the Gulf of Tonkin Resolution (August 1964) is often used to mark the official start of the Vietnam War; this congressional resolution authorized the president to wage war without a formal declaration. The war polarized American society. It killed more than 58,000 Americans and over 2 million Vietnamese.

Operation Rolling Thunder: A bombing campaign conducted by the U.S. Air Force against North Vietnam. Run from March 1965 to November 1968, it dropped more bombs on North Vietnam than had been used by the United States throughout World War II. Failed to achieve its aims.

Viet Cong: Also known as V-C or Charlie. The Viet Cong was the military wing of the National Liberation Front, a communist nationalist group in South Vietnam.

Tet Offensive: A surprise January 1968 offensive by the Viet Cong. While U.S. and South Vietnamese forces prevailed, it permanently undermined American public opinion in the war. Contributed to Johnson's decision to not run for reelection in 1968.

Pentagon Papers: Secret documents regarding the Vietnam War leaked to *The New York Times* by military analyst Daniel Ellsberg. They revealed that Congress had been lied to for many years about the war and that the United States had acted contrary to its publicly stated goals.

War Powers Act: Passed by Congress after learning of Nixon's secret bombings of Cambodia, it severely limited the president's ability to wage war without Congressional approval. However, despite violations over the years, Congress has never taken legal action over the issue, and executive authority to wage war has grown substantially since 2001.

The "Affluent Society"

Beatniks: A counterculture movement in the 1950s and early 1960s emphasizing art, philosophy, and social criticism. Jack Kerouac and Allen Ginsberg were notable members.

Counterculture movement: A broad counterculture movement that started in the early 1960s and emphasized civil rights, feminism, gay rights, university reforms, drug law reform, and an anti-war stance. This New Left was hostile to "Old Left," traditional Marxism centered on the labor movement and class struggle.

Equal Rights Amendment: Also known as the ERA. A proposed amendment to the U.S. Constitution that would have guaranteed equal rights regardless of sex. By 1977, it had been ratified by 35 of the 38 states necessary, but faced a backlash from the growing conservative movement. It failed to be ratified by a sufficient number of states by its 1982 deadline.

Suburbanization: Shift in population from cities to areas outside the cities, especially after World War II when the government subsidized new construction of affordable housing.

From the New Frontier to the Great Society

New Frontier: A slate of liberal policy proposals by John F. Kennedy. Few were adopted in his lifetime due to obstructionism by Republicans and conservative Democrats. Reworked and expanded under President Johnson into the Great Society.

Great Society: A series of domestic programs proposed by Lyndon Johnson, expanding on Kennedy's stalled New Frontier proposals. Aimed to expand civil rights and eliminate poverty. Great Society legislation included low-cost medical care for the elderly (Medicare) and for the poor (Medicaid), the Immigration Act of 1965 (which repealed the discriminatory practices of the Quota Acts of the 1920s), career training, low-cost housing, and environmental protections.

The Civil Rights Movement

Brown v. Board of Education: A landmark Supreme Court case that held that segregation of public schools was unconstitutional. Overturned *Plessy v. Ferguson* in the context of education.

Montgomery Bus Boycott: In response to Jim Crow segregation on city buses and Rosa Parks' arrest, Martin Luther King Jr. helped organize a boycott; this caused an enormous blow to the city's revenues, as African Americans made up about 95 percent of bus riders. The Warren Court ruled that segregation on public buses was unconstitutional; the boycott's success led to challenging more Jim Crow laws in the Southern states.

Student Nonviolent Coordinating Committee (SNCC): Local college and high school students who organized collective action such as sit-ins; soon became young leaders within the civil rights movement. Helped form the Freedom Riders, a 1961 group committed to registering African American voters throughout the South.

Civil Rights Act of 1964: A landmark civil rights law that outlawed discrimination on the basis of race, color, nationality, religion, and sex. It prohibited racial segregation.

Voting Rights Act of 1965: Made literacy tests illegal and prohibited states from denying any U.S. citizen the right to vote on the basis of race. The Selma to Montgomery marches contributed to its passage.

Black Panthers: A socialist, black nationalist organization founded in 1966. Famous for their uniforms and for openly carrying firearms. They organized a social safety net for impoverished African Americans in Oakland. Succumbed to ideological schisms, government harassment, as well as the arrests and deaths of their major leaders by the mid-1970s.

Kerner Commission: A commission established by President Johnson to study the 1967 race riots. Concluded the riots had been caused by frustration among African Americans due to lack of economic opportunity. The report was ignored by Johnson.

Social Justice Movements

Hernandez v. Texas: Ruled that Mexican-Americans, along with all other national groups within the United States, had equal protection under the Fourteenth amendment.

United Farm Workers (UFW): Founded in 1962 by César Chávez and Dolores Huerta to protect the rights of farm workers and fight for higher wages. Favored aggressive but nonviolent protests.

League of United Latin American Citizens (LULAC): Founded in 1929; a consolidation of various existing civil rights organizations, which in many ways paralleled the NAACP for African Americans.

Indian termination: The federal government policy that sought to end U.S. recognition of American Indian sovereignty and all federal, state, and local measures associated with that recognition. One key part was the Indian Relocation Act of 1956 (Public Law 959), which encouraged American Indians to leave their traditional reservations and assimilate into urban areas.

American Indian Movement (AIM): Founded in 1968 to address systemic issues facing American Indians: poverty, healthcare, police brutality, unemployment, and the preservation of Indigenous cultures.

Lavender Scare: During the Second Red Scare of the 1950s, Senator Joseph McCarthy and others alleged that homosexuals were threats to America, inherent communist sympathizers, and easy targets for blackmail by the Soviets. Led to President Eisenhower signing Executive Order 10450 in 1953, banning homosexuals from the military, the federal government, and private contractors working for the government. Would not be fully overturned until Bill Clinton's "Don't Ask, Don't Tell" policy for the military in 1995.

Stonewall Riots: Also called the Stonewall Uprising, a series of 1969 protests in response to police raids on the Stonewall Inn, a gay bar in the Greenwich Village neighborhood of Manhattan. The protests grew massively, and participants began to organize themselves into activist groups.

The Nixon Administration

Richard M. Nixon: Thirty-seventh president. Served from 1969–1974. Vice president under Eisenhower. A noted anticommunist, he narrowly lost the 1960 election to JFK. Domestically, Nixon accepted the Great Society programs. Internationally, he pursued a policy of *détente* and *realpolitik*, most famously establishing relations with the People's Republic of China in order to counterbalance the Soviet Union. He also escalated the Vietnam War, secretly bombed Cambodia, and sponsored a coup in Chile. Only U.S. president to resign, doing so over the Watergate scandal.

Drug Enforcement Administration: Created in 1973, the DEA is a federal law enforcement agency operating under the Department of Justice. It enforces the Controlled Substances Act.

Silent Spring: 1962 book by Rachel Carson, a marine biologist and conservationist, which brought widespread public attention to the dangers of pesticides and disinformation campaigns waged by the chemical industry. Helped inspire the modern environmental movement, eventually leading to the creation of the Environmental Protection Agency (EPA) in 1970.

Détente: The act of easing hostility between two or more parties through diplomacy. Advocated during the Cold War by Richard Nixon and Gerald Ford.

Strategic Arms Limitation Treaty (SALT I): The first round of arms control talks. Negotiations took place under the Johnson and Nixon administrations. The treaty was ratified in 1972.

Organization of Petroleum Exporting Countries (OPEC): An organization of oil-producing states, especially ones in the Middle East. In retaliation for U.S. support for Israel in the Yom Kippur War, OPEC targeted the United States and some of its Western allies for an oil embargo. This led to the 1973 oil crisis.

Watergate: A political scandal sparked by Nixon operatives burglarizing the Democratic Party National Headquarters at the Watergate Hotel on June 17, 1972. The burglars were arrested, and an ensuing investigation by *Washington Post* reporters Bob Woodward and Carl Bernstein revealed a vast web of crimes and political corruption. With impeachment over the Watergate scandal certain, President Nixon resigned on August 9, 1974.

Gerald R. Ford: Thirty-ninth president. Served from August 8, 1974, to January 20, 1977. The only person to serve as president not elected as president or vice president. He ended American involvement in Vietnam by allowing the conquest of South Vietnam by the North. Continued the policy of *détente.* Initially popular, his approval ratings sank after he issued an unconditional pardon of Richard Nixon. Narrowly lost reelection to Jimmy Carter.

The Carter Administration

Jimmy Carter: Thirty-ninth president. Served from 1977–1981. The former governor of Georgia, he ran as an outsider in the 1976 presidential election. Served one term. Carter pardoned Vietnam War draft dodgers, established the Departments of Energy and Education, and returned the Panama Canal to Panama. Internationally, he oversaw the Camp David Accords, ended *détente* in response to the Soviet invasion of Afghanistan, and was dogged by the Iranian Hostage Crisis.

Camp David Accords: A 1979 peace agreement reached between Egyptian president Anwar Sadat and Israeli prime minister Menachem Begin, following 12 days of secret negotiations at Camp David. Settled several outstanding Israeli-Egyptian disputes. Widely considered Jimmy Carter's crowning foreign policy achievement.

SALT II: The second round of the Strategic Arms Limitation Talks. Negotiations took place under the Nixon and Ford administrations. In response to the Soviet invasion of Afghanistan, the final 1979 agreement was not ratified by the Senate.

Three Mile Island: The name refers to a March 1979 accident at the Three Mile Island nuclear plant in Dauphin County, Pennsylvania. Led to the decline of the U.S. nuclear power industry.

New Conservatism

Conservatism: Political philosophy adopted by the New Right Republicans in the 1960s and beyond; favored building a more powerful military and establishing economic free enterprise; upheld traditional social values; opposed social programs made popular by the New Deal.

STOP ERA: 1964 campaign led by Phyllis Schlafly and followers of conservative women against the Equal Rights Amendment, arguing that the ERA would force women into the military draft and stop certain gender-specific legal privileges.

TEST WHAT YOU LEARNED

Questions 1–4 refer to the image below.

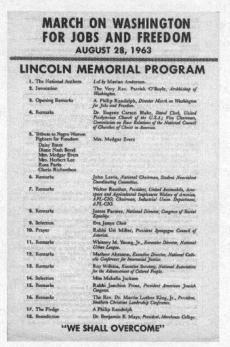

1. The actions of the March on Washington for Jobs and Freedom were most likely the result of an alliance between which of the following?

    (A) African American activists and Southern Democrats

    (B) New Dealers and labor union members

    (C) Supporters of the *Brown v. Board of Education* decision and religious leaders

    (D) Vietnam War veterans and supporters of the *Brown v. Board of Education* decision

2. Which of the following from the latter half of the nineteenth century most clearly parallels the events of the March on Washington?

    (A) The New South

    (B) The Gilded Age

    (C) Radical Reconstruction

    (D) Populism

3. Which of the following actions resulted most directly from the March on Washington?

    (A) Increased federal government regulation

    (B) Expansion of American military presence in Vietnam

    (C) Clashes between hippies and segregationists

    (D) Congressional approval of the Twenty-Fourth Amendment

4. The ideas expressed during the March on Washington most clearly show the influence of which of the following?

    (A) Electoral guarantees contained in the Fifteenth Amendment

    (B) Civil liberties contained in the Bill of Rights

    (C) Belief in separation of power as contained in the U.S. Constitution

    (D) Divisiveness of political parties contained in Washington's Farewell Address

10

Questions 5–7 refer to the excerpt below.

"Our society will never be great until our cities are great . . . [where] we begin to build the Great Society is in our countryside. We have always prided ourselves on being . . . America the beautiful. Today that beauty is in danger. The water we drink, the food we eat, the very air that we breathe, are threatened . . . A third place to build the Great Society is in the classrooms of America . . . Our society will not be great until every young mind is set free to scan the farthest reaches of thought and imagination. We are still far from that goal . . ."

President Lyndon B. Johnson, Great Society speech, May 1964

5. Which of the following movements most likely inspired the ideals set forth in President Johnson's Great Society speech?

   (A) The New Frontier

   (B) The Fair Deal

   (C) The New Deal

   (D) The Progressive Era

6. Which of the following events from the late twentieth and early twenty-first centuries represents a continuation of the ideas expressed in Johnson's speech?

   (A) Negotiations over the SALT I Treaty

   (B) Passage of the Americans with Disabilities Act

   (C) Passage of the USA PATRIOT Act

   (D) Passage of the Affordable Care Act

7. America had addressed multiple reforms leading up to Johnson's speech. The Great Society added which of the following reforms?

   (A) Deregulation of business and industry

   (B) Civil rights and civil liberties

   (C) Economic equality

   (D) Desegregation of the military

10

Questions 8–10 refer to the excerpt below.

"And so tonight—to you, the great silent majority of my fellow Americans—I ask for your support. I pledged in my campaign for the Presidency to end the war in a way that we could win the peace. I have initiated a plan of action which will enable me to keep that pledge. The more support I can have from the American people, the sooner that pledge can be redeemed; for the more divided we are at home, the less likely the enemy is to negotiate in Paris. Let us be united for peace. Let us also be united against defeat. Because let us understand: North Vietnam cannot defeat or humiliate the United States. Only Americans can do that."

President Richard Nixon, Silent Majority speech, November 1969

8. The ideas expressed in the excerpt were most directly supported by

    (A) counterculture groups

    (B) national guardsmen

    (C) construction workers

    (D) CEOs of large corporations

9. Which of the following contributed most directly to sentiments expressed in the excerpt?

    (A) The 1968 antiwar protests in Chicago at the Republican National Convention

    (B) President Johnson's escalation of the Vietnam War

    (C) President Nixon's completion of the Vietnamization program

    (D) The execution of William Calley for the My Lai Massacre

10. President Nixon asserted that "only Americans can do that" in order to express opposition to which of the following groups?

    (A) Radical feminists

    (B) Advocates of black power

    (C) Political supporters of President Johnson

    (D) Students for a Democratic Society

Part B: Key Terms

This key terms list is the same as the list in the Test What You Already Know section earlier in this chapter. Based on what you have now learned, again ask yourself the following questions:

- Can I define this key term and use it in a sentence?
- Can I provide an example related to this key term?
- Could I correctly answer a multiple-choice question about this key term?
- Could I correctly answer a free-response question about this key term?

Check off the key terms if you can answer "yes" to at least three of these questions.

The Early Cold War

- ☐ Cold War
- ☐ Harry S. Truman
- ☐ Truman Doctrine
- ☐ Marshall Plan
- ☐ Berlin Airlift
- ☐ North Atlantic Treaty Organization (NATO)
- ☐ Warsaw Pact
- ☐ National Security Act

Cold War Policy in Asia

- ☐ Korean War

The Second Red Scare

- ☐ Second Red Scare
- ☐ McCarthyism

American Foreign Policy and Attitudes in the Cold War

- ☐ Dwight D. "Ike" Eisenhower
- ☐ Brinksmanship
- ☐ Massive retaliation
- ☐ U-2 Incident
- ☐ John F. Kennedy
- ☐ Bay of Pigs
- ☐ Berlin Wall
- ☐ Cuban Missile Crisis
- ☐ Space Race
- ☐ Military-industrial complex

The Vietnam War

- ☐ Geneva Convention
- ☐ Domino theory
- ☐ Lyndon B. Johnson
- ☐ Vietnam War
- ☐ Operation Rolling Thunder
- ☐ Viet Cong
- ☐ Tet Offensive
- ☐ Pentagon Papers
- ☐ War Powers Act

10

The "Affluent Society"

- ☐ Beatniks
- ☐ Counterculture movement
- ☐ Equal Rights Amendment
- ☐ Suburbanization

From the New Frontier to the Great Society

- ☐ New Frontier
- ☐ Great Society

The Civil Rights Movement

- ☐ *Brown v. Board of Education*
- ☐ Montgomery Bus Boycott
- ☐ Student Nonviolent Coordinating Committee (SNCC)
- ☐ Civil Rights Act of 1964
- ☐ Voting Rights Act of 1965
- ☐ Black Panthers
- ☐ Kerner Commission

Social Justice Movements

- ☐ *Hernandez v. Texas*
- ☐ United Farm Workers (UFW)
- ☐ League of United Latin American Citizens (LULAC)
- ☐ Indian termination
- ☐ American Indian Movement (AIM)
- ☐ Lavender Scare
- ☐ Stonewall Riots

The Nixon Administration

- ☐ Richard M. Nixon
- ☐ Drug Enforcement Administration
- ☐ *Silent Spring*
- ☐ Détente
- ☐ Strategic Arms Limitation Treaty (SALT I)
- ☐ Organization of Petroleum Exporting Countries (OPEC)
- ☐ Watergate
- ☐ Gerald R. Ford

The Carter Administration

- ☐ Jimmy Carter
- ☐ Camp David Accords
- ☐ SALT II
- ☐ Three Mile Island

New Conservatism

- ☐ Conservatism
- ☐ STOP ERA

10

Next Steps

Step 1: Tally your correct answers from Part A and review the quiz explanations at the end of this chapter.

1. C
2. C
3. A
4. B
5. C

6. D
7. B
8. C
9. B
10. D

_____ out of 10 questions

Step 2: Count the number of key terms you checked off in Part B.

_____ out of 64 key terms

Step 3: Compare your Test What You Already Know results to these Test What You Learned results to see how exam-ready you are for this period.

For More Practice:

- Read (or reread) the comprehensive review for this period in Chapter 19.

- Go to kaptest.com to complete the online quiz questions for 1945–1980.

  ○ Haven't registered your book yet? Go to kaptest.com/moreonline to begin.

ANSWERS AND EXPLANATIONS

Test What You Already Know

1. A

The participation of the United States in the United Nations, NATO, and other security organizations led to the creation of a large standing military. The Cold War, which spurred NATO's creation, fostered an ongoing arms race after World War II. Thus, **(A)** is correct. Eisenhower warned about this "military-industrial complex" in his farewell speech, noting the dangers of allowing this complex to influence U.S. policies for the sake of its own self-interest. (B) is incorrect because the development of the limited welfare state in the New Deal, which represented the government's increased involvement in the economy, did not focus on military matters. While minorities' opportunities indeed expanded after the *Brown* decision, Eisenhower discussed how America's role as a global military power could impact domestic politics; thus, (C) is incorrect. The Korean War highlighted the importance of internationalism to the United States. Thus, (D) is incorrect.

2. D

The Vietnam era protests challenged the prevailing power and attitudes in Washington regarding the use of American military power in Southeast Asia, just as Eisenhower cautioned the nation's use of the built-up military. **(D)** is correct. The elimination of factory jobs resulted from economic problems; (A) is incorrect. Lyndon Johnson's Great Society programs did not challenge America's use of its military; instead, the Great Society included domestic programs such as Medicare, civil rights legislation, and federal aid to education. Thus, (B) is incorrect. The development of a homogeneous mass culture resulted from the economic and social stresses of the Great Depression and World War II, eliminating (C).

3. C

Well before President Eisenhower delivered his farewell address, the debate about national security policy elicited concerns about personal liberty. After 1991, concerns over the Cold War eventually gave way to concerns over global terrorism. New military technologies, surveillance techniques, and other methods of securing the nation and its citizens have been developed since 1945. However, the policies behind their use have been challenged because of their effects on individual privacy, liberty, and national identity; **(C)** is correct. Eisenhower's speech focuses on the federal government's responsibility to protect the society without restricting the people's liberty, not the government's role in the economy. Thus, (A) is incorrect. The "military-industrial complex" was Eisenhower's way of warning America that its militarized economy, not the relationship among federal branches, could influence domestic rather than foreign policy; thus, (B) and (D) are both incorrect.

4. D

Congressional investigations of the U.S. entry into World War I led to accusations that American munitions manufacturers had helped push the country into the war. This contributed to America's noninterventionist sentiment in the 1930s; therefore, **(D)** is correct. The first Red Scare stemmed from the social issue of anti-immigrant and nationalistic sentiments after World War I; (A) is incorrect. The economic collapse during the Great Depression was caused by a number of reasons pertaining largely to the economy: decreased production, increased unemployment, inflated stock prices, and large bank loans; (B) is incorrect. The United States intervened in Latin America in order to ward off European intervention in the Caribbean, as outlined by the Monroe Doctrine, and to advance its own economic interests. Thus, (C) is incorrect.

5. A

The 1975 Apollo-Soyuz mission represented a period of mutual coexistence, or *détente*, between the United States and the Soviet Union during the Cold War. Likewise, negotiations between President Reagan and Soviet leader Gorbachev during the Cold War that resulted in the 1987 Intermediate-Range Nuclear Forces (INF) Treaty demonstrated this same sentiment. Thus, **(A)** is correct. The United States and its allies adopted the containment policy to prevent the spread of communism; this policy directly led to conflict with the Soviet Union, making (B) incorrect. NATO was created in order to provide collective security against the Soviet Union, making (C) incorrect. The early 1960s were marked by escalating tensions between the United States and the Soviet Union amid repeated failures at diplomacy, culminating in the Cuban Missile Crisis; (D) is incorrect.

6. A

Because the space race became part of the Cold War tensions between the United States and the Soviet Union, U.S. government expenditures for space missions and exploration became associated with the cost of the Cold War. As the United States faced a series of economic crises at the end of the twentieth and beginning of the twenty-first centuries, federal expenditures for NASA and its programs came into question. Thus, **(A)** is correct. The images symbolize a collaborative science mission between two foes, not the separation of powers as outlined in the U.S. Constitution. Thus, (B) is incorrect. The images do not prompt an immigration debate, making (C) incorrect. The images focus on the space race rather than on the arts; (D) is incorrect.

7. C

William Levitt promoted suburban growth by building the largest planned-living community in the United States on farmland in Long Island, New York, in 1947. Development of the interstate highway system, road construction, and increased car ownership encouraged suburban development. Therefore, **(C)** is correct. Low-cost single-family homes, the hallmark of suburbanization in the post–World War II years, brought home ownership to millions of Americans, eliminating (A) and (D). What some historians have called an Age of Affluence, the 1950s and early 1960s, saw a rising middle class and new opportunities for economic and social mobility. Thus, (B) is incorrect.

8. B

The Servicemen's Readjustment Act of 1944, commonly referred to as the GI Bill, included a low-cost mortgage benefit that allowed veterans to consider home ownership. In the case of Levittown, one of the reasons the homes were built quickly and inexpensively was to meet the needs of a booming population of war veterans' families. Thus, **(B)** is correct. As more Americans moved away from cities and took to their cars, more than 170 U.S. transit companies failed between 1950 and 1970; (A) and (C) are incorrect. Racial fears, among other factors, prompted many white Americans to flee to suburbia. Critics argued that suburbanization contributed to the cultural conformity of the 1950s, including whites-only deed restrictions. Thus, (D) is incorrect.

9. D

In the post–World War II years, the move to the suburbs, GI Bill benefits, a rising middle class, and the baby boom contributed to increased demand for higher education. A college education was increasingly seen as an achievable goal to enhance economic and social mobility, which matches **(D)**. The new suburbia emphasized conformity, which eventually led to a diverse cultural backlash by many of the children raised in it during the 1950s; (A) is incorrect. The Democratic Party ended its dominance with the 1952 presidential election, making (B) incorrect. The passage of new immigration laws in the 1960s largely resulted from the civil rights movement as activists fought to rid the nation of discrimination and racism. Thus, (C) is incorrect.

10. A

The construction techniques of Levittown borrowed many ideas from the Ford assembly-line methodology, using mass production to develop a limited number of house options. Thus, **(A)** is correct. Electronic computers were still extremely primitive in 1951, and their use had not yet expanded into urban design and planning to any notable degree. Thus, (B) is incorrect. Suburbanization fostered the ideal for white nuclear families with gender-specific roles that called for men to work and women to stay home; this makes (C) incorrect. The television became the new mass medium in the 1950s, which is the mid-century rather than the early twentieth century. Thus, (D) is incorrect.

Test What You Learned

1. C

The purpose of the March on Washington for Jobs and Freedom was to take a stand for civil and economic rights for African Americans. In the 1950s and 1960s, many leaders of the civil rights movement came from African American church leadership. **(C)** is correct. (A) is incorrect because Southern Democrats resisted the *Brown* decision. While the labor union movement assisted the civil rights movement in its support for social and economic justice for all, unionists offered support for the march only insofar as it concerned jobs. Likewise, many of the New Deal programs and its supporters discriminated against African Americans; thus, (B) is incorrect. American troop levels in

Vietnam were only just ramping up in this period, so there were not yet many veterans of the conflict. Because these veterans would be only a small fraction of the march's participants, (D) is incorrect.

2. C

The Radical Republican program for Reconstruction called for greater economic and political equality for the freedmen. Often referred to as an "unfinished" revolution, many of the issues and goals of the Radical Republicans, including equal treatment in public accommodations, did not become public policy until the modern civil rights movement of the 1950s and 1960s. Therefore, **(C)** is correct. In the 1880s, Southern merchants and manufacturers led the campaign for a New South that would encourage Southern industrialism by providing breaks for businesses and promising cheap labor. This resulted in oppression for African Americans, making (A) incorrect. (B) is also incorrect; the Gilded Age refers to rapid industrialization and urbanization that resulted in materialism and political corruption. Populism called for economic and political reform to benefit farmers and the common people, eliminating (D).

3. A

The March on Washington campaigned for passage of the Civil Rights Act, which was delayed in Congress. The March on Washington and other marches helped spur the passage of the Civil Rights Act of 1964 and the Voting Rights Act of 1965 during the Johnson administration. Thus, **(A)** is correct. When North Vietnamese allegedly fired on ships of the U.S. Navy in the Gulf of Tonkin in 1964, Congress authorized President Johnson to deter North Vietnamese aggression at all costs; thus, (B) is incorrect. The hippie subculture was still gestating in August 1963; they were primarily opposed to the Vietnam War and, while sympathetic to fellow liberal activists, were not major players in the civil rights movement. Thus, (C) is incorrect. The Twenty-Fourth Amendment had been passed by Congress in 1962, a year prior; (D) is incorrect.

4. B

The Bill of Rights contains the First Amendment, which guarantees freedom of speech, freedom to assemble, and the right to petition the government for redress of grievances. The 1963 March on Washington sought to do all of these things; **(B)** is correct. The Fifteenth Amendment recognized African Americans had the right to vote, but the march itself was built on rights preserved in the First Amendment as detailed above. Thus, (A) is incorrect. The separation of power in the U.S. Constitution outlines a system of checks and balances by creating three branches of government. This march was not concerned with that system, but rather with pressuring the leaders of that system to advance civil rights reform; (C) is incorrect. (D) is also incorrect; Washington warned against the dangers of political parties after the rise of the Democratic-Republicans and Federalists during the French Revolution. He did not address African American rights.

5. C

Historians have identified Lyndon Johnson's Great Society as the continuation or attempt at completion of ideas established during the New Deal by the Franklin Roosevelt administration. Thus, **(C)** is correct. Johnson reportedly found the New Frontier too timid in its proposals, and he instead harkened back to the wide-ranging reforms of the New Deal era. Thus, (A) is incorrect. The Fair Deal, a proposal by President Truman laid out in his 1949 State of the Union address, was a continuation of the New Deal. Most notably, it advocated for universal health care. Johnson and Truman were both inspired by the same source, the New Deal. Thus, (B) is incorrect. The Progressive Era, while sharing some ideas of the New Deal, was also greatly concerned with ideas like antitrust legislation, prohibition, eugenics, and weakening party bosses. Johnson's Great Society did not concern itself with those issues. Thus, (D) is incorrect.

6. D

The Affordable Care Act, passed in 2010, ties into a long-time goal of the Democratic Party to pass health care reform. President Truman's proposal for universal health care under the Fair Deal, President Johnson's creation of Medicare and Medicaid, and the failed effort by the Clinton administration to reform health care are all continuations of the same idea, which LBJ expressed in the excerpted speech. Thus, **(D)** is correct. The SALT I Treaty involved arms control with the Soviet Union, which LBJ did not comment upon; (A) is incorrect. While disability rights would echo the general sentiments of LBJ, they were not repeatedly advocated across multiple Democratic administrations like health care was. Thus, (B) is incorrect because it lacks the same degree of strong continuity. LBJ did not comment on national security, making (C) incorrect.

10

7. B

The Great Society brought civil rights and civil liberties to the forefront of the social issues that America was facing during the 1960s. The Civil Rights Act of 1964 and the Voting Rights Act of 1965 were the centerpiece laws that codified and reinforced the provisions of the Fourteenth and Fifteenth Amendments. Thus, **(B)** is correct. Deregulation did not become a major reform concept until the Carter and Reagan administrations; (A) is incorrect. The Great Society is often called the War on Poverty, so (C) is incorrect. President Truman desegregated the U.S. armed forces in 1948 with Executive Order 9981; (D) is also incorrect.

8. C

In the late 1960s, construction workers, or "hard hats," were the group most outspoken and critical of antiwar protesters. This is most famously demonstrated by the Hard Hat Riot in New York City in May 1970, where 200 construction workers attacked approximately 1,000 antiwar protestors. Thus, **(C)** is correct. Counterculture groups were largely antiwar; (A) is incorrect. Events such as the Hard Hat Riot symbolized the split between labor unions, traditional allies of the New Deal coalition, and the burgeoning New Left, which would have long-ranging political implications. By comparison, national guardsmen and CEOs were not organized as a comparably cohesive political and cultural force. Thus, (B) and (D) are incorrect.

9. B

The excerpt features President Nixon implying that only the antiwar movement can "defeat or humiliate" America.

The antiwar movement did not gain strength and attract widespread popular attention until it became evident that President Johnson's escalation of the war in 1966 and 1967 was not bringing about a military victory. Controversy and dissent grew dramatically after the Tet Offensive in early 1968. Thus, **(B)** is correct. The Democratic Party held its convention in Chicago in 1968, not the Republicans; (A) is incorrect. Vietnamization began in 1969 and ran through 1972. Given the excerpt is from a speech dated to late 1969, Vietnamization could not have been completed yet; (C) is incorrect. Neither William Calley nor any of the other soldiers involved in the My Lai Massacre was executed; due to overwhelming public support, Calley only served three and a half years of house arrest. (D) is incorrect.

10. D

Those most disillusioned by the war in Vietnam were the Students for a Democratic Society (SDS), a group that organized the first widespread student antiwar protests. Later, a faction of SDS gave rise to the Weathermen, a domestic terrorist organization. Therefore, **(D)** is correct. Radical feminists and black power supporters, while typically viewing the Vietnam War in a negative light, had concerns that were more focused on U.S. domestic affairs rather than foreign policy; (A) and (B) are incorrect. Supporters of President Lyndon Johnson would have echoed his hawkish stance and thus would not have opposed Nixon's stance; (C) is incorrect.

CHAPTER 11

Period 9: 1980–Present

LEARNING OBJECTIVES

After studying this time period, you will be able to:

- Chart the development of, and changes in, American politics

- Describe how reformers and activists have changed American society

- Explain the development of economic patterns and the government's response to economic issues

- Explain how technological developments have impacted American economy and society

- Explain the reasons for migration to North America and immigrants' effects on society

- Explain the causes and effects of U.S. economic, diplomatic, and military initiatives in North America and globally

- Describe the effects on American life of differing interpretations of the Constitution

TIMELINE

Date	Event
1980	Ronald Reagan defeats Jimmy Carter to become president.
1981	Sandra Day O'Connor becomes the first woman to serve on the U.S. Supreme Court.
1984	The Iran-Contra scandal is revealed.
1985	Mikhail Gorbachev becomes the leader of the Soviet Union.
1987	Stock markets around the world crash on Black Monday.
1988	George H.W. Bush is elected president.
1989	The Berlin Wall is torn down.
1991	The Soviet Union collapses. Boris Yeltsin becomes the president of Russia. The Persian Gulf War takes place to expel Iraq from Kuwait.
1992	Bill Clinton is elected president.
1993	President Clinton promotes economic globalization by signing NAFTA, the North American Free Trade Agreement.
2000	George W. Bush is elected president.
2001	On September 11, terrorists attack New York City and Washington, D.C. The United States leads an invasion in Afghanistan to battle al-Qaeda.
2003	The United States invades Iraq to look for weapons of mass destruction and to remove Saddam Hussein from power.
2008	Barack Obama is elected the first African American president. A major financial crisis upsets the global economy.

TEST WHAT YOU ALREADY KNOW

Part A: Quiz

Questions 1–3 refer to the chart below.

Top Ten Countries	2010	2000	1990
Mexico	11,711,103	9,177,487	4,298,014
China	2,166,526	1,518,652	921,070
India	1,780,322	1,022,552	450,406
Philippines	1,777,588	1,369,070	912,674
Vietnam	1,240,542	988,174	543,262
El Salvador	1,214,049	817,336	465,433
Cuba	1,104,679	872,716	736,971
South Korea	1,100,422	864,125	568,397
Dominican Republic	879,187	687,677	347,858
Guatemala	830,824	480,665	225,739
All of Latin America	21,224,087	16,086,974	8,407,837
All Immigrants	39,955,854	31,107,889	19,767,316

Place of Birth for the Foreign-Born Populations in the United States, United States Census Bureau

1. Which outcome most directly resulted from the demographic information in the chart?

   (A) Shifting of political power to southern and western states

   (B) Greater consensus on the direction of American foreign policy

   (C) Growth in the power of organized labor in the Northeast

   (D) Decline in the number of clashes between conservatives and liberals

2. Which of the following events from United States history most clearly parallels the situation illustrated in the chart?

   (A) Growth of a cotton economy in the antebellum period

   (B) Rise of an industrial culture in the Gilded Age

   (C) Great Migration of the post–World War I period

   (D) Suburbanization of the post–World War II period

3. The trends expressed in the chart most directly reflect which of the following continuities in United States history?

   (A) Debates about the spread of American ideals abroad

   (B) Debates about the relationships among the three branches of the United States government

   (C) Debates about gender equality

   (D) Debates about national identity

Questions 4–7 refer to the excerpt below.

"Mr. Speaker, our Contract With America states the following:

On the first day of Congress, a Republican House will require Congress to live under the same laws as everyone else; cut committee staffs by one-third; and cut the congressional budget. We kept our promise.

It continues that in the first 100 days, we will vote on the following items: A balanced budget amendment—we kept our word; unfunded mandates legislation—which will be signed in the Rose Garden by the President today; line-item veto—we kept our promise; a new crime package to stop violent criminals—we kept our promise again; national security restoration to protect our freedoms, which we passed; Government regulatory reform—we kept our promise; commonsense legal reform to end frivolous lawsuits—we kept our promise; welfare reform to encourage work, not dependence—we are working on this today and tomorrow; family reinforcement to crack down on deadbeat dads and protect our children; tax cuts for middle-income families; Senior Citizens' Equity Act to allow our seniors to work without Government penalty; and congressional term limits to make Congress a citizen legislature.

Mr. Speaker, this is our Contract With America."

Address by Rep. John Boehner to the
House of Representatives, March 22, 1995

4. Which of the following groups would be most likely to support the passage's perspective?

   (A) Union leaders from the Sunbelt states

   (B) Supporters of 1980s Reagan federalism

   (C) Proponents of 1960s federal programs

   (D) Internet social media users

5. The Contract with America expressed concerns that most closely resemble the goals associated with which of the following historical periods in the United States?

   (A) The era of Manifest Destiny

   (B) The American Civil War

   (C) The Progressive Era

   (D) Lyndon Johnson's Great Society

6. The beliefs expressed in the Republican Contract with America most directly led to political conflicts from the 1990s to the present over

   (A) immigration policy

   (B) globalization and loss of American jobs

   (C) size and scope of social safety net programs

   (D) dependence upon fossil fuels

7. The reasoning expressed in the Republican Contract with America most directly reflects which of the following continuities in the history of the United States?

   (A) Debates about the cost of involvement in foreign wars

   (B) Debates about the changing relationship between state and local governments

   (C) Debates about separation of powers

   (D) Debates about the values that guide the political system

Questions 8–10 refer to the excerpt below.

"Tuesday, September 11, 2001, dawned temperate and nearly cloudless in the eastern United States. Millions of men and women readied themselves for work. Some made their way to the Twin Towers, the signature structures of the World Trade Center complex in New York City. Others went to Arlington, Virginia, to the Pentagon. Across the Potomac River, the United States Congress was back in session. At the other end of Pennsylvania Avenue, people began to line up for a White House tour.

. . .

The details of what happened on the morning of September 11 are complex, but they play out a simple theme. NORAD [North American Aerospace Defense Command] and the FAA [Federal Aviation Administration] were unprepared for the type of attacks launched against the United States on September 11, 2001. They struggled, under difficult circumstances, to improvise a homeland defense against an unprecedented challenge they had never before encountered and had never trained to meet."

9/11 Report, National Commission on Terrorist Attacks Upon the United States, 2004

8. Which of the following twentieth-century events most closely parallels the September 11 attacks and their aftermath?

   (A) The Banana Wars

   (B) Woodrow Wilson's call for the defense of democracy in 1917

   (C) The shift to all-volunteer armed services in 1973

   (D) Opposition to the war in Vietnam in the 1960s and 1970s

9. The events of September 11 most directly led to

   (A) sustained economic growth

   (B) increasing Cold War tensions

   (C) strengthening of World War II–era international coalitions

   (D) a growth in executive power

10. The events of September 11 most directly relate to which of the following continuities in United States history?

   (A) Debates about the impact of airline deregulation

   (B) Debates about economic globalization

   (C) Debates about domestic security and civil rights

   (D) Debates about federalism and states' rights

Part B: Key Terms

The following is a list of the major people, places, and events for 1980–Present. You will likely see many of these on the AP U.S. History exam.

For each key term ask yourself the following questions:

- Can I describe this key term?
- Can I discuss this key term in the context of other events?
- Could I correctly answer a multiple-choice question about this key term?
- Could I correctly answer a free-response question about this key term?

Check off the key terms if you can answer "yes" to at least three of these questions.

The Reagan Administration

- ☐ Ronald Reagan
- ☐ Reagan Revolution
- ☐ Iran-Contra scandal

The End of the Cold War

- ☐ Strategic Defense Initiative (Star Wars)
- ☐ Glasnost
- ☐ Perestroika
- ☐ George H. W. Bush

The Clinton and George W. Bush Administrations

- ☐ Bill Clinton
- ☐ Contract with America
- ☐ Personal Responsibility and Work Opportunity Reconciliation Act of 1996
- ☐ George W. Bush
- ☐ No Child Left Behind Act

Domestic and International Terrorism

- ☐ Oklahoma City Bombing
- ☐ Al-Qaeda
- ☐ Department of Homeland Security
- ☐ Weapons of mass destruction

The Obama Administration

- ☐ Barack Obama
- ☐ Affordable Care Act (Obamacare)

Ongoing Demographic Shifts

☐ Immigration and Control Act

☐ California Proposition 187

☐ Sun Belt

☐ Rust Belt

☐ Affirmative action

Technological Advances

☐ Internet

☐ World Wide Web

Globalization and the United States

☐ North American Free Trade Agreement (NAFTA)

☐ International Monetary Fund

☐ 2008 Financial Crisis

☐ Great Recession

11

Next Steps

Step 1: Tally your correct answers from Part A and review the quiz explanations at the end of this chapter.

1.	A	6.	C
2.	B	7.	D
3.	D	8.	B
4.	B	9.	D
5.	C	10.	C

_____ out of 10 questions

Step 2: Count the number of key terms you checked off in Part B.

_____ out of 29 key terms

Step 3: Read the Key Takeaways in this chapter.

Step 4: Consult the table below and follow the instructions based on your performance.

If You Got...	Do This
80% or more of the Test What You Already Know assessment correct (8 or more questions from Part A and 23 or more key terms from Part B)	• Read definitions in this chapter for all the key terms you didn't check off. • Complete the Test What You Learned assessment in this chapter.
50% or less of the Test What You Already Know assessment correct (5 or fewer questions from Part A and 15 or fewer key terms from Part B)	• Read the comprehensive review for this period in Chapter 20. • If you are short on time, read only the High-Yield sections. • Read through all of the key term definitions in this chapter. • Complete the Test What You Learned assessment in this chapter.
Any other result	• Read the High-Yield sections in the comprehensive review of this period in Chapter 20. • Read definitions in this chapter for all the key terms you didn't check off. • Complete the Test What You Learned assessment in this chapter.

ESSENTIAL CONTENT

Key Takeaways: 1980–Present

1. President Reagan's victory in 1980 was a defining moment for the new conservative movement that had gained strength in the 1970s. Led by Reagan, conservatives promoted tax cuts and the deregulation of many private industries.

2. Through an increased military buildup and a more assertive foreign policy, the Reagan administration sought to end the Cold War. Ultimately, this stronger interventionist U.S. policy, coupled with economic trouble and political changes in Eastern Europe and the Soviet Union, brought the Cold War to an end.

3. Advances in science and technology soared to new heights, especially in the 1990s. Developments in digital technology and the birth of the Internet revolutionized the economy and transformed the world, leading to a new era of globalization.

4. The United States continued to see large shifts in demographics and populations. Intense debates continued over social issues such as immigration, race, gender, family structures, and diversity.

5. Conflict in the Middle East increased. After the September 11 attacks on the World Trade Center and the Pentagon, the United States engaged in military action against Afghanistan and Iraq. The War on Terrorism presented new challenges for U.S. leadership and led to changes in both domestic and foreign policy. Efforts to improve security led to new debates in America over the issue of civil liberties and human rights.

Key Terms: 1980–Present

Remember that the AP U.S. History exam tests you on the depth of your knowledge, not just your ability to recall facts. While we have provided brief definitions here, you will need to know these terms in even more depth for the AP exam, including how terms connect to broader historical themes and understandings.

The Reagan Administration

Ronald Reagan: Fortieth president. Served from 1981–1989. Former two-term governor of California, he heralded a shift within the Republican Party toward an ideological conservatism. Domestically, he oversaw massive tax cuts, economic deregulation, and increased defense spending. Internationally, he took a hawkish line with the Soviet Union while also negotiating arms limitations. His final years in office were dogged by the Iran-Contra scandal.

Reagan Revolution: A significant pivot point in U.S. political history, where the New Deal ideology of the 1930s was replaced by a socially conservative, free market ideology. Began with the 1980 election of Ronald Reagan. The New Democrats of the 1990s were a response to the Reagan Revolution, as left-wing policies were perceived to be unpopular with modern voters.

Iran-Contra scandal: A scandal in which the Reagan administration secretly sold arms to Iran in exchange for the release of Americans hostages. The profits from that sale were then used to illegally support right-wing insurgents in Nicaragua. Led to calls for Reagan's impeachment. In late 1992, President George H. W. Bush pardoned those under trial for their parts in Iran-Contra.

11

The End of the Cold War

Strategic Defense Initiative (Star Wars): A proposal by Ronald Reagan to intercept incoming nuclear missiles using lasers fired from orbital platforms. Popularly known as Star Wars, it was considered technologically infeasible by scientists.

Glasnost: ("openness") A policy instituted by Gorbachev, it allowed Soviet citizens to publicly criticize the government and discuss social problems in the hope of finding solutions.

Perestroika: ("restructuring") Another policy instituted by Gorbachev, it introduced limited free market reforms to the Soviet Union's

socialist planned economy. A key aspect of the Soviet Union's fall.

George H. W. Bush: Forty-first president. Served from 1989–1993. Considered a moderate Republican, his presidency was defined by the collapse of the Soviet Union and the end of the Cold War. He pushed for international cooperation in a New World Order, such as in Operation Desert Storm in the Gulf War (which saw a large American-led multinational coalition expel Iraqi forces from occupied Kuwait). Signed but did not ratify the NAFTA treaty. Breaking his promise to not raise taxes alienated conservatives ahead of the 1992 election.

The Clinton and George W. Bush Administrations

Bill Clinton: Fourty-second president. Served from 1993–2001. Clinton advocated for centrist reform as a New Democrat, signing NAFTA and welfare reform into law, but notably failed to reform health care. Intervened in the Kosovo War. Helped broker the Good Friday Agreement. Impeached in 1998 over allegations arising from his affair with Monica Lewinsky; he was not convicted.

Contract with America: A pledge that listed specific conservative policies the GOP would enact if they gained control of the House of Representatives in the 1994 midterm elections.

Personal Responsibility and Work Opportunity Reconciliation Act of 1996: More commonly referred to as welfare reform, Bill Clinton signed it into law. It stopped open-ended

benefits, instead favoring a limited work-based concept, and shifted control to the states.

George W. Bush: Forty-third president. Served from 2001–2009. He won election after the 2000 recount. The 9/11 attacks defined his presidency. Directed the invasions of Afghanistan and Iraq. Domestically, he signed the No Child Left Behind Act, the Patriot Act, and an expansion of Medicare into law. The final months of his presidency were marked by the 2008 Financial Crisis. He signed the Emergency Economic Stabilization Act of 2008, which bailed out failing banks.

No Child Left Behind Act: Also known as NCLB. Established federal standards in education and test-based performance measurement. Passed in 2001 with bipartisan support. Replaced by the Every Student Succeeds Act (ESSA) in 2015, which reverted standards to the states.

Domestic and International Terrorism

Oklahoma City Bombing: Bombing that destroyed the Murrah Federal Building in

Oklahoma City, Oklahoma, killing 168 people (including infants and children in the building's day-care center). Right-wing extremist Timothy McVeigh and two accomplices were convicted of the terror attack. This was an infamous example of domestic terrorism.

Al-Qaeda: A Salafist jihadist transnational terrorist organization. Formed in 1988 by veteran *mujahideen* fighting against the Soviet Union in Afghanistan. Orchestrated the September 11 attacks, along with other attacks in several other countries over the years.

The Obama Administration

Barack Obama: Forty-fourth president. Served from 2009–2017. A freshman senator from Illinois, he defeated Hillary Clinton in a protracted 2008 primary fight and went on to a landslide general election victory. First African American president. Along with George W. Bush, he oversaw the response to the 2008 Financial Crisis. Signed the Affordable Care Act into law in 2010. His foreign policy was marked by a

Department of Homeland Security: A Cabinet-level department formed in 2002 in response to the September 11 attacks, it consolidated various public security agencies. It has since been criticized on several grounds, ranging from ineffectiveness to violating civil liberties.

Weapons of mass destruction: Typically refers to a nuclear, biological, or chemical weapon that can kill a large number of people in a single action. Also known as WMD.

multilateral approach and the targeted use of military force.

Affordable Care Act (Obamacare): A health care reform act that reduced the uninsured population via expanded Medicaid eligibility and a reworking of the individual insurance marketplace. The Obama administration's signature legislation. Contentious in the 2010s.

Ongoing Demographic Shifts

Immigration and Control Act: A 1986 law signed by Ronald Reagan, which made it a crime to knowingly hire an illegal immigrant. However, it also legalized millions of immigrants who had unlawfully entered the United States before January 1, 1982.

California Proposition 187: Sought to prohibit undocumented immigrants from accessing non-emergency health care and public education. California voters approved it by a 59 percent majority, although an injunction over its constitutionality prevented enforcement. Over the next decade, several other states would pass similar laws.

Sun Belt: A region of the United States comprising California, Texas, Arizona, Florida, and New Mexico. Many people moved to this area to take advantage of the climate and job opportunities.

Rust Belt: A region of the United States centered around the Great Lakes and upper Midwest. The term references the economic decline of the country's former industrial heartland.

Affirmative action: The policy of favoring members of a historically disadvantaged group, usually in the context of employment or education. Came into practice in the United States in the 1960s but has become the subject of increasing controversy. It is banned in several states by law.

Technological Advances

Internet: A worldwide computer network that uses the standard Internet Protocol Suite (TCP/IP). Grew out of ARPANET, a project funded by the U.S. Department of Defense.

World Wide Web: Distinct from but related to the Internet. It is a system by which documents are coded in HTML, identified by URLs, and linked together by hypertext. Invented by Tim Berners-Lee in 1989.

Globalization and the United States

North American Free Trade Agreement (NAFTA): Beginning in 1994, it created a free trade bloc between Canada, Mexico, and the United States. Negotiated by George H. W. Bush and ratified with the approval of Bill Clinton. Opposed in the 1992 election by Ross Perot.

International Monetary Fund: Formed in 1944 at the Bretton Woods Conference, the IMF facilitates global trade to avoid another Great Depression.

2008 Financial Crisis: A global banking crisis that arose from the collapse of the U.S. subprime mortgage market. Resulted in the federal bailout of U.S. banks. Led to the Great Recession.

Great Recession: Downturn of the global economy caused by the 2008 Financial Crisis and lasting through the early 2010s; period of job loss, home foreclosures, and high unemployment.

TEST WHAT YOU LEARNED

Questions 1 and 2 refer to the excerpt below.

"But if these machines were ingenious, what shall we think of the calculating machine. . .? What shall we think of an engine of wood and metal which can not only compute astronomical and navigation tables to any given extent, but render the exactitude of its operations mathematically certain through its power of correcting its possible errors? What shall we think of a machine which can not only accomplish all this, but actually print off its elaborate results, when obtained, without the slightest intervention of the intellect of man?"

Edgar Allan Poe, *Maelzel's Chess-Player*, 1836

1. The technology described in the excerpt most directly foreshadows which of the following developments?

    (A) Social media

    (B) Cable television

    (C) Cell phones

    (D) Personal computers

2. Which of the following was a major contrast between ARPANET and Tim Berners-Lee's World Wide Web?

    (A) The World Wide Web used HTML and hyperlinks.

    (B) ARPANET used HTML and hyperlinks.

    (C) The World Wide Web was initially only meant for military use.

    (D) The World Wide Web was the sole foundation for the modern-day Internet.

11

Questions 3 and 4 refer to the excerpt below.

"It is not just the numbers, Mr. Speaker. That, we could deal with. The fact is that yes, we will have to build more schools; yes, we will have to hire more teachers; yes, there will be pressures for greater and greater resources to address the issue of more people. But then it is what happens even afterwards, in the development of, as I say, these bilingual programs and multicultural programs that have a tendency, unfortunately, I must say this, have a tendency to balkanize America. That is the other difference between the kind of immigration patterns we saw in the early 1900s and immigration patterns today. Instead of pressures within the United States to amalgamate the people who were coming here and bring them into the melting pot . . . something happens in terms of the willingness on the part of a lot of people to accept the greater American dream. We see a tendency to balkanize America, to break ourselves up into separate little enclaves, separated by language and culture."

Rep. Tom Tancredo addressing the House of Representatives, October 18, 1999

3. The excerpt best illustrates which of the following developments?

(A) Debates over the progress made as a nation toward the goal of full equality

(B) Debates over the shortcomings of the American education system

(C) Debates over the importance of preserving an inclusive, unified American identity

(D) Debates over the American national identity being an outdated concept

4. All of the following descriptions are factually accurate. Which twenty-first century development would most weaken the argument in the excerpt?

(A) The high amount of immigration from Mexico and the rest of Latin America

(B) The increasing rate of interracial marriages throughout the United Sates

(C) The 9/11 Attacks on the World Trade Center and the Pentagon

(D) The decline of Spanish usage in the households of second- and third-generation immigrants

Questions 5–7 refer to the chart below.

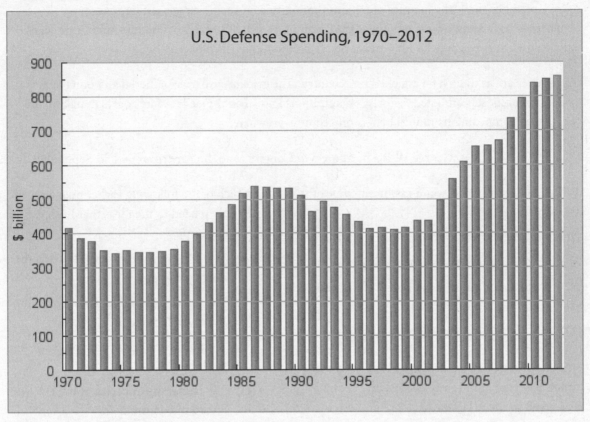

U.S. Defense Spending, 1970-2012. Chart. From usgovernmentspending.com.

5. Which of the following was a direct cause of the defense spending trend between 1980 and 1990 as shown in the chart?

   (A) The breakup of the Soviet Union

   (B) The Reagan administration's military buildup

   (C) The savings and loan crisis

   (D) The Gulf War

6. The Soviet Union's response to the trend illustrated on the chart is best reflected by Gorbachev's proposal for

   (A) *perestroika*

   (B) *glasnost*

   (C) the Star Wars program

   (D) the SALT I treaty

7. Which of the following represents an example of the defense spending trend after 2000?

   (A) The Strategic Defense Initiative

   (B) Support for the Afghan mujahideen

   (C) Support for the Iraqi army

   (D) The diversion of funds to the Nicaraguan Contras

11

Questions 8–10 refer to the excerpt below.

"On September the 11th, enemies of freedom committed an act of war against our country. Americans have known wars but not at the center of a great city on a peaceful morning. Americans have known surprise attacks—but never before on thousands of civilians.

Americans are asking: Who attacked our country? The evidence we have gathered all points to a collection of loosely affiliated terrorist organizations known as al-Qaeda . . . its goal is remaking the world—and imposing its radical beliefs on people everywhere."

George W. Bush, Address to Congress and the American people, September 20, 2001

8. Which of the following was a major outcome of the above speech?

   (A) Unilateral economic sanctions against Iran

   (B) Strict United Nations sanctions against Iran

   (C) Multilateral military intervention in South Asia

   (D) UN-backed military intervention in Iraq

9. Which of the following became a topic of constitutional debate in the early twenty-first century as a result of the 9/11 attacks?

   (A) Curbing of freedom of the press

   (B) Extra-constitutional authority granted to the military

   (C) Suspension of habeas corpus for U.S. citizens

   (D) The civil liberties of American citizens

10. Which of the following earlier policies is most directly related to the ideas that Bush expressed in the excerpt?

   (A) U.S. policy in Vietnam as stated in the Pentagon Papers

   (B) The police action undertaken in South Korea by Truman

   (C) The *détente* policies of Nixon, Ford, and Carter

   (D) The containment policy of the U.S. with regard to communism

Part B: Key Terms

This key terms list is the same as the list in the Test What You Already Know section earlier in this chapter. Based on what you have now learned, again ask yourself the following questions:

- Can I define this key term and use it in a sentence?

- Can I provide an example related to this key term?

- Could I correctly answer a multiple-choice question about this key term?

- Could I correctly answer a free-response question about this key term?

Check off the key terms if you can answer "yes" to at least three of these questions.

The Reagan Administration

☐ Ronald Reagan   ☐ Reagan Revolution   ☐ Iran-Contra scandal

The End of the Cold War

☐ Strategic Defense Initiative (Star Wars)   ☐ Glasnost   ☐ George H. W. Bush
                                              ☐ Perestroika

The Clinton and George W. Bush Administrations

☐ Bill Clinton   ☐ Personal Responsibility and Work Opportunity Reconciliation Act of 1996   ☐ George W. Bush
☐ Contract with America   ☐ No Child Left Behind Act

Domestic and International Terrorism

☐ Oklahoma City Bombing   ☐ Department of Homeland Security   ☐ Weapons of mass destruction
☐ Al-Qaeda

The Obama Administration

☐ Barack Obama   ☐ Affordable Care Act (Obamacare)

Ongoing Demographic Shifts

☐ Immigration and Control Act   ☐ California Proposition 187   ☐ Rust Belt
                                 ☐ Sun Belt   ☐ Affirmative action

Technological Advances

☐ Internet   ☐ World Wide Web

11

Globalization and the United States

☐ North American Free Trade Agreement (NAFTA)

☐ International Monetary Fund

☐ 2008 Financial Crisis

☐ Great Recession

Next Steps

Step 1: Tally your correct answers from Part A and review the quiz explanations at the end of this chapter.

1.	D	6.	A
2.	A	7.	C
3.	C	8.	C
4.	D	9.	D
5.	B	10.	B

_____ out of 10 questions

Step 2: Count the number of key terms you checked off in Part B.

_____ out of 29 key terms

Step 3: Compare your Test What You Already Know results to these Test What You Learned results to see how exam-ready you are for this period.

For More Practice:

• Read (or reread) the comprehensive review for this period in Chapter 20.

• Go to kaptest.com to complete the online quiz questions for 1980–Present.

   ◦ Haven't registered your book yet? Go to kaptest.com/moreonline to begin.

ANSWERS AND EXPLANATIONS

Test What You Already Know

1. A

Many of the recent immigrants to the United States have settled in southern and western states. California, Texas, and Florida are among the most populous states and are therefore among the largest delegations in the U.S. House of Representatives. Thus, **(A)** is correct. The trends in immigration from Asia and the Americas have only minimally affected American foreign policy; thus, (B) is incorrect. Organized labor nationwide has declined in power since 1990, making (C) incorrect. In addition to globalization, mechanization, and the spread of right-to-work laws, mass immigration is sometimes attributed as a cause for the decline in organized labor due to excess manpower resulting in lower wages. (D) is incorrect, as immigration has become an increasingly politically polarized issue since 1990.

2. B

Gilded Age industrialization led to a huge demand for labor. Immigrants from Southern and Eastern Europe poured into the United States at the turn of the twentieth century. They challenged existing immigration patterns, as "new immigrants" no longer came from the once-dominant areas of Northern and Western Europe. Thus, **(B)** is correct. The Antebellum Period refers to a period in the mid-eighteenth century up until the start of the American Civil War. It centered on the plantation economic system. The slave labor involved does not parallel the voluntary labor of modern immigrants; (A) is incorrect. The Great Migration involved African Americans seeking jobs and prosperity in northern and midwestern factories. While their motivation was similar to those of modern immigrants, their migration was internal rather than being an influx of new citizens; (C) is incorrect. The suburbanization of the post–World War II period was another form of internal migration, making (D) incorrect.

3. D

While the turn of the twenty-first century saw greater immigration from Asia and the Americas, over two centuries of European-dominated immigration had seen repeated debates over national identity; **(D)** is correct. For example, the influx of Catholic immigrants from Ireland in the nineteenth century led to a backlash from the majority Anglo-Saxon Protestant population. Nothing in the chart attributes any particular motivation for why these people were immigrating to the United States, and the population is listed in raw numbers rather than by gender; (A) and (C) are incorrect. As previous immigration debates had mainly occurred between rival political factions rather than between branches of government over the extent of their legal authority to regulate immigration, (B) is incorrect.

4. B

Released by the Republicans six weeks before the 1994 midterm elections, the Contract with America represented a wish to continue the limitation of federal power, especially in domestic affairs, begun during the Reagan administration. **(B)** is correct. Unions in Sunbelt states are traditionally weaker compared to those in the North, and they would not welcome the passage's conservative agenda; (A) is incorrect. The Great Society programs would likely be reduced under the Contract's budget reform measures, meaning pro-welfare voters would not be won over; (C) is incorrect. The Internet existed only in a basic form in 1994, limited to basic forums and chat rooms. Modern social media did not yet exist; (D) is incorrect.

5. C

While their specific solutions differ, proponents of the Progressive Era and of the Contract with America both believed that the government was unresponsive to the wishes of the citizenry and needed reform. Thus, **(C)** is correct. Manifest Destiny fostered the territorial expansion of the United States; it did not concern itself with the responsiveness of government, so (A) is incorrect. The American Civil War saw an expansion of the federal government in response to wartime needs rather than a concern over democratic representation; (B) is incorrect. The Great Society programs were concerned with social and economic inequality, not with the responsiveness of government; (D) is incorrect.

6. C

Republican policy, especially since the 1980s, has sought to limit the size and scope of the federal government. Popular welfare programs like Medicare, Medicaid, and

Social Security have proven difficult to reform despite several attempts to do so; **(C)** is correct. The Contract with America did not discuss immigration policy or fossil fuel dependency; (A) and (D) are incorrect. Debates over globalization and the loss of American jobs predate the Contract with America. For example, in the 1992 presidential election, independent candidate Ross Perot campaigned against NAFTA; thus, (B) is incorrect.

7. D

While the Contract with America outlined the role that Congress, especially the House of Representatives, would take, at its core it challenged the concept of "big government." It envisioned an alternative to the values of the New Deal and the Great Society; **(D)** is correct. The document provided makes no reference to the cost of foreign wars or to the relationship between state and local governments; (A) and (B) are incorrect. While the Contract with America promised an adjustment of legislative authority, it did not primarily deal with the separation of powers between the three branches of the federal government; therefore, (C) is incorrect.

8. B

The attacks on 9/11 led to the War on Terror and a belief that the United States should take action against al-Qaeda and like-minded actors who were seen as challenging liberty. This idea echoed Wilson's call to "make the world safe for democracy" ahead of U.S. entry into World War I; **(B)** is correct. The Banana Wars is the umbrella term for a set of military interventions into Latin America in defense of U.S. economic interests, such as those of the United Fruit Company. This does not mirror the moral framework inspired by the War on Terror; thus, (A) is incorrect. President Nixon proposed the all-volunteer military, in part, to undermine the anti–Vietnam War movement, as he felt that affluent youths would cease protesting once there was no risk they themselves would be made to fight. Again, this conflicts with the moral framework of the parallel; (C) is incorrect. The antiwar movement of the 1960s and 1970s would have been skeptical of American interventions abroad, which was an uncommon sentiment in the early days of the War on Terror; (D) is incorrect.

9. D

In the aftermath of 9/11, the Bush administration issued an executive order authorizing military tribunals for noncitizens accused of terrorism. Military interventions in Libya and Syria under the Obama and Trump administrations, respectively, were not authorized by Congress under the War Powers Act, but neither resulted in legal action. **(D)** is correct; these and other actions, in the name of national security, increased executive power. The Dow suffered its worst one-day drop and one-week drop in the immediate aftermath of 9/11, which aggravated a then-ongoing recession; therefore, (A) is incorrect. The Cold War ended with the dissolution of the Soviet Union in 1991; (B) is incorrect. After the invasion of Afghanistan, U.S. armed forces were sent to Iraq with limited international support and over the objections of many traditional allies; thus, (C) is incorrect.

10. C

The September 11 attacks led to increased security across the U.S., including changes to procedures in the nation's airports and law enforcement agencies. Continued reauthorization of the Patriot Act by Congress has increased the debate about the balance of domestic security and civil rights; thus, **(C)** is correct. The 9/11 attacks involved the hijacking and weaponization of jetliners, which is irrelevant to the airline industry's deregulation in the 1980s; (A) is incorrect. While the Twin Towers were targeted in part due to their economic symbolism, that was not a primary motivation for al-Qaeda, and 9/11 did not reflect a debate over economic globalization; therefore, (B) is incorrect. Post-9/11 debates have concerned the federal government's power over both citizens and noncitizens, not its power over the states; (D) is incorrect.

Test What You Learned

1. D

The excerpt describes the basic framework for the personal computer: a machine with multiple abilities, such as calculation, navigation, and computation. Thus, **(D)** is correct. Social media is facilitated by the Internet and personal computer, and it would not arise until around the turn of the twenty-first century. Thus, it is not directly foreshadowed in the excerpt, so (A) is incorrect. Cable television relied on the innovation of the coaxial cable, which is not described in the excerpt; (B) is incorrect. Cell phones also do not involve the technology described; thus, (C) is incorrect.

11

2.   A

Tim Berners-Lee's innovative system of URLs, HTML, and hyperlinks would be the framework for what is now a global system. Thus, **(A)** is correct. HTML and hyperlinks were innovations of Tim Berners-Lee; (B) is incorrect. The World Wide Web was a civilian project created by Tim Berners-Lee while at CERN; (C) is incorrect. ARPA-NET provided the foundation for the modern Internet, in particular with the TCP/IP protocol suite and packet switching. The World Wide Web would build upon that foundation. Thus, (D) is incorrect.

3.   C

Representative Tancredo, while conceding that the material requirements to support immigration are attainable, argued that accommodations for immigrant groups, such as bilingual education, were dividing the nation into separate communities rather than uniting the American people. This debate over the merits and extent of multiculturalism reflects one aspect of the so-called Culture Wars around the turn of the twenty-first century. Thus, **(C)** is correct. Tancredo did not discuss the state of the nation's progress toward the goal of full equality; (A) is incorrect. Although tempting because he singles out bilingual education as a negative, Tancredo's larger point is about the concept of multiculturalism as a whole, of which bilingual education is only one part. So, (B) is incorrect. Tancredo never describes the unified American national identity as being outdated, only suggesting that multiculturalism will weaken it. (D) is incorrect because it is too extreme.

4.   D

In the excerpt, Tancredo advocated the viewpoint that multicultural accommodations for minority groups threatened national unity. He used bilingual education as a specific example of what would lead the United States to "break ourselves up into separate little enclaves, separated by language and culture." In other words, Tancredo felt that unless English was forced onto the children of immigrants in schools, they would never fully adopt the dominant U.S. language. However, despite the widespread availability of bilingual education, Spanish usage in the households of second- and third-generation immigrants has declined in the twenty-first century, as English becomes increasingly dominant with each subsequent generation. Thus, **(D)** is correct. A change in the amount of immigration would not weaken Tancredo's argument about how best to handle immigrants who have already come to the United States;

(A) is incorrect. Tancredo was concerned with immigration, not interracial marriages, which do not necessaily involve marriages with foreign-born individuals; (B) is incorrect. The 9/11 Attacks were perpetrated by foreign nationals, mainly Saudis, not immigrants to the United States, so 9/11 is unrelated to the discussion of immigration and multiculturalism. Thus, (C) is incorrect.

5.   B

Following the Vietnam War, the Iranian Hostage Crisis, and the Soviet invasion of Afghanistan, Ronald Reagan proposed a large military buildup to restore America's prestige and capabilities. This proposal resulted in a notable increase in defense spending during the 1980s up until the gradual breakup of the Soviet Union. Thus, **(B)** is correct. The breakup of the Soviet Union was partly the result, not the cause, of the budget trend illustrated on the above chart. Thus, (A) is incorrect. The savings and loan crisis did not significantly affect the increases in defense spending, as the U.S. national debt increased substantially during the Reagan administration to support this military buildup while simultaneously cutting taxes. Therefore, (C) is incorrect. The Gulf War did not occur until 1990–1991, a decade after this trend began, making (D) incorrect.

6.   A

Perestroika, a restructuring of the Soviet economy to allow for limited free market reforms, was a response to the economic stress the Soviet Union was undergoing in the 1980s, in part due to the Reagan administration's massive military buildup. Thus, **(A)** is correct. Gorbachev's *glasnost* policy was an attempt to moderately liberalize free speech in the Soviet Union as a way to increase government transparency and resolve festering social ills. It was not primarily intended as a fix for the economic stresses partly caused by the U.S. military buildup of the 1980s. Thus, (B) is incorrect. Ronald Reagan proposed the Star Wars program, formally known as the Strategic Defense Initiative (SDI), making (C) incorrect. The SALT I treaty was negotiated in the 1970s, long before Gorbachev came to power, so (D) is also incorrect.

7.   C

After the 2003 invasion of Iraq, the U.S. trained and supplied a rebuilt Iraqi army; **(C)** is correct. The Strategic Defense Initiative (SDI), popularly known as Star Wars, was a missile defense system first proposed by President Reagan in 1983, and the project was cancelled in 1993.

Thus, (A) is incorrect. The United States funded the Afghan mujahideen in the 1980s in order to covertly oppose the Soviet invasion of Afghanistan. This funding ended well before 2000, making (B) incorrect. The funding illegally diverted to the Nicaraguan Contras was not authorized under the defense budget; instead, it was procured from the sale of arms to Iran in exchange for the release of U.S. hostages. This became known as the Iran-Contra scandal in the 1980s; (D) is incorrect.

8. C

President George W. Bush's speech was tantamount to a declaration of war against terrorism. The United States soon led a coalition of Western allies to invade Afghanistan and overthrow the Taliban-led government, which was harboring al-Qaeda. The Middle East is an area located between Western Asia and Egypt in North Africa. Afghanistan, like neighboring Pakistan, is considered part of South Asia. Thus, **(C)** is correct. Iran was not involved in the 9/11 attacks, and its status as a Shia-majority country made it another enemy of al-Qaeda. Thus, (A) and (B) are incorrect. Most legal experts argue that the invasion was technically illegal under international law as it was not explicitly authorized by the Security Council. The Secretary-General of the UN at the time, Kofi Annan, stated in 2004 that he viewed it as a violation of the UN Charter. Thus, (D) is incorrect.

9. D

In the immediate wake of the 9/11 attacks, Congress passed the USA PATRIOT Act, which granted the government the authority to monitor Americans more closely. This authority became the focus of controversy, lawsuits, and reform efforts, as some viewed it as a violation of the Fourth Amendment. Thus, **(D)** is correct. While the press came under fire in the mid-2000s for participating in the Iraq War as "embedded" reporters, this was a voluntary choice on their part and not government censorship. Thus, (A) is incorrect. While the constitutional limits of both executive and judicial power have become matters of increasing debate, the military itself has not been granted extra-constitutional authority or been debated as having such power. Thus, (B) is incorrect. Lastly, (C) is incorrect because, while the suspension of habeas corpus for noncitizens and for unprivileged belligerents was a major issue in the 2000s, habeas corpus rights for U.S. citizens have always been treated by the courts and various administrations as ironclad.

10. B

Truman viewed the invasion of South Korea as an attack on the Free World by an international communist network that wished to enforce its beliefs on the entire world. Bush likewise characterized al-Qaeda as seeking to remake the world. Thus, **(B)** is correct. The Pentagon Papers were secret documents leaked to the press in 1973 that revealed the true goal of U.S. involvement in South Vietnam was to contain the People's Republic of China. Bush did not seek to contain another country's political influence through intervention in Afghanistan. Thus, (A) and (D) are incorrect. The *détente* policy of the 1970s was an effort to seek diplomatic accommodation and peaceful coexistence with the Soviet Union and the People's Republic of China. Bush did not seek coexistence with al-Qaeda after the 9/11 attacks; (C) is incorrect.

PART 3

Comprehensive Review

CHAPTER 12

Period 1: 1491–1607

POPULATIONS IN THE AMERICAS BEFORE EUROPEAN ARRIVAL

Prior to 1492, millions of American Indians lived in the lands stretching from the Arctic Circle in the north to Tierra del Fuego in the south. At least 375 distinct native languages were once spoken in the Americas; some of those languages were spoken by small-scale agricultural societies, others by large-scale empires, still others by nomadic tribes. Political power structures and religious beliefs varied by tribe, but this did not prevent tribes from trading and communicating with each other. Different tribes were often at war with one another to obtain goods, seize captives, or seek revenge for the deaths of family or tribe members, but they also frequently conducted diplomacy and made peace. American Indians did not tend to think of themselves as a single, allied people; the idea of a singular "Indian" was invented by European explorers and colonists. Even when viewed from a regional lens rather than a continental one, obvious distinctions emerge among American Indians.

Mexico and the Southwest

Southern Mexico constitutes one of the major sources of domesticated crops in the Americas. Squash, beans, and cotton were first cultivated there. These crops then diffused throughout the rest of the New World.

The Mexica (also known as Aztec) people occupied territory in Mesoamerica, and the capital city Tenochtitlán was located in what today is Mexico City. A militant warrior tradition characterized their culture. They developed a system of feudalism comparable to what was once found in Japan and Europe. The Mexica were ruled by a single monarch, who exerted power over local rulers. They had an agricultural economy, with cacao beans sometimes used as currency. They practiced *chinampa* agriculture, where farmers cultivated crops in rectangular plots of land on lake beds. A priestly class oversaw polytheistic religious rituals, which sometimes included human sacrifice. Although Mexica society was patriarchal, women were able to own property and agree to business contracts.

In what became the American Southwest, the Pueblo peoples (or Puebloans) established a complex agricultural society. The Pueblo constructed villages of multi-story buildings, using adobe mud, stone, and other local materials for their construction. Their villages hosted hundreds, sometimes thousands, of people. The Pueblo peoples are referred to in the plural because they are a group of related but culturally distinct tribes. For example, there are four distinct Pueblo languages. The Western Pueblos used dry farming, while the Eastern Pueblos used irrigation. Both groups focused on maize (corn), but squash and beans were also cultivated; these crops became known as the **Three Sisters**.

The Great Plains

American Indians of the Great Plains were largely but not exclusively nomadic in character, with an emphasis on hunting and gathering. The American bison, or buffalo, was a vital resource, providing supplies that fostered the continued existence of these tribes. Hunters used spears, bows, and clubs to bring down buffalo. Buffalo skin tepees were a commonplace form of shelter, and buffalo jerky was used as food. Due to this dependence, the tribes followed the buffalo over their seasonal migration. Other animals, such as deer, did provide resources too. However, some semi-sedentary agricultural societies did exist on the Great Plains, such as the Kaw Nation and the Wichita people.

Gender roles in these nomadic tribes were oriented around hunting and gathering, with men and women playing complementary roles. Men would hunt buffalo, trade, and organize tribal political life. Women made clothing and tanned hides, and oversaw the handling of the family tepee as the tribe followed the herd. Plains women typically had the right to divorce, and their overseeing of the tepee could result in a divorced husband becoming homeless.

Plains Indian Sign Language (PISL) served as a way for many different Great Plains tribes to communicate and trade with one another. Its origin is unknown, but PISL was widely in use by the time of the arrival of the first Europeans. PISL was once used from north-central Canada to northern Mexico, from present day Illinois to the Pacific Northwest.

While American Indians of the Great Plains are often associated with horseback riding, this was a post-1492 cultural development. The horse was only introduced into the Americas during the Columbian Exchange.

The Midwest

Some tribes, located in regions such as the Midwest, were nomadic and could easily move to follow food sources or weather patterns. Others settled more permanently; the most notable of these civilizations is the Mississippian culture and their Cahokia Mounds.

Primarily located in the present-day American Midwest, the Cahokia Mounds are remnants of pre-Columbian cities of the Mississippian culture. The Mississippians existed from approximately the eleventh century to the mid-sixteenth century. Cahokia, their largest city, located near present day St. Louis, is believed to have been an important religious center. The Mississippians lacked a writing system, and due to a general lack of contact with Europeans until Old World diseases had thoroughly disrupted their society, little is known about them in comparison to other American Indian civilizations of their era. The Mississippians worked stone and copper. Their agriculture was centered around maize. They participated in trade networks that stretched from the Gulf of Mexico to the Atlantic, from the Great Lakes to the Rocky Mountains.

The Northeast

American Indians of the Northeast utilized companion planting to perfect their method of cultivating crops (maize, beans, and squash); the cornstalks provided a structure for the beans to grow up, and the squash held moisture in the soil. However, these American Indian societies did not maintain livestock or use technology such as plows. They lacked metal tools or machines prior to European arrival in the Americas. Unlike the Europeans, who had developed systems of maritime navigation, natives traveled on large canoes and rafts, which were unable to safely cross open waters such as the Atlantic and Pacific Oceans.

Even though their societies were economically based on land, native populations did not view land as a commodity that could be turned into a profit. Village leaders allocated plots of land to separate families for seasonal use; while these families owned the right to use the land assigned to them, they did not actually own the land itself. Many tribes would claim specific areas for hunting, but anyone could use unclaimed land. This stood in stark contrast to European societies, especially with the English who placed special emphasis on land ownership. Unlike Europeans, indigenous American Indian populations did not focus on accumulating riches or material possessions; instead, they focused on individuals' social statuses within their kinship groups or tribes.

Many American Indian tribes were matrilineal in that tribal rights, tribal responsibilities, and social stations were determined by the bloodline of the mother (as opposed to that of the father). Both genders, however, contributed to decision making. Because men frequently engaged in hunting, women took responsibility for farming as well as household duties. The Europeans viewed American Indian gender roles to be barbaric. Europeans believed that hunting and fishing were leisure activities, which led to their perception that the native men were weak and a poor source of support for the family. Europeans were also upset that women worked in the fields, given that they interpreted agricultural labor as work meant for slaves.

Five Iroquois tribes formed a political confederation called the Great League of Peace, which annually convened with representatives from the five (later six) groups. This league strove to coordinate Iroquois actions, with the goal of collective action. Along with this assembly, each tribe maintained its individual political system and set of religious beliefs.

Pacific Coast

California boasted a diverse multitude of American Indian tribes, with many dozens of languages and related dialects spoken in this comparably small geographic area alone. This diversity is due to the varied and rich landscape of California. Broadly, the many languages can be divided into two families: the Athapaskan languages and Uto-Aztecan. Due to the richness of the land, the native peoples of California never developed much in the way of agriculture; instead, they practiced forest gardening, while also sporadically renewing the land through controlled fires. Acorns were an important food source for many.

The Pacific Northwest enjoyed a diversity and density of population comparable to California, but there were differences. The salmon was important materially and spiritually to various tribes. Shellfish and root crops were also harvested, with the later cultivated in a form of agriculture.

Economically, the potlatch is notable: it is a gift-giving feast practiced by several Pacific Northwest tribes to celebrate major occasions such as births, funerals, weddings, and the transfer of political titles.

> ✔ **AP Expert Note**
>
> **Be able to identify the differences among American Indian societies**
>
> "American Indian" should be understood as an umbrella term, just as "European American," "Asian American," and other similar terms serve as stand-ins for a wide range of regional nationalities. The AP exam will expect you to be able to draw distinctions between various American Indian societies, especially in relation to how they adapted their way of life based on their surroundings (e.g., agricultural practices, stationary vs. nomadic lifestyles, etc.).

THE COLUMBIAN EXCHANGE

High-Yield

Europeans first discovered and explored the Americas as they searched for a sea route to India, China, and the East Indies islands. Europeans originally set their sights eastward to import tea, porcelain, silk, spices, and the other luxury goods that made up the core of international trade.

Christopher Columbus arrived in the Bahamas in October 1492 and subsequently discovered the islands of Hispaniola and Cuba. During Amerigo Vespucci's trips along the South American coast, which lasted from 1499 to 1502, Europeans realized that they had encountered a continent of which they had had no previous knowledge. Columbus's arrival in 1492 prompted the transmission and interchange of plants, animals, diseases, cultures, human populations (including slaves), and technologies between this continent (the Americas) and Europe. This interchange, known as the **Columbian Exchange**, greatly benefited Europeans while simultaneously bringing catastrophe to American Indian populations and cultures.

Destruction by Disease

Wherever European colonists and explorers settled, native populations succumbed to catastrophic epidemics of European diseases, such as smallpox, typhus, cholera, and measles. Three factors contributed to the virulence of the diseases the Europeans introduced to the New World:

1. Foreign trade and invasions exposed Europeans to many ailments.
2. Throughout the Old World, people lived in densely populated cities, which produced and accumulated more waste. Vermin such as houseflies, rats, and roaches infested cities and carried disease-causing microbes.
3. European, Asian, and African populations lived among large quantities of domesticated animals such as cattle, goats, horses, pigs, and sheep. These mammals shared parasites with humans, resulting in new diseases.

Some historians estimate that within one decade of their initial contact with Europeans, disease had killed nearly 50 percent of the American Indians, who lacked immunity to the pathogens brought by Europeans. In some tribes, there were so few survivors that those who remained either lost their tribal identity and joined a neighboring tribe or converted to Christianity and assimilated into European society.

Forced Labor Systems

The intense damage caused to the Native American populations not only inhibited their abilities to repel European encroachment, but also prevented colonists from exploiting natives for labor. To compensate for this lost labor, colonists turned to West Africa, where they began the process of importing slaves. While African slavery had been previously used in Spanish colonies such as Cuba and Hispaniola, the American shift to African slave labor dramatically impacted the Atlantic slave trade.

Ecological Changes

While the natives had carefully altered their natural environment through sustainable hunting, gathering, fishing, forest burning, and field clearing, the Europeans dramatically reshaped the American ecosystem. Because the colonists wanted to continue to use European farming methods in the New World, they imported domesticated farm animals, such as cattle, honeybees, horses, mules, pigs, and sheep, as well as domesticated plants like barley, grapevines, grasses, oats, rye, and wheat. They destroyed forests to obtain lumber and establish farms, and their farming activities, such as plowing and grazing by livestock, caused the naturally rich soil to become dry.

For colonists, there was more land to use than there was labor to develop and harvest it, so they took to building fences around their rather small claimed crop fields. They would then allow their livestock to freely wander the surrounding, unclaimed wilderness, where the animals foraged for wild plants, damaging the natural environment that sustained native populations. The unsupervised livestock also trespassed on native fields and ate these fields' crops. Natives slaughtered and ate the unsupervised livestock, for which the colonists demanded compensation. Upon the natives' refusal, colonizers often reacted by invading and setting fire to American Indian villages.

The introduction of the horse during the sixteenth century had a significant impact on the Great Plains Indians. As runaway horses from Spanish exploration parties made their way into the North American Plains, the Plains Indians learned to tame and utilize the horses. Their hunting became much more efficient, and they were able to follow buffalo migration patterns. As a result, the Great Plains Indians adopted a nomadic lifestyle.

Opposing Worldviews

The natives believed that they were more intelligent and resourceful than the European colonists. While American Indian populations were able to distinguish helpful and harmful resources in nature, Europeans were unable to do so. The natives were impressed by the metal and cloth goods that Europeans brought with them to the New World, but they did not understand why the Europeans would manufacture such goods out of "dead matter" instead of using natural materials.

Europeans had extreme views regarding the natives, perceiving them as either "noble savages" who welcomed the Europeans or as uncivilized brutes who fought them. The Europeans' negative descriptions were based on the natives' different religions, uses of land, and gender roles, which many Europeans perceived as backward. Aside from their perception of indigenous people as "other" because they were nonwhite, Europeans believed that indigenous clothing, architecture, weapons, and technologies were primitive. Because the natives did not keep written records and practiced different systems of governance, the Europeans viewed them as unintelligent and inferior.

> ✔ **AP Expert Note**
>
> **Be able to explain how the Columbian Exchange affected developments in early America**
>
> Contact among Europeans, American Indians, and Africans would drastically impact both sides of the Atlantic World. The official exam will require you to understand multiple implications of this Columbian Exchange. For example, indigenous peoples were devastated by widespread epidemics, which the Europeans brought to the New World. Due to the dwindling indigenous population, the Spanish began bringing Africans to the Americas and forcing them to work as slaves. At the same time, foods and animals were shared among cultures, and sometimes indigenous peoples benefited from this exchange, such as the Great Plains tribes incorporating horses into their lifestyle.

EUROPEAN EXPANSION

French Exploration

Originally, French explorers sought to find gold and discover a northwest passage from the Atlantic Ocean to the Pacific Ocean. Arriving in North America around 1524, the French focused mostly on present-day Canada and the upper northeastern United States. For the majority of the sixteenth century, mostly adventurers, fishermen, pirates, and eventually fur traders sailed along America's eastern coast.

French explorers, such as Jacques Cartier and Samuel de Champlain, cultivated friendly business relations with Native Americans, dealing mostly in beaver pelts. These vast trade networks spanned the upper Northeast down the Mississippi River to current-day New Orleans. Warfare between American Indian tribes worsened as the French traded among warring groups. The French attempted to establish settlements in Newfoundland and Nova Scotia, but these ventures were thwarted by insufficient organization, inadequate finances, and strong resistance by the native populations.

Dutch Exploration

Those living in the Netherlands during the seventeenth century had two unusual freedoms: freedom of the press and widespread religious tolerance. Amsterdam, the Dutch capital, acted as an asylum for European Protestants who encountered persecution in their homelands. Approximately half a million Europeans migrated to the Netherlands during the seventeenth century, and many of these immigrants helped settle the Dutch colonies in the New World. Like New France, New Netherland was originally an economic endeavor, and its population remained small over time.

Spanish Exploration

The **Treaty of Tordesillas**, signed between Spain and Portugal in 1494, decided how Christopher Columbus's discoveries of the New World would be divided. Because the treaty ensured Spain's claims in the Americas, Isabella and Ferdinand were quick to fund explorers' expeditions to gain riches and "civilize" native populations in present-day Mexico, Peru, and the West Indies. In the **Spanish Requirement of 1513**, Spain asserted its divine right to conquer the New World, stating that its main concern was to convert indigenous peoples to Catholicism. The Spanish colonizers wanted to change American Indians into Christian subjects of the Spanish monarchy.

Men such as Vasco Núñez de Balboa, Juan Ponce de León, Ferdinand Magellan, and Hernán Cortés expanded the treasures of Spain with land, gold, and silver. Spanish **conquistadores** enslaved American Indian populations using the *encomienda* **system**, a labor system in which Spaniards were given a group of American Indians by the Spanish monarchy. The Spanish conquistadores were supposed to care for and convert these American Indians, but they essentially enslaved the natives who were supposedly under their protection.

In 1550, the *encomienda* system was replaced with the *repartimiento* **system**, which stated that those living in native villages were legally free and deserving of compensation for the amount of annual labor they completed. This system rendered indigenous slavery nonexistent; natives were allowed land, received compensation, and could not be bought and sold. However, they were still abused by Spanish authorities. By the end of the sixteenth century, the labor in the Spanish empire consisted of the indigenous populations' forced wage labor and intermittent slave labor by Africans in the West Indies and in parts of the mainland.

The promise of finding novel sources of gold prompted Spanish explorers to venture north into the territory that now forms part of the United States. Spain first colonized Florida, in order to create a military base that could prevent pirates from pillaging the Spanish fleet as it sailed from Cuba to Europe, with gold and silver from Mexico and Peru. The Spanish also hoped to prevent intrusions by other European kingdoms, especially France.

In addition to colonizing Florida, Spain sponsored explorations into what is the modern-day south-western United States. These incursions were generally considered failures because they did not yield discoveries of gold or sources of labor. It was not until 1598 that Juan de Oñate led a group of approximately 400 colonists, missionaries, and soldiers to establish a permanent settlement north of Mexico.

English Exploration

In 1585, Sir Walter Raleigh sent approximately 100 male colonists to Roanoke, a small island off of the North Carolina coast, which was then considered to be part of Virginia. This island was surrounded by perilous sandbanks that protected the inhabitants from Spanish discovery and attack; however, these natural defenses also made it difficult for the English ships to deliver supplies or load commodities. In addition, the soil was sandy and arid, which made it unsuitable for farming and harvesting crops. Two years after the initial settlement, Raleigh and his colleagues sent another

94 colonists, including 17 women and 9 children, to Roanoke. These were the first English families to arrive in the New World.

After venturing to the Caribbean to plunder the Spanish colonies, Raleigh and his men returned to Roanoke in August 1590, only to find its inhabitants missing. Thus, Roanoke is also called "The Lost Colony." Though there were no signs of attack by either the natives or the Spanish, the word *Croatoan*, the name of a nearby island, was carved into a tree.

In 1606, the Virginia Company was incorporated by its investors in London, and King James I granted a charter to colonize and govern Virginia. The Virginia Company, its employ, and English colonists arrived in Chesapeake Bay on April 26, 1607.

> **✔ AP Expert Note**
>
> **Be able to explain why Europeans came to North America**
>
> On the exam, you will be expected to know the varying motivations for European settlement in North America. In the beginning, Europeans were searching for a sea route to Asia. Finding the New World instead, Europeans then became motivated to find new sources of wealth. Some, notably the Spanish, were also motivated by a strong desire to convert the native populations to Christianity. European expansion in the Americas was an intense economic, political, and social competition among the various European nations.

 NEXT STEP: PRACTICE

Go to Rapid Review and Practice Chapter 3 or to your online quizzes on kaptest.com for exam-like practice on this topic.

Haven't registered your book yet? Go to kaptest.com/moreonline to begin.

CHAPTER 13

Period 2: 1607–1754

EUROPEAN COLONIZATION IN THE NEW WORLD

The French, Dutch, Spanish, and English colonizers all had different goals in North America. These differences affected the economic, political, and cultural developments of their colonies. They also shaped how the colonizers interacted with the American Indian populations.

French Colonization

Sponsored by a French fur-trading company, Samuel de Champlain founded Quebec as a trading post in 1608. Almost 20 years later, France's New World territories were home to only 240 colonists, and nearly all of these colonists were male. While these Frenchmen benefited from supply ships from their homeland, they also depended upon the altruism of the indigenous populations in order to survive and prosper. Many intermarried with American Indian women, which was one expression of the French preference for alliances rather than conquest.

Later in the seventeenth century, Louis Joliet and the Jesuit Father Jacques Marquette were the first Europeans to locate and map the Upper Mississippi River. By 1682, French explorer Sieur de La Salle reached the Gulf of Mexico, establishing France's claim to the entirety of the Mississippi River Valley region.

Despite this claim, very few white colonists lived in **New France** by 1700. The French government allowed fewer immigrants than other governments because it feared that more significant colonization would undermine its power in Europe and jeopardize its efforts to form a working relationship with American Indians.

Dutch Colonization

Unlike other European nations, the Netherlands had purely commercial ambitions in the New World. In 1609, while employed by the **Dutch East India Company** to find a northwest passage to Asia, the Englishman Henry Hudson sailed into New York Harbor. Dutch merchants soon followed and regularly exchanged goods with American Indians for furs. After a series of short-lived forts on the upper Hudson, the Dutch established their first permanent settlement at Fort Orange, the site of present day Albany, New York. Similar to the French, the largely male colonists and traders often intermarried with the American Indians.

In 1625, the Dutch designated the town of **New Amsterdam** on Manhattan Island as the capital of their New Netherland. New Amsterdam thus acted as their major New World seaport and government headquarters. New Amsterdam's tolerance of religious practices rendered the colony the most religiously and ethnically diverse colony in North America. However, despite the colony's cultural tolerance and favorable location, it failed to attract enough settlers to compete with the populations of England's surrounding colonies. The Netherlands offered a high standard of living, meaning few Dutch wished to live a harsher existence on "the frontier."

England, by contrast, was comparatively impoverished in this period, creating a push factor for migration. In 1664, during the Anglo-Dutch War, the English took control of New Netherland, which today is part of New York, New Jersey, Connecticut, Delaware, and Pennsylvania. In fewer than 20 years under English rule, the New York colony's population grew from 4,900 to 9,800.

Spanish Colonization

In 1610, Spain settled the capital of New Mexico at Santa Fe, which became the first permanent European settlement in the modern-day southwestern United States. By 1680, the small and relatively defenseless New Mexico population numbered fewer than 3,000. It consisted mostly of *mestizos*, descendants with Spanish and American Indian heritage.

As the seventeenth century progressed, the American Indian population dwindled to approximately 17,000. The relationship between the colonial rulers and the indigenous Pueblo population deteriorated as well. The latter half of the seventeenth century saw an intensified Inquisition—the persecution of non-Catholics—in Spain. This was also reflected in Spain's New World colonies, where Franciscan friars attempted to eradicate Pueblo religious traditions by burning their idols, masks, and other sacred objects. These aggressive attempts at religious conversion further alienated the indigenous people.

The start of a prolonged drought, and the Spanish authorities' failure to protect their villages and missionary settlements from Navajo and Apache attacks, contributed to the strife between the Pueblo nation and the settlers. However, as the Pueblos had long been internally divided, the colonists assumed that the Pueblos could never unite against them. In August 1680, a Pueblo man named Popé asserted himself as the head of a coordinated uprising called the **Pueblo Revolt**, which intended to drive the Spanish from the colony and restore the Pueblos' former independence. Two thousand Pueblo warriors attacked isolated farms and missions, killing 400 colonists, including 21 of the 33 Franciscans. The warriors then surrounded Santa Fe, leaving the Spanish with no choice but to abandon the capital. The survivors, along with a few hundred American Indians who had converted to Catholicism, evacuated to the south. In a few weeks' time, nearly 100 years of Spanish colonization in the Southwest was dismantled in the most decisive American Indian victory over Europeans.

English Colonization

Sixteenth-century England was a lesser European power due to its internal turmoil, which had many sources. In 1531, King Henry VIII ended England's alignment with the Catholic Church after the Pope denied the king's request for an annulment of his marriage to Catherine of Aragon. Henry created the Church of England, or the Anglican Church, which was decidedly Protestant. He appointed himself as its head.

It was not until Elizabeth I assumed the throne in 1558 that England began to participate in the competition over the Western Hemisphere. Parliament granted exclusive rights and privileges, known as charters, to Sir Humphrey Gilbert and Sir Walter Raleigh, permitting them to found colonies in North America at their own expense. Raleigh's colony of Roanoke and Gilbert's colony in Newfoundland both failed. **Jamestown** was later established as the first permanent English settlement by the **Virginia Company**.

Between 1550 and 1600, England's population increased from three million to four million, which was not economically sustainable at the time. Additionally, much of the population lived at or below the poverty line. The English believed that land ownership was the basis of liberty, and the New World was advertised as a utopia, where the lower classes could achieve economic independence by obtaining property. Consequently, many people emigrated from England in the seventeenth century, relocating not only to North America, but also to Ireland and the West Indies.

Religion, profit, and prestige all played a role in England's early colonization efforts. Emphatically anti-Catholic, England's government strove to free the New World from the Pope's authority, which was aligned with Spain and France. More significantly, England was still a relatively minor European power at the end of the sixteenth century, but the English believed that they could gain power through colonizing the Americas. England sought to rival France and Spain. Those two nations' respective explorations in present-day Canada and South America left the entirety of the land between the two regions open to England.

INDENTURED SERVITUDE

During the seventeenth century, nearly two-thirds of English immigrants were **indentured servants**. These men and women offered up five to seven years of their freedom in exchange for passage to the New World. They could not marry without their master's permission, they could be bought and sold, and they were often subject to corporal punishment. If indentured servants survived, they received payment in the form of freedom dues and were considered to be free members of society.

Bacon's Rebellion

Bacon's Rebellion of 1676 demonstrated the problems inherent in controlling former indentured servants. Virginia's governor, Sir William Berkeley, ruled the colony based on the interests of the wealthy tobacco planters. While tobacco had initially been lucrative for small farmers, tobacco farming began to spread inland, and the governor gave the best tracts of land to the elite. Former indentured servants who had filled their terms could work as tenants or move to the frontier. In addition, Berkeley advocated for good relations with the remaining American Indians. He disallowed the colonists from settling in areas reserved for the natives, and colonists objected to this regulation.

Nathaniel Bacon, a young, newly arrived member of the House of Burgesses legislative assembly, capitalized on the complaints of his fellow backwoodsmen and mobilized them to form a citizens' militia. In 1676, Bacon's militia raided numerous local American Indian villages, massacring their inhabitants. They then defeated Berkeley's forces and set Jamestown aflame. A short time later, Bacon died of dysentery, and the rebellion was finally crushed. In the aftermath, colonial leaders sought to strengthen racially-coded laws, to avoid repeating the interracial solidarity between black slaves and white indentured servants that had helped provide the manpower for Bacon's Rebellion.

SLAVERY

Atlantic Slave Trade

High-Yield

Spain's New World empire significantly altered the global economy, as the Atlantic Ocean supplanted the Silk Road. Silver and gold from conquests flowed into Spain. Other countries sought precious metals in the New World before shifting toward commodities like furs, tobacco, sugar, and spices. Southern colonies in the Americas developed a plantation economy, which relied on the production of crops such as sugar, rice, and tobacco and depended on agricultural laborers.

Eventually, transatlantic trade networks developed. For example, the **Atlantic slave trade** linked Europe, Africa, and the Americas. Through this Triangular Trade, the New World colonies exported raw materials such as sugar and cotton to England. There, these materials were transformed into rum and textiles. Europeans sold these manufactured goods at African ports in exchange for slaves, who would then be sold in the colonies as farm workers, thus completing the triangle. These enslaved men, women, and children were tightly crammed into ships in order to maximize profits, and many succumbed to dehydration and diseases such as measles and smallpox. Approximately 20 percent of enslaved Africans died before reaching the New World, in what was known as the Middle Passage. Most who survived went to work on plantations in Brazil or the West Indies; in fact, fewer than 5 percent of imported African slaves traveled to the North American mainland.

Slavery in the Americas

Several factors, as well as pervasive stereotypes, made Europeans feel justified in enslaving Africans. Africans were familiar with rigorous agricultural labor. Also, unlike indentured servants, African slaves could not claim the rights of Englishmen and had indefinite terms of labor. In addition, unlike American Indian populations, Africans were largely immune to Old World diseases.

Slavery was especially common in the West Indies. During the first half of the seventeenth century, more English immigrants traveled to the West Indies than to North America, and these immigrants forced African slaves to contribute agricultural labor. In 1619, the first Africans to immigrate to North America arrived in Virginia. They were initially treated as indentured servants, with finite terms of labor, which allowed them to acquire freedom. Although there is evidence of blacks being enslaved as early as the 1640s, it was not until the 1660s that laws of Virginia and Maryland explicitly referred to slavery. From the beginning of African residency in the New World, very strict laws governed their behavior and interactions with whites.

Early Slave Rebellions

During the course of the eighteenth century, many black people, particularly recently enslaved young black men, chanced their lives in resistance to the system of slavery. The first major uprising in colonial America occurred in 1712 in New York City, where a group of slaves burned down colonial houses and killed nine colonists. The colonists responded by executing the conspirators in brutal fashion, using torture, starvation, and burning to send a threatening message to the rest of the slave population.

Another uprising occurred in 1739, when a group of slaves in Stono, South Carolina, took control of a store that stocked various weapons. After arming themselves, they marched toward Spanish Florida, beating drums to signal followers and killing any colonists that they encountered, while chanting "Liberty." This **Stono Rebellion**, with proponents eventually numbering over 100, led to the deaths of more than four dozen colonists and as many as 200 African slaves. It also impelled South Carolina's proprietors to create a stricter slave code.

> ✔ **AP Expert Note**
>
> **Be able to explain multiple causes and effects for a given historical development or process**
>
> One of the historical thinking skills you will be expected to demonstrate on the AP exam is causation, which includes determining causes and effects for a given historical development. For example, you should be aware that multiple factors led to the Atlantic slave trade. Colonies in the South developed a plantation economy based on exporting staple crops such as sugar, rice, and tobacco. Due to the dwindling indigenous populations and a lack of indentured servants, along with predominant racial ideologies of superiority and inferiority, Europeans turned to Africa to find an abundant supply of slaves. An extensive network of slave trading then developed between Africa, Europe, and the Americas.

ENGLISH CONFLICTS WITH AMERICAN INDIANS   High-Yield

Unlike their fellow European colonizers, the English were uninterested in intermarrying with American Indians, converting them into subjects of the crown, or exploiting their labor. Instead, the English wanted their land. While indigenous peoples traded with the colonists and traveled through their settlements, the English sought to remain separate from the American Indians.

Many English colonists recognized that American Indians owned the land which their tribes occupied. The English often obtained these areas by conquering a tribe and subsequently forcing that tribe to agree to a treaty. The recurrent English defeats of the American Indians imbued the colonists with a sense of superiority, which led to the most complete displacement of the American Indians by any of the empires that colonized the New World.

The European invasion deeply affected the American Indians who survived the Old World epidemics. They began to incorporate European products such as woven and metal goods, including guns, into their lives. This dramatically altered the way they hunted, fished, and cooked. As the use of European goods in American Indian cultures increased, traditional skills declined.

American Indians at Jamestown

Prior to British arrival, the area surrounding Jamestown was home to more than 12,000 American Indians, who lived in many small agriculture-based communities. Despite the Virginia Company's instructions to convert indigenous peoples to Christianity, relations between the Jamestown colonists and the American Indians were relatively peaceful. This peace was maintained because John Smith knew that the settlers depended on trading with the American Indians. Soon, however, conflict occurred over resources and food, and John Smith was captured by legendary American Indian chief Powhatan. He was saved from an elaborate, and possibly staged, execution ceremony by Powhatan's favorite daughter, Pocahontas, who brokered peace in 1614.

This peace abruptly ended in 1622, when Powhatan's younger brother Opechancanough planned and executed a surprise attack on Jamestown that killed 347 of the approximately 1,200 Virginia colonists in one day. The remaining settlers destroyed the American Indians and their communities, critically altering the balance of power in the region in favor of the English. Despite these events, the Virginia American Indians continued to trade with the English for the remainder of the seventeenth century.

After another American Indian uprising in 1644, the colonists signed a treaty with the surviving peoples, whose settlements had approximately 2,000 inhabitants. According to this treaty, the American Indians were forced to admit their subjugation to the Jamestown colonial government, relocate farther west, and refrain from entering English settlements without permission.

American Indians in New England

New England's American Indian population was approximately 100,000 when the Puritans arrived. While some settlers, such as Roger Williams, believed that the indigenous people should be treated with justice, most believed that American Indians were unholy "savages" with false gods and rituals. While Puritans claimed that they wanted to convert the American Indians, they did very little to accomplish this; the Puritans primarily viewed them as an obstacle to acquiring land.

The Pequot War

New England's coastal tribes, significantly diminished in population by Old World diseases, initially wanted to ally with the colonists to strengthen their standing against rival tribes. In 1636, however, the Pequot tribe killed an English fur trader. After several weeks of fighting, Connecticut and

Massachusetts soldiers burned the principal Pequot village at Mystic. They killed any who attempted escape, and more than 500 men, women, and children were massacred. In a few months, the entirety of the Pequot tribe had been either killed, sold into Caribbean slavery, or given over as rewards to the native allies of the English. The **Pequot War** opened the Connecticut River Valley to English settlement and signaled the colonists' considerable power to other tribes.

King Philip's War

Also known as Metacom's War, **King Philip's War** was an ongoing battle between English colonists and the American Indian inhabitants of the New England region. This war began in the spring of 1675 when Plymouth colonists captured, tried, and hanged three members of the Wampanoag tribe, to punish these American Indians for killing a tribe member who had served as an informant for the English colonists. In retaliation, American Indian warriors attacked colonial settlements. By the fall, they had attacked over half of the region's towns and fully destroyed a dozen. However, American Indian resistance collapsed by the summer of 1676. Metacom, whom colonists referred to as "King Philip," was executed. The English victory expanded their access to land that was previously inhabited by the American Indians.

> ✔ **AP Expert Note**
>
> **Under the complexities of the early conflicts between European colonists and American Indians**
>
> Some of the major early conflicts include the Pueblo Revolt, the Pequot War, and King Philip's War. As you may recall from earlier in this chapter, the Pueblo Revolt was an uprising of the Pueblo people, led by Popé, against the Spanish colonizers in Santa Fe. The Pequot War and King Philip's War, both of which occurred in New England, resulted from escalating tensions between the English colonists and American Indian populations. It is important to understand that interactions between European colonists and American Indians were complex, often built upon mutual misunderstandings about the other culture's way of life, as well as ongoing conflicts regarding land use, resources, and political sovereignty.

THE DEVELOPMENT OF ENGLISH COLONIAL SOCIETIES IN NORTH AMERICA

The Chesapeake and Jamestown High-Yield

Jamestown, founded in 1607 with an initial population of 104 colonists, was located next to a swamp that contained malarial mosquitoes and pathogens that caused typhoid and dysentery. By the end of the colony's first year, approximately half of the colonists had died. New colonists arrived in 1608, increasing the population; however, after the "Starving Time" winter of 1609 to 1610, only 60 settlers remained.

The colony would have failed completely had it not been for the rigorous leadership of John Smith, whose ironclad rule required colonists to partake in forced labor. Even when Smith returned to England in 1609, due to a gunpowder explosion injury, his successors continued his regime.

The Virginia Company soon decided to forgo its search for gold and instead find a commodity to market in Europe and attract more colonists. To accomplish the latter, the Virginia Company established its use of the headright system in 1618, giving 50 acres of land to any settler who paid for their own—or someone else's—passage to the New World.

In 1619, the Virginia Company established the House of Burgesses, which became the first elected legislative assembly in the New World and served as a political model for subsequent English colonies. However, the House of Burgesses had its limitations; only landowners could vote and only the Virginia Company and the governor could rescind laws.

Early Virginia had minimal familial life. Women who immigrated often came as indentured servants and had to complete their term of service before they could marry and start families. Both married and unmarried women had certain rights, however. If a married woman's husband died before she did, she was entitled to one-third of her husband's property. Unmarried women had independent legal identities and could conduct business.

In 1624, the Virginia Company had not profited from the colony. Despite sending 6,000 settlers, the white population numbered only 1,277 colonists. The company conceded its charter, rendering Virginia the first royal colony whose governor was appointed by the crown.

The Tobacco Boom

In 1611, John Rolfe, an influential Virginian leader, introduced his fellow farmers to tobacco cultivation, which soon became the English colonists' substitute for the gold they had not found. By 1624, more than 200,000 pounds of tobacco were being cultivated in Virginia. In 1664, that amount increased to approximately 15 million pounds.

The crown earned a profit from the crop's taxes. The tobacco boom also fostered an aggressive entrepreneurial spirit and made the colony require more land and more laborers. For the majority of the seventeenth century, these laborers were young men who came to the New World as indentured servants.

Maryland

Maryland was founded in 1632 as a proprietary colony, a colony in which the crown allotted land and governmental command to one person. In Maryland's case, this person was Cecilius Calvert (more commonly known as Lord Baltimore). Lord Baltimore wanted to govern the colony as a haven for his fellow Catholics, who faced persecution in England. The hope was that Protestants and Catholics could harmoniously coexist in Maryland. Even though the colony's population was predominantly Protestant, Lord Baltimore's appointed officials were Catholic. He believed most colonists should have no say in governmental procedures or rulings, even though the Maryland charter guaranteed that all colonists have the same rights and advantages as English citizens.

In 1689, after the ousting of James II, a group of Protestant rebels decided that Lord Baltimore had grossly misled Maryland. This decision prompted William of Orange to revoke the charter and establish a government dominated by Protestants rather than Catholics. After this overthrow, Maryland Catholics were not allowed to vote or hold office, and they would not be free to practice their faith until after the American Revolution.

New England Puritans

Puritanism, which emerged in England during the late sixteenth century, eventually described both a religious code and a societal organization. **Puritans** believed that their religious and social structures were ideal. They thought that the Church of England's ceremonies and teachings were too reminiscent of Catholicism and that true believers ought to read the Bible for themselves and listen to the sermons of an educated clergy.

During the 1620s and 1630s, English citizens thought that Charles I was reinstating ceremonies that resembled those of the recently replaced Catholicism. That shift, coupled with the Church of England's dismissal of Puritan ministers and censorship of their writings, encouraged Puritans to emigrate to the New World. They sought freedom to worship and to live in a society that adhered to their own Christian beliefs and principles.

An important political aspect of the New England colonies was that political power became based in participatory town meetings. These meetings were modeled after the system of church government for Puritans, where each local church was independent. Over time, these meetings evolved into a form of local direct democracy, establishing a strong democratic tradition for the New England states.

The Pilgrims

The first Puritans to arrive in the New World were the Pilgrims, a minority group of Puritan separatists who had completely abandoned the Church of England to form their own independent churches cleansed of any lingering Catholicism. In 1607 and 1608, they immigrated to the Netherlands, but the Pilgrims soon feared that living in Netherlands was corrupting their children. By 1620, 102 Pilgrims sailed for Virginia aboard the *Mayflower* from England. They were blown off course during the journey, but eventually settled in southern Massachusetts and founded the colony of **Plymouth**.

Before arriving in America, the Pilgrims drafted an agreement to establish a secular body that would administer the leadership of the colony. This document, known as the **Mayflower Compact**, was the first written form of government in the modern-day United States.

The Pilgrims founded their colony at an abandoned native settlement. Having landed six weeks before winter without sustenance or livestock, only about half of the Pilgrims survived that winter. The Pilgrims developed a permanent settlement with the help of the local remaining natives. One American Indian in particular, Squanto, had previously learned English after he had been captured and transported to England. Squanto showed the Pilgrims how to plant corn and where to fish. Having survived to the autumn of 1621, the Pilgrims invited their native allies to a harvest celebration, which is now considered to be the first Thanksgiving.

Puritan Society

The Puritans organized themselves into self-governing towns, which each had their own congregational church. The **Massachusetts Bay Company** owners immigrated to America, transforming their commercial charter into a kind of government, to rule the colony without interference or influence from non-Puritan outsiders. Only full church members could vote; to be a full church member, one had to attest to a conversion experience. In 1641, the Massachusetts General Court issued a Body of Liberties that delineated the liberties and duties of Massachusetts settlers as outlined by the social order, which Puritans believed to be a result of God's will. The Body of Liberties allowed for free speech, assembly, and due process under the law, but it also authorized the death penalty for the worship of false gods, blasphemy, and witchcraft.

Puritans believed in domestic male authority as well as in limiting married women's legal and economic liberties. A patriarch's control over his wife, children, and servants was deemed the foundation of social security. A woman's responsibility as a wife and a mother was the basis of her identity. While women were cast lower in sociopolitical spheres, they were considered the spiritual equals of men and were allowed to be full church participants.

The Great Migration

The Massachusetts Bay Company was founded in 1629 by a collective of London financiers. They were advocates of the Puritan cause and wanted to profit from American Indian trade in North America. Thus began the **Great Migration of the 1630s**, during which Puritan families ventured across the Atlantic Ocean, seeking religious freedoms and new beginnings. By 1642, approximately 20,000 Puritans had immigrated to Massachusetts.

The Massachusetts Bay Colony's population grew rapidly, because its colonists had a balanced gender distribution and because its climate seemed hospitable to Western Europeans. By 1700, it is estimated that New England's white population was significantly greater than that of the Chesapeake and West Indies possessions combined.

In 1692, a group of young girls in Salem, Massachusetts, began having fits and complained of being pricked by invisible pins. The girls then began to accuse older, wealthy members of the community of witchcraft, leading to mass hysteria in Salem. By the end of the **Salem witch trials**, 20 people were executed, 5 others died in prison, and the prestige of the traditional Puritan clergy was damaged beyond repair.

Religious Conflict in New England

In 1631, Protestant theologian Roger Williams immigrated to Massachusetts and advocated for the separation of church and state as well as the retreat of colonial congregations from the Church of England. He believed that government involvement in religion amounted to forced worship. Because his theories opposed common European values, Williams was banished from Massachusetts in 1636. He and his followers ventured south and established the colony of Rhode Island. Rhode Island had a more democratic government than Massachusetts did. Also, Rhode Island lacked an established church or a stipulation to attend church.

Anne Hutchinson and her husband followed their minister from England to Massachusetts in 1634. Hutchinson soon started hosting meetings during which she asserted that the local ministers were erroneous in believing that good deeds and church attendance saved one's soul. She believed that faith alone merited salvation. She was soon condemned for this belief, as well as for her claims that God had spoken to her directly rather than through the proper channels (such as the clergy). Banished, she and her followers moved to Rhode Island and then to New York.

The prominent Puritan leader Thomas Hooker founded a settlement at Hartford, Connecticut, in 1636, also after dissenting with the Massachusetts authorities. The **Fundamental Orders of Connecticut**, the first "constitution" in colonial America, fully established the Hartford government in 1639. While it modeled itself after the government of the Massachusetts Bay Colony, the document called for the power of government to be derived from the governed, who did not need to be church members to vote.

The English in New York

After the English seized control of New York from the Dutch, many colonists asserted that they were being denied the given rights of Englishmen. In response to these complaints, an elected assembly was called and drafted in 1683. The **Charter of Liberties and Privileges** mandated elections, in which male property owners and freemen could vote every three years. The charter also reinforced traditional English liberties such as trial by jury, security of property, and religious tolerance for Protestant churches.

The Carolinas

In 1663, Charles II gave eight landholders the right to found an English colony to Florida's north, to block further Spanish expansion. Seven years later, the first settlers in the region established Carolina, which began as a branch of Barbados, the richest plantation island in the Caribbean in the seventeenth century. Because of Barbados's small size, there was not enough land for the next generation, prompting wealthy planters to seek opportunities in Carolina.

Even before arriving, the proprietors issued the **Fundamental Constitutions of Carolina** in 1669. They aimed to create a feudal society composed of nobles, serfs, and slaves. Four-fifths of the land was owned by the planters. Colonial leaders established an elected assembly and a headright system to attract immigrants, who were allowed to own the remaining land. However, they also allowed for religious tolerance, both for Christian dissenters and Jewish people.

Pennsylvania

Pennsylvania was founded by William Penn, who wanted it to be a colony that promoted freedom of religion and a place where American Indians and settlers would be able to coexist in peace. These beliefs stemmed from Penn's membership in the Society of Friends (the **Quakers**). The Quakers advocated that everyone was equal, including women, Africans, and American Indians. Accordingly, Pennsylvania had no established congregation, and Pennsylvanians were not required to attend religious services. Even though personal faith was not monitored by the government, public conduct was; swearing, inebriation, and adultery were outlawed.

Penn owned all of the colony's land and sold it to settlers at low costs, instead of developing a headright system. The religious tolerance, excellent climate, and low cost of land appealed to immigrants from across Western Europe. Pennsylvania's popularity and accessibility resulted in a decline in the number of indentured servants who immigrated to the Chesapeake. This decline resulted in a labor shortfall, which was later filled by African slaves.

Georgia

In the mid-eighteenth century, rice cultivation spread into the land that now encompasses modern-day Georgia. James Oglethorpe, a wealthy reformer, founded Georgia in 1733 as a haven for those who had been imprisoned in England as debtors. London approved the colony in hopes that it would shield Carolina from the Spanish Floridians and their native allies. Georgia's proprietors initially banned slavery and alcohol from the colony, which led to many disputes among settlers. In 1751, however, the colony was surrendered to the crown, which repealed both bans.

CHARACTERISTICS OF ENGLISH COLONIAL SOCIETIES

The social structure of the English colonies closely modeled that of England's towns. Stratification existed in the early years of the English colonies and became more apparent as the seventeenth century came to a close. The influx of more affluent immigrants and the continued development of the plantation economy in the South further increased this economic inequality. The Puritans in New England viewed wealth and success as a sign that one was a member of the elect. In the South, social stratification had been carried over from the old feudal society of England, led by men such as Virginia's governor, Sir William Berkeley.

The middle colonies did not have the same social rigidity as New England and the Chesapeake. Members of the middle classes enjoyed the diversity, acceptance, and religious tolerance of the middle colonies. The elite in New England and the middle colonies were made up mostly of successful merchants. The majority of colonists were involved in agriculture; many were subsistence or tenant farmers.

The division of labor in most English colonies was clearly delineated by gender. Men were mainly responsible for labor outside the home. Women were responsible for care of the homestead and child rearing and had very few rights or legal recourse. Family was very important to the economic and social well-being of colonial societies. On average, colonial citizens married and bore children at a much younger age than Europeans did. More children meant more hands to tend the farm and, therefore, greater earnings for the colonial family.

English Colonial Economies

By the mid-1600s, it became clear to English authorities that they could profit from the New World colonies. **Mercantilism**, the theory that a government should control economic pursuits to further a nation's power, emerged. It defined the role of the colonies: to export raw materials to, and import manufactured goods from, England.

In 1651, the English Parliament, then led by Oliver Cromwell, passed the Navigation Acts, which intended to supersede Dutch control of international trade. According to these laws, colonial commodities such as tobacco and sugar (the most profitable goods) had to be exported to England in English ships and sold in English ports before they could be re-exported to other nations' markets. This helped spur the development of the English shipping industry. Over time, it also led to increasing resentment among politically active American colonial merchants.

Political Changes in England

The year 1688 brought the Glorious Revolution to England, with the overthrow of King James II. Parliament replaced the Catholic monarch with his Protestant daughter Mary II and her Dutch husband, William III of Orange. American colonists became excited, as the removal of James II signaled the end of his repressive measures that limited colonial self-governance. Uprisings in several colonies erupted. With William and Mary now at the helm, American colonists mistakenly believed that Protestant-ruled England would step away from the harsh policies that Parliament had instituted during James II's reign. Unfortunately for the colonists, Parliament continued restricting their ability to establish self-rule. English governors worked quickly to quell the unrest in the colonies, but the relationship between the colonists and their mother country had already been damaged.

The English crown replaced the Massachusetts charter in 1691, demanding that property ownership, not church membership, be the qualification for voting in General Court elections. This led to Massachusetts's status as a royal colony, which forced its inhabitants to follow the English Toleration Act of 1689. This document called for the free worship of most Protestants, not only Puritans.

The Great Awakening

High-Yield

By the early eighteenth century, many colonists had separated from the traditional Calvinist teachings that had once been the cornerstone of the Puritan faith. Moreover, thousands of frontier settlers had little, if any, access to churches and religious services. In the late 1730s, a wave of preachers began delivering sermons that emphasized personal and emotional connections to God. Religious fervor spread across the colonies, with large revivals meeting under tents in the outskirts of towns. This religious movement was called the **Great Awakening**. Preacher Jonathan Edwards is credited with inciting it in 1734, with sermons that encouraged parishioners to repent of their sins and obey

13

God's word in order to earn mercy. He delivered his most famous sermon, "Sinners in the Hands of an Angry God," in 1741.

Emotional sermons evolved after Edwards with other New Light preachers, such as English-born George Whitefield. Whitefield and others traveled through the colonies, speaking to large crowds about the "fire and brimstone" eternity that all sinners would face if they did not publicly confess their sins. Whitefield also undermined the power and prestige of Old Light ministers by proclaiming that ordinary people could understand Christian doctrine without the clergy's guidance.

The Great Awakening affected the colonies in several ways. New sects and divisions arose within the Protestant faith. This helped spur religious tolerance, because no one faith could continue to dominate its competitors. Many universities, such as Princeton, were founded to educate New Light ministers.

✔ **AP Expert Note**

Be able to discuss how religion impacted American life

On the AP exam, you may encounter questions regarding how religion was interwoven into many aspects of American life. For example, it served as a pull factor that drew groups to America and to various colonies, based on government policies and religious tolerance. It was also a unifying factor between many colonists and England; this cultural tie was disrupted during the Great Awakening when, for one of the first times, all of the Thirteen Colonies could claim a common experience. Some historians believe that this common religious experience was one of the foundations of the democratization of colonial society.

NEXT STEP: PRACTICE

Go to Rapid Review and Practice Chapter 4 or to your online quizzes on kaptest.com for exam-like practice on this topic.

Haven't registered your book yet? Go to kaptest.com/moreonline to begin.

CHAPTER 14

Period 3: 1754–1800

THE SEVEN YEARS' WAR

In 1754, the British and the French were vying for power in North America. The French attempted to deter the British from settling farther west by fortifying the Ohio Valley region. The British hoped to thwart French efforts and assert their imperial domination by driving the French from the North American continent. **The Seven Years' War** began in earnest in May 1754, when the governor of Virginia sent Lieutenant Colonel George Washington and his men to reinforce a colonial post in modern-day Pittsburgh. Washington's forces proved weak in the face of a large French and American Indian force and retreated, finally surrendering on July 3, 1754; the French then renamed the post Fort Duquesne. Recognizing that this was not going to be an easy victory, British officials called a meeting in Albany, New York, to devise a defense plan. This Albany Congress, under the guidance of Benjamin Franklin, constructed the **Albany Plan of Union**, which called for a confederation of colonies to defend against attack by European and native foes. However, the colonial assemblies rejected the plan because they were wary of a central consolidation of power. The British government also rejected the plan, as they felt it allowed for too much colonial independence.

British war efforts were ineffective in the early years of the war due to a combination of poor management, internal divisions, and the strength of the French forces and their American Indian allies. This changed under the wartime parliamentary leadership of William Pitt, future prime minister. He shifted British efforts from colonial skirmishes to the capturing of Canada, with key victories in Louisbourg (1758), Quebec (1759), and Montreal (1760). The result was the monumental **Treaty of Paris (1763)**, in which the British took control of French Canada and Spanish Florida, effectively removing France's presence from North America.

> ### ✔ AP Expert Note
>
> **Know the significant political developments of The Seven Years' War**
>
> The Seven Years' War was a major turning point in North America in multiple ways:
>
> - The British emerged as the dominant colonial power in North America.
> - The British determined that the colonial militias were weak and the colonists could not defend themselves.
> - The colonists, conversely, were proud of their ability to fend off French and American Indian forces, and they resented how British military officers had treated their militiamen.
> - Britain was left with a large amount of debt, which the colonists were not willing to help pay off.

EFFECTS OF THE SEVEN YEARS' WAR

Post-War Conflicts with American Indians

The Spanish and French gave up sizable territories to England following the Seven Years' War, resulting in British control of the entire North American continent east of the Mississippi River. The sudden exit of the French shifted the power dynamics between the English and the American Indians, who had primarily allied with the French during the war.

At the close of the war, American Indians in the Ohio Valley refused to relinquish conquered lands, citing harsh treatment by the British. The Ottawa people, led by Chief Pontiac, attacked the new British colonial settlements from the Great Lakes region all the way to Virginia. The damage to forts and settlements was significant, with many lives lost. British forces were sent to protect the colonies, and Pontiac's Rebellion was finally subdued after 18 months of fighting.

To protect the British colonies from further American Indian incursion, King George III signed the **Proclamation of 1763**, barring American colonists from settling west of the Appalachian Mountains. The British saw this as a quick and easy way to make peace with the American Indian tribes of the region. Colonists, however, were incensed by the crown's interference in their ability to take land they had won in battle. Most colonists simply ignored the Proclamation border and settled west in even larger numbers than before the Seven Years' War.

British Measures to Raise Revenue

Saddled with large debt stemming from multiple wars, the British crown sought to leverage the colonies for economic gain. Beginning with the **Currency Act** in 1764, which limited the use of colonial paper money, the British crown looked to the colonies to relieve some of the tax burden on its homeland citizens. Harsher tax collection began with the passage of the **Sugar Act** of 1764, which raised the previous amount demanded on sweeteners (molasses and sugar). In another blow to colonial autonomy, the **Quartering Act** of 1765 required colonial citizens to provide room and board for British soldiers stationed in America. These acts were actually tame in the eyes of the colonists, however, because they were laxly enforced and rarely affected colonists' everyday lives.

It was not until the passage of the **Stamp Act** in 1765 that colonists became truly aware of the impact of British taxation. The act required that all paper in the colonies, from death and marriage certificates to newspapers, have a stamp affixed signifying that the required tax had been paid. The act was justifiable in the eyes of the British Prime Minister, George Grenville, as he felt colonists were being asked to pay only their fair share of the burden of war.

Colonial Reaction to British Measures

Residents in all Thirteen Colonies reacted to the Stamp Act with disdain. The young Patrick Henry, a lawyer from Virginia, expressed popular colonial sentiment when he stood in the Virginia House

14

of Burgesses and accused the British government of usurping the rights guaranteed to colonists as Englishmen. He encouraged his fellow leaders to insist that Virginians be taxed only by Virginians, not by some distant royal authority.

Farther north, James Otis of Massachusetts, the man most associated with the phrase "no taxation without representation," rallied representatives from nine of the Thirteen Colonies to meet in New York as the **Stamp Act Congress**. This body sent word to England that only colonial legislatures had the authority to tax the colonists. Grenville responded by pointing out that because Parliament governed on behalf of the entire British Empire, the colonists did indeed have representation in Parliament, albeit virtual representation.

Colonial Boycott and the Townshend Acts

England's insistence that the colonists had virtual representation did not sit well, and violent reactions soon spread. The **Sons and Daughters of Liberty**, led by Samuel Adams, intimidated tax collectors by attacking their homes, burning them in effigy, and even tarring and feathering them. The Sons and Daughters also ransacked warehouses that held stamps and burned them to the ground. It became fashionable for colonists to quietly protest the Stamp Act by boycotting British goods, wearing homespun clothing, and drinking Dutch tea. The boycotts negatively impacted British trade, and Parliament was ultimately forced to repeal the Stamp Act in 1766. In its place, however, the British passed the **Declaratory Act**, which maintained the right of the crown to tax the colonies in the future.

The new Chancellor of the Exchequer (treasury), Charles Townshend, decided to punish the rebellious colonies by instituting a revenue plan of his own. The **Townshend Acts**, passed in 1767, imposed harsher taxes on the purveyors of imported goods such as glass, paper, and tea. In addition, a special board of customs officials was appointed to enforce writs of assistance, which allowed customs officials to search colonial homes, businesses, and warehouses for smuggled goods without a warrant from a judge. The colonists were slower to react to the Townshend Acts than they were to the Stamp Act, but opposition grew. A series of essays by Pennsylvanian John Dickinson, called "Letters from a Farmer," rekindled interest in the issue of taxation without representation. Samuel Adams was consequently to pen the Massachusetts Circular Letter in 1768, demanding that the Townshend Acts be immediately repealed. The letter was copied and distributed throughout the colonies, sparking the rejuvenation of boycotts of British goods. Wishing to avoid the economic troubles caused by the Stamp Act, the new prime minister, Lord Frederick North, repealed the Townshend Acts in 1770.

Boston's Responses to Taxation

The colonies and Britain maintained relatively peaceful relations between 1770 and 1772, with one notable exception. The residents of Boston were particularly angered by the enforcement of the Quartering Act. Eventually, a crowd of disgruntled Bostonians began to harass the troops guarding the customs house by throwing rocks and frozen oysters. The guards fired upon the crowd, killing five and wounding six protesters. The event became known in the colonies as the **Boston Massacre**.

Aided by the **Committees of Correspondence**, Adams and other colonials circulated letters of protest against British policies. A favorite event of the propagandists was the *Gaspee* **Affair**. The *Gaspee* was a British warship commissioned to capture vessels carrying smuggled goods before they reached the colonies. The *Gaspee* ran aground on the shores of Rhode Island, to the delight of some members of the Sons of Liberty. Dressed as American Indians, the colonists boarded the ship, marched its crew to shore, and set fire to the boat. The event was celebrated and retold throughout coastal colonial towns as a victory for the tax-burdened consumer.

The year 1773 brought renewed conflict to the British colonies with the passage of the **Tea Act**. Even though the new act actually lowered the price of tea, colonists were wary of any British attempt to collect revenue, and they refused to purchase the tea. As a new shipment of tea sat in Boston Harbor awaiting unloading, a group of colonists, again dressed as American Indians, boarded the ship, broke open the crates, and dumped the tea into the water. Colonists were divided as to whether this was a justified protest against oppression or simply a childish destruction of property.

Prime Minister North was not pleased by the news of the **Boston Tea Party** and decided to punish the city. He persuaded Parliament to pass legislation that would close Boston Harbor until the tea was paid for and to revoke the charter of the colony of Massachusetts. This would put the colony under the control of the crown and expand the scope of the Quartering Act, allowing soldiers to be boarded in private homes. In addition, Parliament passed the **Quebec Act** (1774), which allowed the former French region to expand its borders, taking away potential lands from colonists in the Ohio River Valley. Even more offensive to the colonists, the Quebec Act also allowed Quebec citizens to practice Catholicism freely. Enraged, the colonists nicknamed these acts the **Intolerable Acts**.

THE AMERICAN REVOLUTION

`High-Yield`

The Colonies Organize: The First Continental Congress

The Intolerable Acts (also called the Coercive Acts) prompted colonial leaders to quickly organize. Representatives from all but one of the Thirteen Colonies traveled to Philadelphia in September of 1774 to discuss acceptable forms of protest. Delegates' reactions ranged from conservative proposals to radical statements on the liberties of the colonies. One thing was clear: the delegates needed to send a strong message about colonial rights by demanding that Britain repeal the Intolerable Acts. Colonial leaders also urged the colonies to expand military reserves and organize boycotts of British goods in the meantime.

The Continental Congress sent the **Declaration and Resolves** to the king, urging him to correct the wrongs incurred by the colonists while simultaneously acknowledging the authority of Parliament to regulate colonial trade and commerce. The Congress also created the Association, which called for boycott committees throughout the colonies to incur economic damage to Britain. Lastly, the delegates agreed to meet again in May of 1775 if their grievances had not been remedied by the crown. The king and Parliament did not respond to the demands of the **First Continental**

Congress, as doing so would have legitimized the Congress's claim to wield political power. Before the congressional delegates could meet again, war would break out between American militiamen and British soldiers.

The Fight Begins

Having borne the brunt of British punishment, the citizens of Massachusetts were ready to revolt. British general Thomas Gage, now the governor of Massachusetts, ordered his men to seize armaments and arrest rebels in the town of Concord. As the large force of British soldiers marched to carry out his orders, a forewarned group of American militiamen (known as *minutemen* for their ability to be ready at a minute's notice) assembled in nearby Lexington to face the British soldiers. "The shot heard around the world" was fired at that fateful encounter on the Lexington Green. The **American Revolution** had begun. After losing eight men and finding themselves grossly overmatched, the American minutemen retreated. After the British inflicted minimal damage on Concord, however, the minutemen were able to force the British to retreat back to Boston, killing about 250 British soldiers by the day's end.

After fortifying the area around Boston, the minutemen found themselves embroiled in an intense battle for Bunker Hill on June 17, 1775. Even though the colonists lost the battle, they celebrated the massive casualties they were able to inflict on the most powerful military force in the world. Perhaps most importantly, the king officially declared the colonies in rebellion, a proclamation tantamount to a declaration of war. Shortly thereafter, the king hired Hessian mercenaries from Germany, known for their ruthlessness in battle, to invade the colonies. For Patriots, the conflict with Mother England had always been a family affair. When the Hessians entered the picture, the colonists increasingly saw the British motive for war as one of annihilation.

At the beginning of the war, England was the heavy favorite. With the most powerful navy in the world, ample money, and a plentiful supply of recruits, it seemed almost certain that the British would win a quick and decisive victory over the colonists. However, the colonists were able to take advantage of certain British weaknesses. For example, the British troops were a long distance from their own country. Thus, orders from above, munitions, and fresh soldiers took a long time to arrive. The Americans, on the other hand, had leadership with extensive battle experience and a greater understanding of the terrain of the battlefield. However, the colonials, too, faced challenges: infighting among colonies vying for positions of power, sinking morale of the Continental troops due to lack of wages, and shrinking war supplies all threatened to derail the war effort.

The Second Continental Congress

Keeping their promise to reconvene, delegates from all of the Thirteen Colonies met again in Philadelphia in May 1775 to discuss their next steps. Even with skirmishes occurring nearby, the delegates held widely varied opinions regarding the colonial position. Those from the New England colonies tended to be much more radical, insisting on complete independence. Those from the middle colonies wanted to reopen negotiations with Britain. Either way, it was clear that the Continental

14

Congress needed to arrive at a consensus. Virginia's native son, George Washington, was appointed as the head of the Continental Army; this was a strategic move on the part of Northern delegates as the Southern colonies would be inspired to rally behind the war effort. The Congress drew up the Declaration of the Causes and Necessities of Taking Up Arms, which justified the raising of a professional colonial military force and urged King George III a second time to consider colonial grievances. As a last gesture of peace and a preventive measure against total war, the Congress voted to send the Olive Branch Petition to Britain in July 1775. This document reasserted colonial loyalty to the crown and asked King George III to intervene with Parliament on the colonies' behalf. The king, however, refused once again to recognize the legitimacy of the Congress.

In January 1776, Thomas Paine, a recent English immigrant to the colonies, published a pamphlet that would bring the radical notion of independence to the mainstream. Titled *Common Sense*, the pamphlet used **Enlightenment** philosophy to argue that it would be contrary to common sense to allow British injustices to continue. Members of the Congress read the pamphlet with great interest and integrated Paine's arguments into their deliberations in Philadelphia.

As a year of discussion and deliberation came to a close, the **Second Continental Congress** decided that independence was the only acceptable result. On June 7, 1776, Richard Henry Lee called for a resolution declaring the colonies independent of Britain. A committee was then chosen to draft a declaration document that would reiterate the June 7 resolution. Thomas Jefferson and four other delegates quickly set to work on writing the document that came to be known as the **Declaration of Independence**. It contained a preamble that heavily reflected Enlightenment philosophy regarding natural rights, as well as 27 grievances and charges of wrongdoing directed at the crown and Parliament. This declaration was the colonies' official break from England, making the United States a country in its own right.

Independence, Not Dependence

However, the colonies could not mount a unified front against the British. Many historians believe that colonial citizens were divided roughly into thirds: one-third siding with Great Britain (**Loyalists**), one-third actively engaged in the fight for independence (**Patriots**), and one-third remaining neutral. Therefore, one of the major challenges for the new nation was limiting disagreement among its own citizens.

> ✔ **AP Expert Note**
>
> **Understand the varying motivations that influenced colonial loyalties**
>
> The AP exam will expect you to know the political, economic, and social factors that helped determine which side colonists landed on. Patriots were activists for independence from the British Empire. They were mostly young New Englanders and Virginians who did not have significant status in society. Loyalists disagreed with the Patriots and wanted to preserve ties with England. They were often older, wealthy, educated citizens of the Middle or Southern colonies whose allegiance to England benefited their social, economic, and/or political standing. There were also colonists who attempted to remain neutral, or who lived in areas like the West that were relatively unaffected by the war.

The beginning of the war was not auspicious for General Washington. After losing New York City in 1776, Washington made some headway by winning several small battles in New Jersey in 1777. Other American generals, Benedict Arnold and Horatio Gates, are credited with winning the most important battle of the Revolution: the **Battle of Saratoga** (October 1777). American forces were able to cut off the British charge on New England and secure the surrender of British General Burgoyne's army, thus convincing the French of America's military viability. The entry of the French on the side of the Americans in 1778, and the Spanish and Dutch soon thereafter, turned the tide of the war in America's favor.

After surviving one of the coldest winters (1777–1778) on record at Valley Forge, Pennsylvania, Washington's troops took advantage of the depleted British forces and won multiple battles on their march to Virginia. The last major battle of the Revolution was waged at Yorktown in 1781. There, Washington's men, with the assistance of French forces, secured the surrender of British general Charles Cornwallis's regiment. Tired of the strain of the war on their economy, British citizens ousted their Tory government in favor of the Whigs, who were willing to negotiate a peace with the colonists.

At Paris in 1783, the warring sides came together to deliberate and reach a peace settlement. In the **Treaty of Paris (1783)**, the Americans agreed to repay debts to British merchants and promised not to punish Loyalists who chose to remain in the United States. The treaty also included a formal recognition of the United States as a country, and it set the geographic boundaries between the British Empire and the United States. Historians have noted that the Treaty of Paris (1783) greatly expanded the borders of the United States, which now stretched west all the way to the Mississippi River.

✔ **AP Expert Note**

Be able to distinguish between important events, some of which may have similar names.

Two major treaties were negotiated in the eighteenth century, both known as the Treaty of Paris.

The Treaty of Paris (1763):

- **Ended the Seven Years' War (French and Indian War)**
- **Increased Britain's land holdings**
- **Established Britain as the major European power in North America**

The Treaty of Paris (1783):

- **Ended the Revolutionary War**
- **Increased U.S. land holdings**
- **Established the United States as its own sovereign country**

AMERICAN INDIANS DURING AND AFTER THE REVOLUTION

During and after the American Revolution, different American Indian tribes espoused a variety of stances in regard to the burgeoning nation. Some remained neutral, and others sided with Americans. Many American Indian tribes also tried to build political alliances with each other and

14

with Europeans who had a presence in North America. The main goal of these attempted alliances was to keep and protect native land by controlling the migration of white settlers.

During the Revolution, some tribes, particularly those in the mid-Atlantic region such as the Cherokee, attempted, unsuccessfully, to attack frontier settlements and preemptively defend their land. In New England and other northern states, however, many American Indians supported their colonial neighbors during the Revolutionary War, with some even volunteering as minutemen.

One of the most notable conflicts took place in and around the Ohio River Valley after the American Revolutionary War. This conflict has been called several names: the **Northwest Indian War**, the Ohio War, and "Little Turtle's War."

In the Treaty of Paris, the British had officially ceded the lands that would eventually form Ohio and Indiana to the new United States. However, many American Indian tribes still lived in the region, and the British continued to maintain a military presence in the region. The British openly sold firearms and alcohol to the Miami Confederacy, a group of eight American Indian nations whose response to American encroachment on their lands was to terrorize settlers.

The war chief of the Miami Confederacy, Little Turtle, informed Americans that the Confederacy considered the northwestern boundary of the newfound United States to be the Ohio River, not the boundary agreed upon with the British in the Treaty of Paris. In response, the United States sent expeditions in 1790 to quell the increasing violence. What ensued was one of the greatest military disasters in American history, and the single largest American Indian victory over the United States. Little Turtle's troops wiped out U.S. forces at the Battle of the Wabash, an incident more popularly known as St. Clair's Defeat; 632 U.S. soldiers were killed, and dozens more soldiers and camp followers were wounded. The United States military of the day had essentially been destroyed in a single battle.

While the Miami Confederacy paused to deal with poor harvests that year, confident that it had a strong position for peace talks, the United States government undertook several actions. The first Congressional investigation committee was convened to investigate St. Clair's Defeat. George Washington convened the first cabinet meeting to discuss the response to the battle as well. The remnants of the U.S. military were reorganized in the Legion of the United States, whose four sublegions would later form the first four regiments of the modern U.S. Army.

Under the command of General "Mad Anthony" Wayne, a Revolutionary War leader who stressed training of troops and logistics, the Legion would push into the Northwest. The war there would end in 1794, when 3,000 American soldiers won a sweeping defeat of Little Turtle's forces at the Battle of Fallen Timbers. That battle prompted the Treaty of Greenville of 1795, in which 12 tribes ceded vast areas of the Old Northwest to the federal government, including most of what is now Indiana and Ohio. In return, the tribes of the Miami Confederacy were given an initial payment of $20,000 and an annual payment of $9,000.

THE IMPACT OF THE ENLIGHTENMENT

High-Yield

The ideas of political, philosophical, and social thinkers of Europe during the seventeenth and eighteenth centuries had a profound impact on the character and ideologies of many Americans. British philosopher John Locke's theory of natural rights challenged the absolute and divine rule of kings and queens by asserting that all men should be ruled by natural laws (rights derived from basic reason that are independent from any society's laws) and that sovereignty should be derived from the will of those governed. Locke went on to assert that the governed have a responsibility to rebel against a government that fails to protect the natural rights of life, liberty, and property. The emphasis of a social contract between the government and the governed, as well as the concept of majority rule, is clearly reflected in the founding documents produced before and during the Revolutionary period.

Founders, including George Washington, Benjamin Franklin, Thomas Jefferson, and John Adams, were greatly influenced by Enlightenment teachings. With the influence of the writings of philosophers such as the Baron de Montesquieu, who advocated for the **separation of powers**, and Jean Jacques Rousseau, who championed **direct democracy**, enlightened colonials began to emphasize the concept of reason over emotion. This shift in philosophy provided the logical justification for rebelling against a government perceived as directly and deliberately violating their rights.

THE ARTICLES OF CONFEDERATION

Motivated by common political philosophies, colonial leaders set to work building the structures for sovereignty. By 1777, all but three of the colonies had drafted and ratified their own state constitutions. These constitutions attempted to strike a delicate balance between law and order and the protection of natural rights by placing power in the hands of an elected legislature. While the constitutions shared several characteristics of popular sovereignty, such as limiting the power of the governor, states differed widely in other provisions. For example, Pennsylvania's constitution abolished property requirements for voting, while on the other end of the political spectrum, South Carolina imposed much higher property requirements for both voting and holding office.

While colonies were busily forming governments of their own, the delegates to the Second Continental Congress set out to create a national, or federal, government. With slight alterations made to a draft national constitution written by John Dickinson during the First Continental Congress, the **Articles of Confederation** were accepted and sent to the colonies for ratification in 1777. After a dispute between the coastal colonies and inland colonies over the administration of westward lands, the Articles were finally ratified by all of the Thirteen Colonies in 1781. The Articles of Confederation comprised a preamble, 13 articles, and a conclusion, providing a template for government that the infant United States needed. It included the following provisions:

- Each state was sovereign with the exception of specific powers delegated to the confederation government.

- Free inhabitants of each state were entitled to equal rights and could pass unhindered between the states.

- Each state was allocated one vote in Congress and could send a delegation of between two and seven members appointed by state legislatures.

- Only the central government could declare war, make treaties, and borrow money to pay debts; however, it needed nine states to agree before it could do any of these.

- States could not wage war without permission from Congress unless under imminent attack. States could not maintain a peacetime army or navy but were required to keep a ready militia.

- Congress could appoint a president who served no longer than one year per three-year term of Congress.

- To amend the Articles, a unanimous vote was required. To pass laws, a two-thirds majority, or supermajority, was required.

A New Set of Laws

The Articles also established clear policies regarding the settlement and statehood of newly acquired lands to the west. The Land Ordinance of 1785 established the basis for the Public Land Survey System whereby settlers could purchase land in the undeveloped West. In addition, the Ordinance required new townships to set aside a parcel of land reserved for public education and stipulated that the sale of public lands would be used to pay off the national debt. At this time, Congress did not have the power to raise revenue via direct taxation, so this Ordinance created a mechanism for funding public education.

Considered one of the most important legislative acts of the Confederation Congress, the **Northwest Ordinance of 1787** established guidelines for attaining statehood: territories with at least 60,000 people could apply for statehood. If accepted by Congress, the new state would have equal status with other states. Moreover, the Northwest Ordinance banned slavery north of the Ohio River, thereby guaranteeing future free states in the Midwest. In 1803, Ohio was the first state created from the Northwest Territory under the Ordinance.

While these examples show how the Articles provided for the development of the quickly growing nation, the new central government was fraught with complications from the outset. In order to avoid tyranny and abuse of power by the new central government, the Articles did not allow for the taxing of citizens to raise revenue. In addition, the government had no authority to enforce its own laws. While the government could request taxes from the states, it could not enforce tax collection. These apparent weaknesses were deliberate, and they reflected the desire to prevent the reappearance of tyranny so soon after the Revolution; however, by so limiting the strength of the central government, the states created additional challenges. Without tax revenue, large war debts remained unpaid. The American economy was further crippled due to broken trade relationships and a depreciated currency, which drove the new nation into financial crisis. These struggles made the new government appear vulnerable to Europeans and opened the possibility for an invasion by bitter Great Britain or imperialist Spain.

Shays' Rebellion and its Aftermath

While international threats loomed, significant challenges to the strength of the Articles also arose internally. After the war ended, state economies struggled to maintain financial ties with their European business partners; in an attempt to bolster their funds, state governments allowed merchants to impose high demands on customers and borrowers (such as requiring the use of hard currency rather than credit). This strategy was seen primarily in Massachusetts, where the government was dominated by a merchant class that seemingly took advantage of rural farmers to pay off debts.

Angered by these high taxes, debtors' prisons, and continued lack of pay for wartime service, veteran Daniel Shays and a band of Massachusetts farmers rose up during the summer of 1786, demanding tax and debt relief. **Shays' Rebellion** escalated in January 1787 when a mob seized the state arsenal in Springfield. The Massachusetts militia then marched in and quelled the rebellion. Although Shays' Rebellion seemed to be a minor local insurrection, Confederation leaders were concerned about the implications of the event. While Thomas Jefferson saw the rebellion as a sign that "liberty must be refreshed from time to time," other leaders, including George Washington, saw the rebellion as a signal that state constitutions, as well as the Articles of Confederation, must be reformed. With so much emphasis placed on the virtues of a republic, the delegates of Congress had failed to ensure that the states themselves would be able to protect the rights and liberties of their own citizens.

THE CONSTITUTIONAL CONVENTION

High-Yield

To develop provisions for a stronger (and better funded) central government, a convention was called for in Annapolis, Maryland, in 1786. It was sparsely attended, with delegates from only five states, so political heavyweights James Madison and Alexander Hamilton pushed for another convention, this time to be held in Philadelphia the following May. This meeting would become the **Constitutional Convention**.

Postwar Problems

In addition to the economic depression that led to uprisings like Shays' Rebellion, the sovereignty of the United States was also challenged by several European nations and bands of pirates from North Africa. Even though Great Britain promised to respect the sovereignty of the United States, it refused to repeal the Navigation Laws, armed American Indians along the western frontier, and failed to remove troops from posts along the Mississippi River. Spain closed the port of New Orleans to U.S. trade and also armed American Indians in the Southwest. France called for prompt repayment of the war debts owed and further deepened the economic crisis by limiting the ability of the United States to trade in the Caribbean. Taking advantage of the absence of British protection of U.S. shipping in the Mediterranean, North African Barbary pirates attacked merchant ships, often seizing their goods and kidnapping crews.

Because many of these issues were caused or exacerbated by the weak provisions in the Articles of Confederation, 12 of the 13 future states agreed to send delegates to Philadelphia to repair the inadequate Articles. Soon, the meeting shifted from a discussion of the founding document to a construction of a new constitution.

A Secret Meeting

The meeting was composed of well-educated, wealthy men who were familiar with the conventions of republicanism and democracy; most were practicing lawyers and had taken a direct hand in the writing of their own state constitutions. Delegates included Robert Morris, who personally paid over 10 million British pounds to finance the Revolution; Charles Pinckney, who would go on to become governor of South Carolina; and George Mason, who prepared the first draft of the Declaration of Rights in 1776. Some major names did not attend the convention because of overseas business: John Adams was serving as minister to Great Britain; Patrick Henry refused to participate due to his negative feelings about a strong central power; from his desk in Paris, Jefferson approvingly called the meeting a "convention of demigods."

The meeting had been scheduled to begin on May 14, 1787. However, troubles with travel and other engagements kept many delegates from arriving on time. While they were waiting for the others, the delegates from Virginia began working on a proposal that they would present to the full body once it convened. Finally, 55 delegates from all states but Rhode Island met on May 25, 1787, agreeing that all discussions and votes would be kept secret.

Madison Takes Charge

In a unanimous vote, George Washington was elected as president of the convention, but his was by no means the strongest voice at the convention. James Madison, a delegate from Virginia, was well read in the areas of federalism, republicanism, and Lockean theory, and he quickly became the leading voice of the convention. Madison provided the cornerstones for the development of what is now the U.S. Constitution. First, he expressed the need for a central government with power that would exceed the power of the states. Second, he believed in the separation of powers: the executive, the legislative, and the judicial branches of government would be independent of one another but would be held accountable by each. Lastly, Madison outlined the dangers of factions (political parties), saying that a strong national government would have to keep these groups in check. Several of these ideas were widely accepted, but many leaders, such as Thomas Jefferson and George Mason, did not believe that the national government should be supreme to the power of the states and thus able to invalidate state laws. Overall, the members of the convention agreed on several principles; most importantly, they agreed that amending the Articles of Confederation was insufficient and a new constitution must be implemented.

A Great Compromise is Reached

After the decision was made to scrap the Articles and start anew, divisive political, social, and economic issues came to light. First on the agenda was the issue of state representation in the legislative branch. Edmund Randolph and the delegates from larger states sponsored Madison's Virginia Plan, which favored their states. This plan called for representation in both houses to be based solely on population—proportional representation. The smaller states, led by William Paterson, put forth their rebuttal; the New Jersey Plan asked for equal representation, regardless of the number of citizens of a state, in one legislative body (similar to the structure in the Articles of Confederation).

At this point, the discussion was at a standstill, and the convention was close to dissolution. On June 11, Roger Sherman rose with the proposal that membership in one branch of the legislature be based on state population, and the other branch (the Senate) have equal representation for all states, with each state having one vote. At first, Sherman's plan was rejected, but after several more weeks of debate, this **Connecticut Compromise** (also known as the Great Compromise of 1787, or Sherman Compromise) gained support; it was ultimately included in the Constitution. Large states were satisfied because the lower chamber, or the **House of Representatives**, would be composed of members who reflected the population of individual states. Small states were satisfied because representation in the upper chamber, or **Senate**, was composed of membership that was equal regardless of state population. However, large states stood to gain more from this compromise, as revenue bills would originate in the lower chamber, thus possibly easing the tax burden that large states would more likely have to pay.

An Executive Decision and the Three-Fifths Compromise

The delegates also needed to discuss the issue of executive leadership. All of the men present were unwilling to hand the executive branch too much power, but postwar events showed the danger of a weak central authority. After much debate, it was decided that the president would be elected by a representative body rather than by direct popular vote. The delegates worried that the slow diffusion of information would lead to uneducated voters and that citizens would only vote for candidates from their state or region. Several solutions, including election of the president by the House, were proposed and debated; finally, the convention resolved the dispute by choosing to create an **Electoral College**, composed of representatives by state who would cast votes. These delegates believed this would protect the election process from corruption and faction influence. The president was given many more powers than the weak governors of the states. He would command the armed forces, act as chief diplomat, and be able to veto laws made by the legislative branch.

The election of the executive branch was one of the last major issues to be resolved at the convention; however, a major geographic conflict threatened to hold the delegates at an impasse. Southern delegates came from regions with large slave populations. Southerners argued that although these people could not vote, because they were not citizens, they still had to be managed by the state and should thus be counted as part of the population that determined the number of representatives in the House. Delegates opposed to slavery proposed that only free inhabitants of each state should be counted as part of the represented population, which would strengthen non-slave states' standing in the House. The convention considered an amendment proposed to the Articles of Confederation, which would count all noncitizens as three-fifths of their actual number for the purpose of determining tax rates. While that amendment was originally rejected by Southerners because it would hurt them financially, the promise of increased representation led the two sides to agree to this **Three-Fifths Compromise**. Therefore, each enslaved person in the South was counted as three-fifths of a person. In addition, the South conceded to the end of the legal importation of slaves in 1808. Lastly, the Northern and Southern representatives decided on a compromise with regard to trade and taxes by agreeing that Congress could place taxes on imports but not exports.

THE DEBATE OVER RATIFICATION

After the Three-Fifths Compromise, another month of discussion and additional refinement followed. The delegates agreed to assign unresolved questions, including freedom of the press and assumption of war debts, to different committees for resolution. They also finalized several logistical concerns regarding the office of the president, including the length of terms, the office of the vice president, and transfer of specific powers from the Senate to the executive (such as the power to appoint ambassadors).

With their document complete, the delegates to the Constitutional Convention retired to their home states to campaign for **ratification**. Approval from at least nine states was required to ratify the national constitution. As word reached the state governments and citizens that the Articles of Confederation had been thrown out altogether, many feared a return to tyranny. The Constitutional Convention allowed two routes to ratification: a process within the state legislature and a ratifying convention in which delegates were chosen from a state's citizenry to vote on the Constitution. Debate on ratification was generally argued from two sides: those in favor of the Constitution and a strong central government were called **Federalists**, and those in opposition to the Constitution and in favor of strong states' rights were called **Anti-Federalists**.

Several small states, including Delaware and New Jersey, ratified quickly. Pennsylvania was the first large state to adopt the Constitution. By January of 1788, five states had ratified; however, it would take more than two more years for all 13 states to ratify the document, and whether the document would be ratified at all was in question for a significant period of time. Virginia was critical to ratification: it was the most populous state and had the largest concentration of Anti-Federalists, many of them concerned farmers. However, it took less than a month for Virginia's native sons George Washington, James Madison, and John Marshall to persuade Anti-Federalists to ratify the document with the promise of an addition of a **Bill of Rights** that would protect individual freedoms and state sovereignty. To encourage ratification in New York, James Madison, Alexander Hamilton, and John Jay penned a series of 85 powerful essays collectively called the *Federalist Papers*. These papers refuted common doubts about whether a central government could effectively rule such vast territory; one of the more famous letters is Federalist No. 10, which claimed that political parties could not be prevented, but that their influence could be mitigated in a large republic. Soon after New York's vote to ratify, North Carolina and Rhode Island became the last states to ratify the Constitution.

If it had not been for the delay of delegates in arriving to the original convention in May 1787, Federalist Virginians might not have been able to take control of the meeting by presenting their already-prepared Virginia Plan and thus convince the others to discard the Articles. In this respect, the new Constitution and resulting system of federalism was a victory for a very small minority. The addition of the Bill of Rights was the minority's concession to the Anti-Federalists. Congress acted quickly in 1789 to prepare the first twelve proposed amendments. Penned mostly by James Madison, these amendments served to protect states and individuals from possible abuses by the central government. Ten were ratified by the states in 1791, becoming known as the Bill of Rights. There were two additional amendments: the never-ratified Congressional Apportionment Amendment and what became the Twenty-seventh Amendment in 1992.

The 10 Amendments of the Bill of Rights:
1. Freedom of religion, speech, press, assembly, and petition of government for redress of grievances
2. A well-regulated militia and the right to bear arms
3. No requirement for homeowners to quarter soldiers without consent
4. No unreasonable search and seizure
5. Protection from being forced to be a witness against oneself in a criminal case
6. Right to a speedy and public trial by an impartial jury
7. Right to a jury trial and protection from courts overturning a jury's finding of facts
8. Protection from cruel and unusual punishment and excessive fines
9. Acknowledgment that citizens have more rights than those listed here
10. Powers not given to the government or prohibited by the Constitution are given to the states or the people

WASHINGTON'S PRESIDENCY AND THE NEW REPUBLIC

George Washington was instrumental in the adoption of the new Constitution both during and after the Constitutional Convention; while he had expressed some reluctance about taking on the presidency, the delegates had designed the office with Washington in mind. Selected unanimously by the Electoral College, President George Washington took the oath of office on April 30, 1789, in the temporary national capital of New York City. John Adams was sworn in as the first vice president, although the Constitution did not provide a definite job description for that role.

Washington's presidency helped set the precedent for the future of the United States government. For example, according to the Constitution, the president designates departments of the executive branch to assist in government functions. Washington appointed Thomas Jefferson as secretary of state, Alexander Hamilton as secretary of the treasury, Henry Knox as secretary of war, and Edmund Randolph as attorney general. Washington called these four men his *Cabinet* and met regularly with them to confer and gain advice. To this day, presidents regularly call advisory meetings of their Cabinet members.

The smallest section of the Constitution is Article III: the Judiciary Branch. This article applies only to the federal court and is vague with regard to court structure. Therefore, Congress passed the Judiciary Act of 1789, establishing a Supreme Court consisting of one presiding chief justice and five associate justices. The act also provided for the establishment of 13 district courts and three circuit courts of appeal. A clause in the Judiciary Act granted the Supreme Court the power to command any subordinate government authority to take or not take an action that is that authority's legal duty. This clause was declared unconstitutional in the *Marbury v. Madison* case of 1803, as it would grant more power to the Court than permitted by the Constitution. In *Marbury v. Madison*, the Supreme Court ruled that Congress cannot pass laws that are contrary to the Constitution and that it is the judicial system's job to interpret what the Constitution permits.

Hamilton Fixes Finances

Economic problems had plagued the new nation ever since the Treaty of Paris (1783) left the United States saddled with war debts and poor relationships with foreign merchants. Secretary of the Treasury Alexander Hamilton set out to repair the nation's credit and overall financial health at the behest of Washington and Congress. His first Report on Public Credit (1790) recommended that government debts be paid in full in order to create a favorable economic climate; modeled on the British financial system, this structure would pay off government debts with taxes. His Report on Manufactures (1791) promoted the industrialization of the United States and advocated strong protective tariffs for infant industries.

Hamilton's overall financial plan set out to place the United States on firm ground with regard to debt repayment, a stable currency, and a strong federal banking system. The plan aimed to: boost national credit; create a strong financial relationship between federal and state governments; earn revenue through heavy tariffs on imported goods and excise taxes on specific goods; and ensure economic stability by establishing a national bank. Each of these provisions was hotly contested, most strongly by James Madison and the Anti-Federalists. Another controversial provision was Hamilton's suggestion that the federal government assume all state debts. Northern states that had amassed large debts because of the war were thrilled. Southern states, which had successfully paid off most of their debt, did not want to be financially linked to the central government, and opposed contributing to states they suspected had mismanaged their finances. To appease both sides, Hamilton acquiesced to Thomas Jefferson's request to place the nation's permanent capital on the banks of the Potomac River, which straddled the states of Maryland and Virginia.

Geographic tensions were further stoked with the passage of the Tariff Act of 1789, which placed a tariff on imports. Northerners favored a higher rate to protect their manufacturing industry from foreign encroachment, while Southern farmers wanted a lower rate to provide for cheaper consumer goods. Hamilton compromised by setting a rate lower than he preferred while also imposing excise taxes on goods such as whiskey to make up the shortfall in revenue. While the compromise allowed the act to pass through Congress, the excise taxes would become increasingly unpopular in the South.

The **Whiskey Rebellion** tested the new central government's power. Angered by the Federalist government's new economic policies, particularly the excise tax imposed on distilled liquors such as whiskey, farmers in western Pennsylvania turned violent. Much like the Sons of Liberty had done during the pre-Revolutionary era, some of these farmers aggressively protested the tax by tarring and feathering tax collectors or by destroying public buildings, even attacking the home of tax inspector General John Neville. President Washington sent officials to negotiate with the rebels and even rode at the head of an army to suppress the insurgency. The rebels disbanded before the militia arrived, and a fiasco similar to Shays' Rebellion was averted. Even more importantly, the new federal government had proven that it had the power to stop rebellions and maintain peace.

> ✔ **AP Expert Note**
>
> **Be ready to compare and contrast historical developments**
>
> The makers of the AP exam will expect you to be able to make complex connections between historical events. Shays' Rebellion in 1786 and the Whiskey Rebellion in 1794, for example, have multiple similarities but one important difference. Both were both uprisings led by farmers who were upset over what they considered unfair taxation. Shays' Rebellion demonstrated the weakness of the new American government under the Articles of Confederation. The Whiskey Rebellion, occurring during President Washington's administration, was one of the first major tests of the power of the new government, which had been recently established under the U.S. Constitution. In the end, the Whiskey Rebellion protest was quickly suppressed, highlighting the power and necessity of the new federal government.

Disagreement Over the Bank of the United States

The last and most contested part of Hamilton's plan was the establishment of a national bank, the **Bank of the United States**. The federal government would hold the major financial interest in the bank, with private stockholders also contributing. The national treasury would keep its deposits in the bank, keeping the funds safe and available as loanable funds.

Hamilton argued that the "necessary and proper" (or "elastic") clause of the Constitution supported the creation of the bank; this clause holds that Congress has the power to make laws that are necessary and proper to carry out their powers. Hamilton reasoned that the bank would be a reasonable means of carrying out powers related to taxation and borrowing of funds. A "loose constructionist," Hamilton believed that the Constitution granted Congress implied powers beyond those expressly enumerated in the document. Thomas Jefferson, on the other hand, vehemently opposed the bank, stating that the Constitution did not provide for its creation, nor was the bank necessary for the government to carry out its powers. Jefferson was a "strict constructionist," one who believed in the strict interpretation of the Constitution.

While the debate caused Washington to hesitate, he ultimately signed the bill into law. This issue, however, caused the rift to widen between Hamilton and Jefferson, as well as that between the Federalists and Anti-Federalists.

The Rise of the Party System

In fact, Hamilton's financial reforms served as a major impetus for the emergence of a unified opposition party, led by Jefferson and Madison. While Hamilton and the Federalists espoused a conservative ideology that favored strong central government, Jefferson and other liberals championed states' rights and the viewpoint of the common man. The codification of Hamilton's financial plans, many of which would disadvantage Southern farmers, spurred disparate Anti-Federalists to coalesce into a group they named Democratic-Republicans, or Jeffersonian Republicans. The precise date of the party's founding is uncertain, but by the election of 1792, the Democratic-Republicans had vocalized their displeasure with the Treasury department and other Federalist leaders.

Republican Motherhood

Beginning even before the American Revolution and stretching beyond Washington's presidency, a new idea took hold with American women: **Republican Motherhood**. This idea stressed that patriotic women should be raised to both value republicanism and to pass on those republican values to their children. Sons were to be encouraged to serve in government and value liberty. Daughters were encouraged to instill republican values in their own children, receiving more education than was previously common in order to make this a possibility. Many of these newly educated women, instilled with republican values, would later became active in the Second Great Awakening of the nineteenth century; additionally, some would synthesize their political and religious values into abolitionism, forming a major pillar of that cause.

DEVELOPMENT OF FOREIGN POLICY

In addition to building political stability, President Washington and his Cabinet had to respond effectively to the demands of countries around the world. Soon after the new federal government was established, France experienced a revolution of its own. The ensuing political upheaval quickly extended beyond the borders of France and became a world war involving both Britain and the Caribbean. While the American public was largely enthusiastic about potential democratic reforms in their onetime French ally, the **French Revolution** (1789–1793) exacerbated existing political divisions among American leaders. Giving the French revolutionaries assistance as France had done for the Patriots during the American Revolution would strain the already delicate relationship with Britain.

Thomas Jefferson, whose Democratic-Republicans sympathized with the republican ideals of the French Revolution, urged that the United States uphold the provisions of the Franco-American Alliance that had been forged in 1778 during the American Revolution. Alexander Hamilton, on the other hand, understood the necessity of maintaining trade relationships with Britain, and thus called for U.S. neutrality. Washington and many members of his Cabinet agreed that the nation was too young and its military too small to risk engagement in a European war, and thus declared the United States to be neutral in the landmark Proclamation of Neutrality of 1793. Jefferson and Madison responded to the Proclamation with pamphlets decrying the Federalists' neutrality.

Both the French and British ended up violating U.S. neutrality. French minister Edmond Genet recruited American privateers to attack British allies, and the British captured nearly 250 American merchant ships, taking cargo and impressing sailors into military service. These violations led Washington to send Chief Justice of the Supreme Court John Jay in 1794 to negotiate with the British regarding U.S. neutrality. The terms of Jay's Treaty were primarily designed by Hamilton and realized several American economic goals, including the removal of British forts in the Northwest Territory. Britain also benefited, as the treaty gave "most favored nation" trading status to Britain and allowed the British to continue their anti-French maritime policies. Both the Democratic-Republicans and the French were angered by the terms of the treaty, which was authorized for 10 years.

Jay's Treaty also worried Spain, which became concerned about a possible alliance between Britain and the United States. To maintain positive relations with the United States, Spain softened its position on the boundaries between the U.S. and Spanish colonies. President Washington sent statesman Thomas Pinckney to negotiate a settlement of boundary, right of navigation along the Mississippi River, and right to deposit goods for transportation at the Port of New Orleans. The negotiations were successful and essentially removed Spain as a threat to further American settlement in the West. Pinckney's Treaty was unanimously ratified by Congress in 1796.

Upon leaving office in 1797, Washington wrote a letter to the people of the United States, his **Farewell Address**, in which he warned the infant nation to remain neutral with regard to European affairs, to avoid entangling alliances, and to refrain from the formation of political parties.

ADAMS AS SECOND PRESIDENT

Foreign affairs and domestic troubles did not let up as the second president of the United States, **John Adams**, took office. As was provided for in the Constitution, Thomas Jefferson, runner-up in the race for president, became Adams's vice president.

The XYZ Affair

Seeking to halt the incessant seizures of American vessels by the French, Adams sent a delegation to Paris in 1797 to negotiate an agreement. As the delegation arrived in France, it was approached outside of formal diplomatic channels by three French agents only identified as X, Y, and Z. These agents demanded a large sum of money as a loan and an additional bribe from the American delegation just for the opportunity to speak with French officials. The delegation refused to comply, and word of the incident quickly spread across the Atlantic, where the American press dubbed it the XYZ Affair.

Federalists, including Alexander Hamilton, called for immediate military action in response to the XYZ Affair as well as escalating conflicts between French and American merchants. Congress rescinded the nation's treaties with France in July of 1798, and an undeclared naval war, or quasi-war, ensued. Most of the action took place in the West Indies between U.S. sailors and French vessels. From 1798 to 1800, this undeclared naval war strained trade in the Caribbean and was on the verge of escalating into a full-scale conflict. Both sides wished to avoid further conflict, so Adams sent a team of envoys to meet with French foreign minister Charles Talleyrand to negotiate a settlement. The meeting, dubbed the Convention of 1800, ended with the termination of the Franco-American Alliance, an agreement by the United States to pay for damages inflicted on French vessels, and the avoidance of an all-out war with France.

The Alien and Sedition Acts

Emboldened by popular anger over the XYZ Affair, Federalists swept control of Congress in 1798 and began enacting laws aimed at silencing the opposition. The first of these laws were the Alien Acts, which increased the residency requirement for citizenship from 5 to 14 years and gave the president power to detain and/or deport enemy aliens in times of war. The second law aimed at silencing

Democratic-Republicans was the Sedition Act. This law made it illegal to make false statements that were critical of the president or Congress, and it imposed a heavy fine or a threat of imprisonment upon violators, such as editors of newspapers. Jefferson and the Democratic-Republicans were angered by this violation of their right to free speech guaranteed by the First Amendment. Republicans fought back by encouraging states to pass their own statutes to nullify the **Alien and Sedition Acts**. Several states invoked the compact theory: that the federal government was formed because of a compact among states, and thus states should be the final arbiters regarding whether the federal government has acted in good faith. Kentucky and Virginia even passed the **Kentucky Resolution** and the **Virginia Resolution**, overturning the Alien and Sedition Acts in their states. However, no other states followed suit, and the issue of nullification disappeared for a short time.

 NEXT STEP: PRACTICE

Go to Rapid Review and Practice Chapter 5 or to your online quizzes on kaptest.com for exam-like practice on this topic.

Haven't registered your book yet? Go to kaptest.com/moreonline to begin.

CHAPTER 15

Period 4: 1800–1848

THE ELECTION OF THOMAS JEFFERSON

From disagreements over going to war with France, the Alien and Sedition Acts, and increasing debts, the **Federalist Party** lost much of the momentum they had gained leading up to the election of 1800. They resorted to mudslinging during the presidential election, accusing Jefferson of everything from thievery to atheism. These tactics backfired, and the Federalists were swept from both the presidency and Congress. Although **Thomas Jefferson** defeated John Adams in the popular vote, he tied in the Electoral College with fellow **Democratic-Republican Party** member Aaron Burr. It was then up to the House of Representatives to decide who would take the presidency. Still in control of the House, the Federalists debated for four days over the issue. At the urging of Alexander Hamilton, who had long opposed Burr in New York politics and found him to be "without scruple," the House chose Thomas Jefferson as the third president of the United States.

This election was significant because it exposed weaknesses in the recently agreed upon political infrastructure of the nation. First, it showed that the construction of the Electoral College, which allowed electors to vote for two candidates, would not work as intended in an environment with organized parties. Second, the outcome of the election was heavily affected by the three-fifths clause; historians argue that a direct election would have resulted in Adams's victory.

In his first inaugural address, Jefferson stated, "We are all Republicans; we are all Federalists." Jefferson understood that ideology could interfere with the decisions that needed to be made for the betterment of the nation. In this way, Jefferson's presidency was paradoxical: in some cases, he adhered to the letter of the Constitution, while at other times, he adopted a loose interpretation. For example, he kept many of the hallmarks of the Federalist Era intact (such as Hamilton's economic system), but he had the citizenship requirement of the Alien Act reduced to five years and abolished the excise tax. With any decision, he argued that the actions he took were for the good of the nation.

THE LOUISIANA PURCHASE

An apt example of Jefferson's loose interpretation of presidential power was his purchase of the **Louisiana Territory** from Napoleon of France. The United States had enjoyed the right of deposit at the Port of New Orleans since the signing of Pinckney's Treaty in 1795 with Spain, but in 1798, the Spanish revoked the the treaty. In 1800, French military leader Napoleon Bonaparte reobtained the territory under a secret agreement with Spain. The news of France's restored ownership caused unease, as farmers on the western frontier depended on the ability to transport goods on the Mississippi and deposit them for trade in New Orleans, and they feared that France would soon dominate this route. Jefferson, understanding the impact this would have on the economy as well as hazards of engaging in European affairs, dispatched ministers to Paris to negotiate with Napoleon.

In 1803, Jefferson instructed ministers James Monroe and Robert Livingston to offer $10 million for New Orleans and a strip of land that extended to Florida. If the negotiations failed, Monroe and Livingston were to travel directly to London to ask for a transatlantic alliance between the United States and Britain. Much to the American ministers' surprise, the French ministers were offering not only the land Jefferson sought but the entire Louisiana Territory, which stretched from the Gulf of Mexico to the Hudson Bay, and from the Mississippi River to the Rocky Mountains, for the bargain price of $15 million. Napoleon had abandoned his dream of an American empire because of his failure to stop a slave uprising in Haiti; he instead prioritized raising revenue to fund his conquest of Europe. The American ministers jumped at the opportunity to acquire so much land, bringing the deal home for Jefferson's approval.

The president was torn. If he accepted the deal, it would be in direct conflict with his strict views on the Constitution; the document does not specifically provide for the president to negotiate for and purchase land from a foreign power. If he did not accept the deal, however, the Union might be in peril: Napoleon might withdraw the offer, or another country might purchase the land. The president reluctantly sent the deal to the predominantly Democratic-Republican Senate, which quickly approved the purchase.

Lewis and Clark Explore the Land

The Louisiana Purchase doubled the size of the United States for a mere three cents an acre. Both the French and the Spanish were removed as potential threats to U.S. sovereignty, the western frontier now included one of the most fertile valleys in the world, and Jefferson's dream of an agrarian empire was now closer to becoming a reality.

Additionally, Jefferson hoped to find a continuous navigable water route connecting the Missouri River to the Pacific Ocean. To investigate this route, the president appointed a team led by Meriwether Lewis and William Clark to explore the vast territory beginning in 1804. The group traveled a route that began in St. Louis, Missouri, and took them to the Pacific Ocean on the coast of Oregon. They returned to St. Louis in 1806. By keeping meticulous field notes and drawings of the flora and fauna, as well as detailed accounts of encounters with American Indian tribes, Lewis and Clark expanded America's knowledge of the vast new territory and warned of the hardships settlers would face moving west. However, no transcontinental all-water route was found.

THE MARSHALL COURT

A few Federalists were still clinging to power during Jefferson's administration, mostly in the judicial system. In a last-minute piece of legislation before the Congress was to be turned over to the majority Democratic-Republicans, the Federalists squeaked through the Judiciary Act of 1801, in which 16 new judgeships were created. President John Adams worked through the nights of his last days in office, appointing so-called midnight judges who would serve on the bench during Jefferson's administration.

Incensed by the packing of Federalists into lifetime judicial appointments, Jefferson sought to keep these men from taking the bench. He ordered his secretary of state, James Madison, not to deliver the commissions to the last-minute appointees, thereby blocking them from taking their judgeships. William Marbury, one of the midnight judges, sued under the **Judiciary Act of 1789**, which granted the **Supreme Court** the authority to enforce judicial commissions.

Marbury v. Madison

John Marshall, a staunch Federalist, was the sitting chief justice of the Supreme Court. Marshall knew that if the Supreme Court issued a writ of mandamus (an order forcing Madison to deliver the commission), the Jefferson administration would simply ignore the order. On the other hand, if the Court did not issue a writ, then it would seem that the Court was weak compared to the other two branches. As a result, Marshall declared that the Judiciary Act of 1789 was unconstitutional because it exceeded the authority given to the Court by Article III of the Constitution. Marshall went on to state that, as a result, the practice of issuing writs of mandamus was also invalid. This instituted the precedent of judicial review: the ability of the Supreme Court to determine the constitutional validity of legislative acts. From this case and subsequent decisions by the Marshall Court, the power of the Supreme Court was established: it could now check the authority of both the legislative and executive branches.

Even after the rebuke from Marshall and the Supreme Court in the *Marbury v. Madison* decision, President Jefferson was still determined to remove all remaining vestiges of Federalism from the judicial branch. He therefore turned his efforts to the **impeachment** of radical Federalist judges. The House successfully voted for the impeachment of Supreme Court Justice Samuel Chase owing to his highly partisan decisions. The Senate, however, refused to remove Chase because of the absence of any evidence of high crimes and misdemeanors. Jefferson's attempt to push Federalist judges out of the system was unsuccessful, as most remained on the bench for life. The judges did tend to rule more to the president's liking, however, once the threat of impeachment hung heavily over the judicial system. Nevertheless, this episode proved to be the last time that a Supreme Court justice would be impeached, maintaining the precious separation of powers between the legislative and judicial branches.

JEFFERSON'S CHALLENGES

Thomas Jefferson easily won reelection in 1804 and entered a much more difficult presidential term. His authority was challenged by his own former vice president, a threat from within his party, and foreign troubles.

Troubles at Home

Before Jefferson ran for his second term, the Democratic-Republicans decided not to select Aaron Burr as his vice presidential running mate. In 1804, the Twelfth Amendment was added to the Constitution, which called for electors to the Electoral College to specify which ballot was being cast for the office of president and which was being cast for the office of vice president. The tie vote that occurred in 1800 between Jefferson and Burr would not happen again under this new amendment. Burr became very bitter over the snubbing by his own party and the injustice he believed he had endured back in 1800 at the hands of Alexander Hamilton. Seeking retribution, Burr joined forces with a small group of radical Federalists called the Essex Junto. This group had been plotting for a New England state secession from the Union and had originally asked Hamilton if he would run for governor of New York to join in their exploits. Hamilton refused the offer, so the group then asked Burr if he would run. Burr gladly accepted.

Upon hearing the news, Hamilton leaped at the chance to crush Burr's chances of election by leading the opposition faction. Fearing what an ex-Democratic-Republican would do, Federalists in New York chose not to elect Aaron Burr as governor, and the plot faded away. After Burr heard of a snide remark made by Hamilton about his character, Burr challenged his enemy to a duel. Refusing such a challenge would have certainly affected Hamilton's stature as a leader and a man; therefore, the duel was set. Burr shot Hamilton, fatally wounding him, in 1804.

Another issue Jefferson faced was criticism from those who used to back him. John Randolph, one of Jefferson's supporters in the House, opposed Jefferson's abandonment of his once staunch advocacy for states' rights. In 1805, Randolph broke with Jefferson and created the Quids, a conservative wing of the Democratic-Republican Party that wished to restrict the role of the federal government. The Quids stated that Jefferson's decision to pay land companies restitution for illegally obtained land in Georgia (known as the Yazoo land scandal) proved that he was corrupt. This scandal led to a schism within the Democratic-Republican Party that continued to plague Jefferson in his second term.

Troubles Abroad

Foreign troubles also affected Jefferson through his second term. The Barbary pirates from North Africa took advantage of the absence of protective British troops and seized U.S. merchant ships as they traveled in the Mediterranean. Presidents Washington and Adams reluctantly had paid the pirates a protection fee, but Jefferson refused to pay it, and instead sent a small fleet of naval ships to stop the pirates. The U.S. Navy fought the pirates in the Mediterranean Sea for four years in what came to be called the Tripolitan War (1801–1805). Though the Navy was small, it achieved significant victories over the pirates, dissuading foreign nations from attempting to invade the young nation.

A much greater challenge to U.S. authority came with the continued escalation of the **Napoleonic Wars** between Britain and France. While the two countries had been issuing decrees to block trade into one another's ports for years, Napoleon's Berlin Decree in 1806 cut Britain off from trading with the rest of the world and placed America in the middle of the conflict. The British quickly retaliated against France by blockading all ports under French control. The British also ordered all American ships traveling to Europe to stop in Britain first. In 1807, Napoleon retaliated by issuing the Milan Decree, which authorized his navy to seize foreign ships traveling to Europe that had first stopped in Britain.

Americans were growing increasingly concerned over the British practice of impressment and violations of U.S. neutrality. With thousands of American sailors forced into British military service on the high seas, the continued seizures of neutral ships, and a skirmish at sea with a British vessel, Jefferson was compelled to act. In 1807, the British ship *Leopard* fired upon a U.S. ship, the USS *Chesapeake*, right off the coast of Virginia, killing three Americans, and the British impressed four sailors from the *Chesapeake*. Despite the war fever taking hold in America, Jefferson sought to use the power of diplomacy and economic sanctions. Having no interest in going to war or getting involved in European affairs, he hoped that the United States could economically hurt the British, and thus force them to cease violating American neutrality.

Unfortunately, Jefferson's plan was ruinous for the U.S. economy; most of the damage was inflicted on New England merchants and Southern farmers. A vast network of black market goods arose along the Canadian border to circumvent the trade embargo. This led to the passage of harsher enforcement laws that many, especially New Englanders, saw as punitive and oppressive. Congress repealed the **Embargo Act of 1807** but soon replaced it with the **Non-Intercourse Act of 1809**. This law allowed the United States to trade with foreign nations except Britain and France. Like its predecessor, the Embargo Act, it was difficult to enforce and mostly ineffective.

15

THE WAR OF 1812

High-Yield

Prelude to War

James Madison managed to defeat Federalist Charles Pinckney in the presidential election of 1808. He would carry on the legacy of republicanism that Jefferson had left behind; still, international affairs would dominate U.S. politics during Madison's presidency. Congress took up the trade issue again in 1810 and enacted Macon's Bill Number 2, which sought to lift trade restrictions against Britain or France, but only after they agreed to honor U.S. neutrality. Napoleon happily repealed his Berlin and Milan Decrees in the hopes of stirring up tensions between the United States and Britain. Madison had been duped by Napoleon, however, who never intended to honor his promise to remove the restrictions on shipping and trade. The British and French continued their practice of impressment and ship seizures, pushing the United States closer to the brink of war.

A heightened sense of nationalism ushered in the first meeting of Congress in 1811. New young Democratic-Republican congressmen from the South and the West urged a war with Britain to secure a place in the global political structure for the United States. War hawks, such as Henry Clay from Kentucky and John C. Calhoun from South Carolina, insisted that this war would finally clear Britain's influence from North America.

Aside from dealing with the British at sea, the Americans were hoping to eliminate the threat of American Indians, who were armed by the British and continued to cause trouble for western frontier settlers. The **Battle of Tippecanoe** in present-day Indiana caused many members of Congress from the frontier to feel justified in their call for war. Prior to the outbreak of the War of 1812, General William Henry Harrison sought to break up a large native confederacy that a pair of Shawnee brothers, Tecumseh and the Prophet, had organized in the face of an American advance westward. General Harrison and his men successfully repulsed a surprise attack and subsequently burned a tribal settlement at Tippecanoe. Now with the American Indian threat removed in the west, the war hawks looked to conquer Canada.

The British refusal to lift trade restrictions, and immense political pressure, pushed President Madison to ask Congress for a declaration of war in June 1812. Ironically, the British at that very time had repealed the trade restrictions. However, by the time word traveled across the ocean and reached Washington, D.C., the war had already begun.

The War and its Aftermath

Often called the Second War of Independence, the **War of 1812** started disappointingly for the United States. The nation was not prepared to wage war, especially not with the most powerful naval force in the world. The U.S. economy had been devastated by the Embargo Act, and America's military was small, poorly equipped, and under-trained. The U.S. Navy was also no match for the British navy; while U.S. ships were able to outmaneuver the British in the Great Lakes region, the American invasion of Canada was a debacle.

Because Napoleon was no longer a threat in Europe by 1814, the British were able to focus their attention on North America. The Americans repelled a British attack on New York, but could not save Washington, D.C., from being burned to the ground in August of 1814. The Americans did have some notable victories, though. For example, U.S. soldiers valiantly held Fort McHenry through a night of bombing by the British Royal Navy in Chesapeake Bay, inspiring Francis Scott Key, who was being held prisoner on a nearby British ship, to write "**The Star-Spangled Banner.**"

The formidable General Andrew Jackson led American troops through Alabama to New Orleans and successfully prevented the English from gaining control over the Mississippi River at the **Battle of New Orleans**. Interestingly, the battle, while an impressive victory for the Americans, was completely unnecessary, as it was fought two weeks after the signing of the peace treaty that ended the war. Nonetheless, Jackson emerged as an American war hero.

The **Treaty of Ghent** that ended the War of 1812 was signed by American envoys and British diplomats in Belgium on December 24, 1814. The provisions of the treaty provided for the end of the fighting, the return of any conquered territories to their rightful owners, and the settlement of a boundary between Canada and the United States. Essentially, the war ended in a draw—neither side gained any major concessions, restitution, or apologies. Most Americans were pleased, however, because they had expected to lose territory. Despite their complaints, the war did allow manufacturing, especially in New England, to flourish. The country became a bit more independent from European markets. In effect, this was the beginning of America's Industrial Revolution.

IDEOLOGICAL DIVIDES IN THE UNITED STATES

A very serious ideological split divided the nation during the War of 1812: a split between the Federalists and the Democratic-Republicans, which was essentially a split between New England and the rest of the nation. New England states were vehemently opposed to the war effort and the direction in which Democratic-Republicans were taking the nation.

During the winter of 1814–1815, a radical group of New England Federalists met at the **Hartford Convention** in Hartford, Connecticut, to discuss ways to demand that the federal government pay them for the loss of trade due to the Embargo Act and the War of 1812. The group also proposed amending the Constitution to: limit the U.S. president to one term; require a two-thirds vote to enact an embargo, declare war, and admit new states; and repeal the Three-Fifths Compromise. Some even suggested secession from the Union. However, news of the signing of the Treaty of Ghent and Jackson's victory at New Orleans swept the nation. With the war now over, the Federalists were labeled unpatriotic. The Hartford Convention was basically the end for the Federalist Party, which was routed by Democratic-Republican James Monroe in the election of 1816. These ideological divisions would remain intense as the nation moved into the 1820s and began to expand farther westward.

The Missouri Compromise

High-Yield

As the nation expanded westward and new states entered the Union, the debate raged over whether or not to allow slavery in these states. New states in the southern half of the frontier justified slavery by expressing the economic need for a large, stable workforce; those settling in the North had less need for slaves. The issue came to a head in 1819 as Missouri applied for statehood.

A delicate balance existed in the Senate in 1819, with 11 free states and 11 slave states represented. This balance was extremely important to the Southern states because they had less representation in the House due to greater population growth in the North. As long as the balance was maintained in the Senate, Southerners could still block bills passed by the House that could hurt them. However, with Missouri now vying for statehood, each side was forced to consider the possibility of this balance being tipped in the opposite direction.

James Tallmadge of New York proposed an amendment to Missouri's bid for statehood. After the admission of Missouri as a state, the Tallmadge Amendment would not have allowed any more slaves to be brought into the state and would have provided for the emancipation (freeing) of the children of Missouri slaves at the age of 25 years. Southerners were outraged by this abolition attempt and crushed the amendment in the Senate.

At this time, Henry Clay of Kentucky proposed three bills that would together make up the **Missouri Compromise** of 1820. The compromise allowed for the admission of Missouri as a slave state, while also admitting Maine as a free state to maintain the balance in the Senate. In addition, slavery would not be permitted in states admitted above the latitude 36° 30' (with the exception of Missouri, which lay above the line). Clay's compromise was accepted by both North and South and lasted for 34 years, earning him the title the Great Compromiser.

MONROE AND THE ERA OF GOOD FEELINGS

With a renewed sense of national pride, Americans elected **James Monroe** as their president in the election of 1816. However the Era of Good Feelings was not always as harmonious as the optimistic name ascribed to Monroe's two-term presidency. The period was rife with tension regarding tariffs, slavery, and political power within the Democratic-Republican Party.

Owing to the collapse of the Federalist Party, Monroe handily defeated his opponent in 1816 and easily won reelection in 1820. He ushered in an age of intense patriotism and reverence for the American heroes of the past. Nevertheless, Monroe's presidency also included difficult financial times, controversy regarding slavery, and uncertainty about the future that accompanied America's expansion.

The Monroe Doctrine

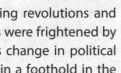
High-Yield

During Monroe's presidency, many Latin American countries were experiencing revolutions and were leaning toward more democratic forms of government. European powers were frightened by the possibility of losing influence in the Western Hemisphere because of this change in political structure. Britain, for example, hoped to ally with the United States to maintain a foothold in the region. While some former American leaders urged President Monroe to enter the alliance in order to keep the British in check, Secretary of State John Quincy Adams was not convinced. He believed that the alliance would hinder U.S. expansion.

In response, he wrote President Monroe's annual address to Congress in 1823, now known as the **Monroe Doctrine**, which included a warning to the European powers to stay out of the Western Hemisphere. It quickly became the basis of U.S. foreign policy from that point forward. The doctrine called for nonintervention in Latin America and an end to European colonization. Though the United States did not actually have a strong enough military to defend the doctrine if necessary, it remained firm and adhered to the doctrine throughout the nineteenth and twentieth centuries.

A New Tariff and its Opposition

Coupled with this revival of patriotism was a strong desire to protect all things American, especially the burgeoning industrial economy. To prevent cheap British goods from flooding the market and injuring American manufacturing, Congress passed the **Tariff of 1816**, which imposed a 20 percent duty on all imported goods and became the first truly protective tariff in American history. However, the passage of the tariff did not go over well in all areas of the United States.

A sectional crisis emerged, with three men leading the charge for their respective constituents. John C. Calhoun spoke for the South, saying that the tariff limited the foreign market for Southern goods by inhibiting international trade. Speaking for the North was Daniel Webster, who complained that New England had not developed enough to withstand interruptions in its ability to trade freely with Britain. Lastly, Henry Clay of Kentucky argued on behalf of American mill and iron industries, stating that the tariff, along with his **American System**, would help establish manufacturing and bring in much needed revenue for internal improvements in the South. Clay's American System included the recharter of the Bank of the United States, protective tariffs, such as the one passed in 1816, and improvements on American infrastructure, such as turnpikes, roads, and canals.

> ✔ **AP Expert Note**
>
> **Be able to explain how events such as the War of 1812 shaped American national identity**
>
> On the AP exam, you will see questions about how the identity of newly-independent America developed. After the War of 1812, America entered into the Era of Good Feelings: a period of national unity, which lasted through the 1820s. Americans felt a true sense of patriotism, and heroes such as Andrew Jackson emerged. The patriotic expression of ordinary people manifested itself in their willingness to buy American products and to support measures such as the Tariff of 1816, rejecting British imports. National pride likewise made Clay's American System quite popular with the American people.

Trouble with the Bank of the United States

Though President Monroe supported the creation of the **Second Bank of the United States** and the tariff, he strongly opposed national spending on internal improvements. Monroe believed that the Constitution did not expressly provide for the federal government to allocate monies to fund public works projects within the states. Therefore, he repeatedly vetoed bills that provided funds for road or canal building.

The Panic of 1819 threatened the Era of Good Feelings that Monroe had enjoyed in his first presidential term. The Second Bank of the United States (BUS) caused this financial crisis; it overspeculated on land in the West and attempted to curb inflation by pulling back on credit for state banks. Typically, countries experience inflation during wartime and then a period of recession after a war. After the War of 1812, demand for American agricultural goods abroad fell sharply, forcing the BUS to demand payment from state banks in hard specie (coin). Unfortunately, frontier banks had limited amounts of currency due to issuing many loans to farmers. Thus, these western or "wildcat" banks could not pay back the BUS in specie, and the amount of currency in circulation became dangerously low. The BUS demanded that western banks foreclose on farmers who could not pay back their debts, resulting in a significant rise of landless farmers. Western banks were deemed evil by frontier farmers and poor citizens, who were particularly hard hit by the depression. Despite all of these events, James Monroe was reelected for a second term in 1820.

THE RISE OF THE TWO-PARTY SYSTEM

As the United States emerged from the Panic of 1819 and underwent massive economic and social changes in the 1820s, the old aristocratic tendencies transplanted from England were soon replaced by a new democratic spirit.

Changes in the Electoral Process

Americans across the nation favored political equality for white American men. More and more men from the middle and lower classes became involved in the political process by voting, campaigning, and running for office. By 1820, many states had adopted universal male suffrage, eliminating the property-owning requirement to be able to vote. Sometimes called the **Rise of the Common Man**, this era signaled a retreat from exclusive rule by the well-to-do and a shift to a more democratic society.

Another significant change was that nominating caucuses were replaced by nominating conventions, in which large groups of people chose their party's candidates. The state representatives to the Electoral College, who had once been chosen by state legislatures, were now chosen by the state's voters. This popular election of electors led to a new democratic system in which presidential candidates now had to run national campaigns and in which political parties had to grow to manage the task.

The Mudslinging Election of 1824

The election of 1824 pitted four candidates from the Democratic-Republican Party against each other for the presidency: John Quincy Adams, Henry Clay, William Crawford, and Andrew Jackson. The campaign was ugly, with Jackson and Adams both defaming, or "slinging mud," on each other's reputations. In the end, Andrew Jackson won the greatest number of popular votes; however, with the votes split four ways, no one man had a majority of electoral votes. Therefore, it fell to the House of Representatives to choose the president. Henry Clay used his influence to make **John Quincy Adams** president. When President Adams then appointed Clay as his secretary of state, the Jackson camp accused President Adams of corruption.

In 1828, **Andrew Jackson** again ran for president. On one side were the **Democrats**, who supported Jackson, and on the other were the **National Republicans**, who supported Henry Clay. The National Republicans eventually became the Whig Party in 1836. Whig ideology, which was very similar to the platform of the old Federalist Party, was specifically crafted to oppose Andrew Jackson. Thus, the two-party system was reborn.

CHALLENGES TO FEDERAL AUTHORITY

Supreme Court Chief Justice John Marshall continued to make his mark on American politics in the 1820s and 1830s. Still holding strong to his Federalist tendencies, Marshall continued to increase the power of the federal government over the states.

Federal and State Power

In 1819, the Supreme Court heard the case of *McCulloch v. Maryland*, which challenged the doctrine of federalism. The case involved the state of Maryland attempting to collect a tax from the Second Bank of the United States. Marshall invoked the "necessary and proper" clause of the Constitution to rule that the federal government had an implied power to establish the bank. He also declared that the state had no right to tax a federal institution; he argued that "the power to tax was the power to destroy" and would signal the end of federalism. Most importantly, the *McCulloch v. Maryland* ruling established that federal laws were the supreme law of the land, superseding state laws.

The Death of the Bank of the United States

As a proponent of the common man, Andrew Jackson sought to separate government from the economy once and for all. He believed that to ensure the success of every American, the government needed to stay out of economic affairs. This issue came to a head as the charter for the Bank of the United States (BUS) was set to expire in 1832. Jackson's key opponent, Henry Clay, favored the BUS and encouraged Congress to pass a rechartering bill. Jackson vetoed the bill and vowed to kill the BUS, which he considered a monopoly.

Jackson also came up with a plan to end the BUS once and for all. All federal funds were removed from the BUS and deposited in various state banks, which opponents dubbed "pet banks." When domestic prices for goods and land subsequently jumped and threatened to destroy the economy, Jackson issued the Specie Circular, which required the payment for purchase of all federal lands be made in hard coin, or specie, rather than banknotes. This caused the value of paper money to plummet and eventually led to the **Panic of 1837**. However, Jackson did succeed in killing the BUS. The United States did not have another federal bank until the creation of the National Banking System during the Civil War.

The Nullification Crisis

Both John Quincy Adams and Andrew Jackson faced stiff opposition to tariffs passed during their presidencies. The **Tariff of 1828** came about in response to New England merchants who had been pushing for stronger protection from foreign competitors. However, the new tariff was incredibly damaging to the Southern economy, causing Vice President John C. Calhoun to secretly write "The Southern Carolina Exposition," which outlined the anger of the South. Calling the tariff the "Tariff of Abominations," Calhoun recommended that the Southern states declare it to be null and void if the federal government refused to lower the duty requirement.

In an attempt to appease the South, Jackson signed into law the **Tariff of 1832**, which lowered the tariff from 45 percent to 35 percent. The attempt failed and Calhoun resigned from the vice presidency in response. South Carolina voted to nullify the Tariff of 1832 and threatened to secede if Jackson attempted to collect the duties by force. In response, Jackson encouraged Congress to lower tariffs even more. However, he also asked Congress to pass the Force Bill, which gave the president the power to use the military to collect tariffs. This signaled to the South that their threats would not be tolerated. In response, South Carolina rescinded the nullification. Jackson had successfully protected the power of the federal government and averted a civil war; however, the tensions between the North and the South would continue to escalate.

Jackson's Government of the People

Andrew Jackson was a champion of states' rights, as long as the nation was not in danger. He believed that to protect the rights and guarantee the success of the common man, the president should exercise all due power. Therefore, Jackson vetoed more bills than the previous six presidents combined. States' rights were a hot topic, as illustrated by the nullification crisis. As Jackson increased the power of the presidency, he sometimes sought to expand democracy, but only when it served his interests.

During Jackson's presidency, as in no time before, everyday Americans participated in the workings of the political system. Voter turnout increased, and new civil service opportunities arose for Jackson supporters. Andrew Jackson was a proponent of the **spoils system**, in which he appointed those who supported his campaign to government positions. Many felt that this practice bred corruption and tainted the political process. Nonetheless, Jackson created jobs and appointed many friends to his unofficial Cabinet, earning it the name "Kitchen Cabinet" from critics.

Jackson also believed in rotating officials to discourage complacency and encourage fresh opinions. He felt that all men were equal, so it was unnecessary for someone to hold office indefinitely. This belief opened the door for many common men to take an active role in governmental affairs. Notably though, Jackson, the "champion of the common man," did not include all Americans, such as women, African Americans, and American Indians, in his vision of democracy.

Jackson and the American Indians

Jackson understood the positive impact continued western expansion could have on the country and wished to open up the frontier to settlers who longed to move there. However, large groups of American Indians already lived on this land. Jackson believed that the solution was to move the natives to land set aside for them west of the Mississippi in what is now Oklahoma and Kansas. The **Indian Removal Act**, signed into law in 1830, provided for the immediate resettlement of American Indians living in Mississippi, Alabama, Florida, Georgia, and present-day Illinois. By 1835, some 100,000 Cherokee, Chickasaw, Choctaw, Creek, and Seminole American Indians had been forcibly removed from their homelands.

The Cherokee Nation refused to leave without a fight and took its case against the state of Georgia to the U.S. Supreme Court. The Court ruled in ***Cherokee Nation v. Georgia*** (1831) that the tribe was not a sovereign foreign nation and, therefore, had no right to sue for jurisdiction over its homelands. In another American Indian removal case, however, the Marshall Court ruled in favor of the Cherokee. In ***Worcester v. Georgia*** (1832), the Supreme Court ruled that the state of Georgia could not infringe on the tribe's sovereignty, thus nullifying Georgia state laws within Cherokee territory. President Jackson was incensed and allegedly said, "John Marshall has made his decision; now let him enforce it." Jackson believed that as president, it was his duty to enforce the Constitution as he interpreted it. Unfortunately for the Cherokee, the federal government did nothing to come to their aid.

By 1838, all of the Cherokees had been forcibly removed from the state of Georgia and relocated to territory in Oklahoma that had been set aside for them. Of the 15,000 people who embarked on the journey, 4,000 died, leading the Cherokee to name this tragic event the Trail of Tears.

RELIGIOUS REVIVAL AND REFORM MOVEMENTS

The Second Great Awakening

High-Yield

The **Second Great Awakening** started in the 1790s when Protestant traditionalists, such as the Calvinists, sought to regain the hearts and souls of the growing population. Its origin was complex. The rationalism that had characterized the late Enlightenment period provoked counter-sentiments that hearkened back to fundamentalist strains of Christianity. Greater social and geographic mobility left many Americans without connections to a long-standing community, and churches filled that void. The vulnerability of families in the market economy, along with the appeal of relationships outside the family sphere, led to greater religiosity among women. Free blacks and slaves alike were inspired by religion to demand an end to slavery.

Religious revivalism reached its full fever pitch in the 1820s, with the preaching of Presbyterian minister Charles G. Finney. Like Jonathan Edwards of the First Great Awakening, Finney appealed to his audience's emotions, rather than to their reason. His "fire and brimstone" sermons became commonplace in upstate New York, where listeners were instilled with a fear of Satan and an eternity in Hell. Finney insisted that parishioners could save themselves through good works and a steadfast faith in God. Harry Hosier (better known as "Black Harry"), a former slave who had become a freedman sometime around the American Revolution, was one of the era's most famous and influential orators, popular with black and white audiences alike. His sermons championed the working man and called on congregants to reject slavery. Hosier was also famous for being able to recite long passages from the Bible by memory, a feat made more notable by Hosier being illiterate.

Many of the new religious converts believed in perfectionism, or the idea that people could reach a level of perfection that resembled the life of Jesus through faith, hard work, education, and temperance. In its earliest stages, this antebellum social reform movement operated on a local level, seeking only to affect individual morals. However, reformers soon decided that to make their work effective, they would have to influence politics on a local, state, and national level.

> **✔ AP Expert Note**
>
> **Be able to distinguish between the First and Second Great Awakenings**
>
> The first Great Awakening of the 1730s and 1740s was born from the sermons of Jonathan Edwards and George Whitefield. This new wave of religious fervor resulted in an increase in the number of church denominations and churchgoers. Whereas the First Great Awakening was a reaction to the Enlightenment, the Second Great Awakening in the early 1800s was more of a reaction against secular beliefs and lifestyles. Through church revivals, or "camp meetings," and inspirational sermons, the Second Great Awakening sparked a great number of reform movements, most notably movements for temperance, public education, women's rights, and abolition.

Temperance and America's Health

The evils of alcohol were one of the first issues of concern of antebellum reformers. Revival preachers joined forces in the mid-1820s to form the American Temperance Society. While their initial goal was to encourage drinkers simply to limit their alcohol intake, the movement soon evolved to demand absolute abstinence, as reformers began to see the negative effects that any alcohol consumption had on people's lives. The movement quickly earned the support of state leaders as decreased alcohol use resulted in fewer on-the-job accidents and more overall productivity. The Maine Law, passed in 1851, completely prohibited the manufacture and sale of alcoholic beverages in Maine. Soon after, 12 other states passed similar laws, either severely limiting the sale of alcohol or prohibiting it altogether. The most active members of temperance societies tended to be middle-class women. When abolitionism gained momentum in the 1850s, many of these women also joined the movement to end slavery.

General health became an important target for reformers. In addition to curbing the consumption of alcohol, reformers also reformed insane asylums and brought increased attention to healthier diets. These advancements were indicative of additional smaller reform movements that developed during this time to assist Americans along their path to "perfection."

Dorothea Dix was a well-known reformer who fought for the humane treatment of the nation's mentally ill population. Her efforts led to the creation of mental institutions where patients were given access to proper treatments. Connected to the asylum reform movement was the crusade to change the penal system in the United States. As a result, some prisons instituted programs that taught prisoners job skills and increased access to religious services.

To cleanse the body and soul, men such as Reverend Sylvester Graham, who inspired the creation of the Graham Cracker, and John Harvey Kellogg, inventor of the corn flake, espoused the importance of healthy diets. Dr. Kellogg established the Battle Creek Mental Institution to put his ideas about diet and health into practice.

The Cult of Domesticity

High-Yield

After the market revolution and transportation boom of the 1820s, the nature of "women's work" shifted. In many American homes, it was no longer necessary for women to work in both the fields and the home. The growth of industry moved men out of the fields and into factories, while women were left to tend the home and children. Children, too, became less important to the overall well-being of the family, as they were no longer required to work in the fields alongside their parents. Thus, the birthrate dropped into the 1860s among middle-class Caucasian families. In this age of moral perfectibility, women's roles were clearly defined as homemakers and mothers, hence the term **cult of domesticity**.

The cult of domesticity was not the only influencing fact on women's lives, however. Some women, mainly in the North, were able to work outside the home in mills and factories. Workplace opportunities for women were due in part to the advances in technology, especially Eli Whitney's development of interchangeable machine parts, which allowed for efficient mass production in Northern factories.

Women also began to play a large role in driving social change, especially fighting for abolition and suffrage. In 1837, **abolitionists** Sarah and Angelina Grimke voiced their opposition to male dominance within the abolition movement, thus starting a dialogue about women's roles. Soon after, Lucretia Mott, Elizabeth Cady Stanton, and Susan B. Anthony organized a meeting of feminists at Seneca Falls, New York, to discuss the plight of women in the United States. The women at Seneca Falls drafted the **Declaration of Sentiments,** modeled after the Declaration of Independence, to declare that "all men and women are created equal" and to demand suffrage for women. Much like the earlier temperance movement, the women's crusade soon became eclipsed by the abolitionist movement and did not resurface until closer to the turn of the twentieth century.

The Abolition Movement and Slave Resistance

The most politicized of all of the antebellum reform movements was the abolition movement. Influenced by the teachings of the Second Great Awakening, abolitionists believed that slavery was sinful and, therefore, must be eliminated. In 1831, William Lloyd Garrison began publishing *The Liberator*, a newspaper dedicated to ending slavery. Garrison also founded the American Antislavery Society in 1833 to oppose slave traders and owners. Garrison's radicalism soon alienated many moderates within the movement when he claimed that the Constitution was a pro-slavery document. Garrison's insistence on the participation of women in the movement led to division among his supporters and the formation of the Liberty Party, which accepted women, and the Foreign Antislavery Society, which did not.

Free African Americans had their own leadership within the abolition movement with Harriet Tubman, Sojourner Truth, and Frederick Douglass. Douglass, a former slave, published *The North Star*, an antislavery journal that chronicled the ugliness of slavery and argued that the Constitution could be used as a weapon against slavery. Thus, Douglass argued for fighting slavery through legal means in contrast to some other radical abolitionists, who advocated varying degrees of violence to achieve abolition. Tubman and Truth, along with many others, helped enslaved Africans escape bondage through an elaborate network called the **Underground Railroad**.

Some, however, chose to take matters into their own hands. Nat Turner, an enslaved African American from Virginia, organized a massive slave uprising in 1831, in part motivated by religious visions. **Nat Turner's Rebellion** resulted in the deaths of over 50 white men, women, and children, and the retaliatory killings of hundreds of slaves. While the most famous and largest-scale slave uprising in North America, Nat Turner's Rebellion was unusual for happening at all. Only around 250 slave uprisings were documented in the United States prior to the Civil War. Plantation owners attributed this stability to "loyalty" from their slaves, but in reality it was due to the sheer brutality with which any hint of rebellion was met. Slaves who rebelled would not merely be executed, often in especially brutal ways, but their families were often at risk as well. Southern whites had a long-standing paranoia about slave uprisings, and they aggressively punished any hint of dissent.

Surviving testimonies from escaped or freed slaves document multiple forms of active and passive resistance that slaves employed against their masters. Some slaves would refuse to work or would work slowly in protest. Because slaves were legally property, family ties such as marriage were not recognized. Husbands and wives, brothers and sisters, parents and children could and were broken apart to be sold as individuals. Yet, family ties endured; one method of building resilience was naming children after lost or dead relatives to keep their memory alive.

Education was forbidden, for fear of slaves organizing revolts, but many enslaved Africans found teachers in church or inside the plantation houses, where white women and children sometimes taught them to read and write. Culturally, slaves practiced syncretism, blending Christianity with traditional African rites and spiritual beliefs. Slave preachers emphasized the Old Testament of the Bible, comparing blacks to the enslaved Hebrews and emphasizing the hope of liberation, even while white preachers emphasized Biblical passages that stressed slaves' obedience.

ECONOMIC AND SOCIAL REVOLUTION

Between 1820 and 1860, a massive jump in America's population, along with advances in transportation, led to the creation of a national market economy. The development of national roads, canals, steamboats, and railroads helped bring people, raw materials, and manufactured goods to regions of the country that had previously been unreachable.

By far the most consequential economic development in this period was the **Market Revolution**, the shift away from localized economies and small-scale farming. The American economy now became one of interlocking, specialized regions. The South generated cash crops for export and raw materials like cotton for industry. The North hosted the factories that processed the raw materials into goods, such as textiles. The West (Midwest in present-day terms) generated the food to feed both the North and the South. All of these goods were transported on an increasingly complex series of roads, bridges, canals, and eventually railroads.

Transportation Advances and National Changes

Turnpikes, or toll roads, were the first transportation advance that served to link many towns in the eastern United States. Most turnpikes were built with private funds, because there was much opposition to the use of federal funds for internal improvements (such as opposition to Clay's American System).

Water travel also underwent important changes, especially when Robert Fulton invented the steamboat in 1807. Before the steamboat, river travel was done by flatboats or keelboats. The steamboat allowed goods and people to be transported easily both upstream and downstream. The Erie Canal, completed in 1825 with funds provided by the state of New York, linked the Great Lakes with the Hudson River. As a result, the cost of shipping dropped dramatically, and port cities along the length of the canal and its terminal points began to develop and flourish.

Finally, the advent of the railroad brought an even cheaper method of transportation to the country, and further connected the regions of the United States. The railroad could quickly traverse mountains and plains, and it soon became the most dependable and convenient means of traveling and shipping freight.

While these developments in transportation made life easier, cheaper, and served to connect the nation, there were notable adverse social and political consequences. Socially, divisions between rich and poor became much more distinct as manufacturers and plantation owners grew in prestige.

Politically, regional divisions sowed dissent that would soon develop into sectionalism. Because manufacturers in the North did a large amount of business with the West, more resources were invested into linking the two regions. The South, on the other hand, was largely cut off from the rest of the country because the resulting railroad network rarely connected with the few Southern railroads that did exist. This division heightened the tension between the North and the South politically and economically, which would continue to escalate through the 1850s.

Immigrants and the National Social Structure

The changes in the economic climate were also accompanied by a shift in demographics that altered the social fabric of the United States. In the mid-1840s, a potato famine in Ireland and tough economic and political conditions in Germany led to an influx of immigrants to the United States. Between 1830 and 1860, Irish immigrants accounted for the single largest immigrant population in Boston and New York City. At the same time, approximately 1.5 million displaced German farmers immigrated to America, often settling on the western frontier to continue farming.

Many Americans were unhappy with the influx of immigrants, and those who fought against the rights of foreigners became known as nativists. In 1849, a wing of the nativist movement became a political party called the **American Party**, or the Know-Nothing Party. The group opposed immigration and the election of Roman Catholics to political office. The members of the party met in secret and would not tell anyone what they stood for, saying, "I know nothing," when asked.

As more and more immigrants arrived and advances were made in technology, transportation, and business, the nation continued to change politically, socially, and economically. These changes would challenge Americans in all walks of life and would soon place enormous burdens on those leading the country.

Further Development of Regional Economies

The Industrial North and the Agricultural Northwest

Improvements in transportation spurred massive economic growth in the North. Industrial growth was led by the creation of a robust textile industry. As manufacturing of other goods also developed, the populations of northern cities experienced massive expansion as well. Unfortunately, the nation's urban areas did not have the necessary infrastructure to support the rapid influx of people, and, as a result, these urban immigrants suffered from overcrowding, disease, and rising crime rates.

Ohio, Indiana, Illinois, Michigan, Wisconsin, and Minnesota made up the Old Northwest region, which was closely tied to the industrial North by way of rail lines and canals. Economic production in this area mainly consisted of corn and wheat farming. Shipping of grains and food crops to the northern cities of New York, Boston, and Philadelphia helped spur the growth of the river and Great Lake port cities of St. Louis, Cleveland, and Chicago.

King Cotton and the Agrarian South

The plantation economy of the South that is now synonymous with antebellum southern culture was established long before the economic regionalization of the United States began. Cotton, the major cash crop of the South, was made even more lucrative with the invention of Eli Whitney's cotton gin in 1793. This invention sped up the process of removing the seeds from raw cotton, making cotton the number one cash crop of the South. Plantation owners switched from growing tobacco to growing cotton to keep up with increasing demands from domestic and overseas markets.

King Cotton also caused an expansion of slavery, from one million slaves to four million in 50 years, because more workers were needed to work the fields. As the population of enslaved Africans increased, slave owners and other white Southerners began to fear the possibility of slave revolts. In some slave states, codes were incorporated into the laws to regulate enslaved Africans. Known as slave codes, these laws were aimed at oppressing enslaved Africans, discouraging free blacks from living in the South, and preventing slave revolts.

The Frontier and Western Lands

Beyond the Mississippi River lay a vast territory that many Americans either longed to settle or wanted to avoid. Besides the writings of Lewis and Clark, little was known of this western region except its dangers. American Indians who had been pushed west had settled in large numbers on the Great Plains and caused great concern for settlers moving into the frontier. Those who did settle in the West built log cabins or mud-thatched homes along rivers, streams, or lakes and lived off the land until farms could be established. The West was unique in that its inhabitants tended to be more open to change than their counterparts in either the North or South. Granting women and African Americans more opportunities and having a more open governmental system were just some of the ways that the West differed from the East.

✔ **AP Expert Note**

Be able to identify attributes of regional economies

The national market economy led to increased distinctions between the various regions in America:

- The West became an agricultural center, responsible for growing the grain that fed much of the nation.
- The East emerged as the industrial powerhouse, with various factories dotting the landscape.
- The plantation economy continued to grow in the South.

These differences are important to keep in mind, as they also contributed to sectional tensions in the years leading up to the Civil War.

NEXT STEP: PRACTICE

Go to Rapid Review and Practice Chapter 6 or to your online quizzes on kaptest.com for exam-like practice on this topic.

Haven't registered your book yet? Go to kaptest.com/moreonline to begin.

15

CHAPTER 16

Period 5: 1844–1877

THE IMPACTS OF MANIFEST DESTINY

Journalist John O'Sullivan coined the phrase **Manifest Destiny** in 1845 to describe the belief that it was God's will for the United States to expand westward. Settlers sought opportunities to spread American values across the trans-Mississippi West, driven by Manifest Destiny, as well as by the market revolution, transportation advancements, and increased nationalism.

By 1840, thousands had moved into what is now Texas, with a few braving the trail to present-day Oregon. Throughout the 1840s, a flood of settlers began traversing the dangerous **Oregon Trail**. Families traveled up to six months in caravans, covering only about 15 miles per day with good weather. While living on the trail, some women began to run prayer meetings and schools to maintain some vestiges of home. Women also began to take on new roles outside of homemaking and childcare, such as repairing wagons and tending to livestock.

Interactions with American Indians

As American settlers moved west, they encountered American Indian tribes, who had lived in the Great Plains region for centuries. Although there was occasional conflict between American Indians and American settlers, there were no large-scale clashes or battles. The lives of the Plains tribes, however, were dramatically altered by the increasing presence of the Sioux Indians. The Sioux had gradually moved westward since the mid-eighteenth century due to the spread of guns and horses, which they used to fight for territory and hunt buffalo. By the early nineteenth century, the Sioux had gained control over much of the Great Plains. However, they were unable to maintain their control of the land due to relentless westward expansion by American settlers.

In contrast to the experiences of Plains tribes, California tribes faced an organized extermination campaign by U.S. authorities. Between 1846 and 1873, the American Indian population in California plunged from approximately 150,000 to 30,000. Between 5,000 to 16,000 native peoples were directly killed in hundreds of massacres, while thousands more natives suffered due to disease and eviction from their ancestral lands. The new state government of California sided with settlers and gold prospectors over native claims to land. Between 1850 and 1863, a kind of legalized slavery for American Indians was authorized under the California Act for the Government and Protection of Indians. By the mid-1860s, the reservation system and assimilation of American Indian children via schooling became the preferred approaches.

The Politics of Expansion

Westward expansion became a major political issue when **Martin Van Buren** was elected president in 1836. Van Buren's presidency was marred by an economic depression resulting from the policies of his predecessor, Andrew Jackson. The **Panic of 1837**, much like the Panic of 1819, was caused by overspeculation on western lands, faulty loans from "wildcat" western banks, the absence of a national bank, and Jackson's Specie Circular, which decreed that all federal land be paid for in gold or silver. These factors placed enormous strain on the economy, and the impact of the depression lasted until the early 1840s.

Van Buren fought for reelection in 1840 against **Whig Party** candidate **William Henry Harrison**, hero of the Battle of Tippecanoe. Mudslinging was fierce in the election, with Whigs blaming "Martin Van Ruin" for the economic crisis and Democrats accusing Harrison of being an alcoholic. The lively campaign saw the Whigs cart model log cabins to towns and distribute hard cider to boast of Harrison's poor background. His "Tippecanoe and Tyler, too" ticket easily defeated Van Buren in 1840. However, Harrison fell ill and died only a month into his term, leaving his vice president **John Tyler** to succeed him.

Americans still harbored hatred for the British after the Revolutionary War and the War of 1812. British presence along what is now the Canadian border provoked tension, with conflict occurring when British lumber companies proposed building a road across contested land. In 1838, a group of British North American lumberjacks collided with Maine militia forces, and the lumberjacks took control of the Aroostook River Valley. The threatened war was quickly averted, as Secretary of State Daniel Webster and the British Foreign Minister Ashburton negotiated terms to settle the boundary dispute. The Webster-Ashburton Treaty (1842) divided the contested territory between the United States and Britain and settled the northern boundary of Maine.

The conflict between the United States and Britain would not end with this treaty, however. The British had enjoyed a profitable fur-trading business in the Oregon Territory and believed their business interests granted them claim to the region. Conversely, the United States contended that it had first found and settled the region and could therefore rightfully claim it. The most ardent proponents of expansion demanded that the United States take the entire territory up to the 54°40' parallel, which ran along the southern shore of Alaska. As the ideology of Manifest Destiny swept the nation and the election of 1844 crept closer, Democrat **James K. Polk** sought to capitalize on the expansionist spirit with a campaign promise to extend the U.S. border up to Russian-controlled Alaska, using the slogan "Fifty-four forty or fight!" By the time he took office, Polk softened his demand for the entire Oregon Territory and was willing to negotiate with Britain. The border was drawn at the 49th parallel, which ceded what is now British Columbia, including Vancouver Island, and it granted navigation rights on the Columbia River to the British. Though the agreement represented a loss of U.S. territory, the Mexican-American War had erupted by this time, overshadowing concerns over the entrance of new free territories into the Union.

Texas Joins the Union

During this time, the status of Texas became a source of conflict. In 1821, Texas was officially a northern region of the newly independent Mexico. Mexico had attracted many American farmers and ranchers with cheap land and relative freedom from government intrusion. By the 1830s, Americans and slaves outnumbered Mexicans in the region. Mexico decided to regulate the Texans more strictly by banning slavery and demanding that all residents become Catholic. American settlers refused to abide by the new laws, and tensions escalated. In 1834, Antonio Lopez de Santa Anna became the military dictator of Mexico and attempted to force American settlers to follow Mexican law. The settlers, led by Sam Houston, staged a revolt in 1836 and declared Texas a republic independent of Mexico.

In present-day San Antonio, Santa Anna's forces attacked the Alamo, killing all Americans stationed there, and they marched to the San Jacinto River. There, a force led by Houston successfully captured Santa Anna. The Mexican dictator was forced to sign a decree granting independence to the Republic of Texas (Lone Star Republic). Houston was chosen to lead the new country, and he quickly applied for annexation, or adoption as a state into the Union. His petitions were initially rejected by Jackson and Van Buren, who feared tipping the balance in the Senate to favor slave states. Despite Tyler's support for annexation, Congress rejected his bid to bring Texas into the Union in 1844.

The presidential election of 1844 brought expansion and the fate of Texas to the forefront. Outgoing President Tyler saw the election of the expansionist candidate Polk as a mandate to drive the annexation of Texas through Congress. A joint resolution was passed to accept Texas's bid for annexation, which angered the Mexican government.

THE MEXICAN-AMERICAN WAR   `High-Yield`

President Polk was forced to react quickly to the impending crisis between Mexico and the United States, because Mexico had ended the diplomatic relationship between the countries and demanded the return of Texas. Polk sent special envoy John Slidell to Mexico City to inform the Mexican government of U.S. desires to draw the Texas border at the Rio Grande, rather than the Nueces River farther south, and to purchase California. In anticipation of Mexican resistance to Slidell's proposal, Polk amassed the U.S. Army, led by Zachary Taylor, along the disputed southern border of Texas at the Rio Grande River in January of 1846. In April, a Mexican force allegedly crossed the border and attacked Taylor's men, killing several American troops. Despite opposition from a small group of Whigs led by Abraham Lincoln, a large majority of Congress voted to declare war on Mexico. The **Mexican-American War** took place from April 1846 to February 1848, but it remained deeply controversial.

The war caused dissension among the many Americans who opposed the fighting on principle. Many Whigs and Northerners accused Polk of falsely claiming that American blood had been shed on American soil when the Mexican force crossed the Rio Grande. To them, the Texas-Mexico border lay some miles north at the Nueces, not at the Rio Grande. Furthermore, the issue of slavery expansion resurfaced. Transcendentalists, such as Henry David Thoreau and Ralph Waldo Emerson, protested the war by refusing to pay taxes. Sectional tension grew in Congress, as Representative David Wilmot proposed an amendment to a bill that would forbid slavery in any new lands acquired by the war with Mexico. The final bill passed in the House but failed in the Senate. This bill, the

16

Wilmot Proviso, signaled the start of an even deeper crisis that would pit the North against the South over issues of slavery's expansion, states' rights, and government representation.

After quick, decisive military victories by the United States in California and Texas, the Mexican-American War ended in September 1847. California had been declared independent as the Bear Flag Republic under the leadership of John C. Fremont, and Texas had been gained as the United States successfully overtook Mexico City. A peace was settled by the Treaty of Guadalupe Hidalgo in February 1848. The treaty granted California and most of the Southwest (including current-day New Mexico, Arizona, Utah, and Nevada) to the United States. The U.S. government agreed to pay war reparations in the sum of $15 million to the Mexican government. Despite continued bitter debate over the expansion of slavery, the treaty was ratified, officially ending the war.

> ✔ **AP Expert Note**
>
> **Be able to explain the impact of the Mexican-American War on the growing tension between the North and South**
>
> The Mexican-American War was controversial throughout its duration, as many Americans were divided on whether the United States should have entered the conflict at all. After gaining large new territories following the Mexican-American War, the United States was faced with a new problem: the question of whether slavery would be allowed in the new territories. Each side, the North and the South, feared that the political balance of free states versus slave states would tip toward the opposing side. Whether slavery would be allowed or banned in places such as California, Utah, New Mexico, and Nebraska was open to bitter debate.

CONTINUED DEBATE OVER SLAVERY

In 1853, President Franklin Pierce completed the Mexican cession through the **Gadsden Purchase** from Mexico, acquiring the Mesilla Valley in southern New Mexico and Arizona. During this purchase, the controversy over slavery escalated nationwide; the debate was political, social, economic, and, for many, moral.

Fueled by the religious passion inspired by the Second Great Awakening, abolitionists spoke out about the evils of slavery. After Nat Turner's Rebellion, however, some Southerners expressed concern over how the nation would handle the sudden release of African American slaves. Proslavery advocates in the South defended the "peculiar institution" against their Northern opponents. Some defenders used Biblical passages to justify slavery, while others maintained that the "family-like" atmosphere slave owners provided for African Americans was preferable to freedom. A large movement of proslavery defenders, led by George Fitzhugh, detailed the happy lives of Southern slaves who were clothed, fed, and housed by benevolent slave owners. Fitzhugh argued in his book *Cannibals All* (1857) that African American slaves were much better off than the "Northern wage slave," who was not provided with basic living needs for himself and his family.

The First Attempts at Compromise

In the election of 1848, a new political party was introduced: the **Free Soil Party**. Inspired by the Wilmot Proviso, antislavery advocates from various political parties founded the Free Soil Party to oppose the expansion of slavery into the new Western territories. Martin Van Buren ran for president as a Free Soil candidate in 1848 against the Whig **Zachary Taylor** and the Democrat Lewis Cass. Cass advocated the use of popular sovereignty to resolve the slavery issue in the new territories, which would enable citizens of the territories to vote on whether slavery would be permitted. Taylor won the election, largely due to the emergent Free Soil Party taking many Northern Democratic votes from Cass.

The discovery of gold in California at Sutter's Mill in 1848 began the **Gold Rush** in the following year, bringing an influx of people to the West. In response to its growing population, California quickly drafted a constitution to gain statehood. This constitution forbade slavery, which would again alter the balance in Congress. Although Taylor was proslavery, he recognized the importance of adding California to the Union. His support for adding California sparked intense debate in Congress, as radical Southerners warned of possible secession.

Henry Clay, the Great Compromiser, again came up with a plan, the **Compromise of 1850**, to avert a national crisis. His plan would:

- Admit California as a free state
- Divide the Mexican cession into the New Mexico and Utah Territories with popular sovereignty serving as the basis for determining the status of slavery
- Ban the slave trade in Washington, D.C.
- Enact a stricter **Fugitive Slave Act**
- Give Texas monetary compensation for that state's willingness to drop its claims to part of New Mexico's territory

As the debate intensified, Henry Clay, John C. Calhoun, and Daniel Webster led with impassioned speeches on the Senate floor. Clay and Webster supported compromise, while Calhoun opposed. Calhoun argued that this was an issue of states' rights, not morality, and the federal government should not intervene. Webster believed the compromise could save the divided Union and urged Northerners to be more conciliatory.

Many disagreed with even the idea of compromise. Northern radical William H. Seward argued that slavery should be banned on moral grounds. President Taylor, though himself a slaveowner, rejected the expansion of slavery on the idea it was economically unworkable in the West. Escalating tensions made compromise appear nearly impossible until President Taylor's sudden death in July 1850. His successor **Millard Fillmore** was more receptive to compromise, and he advocated for a solution that would address each side's primary concerns. Henry Clay drafted the Compromise of 1850, and the young senator Stephen A. Douglas helped garner enough votes. As each piece of the bill passed, President Fillmore stood by to sign it into law.

The Compromise of 1850 alleviated some of the tension between the North and South, delaying the Civil War for another decade. The North had gained a political and economic advantage with the admission of California as a free state. However, many Northerners opposed parts of the

16

compromise: namely, the use of popular sovereignty in Western territories and the strict Fugitive Slave Act, which punished those who harbored fugitives and gave federal commissioners the power to re-enslave those who escaped.

To circumvent the Fugitive Slave Act, abolitionists established the Underground Railroad to assist slaves escaping to the North. The harsh new laws also prompted Harriet Beecher Stowe to write *Uncle Tom's Cabin* (1852), which expressed Northern abolitionist frustrations with the Fugitive Slave Act. In the North, the novel quickly gained fame and convinced many that slavery was morally wrong. Meanwhile in the South, the commitment to protecting the institution of slavery intensified.

The Kansas-Nebraska Act

In the election of 1852, both campaigns largely avoided discussing slavery, which was the most pressing issue of the time. The Democrat **Franklin Pierce** was elected president, weakening the Whig Party even further. The increasing sectional tension became even more problematic, particularly because the Democrats gained control of both the executive and legislative branches.

In 1854, Democratic senator Stephen A. Douglas of Illinois proposed a new bill to address the slavery issue in the Nebraska Territory. This bill would divide the territory into two regions, Nebraska and Kansas, and each would vote by popular sovereignty on the issue of slavery. It was presumed that Nebraska would become a free state, while Kansas would become a slave state. Douglas's motivation was not only political, but also economic: he was a speculator in Western territories and required Southern support for a transcontinental railroad. His bill garnered Southern support, because both Kansas and Nebraska were above the 36° 30′ line of the Missouri Compromise. Douglas was able to push his bill through Congress, and President Pierce signed it into law in 1854.

The **Kansas-Nebraska Act** rekindled much of the controversy that had been quieted by the Compromise of 1850. By repealing the Missouri Compromise, Northern Democrats believed the Union had given too much to the South regarding the slavery issue. The new **Republican Party** emerged from the renewed sectional tension and was founded by antislavery Whigs, Democrats, Free-Soilers, and Know-Nothings from the North and West. Although the Republican Party lost the 1856 presidential election to Democrat **James Buchanan**, the popular John C. Fremont garnered many votes and won 11 of the 16 free states in the Electoral College.

Prior to the election of 1856, violence erupted between proslavery and antislavery groups in the Kansas territory. In response to the Kansas-Nebraska Act, there was population influx in Kansas, as many abolitionists and proslavery farmers wanted to vote on the slavery issue for the state. Henry Ward Beecher and other abolitionists helped antislavery settlers move to Kansas in response to the proslavery "border ruffians" moving across the border from Missouri. Violence inevitably broke out between the groups, giving the territory the name Bleeding Kansas.

In Kansas, the Missouri border ruffians drafted a proslavery constitution, protecting slaveholders and excluding free blacks from the bill of rights. This Lecompton Constitution caused intense debate in Congress, as President Buchanan supported it and Senator Douglas vehemently opposed it. Antislavery forces boycotted the ratification process, prompting a revote; this was then boycotted by the proslavery forces, allowing Kansas to be admitted to the Union as a free state.

The *Dred Scott* Decision

`High-Yield`

The Supreme Court's controversial decision in the **Dred Scott v. Sandford** case added fuel to the already raging debate over slavery. Dred Scott, a slave in Missouri, spent years in Wisconsin and Illinois with his master. After his master's death, Dred Scott, with financial assistance from Northern abolitionists, sued for freedom with the argument that he had spent time on free soil. In *Dred Scott v. Sandford*, the Court ruled that the 36° 30' provision of the Missouri Compromise was unconstitutional and that all African Americans (free or slave) were not citizens, thus making them ineligible to sue in federal court. Chief Justice Roger Taney argued that the Founding Fathers did not intend to give African Americans the protections of citizenship granted by the Constitution, so Scott had no right to sue in federal court. Taney also ruled that Congress had no right to deny citizens of their individual property, and therefore the Missouri Compromise was unconstitutional for stripping slave owners of their rightful property once they moved north. Southerners were encouraged by the decision, while Northern Democrats and Republicans were horrified.

Harper's Ferry

John Brown, a radical abolitionist who claimed he was following orders from God, gathered his followers to raid the federal arsenal at Harper's Ferry, Virginia. Brown planned to arm slaves on surrounding plantations with the hope of generating a slave rebellion and overthrowing the institution of slavery. In October 1859, Brown led a march to Harper's Ferry and seized the arsenal. Eventually, Brown and his followers were captured by the Virginia militia, tried for treason, and hanged. In the North, Brown was a martyr in the eyes of some abolitionists; in the South, he was seen as a dangerous psychotic who represented Northern abolitionists. In response to the raid on Harper's Ferry, Southerners formed citizen militias to counteract possible slave uprisings and became even more suspicious of the North's intentions.

> ✔ **AP Expert Note**
>
> **Know the factors that exacerbated existing sectional tensions**
>
> The AP exam will expect you to be able to string together the multiple factors that contributed to the outbreak of the Civil War. The Missouri Compromise of 1820 temporarily alleviated the sectional crisis over slavery, dictating that new territory in the North would be free, while new territory in the South would continue to have slavery. This Missouri Compromise held for 34 years until it was repealed by the Kansas-Nebraska Act of 1854. The violence that occurred shortly after the Kansas-Nebraska Act demonstrated how volatile regional tensions had become. The Compromise of 1850 would alleviate some of this tension, but only for another decade or so.

16

THE RISE OF LINCOLN AND THE ELECTION OF 1860

Republican **Abraham Lincoln** gained national attention in the Illinois Senate election of 1858, in which he was pitted against the powerful Democrat Stephen A. Douglas. Lincoln, an eloquent orator, challenged Douglas in a series of public debates. The most well-known debate occurred in Freeport, Illinois, where Lincoln challenged Douglas to rationalize the concept of popular sovereignty with the decision of the *Dred Scott* case. Douglas's response, also called the **Freeport Doctrine**, stated that territories would have to pass and enforce laws to protect slavery. In essence, he argued that *Dred Scott* would still be the law of the land but that, by willfully choosing to not arm themselves with the means to police the issue, territories could still technically be free soil. This attempt to appease both wings of the Democratic Party alienated supporters in the South. Although Douglas was able to keep his Senate seat, his chances of winning the 1860 presidential election dwindled. These debates also brought the previously unknown Lincoln into the spotlight as a possible Republican candidate for the upcoming election.

The nominating conventions for the election of 1860 revealed the country's deepening divisions. At the Democratic Convention, Southerners protested the nomination of Stephen A. Douglas, whom they considered a traitor. It became clear that the party would not be able to nominate a single candidate, so the party split and Northerners nominated Douglas, while the Southerners chose John C. Breckenridge. The Republicans decided against the radical William H. Seward and instead nominated the more moderate Abraham Lincoln. In addition to barring the extension of slavery into the new territories, the broad Republican platform promised a protective tariff, immigrant rights, a transcontinental railroad, federal financing for infrastructure improvements in the West, and free homesteads for citizens. During the campaign, Southern Democrats warned that they would leave the Union if Lincoln were elected. Some remaining Whigs and moderates, concerned that Lincoln's victory would end the Union, formed the Constitutional Union Party, which nominated John Bell of Tennessee as its candidate. The party hoped to garner enough Republican votes to prevent the Southern states from seceding.

Lincoln won about 40 percent of the popular vote and 180 electoral votes. Breckenridge carried the South, but only managed to earn 72 electoral votes. Although the South still maintained control of the legislative and judicial branches, secession appeared inevitable.

The Secession of the South

The South Carolina legislature declared its intention to secede from the United States just days after Lincoln's election. By February 1861, six more states had joined South Carolina to form the **Confederate States of America**, with **Jefferson Davis** as its president. As a final attempt at compromise, Kentucky senator John Crittenden proposed an amendment to the Constitution to extend the Missouri Compromise line to the Pacific border, with slavery prohibited north of the line and protected south of it. President-elect Lincoln rejected the compromise, as the extension of slavery opposed Republican beliefs.

Southerners felt that leaving the Union was politically justified, as the states had voluntarily entered the Union to begin with and therefore had the right to leave. Considering the philosophies of John Locke and the American Founding Fathers, Southerners believed it was their responsibility to over-throw a government that no longer protected its citizens' rights to life, liberty, and property. The South drew upon the Kentucky and Virginia Resolutions, as well as speeches by South Carolina's John C. Calhoun regarding nullification and the strength of the Union. The South assumed that the North would allow it to leave the Union peacefully, as the regions were already economically independent. However, the South miscalculated the North's willingness to allow the dissolution of the Union.

THE CIVIL WAR

High-Yield

Regional Advantages and Disadvantages

Long before the first shots of the **Civil War** were fired on **Fort Sumter** in April 1861, the North and South had already become distinctly different regions. Now that each region was preparing for war, each had to take advantage of its strengths and exploit the weaknesses of the enemy.

The Confederacy was faced with fighting a defensive war on its own territory. This, combined with high troop morale, well-trained generals, and access to the coast, gave the South an advantage at the beginning of the war. The Union, on the other hand, was fighting an offensive war. This required many more men and munitions, both of which needed to be moved long distances to the front lines.

However, the sheer size of the North's population was a strong advantage for the Union troops. Since the Compromise of 1850, the North's economy had grown in the industrial and financial sectors; Northerners controlled the nation's banks, railroads, and factories. To pay for the war, the Union levied the first-ever income tax, raised excise taxes and a protective tariff, and issued paper money called "greenbacks" as a wartime currency.

Largely an agricultural region, the South was at a distinct disadvantage in accessing manufactured goods necessary to fight a war, such as weapons and uniforms. As the war continued, Confederate soldiers lacked basic equipment, including shoes, blankets, and clothing. Union forces destroyed Southern railroad tracks, limiting the Confederacy's ability to transport men, supplies, or goods for manufacture. The Confederacy heavily relied on worldwide demand for cotton to keep it afloat during the war, and it sought foreign assistance. The French and British, however, saw a diplomatic alliance with the Confederacy as a liability for a future relationship with the United States and refused to directly support the Confederate war effort. Worldwide demand for cotton fell in the mid-1860s, forcing the Confederacy to issue war bonds, raise duties on farm goods, and even overprint their paper currency, which caused rampant inflation.

Finding Soldiers to Fight

Desertion was common on both sides of the conflict. The Union army originally consisted almost entirely of volunteers. As the pool of volunteers began to dwindle, the Union enacted the first

16

federal law to draft young men to military service in 1863. The draft caused conflicts in the North, most notably the New York Draft Riots, in which hundreds were killed, and entire city blocks were destroyed by fire. The rioters, who were primarily Irish immigrants, feared that newly emancipated African Americans would undercut them in the labor market, and they resented that wealthy men were able to buy exemptions from the military draft. Some African American soldiers fought for the North early in the war; those numbers increased significantly after the Emancipation Proclamation.

The South also relied on volunteers to fill its ranks. With a smaller population to draw from, the Confederacy was forced to implement a draft a year earlier than the North. Class and regional divisions were much more evident in the South, as wealthy planters were able to purchase a substitute to fight on their behalf. Fear of arming slaves kept the Confederacy from using African Americans until the end of the war.

Dissension within the Union

Abraham Lincoln was aware of the tenuous relationship between the North and the border states, as well as the necessity of keeping them in the Union. Delaware, Maryland, Missouri, and Kentucky each decided to remain in the Union, despite their slave-holding status. However, there were still citizens in these states opposed to the war. Citizens' militia groups sympathetic to the Confederate cause were active during the war and were monitored by Union forces.

Dissent was also evident within Congress. Speaking of the unjust nature of the war and their concern over the disruption of Western trade routes, a group of Northern Democrats referred to as the Copperheads lashed out at President Lincoln's broad use of executive power and demanded an immediate end to the war. Despite heated debate, Lincoln continued to use the powers of the executive branch throughout the war.

Military Engagement and Foreign Influence

The Union hoped a quick, powerful attack on Virginia would severely weaken the Confederacy at the outset of the war. However, the Union's military leadership underestimated the Confederates' drive to fight back. The first major battle of the Civil War showed both sides that there would be a long, bitter fight ahead.

In July 1861, federal troops marched about 25 miles from Washington, D.C., south to Manassas, Virginia. There, Confederate troops stood ready for the oncoming attack. Early in the **Battle of Bull Run** (also known as the Battle of Manassas by the Confederacy), Union forces appeared to have the upper hand; however, the arrival of more Confederate soldiers led by General "Stonewall" Jackson forced Union troops to retreat to Washington. While this battle showed the North that this would be a long and bloody war, Southerners felt emboldened by their victory.

The Union army, led by General Winfield Scott, drew up a new four-phase plan to gradually wear down the Confederacy. In the first phase, the Anaconda Plan, the Union navy blockaded all Southern ports in order to cut off their supplies and trade. In the second phase, the navy split the Confederacy in half by taking control of the Mississippi River. In the third phase, the Union cut through Georgia, and then traveled up the coast to the Carolinas. And finally, in the last phase, the Union captured the Confederate capitol at Richmond.

The Second Battle of Bull Run and Antietam

President Lincoln grew impatient as the Eastern Union commander general George McClellan refused to send untrained men into battle. Eventually, McClellan launched his troops into the peninsula region of Virginia in March 1862; however, the Confederate general Robert E. Lee forced the Union army to retreat after seven days. As Union leadership in the East changed, General Lee took advantage of the transition by engaging Union troops again at Manassas in the **Second Battle of Bull Run**. This time, Union General John Pope was sent back across the Potomac in retreat.

Now, with two decisive victories, and with the hope that a third win would bring foreign aid, Lee confidently led his troops into enemy territory in Maryland. With McClellan's return to Union leadership and advanced knowledge of Lee's plans, Union forces were able to cut Lee off at **Antietam** Creek. The bloodiest battle of the war ensued, as more than 22,000 men were killed or wounded. Lee's men were eventually forced to retreat to Virginia. However, General McClellan failed to pursue the retreating Confederates, which enraged President Lincoln. Lincoln promptly relieved him from his command, replacing him with General Ambrose Burnside.

At the **Battle of Fredericksburg** in December 1862, Lee defeated the aggressive Union general Burnside, who was then replaced by General Joseph Hooker. Aside from land battles, 1862 also saw a revolution in naval warfare with the launching of steam-powered warships, the ironclads: The South's CSS *Merrimac*, touted as a ship that could sink wooden naval ships with one blast, posed a grave threat to the Union blockade. The Confederates had not, however, accounted for the Union having its own ironclad, named the USS *Monitor*. In a five-hour battle in March 1862, the ironclads fought to a draw. After this battle, the navy no longer depended on wooden ships.

Union Victories

Control of the Mississippi River was at the center of the fighting in the Western region. Union general Ulysses S. Grant led troops through Kentucky and Tennessee, fighting a bloody battle at Shiloh in April 1862. By the spring of 1863, Grant controlled the port city of New Orleans and almost the entire Mississippi River region. To consolidate control of the region, Grant launched an attack on Vicksburg, Mississippi. Union forces lay siege for seven weeks to the fortified city, and after successfully defeating it, they controlled the entire Mississippi River region.

Meanwhile, fighting continued in the Eastern theater. Jackson's men successfully defeated Union General Hooker at Chancellorsville by flanking Northern forces. Despite the victory, the Confederates suffered great losses of over 13,000 men. In addition, Jackson was killed by friendly fire in a devastating blow to the Confederacy. In a last-ditch effort to invade the North, garner the support of foreign powers, and perhaps force the Union to negotiate for peace, Lee launched an invasion in Pennsylvania. The two armies converged at the small town of Gettysburg in southern

16

Pennsylvania. The **Battle of Gettysburg** was the most significant battle of the war. Fought from July 1 to 3, 1863, Gettysburg was the bloodiest battle, with over 50,000 men killed. Lee could not recover from the losses suffered and retreated to Virginia. The Confederacy would never regain the offensive after Gettysburg. Lincoln's poignant **Gettysburg Address** cemented the battle's place in American memory.

General Grant chose William Tecumseh Sherman to lead Union troops through the South. After winning the battle of Kennesaw Mountain in Georgia, Sherman's army captured and destroyed Atlanta in September of 1864. Sherman then marched to South Carolina and ordered troops to burn and destroy fields, homes, and cities as they marched through Georgia. His goal was to inflict misery on Southerners so they would be compelled to surrender. This strategy made the Civil War the first modern "total war," with citizens as targets. Sherman was able to capture Savannah, Georgia, in December 1864 and Columbia, South Carolina, in February 1865. By this time, Grant's forces in Virginia were on the verge of victory.

Southern Surrender

Lee's troop strength had worn thin by the time his army evacuated the Confederate capital of Richmond, Virginia, in April 1865. Knowing that the end was near, Confederate leaders hoped to negotiate with President Lincoln for peace terms. While Jefferson Davis still clung to the dream of Southern independence, Lincoln refused anything short of an unconditional surrender of the South and a restoration of the Union. General Lee, surrounded by General Grant's forces west of Richmond, agreed to surrender. On April 9, 1865, the Confederate Army of Northern Virginia officially surrendered in the parlor of the house owned by Wilmer McLean at Appomattox Court House in Virginia.

> ✔ **AP Expert Note**
>
> **Be able to assess why the Union was able to prevail over the Confederacy**
>
> Overall, the Union had greater manpower and more resources than did the Confederacy. Despite the military prowess of Confederate leaders, the South's infrastructure was largely destroyed, which would allow for key military victories for the Union army. Under the leadership of Lincoln, the Union was also successful in persuading Europe to not get involved. Additionally, after the Emancipation Proclamation, many slaves left the Southern plantations and joined the Union. These former slaves played a significant role in the ultimate victory over the South.

THE END OF SLAVERY

As a politician, Abraham Lincoln had been extremely cautious regarding the issue of slavery. As president, Lincoln was a master at gauging public opinion and reacting accordingly. Therefore, he understood that he needed to connect with all types of American voters, including residents of the border states and prejudiced Northerners. He calculated the timing of his speeches and actions to coincide with the waves of public opinion and military victories.

16

In the early years of the war, the federal government passed Confiscation Acts designed to allow Union troops to seize enemy property that could be used in an act of war. Slaves fit under the loose definition of property and could, thus, be confiscated. The second of these acts freed slaves in any territory that was currently in rebellion against the Union. These were the first steps in the emancipation of slaves.

After the Battle of Antietam in September 1862, President Lincoln properly calculated that the nation was ready for a shift from an "offensive war" to save the Union, to a "total war" to rectify a moral wrong. As promised, the president issued the **Emancipation Proclamation** on January 1, 1863. The proclamation applied only to slaves living in Confederate states; slavery in the border states was still legal. Despite its limitations, the proclamation did much to bolster the morale of Union troops and supporters at home. However, many in the North (particularly those in the border states) felt that Lincoln had gone too far. Moreover, many Union soldiers felt betrayed by the proclamation, believing they had been duped into fighting a war for emancipation, instead of merely for the Union's preservation. Nevertheless, the next great step toward emancipation had been taken.

The only remaining obstacle to freedom for slaves was the Constitution. Since its ratification, differing interpretations of the document either ignored the slavery issue or protected the institution and slave owners. President Lincoln would need an amendment to the Constitution to fully achieve emancipation and free slaves in the border states. The president worked tirelessly to garner enough votes in Congress to secure passage of the **Thirteenth Amendment**, which abolished slavery in the United States. Tragically, President Lincoln died before the amendment was ratified; he was assassinated by John Wilkes Booth on April 14, 1865, while attending a play in Ford's Theater.

Even before ratification of the Thirteenth Amendment, thousands of freed slaves had flocked to the North in search of refuge. Many joined the Union army, serving in segregated units, while others worked in supporting jobs along the battlefields. In fact, President Lincoln eventually credited the 180,000 African Americans who fought for the Union with having turned the tide of the war. However, full-scale efforts to assimilate former slaves into American society were not made until after the war ended.

CONSEQUENCES OF THE CIVIL WAR

There were multiple social, political, and economic consequences resulting from the Civil War. No part of America was left untouched, as the war of "brother against brother" had raged on for four long and bloody years. Both sides lost a generation of young men to death and injury, a loss from which it would take many years to recover. Approximately 620,000 men had lost their lives in the war, and over a million more had been wounded.

During and after the war, many women struggled with poverty, as they suddenly became heads of the household due to death of or desertion by their husbands. With men away fighting, women played a critical role on the battlefield as nurses and behind the lines as volunteers in hospitals.

The Civil War opened doors for women and gave many the courage to fight for suffrage rights at the turn of the twentieth century.

In 1865, the United States gained about four million new citizens instantly. With the ratification of the Thirteenth Amendment, these newly freed African Americans now had to find a place in the American social structure. Southern whites came to the realization that their way of life would be forever altered, and they struggled to find peace among the chaos.

During the Civil War, President Lincoln exercised his executive power to limit Americans' civil rights and liberties to protect the Union. He enacted a **suspension of the writ of habeas corpus**, which meant that the federal government could hold an individual in jail with no charges levied against him or her. For many traitors, this meant long jail terms with no charges ever filed. Lincoln intended for this suspension to be only temporary, and the constitutional right would be restored after the war was over.

The major long-term effect of the Civil War was a shift of political ideology away from protection of states' rights toward preservation of the Union and the federal government's authority. The concept of democracy had expanded, as new African American citizens were guaranteed the rights and protections of the Constitution. Much to the chagrin of many European conservatives, America's democracy had survived a major challenge and appeared more powerful than ever.

Economically, the war was devastating for the South. Its infrastructure and industry stood in ruins. Jefferson's dream of an agrarian empire soon faded as the energy of the country shifted toward industrialization. During the recovery phase, many Northerners moved South to help newly freed African Americans in their transition and to help organize the reconstruction of Southern governments.

The West benefited from wartime acts designed to stimulate settlement on the frontier. The Homestead Act of 1862 granted 160 acres to any family that would agree to farm it for at least five years. The Morrill Land Grant Act gave federal lands to states for the purpose of building schools that would teach agriculture and technical trades. Perhaps most significantly, the **Pacific Railway Act** approved building a transcontinental railroad that would transform the West by linking the Atlantic Ocean with the Pacific.

RECONSTRUCTION

As the Civil War ended, the federal government was confronted with the issue of the economically and physically destroyed former Confederacy. Questions abounded about the treatment of Confederate leaders, the readmission of former Confederate states into the Union, and the assimilation of four million former slaves into the social fabric of the nation. The decision-making process was hindered by the traditional American fear of a large, powerful federal government. However, it became clear that **Reconstruction** would only be possible with strong federal leadership. The

16

enormous task of reconciling the North and South fell upon the shoulders of President **Andrew Johnson** and Congress.

Before his assassination, President Lincoln had formulated some provisions for the rebuilding of the Union. His Proclamation of Amnesty and Reconstruction, also known as the **Ten Percent Plan**, was issued in 1863 as a way to bring Southern states back under the wing of the federal government. The plan reestablished state governments and required at least 10 percent of the states' voters to swear an oath of loyalty to the United States and the Constitution. Lincoln was also prepared to grant complete pardons to any former Confederate, but required an oath of allegiance and agreement to eliminate slavery.

Fellow Republicans were displeased with Lincoln's plan and decided to pass their own legislation to create more obstacles to readmittance of former rebellious states. The **Wade-Davis Bill** was passed by both houses in 1864. It required that 50 percent of Southern state voters take the loyalty oath, and it allowed only those citizens who had not been active members or supporters of the Confederacy to approve of the new state constitutions. Exercising his executive power, Lincoln pocket-vetoed the bill by refusing to sign it.

Regarding assistance of newly freed slaves, white Americans were typically reluctant to provide much assistance. Many Americans believed that to reap the benefits of a democratic society, all one needed to do was work hard. Therefore, they felt that African Americans should earn their new place in society. However, freed slaves struggled to transition, and the federal government intervened. In order to help manage and assist the newly emancipated slaves, the federal government created the **Freedman's Bureau** in 1865. The bureau provided assistance in the form of food, shelter, and medical attention to African Americans. Eventually, the bureau would establish schools across the South to help educate large numbers of former slaves. The Freedman's Bureau struggled as Congress refused to increase its funding, which expired in 1872.

After Lincoln's assassination, it appeared that President Johnson would continue his predecessor's basic Reconstruction plan, with some added conditions on former Confederates. Keeping Lincoln's Ten Percent Plan, Johnson added the disenfranchisement of some former Confederates, namely those who had been in leadership positions or who had assets of $250,000 or more. Johnson retained his right to grant full pardons to these former Confederates, which he exercised freely with Southern elites. As a result, many former Confederate leaders and wealthy plantation owners were back in Congress as early as the end of 1865.

Johnson was not close with Republican members of Congress, who felt that Johnson was too friendly with the old Confederate guard and were angered by his continual refusal to support African Americans' rights. With the upcoming congressional elections of 1866, Johnson traveled the country in his "swing around the circle" tour, lodging attacks on his opponents who were running for congressional reelection. These opponents countered with accusations of alcoholism and anti-Unionism.

16

In return, Republicans running for office resorted to emotionalism by "waving the bloody shirt," or invoking the pain of the Civil War, in an attempt to turn Northern voters against Democrats. The election yielded a Republican victory, with moderates and radicals gaining more than a two-thirds majority in both houses. The Republicans in Congress felt they had better ideas for Reconstruction. Fearing a return of the Southern Democratic contingency, they became increasingly radical.

While Congress was on hiatus, Southern legislatures adopted **Black Codes** in response to legal emancipation. These codes restricted the actions, movements, and freedoms of African Americans. Under these codes, African Americans could not own land, so they were tied instead to small plots leased from a landowner. This began the system of **sharecropping**. Sharecroppers would lease land and borrow supplies to till their plots, while giving a significant portion of their harvest to the landowner as payment for the loan. The exploitative system ensured that farmers were never able to harvest enough to pay the landlord and feed their families. Generations of African Americans remained tied to their plot of land until the civil rights movement of the 1950s and 1960s. Having refused to sign legislation that would revive the Freedman's Bureau and protect African Americans from the Black Codes, Johnson prepared for a fight with Congress.

The Fourteenth Amendment

Radical Reconstruction occurred as many former Confederates took office. Republicans were furious that these former rebels were allowed to rejoin Congress, and they were further angered by Johnson's backtracking on civil rights. After they modified the bill to restore the Freedman's Bureau, Radical Republicans set out to protect the civil rights of African Americans. The **Civil Rights Bill of 1866** was designed to end the Black Codes by giving African Americans full citizenship. As expected, Johnson vetoed the bill, and Congress overturned his veto. Many Republicans were concerned that a future return of a Democratic majority might mean the end of the bill they had worked so hard to pass. Therefore, they needed a more permanent solution to the civil rights problem.

Proposed by Congress in 1866 and finally ratified in 1868, the **Fourteenth Amendment** protected the rights of all U.S. citizens, granted all African Americans full citizenship and civil rights, and required states to adhere to the due process and equal protection clauses of the Constitution. Furthermore, Republicans added some provisions aimed directly at the former Confederacy, which disallowed former Confederate officers from holding state or federal office and would decrease the proportional representation of any state that denied suffrage to any able citizen.

Radical Republicans directly challenged President Johnson when they rejected his Reconstruction plan and instead passed the Military Reconstruction Act of 1867. The Military Reconstruction Act placed the South under martial law, dividing the South into five districts that would be governed by a Union general stationed in each. The act further tightened the readmission requirements of former Confederate states by requiring petitioning states to ratify the Fourteenth Amendment and provide for universal manhood suffrage.

The impeachment crisis began when congressional Republicans passed the Tenure of Office Act in 1867, disallowing the president from discharging a federal appointee without the Senate's consent.

With the act, Republicans in Congress attempted to protect their positions from Johnson. The president chose to ignore the act and fired Republican secretary of war Edwin Stanton. The House of Representatives promptly submitted articles of impeachment to the floor by charging Johnson with 11 counts of "high crimes and misdemeanors." He was impeached by the House, but the Senate failed to convict Johnson by only one vote.

The Fifteenth Amendment

Johnson did not run for the presidency in 1868, and the Republican nomination went to the Civil War hero **Ulysses S. Grant**, who won with a large boost from the African American vote. During his tenure, radical Republicans such as Representative Thaddeus Stephens and Senator Charles Sumner continued pushing for the protection of civil rights in Southern states. The **Fifteenth Amendment**, ratified in 1870, barred any state from denying a citizen's right to vote on the basis of race, color, or previous servitude.

The last of the Reconstruction-era civil rights acts was passed in 1875. The **Civil Rights Act of 1875** made it a crime for any person to be denied full and equal use of public places, such as hotels, rail cars, restaurants, and theaters. Unfortunately, this act lacked any wording to enforce it, and it was therefore ignored by most states, both Northern and Southern. It took another 90 years before Congress penned an enforceable civil rights act.

> ✔ **AP Expert Note**
>
> **Be able to make connections across time periods**
>
> On the AP exam, you will be expected to identify how historical developments from different time periods are connected. Practice this skill by tracing the impacts the Fourteenth and Fifteenth Amendments would have in the future. The Fourteenth Amendment provided African Americans citizenship, equal protection, and due process. The Fifteenth Amendment provided them the right to vote. In later time periods, these amendments came into play with the U.S. Supreme Court cases of *Plessy v. Ferguson* (1896) and *Brown v. Board of Education* (1954). Many of the protections provided by the Fourteenth and Fifteenth Amendments were largely ignored in the South and would not be realized until the passage of the Civil Rights Act in 1964 and the Voting Rights Act in 1965.

The Ongoing Women's Suffrage Movement

The Fourteenth Amendment introduced the word "male" as a qualifier for voting into the Constitution, while the Fifteenth Amendment explicitly extended voting rights to all men. In other words, "universal manhood suffrage" constitutionally cemented the idea that men were legally superior to women. There was a fear that future court decisions might go further, ruling that women's suffrage itself was unconstitutional on those grounds. The Fourteenth and Fifteenth amendment split the women's suffrage movement in two, leading to decades of bitter partisanship between the two wings.

One faction opposed the Reconstruction amendments on the grounds that voting rights for women and blacks should not be separated. Additionally, some suffragists such as Elizabeth Cady Stanton saw the idea of *all* people having an inherent right to vote as odious, preferring to restrict voting to the "right sort" of men and women (educated, middle- to upper-class); such disdain was not universal among this faction, and it became a moot point after the passage of both amendments. Suffrage for women would be on universal grounds, whatever anyone preferred. This faction went on to form the **National Woman Suffrage Association (NWSA)** in 1869. The NWSA, an all-female organization, favored a federal solution to women's suffrage, namely an amendment. They also supported individual rights for women. Overall, the NWSA was the more liberal in nature of the two splinter groups.

The other suffragist faction accepted that the Reconstruction amendments disadvantaged women, and thought it unfortunate, but held that the needs of former slaves were paramount, even if only male former slaves were protected. Frederick Douglass held the latter view; despite supporting women's suffrage, he saw the matter as a more critical one for blacks. This faction went on to form the **American Woman Suffrage Association (AWSA)** in 1869. In contrast to the NWSA, the AWSA favored a state-by-state effort at securing women's suffrage, accepted male members, and remained focused on suffrage to the exclusion of other issues. It was also more conservative in nature.

Freedmen in the Postwar South

Reconstruction was a turbulent period for African Americans in the South; many were never even told they had been emancipated. Slaves would be freed by Union armies marching through their region and then re-enslaved as soon as the soldiers left. Some plantation owners simply refused to recognize the Thirteenth Amendment. Slaves themselves varied in their response to their newfound freedom. Some joyfully began a new life; others were reluctant to exercise their new freedom and initially remained with their masters. Still others reacted with violence when freed. Eventually, all slaves in the South were freed under federal martial law.

Once free, many went in search of a new life or to find family members and friends. As many as 25,000 former slaves uprooted their families and moved toward Kansas between 1878 and 1880. These migrants called themselves Exodusters, because they believed that their promised land lay somewhere in the West. Word of their travels, as well as rumors about the federal government designating the entire state of Kansas for former slaves, spread through the vast church networks connecting formerly enslaved families across the South. Church became the central focus for most African Americans during the postwar period; it was there that they could form a community with other African Americans.

Southern Governments

Despite being under federal martial law, Southern states hoped to return to statehood and quickly regain some stability. For Republicans on Capitol Hill, recognition of these state governments' legitimacy depended on how quickly they met the federal government's demands. African Americans soon realized the power of the vote, taking control of the lower house in South Carolina and seating several black representatives and senators in Congress. However, whites still maintained majority control of all other upper and lower houses and the governorships in all Southern states.

The Democrats remained the party of choice for Southerners, although the Republican Party did gain some strength through freedmen and Northerners who moved south. Southern Democrats named Southern Republicans scalawags, a derogatory term that meant they were pirates who sought to steal from state governments and line their own pockets. Northern Republicans who moved south to seek their fortunes were called carpetbaggers, a term that came from the stereotype of the Northerner who packed all of his worldly possessions in a suitcase made from carpet. Many white Southerners resented any intrusion by Northerners, even if they were in the South to aid in the rebuilding.

Although tensions ran high during the military Reconstruction period, Southern governments did manage to piece together several successes. Reconstruction Southern legislatures created a system to provide state-funded public education. Southern infrastructure was given a boost, with the public rebuilding and improvement of roads, rail lines, and waterways; hospitals and prisons were also modernized. Republican legislatures funded these improvements through better tax codes and collection services.

Even with these improvements, Southerners remained suspicious of the Republicans. There were accusations of Republicans taking advantage of the weak Southern system by siphoning off monies. Many legislators were alleged to have arranged for government contractors to give them monetary gifts in return for contracts. Others allegedly received bribes from companies and individuals who sought to cheat the system. Grant administration scandals did not improve the Southern perception of Republicans.

Despite ratification of the Fourteenth and Fifteenth Amendments, racism still existed, and angry whites in the South sometimes resorted to violence to intimidate blacks. One of the most infamous examples was the **Ku Klux Klan (KKK)**, an underground society of whites who ruthlessly and successfully used terrorist tactics to frighten both white and black Republicans in the South. Congress sought to abolish the Klan with the Force Acts of 1870 and 1871, which authorized the use of federal troops to quell violence and enforce the Fourteenth and Fifteenth Amendments. While these acts were moderately successful in limiting the Klan's activities, the group continued to exist, resurfacing in the 1920s in response to an influx of Southern and Eastern European immigrants.

A growing movement sought to restore political control of the South to Southerners. This movement was fueled by increasing resentment of federal rule of the South. Those who wished to return control of the South to Southerners came to be known as Redeemers.

The Compromise of 1877

The election of 1876 remains one of the most controversial in American history. Republican **Rutherford B. Hayes** became president after a series of events. When the polls closed and the votes were counted, Democrat Samuel Tilden had won the popular vote. However, the electoral votes of three Southern states that Tilden would need to win the presidency were contested; within each state, both parties claimed their candidate had won. A federal commission was appointed to investigate and decide who should take the contested votes.

The commission was made up of both Republicans and Democrats, and in-fighting between the parties on the commission led to the Democrats threatening a filibuster that would send the decision to the House of Representatives for a vote. As the Democrats held the majority, the Republicans changed their tactics, and the outcome of the election was ultimately decided by an unwritten negotiation. The Compromise of 1877 provided that Rutherford B. Hayes would become president only if he agreed to remove the last remaining federal troops stationed in South Carolina, Florida, and Louisiana. The end of martial law in the South signaled the end of Reconstruction in the United States.

The Impact of Reconstruction

Historians today still cannot agree on the overall impact and effectiveness of Reconstruction. It is clear, however, that white Southerners emerged from the Civil War and Reconstruction embittered and angry, as they believed that their way of life had been forever altered. Southerners were also angry about the federal government's protections provided to African Americans, as well as the Northerners' interference in Southern politics and daily life. As a result, many white Southerners turned radical in their resentment of African Americans and Northerners.

It is evident that President Lincoln, President Johnson, and Congress had no clear plan regarding how to change the postwar South. Republicans seemed to enter Reconstruction with an idealistic mindset and left exhausted by the reality. By offering pardons and quick readmittance for former Confederate states, it was hoped that the South would readily rejoin the Union. Republicans in Congress, however, wished to protect the rights of African Americans, while also advancing their own political agenda.

Unfortunately for African Americans, it was the political agenda of Republicans that would ultimately stand in their path to realizing full rights and protections. Though African Americans were no longer held as slaves, they were widely relegated to inferior positions through economic, political, and social restrictions of their rights. Most found themselves trapped in poverty due to the sharecropping system and disenfranchised despite the rights guaranteed them in the Fourteenth and Fifteenth Amendments. In many respects, the prewar South was revived by the actions of Republicans who had sought to dismantle it. The social and political atmosphere of the postwar South lasted well into the next century.

 NEXT STEP: PRACTICE

Go to Rapid Review and Practice Chapter 7 or to your online quizzes on kaptest.com for exam-like practice on this topic.

Haven't registered your book yet? Go to kaptest.com/moreonline to begin.

CHAPTER 17

Period 6: 1865–1898

THE INDUSTRIALIZATION OF AMERICA

Significant economic and social changes transformed the United States in the years following the Civil War, including the rise of big business, a shift from farming to wage labor, an influx of immigrants from many countries, and the growth of cities.

The Transcontinental Railroad

High-Yield

During the Civil War, railroad building in the West increased as railroad companies sought to earn profits by transporting goods and people between the rapidly growing towns and cities within the region, as well as between the East and the West. To facilitate cross-country rail travel, the U.S. government subsidized the building of the **Transcontinental Railroad**, and gave huge land grants to rail companies building rail lines throughout the West.

At this time, the railroad industry was already booming in the East, with men such as Cornelius Vanderbilt leading in the modernization of older tracks. Vanderbilt had amassed a fortune in the steamboat business and invested this fortune in the consolidation of many smaller rail lines under one company, the New York Central Railroad. Before Vanderbilt's domination of the industry, there were dozens of small rail lines with varying widths of rail, mostly constructed of iron. Steel rails were safer because they did not rust and were stronger, allowing trains to carry heavier loads. By connecting the smaller lines and converting all lines to common-gauge steel rails, Vanderbilt linked major cities on the East Coast and in the Midwest.

The western half of the Transcontinental Railroad was constructed by the Congressionally appointed Union Pacific Railroad and Central Pacific Railroad companies. The federal government gave the railroad companies generous land grants and federal loans for each mile of track that was laid. The Central Pacific Railroad, led by Leland Stanford, set out to build the most difficult stretch of rail from Sacramento, California, through the Sierra Nevada mountains and eastward. The Union Pacific Railroad began building its portion of the transcontinental railroad from Omaha, Nebraska, moving westward. The rail lines of the Central Pacific and Union Pacific finally met on May 10, 1869, at Promontory Point, Utah, just north of the Great Salt Lake. Chinese laborers built most of the Central Pacific's line, while Irish American workers and Civil War veterans built most of Union Pacific's portion of the tracks. The completion of the Transcontinental Railroad linked the nation from sea to sea by both rail and telegraph. This railroad accelerated the development and eventual closure of the frontier.

The growth of the railroads had a major influence on the growth of the national economy, mainly: enormous consumption of steel, employment of thousands of workers, and transportation of raw materials to factories and finished goods to consumer markets. Between 1865 and 1890, railroads grew from 35,000 miles of track to 167,000 miles.

Despite this growth, the impact of railroads on the economy was not always positive. Wishing to reap the rewards of land and money, some railroad owners defrauded the federal government. Men such as Jay Gould earned the nickname **robber barons** as they artificially inflated the value of their company's stock, sold the stock to the public, and pocketed the profits. The company would then go bankrupt, leaving stockholders with nothing. Additionally, competition among rail lines was fierce, leading to dishonest business practices. Many companies offered rebates or kickbacks to certain high-volume customers while charging exorbitant rates to smaller shippers, such as farmers.

Advances in communications technology were also important in facilitating the flow of information across the nation and internationally. Transatlantic cable lines improved the speed of telegraph communication between the United States and Europe. Western Union, which controlled 80 percent of the telegraph lines in the United States, operated nearly 200,000 miles of telegraph routes from coast to coast. The telephone, patented by Alexander Graham Bell in 1876, also increased the speed of communication within the United States. By 1880, there were 50,000 telephones in use in the United States, including one at the White House. By 1900, that number had increased to 1.35 million.

Monopolies and Industrial Consolidation

`High-Yield`

The hands-off approach of the federal government toward big business helped to fuel the growth of large business ventures after the Civil War. The United States experienced a second industrial revolution, as the industrial sector of its economy shifted from light manufacturing to heavy industry, with steel, oil, and heavy machinery driving growth.

Birth of the Steel Industry

The continued growth of the railroad industry after the Civil War served as one stimulus to growth of the steel industry, because new rails and locomotives were made of steel. The Bessemer process, developed by an English inventor, revolutionized steel production by making it faster and cheaper. The increased availability and affordability of steel caused its use to increase in many industrial applications.

A young Scottish immigrant named Andrew Carnegie saw a future in the production of steel and the modernization of the steel industry. Carnegie advanced to management in the railroad business in the 1860s, focusing on innovation, investment in technology, operating at full capacity, and keeping costs (including wages) low. As a result, **Carnegie Steel Company** grew rapidly, and Carnegie soon was responsible for supplying over half of the world's steel.

However, steel production alone was not responsible for Carnegie's success. Carnegie acquired other companies in order to achieve control of every aspect of the production process for steel, from the mining of the ore to the distribution of the finished product. This strategy, called **vertical integration**, was new to manufacturing. When Carnegie retired from the steel business in 1901, he sold his company to J. P. Morgan, who then combined it with other steel companies to create **U.S. Steel**, the country's first corporation with a capitalization of over one billion dollars.

Growth of the Oil Industry

Meanwhile, the discovery of oil in northwestern Pennsylvania in 1859 would revolutionize many other industries throughout the world. Kerosene soon emerged as the fuel of choice for lighting, and the internal combustion engine would make work such as mining and farming faster.

A young businessman saw the potential in this "black gold" and soon joined Carnegie as one of the nation's wealthiest men. John D. Rockefeller invested in 1863 in a refinery in Cleveland, Ohio, which was then the center of petroleum refining. He proceeded to acquire competitors in order to achieve control over the refining business. He would generally invite a target competitor to merge their company into his organization. If his invitation was rejected, he would seek to put the company out of business. Rockefeller's strategy was to control one aspect of the production process of oil: the refining stage. His **Standard Oil Company** eventually controlled 95 percent of the refineries in the United States through consolidation. This business strategy is called **horizontal integration**.

Rockefeller offered an opportunity for stockholders in competing oil companies to enter a **trust**, in which they would sell him their shares of stock and control in exchange for trust certificates. The board of trustees would then control the business transactions of the now consolidated companies, driving other competitors out of business. Rockefeller was able to undercut his competition by cornering the market and driving prices dramatically downward. As a result, Americans were buying Standard Oil products whether they wanted to or not, as smaller companies were either aggressively taken over or driven out of business altogether. Taking a cue from Rockefeller's success and the government's passivity, other American industries developed trusts, creating a ruthlessly competitive business environment.

Financing and Organizational Structure

These enormous corporations had a large appetite for capital. Investment bankers, most notably J. P. Morgan, helped the railroads and other major corporations raise capital. Similar to modern-day investment bankers, J. P. Morgan would analyze a business and frequently suggest changes intended to improve the financial stability of the business, which helped build confidence among investors. He would also require that a representative of his firm be added to the company's board. With respect to railroads seeking capital, he often found it beneficial to combine smaller separate rail lines into larger, centrally controlled systems.

17

The **Panic of 1893** threw several financially overextended railroads into financial ruin, threatening the industry and the economy as a whole. J. P. Morgan and several other Wall Street financiers rushed to wrest control of the failing rail lines and merge them into single companies. The railway system then ran more smoothly, and shipping rates were consistent across the country. However, the governing boards of these companies were dominated by a few powerful men. Morgan created regional **monopolies** that controlled almost two-thirds of the rail traffic in the United States.

Hoping that states would control the practices of big business as needed, the federal government was reluctant to intervene in growth of major industries. Adhering to the principle of **laissez-faire**, articulated by the economist Adam Smith in his treatise *The Wealth of Nations*, American lawmakers believed that natural market forces, not government regulations, should control the marketplace. It soon became clear, however, that the growth of monopolies was keeping any natural competition from occurring. Demands made by small businesses, farmers, consumers, and even some big businesses eventually pushed Congress to act.

Social Darwinism and Imperialism

The growing economic inequality of this era was often justified in terms of **Social Darwinism**, which attempted to apply the principles of Darwinian evolution to human society. According to proponents of this theory, humans either prospered or failed because, as is the case in nature, only the strong survive as they are able to dominate the weak. Therefore, the man who owned a factory was "fitter" than the countless men, women, and children who worked in it, and thus had the moral superiority to impose their economic and political will on those workers.

The theory of scientific racism also developed during this period to explain differences between nations. These theorists assumed that humans consisted of several distinct racial groups and that European racial groups were intellectually and morally superior. Sub-divisions within Europeans existed. For example, a person of English ancestry was considered superior than one of Irish or Italian heritage, who were not considered truly white. These ideas were often used as justification for the exploitative and cruel treatment of immigrants, American Indians, and African Americans.

Just as economic interest in exploiting American Indian land had driven U.S. foreign policy in North America since 1776, the powerful business interests of this era spurred politicians to look abroad for new lands and new resources. Sometimes this took the form of direct annexation, such as with the Kingdom of Hawaii and its lucrative sugar plantations, but increasingly the United States favored access to foreign markets and resources rather than outright control.

This reluctance for annexation in favor of indirect economic control was due to three aspects. First, Americans had a lingering disdain for empire. The United States, barely a century old, had fought for its own independence from the British Empire. Second, annexing foreign lands increasingly meant accepting nonwhite citizens. The peoples of Cuba or Latin America could not be exterminated or segregated on remote reservations like American Indians had been. Annexation would lead, eventually, to statehood and political power for nonwhites. The racism of this era made that prospect unpalatable. Third, Americans were reluctant to maintain the large standing army necessary for a major empire. From 1781 until the advent of the Cold War, the American people viewed a large peacetime military as odious. Such an army could march on Washington and seize power, snuffing out democracy in a country that prided itself on its system of government in a world still largely run by monarchies.

> ✔ **AP Expert Note**
>
> **Be able to assess how the American economy was transformed during this period**
>
> In the second half of the nineteenth century, the American economy changed from one based primarily on local businesses and farming to a national economic system dominated by large corporations in major sectors such as oil, steel, and railroads. Going into the AP exam, you should be ready to summarize large changes like this clearly and concisely.
>
> Factors contributing to America's economic transformation included:
>
> - Development of transportation and communication systems that linked different regions of the nation
> - Growth in the industrial workforce from foreign immigration and the migration of citizens to large cities
> - Development of technology that increased productivity
> - The creation of financing and organizational structures that supported the growth of large businesses

INDUSTRIALIZATION AND ORGANIZED LABOR   High-Yield

This second industrial revolution was dramatically different from the first, which had occurred after the Revolutionary War. During the second industrial revolution, demand for skilled artisans decreased, and industrialists employed more unskilled workers. Increased demand for manufactured goods meant longer and harder hours for the American factory worker.

Labor Conditions

Conditions were often dangerous for workers; for example, in steel mills, white-hot molten steel was poured day and night by men who had been on the job for 12 hours or more. In many industries, laborers worked six days per week, 10 hours per day. Wages for unskilled workers were low, and many managers did not hesitate to reduce wages in order to increase profits.

As a consequence, American laborers sought safer working conditions and better wages. One of the earliest attempts by laborers to secure their rights also became one of the most violent. The **Great Railroad Strike of 1877** began when railroad workers in Martinsburg, West Virginia, who had suffered two wage cuts in the previous year, took control of the trains at the station and said that no trains would move until their pay had been restored. The state National Guardsmen were called in, but most militia members were sympathetic to the workers, along with local residents. The strike spread quickly by word of mouth. There were violent conflicts and physical damage to railroad equipment in several areas, including major cities, such as Baltimore, Newark, Pittsburgh,

St. Louis, and Chicago. National rail traffic was impacted, causing economic disruption. Ultimately, President **Rutherford B. Hayes** authorized the use of federal troops to break the strike. In the end, more than 100 workers were killed in clashes with federal troops, and the strikers gained nothing. However, the scale of the strike, with more than 100,000 workers participating, showed that many workers were unhappy with working conditions.

Factory owners were generally hostile to attempts by labor movements to seek changes in wages and working conditions. Organized protests were often met with indignation and resistance. Cheap replacement laborers were easy to hire as strikebreakers. Factory owners would also often hire private police forces, who would inflict violence on strikers if they attempted to protest. Other methods included locking out workers before a strike even started, blacklisting difficult workers from being hired, or forcing prospective employees to sign a yellow-dog contract, in which the workers agreed to not join a union. Factory owners took advantage of government methods, such as obtaining court orders to ban strikes or gaining permission to fire all striking workers.

Union Attempts to Protect Workers' Rights

The first attempt to organize all workers across the entire country was the **National Labor Union**. Founded in 1866, it sought a broad range of goals, including better working conditions, higher wages, an eight-hour workday, monetary reform, and equal rights for women and African Americans. Members included skilled and unskilled workers as well as farmers, groups that had different, and sometimes incompatible, needs. The impact of the devastating economic **Panic of 1873** contributed to the decline of the National Labor Union, as did the failure of the railroad strike in 1877.

The next major effort to organize workers was the **Knights of Labor**, which was initially formed as a secret society in 1869 under the leadership of Philadelphia tailor, Uriah Stephens. In 1878, the organization held its first national assembly. In 1879, Terence V. Powderly became leader and continued to grow the number of members. Under his leadership, the union went public in 1881. One of the union's strengths was that it was a broad industrial union: all wage workers (skilled, unskilled, women, and minorities) were invited to join. Powderly and his followers advocated for both economic and social reforms, such as the development of labor cooperatives, an eight-hour workday, and government regulation of business. They preferred use of arbitration to settle disputes between labor and management, rather than violent strikes.

Unfortunately for the Knights, the organization was unfairly blamed for the **Haymarket Square Riot**. On May 4, 1886, a rally in support of the eight-hour day, held in Haymarket Square in Chicago, turned violent. When police began to break up what had been a peaceful public meeting, someone in the crowd threw a bomb at the police, and police fired into the crowd. Several dozens of people were killed, and many more were injured. Rumors circulated that an anarchist with ties to the Knights had thrown the bomb in an attempt to begin the overthrow of the government. Many Americans came to believe that the Knights were an anarchist movement that intended to take over their country. Membership declined significantly, and the union was dissolved in 1893.

Some of the former Knights left to join Samuel Gompers and his **American Federation of Labor** (AFL), which was founded in 1886. The AFL was a federation of twenty craft unions (unions of skilled workers, each representing a particular trade). The AFL chose to concentrate on what they considered to be basic economic issues, such as the eight-hour work day and higher wages, rather than get involved in social change. Because the AFL was made up of skilled, rather than unskilled, laborers, Gompers was able to negotiate with employers more effectively; his workers could not be as easily replaced by scabs if a strike were called. Gompers utilized the tactic of collective bargaining to make modest gains for workers, particularly through the establishment of closed shops, or businesses in which all employees had to be members of the union.

Government Support of Strikebreaking

The end of the nineteenth century was difficult for organized labor, as the government decisively sided with big business. One type of support was the practice of **strikebreaking**. In 1892, a major incident occurred at the Homestead factory of the Carnegie Steel Company. When the factory manager, Henry Clay Frick, reached a standoff with the Amalgamated Association of Iron and Steel Workers regarding working conditions, he ordered a lockout of the workers. The workers went on strike, and Frick hired 300 private Pinkerton detectives to protect the plant and enable strikebreakers to enter and restart the steel operations. After an exchange of gunfire between the Pinkerton men and the workers, nine strikers and seven Pinkerton men were dead and many more people were wounded. The governor of Pennsylvania sent in 8,000 members of the state militia to assist replacement workers to enter the mill, and the Homestead Strike was over.

The Pullman Palace Car Company, which manufactured sleeping cars for the railroads, constructed a "model town" for its employees. When management, impacted by the economic downturn of 1893, terminated half the workers and announced a 25 percent wage cut, Pullman Car workers went on strike. The group received assistance from the American Railway Union under the leadership of Eugene V. Debs. Rail workers across the nation joined the Pullman strikers by refusing to load, link, or carry any train that had a Pullman car attached. In effect, all rail traffic came to a halt. To encourage the federal government to intervene, the rail owners pointed out that the same trains that carried Pullman cars also pulled U.S. mail cars. They claimed that the strikers were impeding the flow of mail and, thus, violating the laws protecting interstate commerce. President **Grover Cleveland** encouraged the filing of an injunction to demand the workers stop striking and to get the mail running once again. Debs and his union leadership refused to abide by the court's ruling and were eventually arrested and jailed. The U.S. Army helped ensure the delivery of mail and end the strike.

Organized labor was dealt yet another blow when the Supreme Court ruled in *In re Debs* (1895) that the use of court injunctions to break strikes was justified in the support of interstate commerce. In effect, the federal government had permitted employers to refuse to negotiate with labor unions.

EXPANSION AND CONFLICT IN THE WEST

American identity was greatly influenced by the existence of the frontier, as well as by the way Americans interacted with and developed that frontier. As the Civil War ended and the expansionist goals of Manifest Destiny were complete, the frontier was closing. There was no longer any part of the continent untouched by Americans.

The Gold Rush and Currency Issues

With the discovery of gold at Sutter's Mill in Northern California in 1848, thousands rushed to the region to pan the rivers and mine the hills to find their fortunes. The cities of San Francisco and Sacramento sprang up practically overnight. California also experienced a flood of Chinese immigrants who came in search of gold and work opportunities. Those who came found little gold, but instead found discrimination and poverty.

At most sites, the easily discovered gold and silver were quickly recovered. In order to access more deeply buried metals, though, mining tunnels had to be dug, which required major capital (often from eastern investors). Many individuals who did not find precious metals on their own ended up employed as miners under dangerous working conditions. Hydraulic mining, which gored mountainsides and polluted lakes, rivers, and streams, had a long-term adverse impact on the environment of the West.

Later, there were other discoveries of gold across the West in Colorado, Arizona, and South Dakota. In 1859, the Comstock Lode of silver ore was discovered in Nevada, prompting a silver rush. The discovery and mining of gold and silver had an impact on the economy and value of currency, because the value of both metals fluctuated as more sources were discovered. The money supply was tied to the gold standard, which limited the circulation of currency. As the country rebounded from multiple economic panics, it was clear to those who needed cash the most—farmers and other debtors—that the nation would have to adopt a bimetal standard or use paper currency in place of its limited hard coin. Some, such as those in the Populist Party, argued for the unlimited coinage of silver to loosen up the money supply. Others, such as those in the **Greenback Party**, looked to paper money unbacked by hard currency as the answer to the country's economic woes. Whether currency should be based on gold or silver would continue to be a contentious political issue in the last part of the nineteenth century.

Agricultural Changes

With the completion of the Transcontinental Railroad and other rail systems, it became profitable to ship beef to Eastern markets. Wild cattle had lived for centuries in the Spanish territory that became Texas; it was estimated that five million longhorn cattle could be found along the Texas frontier at the end of the Civil War. These Texas longhorn cattle became the most prized cattle in the United States. Open grasslands were converted into enormous cattle ranches in Texas, Kansas, and Nebraska. Trails were created for transporting the cattle on long drives from deep inside Texas to the rail junctions of Dodge City, Kansas; Abilene, Texas; Denver, Colorado; and Cheyenne, Wyoming. American cowboys and Mexican *vaqueros* drove thousands of cattle along these trails to the immense profit of the cattle owners. However, overgrazing and the proliferation of fences put up by settlers created barriers to the long drives. Cattle ranchers eventually turned to enclosing their herds, selectively breeding, and hiring only local ranch hands to tend their cattle.

The **Homestead Act of 1862** provided a settler with 160 acres of land if he promised to live on it and work it for at least five years. At one point, public lands were being almost given away to encourage Americans to settle and improve the frontier. About 500,000 families took advantage of the Homestead Act, while many more bought land from private purveyors. Unfortunately, the parcels of land on the Great Plains were difficult to farm successfully, owing to lack of rain and hard-packed soil. Many homesteaders left the land behind and returned home. Those who remained were often called sodbusters, as they attempted to farm the land that they were given. Life was difficult on the Plains; drought was always a problem, and plagues of insects were a constant nuisance. About two-thirds of the original homesteaders left the Great Plains, draining the region of half of its population by the turn of the twentieth century.

THE FARMER'S PLIGHT

The already-troubled farming sector of the U.S. economy was further damaged by falling prices for farm products (due to overproduction of crops) and changing demand in the domestic and international markets. Early examples of agribusiness, such as large-scale cash crop farms, became profitable, while small family farms were failing. Improved machinery meant that fewer workers were needed for soil preparation, planting, and harvesting; **mechanized agriculture** began to take over. As a result, small farmers could not keep up with their large competitors in both buying expensive equipment and bringing goods quickly to market.

Midwestern farmers decided to fight their dilemma by organizing together. In 1867, Oliver H. Kelley created the **National Grange of the Patrons of Husbandry** as a kind of fraternity of farmers and their families. The Grange sought to break the hold of railroad owners and middlemen who kept raising the cost of farming by charging exorbitant prices for shipping and storage. By the mid-1870s, there were Grange meetings across the country. Grangers organized farm cooperatives, or member-owned businesses that sold farm products directly to the buyer, which cut out the middleman. Due to the Grangers' political clout and expert lobbying, Granger laws were passed in many states, regulating the rates farmers could be charged for shipping by rail or for using silos. The Grangers also played an important part in the rise of the Populist Party.

The Supreme Court intervened with the case **Munn v. Illinois** (1877) by ruling that a state had the right to regulate the practices of a business if that business served the public interest. Because railroad transportation was very much in the public's interest, according to the Court, state regulation of rates was appropriate. Despite these successes on the state level, federal laws still protected interstate commerce and allowed railroad companies to raise their long-haul rates in order to offset the losses on short hauls. A prime example was the 1886 Supreme Court case of *Wabash, St. Louis and Pacific Railway Company v. State of Illinois*, in which the Court ruled that states could not control interstate commerce.

Congress responded by passing the **Interstate Commerce Act** in 1887 and creating the Interstate Commerce Commission (ICC), which would regulate and investigate railroad companies that participated in interstate rail trafficking. However, the ICC lacked enforcement powers and remained essentially a "paper tiger." Farmers did not gain much from the formation of the ICC, as they lost

17

most of the cases brought before it. Nonetheless, farmers kept up the fight through the end of the nineteenth century as economic issues and railroad trusts made tough times even tougher.

IMPACTS ON AMERICAN INDIANS IN THE WEST

In 1865, some 400,000 American Indians lived freely in the trans-Mississippi West. Some tribes had lived in the region for thousands of years, while others had been forced westward, away from their ancestral homelands, by the push of white settlement.

In the upper west part of the country, Sioux Indians were able to control much of the territory because of devastating European diseases that had removed potential resistance by other American Indian tribes. The Sioux were able to drive further resistance away through their aggressive war-ring tactics. When the Sioux attempted to wipe out the Pawnee tribe, the Pawnee Indians pleaded with the United States government for assistance. In response, the federal government created boundaries throughout the West that designated the land held by each tribe. These first attempts at a reservation system failed, however, as the white leaders in Washington were ignorant of the nomadic nature and tribal leadership systems of many American Indians of the Great Plains.

From the end of the Civil War to 1890, more and more American Indian tribes were waging conflicts with one another and with incoming white settlers. At the same time, white settlers' tactics were becoming increasingly aggressive. In 1864, in Sand Creek, Colorado, the state militia massacred 400 unarmed natives who had been promised protection. The discovery of gold in the Black Hills of the Dakotas sparked additional conflict. White gold miners refused to stay off the land, despite the fact that treaties had designated the region as native land. The 1870s saw additional conflict with the Red River War and the Second Sioux War. The most notable battle of this period is the **Battle of Little Bighorn**. Colonel George Custer marched his column of men deep into Sioux territory only to discover some 2,500 Sioux warriors waiting for them at the Little Big Horn River. Custer and his men were destroyed by the Sioux, who were later hunted and killed by U.S. Army reinforcements.

In 1870, the Dakota Sioux began a movement, known as the Ghost Dance movement, intended to bring about a rebirth of native tradition and a repulsion of white incursion. As part of the U.S. government's efforts to suppress the movement, the respected Sioux leader Sitting Bull was killed. In December 1890, over 200 American Indian men, women, and children were massacred in the **Battle of Wounded Knee**. Bloody conflicts such as these continued throughout the end of the nineteenth century, as many other tribes (such as the Nez Perce led by Chief Joseph and the Apache led by Geronimo) were forced to fight for their land and their lives.

Warfare was not the only factor affecting the American Indians living on the Great Plains. Plains tribes depended on the buffalo for meat, clothing, and fuel. As the railroad made its way across the West, mass killing of the buffalo ensued; buffalo coats became fashionable, and the buffalo hunt became a popular public spectacle. As a result, the American buffalo became an endangered species, with only a few surviving in the nation's zoos and preserves.

While there was heated debate over the government's treatment of American Indian tribes, it seemed that no one could decide what to do now that the damage had been done. Many believed that the tribes needed to be assimilated into American society and forced to give up culture and traditions. In an attempt to "civilize" American Indians, the federal government enacted the **Dawes Severalty Act** of 1887, which stripped tribes of their official federal recognition and land rights and would only grant individual families land and citizenship in 25 years if they properly assimilated. Former reservation land was sold, and the proceeds funded "civilizing" ventures for natives, such as so-called Indian Schools that taught native children how to dress and behave like whites. In reality, these schools were rampant with abuse and neglect. This forced-assimilation policy remained the federal government's way of dealing with American Indians until 1934. The Dawes Severalty Act destroyed tribal organizations and stripped American Indians of the land they had been legally granted via treaty by the U.S. government.

THE NEW SOUTH

The South struggled to recover and suffered from slow economic progress after the Civil War. Southern leaders promoted a **New South** that embraced an industrialized economy; however, postwar economic recovery came with strings attached, as the North had financed a major portion of the South's war debt. Therefore, Northerners owned a majority of the industry that was being revived in the South.

Economic Hardship

Southern citizens remained some of the most impoverished in the nation. The majority of Southerners, both black and white, subsisted as sharecroppers and small farmers. Owing to the South's steadfast belief in the plantation economy, and the lack of education and industrialization, growth and innovation moved more slowly than in the North.

As in the antebellum economy, cotton remained a major cash crop for the South, and more and more farmers converted land to till cotton. They eventually glutted the worldwide marketplace with the fiber, driving the price to an all-time low in the 1890s. As a result, many small farmers lost their land because of their inability to pay back debts. Most farmers, tenant or landowner, remained tied to the land because of the use of crop liens; these allowed farmers to pay for goods on credit, which would be paid back with the harvest of their next crop. A poor harvest could drive a farmer deeper into debt.

Plessy v. Ferguson and Jim Crow Laws   High-Yield

After the North removed federal troops in 1877, without establishing a support system for African Americans, white Southerners sought to enact policies that would create two distinct societies as they were before the war: one black and one white. The Supreme Court aided the South's ability to discriminate through several decisions that more or less dismantled Reconstruction protections of African American civil rights. In the *Civil Rights Cases* ruling of 1883 regarding the Civil Rights

Act of 1875, the Supreme Court decided that Congress had no jurisdiction to bar private citizens (e.g., business owners of hotels, railroads, and theaters) from practicing discrimination. The Court stated that private acts of racial discrimination were private wrongs that the national government was powerless to correct by means of civil rights legislation.

In 1896, the landmark case of ***Plessy v. Ferguson*** was brought before the Supreme Court. In this case, a mixed-race man, Homer Plessy, refused to give up his seat on a whites-only railroad car in the state of Louisiana and was arrested. He sued, claiming that his civil rights had been violated. Justice Henry Brown delivered the opinion of the Court, which ruled that because a car was provided for African American passengers, the state of Louisiana had not violated the Fourteenth Amendment. The justices used the "separate but equal" doctrine to justify their decision. The South had now been given de facto permission by the U.S. Supreme Court to discriminate on the basis of color in all public places. **Jim Crow laws**, which segregated public facilities from drinking fountains to hotel rooms, were immediately adopted by cities across the South.

Discrimination did not end with Jim Crow. Southern states worked to disenfranchise African American voters through the use of literacy tests, poll taxes, and grandfather clauses. Grandfather clauses would allow a man to vote only if his grandfather had voted in an election before 1865 (that is, before Reconstruction). African Americans were not allowed to serve on juries and were subject to harsher penalties when convicted of crimes than their white counterparts. A new form of terrorism and intimidation developed in the postwar South: lynching, or the killing of a person by a mob. Often, the lynching would be publicized in advance so crowds of whites could gather to witness the event.

In response, many African Americans left the South. In the early twentieth century, millions of African Americans moved from southern to northern cities, a trend which was dubbed the Great Migration. African American leaders who remained in the South, such as self-educated former slave Booker T. Washington, offered various views on how African Americans could succeed. Washington advocated for the education of African Americans to allow them access to the growing economy. His Tuskegee Institute in Alabama was founded to instruct African Americans in the industrial arts and the skills to work within the system. With the turn of the twentieth century, more radical African American thinkers would criticize Washington's stance of assimilation.

> ✔ **AP Expert Note**
>
> **Be prepared to answer exam questions about Supreme Court cases dealing with rights for African Americans**
>
> *Dred Scott v. Sandford* (1857): Declared that because slaves were considered property, they could not be considered citizens. This decision extended federal protection to slaveholders.
>
> *Plessy v. Ferguson* (1896): Upheld segregation laws and the notion that as long as African Americans were provided "separate but equal" facilities, their constitutional rights were not violated. This decision perpetuated the Jim Crow system for decades to come.
>
> *Brown v. Board of Education of Topeka, Kansas* (1954): Ended the practice of racial segregation in public schools and overturned *Plessy v. Ferguson*. This decision rejected the Jim Crow system and was a significant victory for civil rights.

17

URBANIZATION AND SOCIAL CHANGE

Immigrants and the City

Both push and pull factors brought millions of new immigrants to the United States in the years 1880 to 1924. Poverty, overcrowding, and religious persecution pushed immigrants from Southern and Eastern Europe. Stories of opportunity and freedom pulled them to cities such as New York, Chicago, and Boston. Clipper ships gave way to large ocean liners, which could carry both freight and passengers across the Atlantic relatively quickly. Cheap steerage-class tickets could be purchased for as little as 20 dollars. For some families, this was still a life's savings, but nonetheless, families from Italy, Poland, and Russia gathered as much money as they could to take the one-way trip to America.

Immigrants flocked to American cities, where they could find affordable housing and abundant factory jobs. To handle the massive influx of people, landlords converted single-family homes into apartments. The city of New York held a contest in 1879 for the best building design for urban dwellings. E. Ware won the contest with his "dumbbell tenement," which conformed to a law requiring windows for every dwelling. The design included windows into an internal airshaft that was supposed to aid the distribution of fresh air through the apartments, but in the end only helped the spread of infectious diseases, as more and more people were crammed into the buildings. New apartment buildings were built up rather than out, as land was at a premium and steel made taller buildings possible.

Ethnic neighborhoods developed in New York, Chicago, Philadelphia, and other American cities. Ethnic groups often formed tight community bonds based on common language, customs, and foods. Even though immigrants were forced to live in cramped, unhygienic conditions, these urban neighborhoods served as welcoming communities for the people who shared them.

With the change in the inner-city populace, affluent and middle-class white Americans began to move to burgeoning suburban neighborhoods. This exodus into the suburbs was aided by the expansion of trolley car lines and subway services that could take them to their jobs in the city.

A Backlash Against Immigrants

The "new" immigrants were markedly different from the "old" immigrants who had come to the United States in the 1820s and 1830s. Southern and Eastern European immigrants were often Catholic, Jewish, or Greek Orthodox Christians; the old immigrants were predominantly English Protestants, although large numbers of Irish and Germans had begun to arrive in the mid-1840s. On the West Coast, Chinese immigrants continued to arrive in Los Angeles and San Francisco, prompting the passage of the Chinese Exclusion Act of 1882 to restrict Chinese immigration to the United States. Soon, Congress passed other acts aimed at restricting the tide of immigration flooding American cities.

Many **nativists**, much like the Know-Nothings during the first wave of immigration, feared domination by a population loyal to the Pope, the head of the Roman Catholic Church. Labor unions feared a loss of jobs to an eager immigrant work pool who would accept lower wages and worse working conditions. In response, the American Protective Association was formed in 1887 to oppose the election of any Catholic to public office. The Reverend Josiah Strong echoed the sentiments of many Americans in his book *Our Country* (1885), in which he derided cities as a menace to American morality and social order. The tide could not be stemmed, however; by the turn of the twentieth century, one out of every three New Yorkers was foreign-born.

✔ **AP Expert Note**

Be able to compare immigration during this time period with earlier immigration trends

From 1820 to 1860, immigrants to America primarily came from Northern and Western Europe. Irish immigrants settled mainly in the Northeast, and many worked low-wage, menial jobs. Germans settled mostly in the Midwest, and worked largely as farmers and artisans. One response to the surge of immigration was nativist movements such as the American Party, also called the Know-Nothing Party, which called for an end to immigration.

Immigration again surged after 1880. But there was a significant shift: immigrants primarily came from Central, Southern, and Eastern Europe, the Middle East, and other parts of Asia. Greeks, Italians, Jews, and Slavs tended to settle in the Northeast (particularly in New York). The large number of Chinese immigrants settled mainly in the West, often working for the railroads or mining companies.

Urban Political Machines

Politics in America's large cities was mired in corruption. Large, disciplined political groups called "machines" controlled party politics in cities such as New York, Chicago, and Baltimore. The most famous of these machines, Tammany Hall in New York City, was led by Boss Tweed. Tweed and his fellow Irish gave aid to small business owners, immigrants, and the poor in exchange for votes. **Political machines** often provided coveted city jobs to those who promised to vote for their candidates. They also found housing for newly arrived immigrants and provided various forms of support to needy families, such as distributing turkeys at Thanksgiving, handing out clothes, and providing job search assistance.

Not all members of this machine were honest in their intentions. George Washington Plunkitt, a lower boss in Tammany Hall, would pocket large sums of taxpayer money. Plunkitt would also gain advance notice of a city project from an insider sitting on the planning board, and then buy the land for the proposed project and sell it to the city for as much as three times its original price. By 1870, the Tweed ring had bilked New York City taxpayers out of over $200 million. Urban citizens did not complain, however, as the political machines took care of them and threatened to harm those who spoke against them.

The end of the Tweed ring began in 1871 when a story ran in the *New York Times* alleging fraud, bribery, and graft by the political machine. Thomas Nast, a political cartoonist for *Harper's Weekly*, became Tweed's archenemy as he drew scathing commentaries regarding the machine's corruption and greed. After avoiding criminal conviction on a number of occasions, Tweed fled to Spain in 1876 and was eventually captured by Spanish police, who recognized him from the Nast cartoons. Tweed finally was imprisoned in the United States, where he died of heart failure in 1878.

A WAVE OF REFORM IN THE GILDED AGE

The deplorable living conditions of poor urban immigrants and the greed of political machines spurred a new wave of reform, which would not fully take hold until the turn of the twentieth century, during what was termed the **Gilded Age**. The reformers were white, well-educated, middle-class Americans who were as concerned about a possible violent uprising of the poor and working class as they were about the well-being of the less fortunate.

The Social Gospel Movement

One of the most influential reform movements of this era was the **Social Gospel** movement. Leaders such as Walter Rauschenbusch believed that Christians had an obligation to improve the lives of those less fortunate, such as the citizens in the poorer areas of New York City. Rauschenbusch's work encouraged many middle-class Protestants to join reform efforts and bring on the Progressive movement.

Akin to the Social Gospel movement was the **settlement house movement**, which was begun by young, college-educated, middle-class women. In an age when women were expected to adhere to a strict ideal of femininity, young female activists sought to better society through volunteerism, as they could not become involved in the political process. The most famous of the settlement houses was Hull House in Chicago (1889). The goal of its founder, Jane Addams, was to have immigrants live with college-educated people in order to ease their transition into American society. Settlement house guests were taught courses in English, hygiene, and cooking. Addams and others also pioneered some of the first instruction in child care. Many other settlement houses modeled themselves after Hull House in this period. Moreover, settlement houses soon became a meeting place for young women activists.

The Temperance Movement

The Victorian ideal of strict moral decorum and the concern over Catholic influences led to the revival of the **temperance movement**, which had been overshadowed by the abolitionist movement in the antebellum years. The Woman's Christian Temperance Union (WCTU) was founded in 1874. In 1879, Frances Willard became President of the WCTU and gave the movement new life by adding a focus on lobbying for laws to prohibit the sale of alcoholic beverages. The group believed that prohibition would diminish threats to women and families that they saw as the direct result of alcohol overconsumption: domestic violence, misspent wages, and adultery. Under Willard's leadership, the WCTU provided an array of services for families. In 1894, the organization also endorsed women's suffrage.

The Anti-Saloon League followed in 1893, gaining more success as states across the country agreed to shutter bars. The most well-known WCTU member, Kentucky-born Carrie A. Nation, was inspired by the death of her alcoholic husband to travel across the United States, smashing bars with her trademark hatchet. Nation believed she was doing the work of God as she wreaked havoc across the Midwest. She was arrested over 30 times and became so well known that she sold pewter hatchet

17

pins to pay her jail fines. Nation also crusaded against the evils of smoking tobacco, fought for women's suffrage, and railed against the restrictive and sometimes dangerous women's fashions of the day.

Opinions on Wealth

The economic divide between the rich and poor grew steadily wider as the nineteenth century drew to a close. Some Americans sought to apply Charles Darwin's theory of evolution and the idea of survival of the fittest in an effort to explain people's differing economic and social standings within society. Social Darwinists, such as Yale's William Graham Sumner, argued that wealth belonged in the hands of those who were most fit to manage it. Many of Sumner's followers also believed that giving assistance to the poor went against the natural order.

Andrew Carnegie developed the philosophy, the **Gospel of Wealth**, which asserted that wealth was a result of God's will and that, in turn, the wealthy had an obligation to give money away to better society. Carnegie had become one of the nation's wealthiest men, and in retirement, he set an example of philanthropy by giving away much of his immense fortune to establish universities, open libraries, and fund museums and other cultural institutions. In addition, Carnegie believed that wealth would benefit the lower classes via the spending and good nature of the rich and would, therefore, benefit society as a whole.

By the end of this period, 90 percent of America's wealth was controlled by only 10 percent of the population. Many lower-class Americans subscribed to the rags-to-riches myth propagated by the novelist Horatio Alger, whose novels, such as *Ragged Dick*, were intended to inspire the poor to become wealthy industrialists. Similarly, John D. Rockefeller stated that his Puritan work ethic was solely responsible for his success. In reality, even though opportunities for incredible success were available, Americans faced nearly insurmountable barriers in trying to achieve them.

Cultural Changes

A Growing Middle and Working Class

As American workers moved from farms to factories, the middle class expanded, and cities grew to accommodate them. Managerial positions developed because factories required people to make sure that human capital was working efficiently to increase profits. To support these managerial positions, clerical workers grew in number. However, female clerical workers earned significantly less than their male counterparts. As the middle class grew, so did the professional service industry in the areas of medicine, law, and education.

The segment of the American society with the greatest growth was the working class, however. Blue-collar workers, who often toiled 10 to 12 hours a day for barely enough money to scrape by, made up nearly two-thirds of the population of the United States by the end of the nineteenth century. For the most part, factory work was reserved for men.

The Changing Roles of Women

The industrial age brought women more independence, along with more difficulties. Despite newfound freedom, women were still denied the right to vote. The women's suffrage movement had not found support during Reconstruction, when the issue of African American suffrage had taken precedence over women's suffrage in the adoption of the Fifteenth Amendment. Activists Elizabeth Cady Stanton and Susan B. Anthony formed the **National American Woman Suffrage Association** (NAWSA) in 1890, combining the once rival National Woman Suffrage Association and American Woman Suffrage Association to fight for a woman's right to vote. The NAWSA organized several hundred state and local chapters.

While gains for women were slow to come, a number of western states had already allowed women to vote prior to 1900. Wyoming was the first state to offer women full suffrage, doing so in 1869 in part to attract female settlers. As a rule of thumb, by 1919 most states west of the Mississippi River offered either full or limited women's suffrage, while most states east of the Mississippi River offered little to no suffrage The Nineteenth Amendment, guaranteeing women's suffrage, would be formally adopted in August 1920.

Changes in Education

Publicly funded high schools and compulsory elementary attendance laws increased the literacy rate of Americans to almost 90 percent by the beginning of the twentieth century. Technical schools were established across the country to train new educators to keep up with rising demand for qualified instructors. Higher education, already improved by the Morrill Land Grant Act of 1862, was further strengthened by the Hatch Act of 1887 and the philanthropy of men such as Carnegie, Rockefeller, Stanford, and Vanderbilt. Universities also professionalized the areas of medicine, law, and sociology by requiring research and practice to obtain a degree.

Achievements in the Arts

Reacting to the Romanticism of the antebellum and Civil War eras, realist writers and artists sought to portray the conditions industrialized Americans were facing. Bret Harte enthralled Americans with his stories of the Gold Rush and Wild West. One of the most famous and prolific of the realists was Mark Twain (born Samuel Clemens), who captured the ruggedness of the frontier and of the South with humor and satire. It was Twain who coined the term Gilded Age for the mid to late nineteenth century.

Later in this era, authors turned to stories of human nature and emotion in novels such as *The Red Badge of Courage* by Stephen Crane and *Sister Carrie* by Theodore Dreiser. Many visual artists, such as Winslow Homer, remained tied to the romantic spirit of the Hudson River School and produced lush American landscapes and marine scenes, while others broke away from tradition and redefined American art. James Whistler and Mary Cassatt experimented with abstract color and composition in their works, which were heavily influenced by their time spent in Europe.

17

The music scene changed as new music traveled from communities in the South to northern cities such as Chicago. Jazz developed from a blending of African American, European American, and European musical traditions.

Informing and entertaining the urban masses was now big business in cities such as New York and Chicago. Daily newspapers like Joseph Pulitzer's *New York World* and William Randolph Hearst's *New York Journal American* fought over circulation numbers in the city with their sensationalized stories and low prices. Magazines also hit the newsstands in search of readership. *Ladies' Home Journal*, *McCall's*, and *Vogue* all sought to reach women through advertisements and fashion tips.

As America's urban centers grew, cultural and intellectual endeavors were given new life, and cultural changes abounded. American identity had undergone a major transformation in the years following the Civil War, and it would continue to shift and evolve in the coming decades.

 **NEXT STEP: PRACTICE**

Go to Rapid Review and Practice Chapter 8 or to your online quizzes on kaptest.com for exam-like practice on this topic.

Haven't registered your book yet? Go to kaptest.com/moreonline to begin.

CHAPTER 18

Period 7: 1890–1945

THE "FORGETTABLE" ADMINISTRATIONS

Politics in the post-Reconstruction years were marked by the lackluster performances of presidents **Rutherford B. Hayes**, **James Garfield**, and **Chester A. Arthur**. All three were elected to one term each from the years 1876 to 1884, but none did much to earn a place in the nation's collective memory.

After the "big" government of the Reconstruction era, many in Washington, D.C., sought to limit the role of the federal government. This was not so much about ideology as about concerns over job security. The spoils system got a makeover during the Gilded Age as leaders in both parties played the game of party patronage, much as the political machines did in large cities. For example, the Republican party during this time was composed of three major factions: the Stalwarts supported the party patronage system, the Halfbreeds opposed it, and the Mugwumps remained neutral on the issue and sought modest reforms.

The presidency was not immune from the patronage that plagued the parties at the national level. After a less-than-stellar term by Hayes, the Republican party chose to run Halfbreed party member James Garfield for president with Stalwart Chester A. Arthur as his running mate. After winning the election, Garfield quickly set to work appointing party loyalists to coveted civil service positions. As Garfield prepared to leave for his vacation in 1881, an irate civil service job seeker shot him. Garfield hung on for nearly three months, finally succumbing to infection from the wound.

Arthur began to separate himself from his Stalwart pals as he took the presidency. Unfortunately for him, the Republican party chose another candidate for the next election: Senator James Blaine. Blaine did not succeed in winning the election of 1884, as his image had been tarnished by his connection to the Crédit Mobilier and other scandals. Instead, **Grover Cleveland** became the first Democrat to take office since before the Civil War.

Some accomplishments were made during the "forgotten" administrations, such as passage of the Pendleton Civil Service Act of 1881, which reformed the corrupt patronage system. No longer could political cronyism secure government positions; all potential civil service employees had to take an exam to prove their worthiness.

AGRARIAN DISCONTENT

Grover Cleveland did not win a second term in 1888, in part because of his support for a lower tariff that would benefit southern and western farmers. The Republicans were able to rally the votes of northern business owners to gain the upper hand in the Electoral College. The new president, **Benjamin Harrison**, presided over a unified government for two years with Republicans also in control of the legislative branch. The unification was short-lived, however, as midterm elections gave control of Congress back to the Democrats.

The Birth of the Populists

Republicans also had competition from a rising third party. Taking a cue from the earlier Grange movement, farmers joined forces in several states across the country to form the Farmers' Alliance. The Alliance gained membership, successfully seated senators and governors in several midwestern states, and eventually morphed into the **Populist Party**. Having drafted their political platform in Omaha, Nebraska, in 1892, the Populists advocated for:

- The unlimited coinage of silver

- A graduated income tax

- Public ownership of railroads, telegraph, and telephone lines

- Government subsidies to assist in stabilizing agricultural prices

- An eight-hour workday

- The direct election of U.S. senators

- Increased voter power with the use of the initiative, referendum, and recall

Even though the Populists made an impressive showing in the election of 1892, they failed to win. Vying for office were President Harrison and former President Cleveland. The Democrat Cleveland became the only president in history to win a second term after leaving the office for a term.

Panic and Protest

The Democratic celebration would be short, however, as the country was soon gripped by an economic depression, triggered by the **Panic of 1893**. Again, railroads and overspeculation by investors artificially inflated the price of stocks, which took a tumble and did not recover for almost four years. Investors began trading in their silver for more valuable gold, depleting the already dangerously low supply of gold.

To mitigate the crisis, President Cleveland brokered a loan from the wealthy investment banker J. P. Morgan for a sum of $65 million and repealed the Sherman Silver Purchase Act. While these actions temporarily solved the gold shortage, they did much more to damage the president in the eyes of the American public, which already was wary of Washington's dealings with big business.

The depression brought protesters to Washington under the leadership of Populist Jacob Coxey, whose army of jobless and homeless Americans proposed federally funded public works projects to employ those who needed work. The government did not listen but rather arrested the group for trespassing. Coxey's radical ideas, however, would soon become the cornerstone of policy for a future president who looked to emerge from an even greater depression.

Gold Versus Silver in the 1896 Election

With the economic crisis and the currency and tariff issues still raging, candidates traveled across the country to tout their remedies for a renewed nation before the election of 1896.

The Democrats were split over the gold and silver controversy with gold advocates like Grover Cleveland on one side and pro-silver advocates without a leader on the other. The young William Jennings Bryan of Nebraska wowed the crowd at the Democratic National Convention with his famous "Cross of Gold" speech, which made him the spokesperson for the pro-silver advocates.

In essence, the Democrats adopted the old Populist platform, and they nominated Bryan as their candidate for the 1896 election. Cleveland and his followers were disgusted with the new party direction and left to make their own run for the presidency. The Republicans nominated **William McKinley**, a friend to labor and a proponent of the gold standard, as their candidate. With the Democratic ticket split and McKinley's use of the media, the Republicans easily took the presidency. Fortunately for McKinley, the country was finally on an economic upswing, and world events would soon turn American's attention away from domestic issues.

NEW IMPERIALISM

The expansion of the United States was traditionally limited to the North American continent. However, with the closing of the western frontier, many Americans felt that Manifest Destiny had still not been fulfilled. The late nineteenth century in particular saw a rise in imperialism due to three factors. First, the great powers of the era increasingly competed with one another to gain more colonies as a form of national prestige. Second, U.S. business interests were increasingly dependent on foreign trade and resources. Third, militarism grew increasingly popular, as war was seen as inherently positive.

Areas of Expansion

Imperialism was not a new idea. European nations had been establishing new colonies as early as the mid-1800s in places such as Africa and Asia. It was this early expansion that led President Monroe to unveil his Monroe Doctrine in 1823. This **new imperialism** was spurred by an aggressive foreign policy stance, the desire to find new markets in which to sell American goods, and Social Darwinism.

The United States first set its sights on Alaska, a region on the northwestern edge of North America, then held by Russia. In 1867, Secretary of State William H. Seward brokered a deal to purchase the

18

land from Russia for a sum of $7.2 million. At the time, Seward was seen by many as a laughing-stock, and Alaska was nicknamed "Seward's Folly." Not until the twentieth century, when oil drillers found that Alaska was rich with fossil fuel, would Americans realize the great deal they had gotten.

One proponent of overseas expansion was U.S. Naval Captain Alfred Thayer Mahan. His book *The Influence of Sea Power upon History* (1890) focused on the idea that the United States needed to pour money and resources into building a powerful, world-class navy to become a major world power broker. To do this, Mahan contended that the United States would need to occupy sites around the world to establish refueling stations and naval bases. The most logical areas for such bases were Hawaii and Cuba. Mahan also advocated the building of a canal across the Isthmus of Panama to provide a quick route between the Pacific and the Atlantic.

Annexing the Hawaiian Kingdom

Since its founding in 1795, the Kingdom of Hawaii had existed as an internationally recognized sovereign state. From 1820 to 1898, the U.S. government even had a form of ambassador to the kingdom known as the United States Minister to Hawaii. However, the rapid growth in sugar plantations on the Hawaiian Islands led to massive American financial investment. The ideal properties of Pearl Harbor as a naval port also interested the United States, both in terms of basing for the U.S. Navy and in denying Pearl Harbor to potentially hostile European powers. In 1887, the U.S. government began leasing Pearl Harbor.

However, taxes and tariffs cut into the profits of American-born and British-born sugar plantation owners. After they sponsored a series of rebellions and coups, with the aid of mid-ranking U.S. military and diplomatic personnel, the Kingdom of Hawaii was finally overthrown in 1893. Its last sovereign was Queen Lili'uokalani.

The United States did not immediately annex Hawaii. President Cleveland called for an investigation into the overthrow, casting doubt on its legitimacy. A Congressional report found that U.S. personnel in Hawaii had abused their power. Even so, the illegal effort against the Hawaii monarchy proceeded, and a Hawaiian Republic was declared. Eventually, in 1898, amid a rising tide of imperialism, President McKinley authorized the annexation of Hawaii.

The Spanish-American War

High-Yield

As trouble reared its head on the Spanish-held island of Cuba, the debate regarding overseas expansion shifted to the Caribbean. Americans had moved to Cuba after the Civil War to establish large sugar plantations on the lush, tropical island. Cuban natives had been growing more and more irritated by the presence of American and Spanish foreigners, who amassed huge fortunes while natives toiled on the plantations. The Spanish sensed the seeds of revolt and reacted by gathering the Cuban natives into central locations under direct Spanish control. Many Cubans died as a result of this effort to rid the country of revolutionaries.

Americans heard of the atrocities, both real and sensationalized, from the American popular press. Papers, such as Hearst's *Journal* and Pulitzer's *World*, radically altered the truth of stories coming out of Cuba in the effort to sell papers. This kind of writing was dubbed "yellow journalism." As a result, many Americans and Cuban immigrants in the United States grew increasingly concerned about the events in Cuba. However, Presidents Cleveland and McKinley did not favor intervention. Popular opinion on Cuba began to shift toward war when, in 1898, a letter was leaked to Hearst's *Journal*. In this letter, Dupuy de Lome, Spanish minister to the United States, insinuated that President McKinley was corrupt. Americans immediately took this as an insult from the Spanish.

The next event made war inevitable in the eyes of most Americans. On February 15, 1898, the USS *Maine* exploded in Havana Harbor under mysterious circumstances. The ship had arrived in the Cuban harbor to provide protection and act as an escape vessel for the Americans currently living on the island. The ship exploded while anchored in the harbor, killing 260 sailors and injuring many more.

The Spanish immediately responded by denying any role in the tragedy. The Americans sent a team to investigate the wreckage and declared that a submarine mine had sunk the ship. Hearst and Pulitzer blamed the Spanish for the tragedy, further fanning the flames of war. Americans cried "Remember the *Maine*!" to push President McKinley to declare war on Spain. The president was reluctant to issue the war decree without some caveats. The Teller Amendment was added to the war declaration to assure Cuba and the world that the United States intended to grant Cuba its independence once the war ended.

The **Spanish-American War** officially began on April 11, 1898. Fighting did not begin in Cuba but rather in the Spanish colony of the Philippines. U.S. Naval Commodore George Dewey was sent with his fleet to Manila Bay and opened fire on May 1. This naval battle was short-lived; the U.S. Navy was able to rout the Spanish fleet in a matter of hours. But as the battle made landfall, it was not quite as easy. Many Filipinos fought to oust both the Spanish and American forces. The United States was able to convince the Filipino revolutionary Emilio Aguinaldo to assist in the fight against the Spanish in exchange for independence after the war's end. As a result, the American and Filipino fighters were able to take Manila by August.

The fight in Cuba would be much more difficult, partly because of tropical diseases and the inexperience of the American forces. Most American casualties were attributed to diseases, with just 10 percent due to actual combat. The most celebrated American battle was for the high ground of San Juan Hill. Theodore Roosevelt and his volunteer force of college students, cowboys, and adventurers, called "the Rough Riders," were able to take the Hill with the heavy assistance of the Fourteenth Regiment Colored Calvary.

After the United States claimed victory in Cuba on July 1, the United States invaded the Spanish colony of Puerto Rico. Unwilling to fight any longer, the Spanish signed a cease-fire with the United States in August 1898. The resulting peace treaty called the **Treaty of Paris of 1898** gave the United States Guam and Puerto Rico. The most difficult decision was what to do with the Philippines. President McKinley could give the Philippines its independence as promised. Instead, he decided that the United States would take the Philippines and deal with the independence issue at a later date.

18

Problems with the New Expansion

The debate over imperialism intensified with the end of the Spanish-American War. Anti-imperialists, such as William Jennings Bryan, even formed an organization to publicly oppose U.S. expansion. Citizens living in newly conquered territories brought cases regarding their constitutional rights to the U.S. Supreme Court. In 1901, the court ruled in the *Insular Cases* that the Constitution and its protections did not follow the flag. In other words, a citizen in a conquered territory did not necessarily have the protection of the Constitution. It was up to Congress to decide the rights of the peoples in the newly conquered territories.

As Cuba set to draft its constitution, the United States ignored the Teller Amendment and its promise to give Cuba independence. Thus, the United States issued the Platt Amendment in 1903, which Cubans would now have to incorporate into their new constitution. The provisions of the Platt Amendment were that Cuba had to have all treaties approved by the United States, the United States had the right to interfere in Cuban affairs both politically and militarily, and the United States would be given access to naval bases on the island. In essence, the Cubans had not gained their independence at all.

The United States then turned its attention to other parts of the world. The Filipinos, under the leadership of the once-American ally Aguinaldo, revolted against the American presence. Guerrilla warfare broke out between the Filipino revolutionaries and Americans on the islands in 1899. Aguinaldo and his fighters were finally subdued by the Americans in 1901, when the leader was captured. The Philippines did not gain its independence until 1946.

China was another area of interest for Americans, especially investors. Japan and European nations had already carved China up into spheres of influence in which they basically controlled the economic dealings of specific regions. Hoping to get a piece of the action, Secretary of State John Hay announced the **Open Door Policy**. Under the Open Door Policy, China would be open and free to trade equally with any nation. The policy was wildly popular in the United States, but unsurprisingly, was denounced and resisted in China. In 1900, a young group of Chinese nationalists revolted against the Open Door Policy and foreign intervention. The Boxer Rebellion sought to remove all foreigners from China by force. The Boxers killed some 200 whites; a multinational force, including U.S. forces, was sent to Peking and ended the rebellion.

The Panama Canal

The canal that Mahan had suggested became a reality once Americans and Europeans built one across the Isthmus of Panama. Construction of the Panama Canal was begun by the French. Unfortunately, the construction effort was plagued with setbacks: workers fell to disease due to the tropical climate, and engineering troubles ensued due to geography.

The United States was more than willing to take over the building of the canal, but several issues stood in the way. The United States needed to secure the right to build the canal from Colombia because the canal would go right through the country. The nation of Panama would have to be created quickly.

In secrecy, and with the aid of the French, President **Theodore Roosevelt** raised a revolutionary force to fight for Panamanian independence from Colombia. The revolution ended as quickly as it began; Roosevelt immediately recognized the new nation. It came as no surprise that the Panamanian government quickly signed an agreement to allow the United States to build the canal. Construction was completed in 1914.

Critics of Roosevelt's policy regarding Panama branded his actions "big-stick diplomacy" because he often threatened to use military force while negotiating peacefully. Latin American countries were becoming increasingly alarmed at the way the "Colossus of the North" was flexing its muscles throughout the region.

The Roosevelt Corollary and Relations Abroad

President Roosevelt had his own imperialist aims aside from the Panama Canal. The president was growing increasingly concerned over problems he was having with attempts by Britain and Germany to collect debts from Venezuela. In order to try to protect Venezuela from European intervention, President Roosevelt amended the Monroe Doctrine with the **Roosevelt Corollary**, which stated that the United States would come to the aid of any Latin American nation experiencing financial trouble. In essence, the United States gained total control of Latin America through the corollary.

Under this new imperialism, the United States used force to "protect" the Dominican Republic and Cuba from political chaos. Roosevelt also intervened in the Russo-Japanese War of 1904. Russia and Japan were feuding over land and ports in Korea and Manchuria. Roosevelt did not want either nation to win control over the region and approached Japan to assist in the settlement of the war. The Treaty of Portsmouth was signed in 1905 to end the war. A year later, Theodore Roosevelt won the Nobel Peace Prize for his role in negotiating the treaty.

U.S.-Japanese relations were not harmonious at the end of the Russo-Japanese War. An influx of Japanese immigrants flooded the city of San Francisco to escape financial crisis in their homeland and to start life anew. White San Franciscans were concerned about the presence of the Japanese in their city, and they began passing restrictive laws aimed directly at the incoming immigrants, such as banning Japanese children from attending public school.

The Japanese were enraged at the discrimination, and Theodore Roosevelt decided to step in. The president was able to craft a Gentleman's Agreement between the San Francisco School Board and the Japanese government. The school board would allow Japanese students to enter public school if the Japanese government would help stem the tide of immigrants coming to California. From this point on, U.S.-Japanese relations were amiable but strained.

Taft and Wilson on Imperialism

President Taft used a different approach to foreign relations. Taft's "dollar diplomacy" encouraged American businesses to send their dollars to foreign countries, such as those in Latin America, to weaken European bonds and strengthen ties with the United States. However, when these American investments were endangered, Taft on several occasions sent U.S. forces to invade Latin American countries and protect American interests. These actions further alienated the United States from Latin America.

President Wilson, in contrast, believed imperialism was immoral; however, he also believed in the superiority of American democracy and thought it was his duty to spread that ideal to nations under threat of totalitarianism. This policy became known as moral diplomacy. As a result, Wilson sent troops to invade Nicaragua and the Dominican Republic and purchased the Virgin Islands. Wilson also intervened in the Mexican Revolution to capture the revolutionary Pancho Villa after he had killed Americans in Mexico and New Mexico. The United States was finally forced to withdraw from the civil war in Mexico in 1917. However, a much larger war was in progress that would soon trouble President Wilson.

THE PROGRESSIVE ERA

Much like the reformers of earlier times, Progressives were largely white middle-class Protestants who hoped to better society. They gained inspiration from earlier reformers such as those of the Social Gospel movement. The nation was changing at an alarmingly rapid rate, and reformers sought to preserve moral values while altering the social, economic, and political fabric of the country at the same time. This reform movement increasingly included women, African Americans, and organized labor, as people who had rarely been allowed to speak gained voices as never before.

The **Progressive Era** began in the 1890s and lasted until the beginning of U.S. involvement in World War I in 1917. The movement was a big tent, with different factions advocating different projects. These causes included: antitrust reform, securing women's suffrage, constitutional reform, food and drug regulation, ending child labor, anti-corruption journalism, and reforming education.

Progressivism took hold in local and state politics long before it reached the national level. As early as 1888, voters in Massachusetts were using a "secret ballot" to vote in elections. Under the leadership of Governor and later U.S. Senator Robert "Fighting Bob" La Follette, Wisconsin became the model for increased voter power at the ballot box. It was the first state in the union to institute direct primaries, in which state voters nominated their own slate of candidates as opposed to selection of the party ticket by the state legislature.

Wisconsin led the way for other states to adopt reform laws with regard to taxes, representation, and commerce regulation. State governments also led the way in adopting the direct election of U.S. senators, which led to the Seventeenth Amendment to the Constitution in 1913.

During the Progressive Era, city governments looked to right the wrongs caused by political machines and overall voter complacency with massive reforms. Public utilities, such as electric companies and streetcar lines, were forced to act in the public interest.

18

Be prepared to answer questions on how literature can lead to reform.

Earlier in history, the novel *Uncle Tom's Cabin* had an important effect on American public opinion leading up to the Civil War. Similarly, another impactful work of American literature was *The Jungle* by Upton Sinclair. He wrote *The Jungle* to expose the filthy conditions in which meatpacking plants were churning out their products. As a result of the public uproar, Roosevelt worked to establish major reforms that would regulate the food and drug industries.

Roosevelt as a Modern President

High-Yield

The assassination of President McKinley during his second term brought the spirited vice president, Theodore Roosevelt, into office. Reform movements had already established firm roots in local and state politics, but with the executive office now in the hands of the young Roosevelt, the spirit of change had a national champion. Theodore Roosevelt soon became known as the Progressive Era's president as he worked on issues ranging from labor disputes to land conservation. His **Square Deal** involved breaking up harmful trusts, increasing government regulation of business, giving labor a fair chance, and promoting conservation of the environment.

Theodore Roosevelt is often called the first "modern" president in that he actively set an agenda for Congress and expected it to listen to his legislative suggestions. Roosevelt's first test was a coal miners' dispute in eastern Pennsylvania. Past presidents had all sided with business owners at the expense of labor, but, surprisingly, the young president decided to intervene by holding a private meeting in the White House between labor and management. When it was clear that neither side was willing to budge, Roosevelt threatened to take over the mines and run them with federal troops. Reluctantly, the mine owners agreed to lift the lockout, offer a 10 percent pay raise, and accept a nine-hour workday. Roosevelt's willingness to step in on the side of labor garnered him enough support to get him reelected in the election of 1904.

Roosevelt's next major effort at reining in the unchecked power of business interests was breaking up the Northern Securities Company, which Roosevelt considered a harmful trust. The railroad monopoly fought the president by taking its case all the way to the Supreme Court. The Court, however, upheld the president's position. Roosevelt's victory gave him a reputation as a champion trust buster.

This success gave the president reason to seek ways to regulate the railroad industry. Congress passed the Elkins Act in 1903, which gave the Interstate Commerce Commission (ICC) more power to prohibit rail companies from giving rebates and kickbacks to favored customers. The Hepburn Act in 1906 allowed the ICC to regulate rates railroad lines could charge, ending the price gouging that had been the bane of farmers. Along with targeting the rail industry, Roosevelt also sought to destroy other harmful trusts, such as Standard Oil.

Roosevelt had firsthand experience with the dangers of food-borne bacteria. During the Spanish-American War, soldiers had suffered from food poisoning caused by meat that was poorly preserved,

18

chemically adulterated, or spoiled. The meat caused an unrecorded number of illnesses and deaths. To provide more consumer protections, Roosevelt worked to get the Pure Food and Drug Act and the Meat Inspection Act passed in 1906.

The final piece of Roosevelt's Square Deal was conservation of the environment. An outdoorsman himself, Roosevelt sought to protect natural resources from industrialization and human habitation. Under his administration, millions of acres of land were protected after the creation of natural reserves and the National Conservation Commission.

Taft's Presidency

The next Progressive president came into the White House in 1909 after having served as Roosevelt's secretary of war. **William Howard Taft** continued his predecessor's policies of dismantling trusts and regulating business. The Mann-Elkins Act of 1910 placed the regulation of communications directly under the ICC. Taft also saw the ratification of the Sixteenth Amendment to the Constitution, which authorized the federal government to collect an income tax.

Taft's policies were not supported by some within his own party. Progressives were angry at Taft's support of a higher tariff bill, his firing of the popular conservationist Gifford Pinchot after he criticized another Cabinet member, and his open support of conservative Republicans during the midterm elections. As a result, the Republican party was split, with liberal Progressives on one side and conservative "old guard" Republicans on the other. Taft further angered his predecessor, Roosevelt, by ordering the prosecution of an antitrust violation by U.S. Steel, a merger that Roosevelt himself had approved. Roosevelt took the case as a personal attack by Taft. The feud would encourage Roosevelt to seek presidential reelection for a splinter sect of the Republican Party in 1912.

The election of 1912 saw Taft as the Republican candidate, Theodore Roosevelt as the Progressive Republican nominee, and **Woodrow Wilson** as the Democratic contender. The Socialists hoped to make a dent in the election with Eugene V. Debs again running for president. Taft was already faltering with low approval ratings, and Debs's radical views contributed to his lack of appeal among many Americans. Therefore, Roosevelt and Wilson were the primary competitors for the Oval Office. Roosevelt introduced his vision of New Nationalism: a smaller federal government with less big business influence, and more support for entrepreneurs and small businesses. Wilson countered with his New Freedom plan, which proposed that the government take a larger role in regulating business; it also sought to grant women voting rights and to support various federal assistance programs. Thanks to the Republican Party split, Wilson enjoyed an easy win, but not enough to claim a mandate. Many Americans supported the Progressives, a clear indication that the new president needed to take heed.

Journalists and Authors Stir Controversy

Just as newspaper giants Joseph Pulitzer and William Randolph Hearst sought to attract and entertain their readers with sensational stories, a new breed of writers hoped to awaken the reformist spirit. Authors and journalists who wrote articles, essays, and books aimed at exposing scandal, corruption, and injustice were disparagingly called **muckrakers** by Theodore Roosevelt, who felt that they took sensationalism a bit too far.

Nonetheless, these muckrakers were successful in gaining an audience and stirring up concerns among their readers. Magazines, such as *McClure's* and *Collier's*, were the first venues of the muckrakers. Ida Tarbell's series of articles titled *The History of the Standard Oil Company* (1904) caused a stir, as she detailed the ruthless business tactics of John D. Rockefeller. Muckraking moved into fiction and became wildly popular through the early 1900s; a famous example is Upton Sinclair's 1906 novel *The Jungle*, which depicted the poor conditions at a Chicago meatpacking plant. The muckrakers were successful in opening the eyes of many American readers and were moderately successful in gaining the attention of lawmakers and big business.

Wilson Introduces New Policies

High-Yield

Wilson sought to break what he saw as the "triple wall of privilege": high tariffs, unfair banking practices, and predatory trusts. In 1913, he persuaded Congress to pass the Underwood Tariff Bill, which significantly reduced tariff rates and protected consumers by keeping the price of manufactured goods low. To offset the loss of federal revenues from the lower tariff, Wilson used the power of the Sixteenth Amendment to have Congress enact a graduated income tax.

Due to the Panic of 1907, Wilson looked to Congress to address the problem of the money supply. Congress passed the monumental Federal Reserve Act in 1913, which created the **Federal Reserve System**. The new banking system consisted of 12 regional banks that were publicly controlled by the new Federal Reserve Board but privately owned by member banks. The system would serve as the "lender of last resort" for all private banks, hold or sell the nation's bonds, and issue Federal Reserve Notes—otherwise known as dollar bills—for consumers to purchase goods and services. This was the first time since Andrew Jackson eliminated the Second Bank of the United States that the country would have a national bank.

Another of Wilson's goals was to curb the power of monopolies. His first step was to gain passage of the **Clayton Antitrust Act** in 1914, which finally gave some teeth to the weak and ineffective Sherman Antitrust Act of 1890. The Clayton Act strengthened provisions for breaking up trusts and protected labor unions from prosecution under the Sherman Act. Labor leader Samuel Gompers hailed the bill as labor's "Magna Carta."

Wilson's second step in controlling monopolies was the creation of the **Federal Trade Commission** (FTC) in 1914. This regulatory agency would monitor interstate business activities and force companies who broke laws to comply with government's cease and desist orders. Wilson's Progressive legislation after 1914 would be eclipsed by gradual U.S. involvement in the Great War.

AFRICAN AMERICANS AT THE TURN OF THE CENTURY

As mentioned before, the Progressives were largely white middle-class citizens who were interested in reforming American society. African Americans were largely ignored by Progressive agendas at

18

the local, state, and national levels. Progressive President Woodrow Wilson even issued an executive order to segregate federal buildings and named the racist silent film *Birth of a Nation*, which glamorized the history of the Ku Klux Klan, as one of his personal favorites.

Since the end of Reconstruction, the protection of African American civil rights had decreased as the federal government failed to take stands against segregation, disenfranchisement, and lynching. It was up to African Americans themselves to fight for their own rights.

Having risen to prominence during the late 1890s, Booker T. Washington continued to argue that African Americans needed the skills necessary to work within the white world. In essence, he argued that blacks needed to make themselves economically successful before they could become equal to whites. This view came to be known as accommodation. On the other side was Harvard-educated W. E. B. Du Bois, who believed that African Americans should demand nothing less than social and political equality with whites; only then would blacks gain economic success.

In 1905, Du Bois held a meeting in Niagara Falls to discuss possible forms of protest and to formulate a plan of action. This group, called the Niagara Movement, joined forces with other concerned African Americans and whites to form the **National Association for the Advancement of Colored People** (NAACP) on February 12, 1908. Founding members answered what they deemed the "call" to end all racial discrimination, segregation, and disenfranchisement. The NAACP became so influential that it pushed President Wilson to make a public statement condemning lynching in 1918.

The activism of the NAACP and Booker T. Washington was spurred by the increase in discriminatory practices throughout the country. Beginning around 1910, a **Great Migration** occurred as millions of African Americans moved away from the South. Just as the northern cities had lured European immigrants during the 1880s, the promise of factory work and less discrimination brought blacks to urban centers. Unfortunately, northern African Americans experienced horrible living conditions, low-paying jobs, and racial discrimination. African Americans would find the fight against discrimination nearly as difficult in the North as it was in the South.

WOMEN'S ROLES AND SUFFRAGE

Many Progressive politicians were not so liberal as to believe that women should have a voice in politics. Still, women's roles in the United States continued to shift as industrialization took hold in more parts of the country. No longer was it necessary for most American families to have many members to care for the family farm. Very few urban families had more than two children; thus, the role of the woman as mother and homemaker changed.

Entering the Workforce and the World of Academia

More and more women entered the workforce as factory jobs opened up. Women were mainly involved in the textile industry, working in spinning mills or large garment factories. Other women found work as telephone or telegraph operators, secretaries, or typists. Some women entered the world of academia, as women's universities opened across the nation. Not all women could afford to attend college; they had to enter the workforce to help support their families. Some even broke through the male-dominated world of labor unions to promote better working conditions for women.

The International Ladies' Garment Workers Union (ILGWU) organized women who worked in sweatshops in cities like New York and Chicago. On March 25, 1911, the unspeakable happened in a New York City sweatshop. The Triangle Shirtwaist Factory was housed in the top floors of the Asch building, where women and girls, some as young as 15 years old, were crammed inside. Windows, doors, and fire exits were completely blocked by people, machines, and trash cans. That night, just before closing, a fire broke out on the ninth floor. With no way to escape, many of the young women died in the building, while others jumped from windows to the pavement below.

After the flames were finally tamed, the fire had taken 146 of the 500 employees' lives. The ILGWU organized protest rallies to inform others around the country of the tragedy. As a result, the state of New York made massive reforms in the conditions of its garment factories. This victory was bittersweet, however, as the owners of the factory were later acquitted of any wrongdoing, even though they had known the exits and fire escapes were all locked.

Active among the railroad workers and coal miners, female activist Mother Jones traveled the country protesting and lobbying for the rights of all workers. Even as she lost her ability to write and walk without assistance, Mother Jones continued to fight for labor rights up until her death at the age of 93 in 1930.

The Women's Suffrage Movement

High-Yield

College-educated women were emboldened by the successes of their male Progressive counterparts and looked to improve their standing in the United States. The National American Woman Suffrage Association (NAWSA) gained a new president in 1900 with the election of Carrie Chapman Catt. Catt was an outspoken advocate of women's suffrage. She believed that women could only guarantee protections for themselves and their children through voting.

The NAWSA would soon have some inner conflict, as more radical members of the group wanted to push for more immediate action. Led by Alice Paul, this splinter group left the NAWSA to form the **National Woman's Party**. The women in this group often picketed important sites, such as the White House and the Capitol, to demand the right to vote. Arrests occurred, and the women were known for going on hunger strikes while in jail.

President Woodrow Wilson was disgusted with these militant protesters, who would chain themselves to the White House gates, yell insults at the president, and carry signs intending to embarrass the chief executive. He did, however, listen to Carrie Chapman Catt, who skillfully used the American mobilization for entrance into World War I to advance her cause. She claimed that armed with the vote, American women would support their president and country as it entered the worldwide crisis. Her message, delivered on the eve of the congressional vote on women's suffrage, hit home. President Wilson gave his public support for the amendment.

Because of such efforts, the **Nineteenth Amendment**, which granted women the right to vote, was ratified in 1920. Catt formed the League of Women Voters to assist these new voters, while Paul continued working with the National Woman's Party and shifted her focus to the Equal Rights Amendment (ERA), which repeatedly failed passage and finally succumbed in the early 1980s.

> ✔ **AP Expert Note**
>
> **Be able to evaluate the significance of the ratification of the Nineteenth Amendment**
>
> For the first time in American history, women could vote in elections and participate in political activities. Women would be able to serve in governmental positions and gain more opportunities in the workplace. Beginning with the Seneca Falls Convention in 1848, the success of the women's suffrage movement in 1920 was a turning point in American history.

WORLD WAR I

For the United States, there was no desire to enter the Great War, yet Americans were affected by the war in the early years. The outbreak of war in Europe had devastating effects on the American economy. As European nations looked for debt repayment in the form of gold and silver, a deep recession was spurred by the drain of hard currency. There was also a loss of profitable overseas markets for U.S. products. However, by 1915, Britain and France looked to the United States to supply them with munitions for war, giving the economy a much-needed boost.

U.S. neutrality was severely tested after both Britain and France imposed naval blockades against the Germans. The Germans had a new weapon that they would use to terrorize shipping traffic across the Atlantic. The German U-boat (a type of submarine) would strike ships as they crossed the Atlantic, whether civilian or military.

The Germans claimed that these ships might be carrying munitions for Britain or France and must be stopped. By September 1915, German U-boats had sunk 90 ships in the Atlantic and surrounding waters. One such ship was the British luxury liner *Lusitania*. Almost 1,200 people died (including about 130 Americans) as the ship was sunk off the coast of Ireland. Wilson, still not wishing to enter the war, issued a stern warning to the Germans to cease submarine warfare on unarmed ships. After the sinking of another liner that cost the lives of two Americans, the Germans finally agreed to stop this type of attack.

The Germans' promise was short-lived. In March 1916, the Germans attacked the French passenger liner *Sussex*, killing four Americans. Wilson issued the Sussex ultimatum, in which he warned the Germans to stop submarine warfare or the United States would break off all diplomatic relations with Germany. This move clearly signaled America's willingness to go to war. Germany again agreed to stop submarine warfare but only if the United States convinced Britain to lift its blockade.

18

In January 1917, an announcement came from Germany that it would, again, start unrestricted submarine warfare and would sink any ship entering the war zone, including American ships. Wilson immediately broke off relations with Germany. On March 2, 1917, Wilson received word that a British agent had intercepted and decoded a letter from the German Foreign Secretary Zimmermann to the German ambassador to Mexico. This **Zimmermann Telegram** contained a promise from the German government to the Mexican president that if his country assisted Germany in a possible war against the United States, Mexico would be given back the territory lost in the Mexican War. Wilson had the ammunition he needed: the security of the United States had been directly threatened. After the news of the telegram and the German sinking of four unarmed American merchant vessels, the United States was now poised to enter the Great War.

✔ **AP Expert Note**

Know the factors that led the United States to engage in World War I

Political alliances all over Europe, increasing militarism, and extreme nationalism made war inevitable after the assassination of the Archduke Franz Ferdinand of Austria-Hungary by a Serbian nationalist in 1914. Initially, President Wilson sought to keep the United States out of the affairs of Europe, and the American public was very hesitant of becoming entangled in an international conflict. However, aggressive actions by the Germans, including naval attacks and the Zimmermann Telegram, eventually drove the United States to enter World War I.

Impact of the War at Home

The United States was woefully unprepared for war. It was Woodrow Wilson's idealism, stubbornness, and belief in American exceptionalism that led the country through the crisis. Wilson truly believed that the Great War was the "war to end all wars."

In advancing his postwar vision, Wilson delivered his Fourteen Points speech to Congress on January 8, 1918. Wilson's points provided for:

- Abolition of secret treaties

- Freedom of the seas

- Economic freedom

- Reduction of arms

- End of colonization

- Freedom of self-determination for all peoples

- Formation of an international organization for collective security

The United States mobilized for war reluctantly. The country was aided by the formation of the Committee on Public Information, headed by George Creel. This department was given the task of gaining the support of Americans for the war through a massive propaganda machine. Posters, speeches, and "liberty leagues" throughout the country encouraged Americans to buy war bonds and support the war effort. Herbert Hoover headed up the U.S. Food Administration, which encouraged Americans to have meatless Mondays, to grow victory gardens, and to limit the amount of food they ate. Americans also renamed German foods, such as frankfurters (liberty sausages) and sauerkraut (liberty cabbage). American factories soon found themselves under the War Industries Board, which sought to control production, wages, and the prices of goods.

Raising an army was another difficult task for the government. In response, Wilson urged the passage of the Selective Service Act (1917), which authorized the conscription of American males into military service. Within months of its passage, the army had enough men to relieve the Allied forces overseas.

Americans experienced a curbing of their civil liberties during wartime. Mostly aimed at German Americans and antiwar protesters, the Espionage Act of 1917 and Sedition Act of 1918 limited the right to free speech. Socialists, such as Eugene V. Debs, were targeted, arrested, and jailed. In the pivotal ruling of *Schenck v. United States*, the Supreme Court upheld the Espionage Act by stating that Congress could limit the right of free speech if it represented a "clear and present danger" that would bring about evils the government was seeking to stop. Unfortunately, the war years were an ugly time for civil liberties; many Americans served jail time for wartime crimes.

Negotiating Peace at Versailles

As the fighting ended and it was time to negotiate peace, President Wilson hoped to promote his Fourteen Points in the treaty talks at Versailles, located just outside of Paris. The president had lost some pull at home, however, as the 1918 midterm elections brought a narrow Republican majority to Congress. Wilson infuriated the legislative branch when he traveled to Versailles without any Republicans; this would later haunt him when he worked to get the treaty ratified by Congress.

The peace conference began on January 18, 1919, with the "Big Four": Woodrow Wilson, Georges Clemenceau of France, Vittorio Orlando of Italy, and David Lloyd George of Great Britain. Germany and Russia were conspicuously absent from the meeting. Being a rather stubborn idealist, Wilson was determined to see his Fourteen Points come to fruition, especially his fourteenth point (the call for the creation of a **League of Nations**). The other European leaders were interested in exacting reparations from Germany, which they believed was responsible for the war. This made Wilson's job difficult, and he had to compromise to see his ideas become a reality. One of the first areas of compromise was the idea of mandates, in which conquered territories would be put under the trusteeship of the League.

Eventually, Wilson would have to compromise on most of his Fourteen Points and give in to the desires of the European powers to assign full blame for the war and its consequences on Germany. Woodrow Wilson did get his League of Nations, and Article X of the League's charter called for members to stand at the ready if another member nation's sovereignty was being threatened.

It was Article X, along with other mistakes Wilson made in the eyes of the Republicans, that would derail ratification of the Treaty of Versailles in the United States. One of the most outspoken opponents of the president and of the treaty was Republican senator Henry Cabot Lodge. Those who were opposed to ratification of the treaty fell into two camps: the reservationists and the irreconcilables. Lodge and his reservationists would agree to ratify the treaty only if reservations, such as the ability to leave the League and international acceptance of the Monroe Doctrine, were added to the League's covenant. The irreconcilables, led by Senators Hiram Johnson and William Borah, refused to ratify the treaty under any circumstances. Wilson had to act quickly to save the treaty and the League of Nations. He traveled across the United States to speak directly to the American public about the treaty and its importance. While in Colorado, the president collapsed from exhaustion. A few days later, he suffered a stroke, which left him partially paralyzed and unable to meet with his Cabinet for seven months.

The Senate voted on the treaty twice in 1919, both times failing to ratify it. Eventually, the fight over the treaty turned on whether or not it would be accepted with or without reservations. Democrats were split: some voted with the reservationists, while loyal Wilson supporters voted to reject the treaty rather than accept it with reservations. The election of 1920, in Wilson's eyes, would be a "solemn referendum" on the treaty, as he hoped Americans would give his Democratic Party a majority in Congress and continued control of the White House.

It was the Republicans, however, who dominated the election. The United States did not officially end its war with Germany until 1921 and never ratified the Treaty of Versailles. As a result, the United States did not join the League of Nations, which weakened the organization.

POST-WORLD WAR I RECOVERY

Returning from war was a difficult transition for American soldiers. The federal government did not have any plans for helping war veterans reestablish themselves in civilian life. The realities of trench warfare and the horrors of war left many veterans scarred both physically and mentally. Many American veterans returned from Europe with missing limbs, facial disfigurements, and shell shock (now called post-traumatic stress disorder). While most war veterans found work quickly when they returned home, they displaced thousands of women and African Americans who had held these jobs during the war years.

Troubles Abroad and the Red Scare

High-Yield

Tensions rose as society shifted from wartime to peacetime. Aside from the end of the war, other developments in Europe alarmed Americans and caused social unrest as the country entered the 1920s.

The 1917 Bolshevik Revolution in Russia frightened middle- and upper-class Americans, as the Bolsheviks overthrew the Provisional Government of Russia and pledged to destroy capitalism. Socialists and anarchists in the United States had been persecuted throughout the war, and their problems intensified as fears over communism rose. Attorney General A. Mitchell Palmer fanned the flames of unrest after a series of bombings, including one that occurred in his neighborhood and was attributed to anarchist groups. Palmer immediately ordered the rounding up of suspected anarchists, socialists, aliens (usually Russians), and agitators and started what is known as the **Red Scare**. During the Palmer Raids, some 6,000 people were arrested in a two-month period, and 500 were deported on "Soviet Arks," which sent the passengers back to Europe.

Labor and Race Issues

Fears of a socialist or communist takeover spilled over into labor conflicts, which peaked in 1919. Organized labor felt the need to protect workers as the nation fell into a recession. Many companies had to lay off employees and drastically cut wages. As labor strikes grew increasingly violent, many Americans began to believe the labor unions were being infiltrated and funded by communist groups. As a result, the federal government began to take a hard-line stance against strikes, especially in cases where the public safety was at risk.

Racial issues also came to the surface as the nation moved into the new decade. Many African Americans were fired in favor of war veterans returning from Europe, and they also faced a backlash due to growing resentment about African American economic and social gains. Riots, fueled by ongoing racial tensions, broke out in such cities as Chicago, Baltimore, and Omaha.

AMERICAN BUSINESS AND CONSUMERISM

Big business continued to enjoy the government's laissez-faire policies as the country entered the 1920s. Presidents Harding, Coolidge, and Hoover all sang the praises of wealthy businessmen and insulated them from litigation. After a brief recession in 1921, a booming economy complemented this attitude. The country emerged from World War I as a creditor nation, and American industrial production rose dramatically in response to worldwide demand for manufactured goods. Despite losses that labor endured in 1920 and 1921, workers' wages actually were higher than they ever had been.

This did not mean the work of organized labor was finished. The labor movement suffered setbacks during the 1920s. Business owners fought for the end of the "closed shop" in which all employees had to become members of the union, sinking union membership to an all-time low. Although the standard of living for the average American was higher than in any other nation, not all Americans enjoyed this prosperity. The poor, including many rural tenant farmers, struggled to make ends meet on incomes that were well below the poverty level. Farmers also suffered from a drop in the price of crops and heavy debt.

Ford and Changing Consumerism

Manufacturing fully benefited from the prosperity of the new era. American productivity was greater than ever, owing to advances in technology and the management systems of men like Frederick W. Taylor and Henry Ford. Many applied Taylor's principles of scientific management to make factory production faster and more efficient, such as Henry Ford did with his automobile factory assembly lines. By specializing the work that employees were hired to complete, Ford's factory could make cars at a speed previously unthinkable. Ford's goal was to create an automobile that would be priced such that an average American family could purchase one.

By 1929, there were about 30 million automobiles in the nation, compared to barely one million before World War I. The car revolutionized American life economically and socially. Because of the increased demand for automobiles, related industries like steel, rubber, petroleum, and road construction experienced booms. Suburbs grew because it was now possible for middle-class families to move outside of the city limits and still commute to work in the city.

America's new prosperity, coupled with massive production of low-priced goods and the birth of modern advertising, led to the growth of a mass-consumption society. New appliances that took advantage of the increasing availability of electric power, such as refrigerators, vacuum cleaners, and electric stoves, became the must-have products of Americans seeking to keep up with the rising standard of living.

Hoping to leave the stubborn, idealist presidency of Woodrow Wilson behind, Americans elected Republican **Warren G. Harding** president in 1920. Harding promised Americans a return to "normalcy," a word he popularized to assure citizens that his administration would renew an interest in domestic prosperity and leave intervention in world affairs behind. The Progressive agenda was now a memory.

A Scandalous Presidency

Harding's election began 12 years of conservative Republican rule. A poker-playing, handsome man from Ohio, Harding was a change from the more dour Wilson. Harding desired to surround himself with men who were familiar to him and capable of assisting with running the country. Harding's cabinet, dubbed the Ohio Gang (or the Poker Cabinet), was made up of old friends from the president's home state who were knowledgeable in the areas in which they served. Some of his friends did more harm than good, however, as Harding's presidency soon became mired in scandal. As a result, Harding's administration would be labeled as dishonest, and it eventually gained the reputation among some historians as one of the worst presidencies in American history. While on a goodwill tour of the Pacific Northwest, President Harding fell ill and died of pneumonia in August 1923, leaving his vice president, **Calvin Coolidge**, to take over.

Harding's Foreign Policy

In addition to dodging scandal, Harding ignored foreign policy issues and renewed the isolationist spirit. The United States worked to avoid having the delicate postwar peace disturbed by other countries. A naval arms race had been developing since the end of World War I among the United States, Britain, and Japan. To keep the peace, Secretary of State Hughes organized the Washington Naval Conference in 1921 and 1922 to address disarmament issues. Several treaties were signed among the countries present—Belgium, China, France, Portugal, Japan, Italy, the Netherlands, and the United States—to limit the expansion of arms and build territorial respect among all present.

The United States also sought to provide economic aid to Germany so Germany could pay its World War I reparations to Britain and France, thus enabling those nations to repay the United States for their war debts. In 1924, Charles Dawes crafted a loan program that would enable Germany to pay its war reparations, thus lessening the financial crisis in Europe. The **Dawes Plan** was successful until the program ended with the U.S. stock market crash in 1929.

Coolidge and Hoover Take Office

After taking the oath of office as president of the United States in his parent's farmhouse in Vermont, Calvin Coolidge set out to promote the idea of limited government. Less than a year after taking the oath, Coolidge won the presidency in his own right in the election of 1924. "Silent Cal" was a man of few words who worked very little as president. Where Woodrow Wilson would often put in 12- to 15-hour days, Coolidge would rarely work more than 4 hours each day.

Aside from the growth of big business aided by Coolidge's inaction, he became mainly known as a president who refused to pay World War I veterans their promised bonuses and twice vetoed the McNary-Haugen Farm Relief Act, which would have assisted farmers who badly needed price supports. His announcement that he would not seek reelection did not surprise the Republican Party, which had **Herbert Hoover** waiting in the wings to run for office in 1928.

Running against Democrat Alfred Smith, who was a New York Catholic, Hoover won relatively easily on a conservative platform that promised a continuation of prosperity and progress. Unfortunately for the new president, economic disaster befell just eight months after his inauguration. Hoover believed in the strength of the American businessperson. He believed in the idea of **rugged individualism**, which held that anyone could become successful through hard work.

At the end of Coolidge's term, world peace was fostered with the signing of the **Kellogg-Briand Pact** in 1928, which made offensive wars illegal throughout the world. Unfortunately, the pact did not have any teeth: it did not prohibit defensive warfare or provide for punishment of countries that disobeyed the pact. The closest Hoover got to enforcing consequences was in response to Japanese aggression toward Manchuria in 1931. FDR would later initiate the **Good Neighbor Policy** with Latin America.

CULTURE IN THE INTERWAR PERIOD

America's new mobility—aided by the automobile and later by air travel—and the rise of radio and film as forms of mass communication helped spawn a new American sensibility, which would excite some and frighten others.

An Entertainment Boom

Often called the **Jazz Age**, or the Roaring Twenties, the era from 1920 to 1929 experienced a cultural explosion similar to that of the antebellum period. Jazz music began to change as it moved from the Deep South into northern cities like Chicago and Philadelphia. It became the music of choice for the young and the urbanites.

American families had more leisure time and looked to entertainment to fill their evenings and weekends. Commercial radio began in 1920 and expanded with the establishment of the National Broadcasting Company (NBC) in 1924, which reached some five million homes across the country. A radio listener in California was often listening to the same program as someone in New York City. A common cultural identity was established, as Americans listened to comedy, drama, and sports from all corners of the nation.

Movies became wildly popular, and Americans flocked to the theaters. Early films were silent with text on the screen for the actor's dialogue and a live orchestra playing the film's score. The release of *The Jazz Singer* in 1927 began the age of the "talkies," so now audiences could listen to actors converse onscreen. Hollywood became the glamorous entertainment capital of the country. Radio and movies altered the standard for the "true American hero" as movie stars, radio personalities, and professional athletes took the place of presidents and world leaders. Professional sports also gained a large following.

Some Americans were not pleased by the more materialistic mass-consumption society of the 1920s. A group of authors and artists, who were increasingly concerned about the influence of money and conservatism on society, began to express themselves. The Lost Generation was made up of authors and poets, such as F. Scott Fitzgerald, Gertrude Stein, Ezra Pound, and Ernest Hemingway. Artists, including Georgia O'Keeffe and Thomas Hart Benton, reacted to the impact of technology and business by painting realist or early surrealist works that portrayed American themes without the glitter of consumerism.

Harlem, a neighborhood of New York City, became the center of African American culture in the 1920s. This is where African American artists, poets, and musicians gave birth to a movement now called the **Harlem Renaissance**.

Deeply critical of white society in some respects, writers such as Langston Hughes and Zora Neale Hurston wrote poems, essays, and novels expressing the joy and pain of being an African American. Jazz musicians such as Louis Armstrong and Duke Ellington became wildly successful as they traveled the country playing concerts for all Americans. The Harlem Renaissance helped to change the perception of African Americans in particular and fostered a greater social consciousness of the abilities and worth of all Americans in general.

A Conservative Reaction

Many Americans were frightened by the changes occurring around them during the 1920s and sought to protect their communities from perceived moral degradation. Fundamentalists, prohibitionists, and nativists all hoped to stop these changes from impacting American identity.

Fundamentalist Christians had new fuel for their fight when the **American Civil Liberties Union** (ACLU) found a school teacher willing to become its test case regarding a state statute

18

that barred teaching the theory of evolution. John Scopes, a biology teacher in Dayton, Tennessee, was arrested and brought to trial in 1925. The ACLU appointed the famous lawyer Clarence Darrow to represent Scopes, while the state of Tennessee chose the outspoken Christian fundamentalist and former presidential candidate William Jennings Bryan as its counsel. The trial was a spectacle, as newspaper and radio press swarmed the town of Dayton. Darrow got Bryan to fumble and contradict himself as Bryan tried to use the Bible to justify the statute while testifying as a religious expert. In the end, however, Scopes was found guilty. The conviction was later overturned.

Prohibitionists continued to protect their coveted constitutional amendment, although it was ineffective and largely unenforced. Many Americans found ways to skirt prohibition. One way was to visit secret clubs called "speakeasies," where visitors needed to know the password and whisper it, or "speak easy," to gain entrance.

The underground, or bootleg, network of illegal alcohol began first with small-time distillers, who would brew "bathtub gin" for sale to local clients. Soon organized crime took hold of the bootlegging industry and grew in size, influence, and violence. Al Capone, the infamous Chicago crime boss, ran a network of illegal activities that began with alcohol and soon included drugs, prostitution, and illegal gambling. Violent turf wars between rival gangs made Chicago one of the most dangerous cities in the United States. Soon many called for the repeal of the Eighteenth Amendment because it appeared that the "noble experiment" engendered more disgust than respect for the law.

Meanwhile, European immigrants and African Americans continued to move into American cities well into the 1920s, and they were met by a resurgence of the nativist feelings that the Know-Nothing Party had embraced in the 1850s. In response, Congress passed several laws aimed at curbing the tide of immigrants coming from European countries. The Emergency Quota Act, or Immigration Act, of 1921 set a strict limit on individuals from each nation of origin based on the 1910 census. The second was the National Origins Act of 1924, which was directed at limiting Southern and Eastern European and Asian immigrants.

The Ku Klux Klan, the once-powerful racist organization, experienced a rebirth during the 1920s with anger directed not just at African Americans, but also at Jewish people, Catholics, and communists. The new Klan used the terror tactics it had employed in the Reconstruction era, such as cross burnings, beatings, and lynchings. Klan members included government officials and police in many southern and midwestern cities. In 1925, a former Grand Dragon of the Klan was convicted of murder, and the public nature and membership of the Klan dipped significantly.

The case of Nicola Sacco and Bartolomeo Vanzetti illustrated the injustice of nativism. The robbery and murder of a paymaster in South Braintree, Massachusetts, resulted in the arrest of two Italian anarchists, Sacco and Vanzetti. The evidence in the case was contradictory and confused. However, the two were convicted and sentenced to death by electric chair. Many people, such as Albert Einstein and the Italian American community, came to their defense, but to no avail. After multiple appeals, Sacco and Vanzetti were executed in 1927.

The Continued Struggle for Equality

Immigrants were not alone in their struggle for an equal place in American society. American Indians, African Americans, and women continued to fight for basic civil rights and equality. Some had radical solutions to the problems of inequality, while others chose to work within the system to better their lives.

In the early twentieth century, the U.S. government took the approach of assimilation toward American Indian tribes; this process is best illustrated with the Indian Residential Schools. These boarding schools banned young American Indians from speaking their indigenous languages, gave these children European names, and attempted to Christianize them. The goal was famously summarized by one advocate as "Kill the Indian, and save the man."

There were other measures as well. In 1919, citizenship was granted to all American Indian men who had served in the U.S. armed forces during World War I. In 1924, the Indian Citizenship Act made citizens of all American Indians born in U.S. states and territories. By 1924, roughly two-thirds of American Indians were already U.S. citizens through various means, such as marriage and military service. However, as with African Americans of the period, Constitutional rights like voting were sometimes more matters of theory than practice. These reforms would also pave the way for the Indian termination policy of the mid-1940s.

Amid the Harlem Renaissance, a young Jamaican immigrant named Marcus Garvey had formed the Universal Negro Improvement Association and encouraged African Americans to form a separate community from white society. He eventually advocated a Back to Africa movement. Unfortunately for the movement, Garvey was arrested and convicted for tax fraud. Garvey was deported back to Jamaica in 1929, and the Back to Africa movement collapsed. Other African Americans, including W. E. B. Du Bois and members of the NAACP, continued to fight for social justice and equality as the number of lynchings increased in the South.

The cult of domesticity continued to be a reality for American women, particularly those of the middle class. New inventions, such as the vacuum cleaner and the dishwasher, left many American women wondering what to do with their spare time. Some women were referred to as flappers, so named because they were not unlike baby birds flapping their wings and leaving the nest. They cut their hair into short bobs, wore short skirts, rolled down their stockings to reveal their knees, drank alcohol, and danced the Charleston. Their numbers were few, but their behavior was very public and raised concerns among America's conservatives. But this leisure time was not experienced by all women, as lower-class women had to work outside of the home to make ends meet.

Margaret Sanger caused controversy when she advocated the use of birth control, founding the American Birth Control League in 1921. Sanger encouraged young women to openly discuss topics ranging from menstruation to the prevention of pregnancy, and her work centered on the issues of poverty, abuse, and the premature death of young women.

Also of great concern to America's conservatives was the increase in divorce during the 1920s. Now that women were voting, legislators were required to listen to their issues, one of which was maintaining the ability to divorce. As a result of more liberal laws regarding divorce, divorces happened in much greater numbers than before.

THE GREAT DEPRESSION

The United States had experienced economic crises every 20 years or so, usually labeled "panics," from the years 1819 to 1907. Most of these panics were short-lived and corresponded with the natural business cycle. By 1929, the New York Stock Exchange had reached an all-time high, with many stocks selling for more than their actual worth. Millions of Americans sought to get rich quick by gambling their life savings in the stock market. Until late September 1929, this seemed to be a worthwhile risk. In October, the financial bubble burst, and the stock market collapsed.

The worst stock market crash in U.S. history occurred on October 29, 1929, commonly known as **Black Tuesday**. Days before, stock prices had plunged to desperate levels, and a selling frenzy on Wall Street occurred. Investors were willing to sell their shares for pennies on the dollar or were simply holding on to the worthless certificates. The signals of impending doom were clear well before the crash. Americans had spent themselves far into debt by purchasing stocks with loans. Investors also artificially drove stock prices sky-high with over-speculation—gambling that the value of the stocks would continue to rise. An overproduction of manufactured goods, both consumer and industrial, flooded the American marketplace.

When it became apparent to manufacturers that consumer spending was slowing down, especially in the realm of durable goods, they laid workers off or cut wages to maintain their profit levels. Farmers also suffered, as the demand for agricultural goods never rose back to World War I levels. To keep up with technological innovations in agriculture, farmers had to purchase new equipment like tractors on credit, driving them further into debt. This new equipment added another dimension to their problems, as improved methods led to overproduction.

The American banking system suffered as a result of its own risky practices. Overspeculating on property and issuing risky personal loans led to numerous defaults and foreclosures. Bank customers' deposits were not protected from poor banking practices; as the stock market failed, many of these people lost the money they had deposited.

Republican policies of the 1920s did not help the situation at a time when laissez-faire policies reigned supreme. Globally, economic depression was just around the bend—heavy debt burdens, war reparations, and the suspension of loan programs to assist the rebuilding of Europe drove countries like Germany and Britain deeper into recession.

Hoover's Reaction

Initially, President Hoover believed that Europe was the force behind the **Great Depression**. In response, Hoover made a grave mistake, in hopes of protecting American business from further injury, and signed the Hawley-Smoot Tariff into law. The tariff on imported goods increased from

30 percent to almost 50 percent and spurred the retaliation of foreign governments, which passed protective tariffs of their own. Hoover also called for a worldwide debt moratorium to ease the struggle of nations paying back loans and reparations from World War I. Hoover's foreign policy was not his downfall; his inability to adequately address domestic issues was.

A staunch believer in rugged individualism and volunteerism, Hoover was reluctant to give direct aid to Americans who were suffering. When it seemed that something had to be done, Congress created the Reconstruction Finance Corporation (RFC) in 1932. The corporation was eventually given authority to issue loans to assist railroads, banks, and municipalities to prevent them from collapsing. Hoover held fast to his belief that the wealthy are given more to spend so eventually they stimulate the economy and the benefits reach the poor. The RFC benefited only the wealthy instead of those truly in need.

Hoover believed that private charity groups, not the government, should be responsible for assisting the needy. This charity-based solution was not enough for a group of World War I veterans, who marched on Washington in 1932 to demand the early release of bonuses Congress had promised to pay in 1945. The Bonus Army arrived in the nation's capital and set up a makeshift encampment around the Capitol. Many Americans who had become homeless had set up similar makeshift camps, which they named "Hoovervilles" as a jab at the current administration. Eventually, the original campers were joined by thousands more veterans and their families, who protested and marched around the Capitol and the White House. The Bonus Bill, however, was not passed by Congress, and a clash between veterans and local police resulted in the deaths of two marchers. President Hoover called in the U.S. Army to stop the ensuing riot, and soldiers used tear gas and tanks on the unarmed protesters. The U.S. Army also burned the encampment, driving away the veterans. Across the nation, Americans looked on in horror, and many saw Hoover as a coward.

The Great Depression's Effects on American Society

The Great Depression had a profound impact on those who experienced it. Despite new prosperity, many of these Americans were insecure about their personal finances well into the 1940s and 1950s. Americans from all walks of life had to make do with what was available to them. Desperate unemployed businessmen often turned to selling apples on the street for a nickel to avoid having to accept charity. Even with the ingenuity of Americans, soup kitchens and bread lines became an everyday sight across the country as citizens looked for a meal. Many proud Americans were not happy about having to take a handout and did so reluctantly.

The Role of Women

Certain groups of Americans faced special challenges during the Depression. Women were often left with the burden of caring for children alone; many men deserted their families out of shame because they could not find work. Women entered the workforce when possible to supplement meager incomes brought in by husbands and other family members.

That plight was even more difficult for the wives of farmers in the Great Plains region. A severe drought hit the Great Plains, killing most of the crops. The topsoil turned to a fine, powdery dust that blew away with the severe, hot winds that wreaked havoc. The area was called the Dust Bowl, as Plains farmers saw their land literally blow away. With no opportunity to save their land from foreclosure, many of these families packed their belongings onto trucks and sought a new life in the West. California picking companies blanketed the Dust Bowl region with flyers promising jobs, money, housing, and fields of beautiful produce.

As a result, many of these farmers and their families flocked to California and earned the name Okies, as many came from the panhandle regions of Oklahoma or Texas. If they survived the journey, many of these migrants realized upon arrival that they were not in the promised land. Bouncing from migrant camp to migrant camp, Okies experienced discrimination, abuse, and humiliation. Nonetheless, many remained in California, finally settling in its Central Valley region to begin a new life.

Minorities in the Depression

American minority groups fared much worse than whites during the Depression. African Americans struggled to survive, as there was little work available to them. Moreover, because of discrimination all across the nation, many African Americans were not given assistance by their states or cities.

Despite FDR's need for the support of Southern Democrats, several New Deal programs openly accepted African Americans. After a threatened march on Washington by Rail Porters Union president A. Philip Randolph, the Fair Employment Practices Committee (FEPC) was established to prohibit employment discrimination in the defense industry.

American Indians regained self-governance with the Indian Reorganization Act of 1934, which replaced the Dawes Act of 1887, returning lands to the tribes and giving support to Native Americans to reestablish and preserve tribal culture.

Roosevelt and the New Deal

High-Yield

The election of 1932 took place during the worst year of the Great Depression. The Democratic Party looked for a household name to run for president and chose the governor of New York, **Franklin Delano Roosevelt** (FDR). Roosevelt promised Americans a "new deal" and criticized the ineffective policies of the Hoover administration, which included massive government spending that led to a large budget deficit. FDR also promised the repeal of the **Eighteenth Amendment**. Americans responded by overwhelmingly electing him to office. The president-elect had made a name for himself through a career that had begun in state politics during World War I. FDR almost left politics permanently when he was stricken by polio in 1921, which paralyzed him from the waist down. If not for the tenacity of his wife, Eleanor Roosevelt, who nursed her husband to health and campaigned for him when he was ill, he might never have become president.

The "new deal" FDR promised as he campaigned was a mystery to Americans, and the president himself, as he entered the Oval Office. Roosevelt knew that he had three goals, which he labeled the *three Rs*: relief, recovery, and reform. But aside from this, the president had no specific plan of action to release the country from the grip of depression. During his presidential campaign, FDR appointed a group of economists, professors, and politicians he would dub the Brain Trust to advise him on matters of economic and political policy.

The period of 1933 to 1935, which saw the implementation of the first part of the **New Deal**, began with a banking holiday. FDR ordered all financial institutions to close for two days; only those banks that were deemed solvent could reopen their doors on the third day. The other banks' assets were taken over by the federal government. To inform Americans of the Emergency Banking Relief Act passed on March 9, 1933, which reopened solvent banks, the president gave the first of his fireside chats. FDR delivered these weekly radio addresses to inform and soothe an American public that was reeling from the pain of unemployment and poverty.

To shore up the nation's currency, the president took the United States off of the gold standard and recovered all of the gold held by private banks and individuals in exchange for dollar bills. The Glass-Steagall Act prohibited commercial banks from performing the functions of investment banks and paved the way for the Federal Deposit Insurance Corporation (FDIC), which would protect Americans' banking deposits up to $5,000. Now Americans could bank with confidence, knowing that their investments could not be used in high-risk financial ventures and that the government was standing by in case of a banking collapse.

Several acts designed to assist in the relief effort were also passed in this period. Beginning what was called an "alphabet soup" of government agencies, the first hundred days saw the birth of such programs as the Public Works Administration (PWA), designed to employ thousands of Americans to rebuild the country's infrastructure; the Civilian Conservation Corps (CCC), which employed young college- and high school–aged young men to reforest America; and the Tennessee Valley Authority (TVA), which worked to electrify the impoverished Tennessee Valley with hydroelectric power.

The National Recovery Administration (NRA) kick started industrial relief. The blue eagle of the NRA was displayed in the windows of businesses that adhered to the regulations of the agency, which included fair labor practices, price ceilings and floors, and temporary monopolies of companies joining forces to increase production. Before long, however, the blue eagle would be shot down; the Supreme Court ruled it unconstitutional in the case of *Schechter v. United States*. This would be the first in a long series of battles between the president and the Supreme Court over his New Deal policies.

The next program, the Agricultural Adjustment Administration (AAA), was also deemed unconstitutional by the Supreme Court in 1935, but not before it aided many of America's farmers. The AAA paid farmers subsidies to destroy or not use their fields so as to create artificial scarcity, thereby increasing the price of foodstuffs and the profits of farmers.

Be able to explain the impact of legislation passed during FDR's presidency

Within the first three months of taking office, President Franklin D. Roosevelt managed to get Congress to pass an unprecedented amount of new legislation, which would alter the role of the federal government from that point on. FDR's **First Hundred Days** saw the passage of bills aimed at:

- Repairing the banking system and restoring the economy
- Starting government works projects to employ those out of work
- Offering subsidies to farmers
- Devising a plan to aid in the recovery of the industrial sector

As FDR continued to drive more legislation through Congress and further increase the power of the executive and legislative branches, he drew criticism from both ends of the political spectrum.

A Second New Deal

The **Second New Deal**, which ran from roughly 1935 to 1938, focused more on relief and reform. Another round of congressional acts continued to increase the federal government's role in the lives of Americans. To encourage more public works projects and the employment of nontraditional workers, such as artists, writers, and young people, the Works Progress Administration (WPA) employed Americans to build bridges, refurbish parks, write plays, and paint murals. The Social Security Act (SSA), passed in 1935, guaranteed income for retirees, the disabled, and the unemployed. Unfortunately, the law was biased—it did not apply to millions of agricultural and service workers, such as domestics, nannies, and janitors, who were largely African American. Nonetheless, the SSA provided a guaranteed pension to shield many of America's most vulnerable from abject poverty.

Watching the American economy from overseas was the British economist John Maynard Keynes. Keynes questioned laissez-faire policies and argued that demand determined the health of an economy. Even though Roosevelt was willing to experiment with government policies, he was uninterested in tinkering with fiscal and monetary policy. Keynesian theory proposed that instead of attempting to balance the budget and imposing new taxes on an already taxed system, the government should spend that which it did not have—in other words, resort to deficit spending. By the government increasing spending, it would "prime the pump" by spurring an increase in demand that would eventually increase the need for employees. Roosevelt had to do something; the Roosevelt Recession occurred in 1937 and 1938 partly because the president had decided to decrease government spending. FDR then initiated an increase in spending on public works projects and other programs. It should be noted, however, that even during the best times of recovery during the Great Depression, the unemployment rate never dipped below 16 percent. It took mobilization for World War II to finally get the country out of the Great Depression.

18

NEW DEAL SUPPORT AND CRITICISM

The New Deal was largely supported by Democrats, who stood by FDR from the day he took office. Organized labor became an ally of both FDR and the Democratic Party, as the administration continued to support workers and workers' rights through the New Deal.

African Americans also became ardent supporters of the Democrats and FDR as the New Deal continued. President Roosevelt, at the urging of his wife Eleanor, appointed more African Americans to executive department positions than had any president before him. His "Black Cabinet" advised him on issues ranging from the repeal of Jim Crow laws in the South to anti-lynching legislation. Unfortunately for African Americans, FDR needed to maintain the support of Southern Democrats, so he did not sign any legislation designed to end either of these practices.

Changing Party Politics and Anti-FDR Sentiments

The Republicans and Democrats both experienced changes in the makeups of their parties as the role of government changed. Southern Democrats struggled with FDR's liberal values with regard to race and gender relations, while many considered fleeing to the "party of Lincoln." The Republicans were experiencing an influx of conservative northerners and southerners who had been lifelong Democrats but disagreed with FDR's handling of the Great Depression. Supporters argued that the New Deal had been successful in keeping millions of Americans from the clutches of poverty.

FDR had critics both inside and outside his party. Extremists on both ends of the political spectrum charged that the president was either not doing enough or doing too much. Socialists argued that the administration needed to do more for the poor. Conservatives were frightened by the increasing role of the government in every aspect of Americans' lives. Claiming that the New Deal was socialism, anti-Roosevelt Democrats formed the American Liberty League to promote the concerns of big business and advocate for small government. They sought to unseat FDR as he ran for president in 1936.

Some of FDR's critics used the airwaves to reach Americans, much as the president did with his fireside chats. Playing to the fears of the average citizen, Catholic priest Father Charles E. Coughlin attacked the New Deal for being a benefit to only the well-to-do and big business. He was extremely popular, but he eventually digressed into anti-Semitic and fascist tirades before Catholic leaders pulled him from the air.

Before the passage of the Social Security Act, Dr. Francis Townsend advocated a federal pension that would provide $200 per month for every retired American over the age of 60. His plan gathered millions of supporters, who agreed that if retirees were given this pension and required to spend it all within a month, it would stimulate the economy. Roosevelt opted for a much less radical plan, which became the Social Security Act. Townsend criticized the president for not pushing for more.

Within Congress, Roosevelt found a critic in the senator from Louisiana, Huey P. "Kingfish" Long, who advocated for a "Robin Hood" plan, called Share Our Wealth, to take from the rich and give to the poor. His plan would impose heavy taxes on inheritance and estates to fund a minimum salary of $2,000 a year for every American. Long argued that the New Deal was not enough to aid the country's most needy citizens.

Supreme Court Challenges

The Supreme Court embodied another challenge for Roosevelt. Angered by court decisions that had effectively killed the NRA and the AAA, Roosevelt decided that he was going to reorganize the Supreme Court with the hope that his legislation might find a more sympathetic audience. His **Judicial Procedures Reform Bill** (1937) would allow the president to appoint one justice for every seated justice over 70.5 years old. At the time, the bill would have given FDR the ability to seat 6 justices on the court, bringing the number to 15.

Conservative Democrats and Republicans immediately opposed it and dubbed the bill a court-packing scheme, but the bill finally died when some of FDR's biggest supporters refused to back it. Roosevelt eventually was able to make eight appointments to the Supreme Court during his presidency, leaving a liberal legacy on the bench.

After the Roosevelt Recession in 1937, the economy had only modestly rebounded, and high unemployment and poverty remained major problems. Americans voiced their concerns during the midterm elections of 1938, when some Republicans and moderate Democrats replaced supporters of the New Deal. This, coupled with worldwide attention turning to Hitler's actions, signaled an end to the New Deal.

Organized Labor Gains

The **National Industrial Recovery Act** (NIRA), passed during the first New Deal, was the most proactive legislation to date in protecting the rights of workers and organized labor. The provisions of the act were administered by NIRA, which was composed of a board of trustees responsible for setting policy for industry in the United States. The board set maximum work hours, minimum wages, and price floors. It was also responsible for setting production quotas and inventories to prevent overproduction or price gouging. Importantly for organized labor, the NIRA guaranteed labor the right to organize and collectively bargain. No longer was the old yellow-dog contract or iron-clad oath an issue; unions could actively recruit members in factories and workplaces.

To further the gains of labor, the **National Labor Relations Act** of 1935—also called the Wagner Act—strengthened the language of the NIRA. Even though all labor unions fought for the protections of workers, not all agreed upon who should be protected. The American Federation of Labor (AFL) was composed mainly of skilled workers who did not agree that unions should protect all workers. Members of the AFL who wished to extend union membership to all workers broke away and joined other labor groups to form the Congress of Industrial Organizations (CIO) under the leadership of John L. Lewis of the United Mine Workers. The CIO focused on organizing laborers in America's heavy industrial sector, which was made up of steel, automobiles, and mines. By 1938, the CIO was completely independent of the AFL.

During the Second New Deal, the **Fair Labor Standards Act** established a federal minimum wage and set the maximum hours for workers employed by interstate businesses. It also ensured an end to child labor. Some industries resisted unionization. In Flint, Michigan, the United Auto Workers (UAW) organized a sit-down strike of assembly line employees at General Motors in 1936 and 1937. When the government refused to intervene between labor and management, the companies reluctantly went to the bargaining table and formally recognized the UAW as an official party with which to negotiate worker contracts. The UAW did not fare as well at the Ford plant, however, as workers were driven away violently before they could strike. The steel industry was also slow in its recognition of unions, with most plants finally accepting their workers' unions by the arrival of World War II.

INTERNATIONAL PROBLEMS AND WORLD WAR II   High-Yield

Most Americans were not keen on getting involved in another world war because the country had fought in the Great War just two decades earlier. Americans were intensely concerned with the Great Depression, even as Germany's Adolf Hitler continually violated the provisions of the **Treaty of Versailles**.

President Herbert Hoover ushered in the 1930s using diplomacy instead of military force to stave off potential threats around the world. It was clear that Americans were interested in maintaining their distance from world affairs through a policy of isolationism. It was Franklin Delano Roosevelt who gave a name to the relationship with Latin America, promising to be "good neighbors" by staying out of their affairs.

Economically, FDR looked to rid the world of the high protective tariffs that had crippled many nations' economies throughout the Depression. To open up new markets, FDR formally recognized the Soviet Union as a sovereign nation in 1933. But even FDR, occupied with getting the United States out of the Great Depression, could not ignore the crisis that was worsening across both the Atlantic and Pacific Oceans.

Trouble Brews Abroad

Totalitarian regimes had gained power in Europe and Japan during the 1920s and early 1930s because of the impact of the worldwide economic depression. The grim reality of being blamed wholly for the Great War caused many Germans to feel betrayed by their new government. They wanted strong leadership.

Faced with runaway inflation, Germans saw Adolf Hitler as the way to return their nation to power. Italians, too, felt that their government had sold them out to other world powers during the Treaty of Versailles negotiations, as they had lost valuable territories and prestige. Italians found hope in the words of Il Duce, the leader of their Fascist movement, Benito Mussolini. Faced with a trade imbalance that would cripple their island nation, the Japanese also looked for a return to power.

18

The United States watched from afar, not wishing to become involved in a foreign war again. Several neutrality acts were passed from 1935 to 1937 in response to the increasing turmoil and threat of war in Europe and Asia. The United States sat and watched as its allies in Europe and Asia enacted diplomatic policies aimed at keeping these dictators at bay, even as Hitler and Mussolini used the Spanish Civil War as a testing ground for their military tactics.

For his part, President Roosevelt did not make the same mistake as his predecessor, Woodrow Wilson. FDR started increasing military spending in 1938 to begin preparation for war. Part of his pump priming, this increase in government spending ultimately took the country on the road to full economic recovery.

Even as early as 1940, FDR was realistic about the potential of U.S. involvement in a war. He pressured Congress to pass the Selective Service Act, which provided for all American males between the ages of 21 to 35 to register for compulsory military service. This was the first time a peacetime military draft had been initiated, signaling that the president's stance was shifting from isolationism to interventionism.

The Road to War

Mussolini and Hitler understood the fragility of the League of Nations and hoped to take advantage of its weaknesses in their bid to take over Europe and the world. Mussolini first sent troops to invade the African country of Ethiopia in 1935; the League condemned his actions but did nothing to intervene. Hitler invaded the Rhineland, a demilitarized region between France and Germany, in 1936, thus violating the Treaty of Versailles. The year 1937 brought the Japanese invasion of China and a potential U.S.-Japanese war as the Japanese "accidentally" sank an American ship on the Yangtze River.

European leaders were at a loss as to how to handle Hitler's increasingly aggressive actions. He claimed an area of Czechoslovakia called the Sudetenland in 1938. In a bid to keep the peace, British prime minister Neville Chamberlain and French president Édouard Daladier met with Hitler to negotiate a settlement over the disputed territory. Surprisingly, Czechoslovakia was not invited. At the conference, held in Munich in 1938, the policy of *appeasement* was born. Hitler would be allowed to take the Sudetenland in exchange for his promise to not invade any other territories. Hitler agreed, and Chamberlain and Daladier were pleased that they had dodged another bullet.

World War II Begins

The peace was short-lived, however, as Hitler invaded the rest of Czechoslovakia six months later and set his sights on Poland. The general secretary of the Soviet Union, Joseph Stalin, had good reason to want to keep Poland as a neutral buffer zone between Germany and Russia. His country had been invaded through Poland many times throughout its history; he hoped a free Poland would keep his people safe.

18

The world was surprised when it was announced that Stalin and Hitler had signed a secret nonaggression pact in 1939, which freed Germany to invade the western half of Poland with no resistance; the Soviets would take the eastern half. The British and French pledged their support of Poland by stating they would declare war on Germany if the invasion took place. Then, on September 1, 1939, Hitler's forces invaded Poland and started World War II.

As former American allies Britain and France were now engaged in a war with Germany and Italy, the United States took measures to maintain its neutrality while supplying munitions to them. The Neutrality Act of 1939 again proclaimed U.S. neutrality but only in name, not in deed. The act provided for the sale of U.S. weapons to European allies on a cash-and-carry basis only. In other words, countries such as Britain and France would have to pay cash and provide their own transport for whatever war munitions they bought. This would eliminate the need for war loans to allies that could cause problems in a fragile postwar economy and would keep U.S. merchant ships out of the war zone.

September 1940 would bring increased U.S. involvement in the war. The new British prime minister, Winston Churchill, pleaded for more assistance in the face of continual bombings of his country by the German air force (the *Luftwaffe*) and the threat of U-boats in the Atlantic and English Channel. The two sides brokered the Destroyers-for-Bases Agreement, whereby the United States would provide Britain several older U.S. naval ships in return for the right to establish U.S. military installments on British-held Caribbean islands.

Reelection for FDR and Plans with Churchill

With the election of 1940 looming, President Roosevelt broke the precedent set by George Washington and ran for a third term. Running against Republican Wendell Willkie, Roosevelt was able to convince Americans that electing him again was choosing a voice of experience in the face of war. He won the election with 54 percent of the popular vote.

Growing more and more concerned over the fate of U.S. allies, President Roosevelt believed that his reelection was a mandate from the American people to end isolationism and become more involved in the war. He still emphasized diplomacy over military force, but it was clear to many that the president was willing to enter the war if necessary.

In his State of the Union address to Congress in 1940, the president offered his vision of U.S. involvement. FDR argued that offering Great Britain loans to buy U.S.-made munitions would further stimulate the economy and aid in the protection of the Four Freedoms: freedom of speech, freedom of religion, freedom from want, and freedom from fear. His proposal was to end the cash-and-carry program and institute the lend-lease program to provide Britain with U.S. war materials.

FDR arranged a secret meeting with Prime Minister Churchill to discuss postwar aims in response to the secret nonaggression pact signed by Hitler and Stalin. The two men drew up the Atlantic Charter, which declared that the self-determination of peoples and free trade would be the cornerstones of a world free of fascism.

18

Attack on Pearl Harbor

As Hitler continued to conquer Europe, with Paris falling in June 1940, the United States struggled to maintain amiable relations with Japan. Japanese forces remained in China and were poised to take French Indochina, which prompted FDR to cut Japan off from U.S. raw materials. As an island nation with few natural resources, the Japanese relied heavily on imports of American oil. Hoping to secure the removal of Japanese troops from China and Indochina in return for lifting the oil embargo, FDR sent Secretary of State Cordell Hull to negotiate with the Japanese government. Amid the negotiations, the new Japanese leader, General Hideki Tojo, changed course unexpectedly and backed out. Little did Hull know that the general was planning a secret attack on the Pacific fleet that he hoped would cripple the United States.

In the early morning hours of December 7, 1941, the entire U.S. Pacific fleet was attacked at **Pearl Harbor**, Hawaii. The surprise attack killed 2,400 American sailors and wounded 1,200. Eight battle-ships were either sunk or severely damaged, including the USS *Arizona*, which lost 1,100 sailors. Ten other ships were severely damaged and almost 200 planes destroyed in the attack. Immediately, FDR asked Congress to declare war on Japan, and it responded with but one dissenting vote. Three days later, Germany and Italy responded by declaring war on the United States.

WORLD WAR II: A TWO-FRONT WAR

By the time the United States entered the war in Europe, the focus of the Allies had shifted from the western to the eastern front, as Hitler broke his promise to Stalin and invaded Russia through Poland in late 1941. The Soviet leader joined the Allies, and the Big Three of Roosevelt, Churchill, and Stalin agreed to focus on stopping Hitler.

Diplomacy and Conferences

Throughout World War II, the Big Three met to discuss wartime concerns and postwar desires. Meetings in Casablanca, Tehran, Yalta, and Potsdam all yielded agreements and concessions among Britain, the United States, and the USSR that would shape the course of the war and impact the coming Cold War.

The first of these war meetings, which took place in Casablanca in 1943, included only Roosevelt and Churchill; Stalin declined the invitation. During this meeting, they decided to invade Sicily and settle for nothing less than "unconditional surrender" from the Axis powers. November 1943 brought Roosevelt, Churchill, and Stalin together in the Iranian city of Tehran. The seeds of the D-Day invasion were sown here. It was also here that the first disagreements between the Soviet leader and the Western powers came to light. Stalin claimed the right to use Eastern Europe to create a buffer zone between his country and Western Europe. Churchill, on the other hand, demanded a free Europe and the preservation of a unified Germany at the war's end. Roosevelt mediated an understanding between the two by promising peace through the proposed United Nations.

The Big Three met once again at Yalta in February 1945 to finalize the plans for postwar Europe. Stalin agreed to enter the war against Japan within three months of Germany's surrender and signed an agreement to create a free Eastern Europe with free elections. Additionally, the **Yalta Conference** yielded a skeleton framework for the **United Nations** and the division of Germany into four occupied military zones.

Focus on Germany

In Europe, the Allies concentrated on ridding the seas of German U-boats and the skies of the German *Luftwaffe*. The new British invention of radar turned the tide of war, as the Royal Air Force was able to down German planes and the U.S. Navy was able to locate and sink U-boats.

In Africa, the Allies struggled to rout the Germans from the North African region as they cut their way northward under the leadership of the German tank commander, General Erwin "the Desert Fox" Rommel. Operation Torch, led by U.S. general Dwight D. Eisenhower and British general Bernard Montgomery, successfully flanked Rommel in Tunisia in May 1943. Next, the Allies looked across the Mediterranean Sea to the island of Sicily, which they invaded in September 1943. Facing fierce resistance from both Italian and German troops, the United States finally took the island in May 1945.

Understanding the need to liberate Nazi-occupied France, the Allies began planning an invasion of the beaches of Normandy. Operation Overlord, now known as the **D-Day** invasion, was an amphibious landing that required the utmost secrecy and favorable weather conditions. The perfect opening arose on June 6, 1944. General Eisenhower led a multinational force to storm the beaches in northern France. Despite enormous loss of life, the invasion proved to be a success, and the Allies liberated Paris by the end of August. The final Allied push into neighboring Belgium was met with an attack by the Germans in December 1944 at the **Battle of the Bulge**. Even after suffering heavy losses in the battle, the Allies were able to recover and continue their push toward Germany. The British and U.S. air forces were successful in crippling Germany by bombing its urban centers.

With German defeat imminent, Hitler took his own life in April 1945, and Nazi forces surrendered unconditionally on May 7. As Allied troops marched further into Nazi-held territory, they came upon unspeakable horrors. Massive concentration camps were discovered throughout Germany, Poland, Austria, and Czechoslovakia, where much of Hitler's genocidal Final Solution had been carried out.

Focus on Japan

After V-E Day (Victory in Europe Day), the Allies could focus on defeating the Japanese. By the end of 1942, the Japanese had extended their sphere of influence far beyond China and Indochina, occupying the Korean peninsula, the Philippines, Indonesia, and many Pacific islands. The Pacific theater was different from the one in Europe; in the Pacific, the Allies had to rely heavily on naval power and the destruction of the Japanese air force to win.

Earlier in the war, two naval battles in the Pacific had served as turning points for the Allies. In the Battles of Coral Sea and Midway (May 1942 and June 1942, respectively), the Allies were able to stop

18

a Japanese aircraft carrier from reaching Australia. They also broke the Japanese code, enabling them to intercept and destroy four more aircraft carriers. The United States employed the strategy of "island hopping," in which the U.S. Navy would focus only on strategic Japanese-held Pacific islands and surround them to engage the enemy. Eventually, this tactic would lead the Allies to the southernmost Japanese islands.

The Japanese were not about to back down, however, and several other battles raged. By 1945, the United States had come close enough to the Japanese mainland to launch air raids on major cities, such as Tokyo. As the Japanese grew more desperate, sending suicide bombers into U.S. aircraft carriers, new president **Harry S. Truman** believed that the only way to end the war would be to invade Japan. (President Roosevelt had died in April 1945, and the presidency had passed to Vice President Truman.) Not wishing to launch an invasion that would more than likely cost many thousands of American lives, Truman decided instead to use a new secret weapon on Japan.

On August 6, 1945, "Little Boy," an **atomic bomb**, was dropped over the industrial city of Hiroshima, killing 80,000 people instantly. With the Japanese still unwilling to agree to an unconditional surrender, a second bomb, "Fat Man," was dropped on August 9 on the city of Nagasaki. Another 60,000 Japanese were killed immediately. Japan surrendered on September 2, 1945.

WORLD WAR II'S IMPACT ON AMERICAN SOCIETY

World War II impacted Americans from all walks of life. Citizens could not escape war propaganda as they walked to work, listened to the radio, ate their meals, and went to the movies. The **Office of War Information** (OWI) produced radio shows and news reels to keep Americans apprised of events overseas. Many sat riveted as USO shows from overseas featuring Bob Hope and Francis Langford were broadcast across the nation. Movies of the day often glorified American war involvement, reaching audiences of millions. Posters and cartoons were created to encourage compliance with rationing, saving grease, and purchasing war bonds. The OWI aimed to keep American morale high and to increase support for the war.

Women and Minorities During Wartime

Women were specifically targeted by OWI propaganda. As many as five million women joined the workforce during the war in response to propaganda that exalted women's war work. Rosie the Riveter was glorified in songs, posters, and movies as an American heroine and everyday woman, able to work all day and still manage the household. Despite the urging of women such as Eleanor Roosevelt to make women's pay equal to that of their male counterparts, companies typically paid female workers just two-thirds of what male workers earned.

American Indians served the country by enlisting in the armed services and working in thousands of factories across the United States. Most famous were the **Navajo code talkers**, who translated U.S. documents into their native language so that enemy forces could not decipher their content.

America's minority groups also experienced changes in their lives due to the war. Again, African Americans flocked to industrial centers in the North to seek jobs in factories, just as they had during World War I. Racial tensions ensued, and the summer of 1943 saw disturbances in multiple cities. One of these conflicts was the **Harlem Riot of 1943**, which took place after a white police officer shot and wounded an African American soldier. It was one of at least six riots that occurred in that same year across the country, due to tensions between black and white populations.

Mexican Americans, many of whom had moved to Mexico during the Great Depression, were encouraged to return to the United States as migrant farm laborers in the *bracero* program. Under this program, both former U.S. residents and Mexican nationals crossed into the United States to work during harvest season, and many remained north of the border to live permanently. However, tensions between sailors stationed in Los Angeles and Long Beach awaiting deployment to the Pacific theater and young Mexican American men reached a boiling point in the summer of 1943, in what was called the **Zoot Suit Riots**.

The individuals most adversely affected by the war domestically were the Japanese Americans living along the West Coast. Some 100,000 Japanese American citizens were ordered to leave their homes for internment camps located across the West.

President Roosevelt issued **Executive Order 9066** in reaction to the paranoia of the War Department that American citizens of Japanese ancestry might turn against their adopted country to aid Japan in an invasion of the West Coast. Of the 100,000 Japanese Americans interned, only 30 percent were foreign born.

Once these families returned to their homes after the war, they found their property, land, and homes taken over by other families. The Supreme Court upheld the decision to intern these citizens in the case *Korematsu v. United States* (1944), stating that in times of war, the curbing of civil rights was justified and that the court could not second-guess military decisions. The federal government finally agreed in 1988 to apologize formally for internment and pay surviving families $20,000 in restitution.

> ✔ **AP Expert Note**
>
> **Be able to trace the shift from isolationist foreign policy to U.S. involvement in World War II**
>
> One of the skills you will be expected to demonstrate on the exam is your understanding of continuity and change: basically, what has stayed the same and what has changed over the course of history. America's relationship with international wars is a topic that demonstrates change over time.
>
> The United States, in its early years, had avowed an isolationist stance toward international conflicts. While this policy was never completely followed, the world wars led to a definite shift in America's involvement. Then, the United States emerged from World War II as a military superpower and an industrial giant. It would lead in terms of global economic, political, and military dominance. The United States was no longer an isolationist nation and would continue to have an interventionist foreign policy for the rest of the century.

18

Wartime Mobilization

The Selective Service System, having already instituted the draft in 1940, expanded to include all 18- to 64-year-old males when the United States declared war on Japan. In addition, some 260,000 women enlisted as members of the Women's Army Corps (WACs), Women Appointed for Voluntary Emergency Service (WAVES), and Women's Auxiliary Ferrying Squadron (WAFS). These women supported the war effort by flying supply missions, decoding enemy communications, and repairing machines. By the war's end, almost 16 million American men and women had served in some capacity in the war effort.

The Office of War Mobilization took over from the earlier War Production Board to transition the country from a peacetime to a wartime economy. Soon outproducing the Axis powers, U.S. manufacturers devoted most of their productive capacity to making war supplies. Unemployment, the scourge of the nation 10 years earlier, had all but vanished, as Americans went to work to fuel the war machine.

The Office of Price Administration (OPA) and Office of Economic Stabilization set out to keep the wartime economy under control by establishing price floors and ceilings, regulating the tax code, and instituting rationing. Rationing stamps were issued to every American family for goods such as sugar, coffee, and gasoline. Rationing made these goods available to troops overseas and freed up manufacturers to focus on supplying war munitions rather than consumer goods. Because of the lack of consumer goods for sale, American families sank the money they made during the war into savings, which would impact the postwar economy by funding expansion and bolstering consumer spending.

Post-World War II Recovery

World War II certainly made its mark on the United States. The war cost the country 400,000 men and over 800,000 casualties, more than all other U.S. wars combined, excluding the Civil War. Monetarily, the war cost some $360 billion and led to the largest budget deficit in U.S. history. Approximately 55 million people died worldwide, and 38 million were either wounded or missing. To promote peace in the postwar world, the United Nations, chartered in October 1945, set to work to peacefully mediate disputes among nations.

Like most postwar economies, the United States experienced inflation as rationing and price regulations were lifted. Workers struggled to earn wages that kept up with inflation, even though the standard of living for the average American was higher than ever before.

Hoping to avoid the mistakes of World War I regarding returning veterans, Congress acted quickly to create a plan to aid those returning from war. In 1944, Congress passed the GI Bill, which provided funding for a college education, as well as low-interest home and small business loans. For 15 million soldiers returning from war, the GI Bill provided the opportunity to secure a career and purchase a home. Returning GIs married and had babies, leading to a baby boom that lasted from 1945 to 1963.

The war opened doors of opportunity to many other groups as well, forever changing the United States. Women and African Americans felt a sense of hope, as they enjoyed steady employment and increased social standing. President Truman hoped not only to continue the New Deal programs of Roosevelt but also to improve upon them by striving for full employment and increased rights for African Americans. Congress passed the Employment Act of 1946 in an attempt to keep the United States at full employment at all times.

With regard to civil rights, President Truman alienated Southern Democrats by ending racial segregation in the federal government and armed forces. However, Americans elected enough Republicans to give the GOP a majority in Congress during the midterm elections of 1946. Under their leadership, the Constitution was amended to avoid the repeat of a four-term presidency (FDR) by limiting a president to two terms. In addition, Congress passed the Taft-Hartley Act in 1947 in an attempt to garner the support of big business. The bill, which was vetoed by Truman but enacted by a congressional override, outlawed "closed-shop" workplaces, limited boycotts, and allowed the president to obtain an 80-day injunction against any strike deemed a danger to national health or safety. Under Taft-Hartley, organized labor lost much of the ground it had gained during the New Deal.

 NEXT STEP: PRACTICE

Go to Rapid Review and Practice Chapter 9 or to your online quizzes on kaptest.com for exam-like practice on this topic.

Haven't registered your book yet? Go to kaptest.com/moreonline to begin.

CHAPTER 19

Period 8: 1945–1980

THE EARLY COLD WAR

Unsurprisingly, the Grand Alliance between the Soviet Union and the Western Allies did not survive the transition to peacetime. Both sides had mistrusted one another for decades. American democratic capitalism and Soviet totalitarian communism were incompatible, opposing ideologies. Fear of communist and socialist subversion in the United States had driven the first Red Scare. The Western powers had halfheartedly intervened in the Russian Civil War in order to hinder the Bolsheviks, which the latter remembered. The Soviets, in turn, saw themselves at the forefront of history, with an ideological and moral duty to liberate the workers of the world from what they saw as an oppressive capitalist system.

World War II had done little to soothe tensions. Pearl Harbor left the United States worried about potential future surprise attacks just as Operation Barbarossa had worried the Soviets. The continued delays in opening a Western Front, only finally taking place in mid-1944 with the Normandy landings, led Stalin to believe his country had been bled dry in order to weaken both it and Nazi Germany. The USSR suffered over 20 million fatalities compared to 420,000 U.S. fatalities.

Despite his agreement at the Yalta Conference, Soviet leader Joseph Stalin refused to permit free elections in Poland and other Eastern European countries. From 1946 to 1948, many communist leaders were installed by Moscow, with the Soviets taking these countries under their wing as "satellite" nations. This was a clear violation of the agreements reached at the war conferences, where the great powers had set forth to protect the self-determination of peoples. In March 1946, Winston Churchill delivered a speech in Fulton, Missouri, where he said, "An iron curtain has descended across Europe." The iron curtain he spoke of was communism. The **Cold War** had officially begun.

The Truman Administration

Heavily influenced by his top advisers, President **Harry S. Truman** sought to counteract the spread of world communism. Three potential approaches were articulated by the foreign policy community: rollback (regime change), and *détente* (relaxing tensions diplomatically), and containment.

Soviet expert George F. Kennan had penned a 1947 article, "The Sources of Soviet Conduct," in which he outlined his predictions of Soviet world domination if the United States did not act, and advocated for a policy of containment. Kennan stated that the Soviet Union respected force, and would not expand its sphere of influence if met by strong resistance. Thus, the United States and its allies would have to present a strong defensive stance. The Truman Administration used Kennan's article as a guideline for its foreign policy, and containment was first implemented in reaction to communist threats in Greece and Turkey.

In March 1947, President Truman asked Congress for funding to assist Greece and Turkey in repelling a possible communist takeover. Now known as the **Truman Doctrine**, the president's speech explained that the United States had a duty to give financial assistance to free nations under communist threat. The Truman Doctrine passed its first test, as both Greece and Turkey successfully thwarted communism.

In rebuilding Europe, the Truman Administration sought to avoid the troubles that had besieged the region after World War I. Postwar conditions fostered radical political parties, including hard-line communists building momentum in France and Italy. To curb their rise, the Truman administration needed to supply funding to rebuild the economies of Western Europe. It also relied on the CIA. In 1948, for example, the CIA gave over one million dollars to center-right Italian parties; the Soviets likewise supported left-wing parties.

In June 1947, Truman's secretary of state, George Marshall, masterminded a plan to give Western Europe massive amounts of financial assistance to rebuild. Congress readily approved the **Marshall Plan**, which would supply $13 billion in aid over a four-year period. The Marshall Plan proved to be a stunning success. By the early 1950s, mass starvation no longer threatened Western Europe, and two decades of postwar economic growth had begun.

The Berlin Airlift and the Warsaw Pact

By June 1948, Stalin was angered by the economic and political reintegration of what would become West Germany. With Berlin mostly under Soviet control, deep inside the Soviet occupation zone, the Red Army blockaded all land routes into and out of the city. The United States was seemingly trapped. Either it withdrew from the city, losing face with Europe, or else it had to break through Soviet lines with a land invasion in order to resupply Berlin. Truman, however, decided on a third option: to airlift supplies to the city in what became known as the **Berlin Airlift**. The world held its breath while the possibility of another world war loomed. Stalin, not wanting the Soviets to be seen as the aggressors for shooting down humanitarian aircraft, finally reopened the city after 11 months.

President Truman broke a tradition dating from Washington's presidency; he joined an alliance with European countries by forming the **North Atlantic Treaty Organization (NATO)** in 1949. Stalin responded by forming the **Warsaw Pact** in 1955, which provided the same military protection, but at a cost: once a country was a member, it could never leave the alliance. These competing alliances sought to develop superior armed forces and weapons. The Soviets exploded their first atomic bomb in 1949. By 1952, the United States had developed and tested its first hydrogen bomb, which was at least 1,000 times stronger than the bombs dropped on Hiroshima and Nagasaki.

19

The National Security Act and NSC-68

Domestically, President Truman urged the passage of the **National Security Act** in 1947, which created the Department of Defense (formally the Department of War), the National Security Council, and the Central Intelligence Agency (CIA). A permanent peacetime draft was enacted in 1948. A classified report labeled NSC-68, written by the National Security Council, was released just after China "fell" and the Korean crisis was about to begin. The report detailed the Soviet Union's plans for worldwide domination and encouraged an immediate buildup of the nation's military. Whereas the Truman Doctrine had provided for financial support in preventing the spread of communism, NSC-68 now provided the rationale for the use of U.S. troops to achieve containment.

COLD WAR POLICY IN ASIA

To keep Japan from communism, the United States occupied Japan until 1951. The United States took part in writing the new constitution, setting Japan on the course for economic recovery. Japan would have a limited military and a democratic form of government, with the emperor as a ceremonial figurehead. Other regions in Asia would not take to democracy so readily for various reasons.

China Goes Communist

From 1839, the date of the First Opium War, onward into the 1940s, China had suffered what became known as the "century of humiliation." Western powers and Japan intervened in China to satisfy their imperial agendas. The overthrow of the Qing dynasty in 1911 by reformers had resulted in a shaky republic, but also in the fragmentation of the country's military into the Warlord Era. Eventually, the Nationalist (Kuomintang) faction, under the leadership of Chiang Kai-shek (Jiang Jieshi), reunified a large portion of China. The Nationalist regime was deeply corrupt. It was also engaged in a civil war with its largest remaining rival, the Communist Party of China, which was under the leadership of Mao Tse-Tung (Mao Zedong).

During World War II, the United States sent the Nationalists financial aid in order to keep the country from falling prey to the Japanese. Once that support was removed after the war, the Nationalists and the Communists reengaged in their civil war. Many Chinese citizens began to turn to the Communists as they became increasingly disgusted by the corruption, inflation, and inequality under the Nationalists. President Truman sent George Marshall to mediate between the two parties but to no avail. More money was sent to the Nationalists, but much of it was misspent. China finally fell to the Communists in 1949; Chiang and the Nationalists fled to the nearby island of Formosa, now called Taiwan. Americans were taken aback by this spread of communism and blamed Truman for his lack of strength. Another blow to containment came in 1950, when Joseph Stalin and Mao Tse-Tung signed an alliance pact.

The Korean War

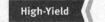

Prior to its forcible annexation by Japan in 1910, Korea had been an independent nation. When Soviet and American forces jointly occupied the peninsula in 1945, splitting the country in two at the 38th parallel, Koreans protested what they saw as another foreign occupation. Efforts at unifying the Soviet northern zone and the American southern zone failed, and each soon established its own government.

Stalin took the lack of American intervention in the Chinese Civil War as a sign that the United States would not care about a smaller theater. He supplied the North Korean army with weapons, and they then invaded the South in June 1950. However, Stalin had miscalculated. President Truman reacted immediately by urging the United Nations Security Council to intervene on behalf of the South Koreans. The Soviet Union, a permanent member of the council, was boycotting the UN at this point over the Nationalists retaining China's seat on the Security Council, so Truman's resolution was not vetoed. The Security Council and U.S. Congress authorized a police action to liberate South Korea. Although Congress did not formally declare war, this conflict is commonly referred to as the **Korean War**.

Meanwhile, North Korean forces were easily driving south across the peninsula. General Douglas MacArthur replied with one of the most daring operations of the twentieth century. He landed an amphibious assault at Inchon, near the 38th parallel, far behind what was now the North Korean lines, and halted the Communist advance. MacArthur was now able to push the invaders all the way back to their border. However, MacArthur exceeded his mandate to liberate South Korea, and he pushed the enemy back almost to the Chinese border. This unsettled the Chinese, who had spent the last century suffering various interventions by foreign powers, and they reacted aggressively. Chinese forces crossed the border, pushing the UN troops back.

At this point, MacArthur was convinced that if he had more resources, such as atomic bombs, he could win the war and possibly liberate China as well. Truman had already called for a limited war and sternly told MacArthur that he was not to make any critical statements of American policy. MacArthur then leaked a letter calling Truman weak, and he went on to unilaterally demand an unconditional surrender of the North Koreans. Truman immediately removed General MacArthur from command in April 1951. MacArthur returned to a hero's welcome, as most Americans could not understand the objectives of containment. Nonetheless, Truman's action signified the supremacy of civilian rule; democratically elected politicians, not generals, controlled U.S. policy.

In the end, the Korean conflict ended in a stalemate, with the original division at the 38th parallel remaining: Communists in the North and Nationalists in the South. Now that the United States had lost two Asian nations to communism, Republicans were beginning to claim that the Democrats lacked what it took to rid the world of communism.

THE SECOND RED SCARE

The tools used to curb alleged communist sympathizers during the **Second Red Scare** were forged well before the Cold War began. The Smith Act of 1940 authorized the arrest of people advocating the U.S. government's overthrow even if they had no intention of ever doing so. The House Un-American Activities Committee (HUAC) was established in 1938 to investigate domestic subversives with either fascist or communist ties.

Paranoia about a potential communist takeover swept the nation in the 1950s, much as it had after World War I. Fueling this fear were actual cases of espionage. HUAC made headlines in 1948 when American communist Whittaker Chambers testified in the case of a State Department employee who had supposedly leaked secrets to the communists. Then-freshman congressman Richard M. Nixon linked Chambers to Alger Hiss, a member of the U.S. delegation to the Yalta Conference. Hiss denied the allegations made against him. Nonetheless, he was convicted and sent to prison for perjury; Hiss had falsely testified under oath that he had never been a member of a communist party.

The FBI successfully uncovered a spy network that led to the arrest of a husband and wife duo, Julius and Ethel Rosenberg. The couple was accused of delivering atomic bomb secrets to the Soviets. The 1951 trial was a press spectacle. Convicted of treason and espionage, the Rosenbergs were executed by electric chair. Soviet archives declassified after the end of the Cold War proved the couple had, in fact, been spies.

Republican senator Joseph McCarthy ceaselessly raised suspicions that communists besides Alger Hiss still worked in the State Department. Playing to the media, McCarthy cast a wide net as he accused many within the Truman administration of anti-American activities. While his accusations were mostly false, Republicans did little to stop him as he helped their chances in the upcoming presidential election. McCarthy soon painted himself into a corner, however. The 1954 Army–McCarthy hearings showed the senator and his staffers in a poor light, as they were caught introducing doctored photos and other fabricated materials into evidence. Public opinion swung against **McCarthyism**. Soon Congress voted to condemn him for conduct unbecoming of a senator.

AMERICAN FOREIGN POLICY AND ATTITUDES IN THE COLD WAR

The Eisenhower Administration

A World War II hero, General **Dwight D. "Ike" Eisenhower** took the reins of the presidency in 1952 with the anti-communist crusader Richard Nixon as his vice president. American foreign policy would now actively support nations that sought liberation from communism through his policy of **brinksmanship**: the United States would push the aggressor nation to the brink of nuclear war, forcing it to back down and make concessions in the face of American superiority. This new approach to foreign policy affected the composition of American armed forces. More emphasis was placed on nuclear and air power and less on conventional forces, in part because the latter's budget proved increasingly burdensome. This led to the policy of **massive retaliation**, whereby the United States would unleash its arsenal of nuclear weapons on any nation that attacked it.

The Eisenhower administration also increased the use of covert means to advance American interests. In 1953, the CIA staged a coup against the democratically elected government of Iran, as they were nationalizing Western oil interests in their country, and reinstalled the Shah. In 1954, the CIA helped overthrow Guatemala's left-leaning government, as it was seen as communist-leaning.

19

The Suez Crisis

When the Egyptian leader Gamal Abdel Nasser asked the United States for assistance in building the Aswan Dam, he was assured the deal would be easy. The United States refused, however, as Egypt had recognized the People's Republic of China as the legitimate government of China. This went against the U.S. policy of supporting the Nationalist government-in-exile in Taiwan. In response, Nasser seized the British-held Suez Canal, both to support the dam's construction and to get rid of the last vestiges of British imperialism in Egypt. The flow of oil from the Middle East to Europe was cut off.

Unbeknownst to Eisenhower, Britain, France, and Israel launched a surprise attack on Egypt and regained control of the Suez Canal. The United States and Soviet Union, in a rare moment of agreement, jointly called upon the UN Security Council to denounce the invasion. They called for the immediate removal of the multinational invaders. The UN complied; Britain and France fell from their role as world leaders, replaced in world opinion by the two superpowers.

The Soviet Union under Khrushchev

Following Stalin's 1953 death, the reformist Nikita Khrushchev came to power. He opened Soviet society to a limited extent. Cultural and entertainment events, along with sports, became widespread. Soviet artists were allowed to travel abroad, and some foreign media was officially allowed into the country. While the Gulag system was not fully wound down until 1960, inmates and family members were now allowed to communicate.

Abroad, the Khrushchev Thaw led to development of reformist wings in the communist governments of Soviet-occupied Eastern Europe. One country, Hungary, saw unrest over political repression explode in a 1956 popular uprising. The Soviet leadership initially allowed events to play out; Khrushchev reformers and Stalinist conservatives debated removing troops and weighed the possibility of a neutral Hungary. When Hungary's new government talked of allowing a multiparty democracy and possible return of capitalism, however, Khrushchev ordered a crackdown. The USSR brutally crushed the Hungarian resistance, killing many. There was no American response. Eisenhower feared that sending in U.S. troops would spark world war, and the concurrent Suez Crisis complicated matters with Western powers invading their own former ally.

In May 1960, the Soviet Union shot down a U.S. U-2 spy plane that had violated its airspace. Khrushchev baited the United States by not revealing the pilot had survived until the Eisenhower administration had publicly claimed the plane had been a simple weather research aircraft. When Khrushchev revealed the pilot was alive and produced evidence that the plane had indeed been a spy plane, Eisenhower suffered great public embarrassment. After the **U-2 Incident**, the tentative thaw ended. The early 1960s would see growing tensions between the two superpowers.

The Cuban Revolution

Communism found a new home just 90 miles off the U.S. coast. In 1959, Cuban revolutionaries led by Fidel Castro overthrew the brutal dictator Batista. A short honeymoon between Castro and the

Eisenhower administration ended when Cuba nationalized all U.S. property on the island. Eisenhower retaliated by severing diplomatic relations. The Cuban leader looked to the Soviets for help, then he set about building a communist state. In late November 1960, Eisenhower approved a covert plan to invade Cuba and overthrow Fidel Castro. However, another president would be in office when that fateful plan was enacted.

The Kennedy Administration

Upon assuming the presidency, Kennedy did not believe that the Eisenhower administration's military would be effective in a world where colonial governments continued to fall in Asia and Africa. JFK's flexible-response military looked to use counterinsurgency tactics and elite special forces units to root out rebels, communists or alleged communists, in nations such as Congo and Vietnam.

The newly inaugurated **John F. Kennedy** approved the invasion of Cuba he had inherited from Eisenhower. It would take place in mid April 1961, with the initial landing at the **Bay of Pigs** (Bahia de Puerco). The invasion proved to be a military and public relations disaster. The United States vastly overestimated the support CIA-trained forces would receive from local Cubans. Kennedy refused to provide the invasion with sufficient air and naval support, not wanting to expose America's overt involvement in the invasion. In the aftermath, Castro's internal position was greatly strengthened, and the defeat of CIA-backed forces bolstered communists and other anti-American groups across Latin America.

Shortly after the Bay of Pigs, Kennedy met with Khrushchev at a summit in Vienna. The two debated the issue of Berlin's final status, and Kennedy refused to remove U.S. troops from the city. The Soviets responded by building a wall around West Berlin to stem the mass emigration of East Germans. President Kennedy did not interfere with the **Berlin Wall**'s construction, but he did travel to West Berlin in 1963 to proclaim U.S. support for Berlin's citizens.

The Cuban Missile Crisis

`High-Yield`

In October 1962, U.S. spy planes discovered that nuclear missile sites were being built on the island of Cuba. While these medium-range and long-range missiles decreased the existing warning time of a nuclear attack on the United States, an acute fear for the American people, these weapons mainly threatened the political balance of power. From the Monroe Doctrine onward, the United States had long seen the Western Hemisphere as its sphere of influence. The appearance of being successfully challenged would have had consequences for U.S. interests worldwide. Indeed, while Khrushchev intended to use the missiles to safeguard communist Cuba from another U.S. invasion, they were also a tool to force concessions from the United States.

Kennedy enlisted a group of advisers, the Executive Committee of the National Security Council (EXCOMM). Headed by his brother, Attorney General Robert F. Kennedy, EXCOMM decided that a naval blockade would be the least dangerous option. After several days of Soviet ships being turned back in the Atlantic Ocean and tense backroom negotiations, Khrushchev agreed to remove the missiles from Cuba, as long as the United States promised never to invade Cuba again and

19

to remove its own nuclear missiles from Turkey. As close as the two nations had been to nuclear war, the **Cuban Missile Crisis** was effective in opening up channels of communication between Washington and Moscow. A direct "red phone," or hotline, was installed so that the world leaders could have immediate contact in the case of emergency.

America's leader would exit the Cuban Missile Crisis with renewed popularity. His counterpart was not so lucky. After several months of plotting, party officials forced Khrushchev to retire in October 1964. Leonid Brezhnev replaced him. A man who favored consensus and rule by committee rather the gambling instincts of his predecessor, Brezhnev reversed the cultural liberalization that had taken place under Khrushchev. Crucially, he attempted no further reforms of the Soviet economy. His 18 years in power saw the Soviet Union suffer economic stagnation and national decline.

U.S. Attitudes

After World War II, Americans traded fear of Hitler and Tojo for fear of nuclear war. U.S. citizens were bombarded with images of nations falling to communist rule and stories of communist spies. Once novelty items, spy gear became popular as Americans hoped to be able to outsmart neighbors who might be Russian double agents.

Yet above all, there loomed fear of the bomb. In August 1949, the Soviet Union exploded its first atomic bomb, roughly five years ahead of Western expectations. President Truman then authorized the development of a more powerful weapon, the thermonuclear bomb. The arms race would only accelerate from there. Soon after two devastating world wars, humankind now possessed the ability to destroy itself.

Bomb shelters became a big business, with Americans spending upward of $5,000 to protect their families (approximately $43,000 today). These underground shelters had provisions for a family of four to survive after a nuclear attack. Children in schools practiced duck-and-cover drills in which they would fall out of their seats, hide under desks, and remain until the all-clear signal sounded. Americans purchased canned goods, bottled water, and Geiger counters. The National Highway Act of 1956, which created the nation's interstate system, looked as if it was intended solely to improve the country's infrastructure, but the 42,000 miles of road were also meant to provide for the quick evacuation of large urban centers and the transport of nuclear missiles.

After the launch of the Russian space satellite *Sputnik* in 1957, Americans were convinced that they had better get moving if they were to keep up with Soviet technology. This began a series of actions referred to as the **Space Race**. Congress responded by allocating millions of dollars to schools and universities across the nation to prepare students in mathematics, science, and foreign languages. Eisenhower also urged the creation of the National Aeronautics and Space Administration (NASA).

The Cold War had a profound effect on the entertainment industry as well. Comic book characters such as Captain America and movies like *The Invasion of the Body Snatchers* fed on the thirst for "commie hunting." Eisenhower himself reacted negatively to Cold War developments in his farewell address. He warned the American people of the **military-industrial complex**, whereby defense contractors and the military would exert too much influence on national policy.

THE VIETNAM WAR

In 1954, the French lost control of its Indochina colony with the final victory of Viet Minh forces at the city of Dien Bien Phu. Although the United States provided the French material aid, such as transport aircraft, it did not offer direct military intervention. Thus, the French were forced to give up the colony entirely. As a result of the **Geneva Convention** (1954), the Indochina region was divided into three nations: Vietnam, Cambodia, and Laos. The convention also decided to divide Vietnam at the 17th parallel, with the communists led by Ho Chi Minh in the north and nationalists led by Ngo Dinh Diem in the south. It was further decided that elections to reunite Vietnam would occur in two years.

Expecting a communist victory, and acting with U.S. support, Diem never allowed those elections. Eisenhower, fearing what he called the **domino theory**, gave economic and military aid to Diem's regime in an effort to keep it from crumbling. This aid included over 900 military advisors by the end of Eisenhower's second term. Eisenhower likened the spread of communism to a chain of dominos. If one nation were to fall, then like a single domino it would topple its neighbor, which in turn would topple its neighbor, and so on.

President Kennedy shared Eisenhower's belief in domino theory. Therefore, as North-backed communist rebels became active in South Vietnam, Kennedy increased U.S. aid. As part of his flexible-response doctrine, Kennedy funneled more advisors into South Vietnam along with special forces that would engage in counterinsurgency. Troop levels increased from approximately 900 at the start of 1961 to over 16,000 by the end of 1963. Following his predecessor's assassination, President **Lyndon B. Johnson** (LBJ) further escalated U.S. involvement.

Diem, a member of Vietnam's Catholic minority, enacted anti-Buddhist discriminatory policies. Buddhists made up more than 75 percent of the country's population. This led to Buddhist monks setting themselves on fire in Saigon as a form of public protest. Just before JFK's death, Diem himself was assassinated in the first of several coups that led to a series of unstable South Vietnamese governments in the early to mid-1960s.

The Gulf of Tonkin Resolution and Escalation in Vietnam

Secretary of Defense Robert McNamara urged President Johnson to take more forceful action to prevent the fall of South Vietnam. In August 1964, Johnson claimed that a North Vietnamese gunboat had carried out an unprovoked attack on two U.S. destroyers in the Gulf of Tonkin off the coast of North Vietnam. The president immediately used the incident to ask Congress for an increase in his authority to wage war in Vietnam without an actual war declaration. The Gulf of Tonkin Resolution is often used to mark the start of the **Vietnam War**. It was later discovered that the U.S. destroyers had actually been assisting the South Vietnamese in attacking their northern neighbor and, thus, the attacks were not unprovoked. Johnson used the Gulf of Tonkin Resolution to widen the war further after his landslide 1964 reelection over Barry Goldwater.

Between South Vietnam's unstable government and the growing communist-backed insurgency, Johnson chose to escalate U.S. involvement. He thought it was not a viable option to back out of Vietnam, as the country would then certainly fall into communist hands. But escalation meant diverting resources from his beloved domestic programs, as funding was needed to fuel the war machine. He hoped the war would be a quick one, and the first-strike, **Operation Rolling Thunder** in 1965, called for bombing raids over North Vietnam. A quick victory was not possible, however, as Ho Chi Minh's Viet Minh and the South Vietnamese **Viet Cong** continued to bounce back with more supplies and more men in the face of the American assault.

The United States relied on air and ground forces to fight in the heavily forested jungles of Vietnam. U.S. tactics focused on destroying the Ho Chi Minh Trail, which linked the South Vietnamese Viet Cong fighters with the North Vietnamese supply lines. The United States dropped more bombs on North Vietnam than were used in all of World War II. The ground war proved grueling. Heavy rain forest canopy and a moist tropical climate made fighting a conventional war impossible. General William Westmoreland developed a controversial *search and destroy* method of rooting South Vietnamese Viet Cong sympathizers out of villages by burning homes to the ground. Finding the enemy proved to be most difficult, however, as the insurgents dressed in the same peasant clothing as ordinary villagers. In an attempt to clear the countryside, the United States uprooted villagers and moved them to cities. Controversy at home escalated as the "hawks" (those who supported the war) and "doves" (those opposed to the war) battled it out in Congress and across America. As the election of 1968 loomed, events in Vietnam would change course.

The Tet Offensive

The Vietnamese Lunar New Year, known as Tet, marked the beginning of a massive Viet Cong offensive that moved the war away from rural areas to the cities of South Vietnam. In January 1968, Viet Cong forces surprised American troops by attacking military bases and regional capitals. Even as General Westmoreland declared that the war was nearly over, it was clear to those watching on television that the communists were not on the back foot. The psychological effect of the **Tet Offensive** changed the course of the war at home. American public opinion shifted against the war, and an increasing minority demanded that the United States immediately pull out of war-torn Vietnam. Having lost almost half of his support in presidential approval ratings, LBJ decided that he would not run for reelection in 1968.

Newly elected President Nixon wished to get the United States out of Vietnam with an honorable peace. Even though he promised during the 1968 presidential campaign that he had a secret plan to end the war, Nixon had no idea how he was going to accomplish this task. Soon after his inauguration, Nixon announced a plan to turn the war over to the South Vietnamese. This process of Vietnamization involved the U.S. military instructing the South Vietnamese how to fight the war on their own. The number of U.S. troops in the country slowly decreased as South Vietnamese troops were phased in. From 1969 to 1972, the number of U.S. troops in Vietnam decreased from over 500,000 to just under 30,000.

Protests, Counterprotests, and Secrets

In 1969, it was revealed that in the year prior, U.S. troops massacred Vietnamese women and children in the village of My Lai. William Calley, the lieutenant in charge of this slaughter, was eventually court-martialed, convicted, and sentenced to life in prison. However, U.S. public opinion overwhelmingly backed the soldiers. Telephone polls showed mass support for Calley, and politicians from George Wallace to Jimmy Carter demanded leniency. Calley would ultimately serve only three-and-a-half years of house arrest. The Vietnam War increasingly polarized American society, and antiwar activists felt estranged from the mainstream. *Ramparts*, a literary magazine whose staffers would go on to found outlets like *Rolling Stone* and *Mother Jones*, featured a boy with a North Vietnamese flag on one 1969 cover with the quote: "Alienation is when your country is at war and you want the other side to win."

Nevertheless, even if some Americans viewed antiwar protests as unpatriotic, many were not pleased with the war's progress. Nixon seemed to be talking out of both sides of his mouth; he wished to reduce the number of troops in Vietnam, but then he escalated the war by secretly bombing Cambodia in 1970 to shut down the Ho Chi Minh Trail. Nationwide protests broke out at news of the secret bombing missions. As a result of two of these protests, four students at Kent State University in Ohio and two students at Jackson State in Mississippi were shot and killed by National Guard troops. A protest in New York City over the Kent State shootings led to a backlash by locals. In what became known as the Hard Hat Riot, about 200 construction workers clashed with approximately 1,000 student protesters.

Then secret documents regarding the Vietnam War under the Johnson administration were leaked to the *New York Times* by a former Defense Department analyst, Daniel Ellsberg. The documents, dubbed the **Pentagon Papers**, revealed that Congress had been lied to about the war in Vietnam for many years. The U.S. goal in the war was not, as publicly stated, the independence of South Vietnam but the long-term containment of China by encircling it with U.S. allies. Among other revelations, the CIA had covertly backed the coup against Diem.

The Vietnam War Ends

Against that backdrop, Nixon had National Security Advisor and later Secretary of State Henry Kissinger meet secretly with the North Vietnamese to negotiate a settlement. Nixon foresaw that the South Vietnamese would not be able to hold the communists off for very long on their own, and he wanted to get out quickly. After the talks stalled, Nixon ordered some of the heaviest bombings yet to get North Vietnam back to the negotiating table. In 1973, the sides returned to the table in Paris to hammer out an agreement. As a result, the North Vietnamese regained control of areas in the South, while the United States agreed to pull out troops in exchange for prisoners of war (POWs).

The last of the U.S. troops pulled out of South Vietnam in March of 1973. Saigon, the South Vietnamese capital, fell to the communist forces in April of 1975. The United States evacuated its diplomatic corps as South Vietnamese sympathizers clung to the skids of U.S. helicopters, which were too few in number to carry them all.

19

The Vietnam War resulted in more than 58,000 Americans killed in action (KIA) with 300,000 wounded and almost 2,500 missing in action (MIA). The Vietnamese lost over two million people, both military and civilian. The United States spent approximately $140 billion on the war through the Eisenhower, Kennedy, Johnson, and Nixon administrations. After learning of the secret bombings of Cambodia, Congress passed the **War Powers Act**, which severely limited the president's ability to wage war without the consent of Congress. However, despite apparent violations over the years, Congress has never taken legal action over the issue, and executive authority to wage war has grown substantially since 2001.

> ✔ **AP Expert Note**
>
> **Be able to connect specific events to larger historical patterns**
>
> The AP exam tests your ability to think like a historian, and one of these skills is being able to detect patterns throughout history. For example, it is more fruitful to study the Vietnam War when you view it not as an isolated war, but through the lens of colonialism and Cold War power struggles. As the colonial empires began to collapse after World War II, the United States sought to keep the resulting newly independent nations aligned with itself rather than with the Soviet Union. American involvement in one such nation, Vietnam, developed over many years.

THE "AFFLUENT SOCIETY"

As President Eisenhower looked to balance the federal budget and maintain the flourishing postwar prosperity, the country as a whole experienced economic growth with little inflation and stable employment rates. The average white American family saw its income more than triple during the decade and enjoyed the world's highest standard of living. Modern conveniences became easier to purchase. "Keeping up with the Joneses," or keeping pace with the prosperity of one's neighbors, became the American mantra. As a result, America experienced a second major consumer revolution as cars, televisions, and household appliances were purchased in large quantities. The mass-consumption culture of the 1920s would be eclipsed by the spending of the 1950s.

Because consumer goods were in short supply during the war, Americans had significant savings to spend. The National Highway Act and the GI Bill fueled the growth of suburbs and the construction industry, as young families moved out of cities and into suburbs. The American Dream was now reality for an increasing number of Americans, but not all. Despite increasing civil rights gains made in the South, African Americans throughout the nation did not share equally in the nation's postwar economic expansion and abundance.

Americans experienced an increase in life expectancy thanks to new medical discoveries. The development of antibiotics in the 1940s improved the chances of surviving bacterial infections. Penicillin, an antibiotic, became widely available to doctors in the United States. It soon became very rare to die from a simple bacterial infection.

Polio was a constant threat to people all over the world. The debilitating disease could cripple children and confine them to a life of pain. Adults, like FDR, were also affected. In 1955, Dr. Jonas Salk

19

discovered how to immunize humans against polio. Using a live strain of the virus, Salk developed a vaccine that would almost eradicate the disease within the United States by the 1960s.

The electronics industry experienced the most growth in this era. As 95 percent of American homes were electrified, the industry worked to keep up with the demand for new and innovative products. Record players, refrigerators, and the new transistor radio revolutionized American life. The first practical electronic computers opened doors for engineers and designers. What once took weeks to calculate, the computer could churn out in a matter of hours. Air travel was no longer afford-able only for the ultra-wealthy, as commercial airlines began to fly Americans across the nation and around the world.

Conformity and Nonconformists

The stereotypical picture of the 1950s usually consists of teenagers sipping ice cream malts and dancing at the sock hop and businessmen in suits coming home to a pipe, newspaper, and doting wife. Television greatly contributed to this image. Sitcoms and advertisements painted portraits of the perfect family, wife, and household. Corporate America affected society as middle-class white-collar workers donned similar clothes and left each day to make enough money to live the American dream. Just as Americans looked to keep up with the mass consumption of goods that surrounded them, many also strove to blend in to this middle-class conformist mold.

Not all Americans bought into the suburban ideal. Women rebelled as conformity to traditional roles created a climate that stifled free thought and individuality. In her book *The Feminine Mystique* (1963), Betty Friedan encouraged women to leave homemaking behind and pursue fulfillment outside of the home. She questioned the notion that women were meant to remain at home to care for family and spoke of opportunities for women to become successful in the business world.

Women of the 1950s were expected to take care of the baby boomer generation as outlined in the baby care book by nationally renowned pediatrician, Benjamin Spock. Homemaking was venerated as a noble profession, and women working outside the home were looked down upon by their more traditional counterparts. Not all women were content with their situation. Alcoholism and depression became burgeoning problems for American women, and the latter was often considered a weakness and left untreated. Sylvia Plath depicted the intense societal pressures facing young women in her seminal 1963 novel *The Bell Jar*.

Many in the academic field questioned the era's conformity by writing essays, books, and research papers. While most Hollywood films celebrated the consumerist/conformist lifestyle of the 1950s, some filmmakers challenged it with movies such as *The Man in the Gray Flannel Suit*, based on the novel by Sloan Wilson. Artists such as Jackson Pollock shocked the world with paintings that did not follow form or function. Novelists of the era often mocked or satirized the American dream, challenging readers to think for themselves. J. D. Salinger's *The Catcher in the Rye* told the adventures of the antihero and nonconformist Holden Caulfield.

The **beatniks**, led by alternative writers such as author Jack Kerouac and poet Allen Ginsberg, encouraged individuality in an age of conformity. Often rebelling against the social standards of

19

the day, beatniks studied art, poetry, and philosophy and openly criticized the society in which they lived. Poetry readings often included free verse, and participants were invited to the open microphone and encouraged to speak their minds. The beatniks provided the mold from which the countercultural movements of the 1960s would be forged.

Countercultural protests

By the 1960s, America's baby boomers were now teenagers hoping to break away from conformity that their parents favored. Many teens grew their hair longer, wore risqué clothing like miniskirts, and listened to rock 'n' roll. Only a small percentage of the youth population was truly involved in the counterculture and antiwar protests. Nonetheless, these students made an impression with their willingness to protest publicly the wrongs they saw in American social, economic, and foreign policy.

College students met in Port Huron, Michigan, in 1962 to form the Students for a Democratic Society (SDS), led by Tom Hayden. The meeting yielded the Port Huron Statement, in which the students demanded the expansion of democracy. This signaled the birth of the New Left, a broad **counterculture movement** that emphasized civil rights, feminism, gay rights, university reforms, drug law reform, and an anti-war stance. This New Left was hostile to "Old Left," traditional Marxism centered on the labor movement and class struggle.

Soon afterward, the Free Speech Movement (FSM) would begin in 1964 on the campus of the University of California–Berkeley. Berkeley students staged sit-ins in administration buildings to protest university policies. They staged teach-ins to hear speeches and lectures regarding issues such as civil rights, communism, and the Vietnam War. Students across the nation took cues from SDS and the FSM to form local activist organizations.

Nothing typified the new youth culture like the 1969 music festival called Woodstock, which took place on a farm in New York State. Hippies gathered at the concert for a three-day party that involved peace, love, and music. Artists such as Jimi Hendrix and Janis Joplin wowed the crowd, and young people found a connection with the work of folk singers such as Arlo Guthrie and Joan Baez, whose protest songs galvanized the counterculture.

The counterculture led to a sexual revolution, in which Americans' views regarding sexual relationships and gender roles softened. With the advent of the birth control pill and the beginnings of the feminist movement in the mid-1960s, some young Americans believed that their parents' sexual mores were repressive. The feminist movement also gained momentum as a result of the counterculture's liberal nature. After the founding of the National Organization for Women (NOW) in 1966 by Betty Friedan, women began to become increasingly vocal in demanding a more equal role in American society. With the Civil Rights Act of 1964 already making discrimination on the basis of gender illegal, women looked to strengthen their rights by amending the Constitution. In 1972, Congress passed the **Equal Rights Amendment**, which would bar states and the federal government from discriminating on the basis of sex. Unfortunately for the women's movement, a backlash to the ERA meant it fell short of the required number of ratifying states and died in the 1980s.

> ✔ **AP Expert Note**
>
> **Be prepared to analyze the women's movement during this time period**
>
> During World War II, women experienced a dramatic increase in employment opportunities. After the war, there was great social and cultural pressure for women to return to the traditional role of homemaker and give up jobs to the returning wartime veterans. With the rise of **suburbanization**, many women became isolated from society. Out of this condition came the women's liberation movement in the late 1960s and 1970s. Though the Equal Rights Amendment did not get ratified, a lot of progress was made in terms of job and college opportunities and moving women into the mainstream of society.

FROM THE NEW FRONTIER TO THE GREAT SOCIETY

In the 1960 election, Democrats chose Senator John F. Kennedy of Massachusetts as their candidate. He chose Texas senator Lyndon B. Johnson as his running mate. The campaign was an uphill battle for Kennedy: a Roman Catholic, an Irish American, and potentially the youngest elected president in history. The choice of Lyndon Johnson as a running mate secured the support of Southerners. Kennedy's youth actually played in his favor, as Americans were drawn to his style and vitality. However, his religion would be a difficult hurdle. Many questioned whether or not a Catholic president could effectively rule the nation without the influence of the Pope. Governor "Al" Smith had lost the 1928 election partly due to this anti-Catholic bigotry. So Kennedy addressed those fears head-on. He assured an audience of Protestant ministers that his religious beliefs would not interfere with his role as chief executive.

Richard Nixon was the Republican candidate in 1960. For the first time, the U.S. presidential debates were televised nationally. These debates sealed the election for JFK. Kennedy's poise and vitality proved effective weapons against the seemingly nervous Nixon. Americans who watched the debates believed that Kennedy had won, while those who listened on the radio gave their nod to Nixon. It was clear that Kennedy would benefit from media coverage, and he used it to his advantage as the election neared. In a narrowly contested race, Kennedy edged Nixon by the slimmest margin ever in an American presidential election.

John F. Kennedy's inauguration marked the start of an era that would deeply affect American society. His domestic policy, named the **New Frontier**, promised equality, full employment, and financial aid to the needy. However, his legislative agenda ran into many roadblocks in Congress. Republicans and conservative Democrats, a coalition that had earlier stalled the New Deal in 1938 and thwarted Truman's attempts to implement universal health care in the late 1940s, repeatedly blocked the president's reforms. Kennedy did have some success in creating the Peace Corps, raising the minimum wage, and advancing urban renewal. Aside from these instances, the majority of Kennedy's domestic legislative initiatives were not passed until after his assassination.

On November 22, 1963, Lee Harvey Oswald shot the president from the window of a book depository in downtown Dallas as the president's motorcade drove by. Americans sat riveted to their

19

televisions as news anchors announced the president's death and the swearing-in of Lyndon B. Johnson (LBJ) aboard Air Force One. LBJ ordered the appointment of a special commission to investigate the assassination of JFK. The Warren Commission, headed by Chief Justice Warren, concluded that Oswald had acted alone in killing the president. Many conspiracy theories abounded after the commission delivered its report.

LBJ and the Great Society

President Johnson did not limit himself to the ideas of the New Frontier, which he personally thought too modest. LBJ espoused a program he called the **Great Society**, which aimed to expand civil rights and declared a War on Poverty. Johnson was heavily influenced by a book by Michael Harrington titled *The Other America*. In it, Harrington explained that 20 percent of Americans and more than 40 percent of all African Americans lived in poverty. Aside from FDR, no other president surpassed the amount of legislation overseen by LBJ.

The Great Society legislation included:

- Low-cost medical care for the elderly (Medicare) and for the poor (Medicaid)

- The Immigration Act of 1965, which repealed the discriminatory practices of the Quota Acts of the 1920s and allowed millions of previously excluded peoples to immigrate to the United States

- The Office of Economic Opportunity (OEO), which oversaw the creation of the Job Corps, a program that provided career training to inner-city and rural citizens

- The Department of Housing and Urban Development (HUD), which provided low-cost housing and federal funding to fight urban blight

- The Bilingual Education Act of 1968

- Various consumer and environmental protection laws

THE CIVIL RIGHTS MOVEMENT

There was a contradiction within America: the country had just fought a world war to liberate people to make their own decisions, but it did not offer that same freedom to many of its own citizens. African Americans had experienced welcoming societies in Europe when they fought in two world wars and wanted that same treatment from their home country.

Discrimination against African Americans was nothing new in American society, and neither were the voices of protest. However, the social climate was changing. In 1947, the Brooklyn Dodgers had broken the color line in professional baseball by drafting Jackie Robinson. President Truman took a step forward by desegregating the armed forces in 1948. The next quarter century would see further reform.

Brown v. Board of Education

As early as the mid-1930s, the NAACP made modest gains in challenging segregation in colleges and universities. However, widespread progress did not occur until the organization found an ideal test case involving a first grader in Topeka, Kansas. Linda Brown had to leave her home an hour and a half early to travel across town to attend an all–African American school. Yet her home was less than a mile from a white neighborhood school. The NAACP encouraged the Brown family to file suit against the Topeka school board on the grounds that Linda's right to equal protection had been violated by its segregation policy. The case made it to the Supreme Court in 1954.

The civil rights movement gained an important ally when President Eisenhower appointed former California governor Earl Warren as Chief Justice of the Supreme Court. Unbeknownst to Eisenhower, the Warren Court would be one of the most liberal in history. The NAACP's Thurgood Marshall—later, the first African American to serve on the Supreme Court—represented the Brown family. He argued that the Fourteenth Amendment guaranteed all citizens equal protection under the law, which translated into equal opportunity. The Warren Court agreed with Marshall, and the ruling in **Brown v. Board of Education** (1954) overturned the 1896 decision in *Plessy v. Ferguson*. The Court decision read that "separate facilities were inherently unequal" and had no place in public education. The Court ordered the desegregation of all public school facilities with "all deliberate speed."

The decision was not well received. Many states claimed they would simply close their public schools if they had to integrate. White families refused to send their children to integrated schools, and some state legislatures even passed laws to resist the ruling. In 1957, the situation came to a head in Little Rock, Arkansas. The state's governor ordered the Arkansas National Guard to bar the entrance of nine African American students into the all-white Central High School. The Little Rock Nine gained admission to the campus by a federal court ruling, but violent protests immediately broke out in the city. President Eisenhower eventually ordered federal troops into the city to restore order and to escort the students safely to their classes. Within a year of the forced integration, all Little Rock public schools had been shuttered; white families sent their children to segregated private schools or public schools outside of the city. It was not until another Warren Court ruling that the Little Rock School Board finally relented and integrated its public schools.

Protests and Community Organizing

Montgomery, Alabama, boasted a population that was almost 65 percent African American. However, segregation meant they drank from separate water fountains, rode at the back of buses, and ate in separate areas of restaurants. Rosa Parks, a recent volunteer for the local chapter of the NAACP, had seen many African Americans arrested and mistreated for refusing to comply with the Jim Crow laws that ruled the bus system. Parks decided enough was enough when, in December 1955, she refused to give up her seat to a white man on a city bus.

Her arrest prompted action. A young minister from Georgia, Dr. Martin Luther King Jr., along with other African American leaders, organized the **Montgomery Bus Boycott** to last until the buses were desegregated. This would be an enormous blow to the city's revenues, as African Americans made up about 95 percent of bus riders. The boycott lasted around 400 days, with the black community organizing car pools and walk buddies for the hundreds of people needing to get to school, work, and home. The Warren Court ruled that segregation on public buses was unconstitutional, and soon the boycott was over. The negotiations between Dr. King and city managers and downtown business owners helped to keep the crisis from exploding into violence. Dr. Martin Luther King Jr. and the Southern Christian Leadership Conference (SCLC) built on the lessons of the Montgomery boycott and began to challenge more Jim Crow laws in the Southern states.

Greensboro, North Carolina, became the stage for a new kind of protest in 1960. Local college and high school students entered a Woolworth's drug store and sat at the whites-only lunch counter, refusing to leave until they were served. Beginning with four students, the sit-in grew to a nationwide effort with a thousand students, who rotated on and off lunch counter seats until the store owners gave in six months later. Several other sit-ins occurred across the nation in motel lobbies, on beaches, at public pools, and in libraries. Students soon became the leaders of the movement, as the **Student Nonviolent Coordinating Committee** (SNCC).

President Eisenhower was a reluctant participant in the civil rights movement, preferring to maintain the support of Southerners and the status quo. He did sign two modest civil rights bills as president, however. The Civil Rights Bill of 1957 sought to ensure that African Americans would be able to exercise their right to vote by supporting a new division within the federal Justice Department to monitor civil rights abuses. Furthermore, a bipartisan report was to be written by representatives of both major political parties on the issue of race relations. By the time the bill was enacted as law, it had been watered down so as to not have much impact. The Civil Rights Act of 1960 gave the federal government authority to monitor local and state elections. After an intense fight in Congress, the final bill was just as weak as its predecessor at protecting African American voting rights.

Pushing Kennedy Forward

In his early days as president, Kennedy was reluctant to take a strong public stand on civil rights for African Americans. Because he needed the support of Southern Democrats to pass legislation, JFK did not want to alienate them. As a result, he did little as the civil rights movement continued to gain momentum. However, circumstances would force Kennedy to take a firmer civil rights stand.

From May to December 1961 the Congress of Racial Equality (CORE) and SNCC initiated a voter registration campaign in the South. The campaigners became known as the Freedom Riders. Mob violence greeted them at several stops, footage of which spread worldwide. Kennedy attempted to strike a balanced response: arranging for the safety of the activists while decrying them as unpatriotic for providing the United States with bad press during the Cold War. Yet the activists persisted. With federal marshals protecting the bus riders as they operated across the South, Kennedy found segregationist Democrats alienated from his administration. Later events compounded the issue. In 1962, for example, JFK sent federal marshals to protect University of Mississippi student James Meredith as he attended the once all-white campus.

In 1963, Dr. Martin Luther King Jr. led a peaceful protest in Birmingham, Alabama. The city had closed all of its public facilities to avoid integration. King and his followers staged a march on Good Friday and were arrested and jailed. While spending two weeks in his cell, Dr. King penned his famous Letter from Birmingham Jail, which explained to other black ministers why he and his followers could not wait for the whites to come around. The nation and world later watched in horror as Birmingham police commissioner Eugene "Bull" Connor had his officers use dogs, fire hoses, and cattle prods to disperse the nonviolent protesters, many of whom were children.

On August 28, 1963, on the centennial of the Emancipation Proclamation, Dr. King organized among the most famous marches in U.S. history: the March on Washington for Jobs and Freedom. Its aim was to advocate for civil rights legislation and pressure President Kennedy to live up to his campaign promises to African Americans in the 1960 election. King delivered his "I Have a Dream" speech, which touched citizens and lawmakers. However, a civil rights bill would not be passed until after JFK's assassination.

The Civil Rights Act and the Voting Rights Act

It fell to President Lyndon B. Johnson to orchestrate the passage of civil rights legislation. A veteran of the Senate, LBJ combined his mastery of parliamentary procedure and hardball negotiation with the widespread public support he received in the aftermath of Kennedy's assassination. The monumental **Civil Rights Act of 1964** outlawed unequal application of voter registration requirements, prohibited segregation of public schools and other public accommodations, and expanded the powers of the Civil Rights Commission established by the Civil Rights Act of 1957. The greatest legislative success of the civil rights movement signaled the end of *de jure* (by law) segregation in America.

Unfortunately, the Civil Rights Act of 1964 did not effectively address many problems associated with African American voting rights. To show lawmakers just how serious this problem was, Dr. King organized a march from Selma to Montgomery in 1965. The march came to a violent end outside of Selma, as state police beat and harassed marchers in front of TV news cameras. This incident helped spur the passage of the **Voting Rights Act of 1965**, which made literacy tests illegal and prohibited states from denying any U.S. citizen the right to vote on the basis of race.

Dissent within the Movement

Even though African Americans had made great strides in securing their civil rights, some within the African American community disagreed with nonconfrontational tactics or objected to the apparent co-opting of their cause by white activitists. Others were not convinced that integration was attainable, or even desirable.

The Nation of Islam followed the teachings of Elijah Muhammad, which were famously delivered by his disciple Malcolm X. Malcolm X openly criticized Dr. King and his followers for having sold themselves out to whites. While not advocating for violence, Malcolm X did encourage his followers to respond to violence perpetrated against them with self-defense. When Malcolm X took his requisite *Hajj* (pilgrimage) to Mecca, however, he returned a changed man in 1964. Abandoning the

Nation of Islam and its message of black separatism, he instead advocated for self-determination for the African American community and cooperation with some civil rights leaders. He maintained his stance on self-defense. Malcolm X summarized his beliefs with the famous "The Ballot or the Bullet" speech, in which he stated that whites would either allow African Americans freedom now or face an armed revolution later. In February 1965, members of the Nation of Islam assassinated Malcolm X.

Meanwhile, the once nonviolent SNCC changed course under the leadership of Stokely Carmichael. In 1966, it rejected integration and advocated Black Power. Carmichael left SNCC for the Oakland–based **Black Panthers**, who openly carried weapons and clashed with police on a regular basis. The Black Panthers organized the community of Oakland to serve as a self-sufficient network, providing free daycare and food for local low-income African Americans. By the mid-1970s, the Panthers eventually succumbed to internal ideological schisms and government harassment, as well as the arrests and deaths of their major leaders.

The Civil Rights Movement in 1968

The latter half of the 1960s was marked by a series of race riots in urban areas, such as in Los Angeles, Chicago, and Atlanta. The Johnson-appointed **Kerner Commission** concluded in 1968 that frustrations over extreme poverty and a lack of opportunity had sparked the riots. Unfortunately for the cause of further reform, the public had grown polarized. Social unrest stemming from the Vietnam War, the riots, and a rise in crime rates all contributed to this backlash.

In April 1968, King was assassinated as he stood on a Memphis motel balcony. In reaction to his murder, riots broke out in over a hundred cities across the country, as African Americans expressed their frustration and anger with society. While King's death spurred the passage of the Fair Housing Act, it also signaled the final breakup of the civil rights movement as it had existed. Many African Americans despaired that substantive change to improve their daily lives was impossible. Many whites fled to the suburbs, and "law and order" politics grew increasingly popular.

> ✔ **AP Expert Note**
>
> **Be able to list the goals of the civil rights movement**
>
> The civil rights movement encompassed multiple attempts to make gains for the African American community. Some of the movement's goals were:
>
> - Desegregation of schools, buses, restaurants, and other Jim Crow–era restrictions
> - Protection of voting rights
> - Protection against violence from the white community, including the police
> - Equal representation under the law

19

SOCIAL JUSTICE MOVEMENTS

In the post-World War II era, the African American community was not alone in seeking redress of long-standing wrongs and injustices. The Constitution promised freedom and equality to all people. These groups sought to make the United States government and its people live up to the Constitution that all held dear.

The Chicano Movement

The Treaty of Guadalupe Hidalgo in 1848 had transformed the national boundary between the United States and Mexico. For many Mexican Americans circa 1945, they had not crossed the border as immigrants at Ellis Island did. The border had crossed them. Mexican Americans faced much discrimination, but the 1950s through the 1970s would see a wave of activism and political reform, as well as a cultural flowering known as the Chicano Movement.

In 1947, the United States Court of Appeals for the Ninth Circuit ruled in *Mendez v. Westminster* (1954) that Mexican Americans in public schools could not be segregated as it violated the Equal Protection Clause. The Supreme Court issued a landmark decision in **Hernandez v. Texas** (1954) that ruled Mexican Americans, along with all other national groups within the United States, had equal protection under the Fourteenth amendment.

Perhaps the best known Latino American rights activist in this period was César Chávez. Born to a family in Yuma, Arizona, Chávez spent his early life as a manual laborer and later joined the navy. Later, he moved to California to work as an activist helping laborers register to vote. In 1962, he co-founded what became the **United Farm Workers** (UFW) union with Dolores Huerta. Chávez favored aggressive but nonviolent protests, and sought to protect the rights of farm workers and fight for higher wages. His famous slogan was "Sí, se puede" ("Yes, we can").

The **League of United Latin American Citizens** (LULAC), founded in 1929, was a consolidation of various existing civil rights organizations, and in many ways paralleled the NAACP for African Americans. For example, it litigated in courts for recognition of basic rights, such as by supporting the *Mendez v. Westminster* case. In 1967, college-aged activists formed the Mexican American Youth Organization (MAYO). In 1970, inspired by Malcolm X and activists such as the Black Panthers, members of MAYO formed Raza Unida Party as a Chicano nationalist organization, although it enjoyed limited success in the Southwest.

The Great Society programs had a tremendous influence on Latino Americans. The Economic Opportunity Act of 1964 and the Equal Employment Opportunity Commission provided tools for activists to fight against economic and workplace discrimination. The Bilingual Education Act of 1968 ended the practice of English-only schooling. The Immigration and Nationality Act of 1965 ended immigration quotas based on country of origin that had existed since the 1920s, paving the way for renewed immigration from throughout the Americas, Asia, and beyond. And, the 1970s were not without reform. In 1975, the Voting Rights Act of 1965 was expanded to protect Americans of all ancestries.

19

Beyond strictly political activism, the Chicano Movement saw a flowering of murals, music, theater, poetry, and other forms of self-expression. Chicano artists fused U.S. and Mexican influences to reflect their joint heritage, and also sought inspiration in pre-Columbian artwork.

American Indian Movement

The mid-century saw the federal government shift to a more proactive approach to assimilation, an approach collectively known as **Indian termination**. This approach was U.S. policy from the mid-1940s into the mid-1960s. Whereas the federal government had previously sought the gradual cultural erasure of American Indian nations, this policy sought to end U.S. recognition of tribal sovereignty and all federal, state, and local measures associated with that recognition. In essence, now that all American Indians were legally U.S. citizens, they would not receive any treatment different from other citizens.

Another aspect of the Indian termination policy was the Indian Relocation Act of 1956 (Public Law 959), which encouraged American Indians to leave their traditional reservations and assimilate into urban areas. This encouragement included paying for transportation expenses, funding for tools and vocational training, medical insurance, and even aid toward purchasing a home. Between 1956 and the 1980s, over 700,000 American Indians migrated to the cities, although not all strictly under this act. Many American Indians faced issues with segregated housing in these urban areas, as well as segregated schools and discrimination.

American Indian activists and their allies lobbied against these measures, and by the mid-1960s convinced President Johnson to shift U.S. policy, ending Indian termination in favor of Indian self-determination. Johnson also supported the Indian Civil Rights Act, which formed Titles II through VII of the Civil Rights Act of 1968. Richard Nixon would make Indian self-determination a bipartisan policy, declaring in 1970 that "We are proposing to break sharply with past approaches to Indian problems." Nevertheless, many issues for the American Indian community remained, ones rooted in centuries of discrimination.

It was against this backdrop that the **American Indian Movement** (AIM) took stage. Founded in 1968 in Minneapolis, AIM sought to address systemic issues facing American Indians: poverty, health-care, police brutality, unemployment, and the preservation of Indigenous cultures. Ironically, while the Indian Relocation Act of 1956 had sought to erase American Indian identities, the relocation of so many American Indians from different tribes into urban areas led to inter-tribal networking. Like-minded people who were once geographically isolated from one another could now work together, forming political activist organizations to lobby for a common cause.

Even though enrollment in the Indian Residential School system would peak in the 1970s, the passage of the Indian Self-Determination and Education Assistance Act of 1975 shifted the system's focus away from cultural assimilation. This reform was made possible thanks to the work of American Indian activists such as at AIM. Other reforms would follow in the 1970s, such as the Indian Child Welfare Act of 1978 (ICWA) and the American Indian Religious Freedom Act (AIRFA).

The Asian American Movement

The term Asian American was coined in the late 1960s by UCLA historian Yuji Ichioka, a second generation Japanese-American who had been interned during World War II. He wished to unite various Asian ethnic groups under a single banner. It also was aimed at displacing the then-common terms Asiatic and Oriental as ethnic descriptions.

The Asian American rights movement in this period was far less successful than many of its counterparts. This was due to multiple factors. Asian Americans at the time did not typically consider themselves as such, and the Pan-Asianism boosted by Yuji Ichioka was still aspirational. Groups such as Chinese-Americans, Filipino-Americans, and Japanese-Americans saw themselves as distinct from one another, sharing little in common.

Another factor was the failure of activists to address local community needs. Asian American activists in this period were typically college students whose focus was on the antiwar movement and other large-scale leftist causes: anti-imperialism, anti-colonialism, international solidarity of the working class, and Third World solidarity. For example, Richard Aoki, a prominent Asian American activist at Berkeley in the late 1960s and 1970s who also led a double-life as an FBI informant, was heavily involved with the Black Panther Party and various far-left groups. This disconnect from local communities meant that Asian American activists were unable to galvanize a mass movement or build much in the way of large-scale political organizations.

The greatest success of Asian American activists during this period was their work with other minority student activists to persuade administrators at San Francisco State University and at Berkeley to establish the nation's first College of Ethnic Studies. These programs would spread throughout the country, in part thanks to groups like the Association for Asian American Studies, which was founded in 1979.

The LGBT Movement

During the Second Red Scare of the 1950s, a **Lavender Scare** took place in parallel. Senator Joseph McCarthy among others alleged that homosexuals had infiltrated the government, in particular the State Department. Gays and lesbians were denigrated as "threats" to America, inherent communist sympathizers, and easy targets for blackmail by the Soviets. Hundreds of employees were fired for suspected homosexuality. In 1953, President Eisenhower signed Executive Order 10450, which banned homosexuals from the military, the federal government, and private contractors working for the government. Executive Order 10450 led to around 5,000 firings; it was partly rescinded in 1973 for civil service workers but not fully revoked until 1995 by President Clinton, who simultaneously instituted the "Don't Ask, Don't Tell" policy for the military.

Frank Kameny, an astronomer for the U.S. Army, was fired in 1957 for being gay. He appealed his firing and, while he failed to overturn the decision, his case was the first U.S. court case that presented sexual orientation as a civil rights matter. Until his death in 2011, Kameny would spend the rest of his life at the forefront of the gay rights movement as an activist and organizer. He would become the first openly gay candidate for Congress in 1971 and would play a major role in convincing the American Psychiatric Association (APA) to change its classification of homosexuality.

In the postwar era, the LGBT movement can broadly be divided into two periods: pre-Stonewall Riots (1945-1969) and post-Stonewall Riots (1969-Present). These periods reflect both a generational and political shift for LGBT activists. The **Stonewall Riots** of 1969 were a major milestone for LGBT activists. They began as a series of spontaneous demonstrations protesting police raids on the Stonewall Inn, a gay bar in the Greenwich Village neighborhood of Manhattan. The protests grew massively, and participants began to organize themselves into activist groups. Often younger and more ethnically and economically diverse than their pre-Stonewall predecessors, these new groups favored confrontational tactics. The first Gay Pride parades in 1970, on the one year anniversary of Stonewall, symbolized the desire of these new activists to live openly and not conceal their sexual orientation from public view.

This period in the early 1970s is sometimes termed the Gay Liberation movement. LGBT activists often found themselves in uneasy alliance with other left-wing groups, be they mainstream or radical, who were at times openly hostile to them on the basis of their sexual orientation. Despite this, LGBT activists created a new space for themselves in the American political landscape. One example would be the 1977 election of Harvey Milk to the San Francisco Board of Supervisors, the first time an openly gay person had been elected in California history. By the late 1970s, however, left-wing political activism throughout the United States had broadly died down as the right wing became ascendant.

THE ELECTION OF 1968

After the Tet Offensive, and facing a vigorous primary challenge from Senator Eugene McCarthy of Minnesota, President Johnson announced that he would not seek reelection. Robert F. Kennedy (RFK) now jumped into the race. The Democratic Party faced a bruising election with no clear leader. The cracks in the New Deal coalition had widened significantly.

Southern Democrats, alienated by their party's shift on civil rights, rallied to Alabama governor George Wallace, who ran under the American Independent Party (AIP) label. The AIP pursued a segregationist agenda, and Wallace hoped to play kingmaker by splitting the Electoral College and forcing the election into the House of Representatives.

Class, race, and Vietnam split the potential Democratic candidates. While Eugene McCarthy primarily attracted college students and upper-middle class whites, Robert F. Kennedy (RFK) attracted working-class whites, Catholics, and African Americans. Vice President Hubert H. Humphrey, a liberal advocate for civil rights long before it had become acceptable in the party's mainstream, was criticized as being too much of an establishment figure by antiwar activists. While the Kennedy name was popular with the general public, LBJ and RFK had a bitter, longtime personal feud. As a sitting president, Johnson had the loyalty of party elites, and he backed Humphrey.

Yet the chaos that seemed in store paled against reality. A long, bitter primary battle between McCarthy and RFK seemingly ended when Kennedy won the California Democratic primary in June 1968. After RFK's victory speech, however, a young Palestinian-born man named Sirhan Sirhan shot and killed the senator as he walked through the kitchen of the Ambassador Hotel in Los Angeles. Grief-stricken at his rival's murder, McCarthy went into seclusion. The Democrats eventually nominated Vice President Hubert Humphrey to the disdain of antiwar activists.

Mayor Richard J. Daley made sure Chicago was prepared for possible trouble when it hosted the Democratic National Convention. Antiwar protesters had mobilized to express their distaste for Humphrey, whom they believed would continue the Vietnam War. A massive number of demonstrators lined the streets of downtown Chicago, with an equal number of police present. Police harassed and beat protesters, resulting in a riot broadcast on national television. This fiasco caused the nation to question the Democratic Party's ability to govern.

The Republicans, meanwhile, gave Richard Nixon another shot at the presidency, in large part due to several years of tireless campaigning the former vice president had done for Republicans in 1964 and 1966. He selected Governor Spiro Agnew of Maryland as his running mate. Nixon campaigned on a platform of "law and order," playing on both race riots in urban areas and on an uptick in the crime rate. He also attacked the liberalism of the Warren Court.

Nixon won the election by a slim margin over Humphrey, while Democrats maintained their majority in Congress. Without a clear mandate from American voters, Nixon would struggle at the start of his presidency.

THE NIXON ADMINISTRATION

Richard M. Nixon had promised the United States change. Hampered by a Democratic Congress, President Nixon attempted to garner more support from across the nation. He appealed to the so-called silent majority: conservative Democrats who were most likely to be either Southern, working class, or elderly citizens, all of whom had become disenchanted by their party's liberalism. Nixon appealed to these voters by attempting to block forced busing of students to integrate public schools and becoming more vocal in his disdain for antiwar protesters. This struck a deep chord with the public. *TIME* magazine would dub "The Middle Americans" as their 1969 "Man of the Year."

Yet despite his battles with Congress, Nixon would often chart a middle path, tacitly accepting the Great Society's reforms in exchange for more maneuvering room in the realm of foreign policy. Although opposed to integration via busing, Nixon declared the *Brown* decision "right in both constitutional and human terms" and oversaw the desegregation of more schools than any president before or since. He also supported affirmative action in 1970 with the "Philadelphia Plan," which required for the first time that federally funded contractors reserve a certain number of jobs for minority workers. Nixon also appointed more women to the executive branch, as mid- and high-ranked staffers, than all his predecessors combined.

19

Economic troubles, however, would be an overriding domestic concern for Nixon. His presidency also saw the emergence of a new economic phenomenon called "stagflation," in which high inflation was coupled with high unemployment. Nixon first attempted to curb inflation by cutting government spending. This proved to be disastrous. Near the end of 1971, Nixon took the United States off the gold standard to bring its currency's value down relative to foreign currencies. This stimulated foreign investment and domestic spending, spurring an economic recovery.

In one area, however, Nixon made a notable change from postwar presidents: emphasizing drug abuse as a major issue. Congress passed the Comprehensive Drug Abuse Prevention and Control Act of 1970. Nixon created the **Drug Enforcement Administration** (DEA) in 1973.

While conservationism had been part of American politics since the late nineteenth century, environmentalism in the modern concept of the term is best traced to the 1962 publication of **Silent Spring**. Written by Rachel Carson, a marine biologist and conservationist, *Silent Spring* brought widespread public attention to the dangers of pesticides and disinformation campaigns waged by the chemical industry. Carson's work helped inspire the modern environmental movement, eventually leading to the creation of the Environmental Protection Agency (EPA) in 1970 under the Nixon administration.

International Issues

`High-Yield`

With military options limited by Vietnam, Nixon would increasingly rely on the CIA, such as with the 1973 Chilean coup that overthrew the country's longtime democracy in favor a U.S.-friendly authoritarian regime. Meanwhile, events in China and the Middle East reshaped the world.

Détente with China and Russia

President Nixon and Henry Kissinger together crafted **détente**, or the relaxing of tensions among the United States, the Soviet Union, and China. In February 1972, shocking the world, the hardline anticommunist Nixon became the first U.S. president to visit the People's Republic of China. He aimed to discuss foreign policy with Mao Tse-Tung. Kissinger and Nixon had also been mediating between the two communist superpowers behind the scenes, as the nations had split over differing opinions about how communism should work in practice. In a rare reversal, Nixon agreed to support communist China's bid to be admitted to the United Nations and officially recognized the Chinese Revolution. Moscow watched this all with fascination, as well as concern.

Nixon also visited Moscow in 1972 to encourage the USSR to sign a nuclear arms limitation treaty. In the **Strategic Arms Limitation Treaty** (SALT I), signed by the United States and the USSR in May 1972, each nation agreed to reduce the number of nuclear missiles in its arsenal in exchange for the United States supplying the Soviets with much-needed grain over the next three years. While not ending the arms race or Cold War, *détente* did much to relieve the tension among the three world superpowers.

The Yom Kippur War and Gas Shortages

In October 1973, on the Jewish holy day of Yom Kippur, war broke out between Israel and a coalition of Arab states led by Syria and Egypt. President Nixon reacted by sending military aid to Israel. The war ended quickly, as U.S. aid greatly bolstered Israeli forces. However, trouble was far from over. The **Organization of Petroleum Exporting Countries** (OPEC) initiated an embargo of oil exports to the United States as punishment for its involvement in the Yom Kippur War. For the first time, gas in the United States was not cheap and plentiful. Americans waited in mile-long lines to purchase the coveted fuel. The effect of the embargo devastated the economy; the nation fell into a deep recession as companies decreased investment, laid off workers, and reduced inventories. Inflation grew at an alarming rate, and there was little the government could do.

The Watergate Scandal

A break-in at the Democratic Party National Headquarters at the Watergate Hotel in Washington, D.C., in June of 1972 would be Richard Nixon's political demise. Through the investigations of *Washington Post* journalists Bob Woodward and Carl Bernstein, the burglars were revealed to be connected to the Nixon administration. Eventually, the journalist duo uncovered evidence that the Watergate break-in was just the tip of an iceberg of illegal activities linked to the Oval Office. As the **Watergate** scandal widened, the president insulated himself with an ever-shrinking circle of supporters. After the revelation of a voice-activated tape system in the Oval Office, Congress insisted that the tapes be released. President Nixon refused by claiming he was protected by executive privilege and fought with Congress for over a year. Just as things could not get worse, Vice President Spiro Agnew was convicted of tax evasion and was forced to resign. Nixon chose Representative Gerald R. Ford as his new vice president.

The Oval Office tapes, finally released owing to a Supreme Court ruling in *Nixon v. United States* in July 1974, contained the "smoking gun" that directly linked the president to the Watergate scandal. Facing certain impeachment and conviction by Congress on the charges of obstruction of justice, abuse of power, and contempt, President Nixon resigned from office on August 9, 1974. **Gerald R. Ford** took the oath of office.

Ford caused a great controversy early in his administration, and he certainly hurt his prospects for securing a second term, when he formally pardoned Nixon of all charges. Ford's biggest challenge was to try to address stagflation. Nothing he attempted worked for very long. President Ford witnessed the final failure of U.S. foreign policy in Southeast Asia, as Saigon fell to the communists in 1975.

19

THE CARTER ADMINISTRATION

The Democrats seized on Ford's ineffectiveness and chose a "Washington outsider" to run in 1976. Former Georgia governor and peanut farmer **Jimmy Carter** was a conservative Democrat from the South whose folksy earnestness appealed to Americans. Carter squeaked out a narrow victory by garnering 51 percent of the popular vote, managing to take 97 percent of the ballots cast by African Americans. The Democrats also were able to secure majorities in both houses of Congress. Carter was thought to be one of the most intelligent presidents ever to serve, but as an outsider, was plagued from the start by his inability to play politics.

Carter upheld his promise to grant amnesty to the 10,000 young men who had fled the country during the Vietnam War draft. He created the Department of Education to address the problems of the nation's public schools and the Department of Energy to try to deal with the nation's energy crisis. The nation's energy woes were coupled with stagflation, and the nation did not emerge from the depths of the economic crisis until the mid-1980s.

Foreign Policy

Domestically, Carter had difficulties eclipsing the troubles he faced in the foreign policy realm, troubles that would eventually torpedo his hopes of winning a second term. Although he did achieve some victories.

Carter's greatest success occurred when he crafted a peace agreement between Egypt and Israel in 1978. He invited Egyptian president Anwar Sadat and Israeli prime minister Menachem Begin to meet at the presidential retreat at Camp David in Maryland. Sadat and Begin discussed peace options while Carter acted as mediator. A peace agreement was signed in September 1978. The **Camp David Accords** served as the first step toward peace in the Middle East since the turmoil that had followed the founding of the state of Israel in 1948. Carter enjoyed another foreign policy success, although controversial at the time, when he negotiated a treaty with Panama in 1977 that relinquished American control over the Panama Canal.

Carter also had to deal with increasing tensions with the Soviet Union. SALT I was set to expire in 1977, so Carter and the Soviets were set to sign a renewal treaty. **SALT II** was negotiated and sat ready for ratification when the USSR invaded the nation of Afghanistan in December 1979. Americans were now certain that the Soviets intended to take control of the precious oil transportation region of the Persian Gulf. The United States immediately ceased supplying the USSR with grain shipments and withdrew SALT II from the table. In protest, President Carter also boycotted the 1980 Olympic Games, which were to be held in Moscow.

The 1979 Iranian Revolution

Unfortunately, events in Iran would come to define the Carter administration. In 1979, a popular revolution led by Islamic fundamentalists overthrew the corrupt Shah, a longtime American ally in the Middle East. Ayatollah Khomeini took power in the resulting theocracy and cut off the flow of petroleum to OPEC, causing yet another gasoline shortage.

As if this were not enough, later that year, Iranian college and high school students stormed the American embassy in the Iranian capital, Tehran, and took the staff there hostage. After a few days, the women and African Americans were released, but 52 white men were held captive for

444 days. President Carter froze Iranian assets in the United States and ordered a rescue mission. However, Operation Eagle Claw proved to be an embarrassing debacle, as eight U.S. servicemen were killed. The Iran hostage crisis came to define the Carter administration, and proved a major political problem for President Carter in the 1980 election.

Energy in the Carter Administration

The 1973 oil crisis led to a consolidation of U.S. energy programs, as a more organized approach was felt needed. Thus, President Carter created the Department of Energy (DOE). Carter encouraged the use of solar power in place of nonrenewable energy sources, and even had solar panels installed on the roof of the White House. He also started the Drive 55 plan to reduce the amount of gasoline consumed by Americans.

Nuclear energy remained a popular alternative power source until 1979, when the plant at **Three Mile Island** in Pennsylvania sent a cloud of radioactive gas into the air. It was soon discovered that in a rush to get the plant online, many shortcuts had been taken that ultimately threatened the safety of Americans living near the plant. After this incident, nuclear power was no longer a palatable option for most Americans. Over fifty planned U.S. nuclear plants would be cancelled in the following decade. No new nuclear plant would be approved for construction in the United States until 2012.

1980 Primary Challenge

A sitting president is rarely challenged for their party's nomination. Yet in 1980, Senator Edward "Ted" Kennedy attempted just that. Carter was seen as a vulnerable figure due to the Iran hostage crisis, unemployment, and stagflation. Carter's infamous "malaise speech" about the ongoing American crisis of confidence was initially well-received by the public, but soon became an albatross around his neck. Carter had spoken of the need to rebuild trust, yet fired his cabinet soon afterward and offered little in the way of concrete solutions. Having drawn attention to public's collective trauma over Vietnam, Watergate, and Iran, he failed to provide visible leadership. In effect, Carter made himself seen like part of the problem rather than its solution.

Yet Senator Kennedy failed to unseat President Carter, who was better able to appeal to southern, midwestern, and Rust Belt voters. Kennedy was associated with northeastern elites, and the 1969 Chappaquiddick incident had tarnished his reputation. The New Deal liberalism that Kennedy espoused was also increasingly out of step with the times. Carter in many ways foreshadowed the rightward shift of the Democratic Party under the Clinton administration; he favored some economic deregulation and other free-market reforms. Yet the primary challenge further weakened Carter, whose approval ratings were akin to those of Nixon during the height of Watergate.

NEW CONSERVATISM

The New Deal's popularity and the advent of the Cold War meant that liberalism became the default mode of thinking in both major parties by the mid-1950s. Political disagreement between the parties existed mainly in terms of priorities and policy approaches, not ideology. Yet just as the 1960s saw the rise of the New Left in the Democratic Party, a similar process played out with the Republicans. This New Right dubbed its philosophy **conservatism**.

In 1953, political theorist Russell Kirk published *The Conservative Mind*, a book which synthesized a canon of politicians from across U.S. history that Kirk viewed as espousing conservative ideas. It inspired William F. Buckley Jr. to found a weekly magazine, *National Review*, which became symbolic of the conservative movement for many decades. This "New Right" rejected the isolationism of the "Old Right," utilizing strident anti-communism to bind together small-government libertarians, business interests, and socially conservative traditionalists.

Conservatism found an early advocate in Senator Barry Goldwater, whose landslide defeat in the 1964 presidential election seemed to outside observers to herald the end of their budding movement. Yet the Goldwater campaign had converted many, and it helped like-minded conservatives to organize and network. This included Ronald Reagan, whose 1964 "A Time for Choosing" speech in support of Goldwater launched his political career.

LBJ's Great Society programs, aimed at ending poverty, became seen as a waste of taxpayer dollars, especially as the funds were perceived to be flowing overwhelmingly into African American communities. The backlash over the Vietnam War also fueled the rise of the conservative movement. While college students stood at the forefront of the antiwar movement, even the youth demographic was not united in opposing the war. To older Americans who had fought in World War II or the Korean War, antiwar protesters were seen as un-American. In his 1966 gubernatorial campaign, Reagan promised to crack down on welfare abuse and "to clean up the mess at Berkeley." Reagan beat his opponent handily.

The 1970s saw two new additions to the growing conservative coalition: union workers and Christian evangelicals. White working-class union workers were culturally alienated from younger Democrats as the New Deal Coalition broke down; they would in the 1980s be termed "Reagan Democrats." Christian evangelicals reacted to several Supreme Court decisions in the 1960s and 1970s, such as banning Bible-reading in public schools and the *Roe v. Wade* decision, by becoming politically organized and active for the first time. The evangelical movement had grown in number in recent years thanks to preachers such as Billy Graham, whose ministry had attracted worldwide interest and who served as a spiritual adviser for several U.S. presidents as well as for Queen Elizabeth II.

Phyllis Schlafly, whose 1964 book in support of Goldwater earned her national attention, led conservative women against the Equal Rights Amendment with the Stop Taking Our Privileges (STOP) ERA campaign. Schlafly and her followers argued that the ERA would force women into the military draft and stop certain gender-specific legal privileges, such as mothers typically gaining primary custody of children during a divorce. The **STOP ERA** campaign was successful, despite the ERA having had the backing of Presidents Nixon and Ford.

By the mid-1970s, Nixon and Ford seemed to embody a style of politics that fostered corruption at home and, through *détente*, immorality abroad. Conservatism continued to gain popularity across the nation. Taxpayers sought to control where their money was spent. Christian fundamentalists became more influential, and Americans broadly looked to traditional family values for strength after the social turmoil of the last decade. Ronald Reagan fought Gerald Ford for the 1976 Republican Party nomination all the way to the convention, only narrowly losing. By 1980, Reagan would not only win the nomination but the general election.

> ✔ **AP Expert Note**
>
> **Be able to explain the goals of the New Right conservatives from the 1960s to the 1980s**
>
> From the 1960s to the 1980s, the New Right conservatives wanted to rollback, not just contain, communism. They believed that building a more powerful military and taking a harder stance against communists abroad would put an end to the Cold War. Socially, many on the New Right desired to uphold more traditional social values and opposed the desegregation efforts of the civil rights movement. Economically, the New Right was decidedly pro-business, believing that the government should not interfere in the marketplace.

 NEXT STEP: PRACTICE

Go to Rapid Review and Practice Chapter 10 or to your online quizzes on kaptest.com for exam-like practice on this topic.

Haven't registered your book yet? Go to kaptest.com/moreonline to begin.

CHAPTER 20

Period 9: 1980–Present

THE REAGAN ADMINISTRATION

Americans overwhelmingly elected **Ronald Reagan**, former movie star and two-term California governor, as the 40th president in 1980. Just as Warren G. Harding had campaigned on returning normality to the United States after the traumas of the 1910s, Reagan promised to do the same for the 1960s and 1970s. His election ushered in the **Reagan Revolution**, a new era of conservative policy-making.

"Reaganism" offered sharp change from the New Deal coalition that had set the tone of government strategy since the 1930s. Reagan promised lower taxes, smaller government, and a stronger military. Helped by the unexpected release of the Iranian hostages during his inauguration, Reagan set forth to enact his agenda.

The new president first aimed to strengthen the economy. Rejecting widely accepted Keynesian demand-side theory, he adopted a supply-side model. Reagan maintained that offering tax cuts and investment incentives to the wealthy would lead to job creation, much like the view championed by Andrew Carnegie in the 1920s. Wealth created this way would "trickle down" to the middle and lower classes. Congress, in 1981, cut taxes by 25 percent over a three-year period. As a result, many federally funded social programs were either cut or eliminated altogether, while defense spending increased at an unprecedented peacetime rate.

President Reagan revised other government policies in the pursuit of economic growth. Clean air standards for automobiles and large factories were lifted. The telephone and trucking industries were deregulated. So was the savings and loan (S&L) industry, which then began making risky investments to increase profits. By the mid-1980s, many of these savings and loan associations were collapsing, and taxpayers would foot the bill for the crisis in this industry.

The specter of a costly strike loomed over the president in August 1981, when the nation's air traffic controllers walked off the job illegally. (Federal employees are forbidden to strike.) In a controversial stand, Reagan fired over 11,000 controllers, the vast majority of the striking workers, and replaced them with military personnel until civilian replacements could be trained. As a result, the air traffic controllers' union was destroyed.

Responding to the perceived weakness of the American military in the post–Vietnam War era, and to the Soviet invasion of Afghanistan, Reagan championed a massive arms buildup.

Reagan had promised to reconfigure the Supreme Court to promote more conservative rulings, and he fulfilled his promise. He seated the first woman on the Court, Sandra Day O'Connor, and he placed conservatives Antonin Scalia and Anthony Kennedy on the bench as well. The nomination of Robert Bork notably failed because of Democratic opposition.

Reagan's Second Term

In 1984, Reagan won reelection in a 49-state landslide. His second term would be marked by continued conservative policies, as Congress worked to lower taxes even further and to limit illegal immigration. But the **Iran-Contra scandal** left a stain on Reagan's presidency.

Congress had prohibited funding of the Nicaraguan Contras, anticommunist right-wing militant groups, due to the Contras' involvement in cocaine trafficking. In a series of clandestine deals in defiance of Congress, senior administration officials secretly sold military equipment to Iran in exchange for the release of American hostages. Money from this negotiation was then covertly funneled to the Contras. While Reagan denied any knowledge of the scandal, he took full responsibility for the actions of his subordinates. Calls for impeachment were ignored by Democratic leaders due to Reagan's personal popularity.

Reagan also witnessed stock markets around the world crash on Black Monday: October 19, 1987. Congress responded by reducing taxes further, fearing a return of recession.

THE END OF THE COLD WAR

High-Yield

After the 1979 Soviet invasion of Afghanistan and the subsequent U.S. boycott of the 1980 Olympic Games, *détente* was a thing of the past. President Reagan promised Americans a stronger military and had some tough words for what he called the "evil empire" of the Soviet Union. The president delivered on his promise of increased defense spending. He also pushed for the **Strategic Defense Initiative**, more popularly known as Star Wars. The system was designed to station satellites in orbit that, with lasers, could defend the United States against nuclear attack. While critics and many in the scientific community spoke of the impossibility of SDI, Reagan used the idea of the system as a scare tactic against the Soviets. The United States shifted its focus to promoting an arms race. This buildup of U.S. military capacity put intense pressure on the Soviet economy as it struggled to keep up.

In 1985, Mikhail Gorbachev came to power in the USSR. He introduced two historic reforms: *glasnost* and *perestroika*. The first, *glasnost*, or openness, allowed Soviet citizens to publicly criticize the government and discuss social problems in the hope of finding solutions. The second, *perestroika*, or restructuring, introduced limited free market reforms to the country's socialist planned economy. Both reforms unintentionally encouraged regional autonomy and nationalism, contributing to the Soviet Union's dissolution.

George H. W. Bush and the Collapse of the Soviet Union

Between Gorbachev's reforms and the toleration of dissident movements like Solidarity in Poland, the Cold War had entered a new phase by the eve of the 1988 election. The question arose of what would happen to the hyper-military ethos Ronald Reagan had developed.

In the election, domestic issues took center stage. The Republicans nominated Vice President **George H. W. Bush**, who went on to handily win the White House. Bush promised to be tough on crime, pointing to Democrat Michael Dukakis, his opponent, as having given convicted murders "weekend passes" from prison. Bush also promised not to raise taxes, a promise he would regret when he later did raise taxes, to the ire of the American public.

Communism worldwide seemed under fire from the moment of George Bush's inauguration. In spring 1989, China experienced pro-democracy demonstrations. On live television, Beijing crushed Tiananmen Square protesters with military force. An unknown number were killed, and many more were imprisoned. In Eastern Europe, the Warsaw Pact countries faced their own challenges. Needing to cut back on military spending, Gorbachev warned those communist governments that the Soviet Union would no longer be providing them assistance.

With the rise of Poland's Solidarity movement and the Romanian government's 1989 collapse, the Iron Curtain was falling. Ronald Reagan's famous words—"Mr. Gorbachev, tear down this wall!"—became a reality after East Germany's fall in October 1989. Despite his attempts at reinvigorating the USSR, Gorbachev watched as his own country fell apart around him. The Soviet republics of Estonia, Latvia, and Lithuania declared their independence in the spring of 1990. Gorbachev was forced from power in late 1991, as the Soviet Union collapsed on Christmas Day. Boris Yeltsin became president of Russia, which joined with the 14 other former Soviet republics to create the Commonwealth of Independent States.

Presidents Bush and Yeltsin immediately began to dismantle the nuclear arms stockpiles that had built up since World War II. They signed START I in 1991, which drastically reduced the number of nuclear warheads possessed by both countries. START II was signed by both men in 1993 to reduce further the number of warheads, with an added promise of U.S. aid to the Russian economy. Both Bush and Yeltsin continued to witness former Soviet republics fall into turmoil.

THE CLINTON AND GEORGE W. BUSH ADMINISTRATIONS

After winning the 1992 election, President **Bill Clinton** worked to reform both health care and welfare. Despite his party controlling both the House and Senate, the drafting and rollout of Clinton's health care bill went poorly. The Democratic Party was not unified on the bill's policies, while the Republicans presented a united opposition. The bill's popularity tanked, as did that of President Clinton. This contributed to the 1994 midterm elections being a Republican landslide. The GOP even won the House for the first time since 1952. The health care bill was dead.

During the 1994 midterm elections, Republicans unveiled their **Contract with America**, which promised to balance the federal budget while still supporting massive military expenditures. They did this by cutting taxes and limiting spending on social programs. Thus, President Clinton and newly elected Speaker Newt Gingrich headed for a showdown. Clinton threatened to veto the Republican budget and force the closure of all government offices until a compromise budget could be drafted. The Republicans were ultimately forced to back down, and Clinton was able to pass a federal budget that better enabled him to pursue his domestic policy objectives. He managed to secure passage of the **Personal Responsibility and Work Opportunity Reconciliation Act of 1996**, which reformed America's welfare system. It delivered on Clinton's campaign promise to "end welfare as we know it."

Much of Clinton's second term was consumed with defending himself against an array of charges of personal and political misconduct. The American economy grew rapidly during the Clinton administration; when he left office, the United States enjoyed a massive budget surplus.

Neither the healthy economy nor Clinton's renewed popularity were enough to carry Vice President Albert "Al" Gore over the threshold to victory in the 2000 election. After a closely contested race that ended only after a multi-week vote recount in Florida, Texas Governor **George W. Bush**, son of George H. W. Bush, was elected as the 43rd president. While the early months of the Bush administration focused on domestic issues, such as education reform with the bipartisan **No Child Left Behind Act**, the 9/11 attacks would change everything.

DOMESTIC AND INTERNATIONAL TERRORISM

Throughout the twentieth century, Americans were primarily concerned with acts of domestic terrorism. A self-declared anarchist assassinated President McKinley in 1901, and other anarchists conducted sporadic bombings over the next two decades. In the 1970s, leftist radicals like the Weather Underground committed other terrorist acts. In 1972 alone, the U.S. experienced over 1,900 domestic bombings. However, by far the most common form of domestic terrorism was committed by white supremacists. Approximately 1,800 African Americans were lynched in the United States in the twentieth century. Many others, like Emmett Till, would be beaten or shot to death.

In 1995, a large bomb destroyed the Murrah Federal Building in Oklahoma City, Oklahoma. The **Oklahoma City Bombing** killed 168 people. Right-wing extremist Timothy McVeigh and two accomplices were convicted of the terror attack. Americans were stunned by the bombing and grieved the loss of so many innocent lives, including the 19 infants and children in the building's day-care center.

Meanwhile, throughout the Cold War, fundamentalist Islamist groups had formed in countries such as Saudi Arabia, Iran, Syria, and Afghanistan. In addition to their own sectarian grudges, many were opposed to American foreign policy and the U.S. military presence in the Middle East. While some were established solely for domestic political purposes, others created networks of terrorist cells. In the 1990s, one such group attacked Americans at home and abroad.

Al-Qaeda, led by Osama bin Laden, a Saudi national, had established a military training camp in Afghanistan to prepare members to attack Western targets. Al-Qaeda began by bombing the World Trade Center in 1993, killing six people but failing to bring the building down. In August 1998, U.S. embassies in Kenya and Tanzania were bombed, killing 224 people, including 12 Americans. In October 2000, a suicide bombing of the USS *Cole* resulted in the deaths of 17 sailors. While each attack was notable, al-Qaeda attracted little lasting attention from most Americans. Soon, however, it would be globally infamous.

September 11 and a New America

High-Yield

September 11, 2001, began as a normal workday in New York City, as employees of the businesses in the World Trade Center rushed off the subways and streets into their offices. At 8:46 a.m. Eastern Time, American Airlines Flight 11 crashed into the World Trade Center's North Tower. Many thought this was a freak accident until approximately 15 minutes later, when United Flight 175 crashed into the South Tower. It was then clear that the United States was under attack. Both towers soon collapsed, killing their occupants and the rescue workers who had rushed in to save anyone they could. Meanwhile, American Flight 77 crashed into the Pentagon and United Flight 93 crashed into a wooded area of Pennsylvania. All flights were immediately grounded and the airspace over the entire country closed to any traffic.

In the end, nearly 3,000 lives were lost in the 9/11 attacks. New York City faced enormous financial damages. The impact on American business was staggering: commercial airlines begged for assistance to avoid bankruptcy, and travel destinations around the country remained empty. Lost, too, was the American people's sense of security. No longer would two oceans seemingly shelter the United States from threats from around the world.

Pledging immediate action, President George W. Bush promised that the perpetrators would be caught and justice served. The U.S. military and a coalition of allies soon invaded Afghanistan. The Taliban, the Sunni Islamic fundamentalist government that ruled the country and sheltered al-Qaeda, was quickly overthrown. Bin Laden, however, would escape justice until 2011. The Taliban persisted as an insurgency, and the Afghanistan War continued through the end of the second decade of the twenty-first century, becoming the longest war in American history.

> ✔ **AP Expert Note**
>
> **Be prepared to analyze American defense policies and their impact on civil liberties**
>
> The September 11 attacks spurred the creation of agencies and laws tasked with combating terrorism. President Bush created the **Department of Homeland Security** in the wake of the attacks, a federal executive department devoted to domestic security, antiterrorism, and disaster management and prevention. The attacks also inspired Congress to pass the controversial Patriot Act in October of 2001. This legislation broadened the scope of law enforcement authority when engaged in counterterrorism operations. Opponents of the Patriot Act have criticized its strengthening of law enforcement power as a threat to civil liberties.

The 2003 Iraq War

In March 2003, the United States invaded Iraq in an effort to remove a potentially threatening dictator and his alleged cache of **weapons of mass destruction**. Saddam Hussein was still in power since the 1991 Gulf War and he refused to cooperate fully with United Nations weapons inspections. Bush convinced Congress and most of the American people that Iraq posed a serious threat to national, and even global, security. The invasion of Iraq was not officially sanctioned by the United Nations and was condemned by many U.S. allies around the world.

Saddam Hussein was quickly removed from power, but weapons of mass destruction were never located. The United States did not remove its forces entirely until 2011. By that point, nearly 4,500 U.S. soldiers had died, mainly during the postwar occupation. Over 100,000 Iraqi civilians are documented as having died during this period. Later threats in the region would see the gradual return of U.S. soldiers.

THE OBAMA ADMINISTRATION

Barack Obama, a freshman senator from Illinois, won the Democratic Party's nomination in 2008 after a spirited primary battle with Senator and former First Lady Hillary Rodham Clinton. He campaigned on a message of hope and bipartisanship. Americans would elect him as their 45th president. Obama was the country's first African American president.

In addition to the challenges of the Great Recession, President Obama aimed to achieve a long-held ambition of the Democratic Party dating back to the Truman administration: reforming health care. Taking lessons learned during the Clinton administration's failed effort, Obama took care to involve Congress in drafting the legislation. After a protracted effort at hammering out a compromise bill and amidst great public debate, President Obama signed the **Affordable Care Act** (ACA) into law in March 2010. More commonly known as Obamacare, it would continue to be a source of intense debate throughout his two terms in office.

The 2010 midterms would see a massive backlash against the Democratic Party's control of the federal government, however. The fiscally-conservative populist Tea Party movement helped fuel a resurgent Republican Party in Congress, as did national discontent over high unemployment and the drawn-out effort to pass the Affordable Care Act. Discontent over the economy and the bank bailouts would also spawn the populist left-wing Occupy Wall Street movement in 2011.

Despite these issues, however, Obama himself remained highly popular with voters. The economy had also began to gradually improve by this point as well. Thus, President Obama would secure an easy reelection in 2012 over Governor Mitt Romney of Massachusetts.

ONGOING DEMOGRAPHIC SHIFTS

The Johnson-era passage of the Immigration Act of 1965 opened the doors to non–northern Europeans who had previously been discriminated against by strict quotas. Cubans fleeing the oppressive dictatorship of Fidel Castro, Vietnamese fleeing communist rule, and Filipinos and Mexicans seeking economic opportunity all came to the United States between 1965 and 2000. While these were the largest groups seeking citizenship, many others joined their ranks from countries such as India, Pakistan, Korea, China, and the Dominican Republic. States such as Texas, California, Arizona, and Florida experienced massive population growth.

From 1965 through 2015, America became more diverse. For example, a full third of Los Angeles residents were foreign-born in 1990. California now had residents from all over the world, with those from Southeast Asia and Mexico predominating. However, this increased immigration also led to a revival of nativism. Aiming to put a damper on illegal immigration, Congress passed the **Immigration and Control Act** in 1986. This measure proved to be largely ineffective. In 1994, **California Proposition 187** sought to prohibit undocumented immigrants from accessing non-emergency health care and public education. California voters approved it by a 59 percent majority, although an injunction over its constitutionality prevented enforcement. Over the next decade, however, several other states would pass similar laws.

✔ **AP Expert Note**

Be prepared to answer exam questions about the causes and effects of population movements

There are multiple push and pull factors that cause people to migrate to or from a country. The period from 1980 onward in America has seen a renewed increase in immigration. After 1965, developing nations, such as those in Central America, replaced Europe as the major source of immigrants. Due to economic hardships in these developing nations, illegal immigration into the United States sharply increased in the later part of the twentieth century. As a consequence, the U.S. population grew, especially in the Southwest, and the nation became increasingly more multicultural.

Americans were also on the move domestically during this period, as many picked up from the former Steel Belt states and moved to the **Sun Belt**. Steel-producing states, such as Michigan, Pennsylvania, and Ohio, became known as the **Rust Belt**, as decreasing domestic demand and increasing competition in the global market led to steel mill closures. Americans flocked to California, Texas, Arizona, Florida, and New Mexico to take advantage of their climates, as well as new job opportunities.

Affirmative Action Debates

Affirmative action, the policy of increasing minority access to jobs and education, first took a blow in 1978 when the Supreme Court ruled in *Bakke v. UC Board of Regents* that the University of California (UC) system's admissions process resulted in "reverse discrimination" such that qualified white applicants were being denied admission in favor of less-qualified minority applicants. Later, in 1996, Proposition 209 was passed, barring affirmative action laws in the state of California. Several other states, such as Michigan, followed suit, enacting laws abolishing affirmative action.

20

The Graying of the Baby Boomers

The "graying" of America began in the mid-1990s and is projected to continue through the 2050s. The number of Americans over 65 will skyrocket as the baby boomers grow older, because improved health care has increased the average lifespan. By 2030, about 25 percent of all Americans will be over 85 years old. The Social Security system, established during the New Deal when both the number of elderly and their expected lifespan were far lower, will be taxed by this development. Health care costs are also expected to greatly increase.

TECHNOLOGICAL ADVANCES

Advances in Health

Through advances in medicine, such as organ transplants, artificial life support, and advanced drug therapy, human life can be greatly extended. Previously deadly bacteria can now be treated with a single regimen of antibiotics. Polio, once a scourge of children everywhere, was eradicated from the Americas by 1994. In an effort to find cures for diseases such as AIDS, cancer, and diabetes, U.S. researchers worked with their colleagues abroad to completely map the entire human genome by 2003. The medical research community has been experimenting with human stem cells in an effort to regenerate damaged cells to cure a variety of illnesses. The use of human embryos in some stem cell research proved to be highly controversial in the United States during the 2000s.

Advances in Communication

The first consumer portable telephones were introduced in 1983, retailing for an eye-popping $3,995 (roughly $10,300 in 2019 dollars). The phones looked like two-way radios and needed frequent charging of a huge battery pack, a far cry from the slim smartphones found worldwide today.

Cable television revolutionized the airwaves in the late 1970s and early 1980s, pushing boundaries with more explicit, complex programming that could afford to appeal to niche audiences. By the late 1990s, prestige shows on cable television had helped give rise to a Golden Age of Television. Standard network stations were likewise eclipsed by their cable counterparts, with CNN rising to fame for its 24/7 coverage of the Gulf War. Satellite communications now meant breaking news from around the globe could be presented to audiences live.

Advances in Computers

High-Yield

A young computer scientist named Bill Gates revolutionized the computer industry with his company Microsoft. As personal computers became more affordable, IBM adopted a form of Microsoft's operating system, MS-DOS, for its personal computer line. More companies entered the business, making consumer software for computers, IBM or otherwise, that ran MS-DOS.

No technological development has affected society more than the **Internet**. Although a primitive military computer networking system (ARPANET) had been expanded to the academic community in the 1970s, it was not until 1989 that English scientist Tim Berners-Lee developed the **World Wide Web**. His system of URLs, HTML, and hyperlinks would establish the framework for what is now a global system, building upon ARPANET's conceptual foundation. By the late 1990s, most Americans had used the Internet. With the spread of Internet use came many new challenges: piracy, identity theft, cyberbullying, doxxing, deepfakes, and more.

ENVIRONMENTAL ISSUES

Issues such as biodiversity, the use of genetically modified organisms, ocean acidification, climate change, resource conservation, and water stress will continue to concern human beings in the foreseeable future. Many of the measures taken to protect the environment have been reversed by later presidents who, in an effort to stimulate the nation's economy, lifted restrictions on waste dumping and pollution emissions.

The nation faces serious choices regarding economic growth, resource conservation, energy sources, and environmental protection in the coming years. For example, the U.S. dependence on fossil fuels has been a running concern since the 1970s. While the United States long sought some form of energy independence, so as to not be reliant on oil imports from areas such as the Middle East, this independence was largely not achieved until the 2010s with the advent of fracking. Long before the 2010s, however, the United States and its allies have sought stability in global oil markets through alliances and security arrangements with governments in the Middle East. Yet fracking and oil drilling both result in more carbon being dumping into the atmosphere, worsening the growing problem of climate change.

One new dimension to environmental issues in the twenty-first century is that industrial factories, the source of many pollutants, are increasingly located overseas in places such as China and India. As with the Ozone Hole problem of the 1980s, tackling global environmental issues requires international agreement. No one nation is the source of any particular problem. Collective action is needed. Yet the differing economic priorities of the countries involved complicates negotiations.

GLOBALIZATION AND THE UNITED STATES

Globalized Economy

High-Yield

President Clinton promoted economic globalization with the **North American Free Trade Agreement** (NAFTA), a treaty with Canada and Mexico that allowed the free flow of goods, services, and jobs in North America. Organized labor, progressive groups, and others hotly contested NAFTA, claiming that jobs being exported to Mexico would harm American workers. NAFTA was signed in 1993, and its value and effects continue to be the subject of debate.

20

Both the 1990s and the 2000s saw recessions that highlighted the potential risks of globalization. In 1997, Asian financial markets collapsed. South Korea, Thailand, and Indonesia experienced severe economic downturns caused by the overvaluing of real estate and by risky investments. Thailand responded by closing banks nationwide, causing a ripple effect across Asia. Bank patrons rushed to withdraw their deposits. Quickly, once-vast fortunes became worthless as currency and stock values crashed in many countries. Exporters to Asia suffered as their supply of goods rose and Asian demand fell. Oil-producing nations found themselves strapped with large reserves of crude and no buyers. The Russian and Venezuelan economies were hit especially hard. The **International Monetary Fund** (IMF) supplied billions in loans to faltering nations. Some economies rebounded quickly, but future economic crises remained a possibility.

The 2008 Financial Crisis

During the early 2000s, there was a bipartisan push to increase homeownership among low- and middle-income Americans. Federal agencies weakened their standards for risk assessment. Looser standards meant many Americans could now take out a mortgage on a new home, but also that they were taking on more debt than they could ultimately pay back. This was not a problem during a period of economic growth, but any downturn meant these Americans would be among the first who would be unable to pay their mortgage.

The demand for housing rose as a result of mortgages being made available to millions more Americans than ever before. This sparked a building boom. However, when the economy finally slowed, the most vulnerable Americans were unable to make their monthly mortgage payments. Now in default, they were evicted from their homes. At the same time, the supply of available housing was now much greater than before the boom. There were more homes on the market than people who could buy them.

These factors combined to severely impact the American economy. By late 2007, the first wave of homeowners began defaulting. Investors in mortgage-backed securities saw their monthly profits dry up. Because the supply of housing far exceeded the demand, individual homes were now worth far less than before the building boom. Thus, the mortgages themselves plummeted in value. Investors lost trillions. This caused further economic turmoil, which caused more Americans to lose their jobs and default on their mortgage payments, which in turn worsened the overall problem. An economic death spiral ensued. More than three million Americans lost their homes in 2008 alone, which was equivalent to 1 out of every 54 households nationwide. This became known as the **2008 Financial Crisis** in the United States, which in turn rippled through the global economy, sparking the **Great Recession**.

Looking Forward

The recent financial crises are just one way in which the United States is more interconnected with the wider world than ever before. Advances in biotechnology, mass communications, and computers have also made the world a much smaller place, bringing excitement and danger along with progress. In this era of globalization, America has seen massive changes domestically as well, all of which have sparked continued debates about population demographics, resources, civil liberties, human rights, and other social issues. America will continue to engage with all of these large and important topics in the years to come.

 # NEXT STEP: PRACTICE

Go to Rapid Review and Practice Chapter 11 or to your online quizzes on kaptest.com for exam-like practice on this topic.

Haven't registered your book yet? Go to kaptest.com/moreonline to begin.

CHAPTER 21

The Free-Response Section

FREE-RESPONSE STRATEGY

Overview

The free-response questions—which include three short-answer questions, one document-based question (DBQ), and one long essay question (LEQ)—are worth 60% of your total exam score.

You have 40 minutes to answer three short-answer questions in Section I, Part B of the exam, which gives you about 13 minutes per question. Section II is 100 minutes long, and it's divided into two parts: the first 60 minutes is the suggested writing time for the DBQ (including a recommended 15-minute reading period), and the last 40 minutes is the suggested writing time for the LEQ.

> ✔ **AP Expert Note**
>
> **Treat Section II as a marathon (and train accordingly)**
>
> 100 minutes can feel like no time at all when you have to write two free-response questions, but it is actually a long time for your brain to maintain sharp focus—especially after you have already spent 95 minutes on Section I. However, if you practice writing, including sticking to the timing and pacing required for Section II, you will build up the necessary stamina and feel much more prepared and confident on the official exam.

Readers will score each individual question according to a rubric. The rubric for the short-answer questions is straightforward: each prompt requires you to complete three tasks, which are worth one point each, for a total of three points for each question. The rubrics for the DBQ and LEQ are a bit more complex and relate to demonstrating certain skills, such as thesis development, contextualization, and use of evidence. (Scoring information and sample rubrics will be provided in the following sections about each specific question type.)

The Kaplan Method for Free-Response Questions

While there are three different kinds of free-response questions on the exam, you can and should approach every prompt using the same Kaplan Method. Employing a methodical, strategic approach will help ensure that you effectively address every part of every question. Just follow these four steps (which spell out AP-AP)!

1. **Analyze the prompt.**
2. **Plan your response.**
3. **Action! Write your response.**
4. **Proofread.**

Let's look at the Kaplan Method steps in more detail.

Step 1: Analyze the Prompt

Take the time to understand each and every part of every prompt—or what the question asks you to do. Analyzing the prompt means thinking carefully about the following components.

- **The content of the question.** Consider exactly what topics the question addresses. Underline key terms and requirements.

- **The action words.** Next, make sure you know exactly what you have to do with the content: *describe, explain,* etc. Consider circling the action words in the prompt so you make sure you do the correct required action. While we often use these action words somewhat interchangeably when speaking, consider carefully how each action word calls for a slightly different treatment of the content. Some examples, from simple to complicated, include:

  - *identify*: point out a trend or piece of information (this task does *not* require providing an explanation)

  - *describe*: fully lay out the details of something

  - *explain*: analyze the *why* or *how* of something (e.g., what causes it, why it's important) using reasoning or evidence

  - *evaluate*: make a determination about a claim and explain your reasoning

- **The source stimulus.** Some questions include a primary or secondary source or sources. Analyze each source stimulus thoroughly, noting components such as topic, main idea, author viewpoint, and author background. You must understand the source(s) to effectively answer the prompt.

Step 2: Plan Your Response

This is the *most important* factor in writing a quality response. Planning is never a waste of time; rather, it is a crucial step to creating an effective response that addresses every part of every prompt. The test makers expect you to take time to plan your responses and have built this into the exam timing, so take advantage of it. Ultimately, planning saves you time by helping you write a focused response. You only have time to write each response once, so make it count!

Here are some tips to help you make your plan:

- Think about what you will write for each part of a prompt. Jot down brief notes—phrases and/or examples—for each part.

- Whenever possible, see if you can come up with specific historical examples to help support your response.

- Double-check the prompt to make sure you didn't skip any required tasks.

Step 3: Action! Write Your Response

After thoroughly completing the pre-writing steps, actually writing the response should be relatively easy: just use the notes you jotted down in Step 2 to write your paragraphs. Be sure to write full paragraphs; lists or outline-style notes will not earn you points on the exam.

As you write, keep in mind that your responses should clearly focus on the required tasks, provide full explanations, and firmly assert your claims. Time is limited, so every word you write should help you earn points. Avoid "filler" and "fluff." The length of your response has nothing to do with your score; the quality of the content and how well it addresses the prompt is what counts.

Finally, make sure you write neatly. Readers can't award points if they can't read what you wrote. Keep in mind that actual people will be reading every word you write, so make them happy by making your responses as easy as possible to read.

✔ **AP Expert Note**

Be strategic with the information you provide

Don't just write as much as you know about the topic of a prompt; rather, respond with information that satisfies each specific requirement. For example, if a free-response prompt asks you to "Briefly explain ONE specific historical effect of the Cold War on United States society," don't waste time writing out *every* effect and *every* detail of the Cold War. Instead, focus on one significant effect on U.S. society, such as McCarthyism's impact on politicians and popular culture. Focus your writing on what the question asks for, and move on!

Step 4: Proofread

Try to leave a minute or two to briskly proofread. Your responses need not be perfect, but you should quickly correct any glaring errors that might distract your readers from your content. If you catch a mistake, just neatly cross it out and write the correction above. There's no time for a complete overhaul of the response, but if you made a plan, there won't be any need for one!

A Note on Timing and Pacing

Now that we've established the Kaplan Method (AP-AP) to apply to every free-response question, let's review timing considerations. You should respond to each prompt for an amount of time that is proportional to the work involved. The three short-answer questions in Section I, Part B should each take approximately 13 minutes each to analyze, plan, write, and proofread.

For Section II, however, you are working over a long total time span (1 hour and 40 minutes), so pacing yourself between two essays will require some effort and practice. Consider wearing a standard wristwatch to help pace yourself in case there is no clock available in the testing room. And just as importantly, practice the free-response sections on the practice tests under timed conditions. It's difficult to anticipate how long each section will feel on the day of the exam, so practicing with a watch will greatly increase your familiarity with the required pacing.

> ✔ **AP Expert Note**
>
> **Remember "AP-AP"**
>
> Recall that the steps of the Kaplan Method for Free-Response Questions spell out AP-AP. Follow all of the steps of this easy-to-remember acronym every time you encounter a free-response prompt, both in practice and on Test Day. By making the Kaplan Method second nature, you won't have to think about what you're doing and can instead focus on the quality of the content you're writing.

SHORT-ANSWER QUESTIONS

Overview

The short-answer part of the test, which appears after the multiple choice questions, consists of four questions—and you must answer three.

Unlike the DBQ and LEQ later in the exam, your response to each short-answer question will be a brief, to-the-point answer to each question's three required tasks. You should use complete sentences, but there is no need to write a thesis or provide any additional information.

The types of short-answer questions will always be the same:

1. **Question 1** is based on a secondary source or sources. You might be asked to describe the difference between two historians' interpretations or provide historical evidence to support a historian's argument.

2. **Question 2** is based on a primary source or sources. You might be asked to describe a perspective expressed in a historical image, such as an advertisement or political cartoon, or to explain a historical event.

3. **Question 3 and Question 4** do not provide sources and include only the three required tasks. You will choose EITHER Question 3 or Question 4. Question 3 will focus on a topic between the years 1491 and 1877, and Question 4 will focus on a topic between the years 1865 and 2001.

Strategy

As is the case for every free-response question, you should follow the AP-AP Kaplan Method. Before walking through a sample prompt step-by-step, let's look at some special considerations for short-answer questions.

- Carefully analyze the source stimulus—which could be a passage or image—on questions 1 and 2. Note key details, look for relevant information in the titles and source information, and paraphrase in your own words the main purpose of the source.

- Since each short-answer question consists of three tasks (a, b, and c), read through all three tasks before you begin planning your response. Some tasks may be related to each other (such as providing multiple historical examples), so you want to be sure you have an understanding of all the required tasks before you dive in.

- Short-answer questions do not require a thesis statement or an organized essay response. Directly and concisely address each required task, using complete sentences, and move on.

- You will choose EITHER Question 3 or Question 4. Read both questions and consider which one you feel more confident about, keeping in mind you'll need to be able to explain each part of your response and provide relevant examples. If needed, quickly begin planning one or both questions to help you determine which question to answer in full.

- You may answer the short-answer questions in any order, as long as you write your responses on the corresponding pages of your response booklet. Begin with whichever question you feel most confident about—be sure you give about a third of your time to each question, since each is weighted the same in your score.

The following is a step-by-step walk-through of a sample short-answer question.

Sample Question

Photograph of National Woman's Party picketers outside the White House, 1917

Using the image, answer (a), (b), and (c).

a) Briefly describe ONE perspective about women's rights expressed in the image.

b) Briefly explain ONE specific historical development or circumstance from 1848 to 1917 that led to demonstrations such as the one depicted in the image.

c) Briefly explain ONE difference between the women's rights movement in the period 1848–1920 and the women's rights movement in the period 1950–1980.

Step 1: Analyze the Prompt

Closely read or analyze the source stimulus, marking important details. If the source is a passage, briefly paraphrase the purpose of the source in your own words to solidify your understanding. If the source is an image, take notes about its details and viewpoint. See below a high-scoring response writer's sample thoughts and notes for the photograph.

- The photo is from 1917 (before the 19th amendment), when Wilson was president.

- The picketers are from their own political party (National Women's Party) and are wearing traditional women's dress.

- The picketers are outside the White House, and the signs address the president and cite "liberty" and the "human spirit." The women are likely picketing for the right to vote.

Look for any additional information that may be provided about the source. For this source, note that the higher-scoring writer included details from the title (the date, location, and group involved) in the notes about the source.

Then read the three parts of the prompt carefully, underlining exactly what each requires. Box, underline, or otherwise mark the action words (which, for this sample prompt, are *describe, explain,* and *explain*). Make sure to respond in a way that fulfills what each action word requires.

Step 2: Plan Your Response

The paragraphs below describe what a high-scoring writer might notice and think about when planning a response. Samples of what that high-scoring writer might write as notes are provided for each part of the prompt.

For Part A, the prompt directs you to describe a perspective about women's rights expressed in the image. Since asked to *describe,* the high-scoring writer would use her notes to find a perspective shown in the image about which she can provide some relevant details.

Part A:

- women in political party and picketing—shows increased political participation

Part B asks for an explanation of a historical development that led to demonstrations like the picketing in the image. The high-scoring writer would brainstorm relevant developments between 1848 and 1917 that are related to the women's rights movement, choosing one for which she can use evidence and/or reasoning to explain how the development led to the picketing in the image.

Part B:

- Seneca Falls Convention
- first major discussion of women's rights, led to more discussions
- Declaration of Sentiments, suffrage debated

Part C requires an explanation of a difference between the women's rights movements in different periods. The high-scoring writer would carefully note the date ranges provided, brainstorm characteristics of each movement, and choose one for which she can use evidence and/or reasoning to explain how the movements differed.

Part C:

- 1848-1920: focused on suffrage, property, jobs; tied w/ issues of abolition, temperance, limits on child labor
- 1950-1980: focused on equal wages, no-fault divorce, reproductive rights, ERA
- different focuses

Step 3: Action! Write Your Response

Just write out the information, using your planning notes. As you write, remember to label each part of your response (a, b, c) and to keep your writing legible. Refer back to the question's action words to make sure you're doing the correct tasks. See the following sample high-scoring response and scoring explanation at the end of this section. One of the best ways to improve your own free-response answers is to read sample responses, thinking carefully about what makes the responses effective and what features you can copy.

Step 4: Proofread

Leave a minute or so for a quick proofread, neatly correcting any errors you catch.

Sample High-Scoring Response

(a) The image reflects the perspective that women in 1917 were participating more in American politics, even if they did not yet have the right to vote in national elections. The women are engaging in the political practice of picketing, addressing the president, and, as the caption indicates, these women are part of a political party which represented women's rights. The women in the photo believed they had the right to participate in the democratic process, even if they did not formally have the national vote yet.

(b) The Seneca Falls Convention of 1848 would have contributed to twentieth-century political demonstrations like the one shown in the photo. The convention was the first major gathering to discuss women's rights, setting the stage for increased focus on women's rights and women's participation in political advocacy. The convention established common goals for the women's movement in the Declaration of Sentiments, and, although not everyone agreed about all of the goals, it began the discussion about women's suffrage in earnest. The suffrage movement, though sometimes taking a backseat to the cause of abolitionism, would grow until the time of the photo and the passage of the nineteenth amendment.

(c) The movements differ in their focuses. The earlier movement emphasized rights for women such as suffrage, job opportunities, and the right to own property, while the later movement, taking place after the nineteenth amendment, emphasized equal pay, no-fault divorce, and reproductive rights. Since the earlier women's movement had succeeded in achieving many of its goals, the later movement focused on additional ways to increase equality for women: now that women could freely work outside the home, they could advocate for fair pay, for instance. The movements also differed in that activists of the earlier movement were often closely tied to other issues of the day, such as abolitionism and temperance.

Sample Response Explanation and Scoring for Question 1: 3 points (1 + 1 + 1)

The following is scoring information an AP reader might use to grade this free-response question. A successful short-answer response accomplishes all three tasks set forth by the prompt. Each part of the prompt is worth 1 point, for a total of 3 possible points.

Part A (1 point)

To earn this point, the response must describe, not merely identify, a perspective about women's rights that is expressed in the photo. The writer of the sample response does so effectively by drawing upon multiple details about the photograph to support a viable perspective about the women's rights movement.

Part B (1 point)

To earn this point, the response must use reasoning or evidence to explain how a historical development or circumstance led to demonstrations demanding women's suffrage. The writer of the sample response effectively describes details of a relevant event, the Seneca Falls Convention, and then explains how this event influenced the event depicted in the photo.

Part C (1 point)

To earn this point, the response must use reasoning or evidence to explain a difference between the women's rights movements of 1848–1920 and those of 1950–1980, specifically addressing a feature of the movements from *both* time periods. The writer of the sample response does so by describing accurate details about both movements and explaining how the cause-effect relationship between the movements led to different focuses, using the example of rights related to jobs and equal pay.

THE DOCUMENT-BASED QUESTION

Overview

Question 1 in Section II is the document-based question (DBQ). It will always include seven documents offering a variety of perspectives on a historical development or process that took place between the years 1754 and 1980. A high-scoring DBQ response will do the following.

- **Thesis:** Make a thesis or claim that responds to the prompt. The thesis or claim must be historically defensible and establish a line of reasoning.

- **Context:** Provide context relevant to the prompt by describing a broader historical development or process.

- **Evidence:** Use *at least six* of the provided documents to support an argument in response to the prompt.

- **Additional Evidence:** Use a historical example not found in the documents as evidence relevant to an argument about the prompt.

- **Sourcing:** Explain how the context or situation of *at least three* documents is relevant to an argument. This could address the relevance of the document's point of view, purpose, historical situation, and/or audience.

- **Complex Understanding:** Demonstrate a nuanced understanding of an argument that responds to the prompt by using evidence to corroborate, qualify, or modify the argument.

While this may sound like a lot factors to keep in mind, the strategies below will help you plan your response in such a way to address all the scoring requirements.

Strategy

As always, use the 4-Step Kaplan Method (AP-AP). Also, consider the following special strategies for the DBQ. Scoring requirements are highlighted in bold.

During Step 1: Analyze the Prompt:

- Use the 15-minute reading period to read the documents and organize them into groups for analysis.

- Feel free to write notes in the test booklet and underline important words in both the source line and the document itself. Nothing in the booklet is read as part of the essay scoring.

- Assume that each document provides only a snapshot of the topic—just one perspective.

- For each document, jot down brief notes to solidify your understanding of the document. The notes will also help you quickly review the documents when you make your plan and write your essay. Take short notes about: the main idea(s) of the source, the purpose of the source (why it was written), and the background of the author and/or the context in which the source was created. Thinking about these factors will help you address the DQB requirements.

- Reread the prompt, thinking about how each of the documents relates to the prompt. Group the documents by their similarities: perhaps they present two or more major viewpoints or can be grouped according to two or more types of changes.

- If the 15-minute reading period has passed and you need a few more minutes to review the documents and organize your thoughts, go ahead! The 15 minutes is a suggested amount of time. That said, you will want to give yourself as much time as possible to write a thoughtful response.

During Step 2: Plan Your Response:

- Making a careful plan can help you make sure you address all the scoring requirements.

- Paraphrase your **thesis** statement. Knowing your claim will make it easier for you to plan an effective argument in your essay. In light of the documents, you must make a claim and/or demonstrate a line of reasoning that responds to the prompt. Avoid statements that are vague or general ("The Vietnam War was very significant") and make a claim that responds to the prompt, uses both the documents and your historical knowledge, and sets up the rest of your essay ("The Vietnam War impacted Americans' perceptions of the U.S. role in international politics, the power of the federal government, and the status of young people, influencing legal and social changes in American society").

- Be sure your thesis or overall plan incorporates a **complex understanding**. You need to demonstrate that you have more than just a basic understanding of the content, so your thesis or overall essay should address complexity in the historical development—perhaps by including multiple variables, by considering both causes and effects, or by making an insightful connection to another time period. See below for a complete list of ways to demonstrate complex understanding.

- Make a note about how you will provide **context** for the topic of the prompt. This may fit well in the introduction or first body paragraph.

- Make a simple outline of your body paragraphs; there will likely be one paragraph for each point you made in your thesis. (For instance, in the above example, there would be a paragraph each about impacts on international politics, the federal government, and the status of young people.) For each paragraph, consider these scoring requirements:

  ○ List the documents you will use as **evidence**—remember that you must use *six or seven* to earn the maximum number of points for using the documents.

- Consider whether the paragraph is a good place to provide **additional evidence**—you must include *one* additional historical example.

- Think about when it would be beneficial to explain **sourcing**, or how a document's context or situation is relevant to the argument—you must do so for *three* documents.

- Finally, review your plan and check off each requirement in your test booklet to ensure you addressed all six.

During Step 3: Action! Write Your Response:

- Nothing is more important in the first paragraph than the clear statement of an analytical thesis. The reader is most interested in seeing a strong thesis as soon as possible.

- Your thesis can be more than just one sentence. With the compound questions often asked by the DBQ, two sentences might be needed to complete the idea.

- Refer to the authors of the documents, not just the document numbers.

- A good idea is to write a concluding paragraph that might extend your original thesis. Think of a way to restate your thesis, adding information from your analysis of the documents.

During Step 4: Proofread:

- Skim for any glaring errors and, if you have time, check again to make sure your response meets each of the DBQ requirements.

✔ **AP Expert Note**

Be prepared to demonstrate complex understanding

The AP exam asks you to analyze sources and develop arguments in a sophisticated way. Demonstrating your complex understanding of the topic at hand is crucial to your success, and here are some ways you can do so.

- Analyze multiple variables
- Employ a complex historical reasoning skill by explaining both similarities *and* differences, both continuity *and* change, both causes *and* effects, or multiple causes
- Explain relevant connections to other regions or other time periods
- Corroborate perspectives across multiple course themes (such as environment, cultural developments, governance, economic systems, social organization, and technology)
- Qualify an argument using other evidence or views

Sample Question

Evaluate the extent of change in United States political parties in the period 1791 to 1833.

Document 1

Source: Alexander Hamilton, leader of the Federalist Party, Opinion as to the Constitutionality of the Bank of the United States, 1791.

The federal government's implied powers are to be considered as equal with the powers explicitly expressed in the Constitution. Then it follows, that as a power of creating a corporation may as well be implied as any other thing, it may as well be employed as an instrument or means of carrying into execution any of the specified powers, as any other instrument or means whatever. The only question must be in this, as in every other case, whether the mean to be employed or, in this instance, the corporation to be erected, has a natural relation to any of the acknowledged objects or lawful ends of the government. Thus a corporation may not be created by Congress for the purpose of superintending the police of the city of Philadelphia, because Congress is not authorized to regulate the police of that city. But one may be created in relation to the collection of taxes, or to the trade with foreign countries, or to the trade between the States, or with the Indian tribes; because it is the province of the federal government to regulate those objects, and because it is incident to a general sovereign or legislative power to regulate a thing, to employ all the means which relate to its regulation to the best and greatest advantage.

Document 2

Source: Thomas Jefferson, leader of the Democratic-Republican Party, Opinion on the Constitutionality of a National Bank, 1791.

I consider the foundation of the Constitution as laid on this ground: That "all powers not delegated to the United States, by the Constitution, nor prohibited by it to the States, are reserved to the States or to the people." To take a single step beyond the boundaries thus specially drawn around the powers of Congress, is to take possession of a boundless field of power, no longer susceptible to any definition.

The incorporation of a bank, and the powers assumed by this bill, have not, in my opinion, been delegated to the United States by the Constitution.

Document 3

Source: Thomas Jefferson, First Inaugural Address, 1801.

But every difference of opinion is not a difference of principle. We have called by different names brethren of the same principle. We are all Republicans; we are all Federalists. If there be any among us who would wish to dissolve this Union or to change its republican form, let them stand undisturbed as monuments of the safety with which error of opinion may be tolerated where reason is left free to combat it.

Document 4

Source: Territorial Acquisitions of the United States, National Atlas of the United States.

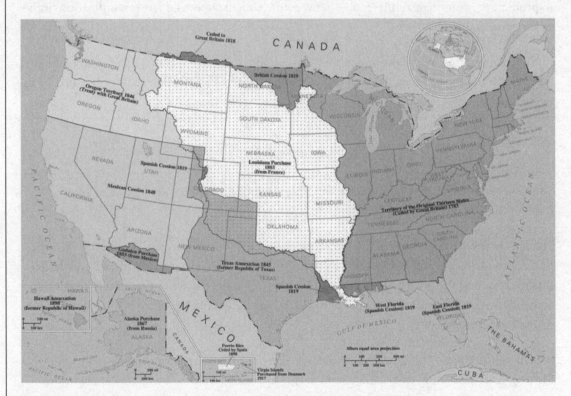

Louisiana Purchase, coordinated by President Thomas Jefferson in 1803, is shown in white

Document 5

Source: Report and Resolutions of the Hartford Convention, meeting of New England Federalists, 1815.

Resolved. That the following amendments of the constitution of the United States be recommended to the states represented as aforesaid, to be proposed by them for adoption by the state legislatures, and in such cases as may be deemed expedient by a convention chosen by the people of each state. . . .

Second. No new state shall be admitted into the Union by Congress, in virtue of the power granted by the constitution, without the concurrence of two thirds of both houses. . . .

Fourth. Congress shall not have power, without the concurrence of two thirds of both houses, to prohibit the commercial intercourse between the United States and any foreign nation or the dependencies thereof.

Fifth. Congress shall not make or declare war, or authorize acts of hostility against any foreign nation, without the concurrence of two thirds of both houses, except such acts of hostility be in defense of the territories of the United States when actually invaded.

Document 6

Source: President Andrew Jackson, leader in Democratic Party, veto message regarding the Bank of the United States, 1832.

The bill "to modify and continue" the act entitled "An act to incorporate the subscribers to the Bank of the United States" was presented to me on the 4th July. Having considered it with that solemn regard to the principles of the Constitution which the day was calculated to inspire, and come to the conclusion that it ought not to become a law, I herewith return it to the Senate, in which it originated, with my objections.

A bank of the United States is in many respects convenient for the Government and useful to the people. Entertaining this opinion, and deeply impressed with the belief that some of the powers and privileges possessed by the existing bank are unauthorized by the Constitution, subversive of the rights of the States, and dangerous to the liberties of the people, I felt it my duty at an early period of my Administration to call the attention of Congress to the practicability of organizing an institution combining all its advantages and obviating these objections. I sincerely regret that in the act before me I can perceive none of those modifications of the bank charter which are necessary, in my opinion, to make it compatible with justice, with sound policy, or with the Constitution of our country.

Document 7

Source: Anonymous member of National Republican* Party, 1832 political cartoon.

The cartoon pictures Jackson standing on the "Constitution of the United States of America,"
"Internal Improvements," and "U.S. Bank."

*By 1832, the National Republicans and other groups had evolved into the Whig Party.

Step 1: Analyze the Prompt

First, read the prompt itself: you'll need to develop an argument about the extent of change in political parties from 1791 to 1833. The prompt uses the verb *evaluate*, so you will need to make a determination about the changes in political parties.

Spend the 15-minute reading period analyzing the documents themselves, thinking for each document about its authorship/historical situation, main idea, and why it was written.

Begin grouping the documents into categories that you can use to help organize your essay. The following is a sample high-scoring writer's notes on the documents:

1. Hamilton - Fed.: federal implied powers equal with explicit powers in Constitution, bank constitutional

2. Jefferson - Demo-Rep.: federal government only has powers delegated by Constitution, bank unconstitutional

3. Jefferson inaugural address: all parties follow same principles

4. Map of territories, feat. Louisiana Purchase - large territory bought by Jefferson

5. Hartford Convention - Fed.: want Congress to have high consensus to take action

6. Jackson - Demo.: veto bank b/c unconstitutional

7. Nat.-Rep. (Whig) cartoon: Jackson like king trampling Constitution w/ vetoes

Groups:

- Fed. & Demo.-Rep. initial views: 1 & 2
- Feds. changing view: 5
- Demo.-Rep. changing view: 3, 4
- new parties & new issues: 6, 7

Step 2: Plan Your Response

Next, take time to plan your response. Focus on formulating a strong thesis, and check your plan against the DBQ requirements. See the sample plan that a high-scoring writer might make. Scoring requirements are written in bold for reference; note that the writer includes all seven documents and plans to use three documents to meet the requirement for sourcing.

- ¶ intro
  - **Thesis:** parties changed ideals & new parties formed w/ new focuses; all devoted to Constitution (**complex understanding:** change and continuity)

- Body ¶1: views of first parties
  - Hamilton (Doc. 1): Fed. pro-bank, loose construction, strong central government
  - Jefferson (Doc. 2): Demo.-Rep. anti-bank, strict construction, powerful states

- Body ¶2: Demo.-Reps. changing ideals
  - Jefferson (Doc. 3): reconcile w/ Feds. (**sourcing 1**)
  - LA Purchase (Doc. 4): shift from strict construction
  - **Add'l Evidence:** Jefferson Embargo Act: shift to strong fed.

- Body ¶3: Feds. changing ideals
  - **Context:** war with Britain, impact on Feds.
  - Hartford Convention (Doc. 5): shift from strong fed.

- Body ¶4: new parties, new issues
  - **Add'l Evidence:** Era of Good Feelings
  - Democrats & Whigs issues: bank, power of president, internal improvements
  - Jackson cartoon (Doc. 7) (**sourcing 2**)

- Body ¶5: continuity: devotion to Constitution
  - (Doc. 3) "same principle"
  - (Docs. 1 & 2) interpretations of Const.
  - (Doc. 6) Jackson claim bank unconst. (**sourcing 3**)

- ¶conclusion: parties shifted in ideologies, new parties based on events, still devoted to Const.

Step 3: Action! Write Your Response

Use your plan to write out your response—if you've taken the time to plan effectively, everything you write should support your thesis.

Step 4: Proofread

Leave a minute at the end to complete a brisk proofread and double-check that you met each of the DBQ requirements.

Sample High-Scoring Response

American political parties experienced major changes through 1833, changing their interpretations of their ideals as they faced the realities of governance and even forming new political parties as concerns evolved over time. Still, all the parties remained rooted in their devotion to the principles of the Constitution.

The first two parties emerged from disagreements about forming a Bank of the United States. Secretary of the Treasury Alexander Hamilton developed a loose construction view of the Constitution, using the implied powers of the federal government in the Constitution to justify his support for a bank (Document 1). Secretary of State Thomas Jefferson argued for a strict construction view, opposing the Bank since it was not explicitly permitted by the Constitution and, he claimed, therefore unconstitutional (Document 2). These philosophies became the foundation of the first two political parties. Hamilton led the Federalists, who championed a strong federal government. Jefferson and James Madison led the Democratic-Republicans, who believed power rested with the states.

However, over time it became clear that the unwavering views of the two political parties needed to moderate if the country were to grow. Jefferson made the first step toward moderation of his political philosophy and reconciliation with the Federalists in his First Inaugural Address (Document 3), stating "We are all Republicans, we are all Federalists." As the newly elected president, perhaps Jefferson felt required to placate his political opponents and didn't fully believe this sentiment, but his time in office would prove that more moderate views were politically expedient. Jefferson and his party had to further adjust their ideals when the opportunity to purchase the Louisiana Territory from France arose in 1803 (Document 4). There was no provision in the Constitution for a president to buy more territory. However, Jefferson moderated his own strict construction views and made the purchase. Later, when American shipping was disrupted during the Napoleonic Wars, Jefferson again showed a shift from his original pro-state view and took the strong federal action of supporting the Embargo Act.

The Federalists also modified their views after war broke out with Great Britain. The Federalists, many of whom were merchants negatively impacted by the war's impact on trade, protested America's involvement. Federalists formulated a set of demands in Hartford, Connecticut (Document 5). By proposing that some government actions require a full two-thirds approval of the states, they were essentially challenging the authority of the federal government and seeking a way for their minority party to gain a greater say in decisions. Thus, the party that had favored a strong central government had now adopted an opposite view based on their circumstances. Both the initial parties changed their ideals when faced with events while governing.

As time went on, new parties emerged that were centered around the new concerns of their times. During the one-party Era of Good Feelings, the Federalist Party essentially ceased to exist, showing that political parties can disappear if their particular focuses are no longer relevant. The Democratic-Republican Party eventually split into two new parties: the Democrats and the Whigs. Although the National Bank was still a divisive issue, these new parties now focused on the issues of the power of the presidency and the role of the national government in modernization. The political cartoon in Document 7, created by a member of the Whigs, demonstrates the Whig view of opposing a strong executive by depicting the Democrat Jackson as a king who literally is trampling the Constitution under his feet. The intent of the cartoon is to mock Jackson as acting more like a king than a president by his excessive use of the veto. That a major facet of the Whig party was its opposing a particular president demonstrates the tendency of early political parties to form and dissolve as issues changed over time.

Despite the changes, all the early parties remained devoted to the principles of the Constitution. As Jefferson indicates in his address (Document 3), the parties have "different names" but are "brethren of the same principle"—the republican form of their government. Likewise, the debates between Federalists and Democratic-Republicans often hinged on how to interpret the Constitution, as shown in both Hamilton's and Jefferson's explanations of the Constitution in Documents 1 and 2. Later, Jackson also based his decision in Document 6 with "solemn regard to the principles of the Constitution." While it is possible that Jackson was merely appealing to the Constitution as an excuse to veto the bank, which he was known to dislike, his words at least show the importance of appearing to honor constitutional principles across party lines.

American political parties developed soon after the Constitution took effect and went through shifts in ideologies and concerns over time. Sometimes changing their views based on what was politically expedient, early parties came in and out of existence based on their particular focuses and current events. Still, their devotion to constitutional principles showed their faith in the new form of government and ensured that the new government would endure and adapt, even when facing political disagreement.

Scoring for Sample Question: 7 points (1 + 1 + 3 + 2)

Category	Scoring Criteria	Notes
Thesis/Claim (0–1 points)	Historically defensible thesis/claim with a logical line of reasoning. The response must make a thesis or claim without restating the prompt itself. The thesis must consist of one or more sentences located in one place, either in the introduction or the conclusion.	A strong thesis should make a claim about changes in political parties by articulating an argument and may identify the categories of analysis that will be used in the essay. The thesis is the last two sentences of the first paragraph. The writer of the sample response claims that political parties changed in two major ways, which establishes the essay's categories of analysis: changing ideals and forming new parties. The writer establishes a complex argument (see Analysis & Reasoning below) by claiming parties experienced both change *and* continuity.

Category	Scoring Criteria	Notes
Contextual-ization (0–1 points)	Broader historical context related to the prompt. The response must connect the topic to historical developments, events, or processes; these can occur before, during, or after the time frame of the prompt itself.	Contextualization for this prompt should explain, not merely mention, broader factors related to changes to political parties. The writer of the sample response does not just briefly mention another event, but rather in the third and fourth paragraphs provides context for Document 5 by describing the impact of the Napoleonic Wars and conflict with Britain.
Evidence (0–3 points)	Use of evidence to support the thesis. The response must utilize the content from at least *three* documents to address the *topic* of the prompt. (1 point) OR The response must use at least *six* documents to support an *argument* based on the prompt. (2 points)	Evidence from the documents must be paraphrased, not merely quoted. The writer of the sample response specifically relates the content of seven documents to the claims about political parties changing ideals, new parties forming, and parties remaining loyal to the Constitution.
	The response must use at least *one* additional piece of historical evidence, beyond what is found in the documents, to support an argument. This additional evidence must be different from what was used for contextualization. (1 point)	The writer offers evidence beyond the documents to support the thesis by using the Embargo Act in the fourth paragraph as evidence of Jefferson acting contrary to his original Democratic-Republican political philosophy, and the Era of Good Feelings in the fifth paragraph as evidence of parties disappearing and emerging over time.

Category	Scoring Criteria	Notes
Analysis and Reasoning (0–2 points)	Complexity of understanding and reasoning. The response must explain, for at least *three* of the documents, how or why the document's purpose, historical basis, point of view, and/or audience are relevant to an argument. (1 point)	Factors' relevance to the argument about changes to political parties should be explained, not just identified. The writer of the sample response uses the role of the viewpoint of Document 3 to qualify the argument about parties changing views over time and the role of the viewpoint of Document 6 to qualify the claim about parties remaining devoted to the Constitution. The writer relates the role of the purpose of Document 7 to the claim that new parties focused on new issues.
	The response must show a complex understanding of the content of the prompt, using evidence to support, qualify, or modify an argument about the prompt. (1 point)	A complex understanding should be incorporated into the overall argument about changes to political parties. The writer of the sample response develops an argument that analyzes both changes *and* continuities by using evidence from the documents in paragraph six to explain how parties over time remained devoted to the Constitution.

LONG ESSAY QUESTION

Overview

The second part of Section II of the AP exam contains three long essay questions—you must respond to one. The long essay question assesses your ability to apply knowledge of history in a complex, analytical manner. In other words, you are expected to treat history and historical questions as a historian would. This process is called historiography—the skills and strategies historians use to analyze and interpret historical evidence to reach a conclusion. Thus, when writing an effective essay, you must be able to write a strong, clearly developed thesis and supply a substantial amount of relevant evidence to support your thesis and develop a complex argument.

The College Board's characteristics of a high-scoring long essay question response are listed below. Note that the requirements are very similar to those of the DBQ; the primary difference is that any requirements related to use of the documents are removed from the scoring requirements for the long essay question.

- **Thesis:** Make a thesis or claim that responds to the prompt. The thesis or claim must be historically defensible and establish a line of reasoning.

- **Context:** Provide context relevant to the prompt by describing a broader historical development or process.

- **Evidence:** Use specific and relevant examples as evidence to support an argument in response to the prompt.

- **Historical Skill:** Use a historical reasoning skill (causation, comparison, or continuity and change) to develop an argument in response to the prompt.

- **Complex Understanding:** Demonstrate a complex understanding of an argument that responds to the prompt by using evidence to corroborate, qualify, or modify the argument.

Strategy

The long essay question may be the most abstract prompt you encounter on the free-response section. It is therefore extra important to use the Kaplan Method in order to organize your ideas and logically think through your response. You must select one of the three long essay questions. While each question focuses on the same reasoning process (for instance, all three questions may test causation), the historical developments and processes tested will be from different time periods: question 2 will focus on the years 1491–1800, question 3 will focus on the years 1800–1898, and question 4 will focus on the years 1890–2001. Choose the option that will best showcase your ability to construct a historically defensible thesis and provide specific, relevant evidence.

As with every free-response question, follow the 4-Step Kaplan Method (AP-AP). Consider the following special strategies for the long essay question. Scoring requirements are highlighted in bold.

During Step 1: Analyze the Prompt:

- Each long essay question will ask you to "evaluate the extent" of some factor in American history. Since you are evaluating, you will need to develop an argument that addresses the prompt. Make sure to read all three prompts carefully. Think of the evidence you could use and the argument you could develop in response to each one, then choose the question you feel most confident about.

- Begin crafting your **thesis** statement. You must have a thesis that makes a claim and introduces the reasoning of your argument. It is not enough to merely restate the question as your thesis; you must take a position. Don't be afraid of making a strong claim; just be sure you can provide relevant evidence to support your assertion. Your thesis may also outline the categories of analysis, or the major points, you will use in your essay.

- Part of developing your thesis should be considering how your essay's argument will demonstrate a **complex understanding**, perhaps by analyzing multiple variables, by considering both changes and continuities, or by making an insightful connection to another time period. See the DBQ section of this chapter for a complete list of ways to demonstrate complex understanding.

During Step 2: Plan Your Response:

- Make short notes that outline each paragraph of your essay, including the points you will make and the evidence you will use to support your points.

- The first paragraph of your essay will likely contain your thesis statement; the thesis may also appear in the conclusion, but placing it in the introduction will make it easier for your readers to follow your essay.

- Consider how you will provide **context** for the essay topic. The context you provide must be more detailed than a brief reference, and should situate the topic of the prompt in relation to developments before, during, or after the time period from the prompt. The introduction paragraph or first body paragraph may be good places to include contextualization.

- In general, each body paragraph should address one point you are making in support of your thesis or one category of evidence you are providing in support of your thesis. Jot down the **evidence** you will include in each body paragraph. To earn the maximum points for use of evidence, you must use examples that support your overall argument—merely listing relevant examples but not explaining how they support your claim will only earn 1 instead of 2 possible points for evidence.

- Confirm that your plan addresses all the essay requirements before moving into the writing step.

During Step 3: Action! Write Your Response:

- There is no "standard" number of paragraphs you must have. You will not be penalized for writing a strong four-paragraph response. Likewise, you will not be rewarded for constructing a weak six-paragraph response. AP readers look for quality, not quantity.

- The first paragraph of your essay should include your thesis and any other organizational cues you can give your reader. There is no need to spend time creating a "hook" or flashy statement for your first sentence or using rhetorical questions. AP graders are reading for the items that are listed on the scoring guide. You will notice that creativity in language and structure is not a listed item, while a well-written and developed argument is.

- Your body paragraphs should follow the "road map" you set in your introduction and thesis. Don't stray from your plan, or you will find yourself straying from the prompt. You have taken the time to make a plan, so follow it! Do not merely list facts and events in a "laundry list" fashion. You must have some element of analysis between each set of evidence you provide. Using transition words, such as *however*, *therefore*, and *thus*, to show shifts in thought can make creating analytical sentences quick and easy. You should practice stringing facts and thoughts together using these "qualifying transitions" in your sentences.

- Beware of telling a story rather than answering the question. Readers are looking for analysis, not a revised version of your textbook. Do not attempt to shower the reader with extra factoids and showy language; focus on developing a well-crafted argument.

- Because this is a formal essay, you should avoid using personal pronouns, such as *you*, *I*, or *we*, and slang words. Because your essay is about history, write your essay in the past tense.

- You should end each body paragraph with a "mini-conclusion" that ties the paragraph back to the thesis. It can serve as a transition sentence into the next paragraph or stand alone. In either case, the reader should be able to tell easily that you are shifting gears into another part of the essay.

- Lastly, write your conclusion. Restate your thesis, but in a new way. Instead of rewriting your thesis word for word, explain why your thesis is significant to the question. Do not introduce new evidence in your conclusion. The conclusion should tie all of the "mini-conclusion" sentences together and leave the reader with a sense of completion. If you are running out of time when you reach the conclusion, you may leave it off without incurring a specific penalty. However, the conclusion can help solidify your entire argument in the minds of your readers, so practice writing timed essays so you can learn the proper timing it takes to write a complete essay (conclusion included).

During Step 4: Proofread:

- Neatly correct any obvious errors.

Sample Question

Evaluate the extent to which the migration of European colonists and the resulting encounters with American Indians affected social patterns in the period from 1495 to 1650.

Step 1: Analyze the Prompt

On the actual exam, you will read three questions and determine which you can answer most confidently. Paraphrase the tasks in your own words to be sure you understand what each requires. For this sample question, note that you will be evaluating how the interactions between Europeans and American Indians impacted societies.

As you choose which question you will answer, begin thinking about what your thesis will entail and how your essay will demonstrate a complex understanding. The notes of a sample high-scoring writer are below.

Thesis (with complex understanding): Spanish, French, and British each used territory differently; result: distinct social patterns

This writer claims that three different countries' approaches to settling territories resulted in different types of social development, but other types of thesis claims are possible. For instance, the thesis could make a single claim about overall social patterns (such as "Europeans' economic goals in the New World and their attitudes of superiority over American Indians resulted in exploitative and hierarchical social structures") or focus on only one or two European nations.

Also begin to consider how you will demonstrate a complex understanding of the material. Since this writer will analyze how three nations' approaches led to different types of social development, the essay will demonstrate a complex understanding by analyzing multiple variables.

Step 2: Plan Your Response

Next, take time to plan your response. Check your plan against the long essay question requirements. See the sample plan that a high-scoring writer might make; scoring requirements are written in bold for reference.

- ¶ intro
  - **Context:** motives for European exploration: new technology, navigation techniques, and trade routes
  - **Thesis** (with **complex understanding**): Spanish, French, and British each used territory differently; result: distinct social patterns

- Body ¶1: Spain
  - goals: wealth and spread Catholicism
  - methods: mining, large-scale agriculture, encomienda, disease/weapons, missions
  - results: forced assimilation, social structure

- Body ¶2: France
  - goal: fur trade
  - method: mutually profitable trade relationships
  - result: alliances

- Body ¶3: Britain
  - goals: permanent settlements, Jamestown, religious freedom (New England)
  - methods: occupying more land for farming, smallpox, Metacom's War
  - results: deaths of indigenous populations
- ¶ conclusion: where Europeans sought permanent settlements or forced labor, resulted in American Indian population decline, upheaval, and threats to tradition

Step 3: Action! Write Your Response & Step 4: Proofread

Use your plan to write each part of the response, and briskly skim for errors when finished.

See the following high-scoring response, and be sure to read the rubric to help you identify what makes this response effective. Think about what features you can incorporate into your own free-response answers.

Sample High-Scoring Response

In the fifteenth and sixteenth centuries, European nations began to claim different regions in the New World. Using new sea technologies such as the astrolabe and improved navigation techniques, Europeans sought new trade routes to the Indian Ocean and Asia. Sailing west and finding new continents instead, the Europeans soon realized the economic potential of the Americas. The Spanish, French, and British each took a unique approach to how they utilized the New World territories in which they settled, resulting in distinct and profound patterns of social development.

The Spanish had two major goals: to gain wealth and to spread Catholicism to the native populations. Realizing the potential to mine precious metals and profit from large-scale agriculture, the Spanish forced American Indians into labor, such as through the encomienda system. Violence and deception were often used to subdue the indigenous populations, aided by the technological superiority of European weapons and the spread of devastating diseases. Although some Spanish came as missionaries with the goal of converting American Indians to Christianity and often protested the abusive treatment of the American Indians, even missions sometimes essentially forced labor and coerced assimilation to Spanish culture. In the long term, a hierarchical social structure developed in the Spanish colonies in which the Spanish-born and their descendants (peninsulares and creoles) dominated those of mixed background (mestizos and mulattos) and especially those of pure African or American Indian heritage. Overall, millions perished between disease and mistreatment, devastatingly weakening traditional cultures but enriching the Spanish.

The French differed from the Spanish in their relationship with the indigenous populations. Using the St. Lawrence River for transportation and trade, the French profited from trading fur pelts, particularly beaver, with the American Indians, and then sending the pelts to Europe. These traders profited from the knowledge and goods of the American Indian populations who lived there, and certainly desired to develop mutually profitable relationships with them. Overall, this more cooperative relationship helped preserve American Indian cultures and led to alliances between the French and different American Indian nations. These alliances benefited the French in later wars with the British.

The British were more interested in establishing permanent communities in North America. Jamestown, Britain's first successful settlement, was economically based. The relationship with the American Indians turned hostile as the number of British settlers increased and they sought to occupy more land for tobacco production. In New England, many of the settlers were Pilgrims or Puritans seeking free expression of their religious beliefs. Here, the British also disrupted American Indian societies and established a relationship of hostility between the groups as the British not only encroached on the native people's land for farming but they also began to spread smallpox, killing a large percentage of the indigenous populations.

Large-scale conflicts broke out; many British and American Indian villages were destroyed during Metacom's War, but it was the American Indian tribes who were largely displaced or eliminated. The British, like the Spanish, resorted to violence to secure their own economic ends and irrevocably disrupted American Indian societies as a result.

Overall, where Europeans sought permanent settlements or economic gain at the expense of the forced labor of others, American Indian societies experienced population decline, upheaval, and ultimately, threats to their traditional lands and traditions.

Scoring for Sample Question: 6 Points (1 + 1 + 2 + 2)

Category	Scoring Criteria	Notes
Thesis/Claim (0-1 points)	Historically defensible thesis/claim with a logical line of reasoning. The response must make a thesis or claim without restating the prompt itself. The thesis must consist of one or more sentences located in one place, either in the introduction or the conclusion.	A strong thesis should make a claim about how the interactions between Europeans and American Indians impacted social patterns by articulating an argument and may identify the categories of analysis that will be used in the essay. The thesis is the last sentence of the first paragraph. The writer of the sample response claims that the different approaches to settlement of European countries led to different types of social development. The thesis also establishes the categories of analysis: the methods and subsequent social developments of the Spanish, French, and British. The writer adds complexity to the argument by addressing how multiple variables—the three approaches to colonization—resulted in different social developments.
Contextualization (0–1 points)	Broader historical context related to the prompt. The response must connect the topic to historical developments, events, or processes; these can occur before, during, or after the time frame of the prompt itself.	Contextualization for this prompt should explain, not merely mention, broader factors relevant to exploration, colonization, or American Indian societies. The writer of the sample response does not just briefly mention another historical development, but rather in the first paragraph situates the colonization of the Americas by describing factors that motivated or enabled European overseas exploration.

Category	Scoring Criteria	Notes
Evidence (0–2 points)	Use of evidence to support the thesis. The response identifies specific examples *relevant to the topic* of the prompt. (1 point) OR The response uses examples to *support an argument* about the prompt. (2 points)	To earn 2 points, the evidence must be used to support an argument about ways in which the interactions between Europeans and American Indians impacted social patterns. The writer of the sample response uses specific historical examples to support each part of the thesis. For instance, in the second paragraph the writer explains how the Spanish practices of using forced labor and spreading their religion resulted in American Indian societies facing forced acculturation and a Spanish-dominated social structure.
Analysis and Reasoning (0–2 points)	Complexity of understanding and reasoning. The response shows historical reasoning to make an argument about the prompt. (1 point) AND The response demonstrates complex understanding, using evidence to support, qualify, or modify an argument about the prompt. (1 point)	Comparison, causation, or continuity and change over time should be incorporated into the overall argument about the ways in which the interactions between Europeans and American Indians impacted social patterns. The writer of the sample response explains how European colonization practices impacted American Indian societies (causation). AND A complex understanding should be incorporated into the overall argument about the ways in which the interactions between Europeans and American Indians impacted social patterns. The writer of the sample response develops an argument that addresses multiple variables by analyzing how each of three different approaches to colonization led to different social results for American Indians.

In this chapter, you've learned about the structure of the free-response sections and the steps to crafting successful responses. To maximize your scoring potential, you'll need to apply what you learned. Practice by responding to the FRQs in the practice exams. You can do this as part of taking a full-length exam, or you can practice an FRQ on its own. Make sure to evaluate your writing using the scoring information provided and to carefully consider whether you met each requirement. If possible, ask someone else to help you fairly assess your work. Then, reflect on which successful qualities you displayed in your responses, as well as which qualities you want to keep working on in your exam prep.

PART 4

Practice Exams

HOW TO TAKE THE PRACTICE EXAMS

The next section of this book consists of three full-length practice exams. Taking a practice AP exam gives you an idea of what it's like to answer AP questions under conditions that approximate those of the real exam. You'll find out which areas you're strong in and where additional review may be required. Any mistakes you make now are ones you won't make on the actual exam, as long as you take the time to learn where you went wrong.

Our three full-length practice exams each include 55 multiple-choice questions, three short-answer questions (including your choice of two prompts for the third question), one document-based question, and one long essay question (your choice from three prompts). You will have 55 minutes for the multiple-choice questions, 40 minutes for the short-answer questions, 60 minutes for the document-based question, and 40 minutes for the long essay question. Before taking a practice exam, find a quiet place where you can work uninterrupted, and bring blank lined paper for the free-response questions. (The proctor will provide lined paper when you take the official exam.) Time yourself according to the time limit given at the beginning of each section. It's okay to take a short break between sections, but for the most accurate results, you should approximate real test conditions as much as possible.

As you take the practice exams, remember to pace yourself. Train yourself to be aware of the time you are spending on each problem. Try to be aware of the general types of questions you encounter, as well as being alert to certain strategies or approaches that help you to handle the various question types more effectively.

After taking each practice exam, complete the following steps.

1. Self-score your multiple-choice section using the answer key immediately following each exam.

2. Read the answers and explanations following each exam. These detailed explanations will help you identify areas that could use additional study. Even when you have answered a question correctly, you can learn additional information by looking at the explanation.

3. Self-score your free-response questions using the rubrics in the answers and explanations section.

4. Navigate to the scoring section of your online resources (kaptest.com/moreonline) to input all of these raw scores and see what your overall score would be with a similar performance on Test Day.

Finally, it's important to approach the exam with the right attitude. You're going to get a great score because you've reviewed the material and learned the strategies in this book.

Good luck!

Practice Exam 1

Practice Exam 1 Answer Grid

1. Ⓐ Ⓑ Ⓒ Ⓓ
2. Ⓐ Ⓑ Ⓒ Ⓓ
3. Ⓐ Ⓑ Ⓒ Ⓓ
4. Ⓐ Ⓑ Ⓒ Ⓓ
5. Ⓐ Ⓑ Ⓒ Ⓓ
6. Ⓐ Ⓑ Ⓒ Ⓓ
7. Ⓐ Ⓑ Ⓒ Ⓓ
8. Ⓐ Ⓑ Ⓒ Ⓓ
9. Ⓐ Ⓑ Ⓒ Ⓓ
10. Ⓐ Ⓑ Ⓒ Ⓓ
11. Ⓐ Ⓑ Ⓒ Ⓓ
12. Ⓐ Ⓑ Ⓒ Ⓓ
13. Ⓐ Ⓑ Ⓒ Ⓓ
14. Ⓐ Ⓑ Ⓒ Ⓓ

15. Ⓐ Ⓑ Ⓒ Ⓓ
16. Ⓐ Ⓑ Ⓒ Ⓓ
17. Ⓐ Ⓑ Ⓒ Ⓓ
18. Ⓐ Ⓑ Ⓒ Ⓓ
19. Ⓐ Ⓑ Ⓒ Ⓓ
20. Ⓐ Ⓑ Ⓒ Ⓓ
21. Ⓐ Ⓑ Ⓒ Ⓓ
22. Ⓐ Ⓑ Ⓒ Ⓓ
23. Ⓐ Ⓑ Ⓒ Ⓓ
24. Ⓐ Ⓑ Ⓒ Ⓓ
25. Ⓐ Ⓑ Ⓒ Ⓓ
26. Ⓐ Ⓑ Ⓒ Ⓓ
27. Ⓐ Ⓑ Ⓒ Ⓓ
28. Ⓐ Ⓑ Ⓒ Ⓓ

29. Ⓐ Ⓑ Ⓒ Ⓓ
30. Ⓐ Ⓑ Ⓒ Ⓓ
31. Ⓐ Ⓑ Ⓒ Ⓓ
32. Ⓐ Ⓑ Ⓒ Ⓓ
33. Ⓐ Ⓑ Ⓒ Ⓓ
34. Ⓐ Ⓑ Ⓒ Ⓓ
35. Ⓐ Ⓑ Ⓒ Ⓓ
36. Ⓐ Ⓑ Ⓒ Ⓓ
37. Ⓐ Ⓑ Ⓒ Ⓓ
38. Ⓐ Ⓑ Ⓒ Ⓓ
39. Ⓐ Ⓑ Ⓒ Ⓓ
40. Ⓐ Ⓑ Ⓒ Ⓓ
41. Ⓐ Ⓑ Ⓒ Ⓓ
42. Ⓐ Ⓑ Ⓒ Ⓓ

43. Ⓐ Ⓑ Ⓒ Ⓓ
44. Ⓐ Ⓑ Ⓒ Ⓓ
45. Ⓐ Ⓑ Ⓒ Ⓓ
46. Ⓐ Ⓑ Ⓒ Ⓓ
47. Ⓐ Ⓑ Ⓒ Ⓓ
48. Ⓐ Ⓑ Ⓒ Ⓓ
49. Ⓐ Ⓑ Ⓒ Ⓓ
50. Ⓐ Ⓑ Ⓒ Ⓓ
51. Ⓐ Ⓑ Ⓒ Ⓓ
52. Ⓐ Ⓑ Ⓒ Ⓓ
53. Ⓐ Ⓑ Ⓒ Ⓓ
54. Ⓐ Ⓑ Ⓒ Ⓓ
55. Ⓐ Ⓑ Ⓒ Ⓓ

SECTION I, PART A
Time—55 minutes
55 Questions

Directions: Section I, Part A of this exam contains 55 multiple-choice questions, organized into sets with corresponding historical sources. Each of the questions or incomplete statements is followed by four suggested answers or completions. Using both the provided sources and your own historical knowledge, select the best answer choice.

Questions 1 and 2 refer to the excerpt below.

"The pueblo communities were now to rid themselves for a time of their Spanish masters, whom they regarded as tyrants. Past efforts to shake off their fetters had only shown how tightly they were riveted. They were required to render implicit obedience, and to pay heavy tribute of pueblo products and personal service. . . . The Spaniards in their later gathering of testimony ignored this element of secular oppression, if, as can hardly be doubted, it existed, and represented the [Pueblo Revolt of 1680] to be founded exclusively, as it was indeed largely, on religious grounds."

Hubert Howe Bancroft, *History of Arizona and New Mexico 1530–1888*, 1889

1. Which of the following contributed most directly to the success of the revolt described in the excerpt?

(A) The diversion of soldiers to fight Iroquois raiders along the border left Spanish authorities unable to suppress an internal uprising.

(B) The widespread famine resulting from flooding in the 1670s generated unrest among the Puebloan population.

(C) The violent and intense competition among various tribes in New Mexico over resources drastically decreased.

(D) The alliance between various Pueblo settlements allowed for a united front against the Spanish colonists.

2. Which of the following later developments had an effect most similar to the conflict described in the excerpt?

(A) The Civil Rights Movement in the 1950s and 1960s

(B) Nat Turner's Rebellion in 1831

(C) The Northwest Indian War in the 1780s and 1790s

(D) Pontiac's Rebellion in the 1760s

GO ON TO THE NEXT PAGE

Questions 3–5 refer to the excerpt below.

"Because no people can be truly happy, though under the greatest enjoyment of civil liberties, if abridged of the freedom of their consciences as to their religious professions and worship; . . . I do hereby grant and declare that no person or persons inhabiting in this province or territories, who shall confess and acknowledge one Almighty God to be the creator, upholder, and ruler of the world, and who professes him or herself to be obliged in conscience to live peaceably and quietly under the civil government, shall in any way be molested or prejudiced for his or her conscientious persuasion or practice. Nor shall her or she be compelled at any time to frequent or maintain any religious worship place or ministry contrary to his or her mind . . ."

William Penn, Pennsylvania Charter of Privileges, 1701

3. What departure from the other colonies in British North America is described in this excerpt?

   (A) Pennsylvania did not have one established faith.

   (B) Settlers in Pennsylvania were required to attend church services.

   (C) Pennsylvania was the first to support religious tolerance for multiple Christian denominations.

   (D) Puritan ideas were banned from the Pennsylvania colony.

4. Which of the following is most similar to the ideas expressed in the excerpt?

   (A) John Locke's influence on the Enlightenment

   (B) The Pilgrims' theological beliefs in founding Plymouth

   (C) John Winthrop's ideal of the "city upon a hill"

   (D) The rights granted in the Maryland Act of Toleration

5. Which of the following documents expressed sentiments most similar to the excerpt?

   (A) The Declaration of Independence

   (B) The South Carolina Exposition and Protest

   (C) The Bill of Rights

   (D) The Alien and Sedition Acts

GO ON TO THE NEXT PAGE

Questions 6–8 refer to the excerpt below.

"With the [cotton gin], a single operator could clean as much cotton in a few hours as a group of workers had once needed a whole day to do . . . Soon cotton growing spread into the upland South and beyond, within a decade the total crop increased eightfold . . . The cotton gin not only changed the economy of the South, it also helped transform the North. The large supply of domestically produced fiber was a strong incentive to entrepreneurs in New England and elsewhere to develop an American textile industry."

Alan Brinkley, *American History: Connecting with the Past*, 2014

6. Based on this analysis, which of the following best describes the political and economic developments of the North and the South in the late eighteenth and early nineteenth centuries?

    (A) The North and the South cooperated politically and economically to develop a successful textile industry.

    (B) Both the North and the South depended upon legislation supporting slavery.

    (C) The North and the South further separated because of rapid industrialization in the North and heavy dependence on agriculture in the South.

    (D) As the South began to develop industrially, it became politically and economically independent of the North.

7. The cotton gin's impact on society is analogous to the impact of all of the following innovations EXCEPT

    (A) the assembly line

    (B) the telegraph

    (C) the sewing machine

    (D) the application of steam power to factories

8. Which of the following was a direct effect of the invention of the cotton gin?

    (A) The invention of the steel plow

    (B) The spread of the plantation system into Northern states

    (C) The development of the Lowell factory system in New England

    (D) The introduction of the factory system in the South

GO ON TO THE NEXT PAGE

Questions 9–12 refer to the map below.

The map depicts Thomas Jefferson's Land Ordinance of 1784.

9. Based on the ideas outlined in this map, Thomas Jefferson intended which of the following?

   (A) Western territories should be evenly divided into free and slave states.

   (B) The United States should create states in the western territories on an equal level with the original Thirteen Colonies.

   (C) Western territories should be sold off in 14 lots to pay off the national debt.

   (D) The United States should purchase New Orleans as an outlet to the sea for the new western territories.

10. Which of the following events prompted American migration into the western territories in the pre-revolutionary years?

    (A) The Proclamation of 1763

    (B) The English victory in The Seven Years' War

    (C) The authorization of writs of assistance

    (D) The passage of the Declaratory Act

11. As Americans began to migrate west of the Appalachian Mountains in the late eighteenth century, which of the following became the settlers' most significant issue?

    (A) The tenuous balance of free and slave states

    (B) The development of industrialization

    (C) The desire for free navigation of the Mississippi River

    (D) The new states' status compared to the original states

12. As the United States grew westward, which of the following was the most significant departure from previous government policies toward American Indians?

    (A) The Treaty of Greenville of 1795

    (B) The Trail of Tears

    (C) The Indian Appropriations Act of 1851

    (D) The Dawes Severalty Act of 1887

GO ON TO THE NEXT PAGE →

Questions 13–16 refer to the excerpt below.

"We owe it, therefore, to candor and to the amicable relations existing between the United States and those powers to declare that we should consider any attempt on their part to extend their system to any portion of this hemisphere as dangerous to our peace and safety. With the existing colonies or dependencies of any European power we have not interfered, and shall not interfere. But with the Governments who have declared their independence, and maintain it, and whose independence we have, on great consideration and on just principles, acknowledged, we could not view any interposition for the purpose of oppressing them, or controlling in any other manner their destiny, by any European power in any other light than as the manifestation of an unfriendly disposition toward the United States."

James Monroe, "Monroe Doctrine" speech, 1823

13. Based on the excerpt, which of the following best describes the change in American foreign policy in 1823?

    (A) An increased involvement in Europe and the extension of the American system into European nations

    (B) An objective to protect the Western Hemisphere against European interference deemed unfriendly toward the United States

    (C) An intention to end European colonialism in the Western Hemisphere

    (D) An intention to overtake and rule nations in the Western Hemisphere previously colonized by European nations

14. The ideals in the Monroe Doctrine augmented the ideals in which of the following previously established American policies?

    (A) The concept of "free trade" in Jay's Treaty

    (B) The provision of "right of deposit" in Pinckney's Treaty

    (C) The idea of "no entangling alliances" in George Washington's Farewell Address

    (D) The acquisition of territory per the Greenville Treaty

15. The United States maintained the foreign policy outlined in the Monroe Doctrine until

    (A) the Mexican-American War

    (B) the Union attempted to keep Britain and France out of the Civil War

    (C) the Spanish-American War

    (D) American participation in World War I

16. The establishment of the Monroe Doctrine was a reaction to

    (A) the outcome of the War of 1812

    (B) attempts by European powers to reclaim Spanish colonies in the Western Hemisphere

    (C) the unsettled results of the Napoleonic Wars in Europe

    (D) European economic encroachment in the Western Hemisphere

GO ON TO THE NEXT PAGE

Questions 17–19 refer to the excerpt below.

"I thank you, Dear Sir, for the copy you have been so kind as to send me of the letter to your constituents on the Missouri question . . . But this momentous question, like a fire bell in the night, awakened and filled me with terror. I considered it at once as the knell of the Union. It is hushed indeed for the moment. But this is a reprieve only, not a final sentence. A geographical line, coinciding with a marked principle, moral and political, once conceived and held up to the angry passions of men, will never be obliterated; and every new irritation will mark it deeper and deeper."

Thomas Jefferson, letter to John Holmes, 1820

17. In the excerpt above, Thomas Jefferson warned about

    (A) the protective tariff

    (B) the need for a geographical line to divide the entire nation

    (C) the economic panic that began in 1819

    (D) the divisive issue of slavery

18. Which event exemplified Thomas Jefferson's fear as described in the excerpt?

    (A) the South Carolina Exposition and Protest

    (B) the passage of the Indian Removal Act in 1830

    (C) the violence of Bleeding Kansas

    (D) the destruction of the U.S. Bank

19. Which of the following best describes why Congress enacted a measure in response to the "Missouri question" in 1820?

    (A) The federal government wanted to maintain the balance of free and slave states.

    (B) Congressmen feared that expansion could worsen the effects of the Panic of 1819.

    (C) The legislative branch was continuing to debate over the protective tariff.

    (D) The federal government feared that expanding west of the Mississippi River would cause the Mexican government to react aggressively.

GO ON TO THE NEXT PAGE

Questions 20–24 refer to the excerpt below.

"Yes, we are the nation of progress, of individual freedom, of universal enfranchisement. Equality of rights is the cynosure of our union of States, the grand exemplar of the correlative equality of individuals; and while truth sheds its effulgence, we cannot retrograde, without dissolving the one and subverting the other. We must onward to the fulfilment of our mission—to the entire development of the principle of our organization—freedom of conscience, freedom of person, freedom of trade and business pursuits, universality of freedom and equality. This is our high destiny, and in nature's eternal, inevitable decree of cause and effect we must accomplish it. All this will be our future history, to establish on earth the moral dignity and salvation of man—the immutable truth and beneficence of God. For this blessed mission to the nations of the world, which are shut out from the life-giving light of truth, has America been chosen; and her high example shall smite unto death the tyranny of kings, hierarchs, and oligarchs, and carry the glad tidings of peace and good will where myriads now endure an existence scarcely more enviable than that of beasts of the field. Who, then, can doubt that our country is destined to be the great nation of futurity?"

John L. O'Sullivan, on Manifest Destiny, 1839

20. Based on the excerpt, what was the purpose of American expansion?

    (A) To promote the ideals of equality and freedom

    (B) To demonstrate American political superiority

    (C) To promote mankind's "only hope" for salvation

    (D) To avoid tyrannical rulers

21. Who of the following would most strongly agree with the sentiments expressed in the excerpt above?

    (A) A male Irish immigrant living in Boston

    (B) A white male squatter from Tennessee

    (C) A female factory worker in New England

    (D) A plantation owner from Georgia

22. The ideals in the excerpt are most similar to the motivations behind

    (A) the annexation of Hawaii

    (B) the takeover of the Philippines after the Spanish-American War

    (C) the acquisition of American Samoa

    (D) the liberation of Cuba from Spanish rule

23. Which of the following events allowed for an almost immediate realization of the goals of Manifest Destiny in the 1840s?

    (A) The Panic of 1837

    (B) The election of war hero Zachary Taylor as president

    (C) The conclusion of the Indian removal policy enacted in the 1830s

    (D) America's victory in the Mexican-American War

24. Which of the following environmental factors further developed the growing division between the North and the South during the antebellum period?

    (A) The discovery of gold in California

    (B) The extensive river systems in the Southwest, which allowed for more internal migration

    (C) The fact that much of the new territory in the Mexican Cession was south of the 36°30' parallel

    (D) The vast western mountains, which enabled the spread of slavery into the southwestern regions

GO ON TO THE NEXT PAGE

Questions 25–27 refer to the excerpt below.

"Resolved, that it is both the part of patriotism and of duty to recognize no political principle other than THE CONSTITUTION OF THE COUNTRY, THE UNION OF THE STATES, AND THE ENFORCEMENT OF THE LAWS, and that, as representatives of the Constitutional Union men of the country . . . we hereby pledge ourselves to maintain, protect, and defend, separately and unitedly, these great principles of public liberty and national safety, against all enemies, at home and abroad; believing that thereby peace may once more be restored to the country; the rights of the People and of the States re-established, and the Government again placed in that condition of justice, fraternity and equality, which, under the example and Constitution of our fathers, has solemnly bound every citizen of the United States to maintain a more perfect union . . ."

Constitutional Union Party Platform, 1860

25. This excerpt addresses which of the following continuing antebellum issues?

   (A) The public debate over slavery

   (B) The failure of compromise

   (C) The debate over the Tariff of 1857

   (D) The split between the Whigs and the Southern Democrats

26. Which of the following was the main reason for the formation of the Constitutional Union Party for the election of 1860?

   (A) To amend the Constitution

   (B) To promote the equality of all citizens

   (C) To avoid secession

   (D) To protect the nation from all enemies

27. The ideas expressed in the Constitutional Union Party platform most directly reflect which of the following?

   (A) Justification for immigration restriction in the 1920s

   (B) The passage of the Progressive Era's amendments to the Constitution

   (C) The Open Door trade policy

   (D) Justification for America's entry into World War I

GO ON TO THE NEXT PAGE

Questions 28 and 29 refer to the image below.

The photograph shows Carey Street in Richmond, Virginia, in 1865

28. The impact of battles in the South, such as the siege of Richmond, affected the outcome of the American Civil War in which of the following ways?

 (A) The destruction of the South's economic infrastructure led to an unconditional surrender following military defeat.

 (B) Angered by the wreckage, the South demanded and won reparations as a condition of surrender.

 (C) Even with the destruction of the South, the Confederate army's access to considerable resources caused the war to last longer than anticipated.

 (D) The Civil War improved the wartime economy because jobs were created to rebuild areas damaged in battle.

29. Which of the following was a strategy in the Union's victory over the South?

 (A) The capture of Richmond, the Confederate capital

 (B) The sea blockade of the South

 (C) The mobilization of free African American soldiers

 (D) The use of formal military training by Union leadership

GO ON TO THE NEXT PAGE

Questions 30–32 refer to the excerpt below.

"The laboring man in this bounteous and hospitable country has no ground for complaint. His vote is potential and he is elevated thereby to the position of man. Elsewhere he is a creature of circumstance, which is that of abject depression. Under the government of this nation, the effort is to elevate the standard of the human race and not to degrade it. In all other nations it is the reverse. What, therefore, has the laborer to complain of in America? By inciting strikes and encouraging discontent, he stands in the way of the elevation of his race and of mankind."

Henry Clews, "The Folly of Organized Labor," 1886

30. Henry Clews's opinion was most likely a reaction to which of the following?

    (A) Rapid industrialization after the Civil War

    (B) Increasing immigration to the United States from Europe

    (C) Lack of work opportunities for Americans in factories

    (D) Incidents such as the Great Railroad Strike of 1877 and the Haymarket Affair

31. Which of the following groups would have most likely supported the sentiments of the previous excerpt?

    (A) The American Federation of Labor

    (B) Opponents of labor unions

    (C) Knights of Labor

    (D) Industrial Workers of the World

32. Which of the following twentieth-century events reflected similar sentiments to the excerpt?

    (A) Creation of the War Labor Board during World War I

    (B) Passage of the Taft-Hartley Act after World War II

    (C) Passage of the Wagner Labor Relations Act of 1935

    (D) Fair Deal proposals regarding labor

GO ON TO THE NEXT PAGE

Questions 33–35 refer to the excerpt below.

"'In our day the market rate determined the price of labor of all sorts, as well as of goods. The employer paid as little as he could, and the worker got as much. It was not a pretty system ethically, I admit; but it did, at least, furnish us a rough-and-ready formula for settling a question which must be settled then thousand times a day if the world was ever going to get forward. There seemed to us no other practical way of doing it.'

'Yes,' replied Dr. Leete, 'it was the only practical way under a system which made the interests of every individual antagonistic to those of every other; but it would have been a pity if humanity could never have devised a better plan, for yours was simply the application to the mutual relations of men of the devil's maxim, Your necessity is my opportunity.'"

Edward Bellamy, the utopian novel *Looking Backward, 2000–1887*, 1888

33. Which of the following best describes the social conditions in the United States when Bellamy wrote the excerpt?

(A) A political desire for economic equality for all

(B) A popular movement for the growth of large unions

(C) An unequal distribution of wealth

(D) A shortage of jobs

34. Which of the following concepts was Bellamy criticizing?

(A) Rapid industrialization

(B) Unlimited immigration

(C) Mechanization of the workplace

(D) Unrestricted capitalism

35. Which of the following groups from the antebellum era espoused ideas most closely resembling those expressed in Bellamy's excerpt?

(A) Utopian communities

(B) Abolitionists

(C) Know-Nothings

(D) Transcendentalists

GO ON TO THE NEXT PAGE

Questions 36–38 refer to the excerpt below.

"I am reminded of that evening in March, four years ago, when I made my first radio report to you. We were then in the midst of the great banking crisis. Soon after, with the authority of the Congress, we asked the Nation to turn over all of its privately held gold, dollar for dollar, to the Government of the United States. Today's recovery proves how right that policy was.

But when, almost two years later, it came before the Supreme Court its constitutionality was upheld only by a five-to-four vote. The change of one vote would have thrown all the affairs of this great Nation back into hopeless chaos. In effect, four Justices ruled that the right under a private contract to exact a pound of flesh was more sacred than the main objectives of the Constitution to establish an enduring Nation. . . .

The Court in addition to the proper use of its judicial functions has improperly set itself up as a third house of the Congress. . . . We have, therefore, reached the point as a nation where we must take action to save the Constitution from the Court and the Court from itself."

Franklin D. Roosevelt, On the Reorganization of the Judiciary, 1937

36. Which of the following motivated Franklin D. Roosevelt's proposal?

   (A) Congress was beginning to question some of the more radical ideas of the New Deal that were introduced in FDR's second term.

   (B) FDR wanted to be able to appoint new Supreme Court justices, because the court had declared some of his key pieces of New Deal legislation unconstitutional.

   (C) The Democratic Party began to react in a negative manner to the radical ideas of the New Deal.

   (D) FDR's second term was not as successful as his first, and he wanted more federal justices to help declare his ideas constitutional.

37. Which of the following groups was generally most loyal to FDR's proposals?

   (A) Liberal Republicans

   (B) Southern farmers

   (C) Union Democrats

   (D) Southern Democrats

38. FDR's relationship with the Supreme Court was similar to which of the following?

   (A) Thomas Jefferson, in reaction to *Marbury v. Madison*

   (B) Andrew Jackson, in reaction to *Worcester v. Georgia*

   (C) Chester Arthur, in reaction to the Civil Rights Cases of 1883

   (D) Grover Cleveland, in reaction to *Plessy v. Ferguson*

GO ON TO THE NEXT PAGE

Questions 39–41 refer to the excerpt below.

"Our psychological and moral perceptions and our ponderous legal machinery had not kept pace with our money-winged, profit-dreaming business development. The industrially strong had been given what they wanted; the industrially weak might keep what they could hold against the subsidized strong. The small investor had a legal remedy, but little real protection. The consumer had less. The competitor had none. As for the worker, male or female, adult or child, skilled or unskilled, he had the right of a freedom of contract, but was not always himself economically free. . . . In 1876 — as now — the American Commonwealths were far behind the leading countries of Europe in laws regulating hours of labor, conditions of work, the prevention of accidents; in laws regulating truck stores, sweatshops, the employment of women, the employment of children."

Walter E. Weyl, economist, *The New Democracy*, 1912

39. Which of the following events best illustrates economist Walter E. Weyl's main argument?

    (A) The development of the theory of Social Darwinism

    (B) The Haymarket Affair

    (C) The domination of the global oil industry by Andrew Carnegie

    (D) The Populist movement

40. Which of the following developments most encouraged monopoly capitalism?

    (A) The assembly line

    (B) The Bessemer process

    (C) The Taylor scientific management system

    (D) Vertical and horizontal integration

41. The government's strongest response to monopoly capitalism was its

    (A) use of the Fifteenth Amendment to encourage further growth of big business

    (B) passage of the Sherman Antitrust Act

    (C) passage of the Clayton Antitrust Act

    (D) ratification of the Hepburn Act

GO ON TO THE NEXT PAGE

Questions 42 and 43 refer to the excerpt below.

"I saw drought devastation in nine states. I talked with families who had lost their wheat crop, lost their corn crop, lost their livestock, lost the water in their well, lost their garden and come through to the end of the summer without one dollar of cash resources, facing a winter without feed or food, facing a planting season without seed to put in the ground. That was the extreme case, but there are thousands and thousands of families on western farms who share the same difficulties. . . .

I shall never forget the fields of wheat so blasted by heat that they cannot be harvested. I shall never forget field after field of corn stunted, earless and stripped of leaves, for what the sun left the grasshoppers took. I saw brown pastures which would not keep a cow on fifty acres."

President Franklin D. Roosevelt, Fireside Chat,
"On Farmers and Laborers," September 1936

42. All of the following resulted from the Dust Bowl in the 1930s EXCEPT

(A) the migration of thousands from drought regions to the West

(B) increased unemployment

(C) the conversion of arid grassland to cultivated cropland

(D) drought conditions for as many as eight years

43. During this time period, many Americans migrated based on which of the following factors?

(A) They were looking for work as the Great Depression gripped their hometowns.

(B) They sought better jobs due to the opportunities created by wartime industry.

(C) They were heading West to take advantage of the New Deal's National Youth Administration program.

(D) Industrial jobs in northern cities attracted impoverished sharecroppers.

GO ON TO THE NEXT PAGE

Questions 44–46 refer to the excerpt below.

"The truth is that the newest immigrants came for many of the same reasons as the old. They typically left countries where populations were growing rapidly and where agricultural and industrial revolutions were shaking people loose from old habit of life—conditions almost identical to those in nineteenth century Europe. And they came to America, as previous immigrants had done, in search of jobs and economic opportunity. Some came with skills and even professional degrees, from India or Taiwan or the former Soviet Union, and they found their way into middle-class jobs. But most came with fewer skills and less education, seeking work as janitors, nannies, farm laborers, lawn cutters, or restaurant workers."

David M. Kennedy and Lizabeth Cohen, *The American Pageant*, 2013

44. Kennedy and Cohen's interpretation of modern immigration can best be described as

    (A) a description of how similar it was to the "old" immigration of the late nineteenth century

    (B) an explanation of how it mirrors Irish immigration in the nineteenth century, as both types of immigration caused a nativist political party to form

    (C) an illustration of many modern immigrants as skilled laborers who usually found work that paid low wages and required little skill

    (D) a recounting of how modern immigrants found little work or opportunity upon arrival

45. Which of the following periods of immigration is most similar to the historical period described in the excerpt?

    (A) The arrival of immigrants following the failed Revolutions of 1848

    (B) The influx of French immigrants during the French Revolution and Napoleonic Wars

    (C) The arrival of Chinese immigrants during the California Gold Rush

    (D) The influx of refugees fleeing the Irish Potato Famine

46. Which of the following groups would have been most likely to oppose Kennedy and Cohen's interpretation of historical immigration?

    (A) The Copperheads

    (B) The Free Soil Party

    (C) The Know-Nothings

    (D) The Progressive Party

GO ON TO THE NEXT PAGE

Questions 47–50 refer to the image below.

"POWER TO THE PEOPLE" (1972)

"Support the Committee to Defend the Panther 21"

47. The image most directly reflects which of the following developments during the late 1960s?

   (A) The widespread mass protests against the Vietnam War

   (B) The uneasy relations between LGBT activists and other left-wing groups

   (C) The radicalization of the Student Nonviolent Coordinating Committee leadership

   (D) The growing hostility among the New Left to the traditional Marxism

48. Which of the following reflects how the Black Power movement's approach differed from previous civil rights strategies?

   (A) The Black Power movement peacefully protested in order to gain credibility and respect among Americans.

   (B) The Black Power movement believed in the principle of integration to gain civil rights.

   (C) The Black Power movement resorted to violence only when provoked.

   (D) The Black Power movement encouraged followers to carry weapons and clash with police.

49. Which of the following most directly led to the rise of the Black Power movement?

   (A) Continued social inequality despite the passage of civil rights legislation in the 1960s

   (B) Jim Crow laws enduring through the end of the 1960s

   (C) The failure of school integration to foster equal opportunity for African Americans

   (D) The disproportionate conscription of African American men to fight in the Vietnam War

50. The Black Panthers' position on equality and civil rights is most similar to

   (A) the work of the suffragists in the nineteenth century

   (B) the concern of progressives over the conditions of tenements in the early twentieth century

   (C) the American Federation of Labor during the late nineteenth century

   (D) the ideas espoused by Malcolm X in his support for the Black Muslim movement

GO ON TO THE NEXT PAGE

Questions 51–55 refer to the photograph below.

The photograph shows a protest against the death sentences of Sacco and Vanzetti, Italian-born American anarchists convicted of murder in 1921

51. The case of Nicola Sacco and Bartolomeo Vanzetti illustrates which of the following debates in U.S. history?

    (A) The injustice of nativism

    (B) The "beyond a reasonable doubt" requirement

    (C) Freedom of the press

    (D) Freedom of speech

52. Which of the following groups at the time would have most likely supported the sentiments shown in the photograph?

    (A) U.S. businessmen

    (B) U.S. lawmakers

    (C) U.S. immigrants

    (D) U.S. soldiers

53. Which amendment most directly provides United States citizens with the ability to engage in the type of protest illustrated in the photograph?

    (A) The Eighth Amendment

    (B) The Fifth Amendment

    (C) The Third Amendment

    (D) The First Amendment

54. Which of the following is a reason the case of Sacco and Vanzetti gained worldwide attention?

    (A) Demonstrators hoped to be arrested to show solidarity with Sacco and Vanzetti.

    (B) American protesters organized demonstrations around the world.

    (C) Demonstrators believed that the courts may have been prejudiced against Sacco and Vanzetti.

    (D) The demonstrations led to changes in the way evidence was gathered.

55. The ideas expressed in the photograph above most directly reflect which of the following continuities in United States history?

    (A) Debates about the judicial system

    (B) Debates about immigration

    (C) Debates about labor practices

    (D) Debates about states' rights

GO ON TO THE NEXT PAGE

END OF SECTION I, PART A

**IF YOU FINISH BEFORE TIME IS CALLED,
YOU MAY CHECK YOUR WORK ON PART A.**

DO NOT GO ON TO PART B UNTIL YOU ARE TOLD TO DO SO.

SECTION I, PART B
Time—40 minutes
3 Questions

Directions: Section I, Part B of this exam consists of short-answer questions. You must respond to Questions 1 *and* 2. For your final response, you must choose to answer Question 3 *or* Question 4. In your responses, be sure to address all parts of the questions, using complete sentences.

"The French and Indian War was the North American conflict in a larger imperial war between Great Britain and France known as the Seven Years' War. The war provided Great Britain enormous territorial gains in North America, but disputes over paying the war's expenses and Britain's authority over the colonies led to colonial discontent, and ultimately to the American Revolution. . . . Unfortunately for the British, the fruits of victory brought seeds of trouble with Great Britain's American colonies. The war had been enormously expensive, and the British government's attempts to impose taxes on colonists to help cover these expenses resulted in increasing colonial resentment of British attempts to expand imperial authority in the colonies. These disputes ultimately spurred colonial rebellion, which eventually developed into a full-scale war for independence."

U.S. Department of State, Office of the Historian, "French and Indian War/Seven Years' War, 1754–63"

"During the negotiations for peace, the French minister for foreign affairs had frankly warned the British envoy that the cession of Canada would lead to the early independence of North America. Unintimidated by the prophecy, England happily persisted. So soon as the sagacious and experienced Vergennes, the French ambassador at Constantinople . . . heard the conditions of the treaty, he said to his friends, and even openly to a British traveller, and afterwards himself recalled his prediction to the notice of the British ministry: "The consequences of the entire cession of Canada are obvious. I am persuaded England will ere long repent of having removed the only check that could keep her colonies in awe. They stand no longer in need of her protection; she [Britain] will call on them [the colonists] to contribute toward supporting the burdens they have helped to bring on her, and they will answer by striking off all dependence."

George Bancroft, historian, *History of the United States of America* (Vol. II), 1886

1. Using the excerpts, answer (a), (b), and (c).

   (a) Briefly describe ONE major difference between the U.S. Department of State's and Bancroft's historical interpretations of colonial discontent with the British.

   (b) Briefly explain how ONE specific historical event or development during the period 1700–1776 that is not explicitly mentioned in the excerpts could be used to support the U.S. Department of State's interpretation.

   (c) Briefly explain how ONE specific historical event or development during the period 1700–1776 that is not explicitly mentioned in the excerpts could be used to support Bancroft's interpretation.

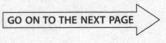
GO ON TO THE NEXT PAGE

Photograph of National Woman's Party picketers outside the White House, 1917

2. Using the image, answer (a), (b), and (c).

   (a) Briefly describe ONE perspective about women's rights expressed in the image.

   (b) Briefly explain ONE specific historical development or circumstance from 1848 to 1917 that led to demonstrations such as the one depicted in the image.

   (c) Briefly explain ONE difference between the women's rights movement in the period 1848–1920 and the women's rights movement in the period 1950–1980.

GO ON TO THE NEXT PAGE

Choose EITHER Question 3 or Question 4.

3. Answer (a), (b), and (c), confining your response to the period 1491 to 1800.

    (a) Briefly describe ONE specific historical similarity between the impact of trade exchanges in the Atlantic economy on Africans and their impact on American Indians.

    (b) Briefly describe ONE specific historical difference between the impact of trade exchanges in the Atlantic economy on Africans and their impact on American Indians.

    (c) Briefly explain ONE specific historical effect of the Atlantic economy on the British colonies in North America.

4. Answer (a), (b), and (c).

    (a) Briefly describe ONE historical similarity between the reform movements of the Progressive Era and the reform movements during the 1960s and 1970s.

    (b) Briefly describe ONE historical difference between the reform movements of the Progressive Era and the reform movements during the 1960s and 1970s.

    (c) Briefly explain ONE specific historical effect of either the reform movements of the Progressive Era or the reform movements during the 1960s and 1970s.

GO ON TO THE NEXT PAGE

END OF SECTION I, PART B

**IF YOU FINISH BEFORE TIME IS CALLED,
YOU MAY CHECK YOUR WORK ON THIS SECTION.**

DO NOT GO ON TO SECTION II UNTIL YOU ARE TOLD TO DO SO.

SECTION II

Time—1 hour 40 minutes

Question 1: Document-Based Question

Suggested reading period: 15 minutes

Suggested writing time: 45 minutes

Directions: Question 1 is based on the following documents. The documents have been adapted for the purposes of this exam.

In your response, you should do the following:

- Make a thesis or claim that responds to the prompt. The thesis or claim must be historically defensible and establish a line of reasoning.

- Provide context relevant to the prompt by describing a broader historical development or process.

- Use at least six of the provided documents to support an argument in response to the prompt.

- Use a historical example not found in the documents as evidence relevant to an argument about the prompt.

- Explain how the context or situation of at least three documents is relevant to an argument. This could address the relevance of the document's point of view, purpose, historical situation, and/or audience.

- Demonstrate a complex understanding of an argument that responds to the prompt by using evidence to corroborate, qualify, or modify the argument.

GO ON TO THE NEXT PAGE

1. Evaluate the extent of change in United States political parties in the period 1791 to 1833.

Document 1

Source: Alexander Hamilton, leader of the Federalist Party, Opinion as to the Constitutionality of the Bank of the United States, 1791.

It is conceded that implied powers are to be considered as delegated equally with express ones. Then it follows, that as a power of erecting a corporation may as well be *implied* as any other thing; it may as well be employed as an *instrument* or mean of carrying into execution any of the specified powers, as any other instrument or mean whatever. The only question must be, in this, as in every other case, whether the mean to be employed, or, in this instance, the corporation to be erected, has a natural relation to any of the acknowledged objects or lawful ends of the government? Thus a corporation may not be erected by Congress for superintending the police of the city of Philadelphia, because they are not authorized to regulate the police of that city. But one may be erected in relation to the collection of taxes, or to the trade with foreign countries, or to the trade between the States, or with the Indian tribes; because it is the province of the federal government to regulate those objects, and because it is incident to a general *sovereign* or *legislative* power to regulate a thing, to employ all the means which relate to its regulation to the best and greatest advantage.

Document 2

Source: Thomas Jefferson, leader of the Democratic-Republican Party, Opinion on the Constitutionality of a National Bank, 1791.

I consider the foundation of the Constitution as laid on this ground: That "all powers not delegated to the United States, by the Constitution, nor prohibited by it to the States, are reserved to the States or to the people." To take a single step beyond the boundaries thus specially drawn around the powers of Congress, is to take possession of a boundless field of power, no longer susceptible to any definition.

The incorporation of a bank, and the powers assumed by this bill, have not, in my opinion, been delegated to the United States by the Constitution.

GO ON TO THE NEXT PAGE

Document 3

Source: Thomas Jefferson, First Inaugural Address, 1801.

But every difference of opinion is not a difference of principle. We have called by different names brethren of the same principle. We are all Republicans; we are all Federalists. If there be any among us who would wish to dissolve this Union or to change its republican form, let them stand undisturbed as monuments of the safety with which error of opinion may be tolerated where reason is left free to combat it.

Document 4

Source: Territorial Acquisitions of the United States, National Atlas of the United States.

Louisiana Purchase, coordinated by President Thomas Jefferson in 1803, is shown in white.

GO ON TO THE NEXT PAGE

Document 5

Source: Report and Resolutions of the Hartford Convention, meeting of New England Federalists, 1815.

Resolved. That the following amendments of the constitution of the United States be recommended to the states represented as aforesaid, to be proposed by them for adoption by the state legislatures, and in such cases as may be deemed expedient by a convention chosen by the people of each state. . . .

Second. No new state shall be admitted into the Union by Congress, in virtue of the power granted by the constitution, without the concurrence of two thirds of both houses. . . .

Fourth. Congress shall not have power, without the concurrence of two thirds of both houses, to prohibit the commercial intercourse between the United States and any foreign nation or the dependencies thereof.

Fifth. Congress shall not make or declare war, or authorize acts of hostility against any foreign nation, without the concurrence of two thirds of both houses, except such acts of hostility be in defense of the territories of the United States when actually invaded.

GO ON TO THE NEXT PAGE

Document 6

Source: President Andrew Jackson, leader in Democratic Party, veto message regarding the Bank of the United States, 1832.

The bill "to modify and continue" the act entitled "An act to incorporate the subscribers to the Bank of the United States" was presented to me on the 4th July. Having considered it with that solemn regard to the principles of the Constitution which the day was calculated to inspire, and come to the conclusion that it ought not to become a law, I herewith return it to the Senate, in which it originated, with my objections.

A bank of the United States is in many respects convenient for the Government and useful to the people. Entertaining this opinion, and deeply impressed with the belief that some of the powers and privileges possessed by the existing bank are unauthorized by the Constitution, subversive of the rights of the States, and dangerous to the liberties of the people, I felt it my duty at an early period of my Administration to call the attention of Congress to the practicability of organizing an institution combining all its advantages and obviating these objections. I sincerely regret that in the act before me I can perceive none of those modifications of the bank charter which are necessary, in my opinion, to make it compatible with justice, with sound policy, or with the Constitution of our country.

GO ON TO THE NEXT PAGE

Document 7

Source: Anonymous member of National Republican* Party, 1832 political cartoon.

The cartoon pictures Jackson standing on the "Constitution of the United States of America," "Internal Improvements," and "U.S. Bank."

*By 1832, the National Republicans and other groups had evolved into the Whig Party.

GO ON TO THE NEXT PAGE

END OF DOCUMENTS FOR QUESTION 1

Question 2, Question 3, or Question 4: Long Essay Question
Suggested writing time: 40 minutes

Directions: Choose Question 2, Question 3, OR Question 4 to answer.

In your response you should do the following:

- Make a thesis or claim that responds to the prompt. The thesis or claim must be historically defensible and establish a line of reasoning.

- Provide context relevant to the prompt by describing a broader historical development or process.

- Use specific and relevant examples as evidence to support an argument in response to the prompt.

- Use a historical reasoning skill (causation, comparison, or continuity and change) to develop an argument in response to the prompt.

- Demonstrate a complex understanding of an argument that responds to the prompt by using evidence to corroborate, qualify, or modify the argument.

2. Evaluate the extent to which the ideas of the Great Awakening and Enlightenment impacted the movement for American independence from 1730 to 1776.

3. Evaluate the extent to which the idea of Manifest Destiny impacted the political development of the United States from 1803 to 1865.

4. Evaluate the extent to which involvement in World War II impacted political development in the United States from 1945 to 1968.

GO ON TO THE NEXT PAGE

END OF EXAM

ANSWER KEY

Section I, Part A

1. D	15. D	29. B	43. A
2. C	16. B	30. D	44. A
3. A	17. D	31. B	45. D
4. D	18. C	32. B	46. C
5. C	19. A	33. C	47. C
6. C	20. A	34. D	48. D
7. B	21. B	35. A	49. A
8. C	22. B	36. B	50. D
9. B	23. D	37. C	51. A
10. B	24. C	38. B	52. C
11. C	25. B	39. B	53. D
12. D	26. C	40. D	54. C
13. B	27. D	41. C	55. A
14. C	28. A	42. C	

Section I, Part B and Section II

See Answers and Explanations and self-score your responses.

Section I, Part A Number Correct: _____

Section I, Part B Points Earned: _____

Section II Points Earned: _____

Sign into your online account at kaptest.com and enter your results in the scoring section to see your 1–5 score.

Haven't registered your book yet? Go to kaptest.com/moreonline to begin.

ANSWERS AND EXPLANATIONS

Section I, Part A

1. D

The Pueblos had long been internally divided, so the Spanish assumed that they could never unite against them. However, a Pueblo man named Pope asserted himself as the head of a large, coordinated uprising that ejected Spain from the region for twelve years. Thus, **(D)** is correct and (C) is incorrect. While there were raids along the border that diverted Spanish manpower, these raids were done by the Apache, not the Iroquois, who are a Northeastern tribe far from New Mexico; (A) is incorrect. Drought and not flooding contributed to the Pueblo Revolt; (B) is incorrect.

2. C

The Northwest Indian War saw an alliance of historically disunified tribes (the Western Confederacy) achieve a massive military victory over a colonizing power (the United States) and temporarily expel its influence from their geographic region. In the long-run, however, both the Western Confederacy and the Pueblo saw defeat once their colonizer regrouped and returned. Thus, **(C)** is correct because it best parallels the arc of the Pueblo Revolt. The Civil Rights Movement did not involve large-scale coordinated military action by the oppressed party against their oppressor; (A) is incorrect. On the other hand, Nat Turner's Rebellion did, but that uprising was unsuccessful and saw no temporary period of self-rule; (B) is incorrect. While tempting, in that Pontiac's Rebellion saw pan-tribal cooperation against a colonizer, (D) is incorrect because this conflict was ultimately a stalemate, and it did not feature a decisive battle where the colonizer was temporarily ejected from the region.

3. A

The Pennsylvania Charter of Privileges, which was formed in 1701, established freedom of religion in Penn's colony of Pennsylvania; **(A)** is correct. The charter required Pennsylvanians to believe in God, but it did not require them to attend church services, so (B) is incorrect. (C) is incorrect because Rhode Island was also founded upon the principle of religious tolerance (in 1631), and Maryland's Act of Toleration (which was passed in 1649) mandated religious tolerance for Christians who were not Catholic. (D) is incorrect because Quakers allowed people of all faiths to live in Pennsylvania, despite the fact that Puritans had previously banished many Quakers from New England colonies.

4. D

Like the excerpt from the Pennsylvania Charter of Privileges, the Maryland Act of Toleration also represented the foundation of religious freedom in the United States. The Maryland Act of Toleration granted equal rights to all residents of Maryland whether they practiced the established faith of Catholicism or Protestantism; **(D)** is correct. (A) is incorrect because John Locke's influence on the Enlightenment was primarily philosophical and political; Locke believed that the people should grant power to their rulers and that the people should have certain natural rights of life, liberty, and property. The Pilgrims founded Plymouth Colony in order to gain the freedom to practice their religious beliefs, but they did not advocate for tolerance of other religions, making (B) incorrect. John Winthrop's vision of Boston as a "city upon a hill" illustrated his hope that Boston could exemplify ideal Puritan living, making (C) incorrect.

5. C

Similar to the Pennsylvania charter's support of religious freedom, the Bill of Rights guaranteed Americans several freedoms (including religious freedom); **(C)** is correct. (A) is incorrect because the Declaration of Independence outlined why America should withdraw from the British Empire; it did not provide colonists with freedoms. The South Carolina Exposition and Protest argued against the Tariff of 1828, making (B) incorrect. The Alien and Sedition Acts actually limited the freedoms of immigrants and noncitizens and prohibited American citizens from falsely criticizing the United States federal government, eliminating (D).

6. C

As the North developed industrially, the political landscapes and economies of the North and the South further diverged; thus, **(C)** is correct. Industrial development primarily occurred in the North, and this development eventually led to the first industrial revolution in the United States; (A) is incorrect. Only the Southern economy depended on the plantation system, which depended on slavery, making (B) incorrect. (D) is incorrect because political and economic interaction and dependence still occurred, albeit to a lesser extent, between the North and the South.

7. B

The introduction of the cotton gin increased the production of tangible (cotton) goods or outputs. The telegraph, on the other hand, had to do with abstract outputs such as increased communication. Therefore, **(B)** is correct. (A), (C), and (D) all had similar impacts as that of the cotton gin, since they also led to production of more tangible products. Like the cotton gin, the introduction of the assembly line increased production in factories and allowed industrialization to develop more quickly. In a similar way, sewing machines enabled the process of making clothing to become faster and less expensive, and steam power was used to increase productivity in factories.

8. C

The Lowell factory system developed in response to the rapid growth of the cotton industry in the South after the invention of the cotton gin. This system, which primarily employed young women, was a textile factory system that emphasized efficiency, productivity, and profits. Thus, **(C)** is correct. (A) is incorrect because the steel plow was utilized to dig through the prairie grounds in the Midwest, not the fields of the South. As industry developed in the Northern states, the plantation system primarily stayed in the Southern states, making (B) incorrect. (D) is incorrect because an extensive factory system did not exist in the South during this time period.

9. B

According to Jefferson's plan, the western territories shown in the map were to be divided into states that would be approximately equal to the original Thirteen Colonies; **(B)** is correct. There is no indication in the map of which territories would be free versus slave states. In fact, when writing the ordinance, Jefferson called for the end of slavery in the western territories; (A) is incorrect. (C) is incorrect because although some land was sold to pay the national debt, this map does not depict that fact. The United States was not able to take control of New Orleans until the signing of Pinckney's Treaty in 1795, eliminating (D).

10. B

After the Seven Years' War, Americans gained confidence that the French and American Indian "menace" west of the Appalachian Mountains was gone. Many Americans then moved west to take advantage of the new territory, making **(B)** correct. The Proclamation of 1763 actually prevented Americans from passing the Appalachian Mountains, eliminating (A). (C) and (D) are incorrect because they are not related to westward migration; writs of assistance were used to allow British officials to search civilian property, and the Declaratory Act affirmed that the British Parliament could enact laws for and tax the colonies.

11. C

American settlers in the western territories needed to use the Mississippi River as a system to transport goods to market. However, the port of New Orleans was under Spanish control, and the American government needed to negotiate use of this port with Spain; **(C)** is correct. This negotiation ended in 1795 with Pinckney's Treaty. (A) and (B) are incorrect because these were not issues in the developing western territories during this time period. The Land Ordinance of 1785 dictated that the new states would be on an equal level with the original Thirteen Colonies, eliminating (D).

12. D

The Dawes Severalty Act of 1887 attempted to reform American Indian tribes in exchange for an allotment of land and American citizenship. However, the American Indians rejected this offer. **(D)** is correct. (A), (B), and (C) are incorrect because they represent previous government policies in which American Indians were forced to accept proposals, often through violence.

13. B

Based on the Monroe Doctrine, the United States would consider any European attempt at interference in the Western Hemisphere as unfriendly toward the United States; the excerpt states that the United States would respond accordingly if such interference occurred. **(B)** is correct. The United States was not attempting to extend its power over other nations or territories; instead, it was attempting to protect against encroachment by European powers, making (A) and (D) incorrect. (C) is incorrect; the excerpt clearly states that the United States "shall not interfere" in "existing colonies . . . of any European power."

14. C

Washington's Farewell Address emphasized the importance of steering clear of alliances with European powers in order to avoid American involvement in a European war; the Monroe Doctrine furthers Washington's ideas by warning the European powers against encroaching upon former colonies in the Western Hemisphere. Therefore, **(C)** is correct. Jay's Treaty was an attempt to settle financial claims between the United States and Britain in response to the British capture of American ships; (A) is incorrect. (B) is incorrect because the "right of deposit" provision in Pinckney's Treaty, which allowed nations to temporarily keep goods in another nation without paying fees, is unrelated to the Monroe Doctrine. The Western Confederacy of American Indians and the U.S. government negotiated the Greenville Treaty regarding the Northwest Territory, and this was unrelated to the European powers described in the excerpt; (D) is also incorrect.

15. D

The United States continued the foreign policy directed by the Monroe Doctrine by refraining from direct involvement in European affairs until the United States declared war on Germany and the Central Powers. World War I became the first time that the United States participated in (what was then considered to be) a European conflict. Thus, **(D)** is correct. The Monroe Doctrine's foreign policy dictated that the United States should not become involved in European conflicts, so the Mexican-American War would not have violated the doctrine; (A) is incorrect. The Union's attempt to keep Britain and France out of the Civil War aligned with the Monroe Doctrine, making (B) incorrect. Although the Spanish-American War involved a European nation, it was not a European conflict; instead, it was a conflict between Spain and the United States prompted by Spanish colonial oppression in Cuba, eliminating (C).

16. B

President Monroe established the doctrine to prevent attempts by European powers to reclaim their former colonies in the Western Hemisphere. **(B)** is correct. The War of 1812 between the United States and Britain did not result in significant changes and concluded several years before the Monroe Doctrine emerged, making (A) incorrect. (C) is incorrect because the United States had little interest in the Napoleonic Wars. The Monroe Doctrine was concerned with European nations attempting to regain their former territories in the Western Hemisphere, not merely with European economic encroachment, eliminating (D).

17. D

Thomas Jefferson's famous "fire bell in the night" letter exemplified his reaction to the Missouri Compromise in 1820. Jefferson feared that the issue of slavery would further divide the nation; **(D)** is correct. (A) and (C) are incorrect because Jefferson did not mention economic issues in the excerpt. The line mentioned in the excerpt had been established by the Missouri Compromise; Jefferson did not warn about the necessity of a line, but rather explained that it could create problems; (B) is incorrect.

18. C

Bleeding Kansas, a series of violent encounters over the issue of slavery in the 1850s, illustrated Jefferson's earlier fear from the excerpt that "every new irritation will mark it deeper and deeper." Thus, **(C)** is correct. The South Carolina Exposition and Protest was a reaction to the tariff issue, not slavery, making (A) incorrect. The Indian Removal Act in 1830 was met with very little opposition from American citizens and was not divisive, eliminating (B). (D) is incorrect because Jefferson's letter did not address the destruction of the U.S. Bank.

19. A

The Missouri Compromise was an effort to maintain a balance between free and slave states. With the addition of Missouri and Maine, there were 12 free and 12 slave states. Therefore, **(A)** is correct. The Panic of 1819 did not affect the admission of Missouri, eliminating (B). The protective tariff did not become a major issue until 1828, making (C) incorrect. (D) is incorrect because Mexico was not yet fully independent from Spain; Mexico had declared independence in 1810, but was not fully independent from Spain until 1821.

20. A

According to O'Sullivan's explanation of Manifest Destiny, American citizens were called upon to expand across North America with the intention of spreading ideals like individual freedom across the hemisphere. **(A)** is correct.

Manifest Destiny, as described in the passage, did not primarily involve a motivation to demonstrate political superiority; rather, America's superiority would arise from its virtues and freedoms. Therefore, (B) is incorrect. (C) is incorrect because the excerpt did not describe Manifest Destiny as the "only hope" for salvation. (D) is also incorrect; the excerpt stated the ability of America to "smite . . . tyranny of kings" but not that America would need to avoid tyrannical rulers.

21. B

This excerpt about Manifest Destiny referred to spreading "universal enfranchisement" and equal rights to all people, but in actuality, this only applied to white male Americans during this time period because only white men (regardless of socioeconomic status) held the right to vote. **(B)** is correct. Irish immigrants to the United States in the 1830s and 1840s encountered discrimination, particularly on the East Coast, making (A) incorrect. (C) is incorrect because women did not have political equality in the United States in 1839. Although plantation owners generally supported Manifest Destiny, they were members of the privileged class and were less likely to believe in the equality of individuals, eliminating (D).

22. B

The U.S. government's motivation behind taking the Philippines after the Spanish-American War was to spread democracy and share its ideals with the indigenous population of the Philippines; **(B)** is correct. The motivations behind the annexation of Hawaii were primarily economic, as the United States government desired to eliminate the tariff issues with sugar crops; (A) is incorrect. The primary motivation for the U.S. acquisition of American Samoa was to gain an island naval base, eliminating (C). (D) is incorrect because the U.S. government did not attempt to spread democracy as it supported the Cubans' attempts to gain liberation from Spanish rule.

23. D

The United States acquired the vast southwestern region of the modern United States through the Mexican Cession, therefore allowing Americans to fulfill the goals of Manifest Destiny and expand westward; **(D)** is correct. The

Panic of 1837, a major financial collapse that resulted in a years-long recession, did not aid United States expansion; (A) is incorrect. (B) is incorrect because rapid westward expansion began before the election of Zachary Taylor. The conclusion of the Indian Removal Act did not immediately fulfill the goals of Manifest Destiny, eliminating (C).

24. C

The Mexican Cession territory was predominantly south of the 36° 30' parallel, causing Southerners to claim that this region should be open to slavery. Controversy ensued because many Northerners did not believe that the arid and mountainous region would be conducive to slavery. Thus, **(C)** is correct. (A) and (B) are incorrect because these issues did not divide the North and the South. While the mountains were a minor point in the Mexican Cession controversy, they were not central to further dividing the North and the South, making (D) incorrect.

25. B

In the years leading up to the 1860 election, a series of failed compromises left the United States deeply divided. For instance, the Compromise of 1850 failed to defuse regional conflicts over allowing slavery in new states. Similarly, the Kansas-Nebraska Act infuriated many Northerners who saw the act as a direct negation of the boundary between slave and free states (as established by the Missouri Compromise). Thus, **(B)** is correct. (A) is incorrect because conservative former Whigs, dissatisfied Southern Democrats, and remnants of the Know-Nothing party formed the Constitutional Union Party to avoid secession over the debate on slavery, but the party did not take an antislavery position. While there was debate over the Tariff of 1857, the two sides did not split across party lines, making (C) incorrect. The Whig party had dissolved by the time the Constitutional Union Party was formed; (D) is also incorrect.

26. C

The purpose of the Constitutional Union Party was to focus on the ideals expressed by the founding fathers in the Constitution and to promote adherence to the laws expressed therein. The party wanted to avoid a civil war at all costs; it was made up of politicians who were predominantly from the border states and feared that a civil war would bring destruction to their states. Therefore, **(C)** is correct. The party's platform was fairly vague, but the founders did not intend to change the Constitution, making (A) incorrect. The party focused its platform on the Constitution in order to maintain the union of states rather than to promote the other patriotic tenets described in the document; (B) and (D) are incorrect.

27. D

President Wilson used similar themes to justify U.S. entry into World War I. Wilson wanted to witness the establishment of a League of Nations to maintain world peace, just as the Constitutional Union Party wanted to maintain peace in the United States. Therefore, **(D)** is correct. The immigration restriction in the 1920s, primarily the Immigration Act of 1924, sought to preserve the ideal of American homogeneity; this emphasis on nativism diverges from the democratic principles of the Constitutional Union Party, making (A) incorrect. Constitutional amendments in the Progressive Era attempted to address issues, including government corruption and urbanization, that were not concerns of the Constitutional Union Party; (B) is incorrect. The Constitutional Union Party did not take a position on international trade, eliminating (C).

28. A

Thinning ranks and few resources left Confederate generals with no option but surrender; **(A)** is correct. Southern citizens were unhappy with the outcome, but authorities in Washington knew the South had no further recourse and rejected any conditions upon surrender, making (B) incorrect. The South's defeat was driven primarily by its army's lack of access to resources; (C) is incorrect. The Civil War weakened the South's economy: working men fought in the Confederate army, infrastructure was destroyed, and resources became sparse; (D) is incorrect.

29. B

As a result of the Union navy's blockade on southern ports throughout much of the war, the Confederacy's economy suffered greatly and Southerners lost access to hard currency. Using only the railroad, Confederates were unable to supply troops with food and munitions or to support Southern infrastructure. These economic and logistical issues had far-reaching effects that ultimately weakened the entire Confederate effort. Thus,

(B) is correct. While Richmond was the center of political and economic activity for the South, the Union army's many attempts to capture Richmond failed; the Union's final siege occurred near the end of the war, making (A) incorrect. African Americans made up only about 10 percent of the Union army; while their contributions were significant, their mobilization was not a key strategy, eliminating (C). Both Union and Confederate leaders received formal military training, so this was not unique to the Union; (D) is incorrect.

30. D

In this excerpt, Clews suggested that American workers enjoy a better work environment than anywhere else in the world; thus, "inciting strikes" was counterintuitive and counterproductive. This sentiment grew in popularity after violent events such as the Railroad Strike of 1877 and the Haymarket Affair, in which workers clashed with police; **(D)** is correct. As a financier and immigrant himself, Clews was unlikely to oppose rapid industrialization or increasing immigration, eliminating (A) and (B). At this time of booming industry, there were many factory jobs available, making (C) incorrect.

31. B

Clews suggested that labor unions were unnecessary because the government was working to support, not degrade, workers; he claimed that unionists' attempts to strike were unproductive. Likewise, opponents of labor unions believed that unions were harmful and took action to suppress them. **(B)** is correct. The American Federation of Labor, Knights of Labor, and the Industrial Workers of the World all supported labor unions and would have opposed Clews's views, eliminating (A), (C), and (D).

32. B

The Taft Harley Act was passed to strip power from labor unions, removing much of the autonomy and power that unions had been granted by the Wagner Labor Relations Act in 1935. Clews was staunchly against labor unions, as demonstrated in this excerpt. Thus, **(B)** is correct, and (C) is incorrect. The War Labor Board was created to develop a cooperative relationship between government policy and labor unions during World War I, and President Harry Truman's Fair Deal proposals attempted to give labor more bargaining power, making (A) and (D) incorrect.

33. C

There was no minimum wage in the nineteenth century, and industrialists made huge profits. Thus, society was characterized by an imbalance in wealth, which matches **(C)**. In this era, workers had little political power and there was not a political movement for economic equality, making (A) incorrect. Labor unions did not enjoy popular support, especially after violent events such as the Haymarket riots, which were associated with unions, eliminating (B). Bellamy was not lamenting the lack of jobs; instead, he was lamenting the lack of economic freedom from which workers suffered, making (D) incorrect.

34. D

Bellamy was criticizing the unrestricted capitalism in which private organizations controlled economic production and could pay workers very little without government oversight. Bellamy proposed a world based on equality of all workers. **(D)** is correct. While rapid industrialization and the mechanization of the workforce were contributing factors to the spread of capitalism in the United States, these were not the target of Bellamy's criticism, making (A) and (C) incorrect. Immigration was a tangential issue to Bellamy's concerns in his work, eliminating (B).

35. A

Bellamy wrote about a future classless society based upon the equality of all; this concept closely mirrors that of utopian communities, making **(A)** correct. Abolitionists supported the end of slavery but not necessarily the equality of all, particularly as this egalitarianism related to labor; (B) is incorrect. Know-Nothings belonged to a right-wing political party opposed to immigrants and the Catholic Church, eliminating (C). Transcendentalists may have held some of the same philosophic beliefs as Bellamy, but they were more focused on the potential of individuals than the potential of collective society; (D) is incorrect.

36. B

The Agricultural Adjustment Act and the National Industrial Recovery Act were both declared unconstitutional by the U.S. Supreme Court. In response, President Roosevelt requested legislation that would allow him to appoint one new Supreme Court justice for each current justice aged 70 years and six months or older. There were six justices that FDR deemed as "too old"; therefore, he wanted to appoint six more. This idea was widely criticized, and even some of his strongest allies in the Democratic Party saw this as an attempt to control the judicial branch of government. **(B)** is correct. While there was opposition to some of FDR's New Deal proposals, Congress was generally supportive in this period due to overwhelming Democratic control of that branch; (A) and (C) are incorrect. The bill that FDR proposed was introduced in early 1937, months after his sweeping reelection victory, eliminating (D).

37. C

Union Democrats were the demographic most loyal to FDR's New Deal; they appreciated the passage of labor-friendly legislation under FDR, such as the Wagner Labor Relations Act in 1935. Thus, **(C)** is correct. Liberal Republicans believed that President Roosevelt was taking too much authority upon himself and the executive branch, eliminating (A). Southern farmers tended to be more conservative and resented government interference in agriculture, making (B) incorrect. Although Southern Democrats supported most of Roosevelt's policies and laws, they believed he was attempting to exercise too much control over the federal government; (D) is incorrect.

38. B

FDR was upset by the Supreme Court's decision to rule many of his key pieces of legislation unconstitutional, and he sought to attack the Court in several ways to regain control over it (as he had promised in his campaign). Andrew Jackson was similarly outraged at the Supreme Court's decision in *Worcester v. Georgia* supporting the Cherokee American Indians' right to their land in Georgia. Jackson reacted by appointing justices that would further his political goal, just as FDR reacted by attempting to appoint more justices to the Court. Thus, **(B)** is correct. Although Jefferson was upset by the decision reached in *Marbury v. Madison*, he complained that the judiciary did not properly uphold the tenets of the Constitution, not that they stymied his policies, making (A) incorrect. Arthur responded to unfavorable rulings in the Civil Rights Cases through intervening in individual cases, eliminating (C). Cleveland applauded the Court's decision in *Plessy v. Ferguson*; (D) is incorrect.

39. B

In this excerpt, Weyl argues that industrialists in the Gilded Age attained vast economic success at such a fast rate that the American legal system and the public's social norms had not been able to adapt. Weyl also points out that workers lacked protections, unlike industrialists. The Haymarket Affair is an example of the social upheaval resulting from these circumstances. The strikes and demonstrations in Chicago over working conditions, as well as friction with police, eventually led to a bombing and deaths. The subsequent trial of the alleged bombers was widely perceived as a miscarriage of justice. Thus, **(B)** is correct. While Social Darwinist theory was used to justify the mistreatment of the lower classes, (A) is incorrect because it only touches upon elite social norms, not those of the working classes. The dynamic of the labor movement involved both groups. (C) is incorrect because Andrew Carnegie supplied half of the world's steel; he did not dominate the global oil industry. (D) is incorrect because the Populists were a left-wing agrarian movement, while Weyl focuses on the consequences of industrialism.

40. D

Vertical and horizontal integration were two types of monopolies that developed under the law during the late nineteenth century; **(D)** is correct. Monopoly capitalism took root before the assembly line was developed (over the course of the nineteenth and early twentieth centuries), making (A) incorrect. While the Bessemer process revolutionized steel production, monopoly capitalism could not have developed without the preexisting legal code that allowed for vertical and horizontal integration; (B) is incorrect. The Taylor scientific management system, termed Taylorism, did not see widespread adoption until the early twentieth century, making (C) incorrect.

41. C

The Clayton Antitrust Act, passed in 1914, added substance to the Sherman Antitrust Act, which had very little in the way of enforcement written into the law. The Clayton Antitrust Act broadened the scope of what were considered anti-competitive business practices and also affirmed workers' rights to engage in peaceful boycotts, strikes, picketing, and collective bargaining. Therefore, **(C)** is correct. The Supreme Court did not interpret the Fifteenth Amendment in such a way as to encourage monopolies;

(A) is incorrect. The Sherman Antitrust Act lacked the scope of the Clayton Antitrust Act, making (B) incorrect. The Hepburn Act dealt solely with railroad regulation and was too narrow to apply to the many industries affected by monopoly capitalism, eliminating (D).

42. C

In the years leading up to the Dust Bowl, farmers inadvertently made lands more vulnerable to wind erosion by plowing the top soil of arid grasslands to grow more crops; this was a cause of the Dust Bowl, not a result. Thus, **(C)** is correct. Choices (A), (B), and (D) are incorrect because they all did result from the Dust Bowl. Many, including the Okies described by Steinbeck, migrated to the West after their land was afflicted by severe drought in the 1930s. Little did they know, those migrating West in search of work were faced with unemployment due to the Great Depression and intense competition for jobs. Additionally, while some areas experienced drought conditions for six years, high plains areas experienced such conditions for as many as eight years.

43. A

After losing their livelihoods in the Dust Bowl to severe drought, many tenant farmers fled to the West with the false hope that well-paying jobs were plentiful there; **(A)** is correct. This migration predated the start of World War II, making (B) incorrect. The National Youth Administration focused on providing jobs and education to younger Americans, which would not have included all migrants, eliminating (C). During the Great Depression, there were few jobs in the North to attract migrants from drought areas; (D) is incorrect.

44. A

According to Kennedy and Cohen, modern immigrant populations are similar to those of the late nineteenth century: they include both highly skilled individuals and people with little to no education who sought opportunities they could not access in their homelands. **(A)** is correct. While some parallels exist between modern immigration and nineteenth-century Irish immigration, only the latter type of immigration incited a nativist third party, the Know-Nothings, to form, making (B) incorrect. The excerpt describes modern immigrants as being a mix of laborers with varying levels of skill and education, not primarily skilled laborers forced to work unskilled jobs; (C) is incorrect. The excerpt discusses a historical parallel and does not argue that modern immigrants are lacking work or economic opportunity, eliminating (D).

45. D

The Irish fled starvation in their homeland during the Potato Famine. Many of these immigrants had little to no skills; they found menial jobs and sent remittances back to family members who had remained in Ireland. **(D)** is correct. The Forty-Eighters were often wealthy and well-educated refugees, fleeing from the failed Revolutions of 1848; (A) is incorrect. Many French immigrants were highly skilled and assimilated into rural agricultural communities, making (B) incorrect. The Chinese came seeking new fortunes but encountered hostility from Californian settlers. In 1882, the Chinese Exclusion Act prohibited additional Chinese immigration, eliminating (C).

46. C

The Know-Nothings formed in response to the nineteenth-century influx of Irish and German Catholics, and they mainly viewed such immigrants as seeking to overthrow democracy. Thus, the Know-Nothings were unlikely to view immigrants as newcomers hoping to find jobs and assimilate into American society; **(C)** is correct. The Copperheads were antiwar Democrats who sought peace with the Confederacy. Irish and Germans in urban enclaves formed Copperhead factions; these immigrants were not opposed to immigration, eliminating (A). The Free Soil Party was a loose collection of activists unified by their opposition to slavery's expansion; however, they lacked a widespread, formal position on immigration, making (B) incorrect. Far from being xenophobic, the Progressive Party of 1948 advocated for the repeal of existing immigration restrictions; (D) is incorrect.

47. C

The image depicts a poster championing the Black Panthers, a group which grew out of the Student Nonviolent Coordinating Committee (SNCC) in the mid-to-late 1960s. Stokely Carmichael, SNCC's chairman in 1966–1967, eventually led a splinter of militant social activists to the newly founded Black Panthers. Thus, **(C)** is correct. While the Black Panthers were against the Vietnam War, their

primary focus was on the lives of African Americans within the United States; (A) is incorrect. The image does not depict or hint at any LGBT activist element; (B) is incorrect. The New Left focused on a variety of social issues, such as civil rights, over the Old Left's fixation on class struggle. The image does not depict any such antagonism between those two groups; (D) is incorrect

48. D

The Student Nonviolent Coordinating Committee (SNCC) changed course under the leadership of Stokely Carmichael. In 1966, it rejected racial integration and advocated Black Power. Carmichael later left the SNCC for the Oakland-based Black Panthers, who openly carried weapons and clashed with police on a regular basis. Therefore, **(D)** is correct. Martin Luther King Jr., who was not affiliated with the Black Power movement, advocated for peaceful protests as a means to gain civil rights, eliminating (A). Unlike other civil rights groups, the Black Power movement did not believe that integration was attainable; (B) is incorrect. Malcolm X encouraged his followers to resort to violence only in self-defense, while the Black Power movement supported the use of violence against police, making (C) incorrect.

49. A

Despite the passage of the Civil Rights Act of 1964 and the Voting Rights Act of 1965, many civil rights activists believed that little progress had been made in alleviating both economic inequality and social injustice in the African American community; **(A)** is correct. By the late 1960s, Jim Crow laws were beginning to disintegrate, making (B) incorrect. For example, the Supreme Court overturned interracial marriage bans nationwide with the *Loving v. Virginia* ruling in 1967. While *Brown v. Board of Education* was a landmark civil rights case, the Civil Rights Act of 1964 and the Voting Rights Act of 1965 were considered wider reaching for all levels of society, eliminating (C). While the Black Panthers objected to the Vietnam conflict, describing it as U.S. imperialism, their focus was mainly on domestic politics in 1967; (D) is incorrect.

50. D

Malcolm X was vocal about his frustration with mainstream civil rights leadership. He expressed the idea that the civil rights movement needed to be more demanding and more forceful; **(D)** is correct. Suffragists and progressives did not support violent resistance, making (A) and (B) incorrect. In the late nineteenth century, the American Federation of Labor was marked by a conservative approach to advocating for labor reform and favored working alongside the capitalist system rather than overthrowing it; (C) is incorrect.

51. A

Sacco and Vanzetti, two Italian anarchists, were arrested for the murder of a paymaster in Massachusetts. Witnesses claimed that the criminals were Italian, which led the government to charge Sacco and Vanzetti. Their case is famous for bringing to light the nativist attitude in America during this time; **(A)** is correct. While people around the globe believed that there was controversial and conflicting evidence that resulted in an unfair trial, the conviction requirement of "beyond a reasonable doubt" was not brought into question, making (B) incorrect. Protesters and the press were not punished for questioning Sacco and Vanzetti's convictions or for publishing stories about the case, eliminating (C) and (D).

52. C

Many immigrants felt that the United States was anti-foreigner, with native-born citizens harboring unfounded suspicions of certain men, such as Sacco and Vanzetti. Therefore, U.S. immigrants would have been the group most likely to support the sentiments shown in the photograph; **(C)** is correct. Many businessmen and lawmakers in the United States would not have been sympathetic to alleged armed robbers, especially Italian-born ones, during the height of the First Red Scare; (A) and (B) are incorrect. Both men had fled to Mexico to avoid the draft during World War I, and they were avowed pacifists, making (D) incorrect.

53. D

Though the demonstration pictured relates to Sacco and Vanzetti and their rights as accused persons, the photograph more directly deals with the freedoms of speech, assembly, and petition. **(D)** is correct; such rights, along with the freedom of religion and the freedom of the press, are protected in the United States by the First Amendment. The Eighth Amendment prohibits cruel and unusual punishments, making (A) incorrect. The Fifth Amendment provides that individuals can be "deprived of life" if due process of law is followed, eliminating (B). The Third Amendment prohibits the quartering of troops; (C) is incorrect.

54. C

Sacco and Vanzetti were Italian, anarchists, and draft dodgers that could have been wrongfully accused, and many around the world believed that there was too little evidence to convict and execute them. Thus, **(C)** is incorrect. While the photograph depicts the protesters urging workers to stand in solidarity with the accused, protesters did not demonstrate in hopes of being arrested, making (A) incorrect. There is no evidence that Americans organized this British demonstration or any other international demonstration, eliminating (B). Demonstrations did not lead to changes in how criminal evidence was collected; (D) is incorrect.

55. A

The Sacco and Vanzetti trial most directly reflects the continuing debate about the effectiveness of the U.S. judicial system in guaranteeing a fair trial based on reasonable evidence; **(A)** is correct. While debates over immigration tie in to the trial and the image urges worker solidarity, neither directly reflects the issue at the heart of the trial, making (B) and (C) incorrect. Debates over states' rights are not expressed in the photograph, eliminating (D).

Section I, Part B

1. A successful short-answer response accomplishes all three tasks set forth by the prompt. Each part of the prompt is worth 1 point, for a total of 3 possible points.

(a) To earn the point, the response must describe a significant difference between the authors' interpretations, specifically addressing the claims of *both* passages. For the first passage, the response should describe the author's argument about how the Seven Years' War led to the American Revolution: disagreements about paying the war's expenses and British attempts to increase its authority in the colonies sparked controversy that eventually led to rebellion. For the second passage, the response should describe the author's argument that France's ceding Canada to the British caused the colonists to no longer feel dependent upon the protection of the British military (from potentially dangerous French and American Indians at the edge of the colonial borders).

(b) To earn the point, the response must identify a specific historical event or development from 1700–1776 and use reasoning or evidence to explain how that event or development supports the author of the first passage's claim that the Seven Years' War and the resulting increases in British authority over the colonies led to the American Revolution. Examples include the Molasses Act of 1733 as evidence of earlier colonial resentment toward British taxation; the Sugar Act and Townshend Acts as evidence of other acts to raise revenue that incurred colonial resistance; and the passage of the Declaratory Act, the so-called Intolerable Acts, and the Proclamation of 1763 as evidence of other resentment-inducing assertions of British authority over the colonies.

(c) To earn the point, the response must identify a specific historical event or development from 1700–1776 and use reasoning or evidence to explain how that event or development supports the author of the second passage's claim that the British acquisition of Canada after the Seven Years' War caused their American colonists to feel they no longer needed British protection. Examples include describing how continuing French possession of Canada might have altered colonial responses to legislation such as the Quartering Act, as presumably the colonists would not have been as resentful of housing British soldiers if they felt threatened by other military forces, and the Quebec Act, as the colonists could not have taken offense at the measures to govern Quebec (such as permitting Catholicism) had Britain not won Quebec from France. The same example(s) could be used for both (b) and (c), as long as a reasonable explanation of how the evidence supports each author's claims is provided.

2. A successful short-answer response accomplishes all three tasks set forth by the prompt. Each part of the prompt is worth 1 point, for a total of 3 possible points.

(a) To earn the point, the response must describe, not merely identify, a perspective about women's rights that is expressed in the photo. Examples include the continuation of traditional/conservative forms of dress while advocating more rights for women, the increasing political involvement of women even without the right to vote in national elections, the equating of women's rights with ideals such as "liberty" and "the human spirit," and the demand for rights in the context of the U.S. stance (and specifically President Wilson's stance) of defending democratic rights in World War I.

(b) To earn the point, the response must use reasoning or evidence to explain how a historical development or circumstance led to demonstrations demanding women's suffrage. Examples include the first large-scale discussion of women's rights in the United States at the 1848 Seneca Falls Convention and its drafting of the Declaration of Sentiments; the extension of the right to vote for women in new western states; the call for the Fourteenth Amendment's protections to apply regardless of sex as well as race; and the development in the nineteenth century of organized women's rights movements and their use of tactics such as conventions, public protesting, and persuasive writing.

(c) To earn the point, the response must use reasoning or evidence to explain a difference between the women's rights movements of 1848–1920 and those of 1950–1980, specifically addressing a feature of the movements from *both* time periods. One example is that the first movement was often more closely tied to other social issues, such as abolition, temperance, and limits on child labor. Another example is the first movement's particular focus on suffrage, which was guaranteed in the nineteenth amendment in 1920. The response could explain different focuses of the movements: civil rights, suffrage, property rights, education, and job opportunities in the first movement and equal wages, no-fault divorce, and reproductive rights in the second movement. The response could explain particular features of the second movement, such as the emergence of the modern women's rights movement, the development of feminism, the formation of the National Organization for Women, the publication of influential works such as Betty Friedan's *The Feminine Mystique*, and the renewed (but unsuccessful) advocacy for the Equal Rights Amendment.

3. A successful short-answer response accomplishes all three tasks set forth by the prompt. Each part of the prompt is worth 1 point, for a total of 3 possible points.

(a) To earn the point, the response must describe a similarity between how the Atlantic economy impacted Africans and how it impacted American Indians. Examples include that both groups were forced into forced labor, as in the Spanish mita and encomienda systems that coerced labor from American Indians and the employment of chattel slavery of Africans throughout the Atlantic coast and Caribbean islands; the devastation to both populations' numbers, as in the widespread deaths in American Indian populations caused by enforced labor systems and the spread of epidemic diseases and the depletion of African communities due to the slave trade; and the persistence in both groups of traditional religions, cultures, and traditions despite Europeans' imposition of European/Christian practices.

(b) To earn this point, the response must describe a difference between how the Atlantic economy impacted Africans and how it impacted American Indians. Examples include that Africans were uprooted from communities and transported across the ocean to become slaves, while displaced American Indians were typically forced off their traditional lands to regions farther west; that more Africans than American Indians were in the slave trade; and that social structures in Africa typically faced upheaval due to kidnappings and the slave trade network, while social structures of American Indians were typically threatened by disruptions from population decline due to diseases.

(c) To earn the point, the response must not just identify, but must use reasoning or evidence to explain why or how the Atlantic economy impacted the British North American colonies. Examples include the development of slave labor plantations in the southern colonies and West Indies; the migration and subsequent increase in population of European settlers as indentured servants or free laborers to participate in the colonial economic systems; the wealth generated for merchants and plantation owners through the Triangle trade; the development of wealthy port cities such as Boston, New York City, and Charleston; and the British imposition of mercantilist policies, which helped contribute to colonists' discontent with British rule.

4. A successful short-answer response accomplishes all three tasks set forth by the prompt. Each part of the prompt is worth 1 point, for a total of 3 possible points.

(a) To earn the point, the response must describe a similarity between the reform movements of the two eras. Examples include the focus on women's rights, democratic participation, and reduction of poverty in both eras; the successful passage of legislation in both eras; and the use of tactics such as protests and persuasive writing to further their causes. The response should describe the similarity in detail, using specific examples when appropriate; for instance, a response about the similar use of tactics could mention *The Jungle*'s role in the Progressive focus on health and sanitation and *The Feminine Mystique*'s role in the feminist movement of the 1960s–1970s.

(b) To earn the point, the response must describe a difference between the reform movements of the two eras. Examples include the different focuses of the movements, such as the Progressives' emphasis on fighting corruption, employing scientific principles, breaking monopolies, and enacting prohibition, and the emphasis in the 1960s–1970s on conservation, civil rights, and protesting the Vietnam War. The eras also differed in the typical groups involved in the movements, as the Progressives tended to include middle class white Americans, while the 1960s–1970s saw more involvement from youth and minorities. Alternately, the response could describe how similar focuses of the eras had different goals: women's rights issues shifted from suffrage to equal pay and access to contraception, democratic concerns shifted from more direct democracy to equal access to voting for all races and a lower voting age, and advocacy for the poor shifted from addressing the living and working conditions created by industrialization to programs started under the Great Society.

(c) To earn the point, the response must not just identify, but must use reasoning or evidence to explain how either of the reform movements impacted American society. Examples of effects of the Progressive movement include the ratification of the Seventeenth, Eighteenth, and Nineteenth Amendments (direct election of U.S. Senators, prohibition, and women's suffrage, respectively) and the passage of regulatory legislation such as antitrust laws and the Pure Food and Drug Act. Examples of effects of the movements of the 1960s–1970s include the passage of civil rights legislation (the Voting Rights Act of 1964 and the Voting Rights Act of 1965), programs created under Johnson's Great Society and its "War on Poverty" (such as Head Start, Medicare, and Medicaid), and the ratification of the Twenty-Fourth and Twenty-Sixth Amendments (abolishing poll taxes and lowering the federal voting age to 18, respectively).

SECTION II

1. *Evaluate the extent of change in United States political parties in the period 1791 to 1833.*

Category	Scoring Criteria	Notes
Thesis/Claim (0–1 points)	Historically defensible thesis/claim with a logical line of reasoning. The response must make a thesis or claim without restating the prompt itself. The thesis must consist of one or more sentences located in one place, either in the introduction or the conclusion.	A strong thesis should make a claim about the extent of change in political parties by articulating an argument and may identify the categories of analysis that will be used in the essay. Example: "American political parties experienced major changes through 1833, altering their interpretations of ideals as they faced the realities of governance, and even forming new political parties as concerns changed over time. Still, all the parties remained rooted in their devotion to the principles of the Constitution." This thesis makes the claim that political parties changed in two major ways, which establishes the essay's categories of analysis: changing ideals and forming new parties. The thesis also establishes a complex argument (see Analysis & Reasoning below) by claiming parties experienced both change *and* continuity.
Contextualization (0–1 points)	Broader historical context related to the prompt. The response must connect the topic to historical developments, events, or processes; these can occur before, during, or after the time frame of the prompt itself.	Contextualization for this prompt should explain, not merely mention, broader factors relevant to American politics in the late eighteenth or early nineteenth century. Examples: An explanation of why political parties were not addressed in the Constitution, such as Washington's warning against them in his farewell address; a description of the conflicts with Britain and France and how it caused disagreement among leaders in government.

Category	Scoring Criteria	Notes
Evidence (0–3 points)	Use of evidence to support the thesis. The response must utilize the content from at least *three* documents to address the *topic* of the prompt. (1 point) OR The response must use at least *six* documents to support an *argument* based on the prompt. (2 points)	Evidence from the documents must be paraphrased, not merely quoted. To earn 2 points, the evidence must be used to support an argument about the changes to political parties. Examples: Documents 1 and 2 to establish the initial views of parties in the First Party System (Federalists and Democratic-Republicans); documents 3 and 4 to support changing views of Democratic-Republicans; document 5 to support changing views of Federalists; documents 6 and 7 to support the emergence of new political parties (Democrats and National Republicans/Whigs) due to shifting concerns over time; documents 1, 2, 3, and 6 to support the continuity of devotion to constitutional principles.
	The response must use at least *one* additional piece of historical evidence, beyond what is found in the documents, to support an argument. This additional evidence must be different from what was used for contextualization. (1 point)	Examples: The use of a description of Whig or National Republican tenants, such as their support of internal improvements, to show how shifting concerns led to the formation of new parties; the use of the Embargo Acts of Jefferson and Madison as examples of strong federal policies by the originally strict constructionist Democratic-Republicans; the use of a description of the "era of Good Feelings" to show how political parties dissolved over time as their particular platforms became less relevant.

Category	Scoring Criteria	Notes
Analysis and Reasoning (0–2 points)	Complexity of understanding and reasoning. The response must explain, for at least *three* of the documents, how or why the document's purpose, historical basis, point of view, and/or audience are relevant to an argument. (1 point)	Factors' relevance to the argument about changes to political parties should be explained, not just identified. Examples: The role of purpose in document 3, which Jefferson delivered as a speech to try to unify members of both parties and smooth the transition in power from a Federalist to a Democratic-Republican president; the role of point of view in document 7, which was created by a political rival of Jackson and may have exaggerated Jackson's actions.
	The response must show a complex understanding of the content of the prompt, using evidence to support, qualify, or modify an argument about the prompt. (1 point)	A complex understanding should be incorporated into the overall argument about changes to political parties. Examples: A description of both change *and continuity* in political parties, such as the continuity of devotion to Constitutional principles as demonstrated in the references to the Constitution by various political parties in documents 1, 2, and 6 and Jefferson's discussion of "principles" in document 3; a description of how political parties underwent similar changes in other time periods, such as the emergence of the Republican party in response to the issue of slavery and the shifting of Republican ideology and base through the twentieth century.

2. *Evaluate the extent to which the ideas of the Great Awakening and Enlightenment impacted the movement for American independence from 1730 to 1776.*

Category	Scoring Criteria	
Thesis/Claim (0–1 points)	Historically defensible thesis/claim with a logical line of reasoning. The response must make a thesis or claim without restating the prompt itself. The thesis must consist of one or more sentences located in one place, either in the introduction or the conclusion.	A strong thesis should make a claim about the ways in which the ideas of the Great Awakening and Enlightenment impacted the movement for American independence by articulating an argument and may identify the categories of analysis that will be used in the essay. Example: "The political theories of the Enlightenment and the sense of religious independence fostered by the Great Awakening had contributed to a sense of autonomy in the colonies for decades before the revolution, making the eventual movement towards independence a logical step for many colonists." This thesis makes the claim that a sense of autonomy had existed before the American Revolution and establishes the categories of analysis: political theories of the Enlightenment and ideas of religious independence from the Great Awakening.

Category	Scoring Criteria	
Contextual-ization (0–1 points)	Broader historical context related to the prompt. The response must connect the topic to historical developments, events, or processes; these can occur before, during, or after the time frame of the prompt itself.	Contextualization for this prompt should explain, not merely mention, broader factors relevant to the Enlightenment, Great Awakening, or American Revolution. Examples: A description of the British government's salutary neglect of the North American colonies due to distance and British involvement in wars with France; a description of how British acts, especially those restricting colonial expansion and commerce after the French and Indian War, were protested by colonists.
Evidence (0–2 points)	Use of evidence to support the thesis. The response identifies specific examples *relevant to the topic* of the prompt. (1 point) OR The response uses specific examples to *support an argument* about the prompt. (2 points)	To earn 2 points, the evidence must be used to support an argument about the impact of the Enlightenment and Great Awakening on the American Revolution. Examples: The Great Awakening creating a cross-colony movement that helped establish a uniquely American identity, the Great Awakening demonstrating the validity of institutions set apart from British control through the establishment of independent churches (such as the Baptists) and the rejection of the established British (Anglican) church. The Enlightenment spreading concepts such as republicanism, consent of the governed, social contract, and natural rights throughout the colonies; the Albany Plan of Union as an early example of an attempt to apply the Enlightenment idea of representative government in the colonies; the inclusion of the ideas of John Locke in the Declaration of Independence.
Analysis and Reasoning (0–2 points)	Complexity of understanding and reasoning. The response shows historical reasoning to make an argument about the prompt. (1 point) AND The response demonstrates complex understanding, using evidence to support, qualify, or modify an argument about the prompt. (1 point)	Comparison, causation, or continuity and change over time should be incorporated into the overall argument about the impact of the Enlightenment and Great Awakening on the American Revolution. Example: An explanation of how the ideas of the Enlightenment were reflected in the arguments used in favor of independence (causation). AND A complex understanding should be incorporated into the overall argument about the impact of the Enlightenment and Great Awakening on the American Revolution. Example: Qualifying the argument by considering alternative perspectives, such as favoring reconciliation with Britain as illustrated in the Olive Branch Petition and the views of Loyalists who remained on the side of Britain throughout the war.

3. *Evaluate the extent to which the idea of Manifest Destiny impacted the political development of the United States from 1803 to 1865.*

Category	Scoring Criteria	Notes
Thesis/Claim (0-1 points)	Historically defensible thesis/claim with a logical line of reasoning. The response must make a thesis or claim without restating the prompt itself. The thesis must consist of one or more sentences located in one place, either in the introduction or the conclusion.	A strong thesis should make a claim about the ways in which Manifest Destiny impacted politics by articulating an argument and may identify the categories of analysis that will be used in the essay. Example: "By increasing the economic differences between the sections of the country and becoming the political battleground for conflicts about slavery, the quest for fulfillment of Manifest Destiny was the primary factor that heightened sectional tensions until civil war erupted." This thesis makes the claim that Manifest Destiny led to civil war by heightening sectional tensions. The thesis also establishes the categories of analysis: economic differences and conflicts about slavery.
Contextualization (0-1 points)	Broader historical context related to the prompt. The response must connect the topic to historical developments, events, or processes; these can occur before, during, or after the time frame of the prompt itself.	Contextualization for this prompt should explain, not merely mention, broader factors relevant to Manifest Destiny, slavery, or politics of the nineteenth century. Examples: A description of factors that spurred westward migration, such as the Louisiana Purchase, the Mexican Cession, the inventions of McCormick's reaper and John Deere's steel plow, and eastern farmers seeking new farmland due to lack of land, rocky soils, or inability to compete with large plantations.
Evidence (0-2 points)	Use of evidence to support the thesis. The response identifies specific examples *relevant to the topic* of the prompt. (1 point) OR The response uses specific examples to *support an argument* about the prompt. (2 points)	To earn 2 points, the evidence must be used to support an argument about ways in which Manifest Destiny impacted politics. Examples: The impact of westward expansion on heightening the differences between regional economies, as western agriculture spurred the development of transportation technologies along the Erie Canal and Mississippi River system and the expansion of railroads, enriching and entrenching industry in the North and a slave plantation (cotton) economy in the South. The impact of westward expansion on political battles over the expansion of slavery and maintaining equal representation of slave and free states in Congress, as occurred in the Missouri Compromise, the Compromise of 1850, the Kansas-Nebraska Act, and *Dred Scott v. Sandford*.

Category	Scoring Criteria	Notes
Analysis and Reasoning (0-2 points)	Complexity of understanding and reasoning. The response shows historical reasoning to make an argument about the prompt. (1 point) AND The response demonstrates complex understanding, using evidence to support, qualify, or modify an argument about the prompt. (1 point)	Comparison, causation, or continuity and change over time should be incorporated into the overall argument about the ways in which Manifest Destiny impacted politics. Example: An explanation of why adding new states and territories spurred conflicts about slavery and how the attempts at compromises failed to eliminate sectional differences (causation). AND A complex understanding should be incorporated into the overall argument about the ways in which Manifest Destiny impacted politics. Examples An explanation of a relevant connection across time periods, such as comparing the political impact of Manifest Destiny to the political impact of the Proclamation of 1763, which halted western migration and contributed to the colonial independence movement.

4. *Evaluate the extent to which involvement in World War II impacted political development in the United States from 1945 to 1968.*

Category	Scoring Criteria	Notes
Thesis/Claim (0-1 points)	Historically defensible thesis/claim with a logical line of reasoning. The response must make a thesis or claim without restating the prompt itself. The thesis must consist of one or more sentences located in one place, either in the introduction or the conclusion.	A strong thesis should make a claim about the ways in which World War II impacted politics by articulating an argument and may identify the categories of analysis that will be used in the essay. Example: "Politically, the most significant change was the permanent and pervasive entry of the United States into international affairs." This thesis makes the claim that the most significant political impact of World War II was in the United States's role in international affairs; this claim establishes the essay's line of reasoning.

Category	Scoring Criteria	Notes
Contextual-ization (0-1 points)	Broader historical context related to the prompt. The response must connect the topic to historical developments, events, or processes; these can occur before, during, or after the time frame of the prompt itself.	Contextualization for this prompt should explain, not merely mention, broader factors relevant to World War II or twentieth-century American politics. Examples: A description of the involvement of the United States in foreign affairs before World War II, such as its relative isolationism from Europe (with the exceptions of the Dawes Plan and the Lend-Lease Act) in the interwar period, exemplified in its refusal to join the League of Nations; a description of the American political landscape before the end of World War II, in which the Democratic President Roosevelt had been elected to four terms and Congress had held a Democratic majority.
Evidence (0-2 points)	Use of evidence to support the thesis. The response identifies specific examples *relevant to the topic* of the prompt. (1 point) OR The response uses specific examples to *support an argument* about the prompt. (2 points)	To earn 2 points, the evidence must be used to support an argument about ways in which World War II impacted politics. Examples: The pervasive entry of the United States into international politics during the Cold War as exemplified by the Truman Doctrine, the arms race, the Korean War, the founding of NATO, and the Vietnam War; the ways in which domestic politics were shaped by fears of communism (the Red Scare, McCarthyism) and renewed advocacy for civil rights after the service of African Americans and women during World War II.

Category	Scoring Criteria	Notes
Analysis and Reasoning (0-2 points)	Complexity of understanding and reasoning. The response shows historical reasoning to make an argument about the prompt. (1 point) AND The response demonstrates complex understanding, using evidence to support, qualify, or modify an argument about the prompt. (1 point)	Comparison, causation, or continuity and change over time should be incorporated into the overall argument about the ways in which World War II impacted politics. Example: An explanation of how the world political situation after World War II led to a profound increase in U.S. involvement in international affairs, especially in the Cold War (change). AND A complex understanding should be incorporated into the overall argument about the ways in which World War II impacted politics. Examples: An explanation of both changes *and continuities* in politics, such as the continuation of Democratic dominance of the presidency (with the exception of the Republican Eisenhower) and Congress that had begun in the 1930s.

Practice Exam 2

Practice Exam 2 Answer Grid

1. Ⓐ Ⓑ Ⓒ Ⓓ
2. Ⓐ Ⓑ Ⓒ Ⓓ
3. Ⓐ Ⓑ Ⓒ Ⓓ
4. Ⓐ Ⓑ Ⓒ Ⓓ
5. Ⓐ Ⓑ Ⓒ Ⓓ
6. Ⓐ Ⓑ Ⓒ Ⓓ
7. Ⓐ Ⓑ Ⓒ Ⓓ
8. Ⓐ Ⓑ Ⓒ Ⓓ
9. Ⓐ Ⓑ Ⓒ Ⓓ
10. Ⓐ Ⓑ Ⓒ Ⓓ
11. Ⓐ Ⓑ Ⓒ Ⓓ
12. Ⓐ Ⓑ Ⓒ Ⓓ
13. Ⓐ Ⓑ Ⓒ Ⓓ
14. Ⓐ Ⓑ Ⓒ Ⓓ

15. Ⓐ Ⓑ Ⓒ Ⓓ
16. Ⓐ Ⓑ Ⓒ Ⓓ
17. Ⓐ Ⓑ Ⓒ Ⓓ
18. Ⓐ Ⓑ Ⓒ Ⓓ
19. Ⓐ Ⓑ Ⓒ Ⓓ
20. Ⓐ Ⓑ Ⓒ Ⓓ
21. Ⓐ Ⓑ Ⓒ Ⓓ
22. Ⓐ Ⓑ Ⓒ Ⓓ
23. Ⓐ Ⓑ Ⓒ Ⓓ
24. Ⓐ Ⓑ Ⓒ Ⓓ
25. Ⓐ Ⓑ Ⓒ Ⓓ
26. Ⓐ Ⓑ Ⓒ Ⓓ
27. Ⓐ Ⓑ Ⓒ Ⓓ
28. Ⓐ Ⓑ Ⓒ Ⓓ

29. Ⓐ Ⓑ Ⓒ Ⓓ
30. Ⓐ Ⓑ Ⓒ Ⓓ
31. Ⓐ Ⓑ Ⓒ Ⓓ
32. Ⓐ Ⓑ Ⓒ Ⓓ
33. Ⓐ Ⓑ Ⓒ Ⓓ
34. Ⓐ Ⓑ Ⓒ Ⓓ
35. Ⓐ Ⓑ Ⓒ Ⓓ
36. Ⓐ Ⓑ Ⓒ Ⓓ
37. Ⓐ Ⓑ Ⓒ Ⓓ
38. Ⓐ Ⓑ Ⓒ Ⓓ
39. Ⓐ Ⓑ Ⓒ Ⓓ
40. Ⓐ Ⓑ Ⓒ Ⓓ
41. Ⓐ Ⓑ Ⓒ Ⓓ
42. Ⓐ Ⓑ Ⓒ Ⓓ

43. Ⓐ Ⓑ Ⓒ Ⓓ
44. Ⓐ Ⓑ Ⓒ Ⓓ
45. Ⓐ Ⓑ Ⓒ Ⓓ
46. Ⓐ Ⓑ Ⓒ Ⓓ
47. Ⓐ Ⓑ Ⓒ Ⓓ
48. Ⓐ Ⓑ Ⓒ Ⓓ
49. Ⓐ Ⓑ Ⓒ Ⓓ
50. Ⓐ Ⓑ Ⓒ Ⓓ
51. Ⓐ Ⓑ Ⓒ Ⓓ
52. Ⓐ Ⓑ Ⓒ Ⓓ
53. Ⓐ Ⓑ Ⓒ Ⓓ
54. Ⓐ Ⓑ Ⓒ Ⓓ
55. Ⓐ Ⓑ Ⓒ Ⓓ

SECTION I, PART A
Time—55 minutes
55 Questions

Directions: Section I, Part A of this exam contains 55 multiple-choice questions, organized into sets with corresponding historical sources. Each of the questions or incomplete statements is followed by four suggested answers or completions. Using both the provided sources and your own historical knowledge, select the best answer choice.

Questions 1–3 refer to the table below.

Old World to New World	New World to Old World
Cattle	Avocados
Chickens	Beans
Cotton	Chocolate
Dogs	Maize (Corn)
Goats	Peanuts
Horses	Peppers
Okra	Pineapples
Pigs	Potatoes
Rice	Rubber Tree
Sheep	Tobacco
Sugarcane	Tomatoes
Wheat	Vanilla

1. The Columbian Exchange most significantly impacted American Indians by

   (A) forcing them off their territories as slave labor was imported from Africa

   (B) decimating their populations with the introduction of new diseases

   (C) separating them from trade routes, which led to mass starvation

   (D) introducing the horse, which disrupted their hunting and agricultural methods

2. The introduction of sugarcane to the West Indies led to

   (A) the importation of slave labor from Africa

   (B) the creation of permanent Spanish settlements, composed of families

   (C) Spain and Portugal's wars over control of the Caribbean islands

   (D) the destruction of many Caribbean islands' ecosystems

3. Which of the following population trends was a significant consequence of the Columbian Exchange?

   (A) African populations increased as a result of the introduction of new weaponry from Europe.

   (B) American Indian populations increased as a result of the introduction of domesticated animals.

   (C) European populations increased as a result of the introduction of new agricultural products from the New World.

   (D) East Asian populations decreased as a result of sending too many crops to the New World.

GO ON TO THE NEXT PAGE

Questions 4–6 refer to the excerpt below.

"We, whose names are underwritten, the Loyal Subjects of our dread Sovereign Lord King James, by the Grace of God, of Great Britain, France, and Ireland, King, Defender of the Faith, etc. Having undertaken for the Glory of God, and Advancement of the Christian faith, and the Honour of our King and Country, a Voyage to plant the first Colony in the northern Parts of Virginia; Do by these Presents, solemnly and mutually, in the Presence of God and one of another, covenant and combine ourselves together into a civil Body Politick, for our better Ordering and Preservation, and Furtherance of the Ends aforesaid: And by Virtue hereof do enact, constitute, and frame, such just and equal Laws, Ordinances, Acts, Constitutions, and Officers, from time to time, as shall be thought most meet and convenient for the general Good of the Colony; unto which we promise all due Submission and Obedience."

Mayflower Compact, 1620

4. The political principles of this document influenced which of the following ideals of the British North American colonies?

   (A) Separation of church and state

   (B) Governance by a constitution

   (C) Rule by majority

   (D) Social equality

5. Which of the following groups would most likely support the political principles of the Mayflower Compact?

   (A) Delegates to the Stamp Act Congress

   (B) Supporters of the Articles of Confederation

   (C) Members of the New Harmony society

   (D) Delegates to the Constitutional Convention

6. The excerpt from the Mayflower Compact most clearly reflects which of the following statements?

   (A) The English were establishing North American colonies based on the *encomienda* system.

   (B) The English were attempting to establish permanent communities in North America.

   (C) The English were prepared to challenge French claims in North America.

   (D) The English were instructing settlers to establish community governments identical to those in England.

GO ON TO THE NEXT PAGE

Questions 7–9 refer to the excerpt below.

"Jamestown stood upon low ground, full of marshes and swamps. The climate, at all times malarious and unhealthy, was at this season made more so than usual by the hot September sun. There were no fresh water springs, and the water from the wells was brackish and unwholesome, making the place especially 'improper for the commencement of a siege.' While the Governor had the advantage of numbers . . . Bacon had the greater advantage of motive. . . . [T]he old man found that there was nothing left for him but a second flight. That night [Berkeley], with the gentlemen who remained true to him . . . stole out of their stronghold in great secrecy, and taking to the ships, 'fell silently down the river.' The fleet came to anchor a few miles away, perhaps that those on board might reoccupy the town again as soon as the siege should be raised, perhaps that they might, in turn, block up the rebels in it if they should quarter there. Bacon found a way to thwart either design."

Mary Newton Stanard, *The Story of Bacon's Rebellion*, 1907

7. What motivated Nathaniel Bacon and his militia to burn Jamestown?

(A) They desired to prevent the House of Burgesses from meeting.

(B) They held grievances against prominent residents of Jamestown.

(C) They wanted to impede the governor and his forces from retaking the town.

(D) They wished to send a message to King Charles II.

8. Which of the following contributed most directly to the outbreak of the conflict in the excerpt?

(A) The government's attempt to boost Roman Catholic immigration

(B) The unequal political power between wealthy plantation owners and frontier settlers

(C) The redistribution of land previously belonging to colonial plantation owners

(D) The mass importation of slave labor from Africa

9. Which of the following events was motivated by a source of conflict similar to that of Bacon's Rebellion?

(A) The Nullification Crisis in South Carolina

(B) The Whiskey Rebellion in Pennsylvania

(C) The Texan Revolution in Texas

(D) Nat Turner's Rebellion in Virginia

GO ON TO THE NEXT PAGE

Questions 10–13 refer to the excerpt below.

"Hark, hark the sound of war is heard,
And we must all attend;
Take up our arms and go with speed,
Our country to defend.

Our parent state has turned our foe,
Which fills our land with pain;
Her gallant ships, manned out for war,
Come thundering o'er the main.

There's Carleton, Howe, and Clinton too.
And many thousands more,
May cross the sea, but all in vain,
Our rights we'll ne'er give o'er.

Our pleasant homes they do invade,
Our property devour;
And all because we won't submit
To their despotic power."

War Song, 1776

10. In studying the song, a historian might deduce that the primary purpose was to

   (A) warn Americans that British troops would be invading the homes of individuals who stood up for their rights

   (B) urge American colonists to be ready to fight the military forces coming from England to enforce British control over the colonies

   (C) inform the colonists who viewed themselves as loyal English subjects that the "mother country" would not win this war

   (D) ensure colonists were aware of the number of soldiers who were en route from England on warships

11. Which of the following represents a major disadvantage the colonists faced while at war with Britain?

   (A) Attacks from American Indians from the West and the British Navy from the East

   (B) The fear of a massive slave rebellion

   (C) The lack of international allies

   (D) The presence of Loyalists throughout the colonies

GO ON TO THE NEXT PAGE

12. The strongest motivation for Americans to "take up arms" against the parent country "who has turned our foe" was

    (A) the passage of taxes and restrictive regulations on the British North American colonies by Parliament

    (B) the continued violation of American freedom of the seas and free trade

    (C) the fear that the English Navy would block American trade with the Spanish and French Caribbean colonies

    (D) the continuous attacks by American Indians on frontier settlements west of the Appalachian Mountains

13. Which of the following best describes the impact of Enlightenment philosophy on the American Revolution?

    (A) Enlightenment ideas justified the colonists' right to rebel against the British based on their entitlement to natural rights.

    (B) Enlightenment ideas protected the right of the colonies to trade freely.

    (C) Enlightenment ideas focused on spiritual and supernatural justifications as to why colonists should revolt.

    (D) Enlightenment theory opposed the Church of England, obligating the colonists to go to war with the British.

Questions 14–16 refer to the excerpt below.

". . . we are enabled this day to add one more step to universal civilization, by removing as much as possible the sorrows of those who have lived in undeserved bondage . . . And whereas the condition of those persons who have heretofore been denominated Negro and Mulatto slaves, has been attended with circumstances which not only deprived them of the common blessings that they were by nature entitled to . . . In justice therefore to persons so unhappily circumstanced, and who, having no prospect before them whereon they may rest their sorrows and their hopes, have no reasonable inducement to render their service to society, which they otherwise might; and also in grateful commemoration of our own happy deliverance from that state of unconditional submission to which we were doomed by the tyranny of Britain."

An Act for the Gradual Abolition of Slavery, passed by the Pennsylvania legislature in 1780

14. The ideas expressed in the excerpt are most consistent with the principle that

   (A) slavery is immoral and should be forbidden

   (B) public education will foster social equality

   (C) religious awakening ought to lead to abolitionism

   (D) prisons must focus on rehabilitation

15. Which of the following groups would have been most likely to agree with the ideals in this excerpt?

   (A) The Locofoco wing of the Democratic Party in the 1830s

   (B) The Liberty Party of the 1840s

   (C) The Free Soil Party of the 1840s and 1850s

   (D) Members of the American Party in the 1850s

16. Which of the following best explains the motivations behind this excerpt?

   (A) The king had forced slavery upon the Americas and was no longer in power over the newly independent states.

   (B) Slavery had been declared illegal in several northern states, and Pennsylvania was pressured to free its slaves.

   (C) After freeing themselves from British rule, Pennsylvanians believed it was morally correct to free those held in bondage within their state and other northern colonies.

   (D) The tyranny of Great Britain had forced slavery onto the people of Pennsylvania; Pennsylvania was now independent and ended the institution.

GO ON TO THE NEXT PAGE

Questions 17–20 refer to the excerpt below.

"The authority given to the Supreme Court by the act establishing the judicial system of the United States to issue writs of mandamus to public officers appears not to be warranted by the Constitution.

It is emphatically the duty of the Judicial Department to say what the law is. Those who apply the rule to particular cases must, of necessity, expound and interpret the rule. If two laws conflict with each other, the Court must decide on the operation of each.

If courts are to regard the Constitution, and the Constitution is superior to any ordinary act of the legislature, the Constitution, and not such ordinary act, must govern the case to which they both apply."

John Marshall, *Marbury v. Madison* decision, 1803

17. According to this excerpt, which of the following has supremacy in American law?

    (A) The executive branch

    (B) The legislative branch

    (C) Writs of mandamus

    (D) The Constitution

18. *Marbury v. Madison* shaped judicial practices by

    (A) establishing the Court's power to review acts of Congress

    (B) empowering the Court to issue writs of mandamus as necessary

    (C) determining that cases can only be closed upon a unanimous vote

    (D) reinforcing the idea that the Court cannot void legislation in conflict with the Constitution without approval from Congress

19. Which of the following pairs of Supreme Court decisions illustrates a similar relationship to *Marbury v. Madison* and the Judiciary Act of 1789?

    (A) *Dred Scott v. Sandford* and *Worcester v. Georgia*

    (B) *Oregon v. Mitchell* and *Schenk v. United States*

    (C) *Plessy v. Ferguson* and *Brown v. Board of Education*

    (D) *Cherokee Nation v. Georgia* and the Missouri Compromise

20. Which of the following presidential actions challenged the main principles outlined in this excerpt?

    (A) Abraham Lincoln's pocket veto of the Wade-Davis Bill

    (B) James Madison's veto of internal improvements in 1817

    (C) James Monroe's issuing of the Monroe Doctrine

    (D) Andrew Jackson's veto of the bill that called for the recharter of the Second Bank of the United States

GO ON TO THE NEXT PAGE

Questions 21–23 refer to the map below.

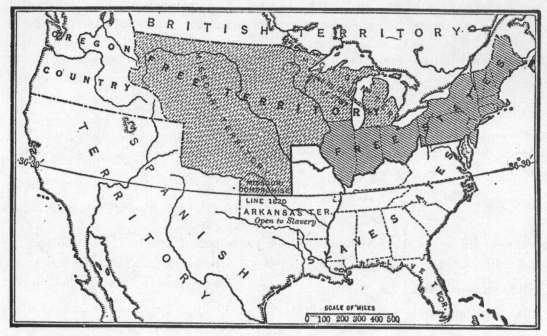

The map depicts U.S. territories as determined by the Missouri Compromise of 1820

21. Which of the following best describes the circumstances in the early nineteenth century that led to the Missouri Compromise?

   (A) Slave territory was beginning to encroach on free territory.

   (B) The United States intended to take Spanish territory in the West.

   (C) The United States was attempting to maintain a balance between free and slave states.

   (D) Free states were hoping to add Oregon Country to their territory and gain access to the Pacific Ocean.

22. Which of the following groups would have most likely objected to the Missouri Compromise?

   (A) Slave owners in the newly emerging cotton-growing states

   (B) New England factory workers

   (C) Poor whites in the South

   (D) Quakers in the Northeast

23. The Missouri Compromise was the center of controversy later in the nineteenth century when

   (A) the debate surrounding slave and free states caused the war with Mexico in 1846

   (B) legislation passed in the 1850s overturned the laws established in 1820, allowing a state to rid its territory of slavery

   (C) the Supreme Court determined the outcome of the compromise to be unconstitutional

   (D) the Free Soil Party began to win elections in the western territories, where it had been determined that popular sovereignty would determine the outcome of a territory's slave status

GO ON TO THE NEXT PAGE

Questions 24–26 refer to the excerpt below.

"And be it further enacted, That when a person held to service or labor in any State or Territory of the United States, has heretofore or shall hereafter escape into another State or Territory of the United States, the person or persons to whom such service or labor may be due, or his, her, or their agent or attorney, duly authorized, by power of attorney, in writing, acknowledged and certified under the seal of some legal officer or court of the State or Territory in which the same may be executed, may pursue and reclaim such fugitive person, either by procuring a warrant from some one of the courts, judges, or commissioners aforesaid, of the proper circuit, district, or county, for the apprehension of such fugitive from service or labor, or by seizing and arresting such fugitive, where the same can be done without process, and by taking, or causing such person to be taken, forthwith before such court, judge, or commissioner, whose duty it shall be to hear and determine the case of such claimant in a summary manner . . ."

Sixth provision, Fugitive Slave Act of 1850

24. The Fugitive Slave Act of 1850 had which of the following immediate effects?

(A) Northern free states created and enacted the first personal liberty laws to protect escaped slaves.

(B) Senator John C. Calhoun declared that slavery was a "positive good" in a speech to the Senate.

(C) Proslavery and free-state settlers flooded into Kansas, sparking the start of Bleeding Kansas.

(D) Use of the Underground Railroad to transport escaped slaves increased significantly.

25. Which of the following pieces of literature was written after the enactment of the Fugitive Slave Act of 1850 in order to raise awareness about the poor treatment of slaves in the South?

(A) *The Liberator* by William Lloyd Garrison

(B) *An Appeal to the Colored Citizens of the World* by David Walker

(C) *Uncle Tom's Cabin* by Harriet Beecher Stowe

(D) *The Adventures of Huckleberry Finn* by Mark Twain

26. The reaction of Northerners to the passing of the Fugitive Slave Act is most comparable to the reaction of the majority of Americans to

(A) the creation of the Monroe Doctrine

(B) the success of Bacon's Rebellion

(C) the passage of the Stamp Act

(D) the Glorious Revolution

GO ON TO THE NEXT PAGE

Questions 27–29 refer to the excerpt below.

"Resolved, That we, the delegated representatives of the Republican electors of the United States in Convention assembled, in discharge of the duty we owe to our constituents and our country, unite in the following declarations:

[Plank] 8. That the normal condition of all the territory of the United States is that of freedom: That, as our Republican fathers, when they had abolished slavery in all our national territory, ordained that 'no persons should be deprived of life, liberty or property without due process of law,' it becomes our duty, by legislation, whenever such legislation is necessary, to maintain this provision of the Constitution against all attempts to violate it; and we deny the authority of Congress, of a territorial legislature, or of any individuals, to give legal existence to slavery in any territory of the United States."

Republican Party Platform, 1860

27. The overall stance of the Republican Party on slavery in the mid-nineteenth century can best be characterized as

(A) supportive of the concept of popular sovereignty

(B) sympathetic toward granting slaves equal rights

(C) opposed to the spread of slavery to new territories

(D) supportive of the passage of the Emancipation Proclamation

28. Which of the following developments in American identity can be most attributed to the ideas expressed in the excerpt?

(A) The formation of a strong connection between the Midwest and the South due to their dependence on slave labor

(B) The increased polarization of the nation as a result of sectional political issues

(C) The creation of a stronger bond between Southern cotton growers and New England factory workers

(D) The generation of a strong economic relationship between the agricultural South and West

29. The concepts presented in the Republican Party Platform of 1860 are most similar to the ideas that drove forward which of the following movements?

(A) The labor movement of the late nineteenth century

(B) The American Temperance Union movement

(C) The women's suffrage movement

(D) The new nativist movement of the turn of the twentieth century

GO ON TO THE NEXT PAGE

Questions 30–32 refer to the image below.

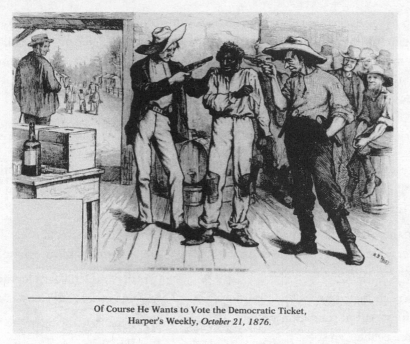

Of Course He Wants to Vote the Democratic Ticket,
Harper's Weekly, *October 21, 1876.*

The political cartoon, from October 1876, depicts voter intimidation in the Reconstruction era.

30. This political cartoon was most likely created in response to

   (A) the use of scare tactics by Radical Republicans in an effort to coerce freedmen into not voting

   (B) the legislation passed by the South that eliminated freedmen's right to vote

   (C) the efforts of certain Southern Democrats, known as Redeemers, to exclude Republicans from Southern politics

   (D) the use of intimidation by white supremacists in an effort to coerce freedmen into voting for certain candidates

31. The rights granted to freedmen during Reconstruction were further supported by

   (A) legislation regarding civil rights that was passed as part of Johnson's Great Society

   (B) policies affecting civil rights that were enacted during the New Deal

   (C) legislation affecting civil rights that was passed in response to the Montgomery bus boycott

   (D) anti-lynching legislation that was written during the Progressive Era

32. Which of the following political actions contributed most strongly to the resolution of the civil rights issue portrayed in the illustration?

   (A) The *Brown v. Board of Education* decision

   (B) The Civil Rights Acts of 1964 and 1965

   (C) The decision to racially integrate the U.S. military

   (D) The *Korematsu v. United States* decision

GO ON TO THE NEXT PAGE

 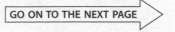

Questions 33–35 refer to the excerpt below.

"The old South rested everything on slavery and agriculture, unconscious that these could neither give nor maintain healthy growth. The new South presents a perfect democracy, the oligarchs leading in the popular movement—a social system compact and closely knitted, less splendid on the surface, but stronger at the core—a hundred farms for every plantation, fifty homes for every palace—and a diversified industry that meets the complex need of this complex age."

Henry Grady, "The Old South and the New," a speech delivered to the New England Society, 1886

33. The ideas expressed in the excerpt best reflect which of the following changes in Southern identity in the nineteenth century?

(A) Following the Civil War, the majority of Southerners came to accept African Americans as citizens with equal rights.

(B) Southerners chose to replace their long-standing hierarchical plantation system with a more egalitarian society.

(C) The post-Reconstruction South began the movement to grant political equality to women.

(D) The South's reliance on the plantation system decreased as it became as industrialized as the North.

34. The concept of the New South as described by Henry Grady would be most strongly counteracted by

(A) the development of the iron and steel industries in Birmingham, Alabama

(B) the industrial development in New Orleans and other Gulf Coast cities

(C) the restructuring of the South's agricultural system

(D) the continuing existence of sharecropping and the crop-lien system

35. Grady's description of the New South most accurately describes the South after

(A) the Antebellum Era

(B) the Great Depression

(C) World War II

(D) the Reconstruction Era

GO ON TO THE NEXT PAGE

Questions 36–38 refer to the excerpt below.

"Herbert has finished his course at the academy, and is about to enter the manufactory as an office clerk. Mr. Cameron means to promote him as he merits, and I should not be at all surprised if our young friend eventually became junior partner. He and his mother have bought the house into which they moved, and have done not a little to convert it into a tasteful home. The invention has proved all that Mr. Cameron hoped for it. It has been widely introduced, and Herbert realizes as much from his own half as Mr. Cameron agreed to pay for that which he purchased. So his father's invention has proved to be Herbert Carter's most valuable legacy."

Horatio Alger, *Herbert Carter's Legacy*, 1875

36. Which of the following cultural trends in the late nineteenth century best illustrates Horatio Alger's message?

    (A) The decreasing labor force inspired Americans to work harder to maintain employment.

    (B) New industrial opportunities became available to Americans.

    (C) With new inventions, Americans could expect a higher level of productivity.

    (D) Americans who worked hard and lived honestly could become successful.

37. Which of the following groups would have been most strongly opposed to the excerpt's main idea?

    (A) Social Darwinists

    (B) Labor union members

    (C) Factory owners

    (D) City dwellers

38. Which of the following historical ideals provides a foundation for the excerpt?

    (A) The Protestant work ethic

    (B) Republican motherhood

    (C) Jeffersonian democracy

    (D) Jacksonian democracy

GO ON TO THE NEXT PAGE

Questions 39–42 refer to the image below.

The political cartoon from 1889, "The Bosses of the Senate," depicts trusts for various industries (steel, copper, sugar, etc.) surrounding the Senate chamber.

39. This political cartoon most directly reflects which of the following nineteenth-century ideals?

   (A) The Social Gospel

   (B) Progressivism

   (C) Populism

   (D) Social Darwinism

40. This political cartoon illustrates which of the following issues of the Industrial Revolution?

   (A) The increased influence of labor unions in the government

   (B) The passage of U.S. Senate legislation promoting fair business practices

   (C) The influence of monopolies and trusts on the U.S. Senate

   (D) The equitable society produced by the industrialized economy

GO ON TO THE NEXT PAGE

41. Which of the following ideas became prominent in twentieth-century American politics?

    (A) New Deal ideas for the redistribution of wealth

    (B) Progressive ideas to break up monopolies

    (C) Populist ideas to directly elect senators

    (D) Great Society ideas that led to voting rights legislation

42. A historian might argue that the ideas depicted in the cartoon most likely led to which of the following twentieth-century events?

    (A) Congress's passing of New Deal legislation to control big business authority

    (B) The government's adoption of a laissez-faire attitude in the 1920s

    (C) Post–World War I to World War II business development

    (D) The government's reaction to the lack of environmental regulation in the 1970s

GO ON TO THE NEXT PAGE

Questions 43–45 refer to the image below.

A DANGEROUS BREW (1904)

*The steam rising from the pot forms human figures labeled Graft, Lawlessness, Anarchy,
Incendiary Press, Dynamite-Persuasion, Riot, Intimidation, Mob Violence, and Boycott.*

43. This political cartoon expresses which of the
following views on labor?

(A) U.S. labor was attempting to politically
dominate America through unions.

(B) U.S. labor was a potential danger to
democracy no matter its organization.

(C) U.S. labor was better off under the
influence of laissez-faire capitalism.

(D) U.S. labor was an internal enemy the likes
of which had already overthrown Czarist
Russia.

44. Which of the following nineteenth-century
events contributed to the American fear of
unionism, socialism, anarchism, and other left-
wing movements of the industrial working class?

(A) The Ku Klux Klan's dominance in parts of
the unreconstructed South

(B) The court case resulting from the Haymarket
Square Riot in Chicago

(C) The events leading to the Homestead Steel
Strike in Pittsburgh, Pennsylvania

(D) Jacob Coxey's March on Washington
protesting outcomes of the Panic of 1893

GO ON TO THE NEXT PAGE

45. Which of the following international events most strongly contributed to the fears of the working class in the United States during the first quarter of the twentieth century?

    (A) The Great Depression

    (B) The Portland Waterfront Strike

    (C) The fallout from World War I

    (D) The Russian Revolution

Questions 46–48 refer to the image below.

The photograph depicts a 1967 Vietnam War protest in Washington, D.C.

46. Based on this photograph, which of the following statements is most accurate?

    (A) For the first time, a large number of American youth protested a political matter.

    (B) American youth opposed the U.S. involvement in the Vietnam War because they were against the military draft.

    (C) American youth were influenced directly by other groups opposed to U.S. involvement in the Vietnam War.

    (D) Youth protests were widespread but did not influence Vietnam War policy.

47. Which event expressed the sentiments of this photograph and had a substantial impact on American politics in the late 1960s?

    (A) The nationwide riots after the assassination of Martin Luther King Jr.

    (B) The antiwar backlash after the assassination of Robert F. Kennedy

    (C) The violent protests at the 1968 Democratic Party Convention in Chicago

    (D) The Woodstock Music Festival with its antiwar sentiments

48. The events surrounding this photograph had which of the following effects on pop culture in the 1960s and 1970s?

    (A) Young adult literature focused more on social justice.

    (B) The visual arts became more oriented toward social causes.

    (C) Television programming became more focused on youth culture.

    (D) Popular music became more focused on antiwar and social themes.

GO ON TO THE NEXT PAGE

Questions 49 and 50 refer to the excerpt below.

"The conditions which brought us as a nation to this point are well-known: two decades of low productivity, growth, and stagnant wages; persistent unemployment and underemployment; years of huge Government deficits and declining investment in our future; exploding healthcare costs and lack of coverage for millions of Americans; legions of poor children; education and job training opportunities inadequate to the demands of this tough, global economy. For too long we have drifted without a strong sense of purpose or responsibility or community.

And our political system so often has seemed paralyzed by special interest groups, by partisan bickering, and by the sheer complexity of our problems . . . I believe we can do better . . . If we have the vision, the will, and the heart to make the changes we must, we can still enter the twenty-first century . . . having secured the American dream for ourselves and for future generations."

President Bill Clinton, Address Before a Joint Session of Congress on Administration Goals, 1993

49. According to the excerpt, which of the following events most affected the United States during the 1990s?

   (A) An economic recession

   (B) Labor unrest that caused massive unemployment

   (C) Record numbers of high-wage jobs being outsourced

   (D) America entering a new era of bipartisan cooperation

50. Which twenty-first century issue was NOT a major concern at the time this speech was given?

   (A) The advent of the Internet

   (B) The North American Free Trade Agreement (NAFTA)

   (C) The War on Terror

   (D) The Soviet Union's collapse

GO ON TO THE NEXT PAGE

Questions 51–55 refer to the image below.

The political cartoon depicts two Rosie the Riveters repairing a warship, with children surrounding them. From the U.S. Office of War Information, circa 1943.

51. Which of the following best describes the political cartoon's role in American society?

    (A) Propaganda to engage women in America's total war effort

    (B) Advertisement to assist women in gaining equal rights

    (C) Criticism of women joining the workforce

    (D) Advocacy for women keeping their jobs after U.S. soldiers' return from war

52. Which of the following groups would have most strongly appreciated this cartoon?

    (A) Shipbuilders who hired women

    (B) Armed forces generals

    (C) Women who had joined the workforce

    (D) Child psychologists

GO ON TO THE NEXT PAGE

53. The ideas expressed in the cartoon most clearly relate to

    (A) the military's commitment to enlist women

    (B) the improved access to consumer goods

    (C) the growing need for childcare in American society

    (D) the shifting roles of women in American society

54. The cartoon most clearly expresses the influence of which of the following events?

    (A) The ratification of the Nineteenth Amendment

    (B) The women's rights movement of the nineteenth century

    (C) The industrialization of society in the nineteenth century

    (D) The growth of trade unions in the nineteenth century

55. Though some Rosie the Riveters left their jobs to return to homemaking following World War II, the number of U.S. women who worked outside the home rose steadily during the 1950s and 1960s. Based on this fact, which of the following conclusions can be drawn?

    (A) The Rosie the Riveters could not sustain their roles as breadwinners without the presence of childcare.

    (B) The war effort contributed to the expansion of jobs for women.

    (C) Women sought higher-education programs in hopes of avoiding the realm of domesticity.

    (D) The Korean War and Vietnam War once again required U.S. women to take up jobs.

END OF SECTION I, PART A

**IF YOU FINISH BEFORE TIME IS CALLED,
YOU MAY CHECK YOUR WORK ON PART A.**

DO NOT GO ON TO PART B UNTIL YOU ARE TOLD TO DO SO.

SECTION I, PART B
Time—40 minutes
3 Questions

Directions: Section I, Part B of this exam consists of short-answer questions. You must respond to Questions 1 *and* 2. For your final response, you must choose to answer Question 3 *or* Question 4. In your responses, be sure to address all parts of the questions, using complete sentences.

"The American Indians' recent history [laid] violent hazards in the way of the [the whites'] 'plan of civilization,' and the most vital and stubborn of the strands took the form of prophetic nativism. Between 1795 and 1815, individual prophets and groups of Indians claiming supernatural inspiration posed direct challenges to those leaders who advocated political and even cultural accommodation to the power of the United States. Insurgent nativists drew upon their histories of intertribal cooperation. They looked to their shared beliefs in the ritual demands of power. Turning to the spirits as well as to their intertribal comrades, they attempted to rally support against those tribal leaders who ceded land to the Americans. Prophetic parties . . . broke with their accommodating countrymen to prepare an intertribal, Indian union against the expansion of the United States . . ."

Gregory Evans Dowd, *A Spirited Resistance: The North American Indian Struggle for Unity, 1745–1815*, 1993

"Some Cherokees believed that 'civilization' was their best protection against forced removal. Consequently, they spoke English, sent their children to school, and converted to Christianity. They established a Cherokee republic with written laws, a court system, and a national police force. They also tried to conform to Anglo-American notions about appropriate behavior for men and women . . .

The Cherokees who are most visible in the historical record succeeded in this transformation. They reacted to the crisis of the late eighteenth and early nineteenth centuries by trying to recreate Cherokee culture and society in ways that accommodated 'civilization.'"

Theda Perdue, *Cherokee Women: Gender and Culture Change, 1700–1835*, 1998

1. Using the excerpts above, answer (a), (b), and (c).

    (a) Briefly describe ONE major difference between Dowd's and Perdue's historical interpretations of American Indian responses to pressures from white Americans.

    (b) Briefly explain how ONE specific historical event or development during the time period 1780–1840 that is not explicitly mentioned in the excerpts could be used to support Dowd's interpretation.

    (c) Briefly explain how ONE specific historical event or development during the time period 1780–1840 that is not explicitly mentioned in the excerpts could be used to support Perdue's interpretation.

GO ON TO THE NEXT PAGE

"THESE are the times that try men's souls: The summer soldier and the sunshine patriot will, in this crisis, shrink from the service of his country, but he that stands it NOW deserves the love and thanks of man and woman. Tyranny, like hell, is not easily conquered; yet we have this consolation with us, that the harder the conflict, the more glorious the triumph. What we obtain too cheap, we esteem too lightly:—'Tis dearness only that gives everything its value. Heaven knows how to set a proper price upon its goods; and it would be strange indeed, if so celestial an article as Freedom should not be highly rated."

Thomas Paine, "The American Crisis," December 1776

"THESE are times that tried men's souls, and they are over—and the greatest and completest revolution the world ever knew, gloriously and happily accomplished. But to pass from the extremes of danger to safety—from the tumult of war to the tranquility of peace, though sweet in contemplation, requires a gradual composure of the senses to receive it. Even calmness has the power of stunning, when it opens too instantly upon us. The long and raging hurricane that should cease in a moment, would leave us in a state rather of wonder than enjoyment; and some moments of recollection must pass, before we could be capable of tasting the felicity of repose. There are but few instances in which the mind is fitted for sudden transitions: it takes in its pleasures by reflection and comparison and those must have time to act, before the relish for new scenes is complete."

Thomas Paine, "The American Crisis: Philadelphia," April 1783

2. Using the excerpts above, answer (a), (b), and (c).

    (a) Briefly describe ONE perspective about the American Revolution expressed in the passages.

    (b) Briefly explain ONE specific historical development or event that led to the writing of the FIRST passage.

    (c) Briefly explain ONE specific historical development or event that resulted from the changes described in the SECOND passage.

GO ON TO THE NEXT PAGE

Choose EITHER Question 3 or Question 4.

3. Answer (a), (b), and (c).

   (a) Briefly describe ONE specific historical similarity between the background or provisions of the Compromise of 1850 and the background or provisions of the Kansas-Nebraska Act.

   (b) Briefly describe ONE specific historical difference between the background or provisions of the Compromise of 1850 and the background or provisions of the Kansas-Nebraska Act.

   (c) Briefly explain ONE historical effect of the Compromise of 1850 or the Kansas-Nebraska Act.

4. Answer (a), (b), and (c).

   (a) Briefly describe ONE specific historical similarity between the domestic response of the United States to the events at Pearl Harbor on December 7, 1941 and the domestic response of the United States to the events of September 11, 2001.

   (b) Briefly describe ONE specific historical difference between the domestic response of the United States to the events at Pearl Harbor on December 7, 1941 and the domestic response of the United States to the events of September 11, 2001.

   (c) Briefly explain ONE international response made by the United States to the events at Pearl Harbor on December 7, 1941 or the domestic response of the United States to the events of September 11, 2001.

END OF SECTION I, PART B

**IF YOU FINISH BEFORE TIME IS CALLED,
YOU MAY CHECK YOUR WORK ON THIS SECTION.**

DO NOT GO ON TO SECTION II UNTIL YOU ARE TOLD TO DO SO.

SECTION II

Time—1 hour 40 minutes

Question 1: Document-Based Question

Suggested reading period: 15 minutes

Suggested writing time: 45 minutes

Directions: Question 1 is based on the accompanying documents. The documents have been edited for the purpose of this exercise.

In your response, you should do the following:

- Make a thesis or claim that responds to the prompt. The thesis or claim must be historically defensible and establish a line of reasoning.
- Provide context relevant to the prompt by describing a broader historical development or process.
- Use at least six of the provided documents to support an argument in response to the prompt.
- Use a historical example not found in the documents as evidence relevant to an argument about the prompt.
- Explain how the context or situation of at least three documents is relevant to an argument. This could address the relevance of the document's point of view, purpose, historical situation, and/or audience.
- Demonstrate a complex understanding of an argument that responds to the prompt by using evidence to corroborate, qualify, or modify the argument.

GO ON TO THE NEXT PAGE

1. Evaluate the extent of change in Americans' views on freedom and equality during World War II from 1939 to 1945.

Document 1

Source: A. Philip Randolph, "The Call to March," published in *The Black Worker*, 1941.

We propose that ten thousand Negroes MARCH ON WASHINGTON FOR JOBS IN NATIONAL DEFENSE AND EQUAL INTEGRATION IN THE FIGHTING FORCES OF THE UNITED STATES.

We believe in national unity which recognizes equal opportunity of black and white citizens to jobs in national defense and the armed forces, and in all other institutions and endeavors in America. We condemn all dictatorships, Fascist, Nazi, and Communist. We are loyal, patriotic Americans, all.

But if American democracy will not defend its defenders; if American democracy will not protect its protectors; if American democracy will not give jobs to its toilers because of race or color; if American democracy will not ensure equality of opportunity, freedom and justice to its citizens, black and white, it is a hollow mockery and belies the principles for which it is supposed to stand.

Only power can affect the enforcement and adoption of a given policy. Power is the active principle of only the organized masses, the masses united for a definite purpose. We loyal Negro-American citizens demand the right to work and fight for our country.

Document 2

Source: President Franklin Delano Roosevelt, Executive Order 9066 authorizing the internment of Japanese Americans, 1942.

Now, therefore, by virtue of the authority vested in me as President of the United States, and Commander in Chief of the Army and Navy, I hereby authorize and direct the Secretary of War, and the Military Commanders whom he may from time to time designate, whenever he or any designated Commander deems such action to be necessary or desirable, to prescribe military areas in such places and of such extent as he or the appropriate Military Commander may determine, from which any or all persons may be excluded, and with respect to which, the right of any person to enter, remain in, or leave shall be subject to whatever restrictions the Secretary of War or the appropriate Military Commander may impose in his discretion.

GO ON TO THE NEXT PAGE

Document 3

Source: Westinghouse Electric & Manufacturing Company's War Production Coordinating Committee, 1942.

GO ON TO THE NEXT PAGE

Document 4

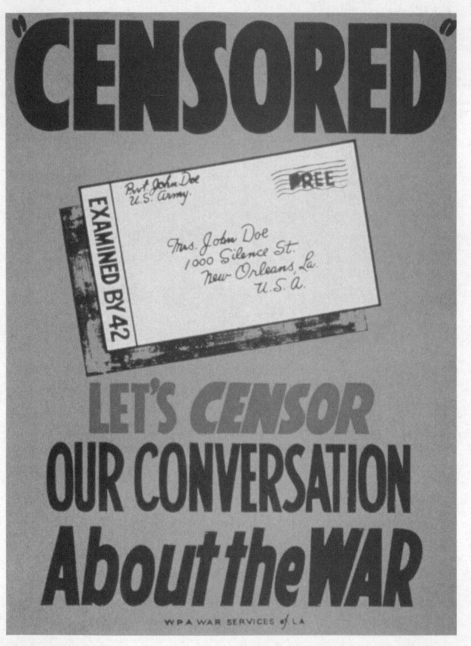

Source: Federal Arts Project of the WPA, War Services Program, 1942.

GO ON TO THE NEXT PAGE

Document 5

Source: Photograph of the Tuskegee Airmen with white commanding officer, 1944.

Document 6

Source: Majority opinion from Supreme Court Case *Korematsu v. United States*, 1944.

Civilian Exclusion Order No. 34 which, during a state of war with Japan and as a protection against espionage and sabotage, was promulgated by the Commanding General of the Western Defense Command under authority of Executive Order No. 9066 and the Act of March 21, 1942, and which directed the exclusion after May 9, 1942, from a described West Coast military area of all persons of Japanese ancestry, held constitutional as of the time it was made and when the petitioner—an American citizen of Japanese descent whose home was in the described area—violated it.

GO ON TO THE NEXT PAGE

Document 7

Source: U.S. Office of Price Administration, 1943.

GO ON TO THE NEXT PAGE

END OF DOCUMENTS FOR QUESTION 1

Question 2, Question 3, or Question 4: Long Essay Question
Suggested writing time: 40 minutes

Directions: Choose Question 2, Question 3, OR Question 4 to answer.

In your response you should do the following:

- Make a thesis or claim that responds to the prompt. The thesis or claim must be historically defensible and establish a line of reasoning.
- Provide context relevant to the prompt by describing a broader historical development or process.
- Use specific and relevant examples as evidence to support an argument in response to the prompt.
- Use a historical reasoning skill (causation, comparison, or continuity and change) to develop an argument in response to the prompt.
- Demonstrate a complex understanding of an argument that responds to the prompt by using evidence to corroborate, qualify, or modify the argument.

2. Evaluate the extent to which the migration of European colonists and the resulting encounters with American Indians affected social patterns in the period from 1495 to 1650.

3. Evaluate the extent to which the market revolution affected internal migration in the United States in the period from 1800 to 1860.

4. Evaluate the extent to which the Great Migration of African Americans affected social patterns in the United States in the period from 1890 to 1930.

GO ON TO THE NEXT PAGE

END OF SECTION II

ANSWER KEY

Section I, Part A

1. B	15. B	29. C	43. C
2. A	16. C	30. D	44. B
3. C	17. D	31. A	45. D
4. C	18. A	32. B	46. D
5. D	19. C	33. B	47. C
6. B	20. D	34. D	48. D
7. C	21. C	35. C	49. A
8. B	22. D	36. D	50. C
9. B	23. C	37. B	51. A
10. B	24. D	38. A	52. C
11. D	25. C	39. C	53. D
12. A	26. C	40. C	54. B
13. A	27. C	41. B	55. B
14. A	28. B	42. A	

Section I, Part B and Section II

See Answers and Explanations, and self-score your responses.

Section I, Part A Number Correct: _____

Section I, Part B Points Earned: _____

Section II Points Earned: _____

Sign into your online account at kaptest.com and enter your results in the scoring section to see your 1–5 score.

Haven't registered your book yet? Go to kaptest.com/moreonline to begin.

ANSWERS AND EXPLANATIONS

Section I, Part A

1. B

American Indians lacked immunity to diseases that were common in Europe. Scholars estimate that anywhere between 50 and 90 percent of people living in the Western Hemisphere at the time of European "discovery" perished; **(B)** is correct. Native people were forced to migrate off their land by Europeans who desired the land for themselves, making (A) incorrect. American Indians were self-sufficient in obtaining food, which eliminates (C). The introduction of the horse benefited American Indians, making (D) incorrect.

2. A

Spanish, and later English, settlers had thousands of slaves work the sugar plantations for up to 14 hours per day in order to maintain constant productivity. This difficult and tedious labor led to a high mortality rate, which in turn required a continuous flow of slave labor into the Caribbean from Africa. Therefore, **(A)** is correct. The Spanish tended to only send men to develop sugar plantations, instead of sending entire families, making (B) incorrect. Spain and Portugal signed a treaty designating geographic areas of influence because Spain had control over the Caribbean islands; (C) is incorrect. (D) is incorrect because the workforce in the West Indies was primarily composed of slaves from Africa.

3. C

Corn and (more significantly) potatoes were imported to Europe as easy-to-grow crops. Countries such as Ireland, the German states, Sweden, and France grew in population as more people were healthier and lived longer. **(C)** is correct. Though Europeans introduced weapons (specifically guns) to the New World, the mass exportation of slaves from Africa to the New World had a decidedly negative impact on this population, eliminating (A). Even though American Indians benefited from the introduction of domesticated animals, the death toll from disease and other factors outweighed this benefit, making (B) incorrect. The exchange of crops and livestock actually improved the diets of East Asian populations; (D) is incorrect.

4. C

The primary principle of the Mayflower Compact was majority rule, which would occur in early New England town meetings; **(C)** is correct. Plymouth Colony was a religious community that lacked separation of church and state; (A) is incorrect. The Mayflower Compact applied to a single community, not to a group of colonies, making (B) incorrect. While the colony pledged to live under the rule of laws, it did not imply the existence of social equality, eliminating (D).

5. D

The delegates to the Constitutional Convention in the summer of 1787 agreed to abide by majority rule in establishing a new, stronger government of the United States. They used majority rule to make compromises as they developed the Constitution; **(D)** is correct. Delegates to the Stamp Act Congress and supporters of the Articles of Confederation were not willing to create a strong central government that would represent majority rule, making (A) and (B) incorrect. The communal society of New Harmony, Indiana, made decisions by consensus, not majority rule, eliminating (C).

6. B

The English were attempting to make inroads in North America as Spain and France were establishing outposts in their growing economic empires. The English hoped that sending families and allowing communities to form a government of laws would help establish stable communities; **(B)** is correct. The British government did not endorse or adopt the Spanish *encomienda* system; (A) is incorrect. The Mayflower Compact was unrelated to occupying French land, making (C) incorrect. The Mayflower Compact was initiated by the Puritan community, to whom the British government did not provide instructions regarding local government, eliminating (D).

7. C

Bacon and his followers laid siege to Jamestown and drove out Governor Berkeley and his forces. Once Bacon and his troops realized that they did not have the resources to hold the capital indefinitely, Bacon instructed his followers to burn Jamestown to the ground; **(C)** is correct.

Bacon himself was an elected member of the House of Burgesses, and he had no reason to keep them from meeting; (A) is incorrect. Although Bacon did hold grievances with wealthy residents, at the time of his occupation of Jamestown he was more concerned with the governor and his forces, making (B) incorrect. (D) is incorrect because Bacon's Rebellion was a localized event and was unrelated to the actions of the king in England.

8. B

The eastern part of Virginia had disproportionately more members in the House of Burgesses than occupants of the western lands did. This state of affairs contributed to feelings of discontent because eastern landowners favored signing treaties to maintain peaceful relations with individual American Indian tribes, while Bacon and his followers favored an aggressive approach to gain access to native lands for settlement. Thus, (B) is correct. The Thirteen Colonies were generally hostile to Catholicism in this period, to the point that Maryland was notable for attempting to establish equal rights for Protestants and Catholics at its foundation. Thus, (A) is incorrect because it is unlikely that Virginia's government would boost Catholic immigration to the colony. Bacon and his rebels sought to settle lands held by American Indian tribes, not redistribute the lands held by plantation owners; (C) is incorrect. Bacon's Rebellion soured colonial planters on the continued use of white indentured servants, as former indentured servants had aided the rebellion. This spurred a shift towards the mass importation of slaves; (D) is incorrect.

9. B

Western Pennsylvanian farmers in the 1790s believed the new excise tax under Alexander Hamilton's financial plan unfairly targeted them and that their interests were not proportionately represented by the wealthy and well-educated representatives in Congress. The resulting Whiskey Rebellion stemmed from this economic conflict between poor landowners and the powerful elite, which is similar to Bacon's Rebellion; (B) is correct. The Nullification Crisis involved a state (South Carolina) opposing the federal government on the subject of tariffs in the 1830s; (A) is incorrect. (C) is incorrect because the Texan Revolution was a conflict between an American territory and another country (Mexico). While Nat Turner's Rebellion consisted of an oppressed class (slaves) rising up against the elite, it did not primarily revolve around economic reasons, making (D) incorrect.

10. B

The lyrics were written to rally Americans to "take up [their] arms and go with speed [their] country to defend" against the thousands of troops the British crown had dispatched to impose control over the American colonies, which they viewed as British possessions. (B) is correct. (A), (C), and (D) do not describe the core message the song is meant to deliver.

11. D

Loyalists made up approximately one-third of the colonial population, and many took up arms and fought alongside the British; (D) is correct. Conflicts with American Indians did not specifically pose a challenge for those fighting for independence, and some American Indians chose to assist the Americans in their fight against Britain, making (A) incorrect. While there was some fear of slave rebellion, slave rebellion was not a major factor during this time; (B) is incorrect. While the colonists did not have international allies at the beginning of the war, they became allies with France in 1778, which provided money, ships, and weapons to the colonists; (C) is also incorrect.

12. A

The English had passed several restrictive acts targeting the Americans, starting in 1765 with the Stamp Act and continuing into the 1770s with the Townshend Act and the Intolerable Acts. Americans believed their "rights as Englishmen" had been violated and that Parliament was taxing them without allowing them representation; (A) is correct. Free trade and freedom of the seas were a result of the American Revolution (rather than a cause), making (B) and (C) incorrect. Many American Indians sided with the colonists, while others joined the British. Either way, this was not a strong motivation for the colonists to go to war, eliminating (D).

13. A

Enlightenment philosophy proclaimed that it is the citizens' duty to revolt if the government does not protect their natural rights (such as freedom, privacy, and life), and the American Revolution hinged on this idea. Thus, (A) is correct. While free trade and economic liberty would come with independence, this was neither the goal of the Revolution nor an Enlightenment idea; (B) is incorrect. Enlightenment philosophies focused on the use of reason rather than spiritual and supernatural justifications, eliminating (C). (D) is incorrect because Enlightenment philosophies promoted religious tolerance.

14. A

Toward the end of the American Revolution, the Pennsylvania Emancipation Act of 1780 called for the gradual emancipation of slaves in Pennsylvania. At this time, some Americans were beginning to realize the hypocrisy of holding slaves while fighting to free themselves from the bondage of British rule; **(A)** is correct. (B) and (D) are incorrect because the public education reform movement and the prison reform movement were not addressed in the Pennsylvania Emancipation Act. The abolitionist movement stemmed from the Second Great Awakening, and while it also focused on ending slavery, it was led by a group who perceived political action as useless and immoral. This group would not have started with political means to further their goals; additionally, they called for the immediate emancipation of slaves, not the gradual emancipation of slaves. Therefore, (C) is incorrect.

15. B

The Liberty Party advocated for the abolition of slavery through legal processes. This movement was a political alternative to the radical abolitionist movement that emerged in the 1830s; **(B)** is correct. The Locofoco wing of the Democratic Party was associated mainly with the state of New York and was labor-friendly and anti-bank; (A) is incorrect. Free Soilers strove to stop slavery from spreading into new territories in order to prevent slaves and freed blacks from competing with white laborers for low-paying jobs, making (C) incorrect. (D) is incorrect because the American Party focused on anti-Catholic and anti-immigrant nativist ideals, not on the emancipation of slaves.

16. C

After the American Revolution, the Pennsylvania Abolition Society formed to outlaw slavery in this colony. Revolutionary leaders found it hypocritical to have slaves, given the fact that they had just freed themselves from the bondage of service to Britain; **(C)** is correct. The Pennsylvania Emancipation Act was drafted by revolutionary leaders who wished to extend their newfound freedom to everyone, making (A) and (D) incorrect. This act was the first of its kind in the nation, which eliminates (B).

17. D

According to *Marbury v. Madison*, the U.S. Constitution is "superior to any ordinary act of the legislature." Ultimately, this court case confirmed the Constitution as the supreme law of the land; **(D)** is correct. *Marbury v. Madison* established judicial review, which called for the Supreme Court to determine the constitutional validity of any legislation, making (A) and (B) incorrect. (C) is incorrect because the Supreme Court ruled that issuing writs of mandamus exceeded the authority granted by the Constitution.

18. A

Marbury v. Madison determined that the Supreme Court is an equal power to the legislative and executive branches by establishing judicial review, which matches **(A)**. (B) is incorrect because this case ruled that the Court cannot issue writs of mandamus based on the Constitution. (C) is incorrect because the Supreme Court only requires a majority vote to rule on a case. The ruling introduced the Court's responsibility to void legislation in conflict with the Constitution, making (D) incorrect.

19. C

Although the Judiciary Act of 1789 granted the Supreme Court power to issue writs of mandamus, the court ruled in *Marbury v. Madison* that this exceeded the authority allotted in Article III of the Constitution. Similarly, *Plessy v. Ferguson* established the precedent of "separate but equal" in 1896, but the court case *Brown v. Board of Education* overturned that decision, stating that separate was inherently unequal and ordering the integration of public schools. Therefore, **(C)** is correct. (A), (B), and (D) are incorrect because the pairs do not involve a court case that overturned the other.

20. D

Although the Supreme Court established the constitutionality of the Second Bank of the United States in the 1819 case *McCulloch v. Maryland*, Andrew Jackson vetoed the bill to recharter this bank. Jackson's veto was not grounded in the Constitution, but rather in his personal opinion that the bank was unconstitutional. **(D)** is correct. (A) and (C) are incorrect because these presidential actions were based on principles stated in the Constitution. (B) is incorrect; Madison vetoed this bill because the Constitution did not grant Congress the power to shape internal improvements, which agrees with the main principles outlined in the excerpt.

21. C

In 1820, the balance of free states and slave states was becoming more and more contentious. Kentucky senator Henry Clay created the Missouri Compromise, which admitted Missouri as a slave state and Maine as a free state in order to maintain the balance and prevent further conflict; **(C)** is correct. (A) is incorrect because the compromise mandated that all new states in the Louisiana Purchase north of the southern boundary of Missouri (except Missouri) be free states. The United States took Spanish Territory in the West by signing the Gadsden Purchase in 1853, so (B) is incorrect. President Polk signed an act that created Oregon Country in 1848, and Congress passed a bill that prohibited slavery in the territory, making (D) incorrect.

22. D

Quakers openly opposed slavery, especially the spread of slavery. Adding a new slave state was not acceptable to those in the early abolitionist movement; **(D)** is correct. (A) is incorrect because the cotton-growing states would have continued to be slave states according to the Missouri Compromise. Factory workers in New England found the compromise to be acceptable because slaves would not create competition for jobs, making (B) incorrect. Poor whites in the South would have welcomed the compromise since it allowed them to keep slaves; (C) is incorrect.

23. C

The Supreme Court *Dred Scott* decision in 1857 declared that slave owners could take their slaves into the western territories because they were property protected by the due process clause of the Fifth Amendment; the decision also declared the Missouri Compromise unconstitutional, which matches **(C)**. (A) is incorrect because it was Polk's desire to expand westward into Mexican territory that led to war in 1846. The *Dred Scott* decision ruled that

Congress, not the states, had the power to prohibit slavery in any territory, making (B) incorrect. (D) is incorrect; the *Dred Scott* decision negated the doctrine of popular sovereignty in the western territories.

24. D

The Fugitive Slave Act of 1850 was one of the more controversial elements of the Compromise of 1850. It required that all escaped slaves in free states be returned to their masters, levied high fees on individuals suspected of helping escaped slaves, and offered rewards for the recovery of escaped slaves. As a result, many free blacks, especially children, were captured and forced into slavery. The passing of this act led to an increased usage of the Underground Railroad to transport captured slaves to free states and Canada, which matches **(D)**. Personal liberty laws, which mandated a jury trial before a fugitive slave could be returned, were passed by the North in response to the earlier Fugitive Slave Act of 1793, so (A) is incorrect. (B) is incorrect because John C. Calhoun's speech occurred in 1837, before the Fugitive Slave Act of 1850 was passed. Bleeding Kansas was a series of violent conflicts that occurred in response to the Kansas-Nebraska Act of 1854, not the Fugitive Slave Act of 1850, making (C) incorrect.

25. C

In 1852, *Uncle Tom's Cabin* illustrated the negative effects of slavery on families and was notable for personalizing the political and economic arguments regarding slavery; **(C)** is the correct answer. *The Liberator* was an abolitionist newspaper founded by William Lloyd Garrison and Isaac Knapp in 1831, which was before the Fugitive Slave Act of 1850, making (A) incorrect. David Walker was an African American abolitionist who published *An Appeal to the Colored Citizens of the World* in 1829, eliminating (B). *The Adventures of Huckleberry Finn* was released in 1884 as a work of satire about past events, not as a piece to educate and inspire people about current events; (D) is incorrect.

26. C

Most Northerners were opposed to the passage of the Fugitive Slave Act of 1850, some expressing their disapproval through both violent and nonviolent protest. The Stamp Act, passed by the British Parliament to raise taxes on the American colonies without their consent, produced a similar response when the majority of American colonists protested; **(C)** is correct. (A), (B), and (D) are incorrect because they refer to events that did not incite such protests among American citizens or colonists. The Monroe Doctrine dissuaded European nations from interfering further in the Americas. Bacon's Rebellion was a conflict between Virginia settlers and Governor William Berkeley. The Glorious Revolution in 1688 deposed King James II of England, who was strongly disliked for being Catholic, and replaced him with William III.

27. C

The Free Soil Party opposed the expansion of slavery into the western territories. Many members of this party were later absorbed by the Republican Party between 1854 and 1856, making **(C)** correct. Republicans attacked the Democrats for actions they took in the name of popular sovereignty, such as the passing of the Kansas-Nebraska Act, eliminating (A). (B) and (D) are incorrect because many Republicans opposed the Emancipation Proclamation and did not want to grant blacks additional rights.

28. B

The Republican Party was most well known in the 1850s for its dedication to keeping slavery out of the territories. This stance drove the North and the South further apart, contributing to the strong sense of regional identity felt by the residents of both regions; **(B)** is correct. During the early nineteenth century, the shift to market production linked the Midwest to the North more closely than the Midwest or West were linked to the South, which still depended on slave labor, making (A) and (D) incorrect. While New England factory workers depended on a consistent cotton crop for their jobs, many began to oppose the use of slave labor as they became more aware of its moral issues; (C) is incorrect.

29. C

The Republican platform mandated that the government ensure each person's right to life, liberty, and property, as outlined in the Constitution. Therefore, because slavery interfered with these rights, it must be illegal. Similarly, the suffrage movement in the United States strove to ensure that women were able to fully utilize their Constitutional rights; **(C)** is correct. The movements in (A), (B), and (D) are incorrect because they were not developed to protect rights promised in the Constitution. The labor movement was a reaction to the free wage-labor market of the late colonial period and was dedicated to protecting the common interest of workers. The American Temperance Union led the crusade against alcohol and drunkenness in the early 1800s. Lastly, the nativist movement of the twentieth century actively opposed granting citizenship and rights to some immigrants, claiming that only immigrants from certain countries were acceptable.

30. D

While the passage of the Fifteenth Amendment in 1870 granted adult male freedmen the right to vote, taking advantage of this right proved to be challenging. This cartoon depicts the intimidation tactics used by the Democratic Party, as part of the Mississippi Plan of 1875, to coerce black Southern voters into voting Democrat; **(D)** is correct. The Radical Republicans strove to secure rights for freed slaves during Reconstruction, so it is unlikely that they would have prohibited freedmen from voting, eliminating (A). The Democratic Party passed new legislation that made voting more difficult for freedmen in the South in 1890, making (B) incorrect. The Redeemers were a coalition of conservative, pro-business Southern Democrats who worked to reestablish white supremacy using bribery and payments to freedmen; (C) is incorrect.

31. A

During the Reconstruction Era, the Thirteenth, Fourteenth, and Fifteenth Constitutional amendments were passed, but freedmen continued to be targeted. The Civil Rights Act of 1964, created under President Johnson's Great Society, prohibited job discrimination and racial segregation in common areas. Similarly, the Voting Rights Act of 1965 eliminated the use of literacy tests, which had prevented minorities from voting. Both of these acts upheld the ideas put forth during Reconstruction, which matches **(A)**. (B), (C), and (D) are incorrect; while each choice denotes important political actions that contributed to the civil rights movement, they did not reinforce rights gained specifically during Reconstruction.

32. B

This political cartoon depicts the intimidation techniques used to coerce black Southern voters into voting for the Democratic Party. Therefore, the correct answer must involve a political action that affected minority enfranchisement. Of the four choices, only **(B)** meets this criteria. The Civil Rights Acts of 1964 and the Voting Rights Act of 1965 codified the integration of society and protected the rights of African Americans to register to vote and participate in the electoral process. The *Brown v. Board of Education* decision stated that laws establishing separate public schools for black and white students were unconstitutional, eliminating (A). Similarly, while the decision to integrate the U.S. military helped to end discrimination, it did not play a role with respect to voting rights; (C) is incorrect. (D) is incorrect because the *Korematsu v. United States* decision, which ordered Japanese Americans into internment camps, resulted in a reduction in civil rights.

33. B

In the excerpt, Grady describes a softer, more communal South that thrives due to increased democracy and equality; **(B)** is correct. (A) is incorrect because most Southerners did not accept African Americans as equal until nearly a century later. (C) is incorrect because the women's rights movement initially began in the Northeast, and Southern states were the last to join. (D) is incorrect; while Henry Grady urged Southerners to adopt a modernized economy based on factories, this transformation did not occur until the mid-1900s. Even then, the South did not reach the same level of industrialization as the North did.

34. D

Henry Grady supported an industrialized Southern society, urging Southerners to abandon agriculture in exchange for a modernized economy based on factories, mines, and mills. The continued existence of sharecropping and the crop-lien system would enable the antebellum plantation system, thereby counteracting the idea of the New South, making **(D)** correct. (A), (B), and (C) are incorrect because each represents a step that would drive the South toward becoming more industrialized, thereby aligning the South with Grady's vision.

35. C

The New South, as advocated by Grady, described a region no longer dependent on slavery or the cotton trade. Rather, this region had modernized and its industrialized economy was thriving. This description fits best with the South of the 1950s, due the growth of industrialization and suburbanization in the region; **(C)** is correct. During the Antebellum Era and the Reconstruction Era, the Southern economy was still highly dependent on cotton and the slave trade, eliminating (A) and (D). During the Great Depression, many people, both black and white, moved to cities in hopes of finding work. While this was a step away from the agriculture-focused society of the Old South, it did not represent the flourishing New South that Grady had pictured, making (B) incorrect.

36. D

The premise in Horatio Alger's stories was that anyone who worked hard and lived an honest life could become a success and live the American Dream; **(D)** is correct. During the 1870s, the labor force expanded immensely, making (A) incorrect. While the Gilded Age provided many new industrial opportunities to Americans and delivered new technologies, such as railroads, Alger's message focused on Americans' abilities to dedicate themselves to a goal and become successful based on their hard work; (B) and (C) are incorrect.

37. B

Labor union members tended to work very hard for long hours, yet due to their working conditions and low wages, they did not become wealthy. Therefore, labor union members would most strongly oppose Horatio Alger's premise that hard work and good character are the only requirements for advancement; **(B)** is correct. Social Darwinists believed that hard work alone would allow a "fit" individual to advance in society and that character was irrelevant to economic output; (A) is incorrect. Factory owners would agree with Alger's positive portrayal of them, making (C) incorrect. City dwellers would have included labor union members, but also others with no stake in industry, so their position would have been mixed; (D) is incorrect.

38. A

The Protestant work ethic was the main theme of Alger's stories and this excerpt. Alger's main characters, as exemplified by Herbert in the passage, were rewarded for their honesty and work ethic; thus, **(A)** is correct. Republican motherhood expressed the idea that mothers were responsible for instilling civic virtue in their children; (B) is incorrect. While Jeffersonian democracy upheld virtue, it focused on the agricultural "yeoman farmer" and disdained the industrialists featured in Alger's work, making (C) incorrect. Jacksonian democracy dealt mainly with extending suffrage to all white males and championing anti-aristocratic reforms, eliminating (D).

39. C

Populism was a pro-agricultural political movement in the late nineteenth century that sought economic regulation and political reform. Populists were critical of the industrialists and the trusts of their era; **(C)** is correct. The Social Gospel dealt with easing the plight of the poor, which is not relevant to the cartoon; (A) is incorrect. Supporters of Progressivism were also critical of trusts, but this movement emerged in the twentieth century, so (B) is incorrect. Supporters of Social Darwinism, or the belief that the strongest members of society should become the most successful, would have disagreed with this cartoon's negative portrayal of wealthy tycoons; thus, (D) is also incorrect.

40. C

The artist promoted the idea that the U.S. Senate was a corrupt body, controlled by the monopolists and trusts; **(C)** is correct. In contrast, labor unions did not significantly influence the U.S. Senate. The U.S. Senate had passed legislation that helped business owners and big industry grow at the expense of workers' safety; (A) and (B) are incorrect. Both of those economic factors contributed to American society being far from equitable in the late nineteenth century, making (D) incorrect.

41. B

The corruption that existed in the U.S. Senate, especially in the late nineteenth century due to the influence of trusts, led to the twentieth-century Progressive movement's demand to break up trusts; **(B)** is correct. The New Deal's redistribution of wealth would be rooted in the public outcry for a response to the Great Depression, not in business interference in government; (A) is incorrect. While the Populists did call for the direct election of senators, that reform was spurred both by a desire for increased democracy and by the gridlock that selecting senators caused state legislatures, making (C) incorrect. (D) is incorrect because the Great Society reforms did not take place until the 1960s, and their ideals were rooted

in the New Deal rather than in the Populist movement of the late nineteenth century.

42. A

The image illustrates a corrupt Senate that is controlled by trusts and monopolies, and Congress's passing of New Deal legislation to control big business authority was its effort to avoid such corruption. Thus, **(A)** is correct. (B) is incorrect, because the government's adoption of a laissez-faire attitude meant that it would not interfere with the economy, which would not have rectified the type of corruption suggested in the image. The New Deal's business reforms were made in response to the Great Depression in an effort to lift the country's economy, eliminating (C). In the 1970s, the government passed landmark environmental regulations to protect the country, but such regulations did not limit trusts and monopolies; (D) is incorrect.

43. C

In the late nineteenth and early twentieth centuries, labor organizers often staged protests and strikes against unsafe working conditions and low wages. This political cartoon illustrates the supposed dangers of labor unions, namely that they lead to social unrest and violence. In other words, labor unions were dangerous, meaning the artist preferred the then-present state of affairs in the United States: traditional laissez-faire capitalism. Thus, **(C)** is correct. (A) is incorrect because the cartoon presents unions as a chaotic element, not one capable of taking over the United States. (B) is incorrect because the cartoon presents labor unions as dangerous, not labor itself. (D) is incorrect because the cartoon is dated to 1904, over a decade before the Russian Revolution of 1917, and a year before the failed Russian Revolution of 1905.

44. B

The Haymarket Square Riot in Chicago, Illinois, led to a significant court case. Eight anarchists were arrested, even though many of them were not present at the incident, for the murder of Chicago policemen. This event led to increased public fear of radical leftists; **(B)** is correct. While the KKK also targeted socialists and union organizers, they were mainly known for attacking African Americans and did not significantly contribute to America's fear of anarchists; (A) is incorrect. The Homestead Steel Strike was a major defeat for unions, which would lessen public fears of them; (C) is incorrect. During Coxey's March on Washington, unemployed workers demanded government relief for the ongoing recession, until federal forces ended the protest. This protest did not significantly contribute to America's fear of radical leftism; (D) is incorrect.

45. D

The Russian Revolution created a panic, or Red Scare, in the United States. Fearing a communist or socialist takeover, European nations deported known anarchists and socialists, many of whom then came to the United States. Numerous labor strikes also occurred in the United States. As a result, many American citizens feared that their nation was heading down the path to revolution; **(D)** is correct. The Great Depression began in 1929, the second quarter of the twentieth century, eliminating (A). The Portland Waterfront Strike was a failure for the labor organizers involved, as their employers did not give into the union's demands; (B) is incorrect. While the aftermath of World War I led to wide social discontent, it did not directly contribute to fear of the working class; (C) is incorrect.

46. D

In 1967, polling indicated that public support for the Vietnam War was at its lowest point. However, the conflict continued until 1975; **(D)** is correct. The American Youth Congress (AYC) had also led widespread youth protests in the 1930s against their own economic exploitation and against the draft, and the AYC had counted over four million members in their ranks by 1939; (A) is incorrect. While many groups opposed the U.S. involvement in the Vietnam War because of the military draft, American youth believed that the war was immoral and accused the United States of having imperialistic goals, making (B) incorrect. The photograph focuses on the protests against the Vietnam War and does not showcase how youth protesters were influenced by other groups, ranging from African Americans to clergy, eliminating (C).

47. C

Although Johnson withdrew from the presidential race in March 1968, protesters still targeted the Vietnam War and the Johnson administration. A nationwide television audience witnessed the protest at the 1968 Democratic Party National Convention as it became violent, which shook public confidence in the Democratic Party's ability to lead the country; **(C)** is correct. (A) is incorrect because the riots following King's death were mainly rooted in the African American community and were not comprised of exclusively youth protesters. While there was an antiwar backlash following Kennedy's assassination, it mainly occurred after Vice President Hubert Humphrey was nominated as the Democratic Party's candidate in the 1968 general election, making (B) incorrect. Woodstock's theme of peace was rooted in the hippie concept of separating from society, contrary to the photograph's depiction of youth protesters being engaged politically, eliminating (D).

48. D

As the 1960s and 1970s progressed, music targeted at youth culture became more prominent in mainstream culture. This music began to reflect the antiwar movement, usually through the genres of folk music and rock and roll; **(D)** is correct. While segments of literature, television, and the visual arts focused on youth culture and explored themes of social justice, young people were merely one segment of their audience rather than an overriding focus. Antiwar sentiments on television risked a backlash from that media's broader audience; for example, the Smothers Brothers variety show was repeatedly censored and finally cancelled because it advocated antiwar ideas. Therefore, (A), (B), and (C) are incorrect.

49. A

In 1993, the United States was in the middle of an economic recession that had created high unemployment and higher-than-average inflation; **(A)** is correct. (B) is incorrect because unemployment from the recession caused labor unrest, not the other way around. (C) is incorrect because low-wage, rather than high-wage, jobs were being exported. Although President Clinton called for a new era of bipartisan compromise, the 1990s would see increasing partisanship; (D) is incorrect.

50. C

The War on Terror began in the late fall of 2001. During the early 1990s, international terrorism by al-Qaeda and comparable organizations was not widely noted in America; **(C)** is correct. (Remember that the question is asking which issue was *not* a factor at the time of Clinton's speech.) (A) is incorrect because the Clinton administration helped promote the Internet, which was then called the information superhighway. The North American Free Trade Agreement and the recent collapse of the Soviet Union were ongoing concerns in 1993, making (B) and (D) incorrect.

51. A

The cartoon depicts two Rosie the Riveters with tools in hand, involved in the difficult work of building a ship. During World War II, the United States entered total war, meaning that nearly every citizen's life was impacted. Men were drafted to fight, and women were recruited to join the workforce to cover the men's duties and responsibilities; **(A)** is correct. While women during this time were working toward gaining equal rights, the Rosie the Riveter figure stemmed from America's need for women to cover men's jobs while they were at war; thus, (B) and (C) are both incorrect. Many women were forced out of their jobs after the war so that returning veterans could be employed again, but this issue is outside the scope of this cartoon; (D) is also incorrect.

52. C

Women who had joined the workforce during World War II to manufacture ships, planes, weapons, and other necessities of war could relate to the depiction of a woman performing physical work while tending her children; **(C)** is correct. Given the time period, managers of female laborers would have been almost uniformly male, and women made up the primary audience for the cartoon; (A) and (B) are incorrect. Given that the cartoon's focus is on women's roles and responsibilities rather than children's, child psychologists would not have appreciated the cartoon as strongly as women would have; (D) is incorrect.

53. D

The cartoon clearly reflects the way women's roles changed as new situations and opportunities presented themselves in American society; **(D)** is correct. The United States military and the economic system of capitalism are irrelevant, making (A) and (B) incorrect. The women are not depicted as being overwhelmed, and the children are not depicted as being neglected or in need of childcare services, so (C) is also incorrect.

54. B

The women's rights movement of the nineteenth century, led by figures such as Susan B. Anthony, focused attention not only on voting rights for women but also on women's roles in society and how these roles developed in the home and in the workplace; **(B)** is correct. The cartoon does not include references to issues such as voting rights or unionization; (A) and (D) are incorrect. Industrialization affected society as a whole, not only the women who formed this cartoon's target audience; (C) is too broad and is therefore incorrect.

55. B

Based on the information provided, and the positive portrayal of women workers in the government-sponsored publication, one can conclude that the role of the Rosie the Riveters contributed to the expansion of jobs for women in the decades that followed; **(B)** is correct. The women depicted in the cartoon are not overwhelmed by their children or in need of childcare; (A) is incorrect. While some women in the 1950s and 1960s were dissatisfied with homemaking in general, many women sought out higher-education opportunities in order to meet potential spouses and return to the realm of domesticity, eliminating (C). Unlike World War II, the Korean War and the Vietnam War were not total wars and did not require the total mobilization of American society to wage them, making (D) incorrect.

Section I, Part B

1. A successful short-answer response accomplishes all three tasks set forth by the prompt. Each part of the prompt is worth 1 point, for a total of 3 possible points.

(a) To earn the point, the response must describe a significant difference between the authors' interpretations of responses to pressures from white Americans, specifically addressing the claims of *both* passages. For the first passage, the response should describe Dowd's claim that the most "vital" response was that of some American Indians who drew on spiritualism and intertribal connections to create a united resistance to settlers who were expanding westward, while also challenging other American Indian leaders who favored "accommodating" the United States and were giving up their lands. For the second passage, the response should describe Perdue's claim that the most historically "visible" of the Cherokees felt that the "best protection" was to assimilate to the ways of the United States and take on customs and ways that whites considered "civilized."

(b) To earn the point, the response must identify a specific historical event or development from 1780–1840 and use reasoning or evidence to explain how that event or development supports the author of the first passage's claim that prophetic nativism—which incorporated spiritualism, intertribal unity, and rejection of white culture—was a strong response to white expansion. An example of American Indian intertribal unity and rejection of white culture is the work of Shawnee chief Tecumseh and his brother, the Prophet, who united various tribes in the Great Lakes region, advocated the rejection of the white people's ways, and led the fight against the U.S. military at the Battle of Tippecanoe. Another example of intertribal cooperation is the united resistance to removal from the Northwest Territory, culminating in the Battle of Fallen Timbers. Note that examples that occurred after 1840, such as cooperation among tribes in the Great Sioux War in 1876, would not earn the point.

(c) To earn the point, the response must identify a specific historical event or development from 1780–1840 and use reasoning or evidence to explain how that event or development supports the author of the second passage's claim that American Indian tribes that incorporated white culture into their traditional cultures were those that became "most visible in the historical record." The response must include an example other than those mentioned in the passage. An additional example about the Cherokee accommodating U.S. culture is their using the American court system in the case *Cherokee Nation v. Georgia* to protest their being forcefully removed from their land. Other examples include the terms of the Treaty of Greenville, in which the Shawnee and other tribes ceded land in the Northwest Territory to the United States, and the Choctaw removal from and ceding of land in the Treaty of Dancing Rabbit Creek.

2. A successful short-answer response accomplishes all three tasks set forth by the prompt. Each part of the prompt is worth 1 point, for a total of 3 possible points.

(a) To earn the point, the response must describe a perspective about the American Revolution that Paine expresses in one or both of the passages. Examples from the first passage include the difficulty of the conflict and the necessity of devotion to the cause, the view that the Americans were fighting for the valuable cause of "Freedom," and the view that the Americans were already serving their own, independent, "country." Examples from the second passage include the view that the revolution was "great" and "complete," and the view that Americans must pause for reflection about the completion of the war. In order to describe the perspective, the response must elaborate on Paine's meaning, for instance, by describing *why* there would be a need for reflection after the war (such as the fundamental change in status in transforming from colonial possessions to an independent nation and the consideration of what type of government should be put in place).

(b) To earn the point, the response must use reasoning or evidence to explain how a historical development or event led to the writing of the first passage, which was written in the early stages of the American Revolution and encouraged devotion despite times of difficulty. Examples of difficulties include the struggle of the Continental Congress to supply the Continental Army soldiers, the continued Tory resistance to the revolution, and British occupation of New York City. Alternately, the response could explain a cause of the American Revolution—such as any of the various acts of Parliament or the early conflicts at Lexington, Concord, or Bunker Hill—or connect the ideals of freedom in the passage to the recently signed Declaration of Independence. Note that the response cannot use an event that occurred after December 1776, such as the difficulties faced by the Continental Army at Valley Forge during the winter of 1777–1778, as an example.

(c) To earn the point, the response must use reasoning or evidence to explain a historical development or event that resulted from the changes described in the second passage, which encouraged a pause for reflection during the conclusion of the American Revolution. Examples include the provisions in the Treaty of Paris that granted the United States independence and set the country's boundaries; and the successes and failures of the Articles of Confederation government (already in effect when the passage was written), which served to unite the former colonies but suffered from various weaknesses, including inability of enforcement, that were already causing concern and debate about the governance of the new nation.

3. A successful short-answer response accomplishes all three tasks set forth by the prompt. Each part of the prompt is worth 1 point, for a total of 3 possible points.

(a) To earn the point, the response must describe a similarity in the background or provisions of the Compromise of 1850 and that of the Kansas-Nebraska Act. The Compromise of 1850 was a set of congressional acts passed in the wake of controversy over slavery in territories acquired after the Mexican-American War; the compromise admitted California as a free state, allowed territories from the Mexican Cession to decide slavery by popular sovereignty, enacted the Fugitive Slave Law, and ended the slave trade in Washington, D.C. The Kansas-Nebraska Act was passed to provide measures to open the two territories to settlement; the act allowed for popular sovereignty, whereby the residents of each territory would vote as to whether slavery would be legal there or not. Examples of similarities between the acts include their basis in the issue of slavery, their creation of new territories, and their inclusion of popular sovereignty.

(b) To earn the point, the response must describe a difference between the background or provisions of the Compromise of 1850 and that of the Kansas-Nebraska Act. Examples include the background of the Compromise of 1850 in the Mexican-American War, while the Kansas-Nebraska Act was motivated by attempts to build a transcontinental railroad; the Compromise of 1850 upholding the Missouri Compromise, while the Kansas-Nebraska Act repealed the provisions of the Missouri Compromise (that slavery could not exist north of a particular boundary); and the Compromise of 1850 involving the admission of California as a free state, while the Missouri Compromise only settled the issue of slavery in admitted territories through popular sovereignty.

(c) To earn the point, the response must identify an effect of either the Compromise of 1850 or the Kansas-Nebraska Act and use reasoning or evidence to explain how the act(s) brought about that effect. Examples of effects of the Compromise of 1850 include delaying the escalation of hostilities that ultimately led to the Civil War, establishing the principle of popular sovereignty, and the polarization of views about slavery, as heightened by northern abolitionists' outrage at the Fugitive Slave Law. Examples of effects of the Kansas-Nebraska Act include its earning the name "Bleeding Kansas" due to the violence that broke out between Free Soilers and proponents of slavery in the territory, including John Brown's raid at Pottawatomie.

Other examples for the Kansas-Nebraska Act include the rising of regional tensions that would eventually lead to the Civil War (with adequate specific details to prevent such a response from being too vague), the physical attack in Congress on Sumner after his verbal attacks on slavery interests in the Brooks-Sumner Affair, the rise of the Republican Party, and the passage of the Wyandotte Constitution that admitted Kansas as a free state.

4. A successful short-answer response accomplishes all three tasks set forth by the prompt. Each part of the prompt is worth 1 point, for a total of 3 possible points.

(a) To earn the point, the response must describe a specific similarity in the domestic responses to the two events. Examples of similarities include the addresses made by presidents (Franklin Roosevelt and George W. Bush) in the aftermath of the attacks, the shifts in public opinion to supporting wars against Japan and terrorism, and the eventual memorialization of the American lives lost in each attack.

(b) To earn the point, the response must describe a specific difference in the domestic responses to the two events. Examples of differences include the intent of the presidents' speeches, as Roosevelt intended not only to comfort the nation but to persuade Congress to declare war on Japan; the extent of mobilization for war; the extent of propaganda use in the ensuing conflicts; and the particular responses to each attack, such as the internment of Japanese Americans after Pearl Harbor and the creation of the Homeland Security Department and expansion of intelligence agencies' powers after 9/11.

(c) To earn the point, the response must use reasoning or evidence to explain how the events at Pearl Harbor or the events on 9/11 led to an international response. Examples of international responses to the Pearl Harbor attacks include the declaration of war on Japan and the subsequent entry into war in Europe after Germany and Italy declared war on the United States, the beginning of the War in the Pacific and early naval battles of the Coral Sea and Midway, and the entry of the United States into campaigns in North Africa and Italy. Examples of international responses to 9/11 include Bush's declaration of the War on Terror, the joint invasion of Afghanistan (Operation Enduring Freedom) to depose the Taliban, the pursuit of al-Qaeda leader Osama bin Laden, and the eventual initiation of the Iraq War to depose Saddam Hussein.

Part 4
Practice Exams

Section II

1. *Evaluate the extent of change in Americans' views on freedom and equality during World War II from 1939 to 1945.*

Category	Scoring Criteria	Notes
Thesis/Claim (0–1 points)	Historically defensible thesis/claim with a logical line of reasoning. The response must make a thesis or claim without restating the prompt itself. The thesis must consist of one or more sentences located in one place, either in the introduction or the conclusion.	A strong thesis should make a claim about the extent of change in views on freedom and equality by articulating an argument and may identify the categories of analysis that will be used in the essay. Example: "Overall, WWII caused short-term limits in liberties and long-term increases in notions of equality, setting into motion movements that would transform what it meant to be an American in the decades to come." This thesis makes the claim that liberty was limited while ideas of equality expanded, which establishes the essay's categories of analysis: limits on liberty and increases in equality. The thesis also establishes a complex argument (see Analysis & Reasoning below) by addressing both causes *and* effects. Other effective arguments could make a claim related to the different groups represented in the documents (African Americans, women, and Japanese Americans) or a claim related to change and continuity in ideas about equality and freedom.
Contextualization (0–1 points)	Broader historical context related to the prompt. The response must connect the topic to historical developments, events, or processes; these can occur before, during, or after the time frame of the prompt itself.	Contextualization for this prompt should explain, not merely mention, broader factors relevant to World War II or the prejudices faced by the groups mentioned in the documents prior to the war. Examples: A description of why the United States entered World War II; a description of the legal and social status of African Americans, women, and/or Japanese Americans before the war.

Category	Scoring Criteria	Notes
Evidence (0–3 points)	Use of evidence to support the thesis. The response must utilize the content from at least *three* documents to address the *topic* of the prompt. (1 point) OR The response must use at least *six* documents to support an *argument* based on the prompt. (2 points)	Evidence from the documents must be paraphrased, not merely quoted. To earn 2 points, the evidence must be used to support an argument about the changes in ideas of equality and freedom. Examples: Documents 1, 3, 5, and 7 to analyze views about equality and documents 2, 4, 6, and 7 to analyze views about freedom; documents 1 and 5 to analyze views affecting African Americans, documents 2 and 6 to analyze views affecting Japanese Americans, document 3 to analyze views affecting women, and documents 4 and 7 to analyze views affecting all Americans; documents 1, 3, and 7 to analyze examples of increases in freedom or equality and documents 2, 5, 4, and 6 to analyze examples of decreases in freedom or equality.
	The response must use at least *one* additional piece of historical evidence, beyond what is found in the documents, to support an argument. This additional evidence must be different from what was used for contextualization. (1 point)	Examples: The use of Roosevelt's issue of Executive Order 8802 to end discriminatory hiring in federal government jobs to support the claim about increases in views of equality during World War II; the increase in female units of the military, such as the WASPS and WACS, to support the claim about increases in views about equality during World War II.
Analysis and Reasoning (0–2 points)	Complexity of understanding and reasoning. The response must explain, for at least *three* of the documents, how or why the document's purpose, historical basis, point of view, and/or audience are relevant to an argument. (1 point)	Factors' relevance to the argument about changes in ideas of equality and freedom should be explained, not just identified. Examples: The role of audience and purpose in document 1, which Randolph delivered to persuade African Americans to participate in a march; the role of purpose in documents 3, 4, and 7, which were created to persuade American citizens to change or monitor their behaviors and attitudes during the war.
	The response must show a complex understanding of the content of the prompt, using evidence to support, qualify, or modify an argument about the prompt. (1 point)	A complex understanding should be incorporated into the overall argument about changes to ideas about equality and freedom. Examples: An explanation of both causes *and* effects of World War II ideas, such as how attitudes about equality in World War II impacted the civil rights movement and women's rights movement of the 1950s and 1960s; an explanation of both changes *and* continuities, such as the continued prejudices demonstrated during the war against Japanese Americans (documents 2 and 6) and African Americans (document 5); a description of a connection to another time period, such as how women's roles in previous wars, such as World War I, impacted their equality after the war.

2. *Evaluate the extent to which the migration of European colonists and the resulting encounters with American Indians affected social patterns in the period from 1495 to 1650.*

Category	Scoring Criteria	Notes
Thesis/Claim (0-1 points)	Historically defensible thesis/claim with a logical line of reasoning. The response must make a thesis or claim without restating the prompt itself. The thesis must consist of one or more sentences located in one place, either in the introduction or the conclusion.	A strong thesis should make a claim about how the interactions between Europeans and American Indians impacted social patterns by articulating an argument and may identify the categories of analysis that will be used in the essay. Example: "The Spanish, French, and British each took a unique approach to how they utilized the New World territories in which they settled, resulting in three distinct patterns of social development." This thesis makes the claim that the different approaches to settlement of European countries led to different types of significant social development. The thesis also establishes the categories of analysis: the methods and subsequent social developments of the Spanish, French, and British. Although this thesis focuses on the differences among the practices of three European nations, other approaches are valid: an effective thesis could make a single claim about overall social patterns or focus on only one or two European nations.
Contextualization (0–1 points)	Broader historical context related to the prompt. The response must connect the topic to historical developments, events, or processes; these can occur before, during, or after the time frame of the prompt itself.	Contextualization for this prompt should explain, not merely mention, broader factors relevant to exploration, colonization, or American Indian societies. Examples: A description of American Indian societies before European contact, such as the Pueblo settlements of the southwest and the villages of the Iroquois Confederacy in the northeast; a description of the factors that motivated or enabled European overseas exploration, such as the development of sea technologies and the search for profitable trade routes.

Category	Scoring Criteria	Notes
Evidence (0–2 points)	Use of evidence to support the thesis. The response identifies specific examples *relevant to the topic* of the prompt. (1 point) OR The response uses specific examples to *support an argument* about the prompt. (2 points)	To earn 2 points, the evidence must be used to support an argument about the ways in which the interactions between Europeans and American Indians impacted social patterns. Examples: The economic and religious motivations of the Spanish leading to forced labor, Catholic missions, large-scale mining and plantation operations, the *encomienda* system, and a hierarchical social structure based on race; the economic motivations of the French resulting in more cooperative fur trade relationships with American Indians in the northeast and facilitating future alliances; the economic and religious motivations of the British leading to displacement of and conflict with American Indians, as in the Pequot War and Metacom's War; the impact of epidemic diseases causing population decline and social upheaval in all American Indian societies.
Analysis and Reasoning (0–2 points)	Complexity of understanding and reasoning. The response shows historical reasoning to make an argument about the prompt. (1 point) AND The response demonstrates complex understanding, using evidence to support, qualify, or modify an argument about the prompt. (1 point)	Comparison, causation, or continuity and change over time should be incorporated into the overall argument about the ways in which the interactions between Europeans and American Indians impacted social patterns. Example: An explanation of how the desire of the French to establish fur-trading relationships with American Indians led to generally cooperative relationships with the American Indians (causation). AND A complex understanding should be incorporated into the overall argument about the ways in which the interactions between Europeans and American Indians impacted social patterns. Examples: Explaining multiple variables that fostered cooperative relationships between the French and American Indians, such as the inability of the French to establish large-scale mining or plantation operations in the northeast and the relatively smaller numbers of French settlers resulting in fewer large settlements; qualifying the argument about cooperative relationships between the French and American Indians by describing the exploitative French sugar plantations on Hispaniola; explaining multiple variables by analyzing how the motives of multiple European nations resulted in different social patterns.

3. *Evaluate the extent to which the market revolution affected internal migration in the United States in the period from 1800 to 1860.*

Category	Scoring Criteria	Notes
Thesis/Claim (0-1 points)	Historically defensible thesis/claim with a logical line of reasoning. The response must make a thesis or claim without restating the prompt itself. The thesis must consist of one or more sentences located in one place, either in the introduction or the conclusion.	A strong thesis should make a claim about the ways in which the market revolution impacted migration by articulating an argument and may identify the categories of analysis that will be used in the essay. Example: "The market revolution increased migration to northern cities and to the West, while migration to and from the South remained relatively unchanged." This thesis makes the claim that the market revolution especially impacted migration in the North and West. The thesis also establishes the categories of analysis: migration to northern cities and migration to the West.
Contextualization (0-1 points)	Broader historical context related to the prompt. The response must connect the topic to historical developments, events, or processes; these can occur before, during, or after the time frame of the prompt itself.	Contextualization for this prompt should explain, not merely mention, broader factors relevant to the market revolution or internal migration. Examples: A description of the American economy before the market revolution, in which most Americans worked on small farms; a description of the involvement of coastal cities in trade relationships of the earlier Atlantic economy.
Evidence (0-2 points)	Use of evidence to support the thesis. The response identifies specific examples *relevant to the topic* of the prompt. (1 point) OR The response uses specific examples to *support an argument* about the prompt. (2 points)	To earn 2 points, the evidence must be used to support an argument about ways in which the market revolution impacted migration. Examples: The importation of the factory system and Eli Whitney's system of interchangeable parts leading to the migration of workers to factory towns and urban factories in the northern and middle states; the increased demand for raw materials and transport of finished goods resulting from factory production leading to the construction of railroads and canals; transportation technologies increasing migration westward by connecting the West with northern markets; the emergence of Chicago as a major railroad hub enabling midwestern and western settlement; new agricultural technologies, such as John Deere's steel plow, encouraging western migration by making farming more productive; steamships enabling settlement and trade networks along the west coast.

Category	Scoring Criteria	Notes
Analysis and Reasoning (0-2 points)	Complexity of understanding and reasoning. The response shows historical reasoning to make an argument about the prompt. (1 point) AND The response demonstrates complex understanding, using evidence to support, qualify, or modify an argument about the prompt. (1 point)	Comparison, causation, or continuity and change over time should be incorporated into the overall argument about the ways in which the market revolution impacted migration. Example: An explanation of how new transportation and agricultural technologies enabled western migration (causation). AND A complex understanding should be incorporated into the overall argument about the ways in which the market revolution impacted migration. Examples: An explanation of both causes *and* effects of western migration, such as the displacement of and conflicts with American Indians in western territories or the sectional conflicts resulting from disputes about slavery in new territories; a qualification of the argument about the impact of migration by describing how the invention of the cotton gin and the demand for cotton from the market revolution entrenched plantation agriculture in the South, resulting in little construction of (and thus no subsequent migration to) factories in the South.

4. *Evaluate the extent to which the Great Migration of African Americans affected social patterns in the United States in the period from 1890 to 1930.*

Category	Scoring Criteria	Notes
Thesis/Claim (0-1 points)	Historically defensible thesis/claim with a logical line of reasoning. The response must make a thesis or claim without restating the prompt itself. The thesis must consist of one or more sentences located in one place, either in the introduction or the conclusion.	A strong thesis should make a claim about the ways in which the Great Migration impacted social patterns by articulating an argument and may identify the categories of analysis that will be used in the essay. Example: "The Great Migration invigorated African American culture and heightened racial tensions; both of these factors would lay the foundation of the modern civil rights movement." This thesis makes the claim that the Great Migration impacted social patterns by establishing the categories of analysis: African American culture and racial tensions. The claim about the civil rights movement addresses events that occurred after the time period of the prompt but introduces a complex understanding of the argument (described under the Analysis & Reasoning category).

Category	Scoring Criteria	Notes
Contextual-ization (0-1 points)	Broader historical context related to the prompt. The response must connect the topic to historical developments, events, or processes; these can occur before, during, or after the time frame of the prompt itself.	Contextualization for this prompt should explain, not merely mention, broader factors relevant to African American migration or the early twentieth century American economy or social structure. Examples: A description of the economic and/or social pressures in the South that prompted African American migration, such as the debt cycle created by sharecropping, the prejudice and violence of vigilante groups, the effective disenfranchisement of blacks through poll taxes and literacy tests, and the discriminatory culture under Jim Crow laws; the growth of American industry due to technological and business innovations of the late nineteenth and early twentieth centuries and the increase in production during and after World War I.
Evidence (0-2 points)	Use of evidence to support the thesis. The response identifies specific examples *relevant to the topic* of the prompt. (1 point) OR The response uses specific examples to *support an argument* about the prompt. (2 points)	To earn 2 points, the evidence must be used to support an argument about ways in which the Great Migration impacted social patterns. Examples: The concentration of African Americans in overcrowded, segregated communities in northern cities; the lower quality of education in black neighborhoods; the racial tension and violence created by prejudice and competition for jobs after World War I, as in the race riot in Chicago in 1919; the development of a vital racial identity in African American communities, as in the Harlem Renaissance; the crossover of African American culture into mainstream American culture, as in the popularity of jazz and jitterbug music.

Category	Scoring Criteria	Notes
Analysis and Reasoning (0-2 points)	Complexity of understanding and reasoning. The response shows historical reasoning to make an argument about the prompt. (1 point) AND The response demonstrates complex understanding, using evidence to support, qualify, or modify an argument about the prompt. (1 point)	Comparison, causation, or continuity and change over time should be incorporated into the overall argument about the ways in which the Great Migration impacted social patterns. Example: An explanation of how the urban communities of blacks resulting from the Great Migration fostered a flourishing of African American culture (causation). AND A complex understanding should be incorporated into the overall argument about the ways in which the Great Migration impacted social patterns. Example: An explanation of both causes *and effects*, as in the impact that black culture and racial tensions would have on the civil rights movement of the 1950s and 1960s.

Practice Exam 3

Practice Exam 3 Answer Grid

1. Ⓐ Ⓑ Ⓒ Ⓓ   15. Ⓐ Ⓑ Ⓒ Ⓓ   29. Ⓐ Ⓑ Ⓒ Ⓓ   43. Ⓐ Ⓑ Ⓒ Ⓓ

2. Ⓐ Ⓑ Ⓒ Ⓓ   16. Ⓐ Ⓑ Ⓒ Ⓓ   30. Ⓐ Ⓑ Ⓒ Ⓓ   44. Ⓐ Ⓑ Ⓒ Ⓓ

3. Ⓐ Ⓑ Ⓒ Ⓓ   17. Ⓐ Ⓑ Ⓒ Ⓓ   31. Ⓐ Ⓑ Ⓒ Ⓓ   45. Ⓐ Ⓑ Ⓒ Ⓓ

4. Ⓐ Ⓑ Ⓒ Ⓓ   18. Ⓐ Ⓑ Ⓒ Ⓓ   32. Ⓐ Ⓑ Ⓒ Ⓓ   46. Ⓐ Ⓑ Ⓒ Ⓓ

5. Ⓐ Ⓑ Ⓒ Ⓓ   19. Ⓐ Ⓑ Ⓒ Ⓓ   33. Ⓐ Ⓑ Ⓒ Ⓓ   47. Ⓐ Ⓑ Ⓒ Ⓓ

6. Ⓐ Ⓑ Ⓒ Ⓓ   20. Ⓐ Ⓑ Ⓒ Ⓓ   34. Ⓐ Ⓑ Ⓒ Ⓓ   48. Ⓐ Ⓑ Ⓒ Ⓓ

7. Ⓐ Ⓑ Ⓒ Ⓓ   21. Ⓐ Ⓑ Ⓒ Ⓓ   35. Ⓐ Ⓑ Ⓒ Ⓓ   49. Ⓐ Ⓑ Ⓒ Ⓓ

8. Ⓐ Ⓑ Ⓒ Ⓓ   22. Ⓐ Ⓑ Ⓒ Ⓓ   36. Ⓐ Ⓑ Ⓒ Ⓓ   50. Ⓐ Ⓑ Ⓒ Ⓓ

9. Ⓐ Ⓑ Ⓒ Ⓓ   23. Ⓐ Ⓑ Ⓒ Ⓓ   37. Ⓐ Ⓑ Ⓒ Ⓓ   51. Ⓐ Ⓑ Ⓒ Ⓓ

10. Ⓐ Ⓑ Ⓒ Ⓓ   24. Ⓐ Ⓑ Ⓒ Ⓓ   38. Ⓐ Ⓑ Ⓒ Ⓓ   52. Ⓐ Ⓑ Ⓒ Ⓓ

11. Ⓐ Ⓑ Ⓒ Ⓓ   25. Ⓐ Ⓑ Ⓒ Ⓓ   39. Ⓐ Ⓑ Ⓒ Ⓓ   53. Ⓐ Ⓑ Ⓒ Ⓓ

12. Ⓐ Ⓑ Ⓒ Ⓓ   26. Ⓐ Ⓑ Ⓒ Ⓓ   40. Ⓐ Ⓑ Ⓒ Ⓓ   54. Ⓐ Ⓑ Ⓒ Ⓓ

13. Ⓐ Ⓑ Ⓒ Ⓓ   27. Ⓐ Ⓑ Ⓒ Ⓓ   41. Ⓐ Ⓑ Ⓒ Ⓓ   55. Ⓐ Ⓑ Ⓒ Ⓓ

14. Ⓐ Ⓑ Ⓒ Ⓓ   28. Ⓐ Ⓑ Ⓒ Ⓓ   42. Ⓐ Ⓑ Ⓒ Ⓓ

SECTION I, PART A
Time—55 minutes
55 Questions

Directions: Section I, Part A of this exam contains 55 multiple-choice questions, organized into sets with corresponding historical sources. Each of the questions or incomplete statements is followed by four suggested answers or completions. Using both the provided sources and your own historical knowledge, select the best answer choice.

Questions 1–3 refer to the excerpt below.

"But as to the great number of their enormities committed by those who style themselves Christians in order to the extirpation of this People, I will hear repeat some of them. . . . I also affirm that I saw with these eyes of mine the Spaniards for no other reason, but only to gratify their bloody mindedness, cut off the hands, noses, and ears, both of Indians and Indianesses, and that in so many places and parts, that it would be too prolix and tedious to relate them. Nay, I have seen the Spaniards let loose their dogs upon the Indians to bait and tear them in pieces, and such a number of villages burnt by them as cannot well be discover'd. . . . They committed many other cruelties, which shook me with terror at the very sight of them, and would take up too much time in the relation."

Bartolomé de las Casas, *A Short Account of the Destruction of the Indies,* 1542

1. Which of the following Spanish practices does de las Casas criticize in this excerpt?

    (A) *Asiento* system

    (B) Headright system

    (C) *Encomienda* system

    (D) *Hacienda* system

2. Bartolomé de las Casas is most known for

    (A) speaking out against the atrocities that the Spanish committed against the native peoples of the Americas

    (B) advocating for the forceful conversion of indigenous people to Christianity by Spanish conquistadors

    (C) suppressing native people in order to gain new land for Spanish Christians wishing to start religious societies in the New World

    (D) starting missions in the New World for native peoples fleeing persecution by Spanish conquistadors

3. Through sharing his disapproval regarding the Spanish treatment of native peoples, de las Casas most likely influenced which of the following?

    (A) The Columbian Exchange

    (B) Spanish conquest of the Inca Empire

    (C) The Black Legend

    (D) Anti-Catholic propaganda

GO ON TO THE NEXT PAGE

Questions 4–6 refer to the map below.

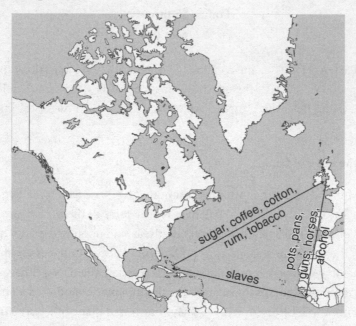

4. Which of the following represents Triangular Trade's impact on the colonies?

   (A) Importation of cotton, tobacco, and sugar to the New World

   (B) Importation of slaves and manufactured goods to the New World

   (C) Importation of rum and gunpowder to the New World

   (D) Importation of lumber and furs to the New World

5. The map most directly illustrates that

   (A) slaves were sent from Africa to Europe in exchange for manufactured goods

   (B) Europe traded manufactured goods in exchange for tobacco, cotton, sugar, and molasses

   (C) slaves were transported by European merchants from Africa to the New World

   (D) European merchants exchanged raw materials for African slaves

6. The Triangular Trade best represents which colonial economic practice?

   (A) Imperialism

   (B) Mercantilism

   (C) Utopianism

   (D) Laissez-faire economics

GO ON TO THE NEXT PAGE

Questions 7 and 8 refer to the excerpt below.

"I was thirty-three years old when the government first plowed up fields for us. . . . New kinds of seeds were issued to us, oats and wheat; and we were . . . taught to plant potatoes. . . . At first we Hidatsas* did not like potatoes, because they smelled so strongly! Then we sometimes dug up our potatoes and took them into our earth lodges; and when cold weather came, the potatoes were frozen, and spoiled. For these reasons we did not take much interest in our potatoes, and often left them in the ground, not bothering to dig them. Other seeds were issued to us, of watermelons, big squashes, onions, turnips, and other vegetables. Some of these we tried to eat, but did not like them very well; even the turnips and big squashes, we thought not so good as our own squashes and our wild prairie turnips. Moreover, we did not know how to dry these new vegetables for winter; so we often did not trouble even to harvest them."

*An American Indian tribe in North Dakota.

Gilbert Livingston Wilson, an ethnographer,
Agriculture of the Hidatsa Indians: An Indian Interpretation, 1917

7. The excerpt best illustrates which of the following developments?

   (A) The introduction of squash, white potatoes, and sweet potatoes to the Americas

   (B) The introduction of agriculture to some American Indian tribes by the U.S. government

   (C) The introduction of wheat, watermelons, and Old World crops to the Americas

   (D) The attempt to "civilize" American Indians under the Indian termination policy

8. Agricultural activities like those described in the excerpt most directly reflected

   (A) the need for developing vaccines for devastating New World diseases

   (B) the ecological and biological perspective on New and Old World interactions

   (C) the ways the New World benefited from the Old World's assistance

   (D) the documentation of American Indians by early European explorers

Questions 9 and 10 refer to the image below.

The engraving depicts a missionary, in the top left, instructing a gathering of American Indians

9. Which of the following groups maintained the most peaceful relations with American Indians?

   (A) English Protestants

   (B) Catholic Jesuits

   (C) Spanish conquistadors

   (D) English explorers

10. Attempts to convert American Indians contributed to which uprising?

   (A) Pontiac's Rebellion

   (B) Battle of Acoma

   (C) The Pueblo Revolt

   (D) Bacon's Rebellion

GO ON TO THE NEXT PAGE

Questions 11–13 refer to the excerpt below.

"Now the onely way to avoyde this shipwracke and to provide for our posterity is to . . . knitt together in this worke as one man, wee must entertaine each other in brotherly Affeccion, . . . soe shall wee keepe the unitie of the spirit in the bond of peace, the Lord will be our God and delight to dwell among us, as his owne people and will commaund a blessing upon us in all our ways . . . that men shall say of succeeding plantacions: the lord make it like that of New England: for wee must Consider that wee shall be as a Citty upon a Hill, the eies of all people are uppon us; soe that if wee shall deale falsely with our god in this worke wee have undertaken and soe cause him to withdrawe his present help from us, wee shall be made a story and a byword through the world, . . . wee shall shame the faces of many of gods worthy servants, and cause theire prayers to be turned into Cursses upon us till wee be consumed out of the good land whether wee are going."

John Winthrop, *A Modell of Christian Charity*, 1630

11. To which group of people is John Winthrop speaking?

    (A) Pilgrims

    (B) Puritans

    (C) Separatists

    (D) Protestants

12. Winthrop and his fleet eventually built which of the following societies in the New World?

    (A) Self-governing towns with one congregational church per town

    (B) Self-governing counties comprised of three towns each

    (C) State-governed towns with a congregational church every 10 miles

    (D) State-governed counties with one church per county

13. Winthrop's vision for his "Citty upon a Hill" was to

    (A) maintain a refuge for people seeking freedom from religious persecution in England

    (B) set an example of rightful living and Puritan values

    (C) create a mission to convert native peoples to Protestantism

    (D) establish a successful center of commerce and economic growth in New England

GO ON TO THE NEXT PAGE

Questions 14 and 15 refer to the excerpt below.

"If they dare come out in the open field and defend the gold standard as a good thing, we will fight them to the uttermost. Having behind us the producing masses of this nation and the world, supported by the commercial interests, the laboring interest, and the toilers everywhere, we will answer their demand for a gold standard by saying to them: You shall not press down upon the brow of labor this crown of thorns; you shall not crucify mankind upon a cross of gold."

William Jennings Bryan, "Cross of Gold" speech, 1896

14. Which of the following was an outcome of Bryan's speech?

    (A) It helped farmers recover from the economic depression of 1893.

    (B) It revived the gold standard in the United States, which had been abandoned since 1873.

    (C) It helped convince the Populist Party to join the Democratic Party in supporting Bryan's candidacy for president.

    (D) It had no significant impact.

15. Which of the following is NOT a correct statement regarding groups who advocated for bimetallism?

    (A) Laborers supported an inflationary monetary policy to increase their buying power.

    (B) Industrialists supported the silver standard to help ensure economic stability.

    (C) Southern and western Americans supported the use of the silver standard to help the regional economies.

    (D) Farmers supported bimetallism because it would help them repay their debts.

GO ON TO THE NEXT PAGE

Questions 16–18 refer to the excerpt below.

"Many courageous fellows were unwilling to come out, and fought most desperately through the palisadoes, so as they were scorched and burnt with the very flame, and were deprived of their arms, in regard the fire burnt their very bowstrings, and so perished valiantly. Mercy they did deserve for their valor, could we have had opportunity to have bestowed it. Many were burnt in the fort, both men, women, and children. Others forced out, and came in troops to the Indians, twenty and thirty at a time, which our soldiers received and entertained with the point of the sword. Down fell men, women, and children: those that scaped us, fell into the hands of the Indians, that were in the rear of us; it is reported by themselves, that there were about four hundred souls in this fort, and not above five of them escaped out of our hands. Great and doleful was the bloody sight to the view of young soldiers that never had been in war, to see so many souls lie gasping on the ground so thick in some places, that you could hardly pass along."

Captain John Underhill, *News from America*, 1638

16. Underhill's message offers an account of which of the following conflicts?

    (A) King Philip's War

    (B) The Powhatan Wars

    (C) The Pequot War

    (D) Pontiac's Rebellion

17. Most conflicts with American Indians in the seventeenth century resulted in which of the following?

    (A) American Indians gaining power over English settlers

    (B) Additional land becoming available for English settlement

    (C) The destruction of English forts by American Indians

    (D) American Indian alliances with the main rival of the English: the French

18. The overall approach of English settlers to New England American Indians in the seventeenth century can best be characterized as

    (A) an effort to befriend the American Indians and encourage their assimilation into English culture

    (B) a strong economic relationship, which was primarily based on coexistence

    (C) a policy of conquest against many tribes, to capture the land the American Indians possessed

    (D) the enlistment of American Indians into militias to fight against the French and Spanish

GO ON TO THE NEXT PAGE

Questions 19–21 refer to the excerpt below.

"Such is the crime which you are to judge. The criminal also must be dragged into the day, what you may see and measure the power by which all this wrong is sustained. From no common source could it proceed. In its perpetration was needed a spirit of vaulting ambition which would hesitate at nothing; a hardihood of purpose which was insensible to the judgment of mankind; a madness for slavery which should disregard the Constitution the laws, and all the great examples of our history; also a consciousness of power such as comes from the habit of power; a combination of energies found only in a hundred arms directed by a hundred eyes; a control of public opinion, through venal pens and a prostituted press; an ability to subsidize crowds in every vocation of life—the politician with his local importance, the lawyer with his subtle tongue, and even the authority of the judge on the bench, and a familiar use of men in places high and low, so that none, from the President to the lowest border postmaster, should decline to be its tool: all these things and more were needed; and they were found in the slave power of our Republic."

Charles Sumner, "The Crime Against Kansas" speech delivered to the United States Senate, 1856

19. Charles Sumner's speech was most likely responding to

   (A) the massacre of proslavery supporters in Kansas, led by John Brown

   (B) the admission of Kansas into the Union as a free state

   (C) the passage of the Kansas-Nebraska Act

   (D) the ratification of the Lecompton Constitution, which secured slavery in Kansas

20. Sumner's incendiary position regarding the survival and expansion of slavery was most likely intended to condemn

   (A) the president of the United States

   (B) the citizens of Kansas and its neighboring territories

   (C) the slave owners and proslavery supporters in the South

   (D) the original framers of the Constitution

21. Sumner's speech to the U.S. Senate had which of the following effects?

   (A) Sumner was immediately expelled from office.

   (B) Sumner was beaten with a cane by Congressman Preston Brooks.

   (C) Sumner was successful in convincing Congress to repeal the Kansas-Nebraska Act.

   (D) Sumner was appointed Secretary of State by President Buchanan.

GO ON TO THE NEXT PAGE

Questions 22–24 refer to the image below.

CAMP MEETING, CIRCA 1819

22. Which of the following groups most benefited from the camp meetings of the Second Great Awakening?

    (A) Congregationalists

    (B) Transcendentalists

    (C) Methodists

    (D) Mormons

23. Camp meetings like those depicted in the image most directly contributed to

    (A) a consolidation of Protestant religious sects

    (B) the founding of universities for the sake of educating preachers

    (C) the development of significant social re- form movements

    (D) a decrease in women's participation in church life

24. Religious activities like those depicted in the image most directly contributed to

    (A) a rise in individualism as a national sentiment

    (B) a greater acceptance of rationalism and empiricism

    (C) an increase in predestination as a popular theology

    (D) a decrease in the number of African Americans practicing Christianity

GO ON TO THE NEXT PAGE

Questions 25–27 refer to the excerpt below.

"Ten years before, Judge Hammond was known as the richest man in Cedarville; and now, the homestead which he had once so loved to beautify—where all that was dearest to him in life once gathered—worn, disfigured, and in ruins, was about to be wrested from him. . . .

I went to one of the county officers, who, on learning the condition of Judge Hammond, took immediate steps to have him removed to the Alms-house, some miles distant. . . . 'Judge Hammond was a selfish, worldly man. . . . His favoring, so strongly, the tavern of Slade, and his distillery operations, turned from him some of his best friends. The corruption and terrible fate of his son— and the insanity and death of his wife—all were charged upon him in people's minds, and every one seemed to turn from him instinctively after the fearful tragedy was completed. He never held tip his head afterward. Neighbors shunned him as they would a criminal. And here has come the end at last. He will be taken to the poorhouse, to die there—a pauper!'

'And all,' said I, partly speaking to myself, 'because a man, too lazy to work at an honest calling, must needs go to rum-selling.'"

T.S. Arthur, excerpt from the novel *Ten Nights in a Bar Room*, 1854

25. The excerpt best illustrates the views of nineteenth century reformers who emphasized

    (A) the merits of laissez-faire capitalism as seen in the success of distillery businesses

    (B) the potential negative outcomes of alcohol sale and consumption

    (C) the cruelties of the conditions within poorhouses

    (D) the adverse effects of prohibition on families and individuals

26. Which of the following was NOT a factor in the passage of the Eighteenth Amendment?

    (A) Anti-German sentiments during World War I

    (B) The need to preserve food for the war effort

    (C) President Wilson urging Congress to support prohibition

    (D) State governments passing similar prohibition laws

27. Which of the following groups was most instrumental in the passage of the Eighteenth Amendment?

    (A) The Anti-Saloon League

    (B) The Massachusetts Society for the Suppression of Intemperance

    (C) The American Temperance Society

    (D) The Order of the Star-Spangled Banner

GO ON TO THE NEXT PAGE

Questions 28–30 refer to the image below.

TAKING THE BULL BY THE HORNS (1903)

28. Which of the following best characterizes Theodore Roosevelt's presidency?

   (A) A direct approach to creating policies

   (B) A laissez-faire approach to economics

   (C) Support for the interests of big businesses

   (D) An emphasis on stimulating the economy by banning trust-busting

29. Which of the following best describes Roosevelt's policies regarding trusts?

   (A) Roosevelt believed that all trusts weakened the economy and must be dissolved to prevent monopolies.

   (B) Roosevelt gained politically from certain trusts which in turn faced less regulation.

   (C) Roosevelt sought to regulate certain trusts and to dissolve more powerful trusts in order to encourage competition.

   (D) Roosevelt believed that trusts were beneficial to the government and did not require regulation.

30. The cartoon was most likely intended to promote

   (A) trusts against the threat of government regulation

   (B) the campaign by Roosevelt to be elected to the presidency

   (C) trusts as being endangered by laissez-faire economics

   (D) the economic reforms of the Progressive movement

GO ON TO THE NEXT PAGE

Questions 31–33 refer to the excerpt below.

"Our greatest primary task is to put people to work. This is no unsolvable problem if we face it wisely and courageously. It can be accomplished in part by direct recruiting by the Government itself, treating the task as we would treat the emergency of a war, but at the same time, through this employment, accomplishing greatly needed projects to stimulate and reorganize the use of our natural resources."

Franklin D. Roosevelt, First Inaugural Address, 1932

31. When Franklin Roosevelt became president, he immediately prioritized the task of

   (A) relieving unemployment

   (B) stabilizing the banking system

   (C) controlling big business

   (D) regulating trusts

32. Which of the following was NOT a major goal of the New Deal?

   (A) Creating employment through rebuilding America's infrastructure

   (B) Regulating and controlling banking policies through government intervention

   (C) Expanding America's overseas empire to import more raw materials

   (D) Reducing overproduction in the agricultural and industrial sectors

33. The Supreme Court ruled the Agricultural Adjustment Act unconstitutional on the grounds that

   (A) Congress could not regulate interstate commerce

   (B) Congress could not regulate agricultural production

   (C) the president did not have the authority to authorize tax breaks for farmers

   (D) the federal government could not pay to relocate farmers from the Dust Bowl

GO ON TO THE NEXT PAGE

Questions 34–36 refer to the excerpt below.

"I stand up here in a more solemn court, to assist in a far greater cause; not to impeach the character of one man, but of a whole people—not to recover the sum of a hundred thousand dollars, but to obtain the liberation of two millions of wretched, degraded beings, who are pining in hopeless bondage—over whose sufferings scarcely an eye weeps, or a heart melts, or a tongue pleads either to God or man. I regret that a better advocate had not been found, to enchain your attention, and to warm your blood. Whatever fallacy, however, may appear in the argument, there is no flaw in the indictment; what the speaker lacks, the cause will supply."

William Lloyd Garrison, "An Address to the American Colonization Society," 1829

34. Which of the following best describes William Lloyd Garrison's view of the Constitution in regards to slavery?

    (A) He claimed that the Constitution banned slaves from society.

    (B) He argued that the Constitution could be used as a weapon against slavery.

    (C) He asserted that the Constitution was a proslavery document.

    (D) He did not believe that the Constitution endorsed or rejected the institution of slavery.

35. The goal of the American Colonization Society was to

    (A) relocate free blacks to Africa

    (B) free slaves in the South through the Underground Railroad

    (C) provide education for free blacks after the Civil War

    (D) use politics to promote the emancipation of slaves

36. Which of the following statements best characterizes the abolitionist movement prior to the Civil War?

    (A) The abolitionist movement became a popular movement that motivated owners to emancipate their slaves.

    (B) The abolitionist movement was generally unpopular throughout the United States.

    (C) The abolitionist movement gained much support in Congress, which issued gag orders on any proslavery laws.

    (D) The abolitionist movement accepted the institution of slavery in the South but opposed its expansion to the West.

GO ON TO THE NEXT PAGE

Questions 37–41 refer to the image below.

Political cartoon from 1869 regarding the women's suffrage movement

37. Which of the following best matches the purpose of the cartoon?

   (A) To inspire women to run for office

   (B) To satirize the women's suffrage movement

   (C) To criticize the government for not granting women suffrage

   (D) To express concerns about the safety of suffragettes

38. Women's suffrage led to which of the following concerns in the nineteenth century?

   (A) Reversal of gender roles

   (B) Reduced size of families

   (C) Domestic violence

   (D) Child labor

39. During the nineteenth century, which of the following groups would have most likely supported the viewpoint expressed in the image?

   (A) The National Woman Suffrage Association

   (B) Attendees at the World's Anti-Slavery Convention in 1840

   (C) The International Council of Women

   (D) The majority of elected politicians in the United States

40. Which of the following movements is most closely related to the debate suggested by the cartoon?

   (A) The states' rights movement of the 1860s

   (B) The labor union movements of the 1890s

   (C) The civil rights movement of the 1960s

   (D) The libertarian movement of the 1980s

41. Which of the following issues in the first half of the twenty-first century most closely parallels the controversy depicted in the cartoon?

   (A) Campaign financing

   (B) Immigration reform

   (C) Universal health care

   (D) Same-sex marriage

GO ON TO THE NEXT PAGE

Questions 42–44 refer to the excerpt below.

"The question of the relation which the States and General Government bear to each other is not one of recent origin. From the commencement of our system, it has divided public sentiment. Even in the Convention, while the Constitution was struggling into existence, there were two parties as to what this relation should be, whose different sentiments constituted no small impediment in forming that instrument. After the General Government went into operation, experience soon proved that the question had not terminated with the labors of the Convention. The great struggle that preceded the political revolution of 1801, which brought Mr. Jefferson into power, turned essentially on it; and the doctrines and arguments on both sides were embodied and ably sustained—on the one, in the Virginia and Kentucky Resolutions, and the Report to the Virginia Legislature—and on the other, in the replies of the Legislature of Massachusetts and some of the other States."

John C. Calhoun, Fort Hill Address, 1831

42. John C. Calhoun's address refers to the Virginia and Kentucky Resolutions, which corresponded with his belief in

    (A) national supremacy

    (B) executive power

    (C) states' rights

    (D) judicial review

43. Calhoun's sentiments in the excerpt led to which of the following?

    (A) The Indian Removal Act

    (B) The Nullification Crisis

    (C) The annexation of Texas

    (D) Nat Turner's slave rebellion in Virginia

44. Calhoun's comment about the "great struggle" was in reference to

    (A) the debate over the Supreme Court's ability to review any laws passed by Congress

    (B) the battle between supporters of states' rights versus those who supported federal power

    (C) the argument over whether or not slaves would be counted for Congressional representation

    (D) the War of 1812 between the United States and Great Britain for control of North America

Questions 45 and 46 refer to the image below.

"LET HER BE HEARD!" (1915)

45. As war broke out in Europe, President Wilson's primary objective was

    (A) keeping the United States neutral and removed from the war

    (B) providing arms and ammunition to the Allied Powers

    (C) mobilizing United States troops to invade Europe

    (D) convincing the American public to support war against the Central Powers

46. Which of the following best describes the reason that the United States ultimately entered World War I?

    (A) The Germans declared British waters to be a war zone.

    (B) The Germans attempted to persuade Canada to become an ally.

    (C) Germany began to practice unrestricted submarine warfare on the open seas.

    (D) The economic depression necessitated the development of arms manufacturing.

GO ON TO THE NEXT PAGE

Questions 47–49 refer to the excerpt below.

"For God's sake, tell me what is the cause of all these commotions? Do they proceed from immorality, British influence disseminated by the [Loyalists], or real grievances which admit of redress? If the latter, why was redress delayed until the public mind had become so much agitated? If the former, why are not the powers of government tried at once? It is well to be without, as not to exercise them. Commotions of this sort, like snowballs, gather strength as they roll, if there is no opposition in the way to divide and crumble them."

George Washington, letter discussing Shays' Rebellion, 1786

47. Shays' Rebellion occurred partially as a result of

    (A) foreclosures on private land in Massachusetts

    (B) high taxes levied by Congress

    (C) mandatory enlistment into the Continental Army

    (D) tensions with Native Americans on the frontier

48. Washington's fear of rebellion sweeping through the nation added leverage to

    (A) Federalist sentiments in Congress

    (B) arguments for amending the Articles of Confederation

    (C) pro-British sentiments throughout America

    (D) the concept of forming alliances with foreign nations to improve America's military forces

49. Which of the following events resulted from factors similar to those of Shays' Rebellion?

    (A) Nat Turner's Rebellion

    (B) Pontiac's Rebellion

    (C) The Whiskey Rebellion

    (D) The Stono Rebellion

GO ON TO THE NEXT PAGE

Questions 50–53 refer to the image below.

Political cartoon depicting Standard Oil, owned by J. D. Rockefeller.

50. The illustration depicts which criticism of businesses such as Standard Oil?

    (A) They paid workers low wages to increase profits.

    (B) They had too much control over the economy and the government.

    (C) They were the subject of government audits.

    (D) They went bankrupt and required taxpayer money for bailouts.

51. The Gilded Age was an economic period characterized by

    (A) strong presidents who controlled private industry through regulatory actions

    (B) legislation that disenfranchised trusts in order to give power back to the federal government

    (C) big business control of government and the American economy

    (D) major advancements in workers' rights and fair wages

52. The Interstate Commerce Act was intended to

    (A) allow railroad owners to ship goods across state lines without inspection

    (B) grant the federal government the power to set standard rates for interstate commerce

    (C) regulate the railroads' control over commerce and rates across state lines

    (D) lower tariffs on certain goods that America needed from foreign countries

53. Trusts in the Gilded Age innovated which of the following business practices in order to gain power?

    (A) Fair wages and work environments that fostered employee loyalty

    (B) Eliminating competitors by partnering with them

    (C) Horizontal and vertical integrations of competition

    (D) Cutting off ties with government representatives

GO ON TO THE NEXT PAGE

Questions 54 and 55 refer to the image below.

Political cartoon from 1918

54. After the Great War, one of America's most significant internal concerns was

   (A) losing its overseas possessions in the Treaty
   of Versailles

   (B) bringing its troops stationed in Europe
   home to the United States

   (C) preventing different governing philosophies from infiltrating American life and
   politics

   (D) integrating returning soldiers back into the
   workforce

55. All of the following were causes of the First Red
Scare that immediately followed World War I
EXCEPT

   (A) American soldiers returning from Europe
   with socialist ideals

   (B) the emergence of workers' unions that opposed America's involvement in the Great
   War

   (C) a fear of American socialism after Russia
   fell to the Bolsheviks

   (D) a series of violent strikes blamed on anarchists

GO ON TO THE NEXT PAGE

END OF SECTION I, PART A

**IF YOU FINISH BEFORE TIME IS CALLED,
YOU MAY CHECK YOUR WORK ON PART A.**

DO NOT GO ON TO PART B UNTIL YOU ARE TOLD TO DO SO.

SECTION I, PART B
Time—40 minutes
3 Questions

Directions: Section I, Part B of this exam consists of short-answer questions. You must respond to Questions 1 *and* 2. For your final response, you must choose to answer Question 3 *or* Question 4. In your responses, be sure to address all parts of the questions, using complete sentences.

> "The railways and steamboats at first did but bring into sharper conflict an already established difference between the two sections of the United States. The increasing unification due to the new means of transport made the question whether the southern spirit or the northern should prevail an ever more urgent one. There was little possibility of compromise. The northern spirit was free and individualistic; the southern made for great estates and a conscious gentility ruling over a subject multitude. Every new territory that was organized into a state as the tide of population swept westward, every new incorporation into the fast growing American system, became a field of conflict between the two ideas, whether it should become a state of free citizens, or whether the estate and slavery system should prevail."

H.G. Wells, *A Short History of the World*, 1922

> "The doctrine of state rights is one that is intimately associated with American history, especially with certain movements and controversies that fell in the period before the Civil War. . . . The kernel of all forms of the state rights doctrine was the desire of the state governments to enhance their power or, at least, to resist encroachments of the federal authority. Since the respective spheres of power of state and nation are defined in the federal Constitution, advocates of state rights, however they may have differed among themselves, all joined in professing a belief in a 'strict construction' of that instrument."

Arthur Meier Schlesinger, *New Viewpoints in American History*, 1922

1. Using the excerpts, answer (a), (b), and (c).

   (a) Briefly describe ONE major difference between Wells's and Schlesinger's historical interpretations of the ideologies and/or events that led up to the Civil War.

   (b) Briefly describe how ONE specific historical event or development during the period 1819–1861 that is not explicitly mentioned in the excerpts could be used to support Wells's interpretation.

   (c) Briefly describe how ONE specific historical event or development during the period 1819–1861 that is not explicitly mentioned in the excerpts could be used to support Schlesinger's interpretation.

GO ON TO THE NEXT PAGE

"Let us say to the democracies: 'We Americans are vitally concerned in your defense of freedom. We are putting forth our energies, our resources, and our organizing powers to give you the strength to regain and maintain a free world. We shall send you in ever-increasing numbers, ships, planes, tanks, guns. That is our purpose and our pledge. In fulfillment of this purpose we will not be intimidated by the threats of dictators that they will regard as a breach of international law or as an act of war our aid to the democracies which dare to resist their aggression. Such aid—Such aid is not an act of war, even if a dictator should unilaterally proclaim it so to be.'"

Franklin Delano Roosevelt, State of the Union Address
("The Four Freedoms" speech), delivered January 1941

2. Using the excerpts, answer (a), (b), and (c).

(a) Briefly describe ONE perspective about American involvement in World War II expressed in the passage.

(b) Briefly explain ONE specific historical development, circumstance, or event that led to the actions advocated in the passage.

(c) Briefly explain ONE specific historical development or event that resulted from the actions advocated in the passage.

GO ON TO THE NEXT PAGE

Choose EITHER Question 3 or Question 4.

3. Answer (a), (b), and (c).

    (a) Briefly describe ONE specific historical similarity between the national governments under the Articles of Confederation and the U.S. Constitution.

    (b) Briefly describe ONE specific historical difference between the national governments under the Articles of Confederation and the U.S. Constitution.

    (c) Briefly explain ONE specific historical reason for a difference between the provisions of the Articles of Confederation and the provisions of the U.S. Constitution.

4. Answer (a), (b), and (c).

    (a) Briefly describe ONE specific historical similarity between the provisions of the treaty that ended the Spanish-American War and the provisions of the treaty that ended World War I.

    (b) Briefly describe ONE specific historical difference between the United States' reasons for involvement in the Spanish-American War and its reasons for involvement in World War I.

    (c) Briefly explain ONE specific historical effect of either the Spanish-American War or World War I.

GO ON TO THE NEXT PAGE

END OF SECTION I, PART B

IF YOU FINISH BEFORE TIME IS CALLED,
YOU MAY CHECK YOUR WORK ON THIS SECTION.

DO NOT GO ON TO SECTION II UNTIL YOU ARE TOLD TO DO SO.

SECTION II
Time—1 hour 40 minutes

Question 1: Document-Based Question

Suggested reading period: 15 minutes

Suggested writing time: 45 minutes

Directions: Question 1 is based on the accompanying documents. The documents have been edited for the purpose of this exercise.

In your response, you should do the following:

- Make a thesis or claim that responds to the prompt. The thesis or claim must be historically defensible and establish a line of reasoning.
- Provide context relevant to the prompt by describing a broader historical development or process.
- Use at least six of the provided documents to support an argument in response to the prompt.
- Use a historical example not found in the documents as evidence relevant to an argument about the prompt.
- Explain how the context or situation of at least three documents is relevant to an argument. This could address the relevance of the document's point of view, purpose, historical situation, and/or audience.
- Demonstrate a complex understanding of an argument that responds to the prompt by using evidence to corroborate, qualify, or modify the argument.

GO ON TO THE NEXT PAGE

1. Evaluate the extent of change in American colonists' political ideas in the period 1765 to 1776.

Document 1

Source: Declaration of Rights and Grievances of the Stamp Act Congress, 1765.

The members of this Congress, sincerely devoted, with the warmest sentiments of affection and duty to His Majesty's Person and Government, and with minds deeply impressed by a sense of the present and impending misfortunes of the British colonies on this continent; having considered as maturely as time will permit the circumstances of the said colonies, esteem it our indispensable duty to make the following declarations of our humble opinion, respecting the most essential rights and liberties of the colonists, and of the grievances under which they labour, by reason of several late Acts of Parliament.

Document 2

Source: John Dickinson, lawyer, "A Warning to the Colonies" *Letters from a Farmer in Pennsylvania*, 1768.

Let these truths be indelibly impressed on our minds—that we cannot be happy without being free—that we cannot be free without being secure in our property—that we cannot be secure in our property, if, without our consent others may, as by right, take it away—that taxes imposed on us by parliament do thus take it away—that duties laid for the sole purpose of raising money are taxes—that attempts to lay such duties should be Instantly and firmly opposed—that this opposition can never be effectual unless it is the united effort of these provinces—that therefore benevolence of temper towards each other and unanimity of councils are essential to the welfare of the whole—and lastly, that for this reason every man amongst us who in any manner would encourage either dissension, diffidence, or indifference between these colonies, is an enemy to himself, and to his country.

GO ON TO THE NEXT PAGE

Document 3

Source: Paul Revere, copper engraving, "The Bloody Massacre Perpetrated in King Street Boston on March 5th, 1770," 1770.

Document 4

Source: Declaration and Resolves of the First Continental Congress, submitted to King George III, 1774.

To these grievous acts and measures, Americans cannot submit, but in hopes that their fellow subjects in Great Britain will, on a revision of them, restore us to that state, in which both countries found happiness and prosperity, we have for the present, only resolved to pursue the following peaceable measures: 1. To enter into a non-importation, non-consumption, and non-exportation agreement or association. 2. To prepare an address to the people of Great Britain, and a memorial to the inhabitants of British America; and 3. To prepare a loyal address to his majesty, agreeable to resolutions already entered into.

Document 5

Source: Olive Branch Petition, submitted to King George III by the Second Continental Congress, 1775.

Knowing to what violent resentments, and incurable animosities, civil discords are apt to exasperate and inflame the contending parties, we think ourselves required by indispensable obligation to Almighty God, to your majesty, to our fellow subjects, and to ourselves, immediately to use all the means in our power, not incompatible with our safety, for stopping the further effusion of blood, and for averting the impending calamities that threaten the British empire.

GO ON TO THE NEXT PAGE

Document 6

Source: Thomas Paine, *Common Sense*, 1776.

Until an independence is declared, the Continent will feel itself like a man who continues putting off some unpleasant business from day to day, yet knows it must be done, hates to set about it, wishes it over, and is continually haunted with the thoughts of its necessity.

No man was a warmer wisher for reconciliation than myself, before the fatal nineteenth of April 1775*, but the moment the event of that day was made known, I rejected the hardened, sullen, tempered ruler of England for ever; and disdain the wretch, that with the pretended title of FATHER OF HIS PEOPLE, can unfeelingly hear of their slaughter, and composedly sleep with their blood upon his soul.

Ye that tell us of harmony and reconciliation, can ye restore to us the time that is past? The last cord now is broken, the people of England are presenting addresses against us. There are injuries which nature cannot forgive; she would cease to be nature if she did.

*Date of the battles of Lexington and Concord

Document 7

Source: David Ramsay, *History of the United States,* 1816.

The style, manner, and language of Thomas Paine's performance were calculated to interest the passions and to rouse all the active powers of human nature. With the view of operating on the sentiments of religious people, Scripture was pressed into his service; and the powers and name of a king were rendered odious in the eyes of numerous colonists . . . Hereditary succession was turned into ridicule. The absurdity of subjecting a great continent to a small island on the other side of the globe was represented in such striking language as to interest the honor and pride of the colonists in renouncing the government of Great Britain. The necessity, the advantage and practicability of independence were forcibly demonstrated.

GO ON TO THE NEXT PAGE

END OF DOCUMENTS FOR QUESTION 1

Question 2, Question 3, or Question 4: Long Essay Question
Suggested writing time: 40 minutes

Directions: Choose Question 2, Question 3, OR Question 4 to answer.

In your response you should do the following:

- Make a thesis or claim that responds to the prompt. The thesis or claim must be historically defensible and establish a line of reasoning.
- Provide context relevant to the prompt by describing a broader historical development or process.
- Use specific and relevant examples as evidence to support an argument in response to the prompt.
- Use a historical reasoning skill (causation, comparison, or continuity and change) to develop an argument in response to the prompt.
- Demonstrate a complex understanding of an argument that responds to the prompt by using evidence to corroborate, qualify, or modify the argument.

2. Evaluate the extent to which Shays' Rebellion shaped the political development of the United States from 1787 to 1791.

3. Evaluate the extent to which the wartime experience of the Civil War shaped the political development of the United States during the Reconstruction era from 1864 to 1877.

4. Evaluate the extent to which the wartime experience of World War II shaped rights movements from 1945 to 1980.

GO ON TO THE NEXT PAGE

END OF SECTION II

ANSWER KEY

Section I, Part A

1. C	15. B	29. C	43. B
2. A	16. C	30. D	44. B
3. C	17. B	31. B	45. A
4. B	18. C	32. C	46. C
5. C	19. C	33. B	47. A
6. B	20. C	34. C	48. A
7. C	21. B	35. A	49. C
8. B	22. C	36. B	50. B
9. B	23. C	37. B	51. C
10. C	24. A	38. A	52. C
11. B	25. B	39. D	53. C
12. A	26. C	40. C	54. C
13. B	27. A	41. D	55. A
14. C	28. A	42. C	

Section I, Part B and Section II

See Answers and Explanations, and self-score your responses.

Section I, Part A Number Correct: _____

Section I, Part B Points Earned: _____

Section II Points Earned: _____

Sign into your online account at kaptest.com and enter your results in the scoring section to see your 1–5 score.

Haven't registered your book yet? Go to kaptest.com/moreonline to begin.

ANSWERS AND EXPLANATIONS

Section I, Part A

1. C

In this excerpt, Bartolomé de las Casas criticizes the *encomienda* system, a labor and behavior control system that Spanish colonists used on native people; **(C)** is correct. De las Casas was a Spanish social reformer and historian who gave up his native slaves and the practice of *encomienda* in 1515. (A) is incorrect because the *Asiento* system was part of the Treaty of Utrecht from which Britain gained the exclusive right to supply slaves to Spanish colonies. The headright system was primarily an English pattern of settlement that involved granting 50 acres of land to settlers, making (B) incorrect. While the *hacienda* system of private land ownership emerged from the *encomienda* system, it is not what de las Casas is discussing in this excerpt, making (D) incorrect.

2. A

Bartolomé de las Casas was an outspoken opponent of the Spanish mistreatment of native peoples in the New World, which matches **(A)**. (B) and (C) are incorrect because de las Cases did not approve of oppressing indigenous people from the New World after 1515. De las Casas attempted to establish towns of free native peoples, not religious missions, eliminating (D).

3. C

The Black Legend was an anti-Spanish historical view that depicted the Spanish as barbaric. Spain's rivals wrote Black Legend propaganda in the sixteenth century to decrease the influence of the Spanish empire throughout the world and often cited works that disapproved of Spanish colonization practices. Thus, **(C)** is correct. (A) is incorrect because the Columbian Exchange refers to the period of cultural and biological exchanges between the New and Old Worlds, which was well underway before de las Casas's writings. De las Casas disapproved of how the Spanish treated native peoples upon colonization, but this disapproval did not directly influence Spain's conquest of the Inca Empire, eliminating (B). While de las Casas criticized the Spanish conquistadors for claiming to be Christians while mistreating the native peoples, he did not influence anti-Catholic propaganda, making (D) incorrect.

4. B

As part of the Triangular Trade, African slaves were shipped to the colonies in the Middle Passage, and colonies received manufactured goods from the Old World. **(B)** is correct. The New World shipped raw materials of cotton, sugar, and tobacco to Europe in the Triangular Trade, making (A) incorrect. The colonies shipped gunpowder and rum to Africa in exchange for slaves; (C) is incorrect. The colonies exported lumber and furs to the Old World, eliminating (D).

5. C

Slaves were transported by European merchants via the Middle Passage on ships across the Atlantic to be sold in the Americas; **(C)** is correct. (A) is incorrect because the slaves were sent to the colonies, not to Europe. European merchants brought manufactured goods to Africa in order to acquire slaves, not raw materials, making (B) incorrect. (D) is incorrect because European merchants exchanged manufactured goods, not raw materials, for African slaves.

6. B

According to mercantilist principles, a nation must export more and import less to strengthen its economy. In the Triangular Trade, the involved regions exported large amounts of goods that they had in abundance in exchange for scarce goods; **(B)** is correct. (A) is incorrect because imperialism is a political practice in which a nation increases its power and territory, often through force. (C) is incorrect; according to utopianism, a nation should pursue a "perfect" state in which no problems exist. Laissez-faire is the economic policy that opposes direct government involvement in market exchange, eliminating (D).

7. C

The New World received crops such as wheat, oats, watermelons, and onions as part of the Columbian Exchange, which revolutionized farming and agriculture across the planet; **(C)** is correct. (A) is incorrect because squash, white potatoes, and sweet potatoes were introduced to the Old World from the New World. (B) is incorrect because the excerpt alludes to the Hidatsa already practicing some form of agriculture, given the references to "our own squashes" and knowledge of drying familiar vegetables for wintertime. (D) is incorrect because Indian termination was U.S. policy from the mid-1940s into the mid-1960s, while the excerpt is dated to 1917.

8. B

The excerpt reflects the ecological and biological interaction of the New World and Old World, a process known as the Columbian Exchange, which included the transfer of plants, animals, diseases, and people. Thus, **(B)** is correct. Though European diseases did decimate indigenous populations in America, there is no mention of such diseases in the excerpt; (A) is incorrect. The excerpt describes how the Hidatsa were unfamiliar with the various crops introduced to them, to the degree that they were unable to harvest and preserve them in a useful way. Thus, (C) is incorrect because the Hidatsa did not benefit from any assistance. (D) is incorrect because the excerpt is dated to 1917.

9. B

Catholic Jesuits constructed communities in which American Indians and Europeans lived among each other. They attempted to convert American Indians with their peaceful displays of faith. Therefore, **(B)** is correct. While Catholic Jesuit missionaries traveled to and lived within indigenous villages as they spread their message, English protestants required American Indians to completely abandon their cultural customs and adopt English ways; (A) is incorrect. (C) is incorrect because Spanish conversion tactics often led to cruel treatment of American Indians. (D) is incorrect because English explorers were intent on economic gain in the New World; their aggressive methods often contributed to strained relations with American Indians.

10. C

In the American Southwest, the Spanish enslaved and mistreated Pueblo peoples in order to convert them to Catholicism. These conditions led to the Pueblo Revolt in 1680, making **(C)** correct. The other rebellions occurred for reasons other than religious conversion. Odawa Pontiac led Native American tribes in a rebellion against the British because they were dissatisfied with postwar policies in the Great Lakes region following The Seven Years' War; (A) is incorrect. The Battle of Acoma began

in 1598 when the Acoma tribe refused to help the Spaniards after their military demanded supplies that would assist in winter survival, eliminating (B). (D) is incorrect because economic problems in the Virginia colony led to Bacon's Rebellion.

11. B

John Winthrop led the first non-separatist Puritans from England in 1630 when he founded the Massachusetts Bay Colony; **(B)** is correct. The sermon in question was given aboard the ship *Arabella* as the future colonists approached their destination. Winthrop encouraged his fellow passengers to serve as an example to the rest of the world in rightful, Christian living. Pilgrims, while similar to Puritans in their Christian beliefs, believed themselves to be separate from the Church of England, making (A) incorrect. Similarly, Puritans were Protestants in that they belonged to the Anglican Church, which was formed in protest to the tenets of Catholicism; however, this term is too broad because Winthrop was speaking to a distinct subgroup of Protestants, eliminating (D). (C) is incorrect because John Winthrop and his fellow passengers did not desire to separate from the church altogether.

12. A

Puritans organized themselves into self-governing towns, which each had its own congregational church; **(A)** is correct. This group of people immigrated to America in part because of religious persecution; Puritans emphasized the need for towns to be organized around a church to ensure that their religious practices and beliefs would not be threatened by the government, eliminating (B). Puritans strongly believed in self-government, making (C) and (D) incorrect.

13. B

Winthrop hoped his colony would become a beacon of Puritan values, showcasing a strong work ethic and pious living based on biblical principles; **(B)** is correct. While the Puritans did leave persecution in England to practice "purified" Anglicanism, (A) does not adequately reflect Winthrop's intentions for the settlement. Rather, it refers to the Pilgrims' motivations to create their settlement at Plymouth. (C) is incorrect; the Puritan belief in predestination limited active attempts of conversion. Though the Massachusetts Bay Colony thrived economically under his governance, Winthrop's vision was primarily concerned with Christian values rather than commerce, making (D) incorrect.

14. C

The Populist movement began to gain momentum in the late nineteenth century as farmers and laborers banded together to oppose exploitation by railroad companies and banks. William Jennings Bryan was selected as the Democratic candidate for president in 1896 and delivered his "Cross of Gold" speech at the Democratic nominating convention. Bryan's speech against big business and in favor of bimetallism was a factor that persuaded the Populist Party to unite with the Democrats in supporting him to run against William McKinley for president; **(C)** is correct. While the speech favored taking action to improve the economy, it did not directly improve economic conditions, making (A) incorrect. The gold standard was put in place in 1873, not abandoned, eliminating (B). Bryan's "Cross of Gold" speech was influential in gaining popularity and support during his election campaign, making (D) incorrect.

15. B

Industrialists favored the gold standard instead of bimetallism because it allowed them to control the financial policies of the economy; therefore, they would not have supported the silver standard. **(B)** is correct. (A), (C), and (D) describe reasons why these groups favored bimetallism. Farmers and laborers tended to favor the silver standard and inflationary monetary policies because such economic strategies placed more money in circulation.

16. C

Captain John Underhill led a colonial militia in the Pequot War, which was an early conflict between settlers and American Indians that occurred in Connecticut. Notably, it led to the deaths of hundreds of Pequot tribe members in the massacre at Mystic River in 1637. **(C)** is correct. King Philip's War and Pontiac's Rebellion both postdate the time span chronicled by the cited document, making (A) and (D) incorrect. While the Powhatan Wars took place during this same time period, *News from America* was a published account of the Pequot Wars, eliminating (B).

17. B

English victories in conflicts with American Indians, such as the Powhatan Wars, the Pequot War, and King Philip's War, resulted in additional land available for English settlement, which matches **(B)**. In each of these wars, English settlers demonstrated power over the American Indians and took their lands, making (A) incorrect. While American Indians attacked colonial settlements in King Philip's War, they did not burn English forts in the Pequot War; (C) is incorrect. The Dutch, rather than the French, were the primary competitors of the settlers in New England during this period, making (D) incorrect.

18. C

As overwhelming numbers of English people flocked to the colonies, the colonists began expanding their territory and displacing American Indians from their land; **(C)** is correct. While the English colonists often traded with and befriended American Indian peoples initially, they eventually began to wage war against them in competition for resources; (A) and (B) are incorrect. The Spanish empire stretched across Latin America, but its presence along the North American eastern seaboard was limited to Florida, and it did not extend to New England; (D) is incorrect.

19. C

According to the Missouri Compromise (1820), slavery was forbidden in the Louisiana territory north of a certain latitude. This was nullified by the Kansas-Nebraska Act of 1854, which proposed that each territory could vote on slavery based on popular sovereignty. While this act had little effect in Nebraska, it led to controversy in Kansas, including acts of violence from both supporters and dissidents of slavery. Senator Charles Sumner made his antislavery speech in response to this act, so **(C)** is correct. Following the act's passage, proslavery forces from Missouri, dubbed "border ruffians," crossed the border into Kansas and terrorized and murdered antislavery settlers. Antislavery sympathizers also carried out attacks in Kansas. In August 1856, John Reid led pro-slavery activists to attack the town of Osawatomie, Kansas. Abolitionist John Brown attempted but failed to defend the town; Brown did not lead an effort to massacre proslavery forces, making (A) incorrect. Kansas's admission into the Union as a free state and the ratification of the Lecompton Constitution occurred after Sumner's 1856 speech (in 1861 and 1857, respectively), eliminating (B) and (D).

20. C

Senator Charles Sumner emerged as an antislavery leader in the late 1840s. Following the passage of the Kansas-Nebraska Act in 1854, Sumner directed his speech to Southern supporters of slavery; **(C)** is correct. In his speech, Sumner referenced the president in a list of vocations that are affected by the evils of slavery, but he was not specifically condemning the president; (A) is incorrect. Because a majority of the Kansas population opposed slavery, Sumner was not condemning the citizens of Kansas, making (B) incorrect. Sumner specifically stated that the people he was referencing "disregard the constitution," making (D) incorrect.

21. B

After the Kansas-Nebraska Act was passed in 1854, Sumner delivered the excerpted speech to Congress. In this speech, Sumner characterized Andrew Butler, a South Carolina senator and a Democrat, as a pimp for slavery. Two days later, Sumner was nearly killed when he was caned by the senator's relative, the South Carolina congressman Preston Brooks; **(B)** is correct. Sumner spent many years recovering from the beating but kept his seat in the Senate and officially returned to it four years later, eliminating (A). (C) is incorrect because the Kansas-Nebraska Act was never repealed. President Buchanan, while morally opposed to slavery, believed it was protected by the United States Constitution, so he tried to maintain peace between proslavery and antislavery factions in the government; (D) is also incorrect.

22. C

Baptist and Methodist forms of Protestantism heavily emphasized the personal aspects of religion. Many individuals underwent personal conversions and joined these denominations during this era of field revivals; **(C)** is correct. Congregationalists gained more members during the First Great Awakening, but the Second Great Awakening did not significantly impact their membership; (A) is incorrect. Though Transcendentalists and Mormons both emerged during the time of the Second Great Awakening, these groups did not participate in large-scale religious revivals, making (B) and (D) incorrect.

23. C

The Second Great Awakening prepared society for future social and religious reform movements, such as abolitionism, temperance, and women's suffrage; **(C)** is correct. The number and diversity of Protestant religious sects increased in the Second Great Awakening; (A) is incorrect. (B) is incorrect because it was a feature of the First Great Awakening, while the Second Great Awakening was more associated with self-taught preachers. (D) is incorrect; women's participation in church life massively increased during the Second Great Awakening, which helped foster various social reform efforts.

24. A

The Second Great Awakening strengthened individualism and self-reliance as national values, as the concept that people can choose their own salvation replaced predestination as popular theology. Thus, individual choices were key to a person's fate; **(A)** is correct and (C) is incorrect. (B) is incorrect because the Second Great Awakening, like the first, was a reaction against the rationalism and empiricism of the Enlightenment. The Second Great Awakening also saw African Americans increasingly adopt Christianity, even founding their own sects; (D) is incorrect.

25. B

Temperance reformers of the late nineteenth century believed that drunkenness destroyed families. The author of this excerpt clearly favors temperance, attributing Judge Hammond's loss of his house, friends, family, and freedom to his "favoring, so strongly, the tavern"; **(B)** is correct. (A) is incorrect because the author only mentions "distillery operations" as contributing to the judge's loss of friends; as a proponent of temperance, the author would not praise any economic success of distilleries. Although the author implies that the judge ending up in a poorhouse is tragic, the passage focuses on the impacts of alcohol consumption, not the conditions of poorhouses; (C) is incorrect. (D) is incorrect because temperance reformers like the author supported the prohibition, or prohibiting, of alcohol.

26. C

President Wilson did not play a significant role in the passage of the Eighteenth Amendment and actually felt that national prohibition would be unproductive and difficult to enforce; **(C)** is correct. Prohibitionists took advantage of anti-German sentiments during World War I to oppose the German-dominated brewing industry, making (A) incorrect. Prohibitionists believed that grain and other agricultural products used in making alcohol should be diverted to the war effort, eliminating (B). Several states had already passed local prohibition laws prior to the Eighteenth Amendment, which was a precursor of national prohibition; (D) is also incorrect.

27. A

The Anti-Saloon League was highly effective in promoting its prohibitionist agenda by using images of saloons to reinforce the negative effects of alcohol consumption; **(A)** is correct. (B) and (C) are incorrect; the American Temperance Society and the Massachusetts Society for the Suppression of Intemperance were earlier organizations from the nineteenth century that advocated for drinking in moderation as opposed to advocating for teetotalism. These organizations did not significantly influence the prohibition movement of the early twentieth century. The Order of the Star-Spangled Banner was not associated with the temperance movement; it was a nativist group that appeared during the nineteenth century as a result of the influx of immigrants, eliminating (D).

28. A

Theodore Roosevelt had a direct and dynamic approach to policy-making as president. During his administration, he spearheaded various reforms and actively ensured that Congress implemented policies; thus, **(A)** is correct. (B) is incorrect; Roosevelt challenged laissez-faire economics. He supported trust-busting in order to limit the powers of big businesses and to reduce the gap between the rich and the poor, eliminating (C) and (D).

29. C

Roosevelt's goal was to regulate trusts as a way to promote competition; **(C)** is correct. Roosevelt's goal was to regulate, not eliminate, large corporations, making (A) incorrect. Roosevelt imposed regulations on many trusts in order to prevent monopolies from taking over the market; (B) and (D) are incorrect.

30. D

The cartoon depicts trusts as a rampaging bull, a threat that must be "taken by the horns" by someone like Theodore Roosevelt, who was at the forefront of the Progressive movement and sought to break up trusts and monopolies. Thus, **(D)** is correct. Roosevelt is not depicted as being the threat, but as the one taking on the threat of the "Trust" bull; (A) is incorrect. Theodore Roosevelt was not originally elected to the presidency; he became president after William McKinley was assassinated, and later won a second term. So, (B) is incorrect. Trusts were a product of weak government regulation of the economy, so they were not endangered by laissez-faire economics. (C) is incorrect.

31. B

When Franklin Roosevelt took office in 1933, the country was in crisis, suffering from the effects of the Great Depression. The president's first priority was to restore people's confidence in the banking system in order to avoid a widespread financial panic. During his first week in office, FDR declared a bank emergency, persuaded Congress to pass the Emergency Banking Act, and deployed federal auditors across the country to determine which banks were solvent and could reopen; **(B)** is correct. While relieving unemployment was an important issue given the high unemployment, Roosevelt prioritized banking immediately after taking office, eliminating (A). Big business and trusts were not a priority for FDR, making (C) and (D) incorrect.

32. C

The New Deal focused on addressing America's internal issues, not on overseas possessions and politics; **(C)** is correct. FDR made concessions to lower tariffs to boost international trade and refused to send delegates to the London Conference designed to stabilize currency. With the New Deal, FDR and Congress attempted to improve the economic well-being of citizens and restore trust in the United States government by creating jobs, reforming banking, and increasing farmers' incomes; (A), (B), and (D) are incorrect.

33. B

The Agricultural Adjustment Act (AAA) was created to help increase farmers' incomes. It provided financial incentives to farmers who agreed to limit production by taking land out of production and/or raising fewer animals. The Supreme Court ruled that the AAA was unconstitutional and cited that the Tenth Amendment forbids Congress from regulating agricultural production; **(B)** is correct. Congress has the authority to regulate interstate commerce, making (A) incorrect. The AAA did not provide tax breaks for farmers; (C) is incorrect. (D) is incorrect because the AAA did not focus on relocating farmers from the Dust Bowl.

34. C

Garrison's radicalism alienated many moderates within the movement when he claimed that the Constitution was a proslavery document; **(C)** is correct. Frederick Douglass, another abolitionist at the time, fought for the end of slavery through legal means and claimed that the Constitution could be used as a weapon against slavery, making (B) incorrect. (A) and (D) are incorrect because Garrison held that the Constitution was in favor of slavery.

35. A

The American Colonization Society, which formed in 1817, advocated for sending free blacks to Africa. The colony of Liberia was created on the west coast of Africa as a place for black American immigrants to live; **(A)** is correct. (B) is incorrect because the society had no involvement with the Underground Railroad. After the Civil War, the American Colonization Society lacked the funds for emigration and focused primarily on educational and missionary efforts in Liberia, making (C) incorrect. The controversial colonization movement did not support emancipation; (D) is incorrect.

36. B

The abolitionist movement was not popular in the years prior to the Civil War. Some abolitionists, such as William Lloyd Garrison and the Tappan brothers, nearly lost their lives because of their views, and Reverend Elijah Lovejoy was killed by an angry mob for speaking out against slavery; **(B)** is correct. Southern slave owners opposed the abolitionist movement, making (A) incorrect. Congress took various actions to oppose the abolitionists, including imposing gag rules on antislavery legislation and petitions, eliminating (C). Abolitionists did not accept the existence of slavery anywhere in the United States; (D) is incorrect.

37. B

Once the women's suffrage movement gained popularity, it attracted significant scrutiny as many citizens, including women, grew concerned about how women could continue to uphold their domestic duties. With its sarcastic depiction of two candidates ("Susan Sharp-Tongue the Celebrated Man-Tamer" and "Miss Hangman for Sheriff") and female voters wearing masculine clothing and smoking cigars, the image is intended to deride the women's suffrage movement; **(B)** is correct. While today "Man-Tamer" might be considered a compliment, contemporaries of this time period would not have found the message to be inspiring, making (A) incorrect. The sentiment of the illustration is focused on societal upheaval, not the rights or safety of women suffragists, eliminating (C) and (D).

38. A

Many Americans worried that women's suffrage would lead to an unwanted reversal of gender roles in society, as represented in the image; **(A)** is correct. While family sizes sharply declined near the end of the nineteenth century, many factors other than women's suffrage influenced this, such as economic depressions and recessions; (B) is incorrect. Suffragettes opposed sexual exploitation, domestic violence, and child labor, and their fierce opposition to each of these ensured that they would not become a serious concern if women were granted the right to vote; (C) and (D) are incorrect.

39. D

During the nineteenth century, elected politicians would have supported the illustration's viewpoint because granting women the right to vote would impact their own political futures; **(D)** is correct. While the National Woman Suffrage Association and the International Council of Women differed in their messages and strategies, neither group would have endorsed the cartoon's unflattering depiction, making (A) and (C) incorrect. Female abolitionists shared many views with suffragists, and they would also have disagreed with the cartoon's unflattering depiction, eliminating (B).

40. C

This political cartoon reflects the debate over extending political rights to a marginalized group of citizens, which reflects the goals of the civil rights movement of the 1960s; **(C)** is correct. While the right of states to grant voting status was an aspect of the suffrage movement, women's voting rights were not a major part of the movement that preceded the Civil War, making (A) incorrect. While labor unions and suffragists shared many political ideals, the labor union movement fought for goals regarding fair wages and safe work environments rather than voting rights; (B) is incorrect. The libertarian movement championed individual liberty like the women's rights movement; however, the broader scope of the libertarian movement advocated for other causes unrelated to civil rights, eliminating (D).

41. D

The issue of whether to legalize same-sex marriage most closely parallels the controversy depicted in the cartoon because it represents the fear of changing gender roles and behaviors upon granting a new right to a specific group; **(D)** is correct. Campaign financing and universal health care are controversies that showcase different concerns than those depicted in the cartoon, making (A) and (C) incorrect. While the issue of immigration reform parallels the cartoon's controversy in that it represents a societal development that some citizens fear, this fear is not based in anxieties pertaining to gender roles; (B) is incorrect.

42. C

The Virginia and Kentucky Resolutions were initiated by Thomas Jefferson and James Madison and passed by the legislatures of the two states in response to the Alien and Sedition Acts of 1798. These resolutions promoted the idea that a state could nullify a federal law if the law violated constitutional rights. Advocates of states' rights supported the resolutions, which matches **(C)**. The views of those who supported a strong central government emphasized national supremacy and executive power, making (A) and (B) incorrect. Judicial review refers to the power of the Supreme Court to rule on actions by Congress and the executive branch. This principle was not yet established in 1798; it was established in 1803 with the Supreme Court's decision on *Marbury v. Madison*, eliminating (D).

43. B

Calhoun's speech provided justification for South Carolina to declare the Tariff of 1832 null and void. South Carolina's action was countered by President Andrew Jackson, who issued a proclamation that a state did not have the power to nullify a federal law. Civil war seemed likely because both sides called up troops. It was only after Henry Clay negotiated a compromise tariff in 1833 that this Nullification Crisis ended; **(B)** is correct. The Indian Removal Act and the annexation of Texas did not involve a crisis over states' rights, but rather the assertion of executive power, eliminating (A) and (C). Government action regarding states rights was not involved in Nat Turner's slave rebellion, making (D) incorrect.

44. B

Calhoun's speech refers to the time period between the implementation of the Constitution and the Revolution of 1800. The "great struggle" involved conflict between supporters of a strong central government and supporters of states' rights. The Alien and Sedition Acts reflected strong central government action, and supporters of states' rights created the Virginia and Kentucky Resolutions in order to nullify the application of those laws in specific states; **(B)** is correct. (A), (C), and (D) are incorrect because those disputes occurred after 1801.

45. A

Wilson's primary objective in the first term of his presidency was to keep the United States out of World War I. In fact, he ran for reelection in 1916 on that very platform. However, as Germany became increasingly belligerent, Wilson's Cabinet, Congress, and the American public challenged America's neutrality; **(A)** is correct. (B), (C), and (D) are incorrect; each represents an action that would have been in direct opposition to Wilson's pledge of neutrality.

46. C

Wilson was able to maintain his neutral stance even after Germany violated several diplomatic pledges by stating that Germany had not committed an overt act that warranted military response. However, once Germany declared that they would practice unrestricted submarine warfare, Wilson was forced to recognize Germany's direct aggression against the United States; **(C)** is correct. Even after Germany declared the waters surrounding Great Britain to be a war zone, Wilson merely warned Germany that they would be held accountable for their actions, making (A) incorrect. (B) is incorrect because while Germany attempted to enlist Mexico as its ally with the Zimmermann Telegram, Germany did not reach out to Canada. During this time, the United States was overcoming a recession and experienced enormous economic growth through 1917, eliminating (D).

47. A

Farm foreclosures and heavy taxation by the Massachusetts legislature culminated in an uprising of farmers and war veterans, making **(A)** correct. Congress lacked the ability to levy taxes and to mandate military service under the Articles of Confederation; (B) and (C) are incorrect. Shays' Rebellion took place in western Massachusetts, not the western frontier, eliminating (D).

48. A

Shays' Rebellion made it clear that the current central government was not strong enough to deal with significant unrest. Washington and other proponents of Federalism used Shays' Rebellion as an example of why a stronger central government was needed; **(A)** is correct. The Articles of Confederation were not amended; instead, they were completely replaced by the Constitution, eliminating (B). While pro-British sentiments were a factor earlier in America's history, they were no longer a threat at this time, making (C) incorrect. America did not reach out to foreign nations to form alliances or for aid; (D) is also incorrect.

49. C

Like Shays' Rebellion, the Whiskey Rebellion of 1794 occurred due to consequences of taxation; **(C)** is correct. In both events, American citizens rose up against the United States government to demand economic relief. Nat Turner's Rebellion and the Stono Rebellion were both slave uprisings, making (A) and (D) incorrect. Pontiac's Rebellion involved conflicts between Native Americans and the British after The Seven Years' War, eliminating (B).

50. B

In this illustration, J. D. Rockefeller's Standard Oil is a monster with strong, far-reaching control of oil fields, ships, and government buildings. At its height, the company controlled 95 percent of America's oil production and distribution in the United States and took advantage of lax government oversight; **(B)** is correct. While Standard Oil and other big businesses indeed paid their workers low wages, the illustration captures the broader characterization that monopolies and trusts were gaining too much control of the economy and the government; (A) is incorrect. During this time, such industries lacked oversight by the government, making (C) incorrect. Rockefeller and his contemporaries, such as William Vanderbilt and Andrew Carnegie, enjoyed much financial success in the Gilded Age, eliminating (D).

51. C

During the Gilded Age, the unprecedented concentration of wealth and power in the hands of a few capitalists drove the proliferation of railroads, the spread of industrialization, and a rise in complex financial dealings. During this time, financial empires were able to control many aspects of the U.S. economy: prices, wages, labor, corporate partnerships, and manufacturing; **(C)** is correct. Although the government gradually began to regulate these trusts, legislation to disenfranchise trusts only gained momentum in the Progressive Era in the early twentieth century, making (A) and (B) incorrect. Even though labor unions emerged during the Gilded Age, they were subject to heavy suppression by both trusts and the government; (D) is incorrect.

52. C

The Interstate Commerce Act was the first major piece of antitrust regulation. Passed in 1886, this act was designed to regulate railroad and interstate shipping rates in order to foster fairness and to eliminate monopolistic practices, such as price-gouging and favoritism; **(C)** is correct. While weak in its enforcement mechanisms, the Interstate Commerce Act was intended to impose limits on railroad owners, making (A) incorrect. Although this act required rates to be "reasonable and just," it continued to allow railroads to set rates, eliminating (B). (D) is incorrect because this act applied to commerce across state lines, not across national borders.

53. C

Industrialists routinely engaged in horizontal or vertical integration to gain control of their industries. **(C)** is correct. Trusts did not attempt to implement fair wages or improved work environments, eliminating (A). Trusts often destroyed other companies by buying them out or lowering prices to eliminate competition; (B) is incorrect. Trusts were able to circumvent government oversight by inserting or buying out trust-friendly government representatives, making (D) incorrect.

54. C

Threats of socialism and communism in America emerged during and after World War I, especially after the Bolsheviks took control of Russia. Labor unions protested the U.S. involvement in the war and its ensuing conscription efforts. In addition, anarchist groups ignited fears that led to widespread xenophobia; **(C)** is correct. The Treaty of Versailles established postwar peace agreements and entailed significant repercussions on Germany. While some American politicians (notably President Wilson) disagreed with such punitive measures, America was not at risk for losing overseas possessions as a result of the treaty, making (A) incorrect. The war's psychological effects on returning troops were more concerning than the logistical concerns of reintegrating war veterans into the workforce or bringing troops back to the United States, eliminating (B) and (D).

55. A

Soldiers returning from Europe had not been introduced to socialist ideals; American politicians were focused on internal threats, making **(A)** correct. The First Red Scare was driven by threats both real and imagined. Such threats included the Russian Revolution, which occurred when radical socialist factions overthrew the longstanding Russian autocracy, and bombings blamed on anarchists in the United States. Labor unions protested America's involvement in the Great War, along with its conscription efforts, and often espoused socialist ideals. Therefore, (B), (C), and (D) are incorrect because each represents a direct cause of the First Red Scare.

Section I, Part B

1. A successful short-answer response accomplishes all three tasks set forth by the prompt. Each part of the prompt is worth 1 point, for a total of 3 possible points.

(a) To earn the point, the response must describe a significant difference between the authors' interpretations of ideologies and/or events that led up to the Civil War, specifically addressing the claims of *both* passages. For the first passage, the response could describe Wells's claim that the differing "ideas" or "spirits" of the North and South, which he classifies as a difference between freedom and the slave system, were the source of conflict. The response could also mention Wells's claims that improved transportation and westward expansion intensified these differences. For the second passage, the response should describe Schlesinger's claim that the issue of state rights, which he defines as states working to increase their power or stop federal "encroachments" of power, were the source of conflict. The essential difference between the claims of the passages is that the first cites regional ideologies and the second cites states rights as contributing to the conflict of the Civil War.

(b) To earn the point, the response must identify a specific historical event or development from 1819—1861 and use reasoning or evidence to explain how that event or development supports a claim made by Wells. For example, the response could support the claim that the difference between the free system of the North and the estate/slave system of the South left "little possibility for compromise" by using the Tariffs of 1828 and 1832 (the Nullification Crisis) as examples of regional differences in commerce, by describing the conflicts over slavery instigated by the Fugitive Slave Act of 1850 and the publication of *Uncle Tom's Cabin*, or by highlighting the intensity of conflict as demonstrated by the caning of Senator Charles Sumner and John Brown's raid on Harper's Ferry. The response could support the claim that the addition of new western states led to conflict by describing the controversies surrounding the Missouri Compromise, the Compromise of 1850, or the Kansas-Nebraska Act. Note that although Wells describes the creation of new states, he does not mention any specific examples of territories or new states, so they may be used as valid examples in a response.

(c) To earn the point, the response must identify a specific historical event or development from 1819—1861 and use reasoning or evidence to explain how that event or development supports a claim made by Schlesinger. For example, the response could support the claim that the doctrine of states' rights contributed to controversy before the Civil War by explaining how the Nullification Crisis or the 1860 election of Abraham Lincoln demonstrated state resistance to federal actions that some southerners perceived as harming some states at the expense of others. Events reflecting the doctrines of states' rights and/or strict construction of the Constitution that occurred before 1819, such as the 1798 Kentucky and Virginia Resolutions, could not be used to earn the point. Note that the same example(s) could be used for both (b) and (c), as long as a reasonable explanation of how the evidence supports each authors' claims is provided.

2. A successful short-answer response accomplishes all three tasks set forth by the prompt. Each part of the prompt is worth 1 point, for a total of 3 possible points.

(a) To earn the point, the response must describe a perspective about American involvement in World War II as expressed in the passage. Examples include the view that the United States must defend the "freedom" of endangered "democracies," the strategy that American support included the production and shipment of military vehicles and guns, and the assertion that aiding democracies facing aggression from dictators did not constitute an act of war (and the determination to provide aid in the face of threats from such dictators).

(b) To earn the point, the response must use reasoning or evidence to explain a historical development, circumstance, or event that led to Roosevelt's speech. Examples of events that would have prompted Roosevelt to pledge aid include the aggressions of Germany and Italy in Europe and Africa and Japan in the Pacific—for instance, the German invasion of Poland, the fall of France to Germany, and the bombing of Britain. An example of circumstances that prompted the speech include Roosevelt needing to motivate American involvement in the war after the preference for isolationism in the years since World War I. Note that events that occurred after the speech, such as the December 1941 attack on Pearl Harbor, cannot be used as examples that led to the speech.

(c) To earn the point, the response must use reasoning or evidence to explain a historical development, circumstance, or event that resulted from Roosevelt's encouragement of American support for countries under threat in World War II. Examples include the continuation of the Lend-Lease program to help supply the Allies and the eventual formal entry of the United States into World War II after prompted to declare war on Japan after the December 1941 attack on Pearl Harbor.

3. A successful short-answer response accomplishes all three tasks set forth by the prompt. Each part of the prompt is worth 1 point, for a total of 3 possible points.

(a) To earn the point, the response must describe a specific historical similarity between the national governments under both documents. Examples include that both documents unified the states by creating a central government that negotiated with foreign nations, settled disputes between states, and contained a legislature composed of representatives from the states.

(b) To earn the point, the response must describe a specific historical difference between the national governments under both documents. Examples include the differences in requirements for passing legislation and amending the government documents, including the

unanimous agreement needed to amend the Articles; the confederate nature of government under the Articles versus the republican nature of government under the Constitution; the higher emphasis on state sovereignty under the Articles; the lack of enforcement or taxation powers under the Articles; the inability of the central government to regulate commerce under the Articles; the unicameral legislature under the Articles versus the bicameral legislature under the Constitution; the lack of executive and judicial branches under the Articles; and the eventual addition of a Bill of Rights to the Constitution.

(c) To earn the point, the response must identify a specific historical reason and use reasoning or evidence to explain why that reason led to the difference between the Articles and the Constitution. One possible example concerns the reason why the writers of the Articles did not grant the central government the power of taxation while the writers of the Constitution did. The Articles were written during the midst of the Revolution, during which Americans were fighting against what they perceived to be the unfair taxation practices of the British government, so they were unlikely to create a central government with strong taxation powers. On the other hand, the Constitution was written after the Articles government had been shown to be unable to fund a military to handle uprisings such as Shays' Rebellion. Another possible example is that the writers of the Constitution decided that the document could be amended by a two-thirds vote in both houses or two-thirds of state legislatures, since the unanimous agreement required to amend the Articles made it nearly impossibly to make adjustments.

4. A successful short-answer response accomplishes all three tasks set forth by the prompt. Each part of the prompt is worth 1 point, for a total of 3 possible points.

(a) To earn the point, the response must describe a specific similarity between the two peace treaties. Examples include that both treaties included a European power ceding territories or former colonies, such as Spain recognizing the independence of Cuba and granting Pacific and Caribbean territories (the Philippines, Puerto Rico, and Guam) to the United States, and Germany ceding regions in Europe and giving up rights to former colonies in Africa and the Pacific; that both treaties recognized the independence of nations, such as Cuba after the Spanish-American War and Czechoslovakia and Poland after World

I; and that both treaties contained provisions that that led to later conflicts, such as conflict in the Philippines after the Spanish-American War treaty granted the territory to the United States and the eventual outbreak of World War II partly due to the economic and political conditions created in Germany by the World War I treaty.

(b) To earn the point, the response must describe a specific difference between the United States' reasons for entering the wars. Examples include the role of isolationism, as many Americans, spurred by reports of abuses by the Spanish to Cubans, were eager to enter the Spanish-American War in the imperialist mindset of the late nineteenth century, but many favored non-involvement in Europe and only reluctantly entered World War I officially; the role of journalism and public opinion, as "yellow journalism" fueled public support for the Spanish-American War despite the mysterious circumstances of the destruction of the *U.S.S. Maine*, while, despite public outcry, the United States did not enter World War I for two years after the German sinking of the *Lusitania*; and the overall reasons for entering the wars, as the United States entered the Spanish-American War with the expressed purpose of helping Cuba gain independence and entered World War I to combat German aggressions and "make the world safe for democracy."

(c) To earn the point, the response must identify an effect of either war and use reasoning or evidence to explain how the war brought about that effect. Examples of effects of the Spanish-American War include the effective ending of the Spanish empire, the increased role of the United States in the Caribbean and the Pacific due to its acquisition of former Spanish colonies, the expansion of U.S. influence in Latin American countries contributing to its future claims of interventionist power in the Roosevelt Corollary to the Monroe Doctrine, the independence of Cuba, the creation of the U.S. territories of Guam and Puerto Rico, and the beginning of the United States' involvement in the Philippines. Examples of the effects of World War I include the creation of the League of Nations (despite the U.S. failure to join); the increase of isolationist and nativist sentiments in the United States; concerns about radicalism after the Russian Revolution leading to a Red Scare; the growth of American factories and urban centers as a result of wartime production, which contributed to the Great Migration of African Americans from the South; the involvement of the United States in the reparations repayment and overall economy of Europe through the Dawes Plan; and the instability in Germany caused by reparations, forced ceding of territory, and the war guilt clause laying the foundations for World War II.